HTML *Goodies*

HTML Color Codes

Aliceblue F0F8FF	Antiquewhite FAEBD7	Aqua 00FFFF	Aquamarine 7FFFD4
Azure F0FFFF	Beige F5F5DC	Bisque FFE4C4	Black 000000
Blanchedalmond FFEBCD	Blue 0000FF	Blueviolet 8A2BE2	Brown A52A2A
Burlywood DEB887	Cadetblue 5F9EA0	Chartreuse 7FFF00	Chocolate D2691E
Coral FF7F50	Cornflowerblue 6495ED	Cornsilk FFF8DC	Crimson DC143C
Cyan 00FFFF	Darkblue 00008B	Darkcyan 008B8B	Darkgoldenrod B8860B
Darkgray A9A9A9	Darkgreen 006400	Darkkhaki BDB76B	Darkmagenta 8B008B
Darkolivegreen 556B2F	Darkorange FF8C00	Darkorchid 9932CC	Darkred 8B0000
Darksalmon E9967A	Darkseagreen 8FBC8F	Darkslateblue 483D8B	Darkslategray 2F4F4F
Darkturquoise 00CED1	Darkviolet 9400D3	Deeppink FF1493	Deepskyblue 00BFFF
Dimgray 696969	Dodgerblue 1E90FF	Firebrick B22222	Floralwhite FFFAF0
Forestgreen 228B22	Fuchsia FF00FF	Gainsboro DCDCDC	Ghostwhite F8F8FF
Gold FFD700	Goldenrod DAA520	Gray 808080	Green 008000
Greenyellow ADFF2F	Honeydew F0FFF0	Hotpink FF69B4	Indianred CD5C5C
Indigo 4B0082	Ivory FFFFF0	Khaki F0E68C	Lavendar E6E6FA
Lavenderblush FFF0F5	Lawngreen 7CFC00	Lemonchiffon FFFACD	Lightblue ADD8E6
Lightcoral F08080	Lightcyan E0FFFF	Lightgoldenrodyellow FAFAD2	Lightgreen 90EE90
Lightgrey D3D3D3	Lightpink FFB6C1	Lightsalmon FFA07A	Lightseagreen 20B2AA
Lightskyblue 87CEFA	Lightslategray 778899	Lightsteelblue B0C4DE	Lightyellow FFFFE0
Lime 00FF00	Limegreen 32CD32	Linen FAF0E6	Magenta FF00FF
Maroon 800000	Mediumauqamarine 66CDAA	Mediumblue 0000CD	Mediumorchid BA55D3

HTML Color Codes (Continued)

Mediumpurple 9370D8	Mediumseagreen 3CB371	Mediumslateblue 7B68EE	Mediumspringgreen 00FA9A
Mediumturquoise 48D1CC	Mediumvioletred C71585	Midnightblue 191970	Mintcream F5FFFA
Mistyrose FFE4E1	Moccasin FFE4B5	Navajowhite FFDEAD	Navy 000080
Oldlace FDF5E6	Olive 808000	Olivedrab 688E23	Orange FFA500
Orangered FF4500	Orchid DA70D6	Palegoldenrod EEE8AA	Palegreen 98FB98
Paleturquoise AFEEEE	Palevioletred D87093	Papayawhip FFEFD5	Peachpuff FFDAB9
Peru CD853F	Pink FFC0CB	Plum DDA0DD	Powderblue B0E0E6
Purple 800080	Red FF0000	Rosybrown BC8F8F	Royalblue 4169E1
Saddlebrown 8B4513	Salmon FA8072	Sandybrown F4A460	Seagreen 2E8B57
Seashell FFF5EE	Sienna A0522D	Silver C0C0C0	Skyblue 87CEEB
Slateblue 6A5ACD	Slategray 708090	Snow FFFAFA	Springgreen 00FF7F
Steelblue 4682B4	Tan D2B48C	Teal 008080	Thistle D8BFD8
Tomato FF6347	Turquoise 40E0D0	Violet EE82EE	Wheat F5DEB3
White FFFFFF	Whitesmoke F5F5F5	Yellow FFFF00	YellowGreen 9ACD32

HTML Ampersand (&) Commands

® ®	± ±	µ µ	¶ ¶	· ·	¢ ¢
£ £	¥ ¥	¼ ¼	½ ½	¾ ¾	¹ ¹
² ²	³ ³	¿ ¿	° °	¦ ¦	§ §
< <	> >	& &	" "	(A Space)	&Ccdil; Ç
&ccdil; ç	Ñ Ñ	ñ ñ	Þ Þ	þ þ	Ý Ý
ý ý	ÿ ÿ	ß ß	Æ Æ	Á Á	Â Â
À À	Å Å	Ã Ã	Ä Ä	æ æ	á á
â â	à à	å å	ã ã	ä ä	Ð Ð
É É	Ê Ê	È È	Ë Ë	ð ð	é é
ê ê	è è	ë ë	Í Í	Î Î	Ì Ì

Ï Ï	í í	î î	ì ì	ï ï	Ó Ó
Ô Ô	Ò Ò	Ø Ø	Õ Õ	Ö Ö	ó ó
ô ô	ò ò	ø ø	õ õ	ö ö	Ú Ú
Û Û	Ù Ù	Ü Ü	ú ú	û û	ù ù
ü ü	« «	» »			

Praise for *Web Site Design Goodies*

"Those looking for design templates and HTML "how-to" will be disappointed. And a good thing too. Instead, Joe Burns provides refreshing honesty and opinion, with intelligent advice on the key elements of Web site design; advice which will still stand you in good stead long after HTML is a distant memory—a Web design guide for life.

Give a man a design template or code list and you've fed him for one Web site. Give him this book, and you've set him on his way to building as many different Web sites as he needs. Instead of a paint-by-numbers approach, Joe uses his personable, conversational style to encourage self-development and design confidence.

At the same time, he provides in-depth comment on important Web site design issues, such as colors, technical wizardry, link placement, fonts, focus, and so forth[me]and uses numerous examples, surveys, and site reviews to back up his points. Anyone who thinks he's done a good job with his Web site would do well to read this book and then reassess his work."

—*Mark Brownlow, VP Content, Internet Business Forum, Inc.;* http://www.ibizhome.com/

Top Notch Design Advice without HTML Getting in the Way

"This is the kind of book that an aspiring Web designer should read before learning HTML. For it is not just another HTML book, in fact it contains no HTML at all. The author presents pages followed by his opinion regarding the design. As Burns is the first to say, his opinions are not infallible; there can be circumstances where you may not want to follow his advice. However, he does know what he is talking about, so do not be hasty towards the contrary position.

I found the book easy to read and the choices for sample sites were well made. Rather than make it easy for himself by picking sites that are awful, in general he chose pages that were quite good. If a site had been atrocious, the problems would have been obvious, even for a beginner. By choosing good ones, he could then point out the "flaws" that are easily overlooked.

This is a book that should be read either before or concurrently with a book that teaches the construction of pages. It is not necessary to know HTML to understand the material and Web pages are like houses; you should first learn to read the blueprints before you start to build the walls."

—*Charles Ashbacher, author of Sams Teach Yourself XML in 24 Hours*

Another Superb Job by Joe Burns!

"I have been working with Web pages for over four years and I have taught Web design classes. I thought I had a good idea of what is involved with the design, setup, and marketing of a Web site. Now I find this book and there are so many things I had never thought of before.

As with other Joe Burns books, this book is an excellent representation of what you can do if you have a little guidance to help you along. Burns is truly remarkable in the ways he is able to present ideas clearly yet make them understandable at the same time.

The book begins with an overview of what things to look for and what ideas to consider when planning and designing a Web site. Then Burns has you consider five questions before you begin the actual design layout, an approach that will help in making a better Web site.

There are other topics like the 10 things you shouldn't put in the Web site, to choosing a server and ISP, to text and color. There is something for beginners and experts alike. Burns also spends time explaining links, images, and visual effects before moving on to counters and Web site promotion.

Overall, there is about everything you need to have to make sure you have a successful Web site right from the start and for years to come. A first-rate book from a first-rate author."

—Michael Woznicki

Praise for Author Joe Burns' HTML Goodies Web Site

From the Web Site Visitors

"I'd like to thank you for your HTML site. Instead of wasting time scouring the Internet, the code and examples on your site have made it so much easier to see my mistakes and to finally create a working Web site."

—Anthony Moore

"... your tutorial, page by page, word by word, told me every other thing I needed to know about Web design. It was like me finding a gold mine. Your language was so impressive and so much direct to the heart, that I always thought you [were] there talking to me, instead of me reading from your site. I saved all the pages of [HTMLGoodies.com and it] became the bible of my Web design."

—Barun Sen

"Thank you so much! Trying to learn how to use tables was causing my brain to pick up smoking. I understand now; thanks for explaining it in English."

— *Elizabeth Rotondi*

"Thanks thanks thanks for the wonderful (easy) primer! I am going day by day, and my page, boring though it is   is really coming along!"

— *Jean Van Minnen*

"... HTML Goodies is a excellent Web site with plenty of GOLD content about HTML Well done on a superbly successful site!"

— *Carl Blythe*

"Thanks for the beautiful pieces of work. I salute you."

—*John J. Lacombe II;* `jlacombe@cpcug.org`;
Organization: Capital PC Users Group

"This is not only a first-rate page, but is also a huge help to me, and, my guess is, many, *many* people like me. These tutorials have helped me create my own page. Once again, thank you. You're terrific."

—*Rose Dewitt Bukater*

"You probably get dozens of thank you notes each day, but I just wanted to add my own to the lot. Since I'm a just starting out in the HTML world, I've been visiting your tutorials a lot. Just wanted you to know I've learned more from your site than from any of the books I've bought!"

—*Dawn C. Lindley*

"Dear Mr. Really Smart cool-happening dude, I would like to thank you because I have made the transition from FrontPage 98 to HTML all because of you. I spent months trying to learn HTML before I learned of your site, and at age 14 I fully understand the ins and outs of HTML 4. My page is in the works and I owe it all to you. =)"

—*Taylor Ackley*

"I just wanted to let you know that you are doing an amazing service to all of us weekend Web masters. Thanks a million! P.S. My Web page looks and feels a thousand times better since I have been following your tutorials."

—*Aaron Joel Chettle; Organization: Seneca College Engineering*

"WOW!!!!...I was always interested in setting up a Web page, but was afraid that it would be too difficult for me to comprehend... So my first introduction to HTML was actually YOUR primers...and WOW!!!!!!! I went through ALL of them this very morning with my mouth hanging wide open...I am still so surprised that I cannot gather any words to describe to you how I feel at this moment."

—Ludwin L. Statie

"I'm an old dog learning new tricks. I will be taking a Web publishing college course come August. I used your primer as a jump start. I really enjoyed your primer and thought it would...help me. I now feel prepared for the college course and not so afraid to 'run with the big dogs."

—Patricia Cuthbertson

From the Media

"If you are just learning, or already know HTML, this site is the only place you'll need. Expert tutorials make learning Web design quick and easy. Definitely check this site out."

—HTML Design Association

"Dr. Joe Burns offers help at all levels—from novice to the expert."

—Signal Magazine; January 26, 1998

"Great stuff. Probably the best overall site reviewed here."

—NetUser Magazine

"If you're looking for information on HTML, you'll find it here."

—USA Today Hot Site; March 23, 1998

"His is a technical site that appeals to an exploding piece of the Internet pie—people building their own Web site."

—PCNovice Guide to Building Web Sites; 1997

"We would like permission to use your Web pages [HTML Goodies] to help teach [building] Web sites."

—San Antonio Electronic Commerce Resource Center; February 10, 1998

From Teachers

"If everyone wrote 'how to' pages and books as well as you, boy—life would be simpler."

—Deb Spearing Ph.D.; University Registrar, Ohio State University

"I am going to use your Goodies [to teach with] this summer! Awesome!"

—Cynthia Lanius; Rice University

"I hope your own students and colleagues appreciate the importance and magnitude of the service you provide to the discipline of communication technology via the Internet. In just a short time, Joe Burns has become a legend on the Internet among those who teach in this field."

—Raymond E. Schroeder; Professor of Communication, Springfield University

"The English classes at Union Alternative High School [are] using Dr. Joe Burns' Web site HTML Goodies as an online text book. Students now have Web pages they are proud of. They have learned to teach themselves unfamiliar subject matter. There is new excitement in the class, self-esteem is up. In a nutshell: We have succeeded. Thank you for helping, Dr. Burns."

—Aaron Wills; English teacher, Union School District, Union, MO

HTML
Goodies

Second Edition

by Joe Burns, Ph.D.

Pearson Technology Group
201 West 103rd Street Indianapolis, Indiana 46290

HTML Goodies Second Edition

Trademarks

Warning and Disclaimer

Acquisitions Editor
Todd Green

Development Editor
Victoria Elzey

Technical Editors
Lindy Humphries
Deborah Claudio

Managing Editor
Thomas F. Hayes

Senior Editor
Susan Ross Moore

Production Editor
Candice Hightower

Indexer
Tim Tate

Proofreader
Wendy Ott

Team Coordinator
Cindy Teeters

Interior Design
Louisa Klucznik

Cover Design
Aren Howell

Layout Technician
Susan Geiselman

Contents at a Glance

Introduction   1

Part I: How to Build a Web Site in 7 Steps   **7**

Primer 1: What You Need to Get Started   9

Primer 2: Flags and Commands   17

Primer 3: Manipulating Text   23

Primer 4: Making a Link to Someone Else   29

Primer 5: Placing an Image on Your Page   33

Primer 6: Manipulating Images   39

Primer 7: Graduation Day   45

Part II: Everything You Need to Know About Text and Graphics   **53**

1 Playing with Text   55

2 Creating Links   77

3 Adding Images and Backgrounds   93

4 Imagemaps   149

Part III: Getting More Control Over the Layout of Your Web Pages   **163**

5 Tables   165

6 Frames   187

7 Link Buttons and Forms   219

8 Cascading Style Sheets and Layers   249

Part IV: Beyond HTML   **281**

9 Behind the Scenes on Your Web Site   283

10 Sound and Video   293

11 Java Applets and JavaScript   311

12 Common Gateway Interface (CGI)   363

13 Explorer-Specific Tutorials and DHTML   383

14 Building Web Site Banners   417

15 Other Stuff You Should Really Know   455

Part V: Appendixes   **513**

A Everything You Need to Know About HTML 4.0   515

B Useful Charts   527

C Valuable Links   537

Index   547

Contents

Introduction   **1**

     About This Book 1

     My Thoughts on Building a Web Site 2

     The Four Basic Rules 2

     The Home Page 3

     Images 4

     Backgrounds 5

     Colors 5

     Text 6

Part 1: How to Build a Web Site in 7 Steps   **7**

P1 What You Need to Get Started   **9**

     What Do I Need to Create a Web Page? 9

     What Is HTML? 10

     Some More Information Before Writing 11

     Creating HTML Documents with a Word Processor 11

     How to Name Your HTML Document 12

     Opening Your HTML Document in a Browser 13

P2 Flags and Commands   **17**

     What Are Flags? 17

     Open and Close Flags 19

     Single Flags 19

     Writing Your First Web Page 20

     So Here You Go! 21

P3 Manipulating Text   **23**

     Heading Flags 23

     Font Size Commands 24

     Centering and Aligning Text 25

P4 Making a Link to Someone Else   **29**

People E-mailing You from Your Page 31

P5 Placing an Image on Your Page   **33**

Inserting the Image 33
Image Formats 35
Where Do I Get My Images? 35
Creating an Active (Clickable) Image 36

P6 Manipulating Images   **39**

Placement on the Page 39
Aligning Text with Images 40
Changing Image Size 41
Making Horizontal Lines of Different Lengths 42

P7 Graduation Day   **45**

How Do I Get an Internet Service Provider? 45
How Much Should I Pay? 46
How Do I Get My Pages on the World Wide Web? 46
Using FTP Software 47
How FTP Works 47
ASCII Versus Binary 48
Rule of Thumb 50
Why Not Send and Save Everything as Binary? 50
What Do Those HTML Assistants Do? 50
Where Do I Go Now? 51

Part 2: Everything You Need to Know About Text and Graphics   **53**

1 Playing with Text   **55**

Text Codes 55
Abbreviation: <ABBR> 56
Acronym: <ACRONYM> 56
Address: <ADDRESS> 56
Bold: <B> 56

Base Font: <BASEFONT> 57
BDO: <BDO> 57
Big: <BIG> 57
Blink: <BLINK> 57
Block Quote: <BLOCKQUOTE> 57
Cite: <CITE> 58
Code: <CODE> 58
Comment: <COMMENT> 58
Delete: <DEL> 58
Definition: <DFN> 58
Division: <DIV> 59
Emphasis: <EM> 59
Font Color: <FONT COLOR> 59
Font Size: <FONT SIZE> 59
Font Face: <FONT FACE> 59
Heading: <H#> 60
Italics: <I> 60
Inserted: <INS> 60
Keyboard: <KBD> 60
Listing: <LISTING> 60
Multiple Columns: <MULTICOL> 60
No Break: <NOBR> 61
Plain Text: <PLAINTEXT> 61
Preformatted: <PRE> 61
Quote: <Q> 61
Small: <SMALL> 61
Sample: <SAMP> 62
Span: <SPAN> 62
Strikethrough: <S> 62
Strong: <STRONG> 62
Subscript: <SUB> 62
Superscript: <SUP> 62
Typewriter Text: <TT> 63
Underline: <U> 63
Variable: <VAR> 63
Wrapping Break: <WBR> 63
XMP: <XMP> 63
Changing Text Colors 63
Changing the Color of All the Words on the Page 64
Changing Color One Word at a Time 65
Changing Specific Link Colors 65

Changing Text Fonts 65
    One More Tip 67
Indents and Lists 67
    Indenting a Paragraph 67
    Bulleted Lists 68
    Numbered Lists 70
    Combining Types of Lists 72
    A Definition List 73
Newspaper Columns 75

2 Creating Links   77

Setting Up a Site 77
    Putting A Site Together 77
Page Jumps 81
    How You Do It 81
    Jumping to a Specific Page Section 83
    The Link Form 83
Active Images (Images That Act Like Links) 84
    Removing the Blue Border Around the Link Image 85
Creating Links That Open a New Browser Window 87
    How Do I Stop It from Happening? 87
How to Create a Dynamic Page 88
    Getting a Page to Change 88
    How to Add Sound 89
So You Don't Want Links Underlined? 90
    Affecting Just One Link 92

3 Adding Images and Backgrounds   93

Grabbing Images Off the Web 93
    How It's Done 94
    Aligning Text with Images 96
    Getting Text to Wrap 96
    Centering an Image in Text 97
    Aligning One Line of Text 99
    Aligning Two Lines of Text Around an Image 100
Using HEIGHT, WIDTH, and ALT Commands 102
    HEIGHT *and* WIDTH *Commands* 102
    ALT *Command* 103
    How Do I Find Each Image's Size? 104

Making Lines with Images 105
   The Image 105
Creating Thumbnail Images 107
   Offering Text Links to Images 108
   Offering Two Images 108
   Offering One Image 109
Loading a Low-Res Version of an Image First 110
   Why Would I Do This? 111
   When Would I Use This? 112
   How Do I Make the LOWSRC *Picture?* 112
Transparent Images 112
   What Is Actually Happening 113
   Where Do I Get a Transparency Program? 113
   Making Transparencies with LView Pro 113
Creating Animated GIFs 116
   Making the GIFs for Your Animation 118
   Making the Animated GIF 120
   Placing an Animated GIF on Your Page 124
Creating Horizontal Lines with the HR Command 124
   Changing the Rule's Width 124
   Changing the Rule's Height 125
   Aligning Horizontal Rules 126
   Horizontal Rules without Shading 126
Backgrounds 128
   Background Image Wallpaper 128
Make Your Own Wallpaper 129
   Easy Wallpapers 129
   Harder, Geometric Wallpapers 129
   One More Thing... 130
Sideline Backgrounds 131
   How You Do It 131
Image Formats On The Web 135
   Image or Graphic? 136
   Forty-four Different Graphic Formats? 136
   What's A Bitmap? 139
   Compression 140
   The GIF Image Formats 142
   JPEG Image Formats 144
   Progressive JPEGs 145
   Which Image Should I Use Where? 146

How Do I Save in These Formats? 147
Do You Edit and Create Images in GIF or JPEG? 147

4 Imagemaps 149

Server-Side Imagemaps 149
The Imagemap Command 150
Making the Map 152
The Image 153
Putting It All Together 154
Client-Side Imagemaps 155
Let's Make a Map! 155
Fake Imagemap 158
The Image(s) 160
Getting It All to Line Up 161

Part 3: Getting More Control Over the Layout of Your Web Pages 163

5 Tables 165

The Simple Table Flags 166
Really Fancy Table Stuff 168
Finally... 173
Advanced Table Commands 174
The COLSPAN Command 174
The ROWSPAN Command 175
What's That WIDTH="nn" Deal? 176
Can I Use COLSPAN and ROWSPAN Commands Together? 177
A Table Within a Table 177
Using Tables to Make an HTML Calendar 179
Adding Color to Your Tables 182
Changing Cell Colors 182
Changing Text Colors 183
Changing Table Border Colors 184
Some Extra Play with Colors 186

6 Frames   187

Advice on Using (or Not Using) Frames 187
Simple Frames 189
   Creating Frame Columns 191
   Adding Frame Rows to the Mix 192
   Combining Frame Columns and Rows 193
Why Use Frames? 195
Dynamics of Frames, NAMEs, and TARGETs 195
   Click a Link in a Frame—Just That Frame Changes
   Pages 196
   Click a Link in a Frame—Another Frame on the
   Screen Receives the Information 196
   Completely Leaving a Frames Page 198
   What About People Who Don't Have Frame-
   Ready Browsers? 198
Advanced Frame Commands 199
   Resizing Frame Window Borders: BORDER="###" 201
   Changing the Space Between Frames 201
   Changing Frame Window Margins 202
   Keeping Your Frame Window Borders in Place 202
   To Offer or Not to Offer...A Scrollbar 203
   A Tip for Filling Multiple Frame Windows with
   One Page 205
Seamless Frames 206
   The Main Frame Command 206
   The Frame Sources 209
Changing Multiple Frame Cells 210
   Frame Order 212
Frames Border Color 213
Frames Yes! Frames No! 214
   No Frames! 215
   Yes Frames! 215
   Examples 216

7 Link Buttons and Forms   219

   How to Make a Link Button 220
   Lining Up Link Buttons 221

Simple Forms 224
   The First Step to Building a Form 224
   The Text Box Form 225
   The Text Area Box Form 226
   The Radio Button Form 228
   The Check Box Form 229
   The Drop-Down Box Form 230
   Send and Reset Buttons for Your Forms 232
Creating a Guestbook 233
   A Basic Guestbook 233
   Simple `Mailto:` *Guestbooks* 235
   Augmenting Your Guestbook Output 235
   Guestbooks with Virtual Pages 236
Image Submit Buttons 237
So You Want a Searchable Database, Huh? 238
   Search Someone Else's Database 238
   But I Want to Search My Site! 240
   But I Want to Search My Site! (Take Two) ... 241
   But I Want to Search My Site! (Take Three) ... 241
`TABINDEX` and a Few Other Neat Tricks... 242
   The Command In Action 242
   Focus `onLoad` 243
   Losing the `VALUE` *Text* 244
Working with Internet Explorer's AutoComplete ... 245
   How It Works 245
   Using AutoComplete on Your Forms (Or Not) ... 247
   I Want the Silly Thing Turned Off Altogether ... 247
   How Do I Erase My AutoComplete Responses? ... 247
   How Do I Clear Just One AutoComplete Response? ... 248

8 Cascading Style Sheets and Layers   **249**

   One Style Sheet—One Page 251
   Hey! Make with the Style Sheet Already, Bub! ... 251
   One Style Sheet—Many Pages 256
   Can I Use These Style Elements on Individual Items? ... 257
Positioning Things Precisely on Your Web Page ... 258
   Positioning an Image 259
   Positioning Text 261
   Can I Set Other Styles? 263

Using Classes and IDs 264
   Setting Up the STYLE *Section* 265
   Setting Up the Classes 265
   Putting the Classes to Work 266
   What About Those IDs? 267
CSS and Forms 268
   Adding a Background Color 270
   Adding a Separate Text Color 270
   Adding a ToolTip on Mouse-Over 271
   Adding Colored Buttons 271
CSS and Cursors? 272
CSS and the Scrollbar 274
   The Main Document Scrollbar 275
   The Textarea Scrollbar 275
   The Scrollbar Color Commands 276
Using Layer Commands 277
   Layering in General 280

9 Behind the Scenes on Your Web Site   **283**

   What the <HEAD> *Commands Actually Do* 284
   Information Regarding the Document 285
   Parts Two and Three 287
Declaring Your Version of HTML 288
Web Pages Without the .html Extension 289
   The Index Page 290
   How to Do It 291

10 Sound and Video   **293**

   Helper Applications 294
   Putting Sound on the Page 295
   Embedding Sound on a Page 295
   More About EMBED 299
RealAudio: A Special Format 300
   RealAudio from Your Site 301
   Creating the RealAudio Sound File 302
   Creating the RealAudio Meta File 302
   RealAudio in the HTML Document 303
   So What's the Downside? 303

Video on the Net 304
   Film and Video 305
   The Trick Is Compression 307
   Getting the Hardware 307
   Video Player Software 308

11   Java Applets and JavaScript   311

Java Applets 312
   How Does Your Browser Know It's a Java Applet? 313
   The Dancing Text Applet 314
JavaScript 320
   Let's Get Started 320
   JavaScript Requirements 323
   JavaScript Troubleshooting 323
Advanced JavaScript Commands 324
   The onMouseOver *Event Handler* 325
   onMouseOver *and Background Colors* 327
   The Alert *Event Handler* 328
   The onClick *Event Handler* 328
   Opening New Windows 333
   Page Inside a Page 336
   A New Window MIDI Trick 338
   Image Flip 339
Using External JavaScripts 342
   The Date Stamp 343
   Browser Choice Script 345
   Shopping Cart 348
Print with JavaScript 354
Saving Grace! 355
   Some Suggestions 356
Pre-Loading Images with JavaScript 357
   Why Pre-Load Anything? 357
   Load 'em 358
Post by Screen Size 359
   Redirection Choice 360
   Internal Page Choice 361

12 Common Gateway Interface (CGI)   363

Using a Hit Counter 364
  Formatting a Counter *365*
  Finding a CGI Counter on the Net *365*
Putting a Counter on Your Site 368
  How This Thing Works *369*
  Creating Directories with FTP *369*
  Creating Directories with Telnet *370*
  Making the CGI Directories *371*
  Grabbing the CGI Script and Modifying It *371*
  Finding the Absolute Path *372*
  Getting the Counter on the HTML Page *373*
  Keeping Others from Using Your Counter *374*
Putting a Guestbook on Your Site 375
  Getting the Guestbook on the HTML Page *375*
  Modifying the CGI Script *377*
  Activating the Guestbook *378*
Billboard Server (BBS) CGI 379
  Grab the CGI *379*
  Altering the Script for Your Server *379*
  The HTML Document *380*
  The BBS.html *Page* *381*
  That's It! *382*

13 Explorer-Specific Tutorials and DHTML   383

  Setting Static Backgrounds *384*
  Specifying Page Margins *384*
  Loading a Background Sound *384*
  Setting Table Properties *384*
Using IE Marquees 386
Using IE Active Channels 388
  Creating an Active Channel Link on Your Page *390*
Using Inline Frames with IE 394
  Adding the IFRAME *Command* *395*
  Adding Multiple Frames *395*
  I Want a Button! *397*
  Adding Invisible Frame Borders *397*
  Altering Inline Frames *399*

Using Dynamic HTML 400
   Is Dynamic HTML Really Being Used? 401
   Using DHTML for an Interactive Game 402
   Using DHTML for Page Transitions 406
So, You Want Your Own Bookmark Icon, Huh? 408
   The Icon 409
   Placing the Icon 410
   Wait! I Don't Have A Domain! 410
Add Your Page to Favorites 411
   Add This Page to Your Favorites 411
   The Code 411
   Only in IE 4.0 or Higher 412
   The Code 412
Setting Your Page as the Browser Home Page 413
   The Code 413
   Alter It 415
   Some Other Changes 415
   How About a Button? 415

14 Building Web Site Banners   **417**

Software Tools Needed 417
   Graphics Program 417
   GIF Animator Program 418
Banner Primer 1: Getting Started 419
Banner Primer 2: Creating New Images 422
   Creating a New Image 422
   Saving the Image 423
Banner Primer 3: Learning to Crop 425
   Cropping an Image 425
Banner Primer 4: Importing Images—Copying and
  Pasting 428
   Copying and Pasting 429
   Performing the Copy 430
   Performing the Paste 431
   Tearing the Ticket 433
Banner Primer 5: Adding Text and Shadows 436
   Text Color 436
   Text Font 438
   Text Size 441
   Adding Shadow 441

Banner Primer 6: Animating the Images 443
   Creating an Animation List 444
   Adding Time Sequence 445
   Creating an Animated GIF 447
Banner Primer 7: Activating the Image—Show Time 448
   Getting Your Banner Out There 448
   Placing Your Banner on a Page 450
   Keeping Track of Visitors 452
   Activating Your Banner 452

15 Other Stuff You Should Really Know   **455**

What Is a Copyright, Anyway? 455
   The Internet Is Public Domain, so Isn't Everything
    Fair Game? 455
   So, Is Making a Link to Another Copyrighted Page
    Against the Law? 456
   How Do I Get My Stuff Copyrighted? 456
   What Do I Put on the Page? 456
   Wait, Don't I Have to Send a Form to the Government? ..457
   How Do I Register with the Copyright Office? 457
   Can I Just Send in a Disk? 457
   Do I Have to Register all My Pages Separately? 457
   How Long Does My Copyright Last? 457
   I'm Just a Kid. Can I Get a Copyright? 458
   The Internet Is Global. What About Someone in
    Another Country Using My Stuff? 458
   What If I Copyright Something and Someone Else
    Copyrights the Same Thing? 458
   I Call My Site "Dog Breath." Can I Copyright That? 458
   This One Site Has a Great Image, But It's Copyrighted.
    Can I Use It? 458
   Can I Use Anything from a Site? 458
   I'll Just Post Everything and Cite to My Heart's Content ..459
   What if I Take the Person's Page and Change It a Little. Can I
    Copyright It? 459
   What Can I Do if Someone Uses My Copyrighted Stuff
    Without Getting Permission? 460
   What Do You Do when Someone Posts Part of HTML
    Goodies Without Permission? 460

Has This Ever Happened? 460

Would You? 460

What if I Use Something I Didn't Know Was Copyrighted? 460

What if I Am Using Something That Is Copyrighted and I Know It? 460

I'm Just a Kid. I Don't Have Anything to Take. Go Ahead! Sue Me! You Can't Do Anything to Me! 461

What if I Don't Take the Image, but Make a Link? 461

I Want Music or Video from My Favorite Group on My Site 461

But I Only Play a Portion, Like in the "Fair Use" Deal 461

I Play My Version of the Song on My Keyboard and Post That 461

I Play a Recording of an Old Beethoven Piece 462

What Is in Public Domain? 462

What if I Scan Something That's Copyrighted? 462

How Can I Be Sure Nothing on My Site Is Copyrighted? 462

Do You Do That? 462

Final Thoughts 463

What Are Cookies? 463

Cookies, Joe? 464

What Do Cookies Do? 464

Getting Back to Cookies… 465

Do You Hand Out Cookies on Goodies, Joe? 466

Temporary Versus Persistent Cookies 466

I Want to See a Cookie 468

What It All Means 468

Is That It? 470

Using META Commands with Search Engines 471

Search Engine…What's That? 471

What You Can Do with META Commands 472

Offering Keywords 472

Offering Your Page Generator 473

Offering a Description of Your Page 473

Author, Copyright, and Expire 473

Where Do I Place These on My Page? 474

What if I've Already Submitted the Pages? 474

How Do I Register My Pages with Search Engines? 474

   Registering Pages—What's That? 474

   It Isn't Always Free 475

   How It's Done 475

Getting Them all the Same: Cross-Platform Tips for
HTML Artists 477

   Tip One: Put Multiple Browsers on Your Computer 477

   *Tip Two: Write for the Browser That Is Pickiest About
Coding* 478

   *Tip Three: Enable the Browser to Decide When Long
Pieces of Text Wrap* 478

   Tip Four: Force Text Issues 478

   *Tip Five: You May Want to Stay Clear of Style Sheets
and Hard Code Most Elements* 478

   *Tip Six: Be Kind to Those Who Are Surfing Without
Images and Use* ALT *Commands* 479

   *Tip Seven: If You Use Imagemaps Offer Hypertext
Links Too* 479

   *Tip Eight: Do Not Use Frames Unless You Have a Very
Good Reason* 479

   *Tip Nine: JavaScript—I Love It, But Don't Get Crazy
with It* 480

   *Tip Ten: Only Use Applets If It Is Necessary—And It
Probably Isn't* 480

   Tip Eleven: Always Use both the EMBED *and*
BGSOUND *Commands* 480

   Tip Twelve: Force Your Page's Layout and Design 480

   Tip Thirteen: Force Your Page's Width 480

   *Tip Fourteen: If Possible, Use Pixels When Forcing
Widths* 481

   *Tip Fifteen: Use GIF Format for Icons and JPEG Format
for Larger Pictures* 481

   Tip Sixteen: Try to Avoid META *Refresh Tags* 482

   Tip Seventeen: Always Double-Align Text and Images 482

   *Tip Eighteen: DHTML Is only Supported by IE 4.0
and Higher* 482

   *Tip Nineteen: When Denoting Colors, Try to Use the
216 "Safe" Colors* 482

   *Tip Twenty: If You Need to Pick a Screen Resolution to
Design for, Choose 640×480* 482

   Tip Twenty-One: Write Simply 482

How Do I Get Advertisers on My Site? 483
   What Do You Have That People Want? 483
   What Is the Magic Number? 484
   How Much Do I Ask For? 484
   Flat-Rate CPM, Click-Throughs, or Impressions? 485
   How Do I Get Started? 485
   How Many Advertisers Should Go on One Page? 487
   Final Thoughts 487
So You Want a Web Ring, Huh? 487
   Web Ring? 488
   Web Ring Method One: Linear Rings 488
   Web Ring Method Two: Generated Rings 488
   Web Ring Method Three: Let Someone Else Handle It! 489
So You Want a Password Protected Page? 491
   Here's What Happens 491
   Do all Servers Work This Way? 492
What Is XML? 492
   What Is It? 493
   DTD—Document Type Definition 493
   Making Your Own Blocks 494
   Two Kinds of XML Pages 494
   Creating the DTD 495
   So Now What? 497
So You Want to Screen Capture? 497
   Be Careful of Violating Copyright Laws! 497
   Here's How You Do It 497
How to Use Telnet 501
   Telnet 501
   Where Do I Find Telnet? 501
   How Does It Work? 502
Writing for Disabled Assistant Browsers 503
   Priority One Tips 504
   Priority Two Tips 505
   Priority Three Tips 505
Charset 506
   The Code 507
   Other Charsets 507
   Why iso-8859-1 Rather Than us-ascii? 508
So, You Want A 404 Error Page, Huh? 509
   You'd Best Ask First 509

Your .htaccess File 509
Let's Edit It 510
Let's Turn It On 511

Part 5: Appendixes — 513

A Everything You Need to Know About HTML 4.0 — 515

Readers Questions Regarding HTML 4.0 516
What Is HTML 4.0? Should I Be Concerned About It? 516
I Use Netscape 4 (or Explorer 4). Does That Mean I
    Should Be Writing in HTML 4.0? 516
What Version of HTML Are We Currently Using? 517
Who Decided We Should All Go to HTML 4.0? 517
Every Time I Hear About HTML 4.0, I also Hear
    About SGML and XML. What Are They? 517
Will You Puh-Leeze Get to HTML 4.0!? 518
New Commands 518
Take Them for a Test Drive 522
Some New Attributes 522
Now Take These for a Test Drive 524
Deprecated Elements 524
Dead Elements 524
That's the Scoop 525

B Useful Charts — 527

Color Codes 527
Non-Dithering Color Chart 527
An Explanation of Hexadecimal Codes 530
Ampersand Commands 532
Here's How It Works 533
ASCII Commands 533

C Valuable Links — 537

Links to Search Engines 537
Ahoy! 537
AltaVista 537
Apollo—The Web's Advertising Catalog 537
BizAds Business Locator 537
ComFind—A Business Directory 538

EuroSeek 538
Excite 538
Galaxy 538
Google 538
Humor Search Comedy Search Engine 538
HotBot 538
Human Search—Real Humans Do the Search for You 538
Go.com 538
Inktomi 538
Internet Sleuth 538
Lycos 539
MoneySearch—Geared to Small Business and
   Investment 539
Nerd World Media 539
PedagoNet—Geared to Teaching and Learning Sites 539
Planet Search 539
Rescue Island 539
SoftSearch—Geared to Finding Software Programs 539
Webcrawler 539
Websurfer 539
What-U-Seek 539
WWWomen—Geared to Finding Sites Regarding
   Women's Issues 539
WWWW (The World Wide Web Worm) 540
Yahoo! 540
Search for Search Engines 540
Beaucoup's Search Engines—Close to 600 at Last Count ..540
Dr. Webster's Big Page of Search Engines 540
Search.Com—From C-Net Central 540
Yahoo!'s Search Engine Page—The Mother Lode 540
Registering with Search Engines 540
@Submit! 540
1–2–3–Register Me! 540
AnsurWeb Services 541
Add Me! 541
Linkosaurus 541
Postmaster 541
Register-It! 541
Submit-It! 541
Sites Offering JavaScripts 541
Danny Goodman's JavaScript Pages 541
HotSyte 541

JavaScript Authoring Guide 541
JavaScript FAQ 541
JavaScript Planet 542
JavaScript World 542
JavaScripts.com 542
Yahoo!'s Java Script Page 542
Pages Offering Java Applets 542
Gamelan 542
Jars.Com—A Massive Site with Links and Reviews 542
Java Boutique 542
Java Centre 542
SneakerChat—Applets for Creating Chat Rooms 542
Yahoo!'s Applet Page 542
HTML Helper Applications 543
MS FrontPage 543
Globetrotter Web Assistant 543
HotDog 543
HoTMetaL 543
HTML Assistant 543
HTMLpad 543
Web Director 543
Yahoo!'s HTML Editors 543
Yahoo!'s HTML Editor Review Page 543
Internet Browsers 544
Cello 544
HotJava—A Java-based Browser from Sun Microsystems ..544
Lynx—A text-only browser 544
Microsoft Internet Explorer 544
Mosaic for Windows 544
Mosaic for Macintosh 544
NetCruiser 544
Netscape Communicator—A Suite of Programs
  Including the Navigator 544
NetTamer—A DOS-based Browser 544
Opera 545
Voyager—Made for the Amiga Computer 545
WinWeb 545
Yahoo!'s Browser Page 545

Index   547

Preface

So you're reading the preface, huh? Good for you. I usually skip over them. It's so hard to pass up jumping right to Chapter 1. I actually do end up reading the preface, but only after I finish the book itself. Strange, yes, but that's what I do.

Hopefully you're not following my out-of-order lead and are reading this first. It helps you a great deal in understanding how this book was put together, why I did all this, and how you can use it to start putting yourself on the Cyberspace road map.

A Little History...

Around 1992, when the World Wide Web was still something most people had never heard about, a new browser called Netscape 1.0 had come out and I started studying for a Ph.D. in communications at a large university in Ohio. During the first couple of weeks of the semester, everyone wanted to get hooked up to the school's Internet server so they could send e-mail around. I was the first to successfully attach. It was more dumb luck than skill.

Of course, that also meant I was the first to be called when someone else couldn't seem to make his connection. After helping three or four people, somehow I was given the moniker "Computer Wizard." It was a totally groundless title, but one I wasn't willing to give up by telling the truth.

Word spread to the computer science department of this great computer guru housed within the communications building. They needed someone to teach a section of basic computers. I nervously accepted. Luckily, it was getting to be Christmas break, which meant a month's free time. I had to teach myself the computer. I traded a guy the use of his computer in exchange for a month of taking care of his cats. When I got started, however, I found I did have a knack for these fancy thinkin' boxes. I began to become consumed by what they could do.

When school started again, the Webmaster asked if I wanted some World Wide Web space on his server. At this stage in my computer learning curve, he might as well have been speaking Lebanese. But it was free. I took it. http://www.cs.bgsu.edu/~jburns was created that afternoon.

I began asking anyone who seemed to have any form of computer knowledge how to go about making a Web page. Very few were willing to offer any help. It seemed that if I were going to learn this HTML language, I was going to have to teach myself.

My first and only home page to this point existed only on a computer disk. It had clean lines and looked good. Later in the same day that the page was finished, I got into a conversation with the head of the computer department, who asked what I had been up to lately. I showed her my page. She asked if I would be willing to teach the HTML summer class.

Sure.

Once again, I had accepted a position I was completely unqualified to perform. I started looking at the source codes of World Wide Web pages, collecting, categorizing, and sub-categorizing the commands and what they did. There wasn't a chance on earth that I was going to remember all this, so I wrote seven tutorials covering seven basic HTML areas. The purpose was to help me remember the required commands while lecturing.

I also collected a handful of images that all looked like little pieces of candy, what my father use to call *goodies*. The name stuck. The first HTML Goodies page went up in June 1994.

I figured it couldn't hurt to register the tutorials with Webcrawler and Yahoo!. I had a hard enough time learning this myself. If I could make someone else's life a little easier, all the better.

A month went by and I received a letter from the Webmaster who had offered me the space in the first place. He was yelling, as much as one can yell in an e-mail letter, that so many people were using my site that it was putting a strain on the server. It seemed that I had built the better mousetrap. People were coming in droves.

The e-mail poured in. People wrote long, emotion-filled, thank you letters, telling me they were happy to have found a site that showed them HTML in a language they could understand. No one had yet taken the time to explain the language in simple English, let alone offer it on the World Wide Web. Others wrote with questions. I started answering them. Within three months of posting the pages, I was answering 20 questions a day and servicing some 50,000 people a month. And they keep coming…

In November 1996, the domain name `htmlgoodies.com` was born. I had my first advertiser not too long after that. AOL was nice enough to buy ad space.

Since then the site has been sold and then resold. At the time of this writing (May 2001), Internet.com owns HTML Goodies. The one thing I am happy with is that through both sales, the new owners basically left me in charge. I have been the sole author since 1994. HTML Goodies is still enjoying many visitors. High schools, universities, and colleges around the nation and the world visit the site heavily. It's fun to watch the visitation numbers jump during finals week. It's not unheard of for HTML Goodies to provide over two million page views a week during that time.

I have received e-mail from Web designers as young as 9 and as old as 84. The e-mail arrives from everywhere you can imagine. It's a great feeling when I hear that I have helped military personnel in Guam, a housewife in Wisconsin, and a student in St.

Petersburg, Russia.

HTML Goodies has also grown beyond just a Web site. Just after this book's first edition came out, I started a weekly newsletter titled, "Goodies to Go!" I'm stilling putting it out and over 200,000 are reading it.

HTML Goodies now supports over 180 tutorials and services over a million people a month. And yes, I still attempt to answer as many e-mail questions as I can. Often, this is just not a lot. I may get to reply to 40, but 200 are still waiting to be read.

This second edition is the culmination of seven years of research, hard work, and an untold number of questions from readers.

What I Believe

The purpose of this book is to enable you to teach yourself to write HTML. Some may suggest that actually learning HTML code is no longer required now that software applications that build the pages for you are available.

Resist. Learn the language.

I believe HTML is an art. My pages are my creations, my art. Learning to build Web pages by clicking buttons in a helper program is not creating.

A Goodies visitor once told me that she created almost her entire site using a software application that did 90% of the work.

However, she saved one page for herself. She placed every command and worried over the modification of every shape and structure. It's her favorite page. She called it her "child" because she sees all her hard work every time she looks at it.

Don't miss that feeling.

About the Author

Joe Burns, **Ph.D.** began writing HTML tutorials in 1994 to be able to remember complex commands while teaching. Less than a month after his first five HTML Goodies tutorials were available, they were the most visited pages on the university Web site. At one point, the tutorials were taken down for a short while because the volume of visitors was putting too much of a strain on the server. The site exploded into millions of visitors in 1996 when seven HTML primers and 10 new tutorials were added to the first five to create HTMLGoodies.com. HTML Goodies is now the largest HTML help site on the Web, supporting over 180 tutorials, hundreds of free images, and numerous bad jokes. The site serves close to 8 million page views a month from a mind-boggling number of users. The site has won over 170 awards, been reviewed favorably in national newspapers and magazines, and continues to grow.

Burns holds a Ph.D. in communications from Bowling Green State University. He's currently a professor of communications at Southeastern Louisiana University, where he lives with his wife and two cats, Mardi and Chloe.

Dedication

This book is dedicated to my wife, Tammy, who always seems to have more faith in me than I ever seem to have in myself.

Acknowledgments

My very special thanks to Dr. Bruce Klopfenstein for making me buy my first modem; Dr. Ann Marie Lancaster for enabling me to teach HTML for the first time; Ben Amerman for setting up the first HTMLGoodies.com; everyone at Wolverine Web Productions (now Go Beyond Media) for helping me create the HTML Goodies hierarchy format; Murray, Jen, Mike (Joe, how the heck are ya?), John, and Brian at EarthWeb for the use of their huge powerful servers and being there just before I gave it all up for good; and my editors, Tim Ryan and Todd Green, for putting up with my rants.

On a personal side, thanks to my mother for being the inspiration for my writing style. I knew if I could write so she understood the concept, I was at the right level. And to my father who instilled in me that a thank you is enough payment for doing something nice for someone else.

Thank you to all the people who would *not* help me learn HTML when I first got started. It was because of you I promised myself that if I ever learned this language, I would do my best to make it so others wouldn't have such a hard time.

Thanks to Lindy who agreed to edit this second edition.

And of course, thanks to everyone who ever visited or wrote an e-mail letter to me over the last six years. It has all been taken to heart to create what you read today.

…and Gus

Tell Us What You Think!

As the reader of this book, *you* are our most important critic and commentator. We value your opinion and want to know what we're doing right, what we could do better, what areas you'd like to see us publish in, and any other words of wisdom you're willing to pass our way.

As the Executive Editor for the Web development team at Que Publishing, I welcome your comments. You can fax, e-mail, or write me directly to let me know what you did or didn't like about this book—as well as what we can do to make our books stronger.

Please note that I cannot help you with technical problems related to the topic of this book, and that due to the high volume of mail I receive, I might not be able to reply to every message.

When you write, please be sure to include this book's title and author as well as your name and phone or fax number. I will carefully review your comments and share them with the author and editors who worked on the book.

Fax: 317-581-4666

E-mail: feedback@quepublishing.com

Mail: Executive Editor
            Web Development
            Que Publishing
            201 West 103rd Street
            Indianapolis, IN 46290 USA

Introduction

About This Book

Have you ever embarked on a new project and found it difficult to get all the information you need? Sometimes it gets to the point where you throw up your hands and scream, "I wish someone would just explain this to me!"

Me too. I had a hard time finding anyone who would just simply tell me how HTML was done, let alone explain it in a language I could understand.

That's why I built the HTML Goodies site and wrote this book. I promised myself that if I ever learned this language, I would do my best to make it easier for the next person. It makes me very happy to say that my HTML Goodies site gets more than two million page views a week from a lot of people like you.

This book is a series of self-contained tutorials written in a very friendly, conversational method. Everything needed is contained within the lesson. Checking in the previous chapters for information is not necessary. If that means I have to offer the same command in three or four different tutorials, I do. And the great thing is that my HTML Goodies Web site has a wealth of code, graphics, JavaScript, and other stuff that you can use for free.

Click Here *This icon gives you the address on a specific page of the HTML Goodies Web site where you can download stuff and see exactly how the examples in the book work.*

I tried to put together the most complete book possible. HTML is covered from the ground up. But even more, I go into what you need to do with the pages you write, what makes a good home page, how to get people to visit you, how to get a domain and sell advertising, and what concerns you should have about copyright. All the color codes and ASCII and ampersand commands are contained, as well as a full list of all available HTML commands for quick reference. It also contains a glossary for some of those more interesting acronyms computer people love to throw around.

You're going to have questions. I know—I answer around 150 a day from the HTML Goodies Web site. I've tried to anticipate your queries and have put them in the sidebars that show up throughout the book. On the Web these types of questions are called *FAQs* (Frequently Asked Questions). The FAQs are all true readers' questions taken straight from the Goodies e-mail box. I bet you see your own questions asked and answered in one or more of these sidebars.

My Thoughts on Building a Web Site

I start with the most asked questions I receive: "What should my Web site look like?" Up until now I thought it would be a bit bold to state my views on home page building because I believe that HTML is an art and telling you how to create your art would be a bit egotistical on my part. But there was nothing good on television this weekend, so here goes:

> I've actually now gone as far as to write an entire book regarding what I feel should be on a Web site. The book is called *Web Design Goodies* (ISBN: 0-7897-2485-5, Que Publishing) and should be available right where you bought this book.

These suggestions are my own thoughts; they are by no means laws or rules. If you want to disregard everything I write, do it. Goodness knows I've been wrong before.

If you are brand new to HTML, some of the suggestions might not make sense right off. But read it through—when you get to the tutorial that explains that part in more detail. You already have an idea on how to use it.

The Four Basic Rules

Above all else, I believe this:

- Offer something worthwhile—Content is the most important part of your Web site. If the reader leaves your page asking herself, "Why did I come here?" the mission has not been accomplished. You have been given this small bit of space with which to post what is important to you. Web sites have become the business cards of the twenty-first century. Tell me about yourself, post your poetry, write a story, show me pictures of your cats, tell me a good joke, show me pictures of your son or daughter, or just tell me what makes you, you. Give me something in return for my time with you. I want to leave your site a little more enriched than when I came.

- Make it easy on me—Don't make me have to search for the items on your page. This is especially important when talking about your hypertext links. Get them up high on the pages. Don't fill up with 20 JavaScripts, 15 applets, 12 scrolling words, flashing lights, and polar opposite colors. Make it so the links are obvious. Use words such as Click Here for This. If the page does scroll, give me a quick way to get to the section I want.

- Answer me—I get letters telling me that it was amazing that I wrote back. If someone writes to you, that is a form of communication. They want you to respond. You have posted this page. You gave people a way to contact you. Talk back.

- Change is good—Work on your page. Update it. Add to it. Fix it when a problem arises. Show me that you are taking as great an interest in your page as you want me to take. Static pages die slow. People just stop coming.

Was that too preachy?

The Home Page

This is your welcome mat. A well-known commercial states that you never get another chance to make a first impression. Here it is. This page should be representative of you, your site, and should immediately guide the viewer. Big graphics aren't needed. Style, page layout, and guidance are what work best.

Make your home page small and simple. It should never be longer than two screens. Get it all onto one if you can. Offering a ton of good information is not a problem. Just don't attempt to offer it all on the home page. In fact, offer none of it. Use the home page as a map to all the great information. Multiple pages are much easier to surf than one big page that melds into a useless block of text. Think of your home page as the body of a spider. Everything comes out from and is attached to it.

The following are the things that bug me most on home pages:

- A home page that is just a logo, corporate, or otherwise.
- The logo is active and you're supposed to click it to go further. Why? Don't get me started.
- A home page that asks if you want frames or no frames. That drives me nuts. Pick one!
- A home page with multiple advertising banners. I like Bannermania, the Internet Link Exchange, and money too, but it just takes too long to load.

- A home page with only text telling me how great the following is going to be. It changes for me or asks me to click to continue to the real home page. This should be outlawed or at least severely punished.
- Ditto with JavaScripts telling the same. The silly thing comes up every time I return to the home page.
- No more double windows please! Just one window is fine, thanks. I don't need the main window and then a second smaller window with other links that open other windows.

Images

Let's be honest. The World Wide Web is what it is today because of images. The ability to place pictures is just the greatest part of this pup. Don't get me wrong. I love images. But I must stay within the limits.

When to use:

- GIF—GIF is a format of little colored dots. After the image is created, no further compression occurs when it is stored. (It occurs when the file is created, but not afterward.) What is transferred is what is displayed. GIF is good for pictures without great detail or many lines. Icons and line art look great in GIF. GIFs can also be saved at 256, or all the way down to two colors, and still look crisp. I think uncomplicated black and white images look best in GIF.
- JPEG—JPEG is a compressed format. That means it is sort of squashed together when it's put away. JPEG saves images using a pallet of 16.7 million colors. That means it is best for images with a great many colors. Scanned photos and very detailed images look best in JPEG.

In terms of images:

- Go with as few as possible to cut down on load time. I know they look great, but waiting for them to load is dull. Learn the value of understatement. Images are support for content. Your site must first have good content. The images simply go to support that good content.
- Always denote every image's height and width. Not a suggestion—do this.
- If at all possible, combine images that sit next to each other into one big image. That helps a lot with load time. If the images need to be different links, make the image an image map.
- As often as possible, offer people the choice of whether to look at large images. Your photos from the last family reunion may be great, but no one outside of your

immediate family sits through 20 50K JPEGs loading into their browser window. Offer links to the images and explain them and people can decide whether or not to view them.

- Go easy on the animation and applet motion. I speak the truth here. One good animation is far better than nine pretty good ones.
- Lose the blue border on active links images. Maybe this is just personal opinion here, but that blue border is annoying, especially on imagemaps. Lose it by placing BORDER="0" into the image command between the IMG and the SRC.
- Use ALT commands. Be nice to those who surf without images.
- I hit on this previously, but it's best to restate it here. Content cannot be replaced by graphics. If what you are offering is dull or not worth someone's time, no amount of graphic support does the trick.

Backgrounds

I love a good background image, no doubt. However, remember that it slows the completion of the page. If you are going to use a background image, ask yourself these questions:

> What does it do for the page? If it visually helps it, great—keep it. Just try to make the background image as small as possible to cut down on load time.

> Does it disrupt the text? If the text is at all hard to read, lose the background or do something to the text. Remember that content, not the image, is the most important part of your site.

Colors

Love 'em! I think the use of color in a Web site is wonderful. The main reason I like color commands is that they are part of the HTML document and they don't tax the server any more than they have to. Just watch a few things:

- Pick complementary colors—your mother taught you how to dress. You know a gross combination when you see one.
- If when you stare at the page, the text appears to be moving around—bad color combination. Enough said.
- Bright primary colors tend to tire the eye. Pastels and calm color combinations work better.
- Try to use color to draw the eye. Get attention through the use of one bright color. If everything on the page is turned up to 11, nothing stands out.
- Just because colors are available doesn't mean you have to use them.

Text

I mean what you write here. This is where I really can't say much. This is your page and you have every right to write what you want, topics or otherwise. I just have one simple rule:

> Brevity is the heart of wit.

Say what you are going to say quickly, with as few words as possible. Looking back over the size of this section, it seems even I have trouble following that rule.

Hopefully, you can take something from this. I truly don't mean to be high and mighty here, but I thought this might be helpful. Even so, feel free to ignore it all. It is your page, after all, and I respect that a great deal.

No matter what you do, I still think these four main points apply:

- Offer something worthwhile. Content is the most important part of your Web site.
- Make it easy on me.
- Answer me.
- Change is good.

Here's to writing great Web pages that make up a great Web site!

Enjoy!

Part I

How to Build a Web Site in 7 Steps

Primer 1   *What You Need to Get Started*

Primer 2   *Flags and Commands*

Primer 3   *Manipulating Text*

Primer 4   *Making a Link to Someone Else*

Primer 5   *Placing an Image on Your Page*

Primer 6   *Manipulating Images*

Primer 7   *Graduation Day*

What You Need to Get Started

Welcome to HTML.

This is Primer 1, in a series of seven, that calmly introduces you to the very basics of HTML (Hypertext Markup Language). I suggest you read the primers one at a time over seven days. By the end of the week, you'll easily know enough to create your own HTML home page and site. No, really you will.

Many people scoff at the notion that they can actually learn this Internet language. I'm still amazed that one of the best-selling lines of computer books calls its readers "dummies." People seem to revel in that title. Some of the smartest people I know love to proclaim themselves "dummies" regarding every aspect of computers. Strangely, I think you'll do a whole lot better at your next cocktail party by handing out your home-page address rather than laughing about how dumb you are regarding the Internet.

You *can* do this!

 Visit this tutorial online at http://www.htmlgoodies.com/primers/primer_1.html.

What Do I Need to Create a Web Page?

I'm assuming that you know nothing about HTML. However, I am assuming you have some computer knowledge. You wouldn't be looking at this page without having some knowledge. To continue with these primers, you need

1. A computer (obviously)

2. A browser such as Netscape Navigator, Microsoft Explorer, Opera, or Mosaic (you probably have one if you've purchased this book)

3. Access to Window's Notepad program or the Macintosh SimpleText program

Those are all you need to create a Web site, but you need a few more things once you've created the site, which are mentioned in Primer 7, "Graduation Day." These help make your site available on the Internet so people can see it. The following FAQ may contain a few questions you have:

FAQs from the HTML Goodies Web Site

Q. I have a Macintosh (or IBM). Will this work on my computer?

A. Yes. HTML does not use any specific platform; it works with simple text.

Q. Must I be logged onto the Internet to do this? More specifically, will learning this throw my cost for online way up?

A. No—to both. You write HTML offline.

Q. Do I need some sort of expensive program to help me write this?

A. No. You write using Notepad, SimpleText, or another word processor. You can buy those programs if you'd like, but they are not essential. I have never used one. In fact, I suggest that, until you learn the language, you stay away from using one. Learn HTML first, then go and seek out an HTML assistant.

Q. Is this going to require that I learn a whole new computer language, such as Basic, Fortran, or some other cryptic, silly-looking, gothic, extreme gobbledygook?

A. Touchy, aren't we? No is your answer. HTML is not a traditional computer language. No programming is involved. Allow me to repeat that. HTML is not some complicated computer language!

What Is HTML?

HTML stands for Hypertext Markup Language. Computer people love acronyms—you'll be talking acronyms ASAP. Let me break it down for you:

- *Hyper* is the opposite of linear. Computer programs in the past had to move in a linear fashion. This before this, this before this, and so on. However, HTML is not like that. It allows the person viewing the World Wide Web page to go anywhere anytime they want.

- *Text* is what you use—real, honest-to-goodness English letters.
- *Markup* is what you do. You write in plain English and then mark up what you wrote. I have more to come on that in Primer 2, "Flags and Commands."
- *Language* because the creators needed something that started with *L* to finish HTML, and Hypertext Markup *Louie* didn't flow correctly. (Because it's a language, really.)

HTML is the language you use to write your Web pages. It tells the browser how you want your text and graphics to be arranged and denotes if something is bold or underlined. HTML is also used to insert images and make words act as links to other pages. It's easy. As I said earlier, you can do this.

Some More Information Before Writing

You actually begin to write HTML in Primer 2. For now I just want to tell you how to go about creating a Web page with HTML.

You write the HTML document with Notepad or with Simple Text. When you are finished, read the document in the browser (such as Netscape Navigator). You create the code first and then view it in the browser. Keep that in mind.

Those who are schooled in HTML are going to immediately jump up and down and yell that you should be using an HTML assistant program (such as HotDog, FrontPage, or Dreamweaver) because it makes it easier. Perhaps, but it also makes it harder to learn HTML because the program does half the work for you. Take my word for it: Use the word processor until you learn HTML, or at least until you complete these primers. Then go to the assistant if you want to. (I even tell you later how to get one.) You'll be far better off for the effort.

Creating HTML Documents with a Word Processor

You should strive to use Notepad or SimpleText, but many have told me that they want to use their word processor. Some are just more comfortable in Word or WordPerfect. Fine.

If you write with the word processor (this does not apply to Notepad or SimpleText), you need to follow a few steps. Here they are:

1. Write the page as you would any other document.
2. Save the document, but the trick is to always choose Save As.
3. Save the page in a specific format when the Save As box pops up. Look at the box when you get into the word processor; there is a place where you can change the file format.

4. If you have an IBM-compatible computer, save your document as ASCII text DOS or just text format.

5. If you have a Macintosh, save your document as text format.

Please remember that it is very important to choose Save As every time you save your document. If you don't, your program may not save as text, but as its default format. In layman's terms, use Save As or you mess up your document.

Notepad and SimpleText save your work as text without being prompted. So all the preceding steps need not be followed. It's almost as if the programs were made to write HTML documents. In fact, I still use Notepad to write some of my pieces.

How to Name Your HTML Document

You must name your document and add a suffix to it. What you name your document is very important. That's the way everything works in HTML. Follow these steps to name your document:

1. Give it a name. If you have an IBM that's not running Windows 95, you are limited to eight letters.

2. Add a suffix. For all HTML documents, add .htm or .html—.htm for PCs with Windows 3.1 and .html for Macintoshes and PCs running Windows 95 or 98.

Let's say I am naming a document I just wrote on an IBM machine and I want to name the document *fred*. I'm using an IBM, so the name of the document must be fred.htm. If it were a Macintosh I would name it fred.html. Please notice the dot (.) before .htm and .html!

Uhhhhhh…Why Do I Do That?

Glad you asked. It's a thing called *association*. It's how computers tell different things apart. .html tells the computer that this file thing is an HTML document. When you get into graphics, the suffix is different. All files are `name.suffix`—always.

Why `.htm` for Some and `.html` for Others?

Older operating systems such as Windows 3.1 can only handle what's known as an 8.3 filename. This means the file can only have an eight-letter name and a three-letter suffix. Macintoshes and PCs with Windows 95 or 98 allow four—or more—letter suffixes. Your browser can read all files, whether they have three- or four-letter suffixes. I would stick with three letters, in case you want to transfer your files to a PC with an older operating system. That's just a suggestion. Feel free to ignore it.

Why Do I Save It as Text or ASCII Text DOS?

You're just full of questions! HTML browsers can only read text. Look at your keyboard. See the letters, numbers, and little symbols such as %, @, and *? That's all considered text. That's what the browser reads.

If you do not save as text or ASCII text DOS, you are saving a lot more than just the text. You are saving your margin settings, your tab setting, bold, italics, and so on. With a browser, you don't want all that—*just the text*! All that other stuff confuses your browser and makes your Web site look a mess.

Remember that if you are using Notepad or SimpleText, the document is saved as text with no extra prompting. Just choose Save.

Opening Your HTML Document in a Browser

When you have your HTML document on the floppy disk or hard drive, you need to open it in the browser using the following steps:

1. Under the File menu (top-left of this screen), you find Open, Open Page, Open File, or other words to that effect.

2. Click those words. In some browsers a dialog box immediately opens. Explorer users, and users of later Netscape versions, need to click the Browse or Choose File button to get to the dialog box. When you get there, switch to the A:\ drive (or the floppy disk for Macintosh users) or C:\ drive depending on where you saved your file and open your document.

3. The browser does the rest.

FAQs from the HTML Goodies Web Site

Q. I opened my document in the browser and saw all the code I wrote instead of the Web page. What gives?

A. Ten bucks says you saved the file with a .txt extension rather than an .htm or .html extension.

One More Thing

You now easily have enough to keep you occupied for the first day. Don't worry. The primers get less wordy after this.

If you are going to do this, I suggest you make a point of learning to look at other people's HTML pages. You say you're already doing that, right? Maybe. What I mean is for you to look at the HTML document that presents the page you are looking at. Don't look at the pretty page; look behind it at the document.

Why Would I Do That?

Let's say you run into a page that has a really neat layout, a fancy text pattern, or a strange grouping of pictures. You'd probably like to know how to do it so you can use it. I'm not telling you to steal anything, but let's be honest—if you see some landscaping you like, you're going to use the idea. If you see a room layout you like, use the idea. That's the point of looking at another page's HTML document.

Here, I give you an Internet URL (that's computerspeak for a Uniform Resource Locator. Non-computer people call it a Web address). The page is located on my site. You can go into the page and look at the HTML I used to make it. The instructions on how to do this are printed right on the Web page.

And by the way, please feel free to look at the HTML code of any of the pages posted on HTML Goodies. Then go ahead and use the code yourself. I want you to. That's what Goodies is for!

 To find out how to view the HTML code behind any Web page, go to `http://www.htmlgoodies.com/book/firstpage.html`.

The following steps tell you how to view the HTML that was used to create a Web page (this doesn't work for AOL, but keep reading):

1. When you find a page you like, open the View menu on your browser. You'll find it way at the top of the browser screen.
2. Choose Document Source from the menu.
3. The HTML document appears on the screen as it was written.

It looks like chicken-scratch right now, but by the end of the week, it looks readable and you are able to find exactly how a certain HTML presentation was performed.

Those of you who use AOL can see the source code by right-clicking the page. You get a little window that offers you the ability to see the code.

That's the primer for today. Get ready to dive in and write your first HTML document. See you tomorrow...or whenever you turn the page.

FAQs from the HTML Goodies Web Site

Q. Should I really use someone else's code? Isn't that against copyright?

A. I didn't tell you to steal code straightaway and paste it to your page (except from HTML Goodies; I gave you permission to do that). Besides, what fun would that be? You are new to HTML. You should take the time to view pages that are already finished and try picking out commands you already know. In addition, seeing how someone else set code helps you build your own pages. That said, don't just copy and paste someone else's code.

Flags and Commands

Hello and welcome to Primer 2. No doubt you've attempted to write a small document on your word processor and save it in the appropriate text format. You remembered to save the document with the `.htm` or `.html` suffix, I'm sure. Good. Now let's move on to today's lesson—you write!

 Visit this tutorial online at `http://www.htmlgoodies.com/primers/primer_2.html`.

What Are Flags?

HTML works in a very simple and very logical format. It reads like you do—left to right and top to bottom. That's important to remember. HTML is written with text—English text. You use a series of *flags* to distinguish this text as bigger, smaller, bold, underlined, and so on.

Think of flags as commands. Let's say you want a line of text to be bold. You put a flag at the exact point where you want the bold lettering to start and another flag where you want the bold lettering to stop. If you want just a word to be italicized, you place a start italic flag at the beginning of the word and an end italic flag at the end of the word. Is this making sense so far?

All flag formats are the same. They begin with a less than sign (<) and end with a greater than sign (>)—no exceptions. The command goes inside the < and >. When you learn

HTML, you are learning the code to perform whatever manipulation you want. The HTML flag for bold lettering is <B>. That makes sense. The following are the flags that turn the word *Joe* bold:

```
<B>Joe</B>
```

Let's look closer at what's happening:

1. <B> is the open bold flag. It turns bold on.
2. Joe is the word being affected by the <B> flag.
3. </B> is the close bold flag. It turns bold off. Notice that the close bold flag is exactly the same as the open flag, except a slash is in front of the B.

FAQs from the HTML Goodies Web Site

Q. Is the close flag for other commands simply the open flag with the added slash?

A. Yup.

Q. Will the flags show up on my page?

A. No. As long as your commands are inside the < and > marks, they perform the command, but are hidden from the viewer.

Q. Your bold flag uses a capital B. Do all HTML flags use a capital letter?

A. The browser doesn't care. In terms of flags, uppercase and lowercase letters are equal, but it is a very good idea for you to make a habit of writing your flags in uppercase letters, as it sets them apart from the normal text.

Q. Must everything have a flag to show up on the page?

A. No. Text with no flags will show up, but the text will not have any special look. It will not be "Marked-Up."

Q. What if I forget to add the close flag or forget to add the slash to the close flag command?

A. That's trouble, but easy-to-fix trouble. It will be obvious if you've not placed an end flag when you look at the document in your browser. All the text that follows the un-ended command will be affected.

Q. Do all HTML flags require both an open and close flag?

A. No. There are exceptions to the rule, but let's stay on those that do require both flags to work.

Open and Close Flags

The majority of HTML flags do require both an open and a close flag (a begin and end flag). Table P2.1 shows a few flags and what they do to text.

Table P2.1   A Few HTML Flags

Effect	Flags	How It Looks
Bold	`<B>Bold</B>`	**Bold**
Italic	`<I>Italic</I>`	*Italic*
Typewriter	`<TT>Typewriter</TT>`	`Typewriter`

Can I Use Two Flags at Once?

You're probably wondering if you can use two flags at once. The answer is yes! One of the neat things about HTML is that you can combine flags to make different effects. Just make sure to open and close both sets of flags, like so:

`<B><I>Bold and Italic</I></B>` gives you ***Bold and Italic***

`<B><TT>Typewriter and Bold</TT></B>` gives you `Typewriter and Bold`

FAQs from the HTML Goodies Web Site

Q. If I use two types of flags (like bold and italic), does it matter in what order they are used?

A. You should try to keep the tags in order. As seen earlier in the bold and italic example, if the bold command is closest to the affected word on the left, it should be closest on the right and if italic is second closest on the left, it should be second closest on the right.

Single Flags

The open and close flags format dominates the majority of the available HTML flags, but some flags stand alone. Table P2.2 shows the three most commonly used single flags, and Figure P2.1 shows how they look on a Web page.

Table P2.2   Most Commonly Used Single Flags

Flag	What It Does
`<HR>`	This command gives you a line across the page. (HR stands for Horizontal Reference.)

Table P2.2   Most Commonly Used Single Flags (continued)

Flag	What It Does
 	This BReaks the text and starts it again on the next line. Remember that you saved your document as text, so where you hit Enter to jump to the next line was not saved. In an HTML document, you need to denote where you want every carriage return with a .
<P>	This stands for Paragraph. It does the exact same thing as the except that this flag skips a line. just jumps to the next line. <P> skips a line before starting the text again.

Figure P2.1

The <HR>, <BR>, *and* <P> *flags.*

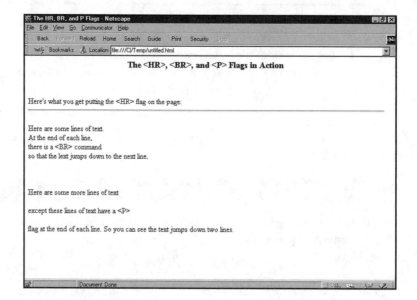

Writing Your First Web Page

So here you go. You're going to write your first HTML page using what you have learned, in addition to two other items. These two items are important to every page that you ever write. Why? Because they are on every page you ever write.

1. You start every page with this: <HTML>. That makes sense. You are denoting that this is an HTML document.

2. Your next command is always this: <TITLE> and </TITLE>. Look at the very top of your browser the next time you have it open. See the blue line way up top? What you write between these <TITLE> commands appears in the blue line.

3. Finally, end every page you write with this: </HTML>. Get it? You started the page with <HTML> and you end the page with </HTML>. That makes sense again.

So Here You Go!

I want you to play around with these commands. Just remember that HTML reads like you do—top to bottom, left to right. It responds where you place the open flag and stops where you place the close flag. Just make sure your commands are within < and >.

The following is a sample page to show you what I want you to do:

```
<HTML>
<TITLE> My first HTML page </TITLE>
<B>This is my first HTML page!</B><P>
I can write in <I>Italic</I> or <B>Bold</B><BR>
<HR>
<B><I>Or I can write in both</I></B><BR>
<HR>
<TT>...and that's all</TT>
</HTML>
```

Notice that I only used the flags I showed you on this page. Yes, it's a simple page, but you're just starting out. Notice the <HTML> and </HTML> at the beginning and end of the page. Notice <TITLE> and </TITLE>. See an open and close flag and how the <P> and <BR> commands are used to go to new lines?

Figure P2.2 shows you what all this looks like when viewed through a browser.

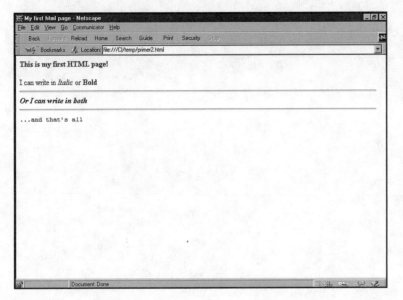

Figure P2.2
How your first Web page looks in a browser.

21

FAQs from the HTML Goodies Web Site

Q. Hey! Where's <TITLE>? I swear I did them, but I don't see them!

A. <TITLE> is probably there, you're just not looking in the right place. Remember, the title appears in the colored bar, usually blue, way at the top of the screen. It doesn't show up on the actual browser window.

Look at the program and then at what it produced. See how the HTML flags denote where text was affected? Good! I knew you would. Now go! Go into the world—or at least to your word processor—and create. Follow the instructions in Primer 1, "What You Need to Get Started," to help you save and then display your first HTML page.

You can do this!

Manipulating Text

How did it go with your first HTML page? I assume it went well. If I don't assume such, I can't go on, and I want to go on. Now you know the basics about placing flags and manipulating text in terms of bold, italic, and typewriter font. That's good. With that knowledge along with the <HR>, <BR>, and <P> commands, you are able to play with text placement. Now, I talk about changing text size.

 Visit this tutorial online at http://www.htmlgoodies.com/primers/primer_3.html.

Heading Flags

Heading flags are used extensively on HTML documents to—you guessed it—create headings! How novel.

The six heading flags are <H1> through <H6>. <H1> is the largest and <H6> is the smallest. Headings need open and close flags, as shown in Figure P3.1.

Heading commands create nice bold text, as shown in Figure P3.1, and are quite easy to use. The format is a simple <H#> and </H#> format. However, they do have one other annoying trait. They like to be alone. When you use a heading command, the text is set alone by default. It's like the heading commands carry a <P> command with them. Getting other text to sit next to it is hard. It acts as if it wants to be, dare I say, a heading. Try a few for yourself.

Figure P3.1
The six heading flags.

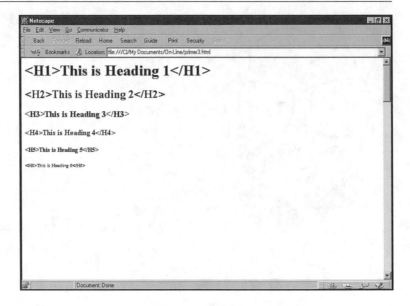

Font Size Commands

Maybe you'd like a little more control over your text size. Well, here it is: the <FONT SIZE> flags. Heading commands are great for text at the top of the page and they're also good for separating your Web page into logical sections of text.

The 12 font size flags available to you are +6 through +1 and -1 through -6. As you probably guessed, +6 is the largest. That's huge. The smallest one is -6. That's a little small. Figure P3.2 shows a few in action. Follow this pattern to place one on your page:

```
<FONT SIZE="##">
```

The ## can be anything from +6 to -6.

Notice that the first flag is actually doing two things:

1. Asking for a new font size.
2. Offering a number with which to denote the font size.

This is what's referred to as an *attribute*. When you have that, you denote the subcommand with an equal sign (=) and enclose it within quotation marks. Look at the preceding code. Do you see the equal sign, and the plus or minus number (##) in quotation marks? That's the attribute.

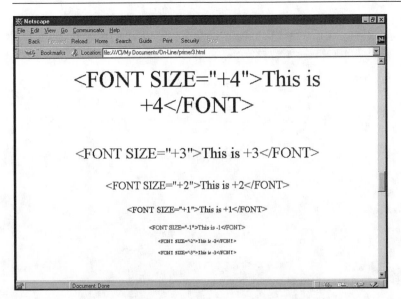

Figure P3.2
Changing font sizes with the <FONT SIZE> *flag.*

Also notice in Figure P3.2 that the close flag for a <FONT SIZE> flag only requires </FONT>. The reason is because FONT is the flag and SIZE is the attribute. You need only close the flag. The attribute need not be closed.

FAQs from the HTML Goodies Web Site

Q. Every so often I come to these pages that have really great text. It's like the letters are made out of steel or blood or other stuff. How do I do that?

A. I think if you look at the source code you'll learn that the text is really an image or series of images rather than a different font. In Primer 5, "Placing an Image on Your Page," I get into how to place images on your page.

Centering and Aligning Text

Because you've already created a few Web pages, you no doubt noticed that the text always starts at the left of the screen. That's the default; it just happens without you doing anything. What if you want your text centered or aligned with the right side of the screen? Can you do that? Yes! (Figure P3.3 shows you some examples).

Getting text to align on the right is a little trickier. You need to set the text aside as a paragraph. This is the format:

```
<P ALIGN="right">text that will go to the right</P>
```

Figure P3.3
Left-aligned, centered, and right-aligned text.

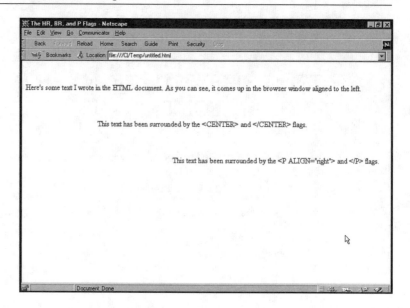

You probably remember that <P> command from Primer 2, "Flags and Commands." Here again is the concept of an attribute. You are setting an attribute of the <P> flag. That alignment command is what pushes to the right. Remember when you use an attribute in the <P> flag, you need to end with a </P> flag.

You center text by surrounding it with simple <CENTER> and </CENTER> commands. This is what it looks like:

```
<CENTER>All text in here will be centered</CENTER>
```

Want to see a live example of text that is centered, right-aligned, and in different font sizes and headings? Point your browser to http://www.htmlgoodies.com/book/ textexample.html.

FAQs from the HTML Goodies Web Site

Q. You say on your site that you should use quotation marks around attributes, but when I look at the code for other people's pages, the quotation marks aren't there. Should I use them or not?

A. I'm a traditionalist in terms of HTML. If you want my opinion, yes, use them. The marks have become required less often with the coming of later-version browsers. I still use them because I think they serve the purpose of setting the commands apart from the rest of the page, if only for my eyes. Just remember that if you use them, use them all the time. Using them now and again easily leads to forgetting to add a closing quotation mark on an attribute. That causes problems.

And Primer 3 comes to an end. Notice that they're getting shorter? Now go and incorporate a few of these `<H>`, `<FONT SIZE>`, and `<CENTER>` commands into a page. To do is to learn. A brilliant man once said that...I think he had a beard, too.

Making a Link to Someone Else

Welcome to your fourth day. Today you learn only one thing—how to create a link to another page. This is a basic format like any of the others you have seen so far.

 Visit this tutorial online at `http://www.htmlgoodies.com/primers/primer_4.html`.

When you learn the format, you can make as many links to other pages as you want. The following line of HTML creates a link to the HTML Goodies home page. Figure P4.1 shows how this link looks on a Web page.

```
<A HREF="http://www.htmlgoodies.com">Click Here To Go To HTML Goodies</A>
```

This is what's happening:

- A Stands for Anchor. It begins the attachment to another page.

- HREF Stands for Hypertext REFerence. That's a nice, short way of saying, "This is where the link is going to go."

- ="http://www.htmlgoodies.com" The *full address* of the site you want to link to. Always use the full address in the link. The one exception is if you are linking to another page within your site. In that case, only use the page's name and .htm or .html extension. Also notice that the address has an equal sign in front of it and is enclosed in quotation marks. Why? Because it's an attribute. Remember that from Primer 3?

- ⬤ `Click Here to Go` Where you insert what appears on your Web page for the viewer to click. Write some text that describes the link.

- ⬤ `</A>` Ends the entire link. Notice I didn't close `HREF`. That's an attribute. You need only close the flag. That's "`A`".

Figure P4.1
A link on a Web page.

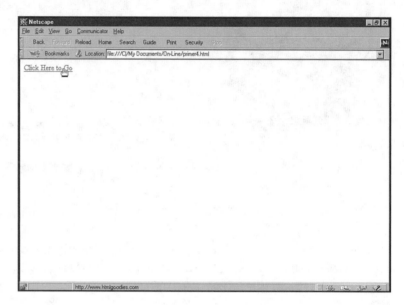

Go ahead and place a link on your page. Now, without clicking, simply lay your pointer on the blue words. The address of the link you created comes up along the bottom of the browser window, in the status bar, where it usually reads "Document Done."

FAQs from the HTML Goodies Web Site

Q. Can I link to any site on the Net?

A. Yes, as long as you have the correct address (URL) in the command. I will say that in very rare instances people have been asked to take their links down, and because the people requesting that the link be taken down own the copyright to their page, they can say who links to it and who doesn't. For example, a link was made to HTML Goodies and the owner wrote to tell me all about it. When I went to see the site, it was all dirty pictures. My HTML Goodies banner was sitting above pictures no one should see! I used my copyright abilities to tell him to take the link down.

Q. I made a link to another site and I keep getting a box that tells me the page doesn't exist. I know it exists!

A. First I would suggest checking your spelling. If you're positive that it's right, you may have corrupted the link by enabling the address to break over two lines. Make sure the address appears on one line in your HTML code. The HTML code can go on two lines, but the address should all run together. If you have a line break in there, the browser may add a space. That puts a space in the address and you've created a Web address that doesn't exist just like the browser told you. Finally, if the address is all on one line, check to see if you have the correct extension. If you have .htm and the page actually ends in .html, that could be it. I know that sounds strange, but it's part of the fun of the Web.

The following is a page with a series of links on it and a link that enables you to write to me. You can look at the source code to see how I did it. Go to `http://www.htmlgoodies` `.com/ book/links.html`.

People E-mailing You from Your Page

You can make it easy for people to send you e-mail from your Web site by using what's known as a `mailto:` command. It follows the same formula as the preceding link. The command places blue wording on the screen that people can click to send you a piece of e-mail. This is the pattern:

```
<A HREF="mailto:jburns@htmlgoodies.com">Click Here To email Me</A>
```

Notice it's the same format as a link, except that in a link you put in an address to jump to. This example sends e-mail to me. To set it up to send e-mail to you, simply delete `jburns@htmlgoodies.com` and substitute your own e-mail address.

The `mailto:` portion of the code calls on the e-mail program contained in your visitor's browser. The browser does most of the work—you are just setting the "trigger" to make it work. Now, if you run this command and it doesn't do what I've described, you may not have the e-mail preferences in your browser set up. If you use Netscape, find the Preferences under the Edit menu at the top of the browser. If you use Explorer, find your Options under the View menu. In there find a place to put in your e-mail address, your real name, and a few other items. Make sure that's all filled in and you are good to go for setting up `mailto:` links.

Figure P4.2 shows what happens when a visitor to your Web site clicks the `mailto:` link.

Figure P4.2
Results of clicking a `mailto:`
link.

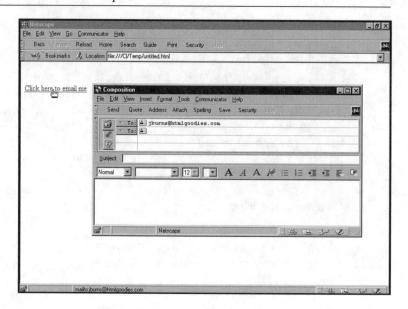

Now put one on your page. Go ahead, click it. I know you're dying to. You get an e-mail page addressed to me, or whomever you address the link to.

FAQs from the HTML Goodies Web Site

Q. I did the link command exactly like you said to. Now everything on the page is blue!! AAAAUUUGH!?

A. If everything on the page is blue, you probably either forgot the `</A>` flag or are missing the slash before the `A` in the end flag. The computer doesn't know when to stop the link without it, so it makes everything a link (which makes everything blue).

And that wraps up Primer 4. The next primer gets into the fun part of the World Wide Web—little pictures.

Primer 5

Placing an Image on Your Page

By now you know enough to write a very nice text-based Web site, but it is the World Wide Web's ability to provide pictures that made it so popular. In this primer you learn how to place a picture on your page as well as how to turn a picture into a link to another page.

 Visit this tutorial online at `http://www.htmlgoodies.com/primers/primer_5.html`.

Inserting the Image

The flag you use to place an image is constant—you use the same format every time. When you are writing your pages, wherever you place the image tag is where the image appears in relation to the items on your page (including text). Technically, images are called "inline" images because they are in the lines of text.

It is not necessary, but it is a good idea to store your HTML files and your image files in the same directory on your hard drive. That way you can call for them by name alone without having to add the entire address. More on that is coming up in Primer 7, "Graduation Day."

Insert an image on your Web page using the following:

```
<IMG SRC="image.gif">
```

Replacing the example name `image.gif` with the name of an actual image I have, joe.gif, gives you the results shown in Figure P5.1. No doubt about it—I'm a handsome man!

This is what's happening:

- ● `IMG`   Stands for image. It basically states that an image goes here.

- ● `SRC`   Stands for source. It tells the browser where to go to find the image. Again, it's best for you to place the image you want to use in the same directory on your hard drive as the HTML page that uses the image. If you do that then you need only call for the image by name. The browser finds it because it is in the same place as the document that is calling for it.

- ● *image*`.gif`   The name of the image. Notice it's following the same type of file format that your HTML documents follow: a name (*image*), a dot, and then a suffix (`gif`).

Figure P5.1
Inserting a picture of me on your Web site.

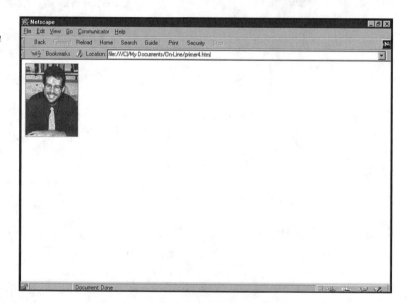

FAQs from the HTML Goodies Web Site

Q. I want the same image to appear on the page 10 times. Do I need to save the image with 10 different names?

A. Nope, just keep calling for it by the same name. The browser displays it again and again.

Image Formats

You can use three basic graphics file formats on your Web pages. Each is denoted to the browser by a different suffix:

- .gif (pronounced *jif*). This is an acronym for Graphics Interchange Format. CompuServe invented the format. A series of colored picture elements (*pixels*) line up to make a picture. Browsers can handle this format quite easily. GIF images are usually logos and icons and other smaller elements with little detail and bold colors. The format is suited well for that type of image.

- .jpeg or .jpg (pronounced *j-peg*). Two names are necessary because Macintoshes and Windows 95/98 have four letters after the dot. jpeg is an acronym for Joint Photographic Equipment Group, the organization that invented the format. The format is unique in that it's a *compressed format*. That's fancy computer talk that means that when the computer is not using a jpeg image, it folds it up and puts it away. For example, if the picture is 10KB when displayed, it may be only 4KB when stored. Nice trick, huh? It saves on hard drive space. JPEG images are best for photographs and detail-rich images.

- .bmp (pronounced *bimp* or *bump*). This is a bitmap. Microsoft invented the BMP format for use in Windows. Microsoft Explorer enables you to display bitmaps by simply using the same image format as described earlier, but I wouldn't do it. Netscape Navigator users can't see the image. It doesn't display in that browser. Go figure.

FAQs from the HTML Goodies Web Site

Q. My image won't show up! All I get is a red X (or a broken image).

A. This is by far the most asked question of the Goodies primers. The image may not be showing up for many reasons. The following are the most common:

1. You have made an error in the code. Look for misspellings (src is the biggest one people mess up) or a missing quotation mark.

2. You have not used the correct image name. Remember, the image name you call for must be the file's exact name of the image. Even the capitalization must be the same.

3. You have included a path in the command such as a:\ or c:\. If so, lose it. Call for the image by name only.

Where Do I Get My Images?

You can draw them with a paint program or create them with a scanner. In addition, premade images are available almost everywhere. The HTML Goodies home page enables you access to over 700 images—for free—and other sites out there offer just as many.

Go to http://www.htmlgoodies.com/images.html *to grab a few free images for yourself.*

Since you've been surfing, you've seen hundreds of images already. If you see something on someone's page that you really like, ask to use it.

Don't just take it. It may be against the law because you may be using something protected by copyright. Ask before you use. I have found most people on the Internet are very giving. Some aren't. If you ask and they say no, just find another image to use.

FAQs from the HTML Goodies Web Site

Q. I found that if I put in the entire address to an image on another site, I can get that image to show up on my site. Woohoo!

A. Woohoo indeed. You might be breaking copyright law. Yes, you can put in a full address and run images off other sites, but did you get permission to do so?

 To see a page with a few images and image links on it, see http://www.htmlgoodies.com/book/imagelinks.html. *Be sure to look at the source code!*

Creating an Active (Clickable) Image

Okay, this gets a little fancy. In the previous primer I showed you how to create a hypertext link. It created blue words on your page that someone could click and then jump to another site. Well, now you're going to set it up, so an image becomes active. The viewer clicks the image instead of the blue words to make the jump. I made a link to my HTML Goodies home page using the preceding image. The following is the format:

```
<A HREF="http://www.htmlgoodies.com"><IMG SRC="joe.gif"></A>
```

Look at it again. See what happened? I placed a basic image command where I would have placed wording. Put one on your page. Lay your pointer on it, but don't click. Notice that the entire image is active. Figure P5.2 shows what you should get.

When you click the image, your browser takes you to the Web address you listed (in this case, my HTML Goodies site). Neat, huh? But what's with that blue line around the image? That's what happens when you activate an image. The browser attempts to turn the link blue like the wording it's replacing, so it places what's known as a *border* around the image. Some people like it. I don't and I know how to get rid of it.

To make the blue border disappear, you must add a subcommand inside the image flag. Make the image command in this format:

```
<IMG BORDER="0" SRC="joe.gif">
```

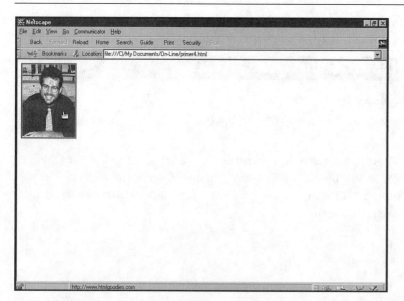

Figure P5.2
An active image.

See what I did? I added a command that denoted that the border should be 0. You can go the other way, too, if you'd like. Make it BORDER="55" if you want; you have a huge border. Note that the number 0 is in quotation marks. Figure P5.3 shows what you get using BORDER="0".

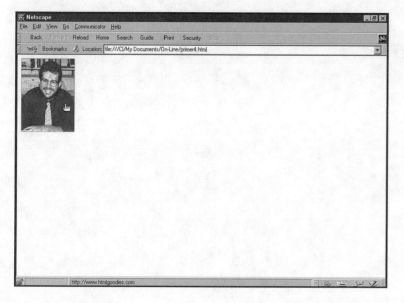

Figure P5.3
An active image with BORDER="0".

Again, place an image on your page. Lay your pointer on the image without clicking. Notice that it is active, but doesn't carry that annoying blue border.

FAQs from the HTML Goodies Web Site

Q. How do I make the border bigger?

A. Instead of BORDER="0", try 2, or 4, or 700. That is a big border.

That brings us to a close. This is a nice way to end this primer because it gives you a hint of what's to come tomorrow in Primer 6, "Manipulating Images." Tomorrow you deal almost exclusively with commands inside of commands, which manipulate your images. You'll truly impress your friends with this one.

Manipulating Images

Just as I believe a primer, Primer 3, was required to explain manipulating text, I also think a primer is needed to explain manipulating images. Believe it or not, manipulating images is easier than manipulating text. Here you go.

 Visit this tutorial online at `http://www.htmlgoodies.com/primers/primer_6.html`. *For some extra examples of manipulating images, see* `http://www.htmlgoodies.com/book/ manipulatingimages.html`.

Placement on the Page

First let's look at placing the image somewhere on the page. The default is left. If you simply place an image command on a page, the image pops up hard lefts. That's all to it. If you want to have an image placed in the center of the page, simply surround the image command with `<CENTER>` and `</CENTER>` flags, like this:

```
<CENTER><IMG ALIGN="right" SRC="image.gif"></CENTER>
```

To get the image to the right of the page, you need to add an `ALIGN` attribute. Figure P6.1 shows what you get using the following command.

```
<IMG ALIGN="right" SRC="image.gif">
```

Figure P6.1
An image aligned on the right side of the page.

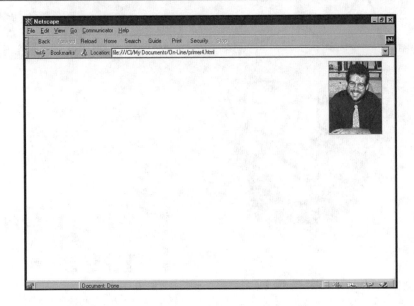

Aligning Text with Images

Images don't always stand alone. You often want text alongside them. To set that up, you simply insert an ALIGN attribute with top, middle, or bottom depending on where you want the text. Figure P6.2 shows what the following examples produce on your page.

```
<IMG ALIGN="top" SRC="htmlgdds.gif"> Text at the top
<IMG ALIGN="middle" SRC="htmlgdds.gif"> Text in the middle
<IMG ALIGN="bottom" SRC="htmlgdds.gif"> Text at the bottom
```

FAQs from the HTML Goodies Web Site

Q. When I use the ALIGN attributes, the text jumps down to under the image after the text reaches the end of the line. I want it to wrap around the image. How do I do that?

A. Use ALIGN="left". Yes, I know the image automatically aligns to the left. Trust me.

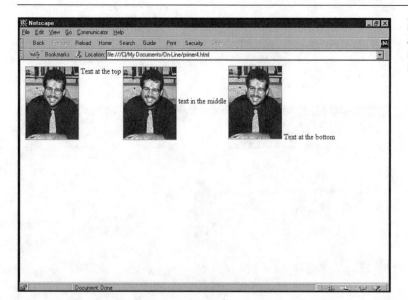

Figure P6.2
Images aligned with the top, middle, and bottom of text.

Changing Image Size

To begin this section, remember that images on a computer are not like photographs. Computer images are made up of a lot of little colored dots all pushed right alongside each other. The little colored dots are known as *picture elements* or *pixels*. Just remember that during this part of the primer numbers refer to pixels rather than inches, centimeters, or the like.

Every image is made up of pixels. This means that you can also measure the size of an image by its number of pixels. For example, the joe.gif image is 154 pixels high by 116 pixels wide. How do I know that? I have a graphics program that tells me so. How would you know? Without a specific program, you might have to play around with the numbers in these commands a little bit, but it's easy to do.

This is what you do. Denote to the image command how many pixels high by how many pixels wide you want. The `joe.gif` image is 50×100 pixels. If I want the image to appear smaller, I ask for the pixels to be smaller, say 25×50. If I want it bigger, I would set the pixels larger, say 100×200. If I want to totally distort the picture, I can do that too.

The following is the format:

```
<IMG HEIGHT="##" WIDTH="##" SRC="image.gif">
```

Notice the HEIGHT and WIDTH attributes nestled right where the U command went before. (Yes, you can also use an ALIGN attribute when using the HEIGHT and WIDTH commands.) Replace the ## with a number of pixels for height and width. Figure P6.3 shows three examples.

Figure P6.3
The same image with different HEIGHT and WIDTH attributes applied to it.

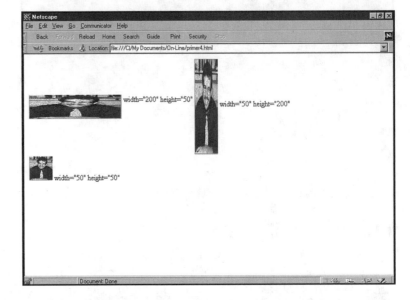

FAQs from the HTML Goodies Web Site

Q. Should I use the HEIGHT and WIDTH attributes even when I don't want to change image size?

A. Yes! You should use the HEIGHT and WIDTH commands every time you place an image. When you want to place an image and not distort its size, enter its actual height and width. That enables the text on your page to load while leaving a space just big enough for the image to load later. Your users thank you for it.

Making Horizontal Lines of Different Lengths

That WIDTH attribute also works on the <HR> flag, except you use percentages to indicate the size. Just put the WIDTH command right after the <HR>, like this: <HR WIDTH="##%">. Replace the ## with a number from 1 to 100 and remember to add the percentage sign. If you don't put in the percentage sign, the WIDTH attribute thinks you mean pixels. Forgetting the percentage sign may give you a line that is only 65 pixels wide rather than 65% of the page, get it? The following commands produce the page shown in Figure P6.4. Notice that

if you want a full-length HR, you can just use the `<HR>` flag—you don't have to put
`<HR WIDTH="100%">` even though that also works.

```
<HR>
<HR WIDTH="80%">
<HR WIDTH="50%">
<HR WIDTH="30%">
<HR WIDTH="10%">
```

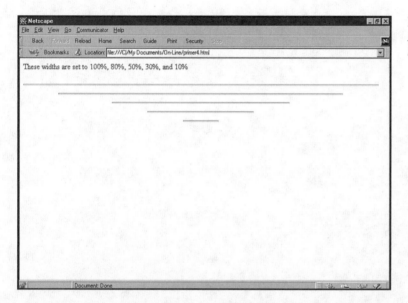

Figure P6.4
*Making lines of different
length with* HR *and* WIDTH.

You get the idea of how to combine all these flags and commands, yes?

FAQs from the HTML Goodies Web Site

Q. Will the HEIGHT command work in the HR command too?

A. Yes, but here you might want to use just the number without the percentage sign. It relates to pixels. You really don't want a line that is 65% wide and 25% high. That would just look goofy.

That wraps it up. Try these in the comfort of your own home under the supervision of an adult. If you are an adult, find a kid who can program the VCR to help you along.

Graduation Day

Congratulations! You have beaten through six days of HTML and struggled with all those silly flags.

This is your diploma:

You Passed!

*May all your
HTML dreams
come true.
--Joe Burns*

So you know it all, huh? Well, not quite. Literally, it's impossible to know everything. I don't come close. HTML is a growing and ever-evolving art. You have the basics. Now you can go on to the major tutorials located in the chapters of this book; you understand them now. First let's talk about how to post your new pages on the Web.

How Do I Get an Internet Service Provider?

Now you need to find a place to post the page you wrote for the World Wide Web. Where should it go? Choose any one of a million places. ISPs (Internet service providers) are popping up everywhere—just graze through your Sunday paper or open your yellow pages under "Internet." You should be able to choose from a bunch.

What you're looking to attain is a bit of space on a server already attached to the Internet. Post your files to that space on the server and then people from all over the world can visit the pages you posted.

How Much Should I Pay?

Depending on what you want, you could pay a great deal or a little bit. I hold an entire domain, `htmlgoodies.com`. I pay a good bit. You shouldn't pay more than between $10 and $30 a month. The following are a few things you should get for your money:

1. You should pay a flat fee for your time on the Net. Do not pay for every second you're using your computer.

2. You should be able to dial a local number to connect.

3. You should get free connection software. This is called FTP (File Transfer Protocol) software. Ask for it specifically by name.

4. The connection should be a SLIP (Serial Line Interface Protocol), PPP (Point to Point Protocol), or another TCP/IP connection that enables you to use a browser on your computer. Ask for one of these specifically.

5. You should get at least 5MB of space on a server for placing your own HTML documents. That's the lowest amount.

6. You should get e-mail, Telnet, FTP, and newsgroup access. Again, even if you don't now know what the terms mean, ask for them.

   You should have access to help, where you talk to a person, not just make contact via e-mail or a help line answering machine.

I cannot recommend or downplay any provider. I think getting a connection to the Net should be a personal choice. Make a point of getting these things listed here, as you can get it all fairly easily.

How Do I Get My Pages on the World Wide Web?

For the world to see your Web page creations, you are going to have to get those HTML and image files from your computer to your ISP's server. When you get an account with an ISP, it gives you your own Web address and tells you what directories on its server you can use to store and display your Web pages. After you have this information, you can begin putting your pages on the Web. This primer tells you how to do it and discusses a few things to watch out for.

 This FTP tutorial can be found online at `http://www.htmlgoodies.com/beyond/ftp.html`.

Using FTP Software

FTP is the concept of moving a file from the hard drive on your local computer to the remote Internet server (probably owned by your ISP), where others can look at it. The process of transferring files from your computer to the server is called *uploading*. Being able to upload files is a basic skill needed to build a Web site. This is easy to do, but sometimes people get confused about why files can sometimes be corrupted when transferring. This primer helps you make sure your files arrive at the server in one piece.

How FTP Works

FTP is actually very basic. You can take about a million different FTP programs from the Internet as shareware or commercial software. I use a shareware program called FTP2000. Figure P7.1 shows what it looks like.

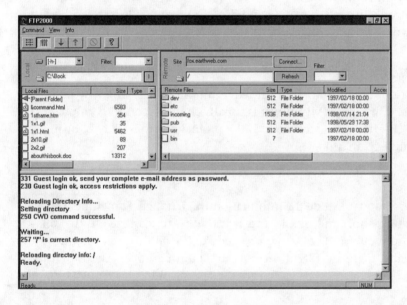

Figure P7.1
The FTP2000 software.

My guess is that you have your own FTP program already. Your ISP should have given you one that is compatible with your server. You should have also gotten full instructions on installing and using it. If not, head to Dave Central's FTP page (http://www.davecentral.com/ftp.html) and grab a few programs for yourself. FTP2000 is there, as well as another favorite, called CuteFTP.

Figure P7.2 shows an illustration of the interface for a generic FTP program. Yours is something like this. The bold ASCII and BINARY at the top are buttons that change the file transfer type.

Figure P7.2
A simplified illustration of what FTP software looks like.

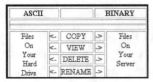

The column on the left that says Files On Your Hard Drive is where a directory that lists all the files on your computer appears. Sometimes this area is labeled `local` files.

The column on the right that says Files On Your Server is where a directory appears that lists all the files found on the part of your ISP's server that you have access to. This is where you place all your Web page files, so others can see them.

The center column of three buttons enables you to click either side of the command to transfer the file between your computer and the server. Sometimes, as with the FTP2000 program, you find no buttons. Instead, you drag and drop from your side to the other; the upload is performed for you.

ASCII Versus Binary

This issue is the main reason for this tutorial. I get letters all the time asking why images (or applets, or JavaScripts) don't work. My answer is usually that the person corrupted or broke the object in the FTP. That usually confounds the problem further. The following sections hold a more in-depth explanation.

ASCII

ASCII stands for American Standard Code for Information Interchange. Sometimes Called *TEXT* or *TEXT DOS*, it is text, short and simple. It is text that is standardized so that all computers everywhere understand it. Look at your keyboard. See all those things, those letters and characters? Actually, there are 128 of them in all (counting upper- and lowercase separately).

Now it gets loopy…

Computers deal with numbers. Period. You see little letters, but the computer doesn't. It sees numbers—1s and 0s to be exact. Each 1 or 0 is called a *bit*, which is short for binary digit. ASCII is a series of seven 1 and 0 number combinations representing letters and characters. (Some computers now use an Extended ASCII, which uses eight numbers.) An extra digit is often added as a check to see if the other seven are correct. This is called a *parity digit* or a *check bit* and it checks to see if the numbers are correct via a mathematical equation involving the other seven numbers. Some ASCII code looks like the following:

```
Symbol ASCII Code Symbol ASCII Code A 01000000 a 01100001 ! 00100001
➡$ 00100100 Z 01011010 z 01111010 ...etc, etc, etc up to 128
```

Notice that only two numbers are involved, 1 and 0. This is what's known as *binary*, two items. What's the difference between the two, you ask? I told you this gets loopy. ASCII code is code for text alone. Those 128 groupings of 1s and 0s represent text, period.

In terms of FTP: If you are FTPing something that only has text, like an HTML document, use your application's ASCII mode. More on why in a moment.

FAQs from the HTML Goodies Web Site

Q. Does my FTP program choose ASCII or binary for me?

A. Maybe. Mine does, but it's still a good idea to force the FTP program's hand and decide for it. Never rely fully on the program to make the choice. Always check and make sure the file is being sent using the correct method.

Binary

Binary is best explained in comparison to ASCII. Sometimes called *Raw Data* or *All Files*, binary also uses the seven (sometimes eight) digit 1s and 0s combinations, but it sees the characters in a different light.

Let's say you are FTPing an image. Yes, it is text, 1s and 0s, but with one major exception— all characters are not equal. If you look at your image (in a text editor), it looks like text. Remember that the computer sees numbers only and characters are a good representation of those numbers. You see, the computer doesn't require that you see what happens to work. Text is there just so you can get a representation of what it is doing.

A binary transfer differs from ASCII in how it treats the characters used. An image needs to not only retain the same characters when it transfers, but it also needs to retain the form. It has to be equally as wide and tall when it arrives at its destination as it was when it left. If it is not, it's corrupted and doesn't work.

For example, when you create an HTML document, you may have noticed that adding a ton of spaces between words did not translate into a ton of spaces in the browser window. In addition, hitting Enter to jump to the next line didn't mean diddly when you posted it. The line broke when it wanted (unless you put in a <BR> command).

The reason for this is you saved the document as text of one form or another. That only saved the letters, nothing else. Hitting Enter didn't matter. Your margin settings weren't saved—only the text was saved. This is why you have to put in flags to make the text do what you want. Only the text goes when you transfer the file over as ASCII, because that's all that is required. Its form is immaterial. You could write your HTML document as one really, really long line. The computer doesn't care. It changes the text off the flags, not by the form it was sent. How pretty you make your HTML document doesn't matter.

Imagine you just finished creating an image. Yes, it's 1s and 0s, but the text is more than just a bunch of numbers; it is in a certain format. Some of the text represents commands for the computer and some represents text that appears on the screen. Still other text represents a jump to the next line. That format must be retained. If you send the image as ASCII, the transfer literally changes the image into a long line of characters—it basically makes it text alone. The different types of commands have lost their meaning. All is now equal. It is corrupted. It does not work.

Rule of Thumb

This goes for both FTP uploading and downloading!

- Use ASCII only for transferring HTML documents.
- Everything else goes binary (or "raw data" or "all files," depending on your program).

Why Not Send and Save Everything as Binary?

You can. Sending an HTML document as binary just tends to mess it up a bit. More than just text is being sent; form is now involved and it may alter what you want. Then again it may not. This is your choice. Finally!

The things I said go for both FTP and downloading! Text is text. Images and applets are quite different.

If you download or transfer something and it fails to work, the smart money is that you corrupted it through one or many of your transfers.

Thanks for stopping by...now go FTP something. Speaking of software, what about those HTML assistants I mentioned in Primer 1, "What You Need to Get Started"?

I knew you'd ask me that.

What Do Those HTML Assistants Do?

They do a good bit, actually. The Help programs are usually set up like a word processor with a whole lot of little buttons to push. Those buttons give you the flags. For instance, you'd click the B button and get the open and close flags to make something bold. They also save the files in the text format required. I use HTMLPad. You can get it here: `http://www.intermania.com/htmlpad/`. This is an IBM program that only gets as involved as you let it. You can use the buttons or not.

A few other HTML assistants that I have heard both good and bad things about are HoTMeTaL, HotDog, FrontPage, and Dreamweaver.

Each is available as shareware, or for a short trial period on the Internet. Links to these and other HTML assistant programs are in Appendix C, "Valuable Links."

Assistants are helpful, but don't get too involved in using one. Remember, this is your page—you do the writing. What fun is using a program that does half the work for you?

Where Do I Go Now?

You've put your foot in the water, so now it's time to dive right into Chapter 1, "Playing with Text," and start learning all the fun details of HTML.

You have the technology. You have the power. Heck, you have this book (and a Web site to go with it). Use my other tutorials and create your own little corner of the World Wide Web.

Go get 'em!

Part II

Everything You Need to Know About Text and Graphics

1   *Playing with Text*

2   *Creating Links*

3   *Adding Images and Backgrounds*

4   *Imagemaps*

Chapter 1

Playing with Text

Text is so important to a Web page. Content is king when it comes to a Web site and that content is created through text. Images are nice. Colors are nice. Backgrounds are nice, but it's my opinion that text is where it's at when it comes right down to the meat and potatoes of a site.

Text Codes

I get letters from new users all the time asking if there are any commands for manipulating text other than <B> and <I>. I usually tell them no and go on.

I'm kidding, of course! The following 40 HTML flags can be used to manipulate text. I thought I'd throw this little deal together, so that you could see all those commands in one place. This is a nice reference for the next time you wish to find just the perfect text format.

Please understand that a few of these commands basically do the same thing. For instance, the <STRONG> command produces basically the same effect as <BOLD>. I'm sure that there's a very, very specific difference between the two, but in seven years of writing more than 5,000 pages, I've never needed <STRONG>.

Each of the tags described here is useful, but this is the only place you'll see many of them in this book. They're just not popular or complex enough to warrant their own tutorial.

Play with these. Put them on your page and *Oooooh* and *Aaaah* at what they do. Use the ones you like and dismiss the ones you don't. These are your pages you're creating.

In each of the following examples, I used the words The Altered Text as the text that the flags affect.

 If you want to see all these in action, point your browser to `http://www.htmlgoodies.com/ tutors/textcodes.html`*.*

Abbreviation: <ABBR>

This is a new command in HTML 4.0, the current accepted version of HTML (see Appendix A "Everything You Need to Know About HTML 4.0"); your browser may not support it yet. It tells browsers and search engines that the text is not a word, but an abbreviation. It also produces a ToolTip—a rollover effect that opens a small text box when the mouse rolls over.

```
<ABBR>The Altered Text</ABBR>
```

Acronym: <ACRONYM>

This is a new command in HTML 4.0. Your browser may not yet support it. The purpose of this command is almost exactly like the <ABBR> flag, except that this flag specifically denotes the text as an acronym, so that the search engine can better categorize it.

```
<ACRONYM>The Altered Text</ACRONYM>
```

Address: <ADDRESS>

This sets text apart as an address. By using the command, search engines and other systems will see the text as being tagged as an address. It adds a little more definition to the text. In addition, it makes the text italicized. Two for one. How about that?

```
<ADDRESS>The Altered Text</ADDRESS>
```

Bold: <B>

This flag simply bolds the text.

```
<B>The Altered Text</B>
```

Base Font: <BASEFONT>

BASEFONT should be used to inform the browser of a default font for the entire body or just a subsection of a page. Which is defined depends on how much text you surround with the start and end flag. BASEFONT will override the browser default font, but not any font setting put directly to text. This would include a FONT FACE flag and attribute.

```
<BASEFONT COLOR="red">The Altered Text</BASEFONT>
```

BDO: <BDO>

This is also a new command in HTML 4.0. Your browser may not support it yet. The BDO command denotes direction. See the following DIR command? RTL means right to left and LTR means the opposite. This comes into play if you are using a language, such as Hebrew, that has text going the opposite of English's left-to-right format.

```
<BDO DIR="rtl">The Altered Text</BDO>
```

Big: <BIG>

This is a great command. This bolds the text and bumps its size up a few pixels from the browser default setting on text not otherwise altered by an HTML flag.

```
<BIG>The Altered Text</BIG>
```

Blink: <BLINK>

Netscape Navigator browsers alone support this command. Hopefully, they'll drop it soon. It makes the text blink on and off, and on and off, and on and off...until you go crazy.

```
<BLINK>The Altered Text</BLINK>
```

Block Quote: <BLOCKQUOTE>

This command can surround a large chunk of text and indent it as a whole. The best way to describe it is it sets text apart in a paragraph format smaller and thinner than the surrounding text.

```
<BLOCKQUOTE>The Altered Text</BLOCKQUOTE>
```

Cite: <CITE>

This works just like the italics command. It sets the text aside in the browser's mind as a being a reference to another written piece. You remember, in high school, when you wrote all those papers?

```
<CITE>The Altered Text</CITE>
```

Code: <CODE>

This sets text aside as code that is to be displayed. The text is placed in a monospace font, which is a bit more blocked (or square) than the normal font. The effect is similar to the <PRE> flag. <PRE> is a simple display, whereas <CODE> sets text aside in the browser's mind to display it as code, rather than just displaying it.

```
<CODE>The Altered Text</CODE>
```

Comment: <COMMENT>

Nothing appears on the page when you use this flag. You see, this flag marks text as a comment. Comments are good ways to make notes to yourself while writing HTML, and to make sure those notes don't appear on your Web site. Surrounding text with the <!-- and --> commands achieves the same effect.

```
<COMMENT>The Altered Text</COMMENT>
```

Delete: <DEL>

Also a new command in HTML 4.0, your browser may not support it yet. It stands for deleted text. The text you mark with the <DEL> tags should get a strikethrough effect.

```
<DEL>The Altered Text</DEL>
```

Definition: <DFN>

DFN stands for definition. It is more for the browsers and search engines than it is for your eyes. Let's say you were searching for the definition of a word via an online search engine. If the pages you were searching through used this command, your search could be limited to definitions. It would produce a much better search than hitting everything.

```
<DFN>The Altered Text</DFN>
```

Division: <DIV>

DIV sets apart a section of the page, so that it can be altered—usually with style sheet commands. You should also take a look at Chapter 8, "Cascading Style Sheets and Layers," for more exciting exploits of the <DIV> flag; the chapter also holds the class, ID, and layering tutorials. It makes great bedtime reading.

```
<DIV>The Altered Text</DIV>
```

Emphasis: <EM>

EM makes the text stand out by making it italic. (I know it seems at this point like many commands do the same thing. They do. Critics of HTML have been pointing this out for a while.) I always use italics rather than emphasis, but to each his own. Some tell me they use both because it helps them keep things straight in their code.

```
<EM>The Altered Text</EM>
```

Font Color: <FONT COLOR>

You've seen this before. Read over Primer 3, "Manipulating Text," for a refresher course. The flag is "FONT". The attribute is "COLOR".

```
<FONT COLOR="red">The Altered Text</FONT>
```

Font Size: <FONT SIZE>

Ditto. For more, see Primer 4, "Making a Link to Someone Else." Hey! That rhymes! Again, this is a flag and attribute.

```
<FONT SIZE="+1">The Altered Text</FONT>
```

Font Face: <FONT FACE>

This changes the text's font face. For more, see the text font tutorial later in this chapter in the section, "Changing Text Colors." That doesn't rhyme, but it is still a flag and attribute.

```
<FONT FACE="arial">The Altered Text</FONT>
```

Heading: <H#>

You can create six levels of headings by replacing the # sign with any of the numerals 1–6. For more information, see Primer 4.

```
<H#>The Altered Text</H#>
```

Italics: <I>

This makes the text italic.

```
<I>The Altered Text</I>
```

Inserted: <INS>

This is also a new command in HTML 4.0 that your browser may not support yet. This tag indicates inserted text. You should get an underline effect with it.

```
<INS>The Altered Text</INS>
```

Keyboard: <KBD>

KBD makes the text look like text typed on an old typewriter.

```
<KBD>The Altered Text</KBD>
```

Listing: <LISTING>

I wouldn't slap this on a brain cell just yet. This is a dead command under HTML 4.0. Use <PRE> instead.

```
<LISTING>The Altered Text</LISTING>
```

Multiple Columns: <MULTICOL>

This sets text apart in multiple newspaper-like columns in Navigator only. Internet Explorer did not support the command as of the writing of this book.

```
<MULTICOL>The Altered Text</MULTICOL>
```

No Break: <NOBR>

When you surround text with the <NOBR> flag, it does not wrap at the end of the line, but keeps rolling right off the right side of the screen.

```
<NOBR>The Altered Text</NOBR>
```

Plain Text: <PLAINTEXT>

No need to know this one cold, either. This is a dead command under HTML 4.0. Use <PRE> instead.

```
<PLAINTEXT>The Altered Text</PLAINTEXT>
```

Preformatted: <PRE>

Use <PRE> to keep text in the same format and shape it appears in when you type it into your Web site. Imagine you've just finished writing a paper that contains a few tables with lines of data. You could go in and add the commands to make an HTML table with the data—or you could just put the <PRE> command before and after the table—it displays as you write it. In fact, you could post the entire paper by using the <PRE> commands.

I don't usually use the flags; I go into the document and format the text for the Web. I think it looks better. When you use the <PRE> command, you get text that looks a little weak compared to other HTML text. Go ahead and place text in <PRE> commands next to straight text in an HTML document: you'll see the difference. All in all, I think formatting the text looks better, but using the <PRE> command sure is fast.

```
<PRE>The Altered Text</PRE>
```

Quote: <Q>

This is a new command in HTML 4.0. Your browser may not support it yet. It is a replacement for the <BLOCKQUOTE> flag. It also has the same properties available that the new SPAN command has.

```
<Q>The Altered Text</Q>
```

Small: <SMALL>

This renders text one size smaller than the browser's default setting.

```
<SMALL>The Altered Text</SMALL>
```

Sample: <SAMP>

SAMP creates very block-style text that is set to equal widths. It sets up neat, straight columns of text if you use it with tables.

```
<SAMP>The Altered Text</SAMP>
```

Span: <SPAN>

The SPAN command works a lot like the <DIV> command. You can set all sorts of parameters with it. For instance, if you are using a version 4.0 browser, you can lay your mouse pointer on the altered text and get a little box with text to pop up, a ToolTip. See the HTML 4.0 tutorial in Appendix A for more information.

```
<SPAN>The Altered Text</SPAN>
```

Strikethrough: <S>

The <S> flag causes text to be marked with a line through it.

```
<S>The Altered Text</S>
```

Strong: <STRONG>

This makes the text bold. This, again, is an instance of two commands producing the same effect. However, I choose to use the <BOLD> flag for all places where I want text to be made stronger.

```
<STRONG>The Altered Text</STRONG>
```

Subscript: <SUB>

This sets text apart as subscript. The 2 in H_2O is an example of a subscript.

```
<SUB>Altered</SUB>
```

Superscript: <SUP>

This flag sets the text to superscript, such as the 8 in 10^8.

```
<SUP>Altered</SUP>
```

Typewriter Text: <TT>

The <TT> flag sets text in a typewriter-style font. Typewriter font makes old-fashioned, bland, blocky text.

```
<TT>The Altered Text</TT>
```

Underline: <U>

This underlines the text.

```
<U>The Altered Text</U>
```

Variable: <VAR>

Text marked with the <VAR> flag is set in a small, fixed-width font.

```
<VAR>The Altered Text</VAR>
```

Wrapping Break: <WBR>

Placing the <WBR> enables no-break text to wrap at the indicated point if necessary.

```
<NOBR>The Altered<WBR>Text</NOBR>
```

XMP: <XMP>

This is also a dead command. You should use <PRE> instead.

```
<XMP>The Altered Text</XMP>
```

Changing Text Colors

You'll need two things to change text colors:

- A color code: These come in either hex or word form.
- A command to change the text color.

I get to the commands in a moment. First, grab yourself a color hex code and a color word code. There are slews of them in Appendix B, "Useful Charts." Any one will do.

Waiting…waiting…waiting…

If you don't feel like flipping through the pages, here's a favorite: blue (word form) that is the same as #0000FF (hex code).

To see the text color tutorial online, head to `http://www.htmlgoodies.com/tutors/` `backgrnd.html`.

Changing the Color of All the Words on the Page

You have the ability to change full-page text colors over four levels:

- `<TEXT="######">` Denotes the full-page text color.
- `<LINK="######">` Denotes the color of the links on your page.
- `<ALINK="######">` Denotes the color the link flashes when clicked on.
- `<VLINK="######">` Denotes the colors of the links after they have been visited.

These commands are placed inside the `<BODY>` container tag. Again, in that position they affect everything on the page. You also need to place them all together inside the same command, along with any background commands you might be using. The following is an example of a `<BODY>` command in which the background is yellow, the text is black, the links are blue, the visited links are green, and the active links are purple. I have used color commands in both word and hex code form.

```
<BODY BGCOLOR="######" TEXT="######" LINK="######" VLINK="######">
```

You can combine them, such as I do here:

```
<BODY BGCOLOR="yellow" TEXT="#000000" LINK="blue" VLINK="green" ALINK="#800080">
```

 Check out `http://www.htmlgoodies.com/book/bgexample.html` *to see these flags in action. Be sure to look at the HTML source code.*

FAQs from the HTML Goodies Web Site

Q. I see that you use a pound sign (#) before your hex codes. Do I have to use them?

A. It depends on if you're a stickler, such as me. Later browsers don't require their use, but I use them anyway. Someone out there may still be using version 1.0 of a certain browser. You should never forbid the browser-challenged from enjoying your page.

Q. I found a great way to use color codes: I set the background color and the color of the visited links to the same color. Then, after the person clicks, the link disappears.

A. Clever. Good tip—if you don't ever want someone to use the same link twice.

 If you want to see the disappearing link in action, go to `http://www.htmlgoodies.com/` `book/disappear.html`.

Changing Color One Word at a Time

You only want to change one word's color (or maybe just a paragraph's color). Once again, you use a color code, either hex or word, to do the trick. Follow this formula:

```
<FONT COLOR="######">text text text text text</FONT>
```

This is a pain in the you-know-where, but it gets the job done. It also works with all H and text-size commands. Basically, if it's text, it will work.

FAQs from the HTML Goodies Web Site

Q. I used three or four different `<FONT COLOR>` commands, but only the first one seems to be working. What did I do wrong?

A. I bet you only have one `</FONT>` command. Remember, every time you use a `<FONT>` command, you need a `</FONT>` command.

Q. I want to use both the `<FONT COLOR>` and `<FONT SIZE>` commands together. Do I need to have two whole font commands?

A. No. Just put both the `SIZE` and `COLOR` subcommands in the same `<FONT>` command, such as : `<FONT SIZE="+#" COLOR="######">`. Then you only need one `</FONT>` command.

 See some examples of using hex and word color codes to change text color at `http://www.htmlgoodies.com/book/textcolor.html`.

Changing Specific Link Colors

You saw earlier that you could affect the color of every link on the page using the `<LINK="####">` flag. You then saw one word affected through `<FONT COLOR="####">`. It would seem that you could use either, or both, to affect the color of only one link, but it isn't necessarily so.

At the time of this writing, only the Netscape Navigator and Microsoft Internet Explorer browser versions 4.0 or higher support the altering of one link's color through the use of `<FONT COLOR="####">`.

Changing Text Fonts

I have been asked time and time again how to get the font face to change. I'm assuming you already know you can change font size through the use of H and FONT number commands. If what I just said is Greek to you, see Primer 3.

See this text font tutorial online at http://www.htmlgoodies.com/tutors/textfont.html.

Figure 1.1 shows what I'm talking about. I have listed a few font face commands that you can use. I simply wrote this tutorial using Word 7.0 and entered every font face available with the little TT next to it (that TT stands for TrueType, by the way). Here are the ones that worked. Follow the format for your page.

Just remember that very old browsers might not process these commands and the text appears unchanged. Moreover, even if the user has a new browser, she must also have all the fonts that you use already installed on her own computer. Changing fonts this way is fun, but not the most reliable thing you can do. The safest fonts to use (because they are the most common on Windows machines) are Arial, Times New Roman, Courier New, and Comic Sans.

Figure 1.1
You can display some fonts on your Web site.

FAQs from the HTML Goodies Web Site

Q. Hey! I tried using your <FONT FACE> flag and it didn't work. I saw the font, but my friend didn't. Is it because we were using two different browsers?

A. Could be, but I doubt it. You see, these font commands only work if the computer reading the page has that specific font loaded onto its hard drive. If it doesn't, you'll get straight text like your friend did. Just be sure to choose more common fonts in the future.

One More Tip

You can now set numerous text font faces for the computer to play with. Here's what I mean:

```
<FONT FACE="modern, arial, veranda">Text Text</FONT>
```

Notice that I have three font faces listed each with a comma in between. Following that format, I suggest numerous font faces in descending order of importance. When the page loads, the browser checks to see if the computer has the first font face listed. If the font face is on the computer, it displays. If not, the browser attempts to find the second font face listed. If it's not there either, the third comes into play. I've seen pages that list up to 10 font faces. That way you're sure to get at least one unless you list 10 really goofy font faces.

Good luck with other fonts. Just remember that not all computers are built the same. What displayed perfectly on your computer might not on someone else's. In fact, Murphy's Law suggests it doesn't.

 Go to `http://www.htmlgoodies.com/book/testfonts.html` *to see if these common fonts display on your computer.*

Indents and Lists

I have received a good many letters asking how I indent paragraphs and bulleted lists. Here's a quick rundown of the hows and whys.

 This tutorial is online at `http://www.htmlgoodies.com/tutors/lists.html`.

Indenting a Paragraph

I simply indent by adding blank spaces. "But my browser ignores my spaces!" you say.

Mine does, too. I can put in 50 spaces, and only one of those spaces display, but I know the way around it. I use this small code to create each of my spaces: .

That thing is an ampersand command, which creates a space as if you pushed the spacebar. I have a whole tutorial on & commands in Appendix B if you would like to see more.

This is what I use when I indent five spaces:

```
     
```

See the five spaces? That's what I do. Look at the View Source of any of my tutorials if you don't believe me. There are other methods, but I like this one. In addition, this method works on all browsers at all version levels. It's a little more work, but you're sure to get your indent when you use my method.

Bulleted Lists

Bulleted lists are nice. Here's why I like them:

- They present information in an easy fashion.
- The bullets look cool.
- They make me happy.

Sorry about that last one. I just needed another item to make a three-item list. Figure 1.2 shows these bullets on a Web site. Here's how you do it:

```
<UL>
<LI>They present information in an easy fashion.
<LI>The bullets look cool.
<LI>They make me happy.
</UL>
```

Don't be put off by the commands; there are actually only two commands being used again and again. Here's what's happening:

- <UL> Stands for unordered list. That means bullets are used rather than numbers.
- <LI> Stands for list item. It denotes the next thing that receives a bullet. Please note that no </LI> is required. The text stays within a confined space and remains indented from the left without your doing anything.

The <LI> does all that good stuff for you, such as make the little black dot. </UL> ends the entire list.

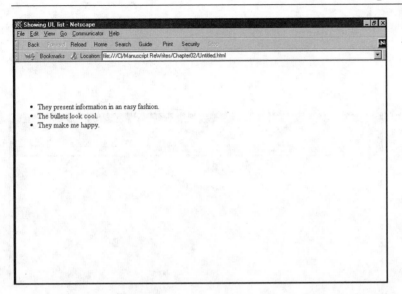

Figure 1.2
A bulleted list.

Using a center command before these commands doesn't center the entire list. It centers each item. That messes up the look of the list. If you would like to move the list closer to the center of the page, simply add more <UL> commands. Just remember that if you use three <UL> commands, you need to offer three </UL> commands. Such as this:

```
<UL><UL><UL>
<LI> list item
</UL></UL></UL>
```

Please note though that using multiple <UL> flags creates different looking bullets. The first <UL> level is a solid dot, the second is a circle, and the third is a square. The preceding example would create a square bullet. It's not quite the same with multiple <OL> flags.

Multiple <OL> lists do not change the text of the numbers or the letters. If you set the TYPE to I, however, it indents each list level.

For more precise control over the spacing you can add an   to bump the text over a little more.

I Don't Like Round Bullets—I Want Squares!!!

Easy there, fellah. You can have your list and squares too. Simply add the command TYPE="square" into your UL command. Figure 1.3 shows what your bulleted list would look like.

```
<UL TYPE="square">
<LI>List Item 1
<LI>List Item 2
<LI>List Item 3
</UL>
```

Figure 1.3
A bulleted list with square bullets.

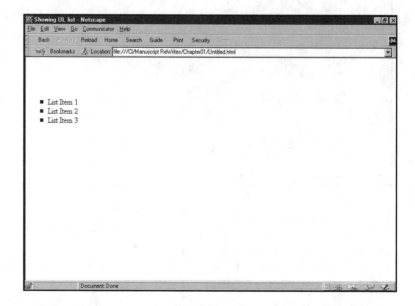

Numbered Lists

If you would like to create a list that numbers the items rather than just bulleting them, HTML can do that for you, too. Yeah, you could just number the things yourself, but that's no fun. It's also time-consuming. Figure 1.4 is an example of a numbered list. Notice it's the same format as the other lists, except <OL> is where <UL> used to be. Nothing to it. The browser continues to count as long as you keep putting <LI> items after the <OL>. By the way, OL stands for ordered list.

```
<OL>
<LI>List Item 1
<LI>List Item 2
<LI>List Item 3
</OL>
```

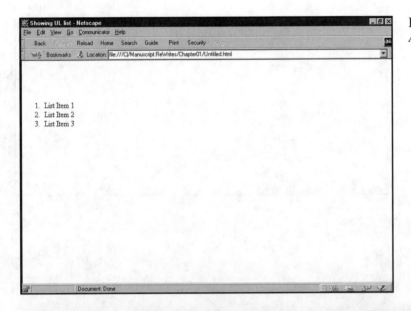

Figure 1.4
A numbered list.

FAQs from the HTML Goodies Web Site

Q. How can I get the list to start at a specific number? I need the list to start at 3.

A. Add the subcommand START="3" to the <OL> flag, so that you get this: <OL_START= "3">. Keep in mind that is a fairly new command and might not work across all browsers.

I Want Roman Numerals!!!

Arabic isn't good enough for you, huh? Well, simply place a TYPE="I" inside the <OL> flag. Notice that is a capital I, not the number 1. See the list in Figure 1.5. Here's how you do it:

```
<OL TYPE="I">
<LI>List Item 1
<LI>List Item 2
<LI>List Item 3
</OL>
```

Figure 1.5
A numbered list with Roman numerals.

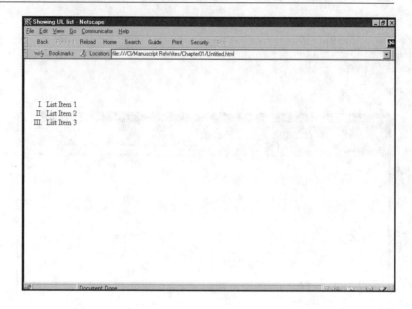

Start the Count After One

Maybe you don't want your count to start at one every time. That's easy to fix. This is an ordered list that starts at four.

```
<OL START="4">
<LI>List Item 1
<LI>List Item 2
<LI>List Item 3
</OL>
```

Try it yourself.

Combining Types of Lists

You can combine lists, but just remember to close each one. You could make an <OL> list and put in a small <UL> under each <LI> command for the <OL>. The following code produces what you see in Figure 1.6:

```
<OL>
<LI>Main Heading
  <UL>
    <LI>List item 1
    <LI>List item 2
  </UL>
<LI>Secondary Heading
```

```
<UL>
   <LI>List item 1
   <LI>List item 2
</UL>
</OL>
```

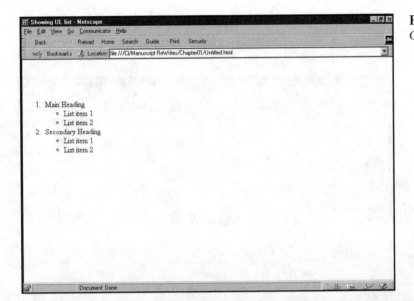

Figure 1.6
Combining types of lists.

FAQs from the HTML Goodies Web Site

Q. I see sites where some of the bullets (little dots) are just circles. How do I do that?

A. My guess is that those little circles were created because the person is using a <UL> list under another <UL> list (as shown earlier). That produces different types of bullets at each level.

 You can check out multiple lists under lists and see the kind of bullets produced by going to http://www.htmlgoodies.com/book/diffbullets.html.

A Definition List

There's one more set of list commands that manipulates the text for you. The previous ones are all single-item lists; each <LI> flag makes one list item (see Figure 1.7). The following tags all work together to create a specific type of list. Here's what the HTML looks like:

```
<H4>Here's What's For Dinner</H4>
<DL>
<DT>Salad
<DD>Green stuff and dressing
<DT>The Meal
<DD>Mystery meat and mashed yams
<DT>Dessert
<DD>A mint
</DL>
```

Figure 1.7
A definition list.

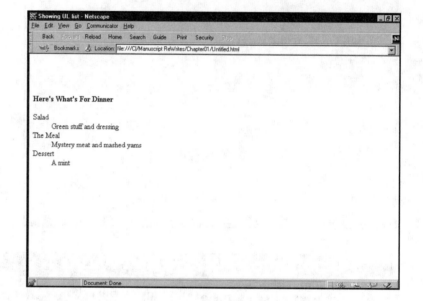

This is what's happening: I used an <H4> command to create a heading.

- <DL> Stands for definition list. It tells the browser that a double-tier list is coming up.
- <DT> Stands for definition term. It's the first tier.
- <DD> Stands for definition description. It's indented and describes the definition term.

It's a nice look, although I haven't run into any place to use it quite yet. I usually go with multiple <UL> lists, one under the other.

Well, that's all I have. You can play with the text all you want inside of these list commands. Bold, italic, and any other text command you want works. Use the list commands to present information to your readers in a fashion smoother than writing long, drawn-out paragraphs with a lot of detail. I use these lists all the time. Enjoy, and happy listing.

Newspaper Columns

Look at Figure 1.8!

Figure 1.8
Creating newspaper-style columns.

Sorry for the drama, but it had to appear newspaper-like. Now onto the matter at hand—how did I get these three nice columns? (Please note that the techniques in this section work in Netscape Navigator browsers only! Internet Explorer browser has to use tables to get somewhat the same effect.) I used a command that looks more like an afterthought than something the HTML know-it-alls created for everyday use.

I used this to get the effect shown in Figure 1.8:

```
<MULTICOL COLS="3" GUTTER="10" WIDTH="90%">
text text text text text, etc., etc.
</MULTICOL>
```

To do this, simply surround a block of text with the commands <MULTICOL> and </MULTICOL>. Then you're off and running.

There are three other subcommands that go with MULTICOL. They all go inside the first MULTICOL as subcommands and affect everything in between:

- COLS="#"   Denotes how many columns your page has. I chose three. I just felt like a trio at the time.

- GUTTER="#"   Denotes the width, in pixels, between the columns of text. I chose the number 25 for this lovely tutorial.

- WIDTH="#"   Denotes the overall width of the columns combined. All the commands that manipulate text shape, such as CENTER and ALIGN, work inside the column. If you center something, it centers inside the column. You knew that.

 To see an example of these commands being used, go to http://www.htmlgoodies. com/book/multicol.html.

FAQs from the HTML Goodies Web Site

Q. How do I make sure that both Netscape and Explorer users can see my newspaper columns, since the <MULTICOL> flag only works in Netscape?

A. Don't use the <MULTICOL> flag. There's no way you can "make" a browser use a command if it doesn't understand it. You need to create this effect via table cells; see Chapter 5, "Tables." That's the only way to ensure it's working across browsers.

Speaking of commands that don't work in certain browsers:

Q. What happens if I use a command that Internet Explorer understands, but Navigator does not? Does the code show up, cause problems, or what?

A. None of the above. The one really nice thing about all the browsers out there right now is that they are very adept at ignoring commands they don't understand. If you have commands that produce something in Internet Explorer, but not in Netscape, go ahead and use them. The Explorer users get to see the effect and the Netscape users never know the commands were there to begin with. Just don't make the commands that work in one browser or the other a crucial part of your page.

I think the <MULTICOL> flag is a bit of an afterthought because a command that jumps you to the beginning of the next column to start a new story or heading does not exist. The flag simply takes text and breaks it into columns. The only real downfall is that you have to keep scrolling the browser window up and down to read the silly thing.

Oh, and in case you were wondering if a <MULTIROW> command exists, the answer is yes. It's called paragraphs. Ha! I kill me!

Chapter 2

Creating Links

Ah links! I see them as the great equalizer. Any site can link to any site. The smallest can link to the biggest. The biggest can link to the smallest, but usually it's the other way around.

Links are great and they're unbelievably easy to create and maintain. Links attach everything to everything. They don't call it a "Web" for nothing.

Setting Up a Site

Answering a ton of e-mail every day enables me to keep an eye on when the new batch of HTML writers comes into the fold. The questions I receive always become more and more difficult, and then all of a sudden they become much simpler. The latest group of people has arrived. With that in mind, I offer this—a popular topic with beginning writers.

 This tutorial is online at `http://www.htmlgoodies.com/tutors/sitelinks.html`.

Putting A Site Together

Okay, you write some pages. Let's say you create a home page. You call it `homepage.html`.

You then create three more pages:

- `links.html`   A page of your favorite links
- `photos.html`   A page of your favorite photos
- `story.html`   A page with one of your best stories

At the moment they are just sitting on your hard drive or floppy disk; `homepage.html` offers links to the three other pages. That is your first site—good start. How do you hook them all together?

HREF *Links*

First, I'm assuming you already have a place to post these pages. If you don't, read over Primer 7, "Graduation Day," for help finding and choosing an Internet service provider (ISP).

Now you have a place for your files. This "place" you have been given is actually a small section of a hard drive on a server somewhere. In computer lingo, you have a directory where you can place your files. Think of this directory like an equal to a floppy disk or a directory on your own hard drive. It's a contained area where the pages (and all the images that go on those pages) are housed.

This is important to remember when you're writing the links that connect the four pages.

FAQs from the HTML Goodies Web Site

Q. I made links like you said, but they don't work. I checked for spelling, but that's all correct. What's wrong?

A. If the spelling and capitalization are correct in reference to the file you're calling for, I would think the problem might be between .htm and .html. Servers sometimes see them as two different files. If the file you are calling for is .htm and you call for .html, the link doesn't work. Check that.

You know what else it may be? The site could be gone. This won't happen with many of the big sites like Yahoo! and HTML Goodies, but if you link to a person's personal site, it may just go away with no warning. It's been known to happen.

On-Site Versus Off-Site Links

First attach to a page outside of your site. This is called an *off-site link*. This is the basic format:

```
<A HREF="http://www.htmlgoodies.com">Click Here</A>
```

Note that the address is a full URL (Universal Resource Locator). It starts with that `http` thing and ends with that `.com` deal.

The format is simple. The A stands for anchor and the HREF stands for hypertext reference. It's a reference to another page, thus the address `http://www.htmlgoodies.com`.

Now let's look at what I call an *on-site* or *internal link*. This is a link that stays within your own site. One of your pages is calling for another one of your pages. This is a link from `homepage.html` to `links.html`. Remember those two from earlier? Here's the format:

```
<A HREF="links.html">Click Here</A>
```

Notice I'm only calling for the page without the full address attached? Why not? I don't need it. To make the point a little stronger, look at the directory structure of Web addresses.

Note

You've probably already read through Primer 4,"Making a Link to Someone Else." If not, give it a once-over pretty soon. It gives you the basic format of a link.

Linking Using Directory Structures

For the sake of continuing this discussion, and because I love to hear myself talk, let's take this little fantasy of mine a bit further. You purchase an account on a server called `www.joeserver.com`. You choose the login `schmoe` when you sign up for your account. This means that your e-mail address most likely is `schmoe@joeserver.com` and your Web site address is `http://www.joeserver.com/~schmoe`. The little squiggly line (~) is called a tilde. It tells the server, "There is one Web directory on this server called `schmoe`—find it."

When you use your file transfer protocol (FTP) program to upload files to your new server, you upload into the directory that was set aside for you; in this case, `schmoe`.

You upload your `homepage.html` page into your directory. The address of that page is now `http://www.joeserver.com/~schmoe/homepage.html`.

See the slash I added and the name? I do that because the `homepage.html` page is now inside your `schmoe` directory.

Think of a directory structure as one item being inside a larger item. For example, a word is inside a sentence, is inside a paragraph, is inside a page, is inside a chapter, is inside a book. If this were written in directory structure format, it would look like this:

```
Book/chapter/page/paragraph/sentence/word
```

Notice that the bigger ones are to the left. The items get smaller as you move to the right. Take this URL for example:

```
http://www.server.com/users/pages/ohio/joe.html
```

The page `joe.html` is inside a directory called `ohio`, is inside a directory called `pages`, is inside a directory called `users`, and is on a server called `server.com`.

That's why the page `homepage.html` is at the end of the address. Make sense?

To Use Full URL, or Not to Use Full URL

If you are linking to a page from your site, you must use the full URL because you are leaving your own directory. In fact, the chances are really good that you are leaving your server altogether. Because of that, you need to offer your HREF attribute the full address to the new site.

When you're staying within your own site you need only call for the page name. You see, your directory is a closed home for all your pages. If you only call for a page or an image through its name (minus the full address), the server looks for the page or the image inside the same home that houses the page that called for it. In other words, servers search a page's home directory by default. That's good to know when you create your links. This means you only have to use the page's name minus the full URL.

If you do choose to use the full URL your internal links might run slower. If you use the full address, a full search process begins when your user clicks a link. First the server is located, next the directory is located, and then the page is located. If you use only the name, the search is already at its destination. The server simply searches itself. Slick, huh?

FAQs from the HTML Goodies Web Site

Q. I've written my pages using the full URL every time. Would you suggest going in and changing them?

A. If the site is working up to your expectations, I wouldn't go to the trouble unless you simply have the time to kill.

Home Page Links

What is written onto `homepage.html` that links the pages together? This:

```
<A HREF="links.html">Click Here for My Favorite Links</A>
<A HREF="photos.html">Click Here for My Photos</A>
<A HREF="story.html">Click Here for My Best Story</A>
```

Now you're all linked. Hey! You made more than a couple of pages. You linked them all together. You made a site.

I have this exact example set up at `http://www.htmlgoodies.com/book/site.html`.

Page Jumps

I get letters about how to do these internal page jumps all the time. They are a great way to enable people to move quickly inside a long page. I have them all over my HTML Goodies tutorials. Stop into any of them; at the top and bottom there are hypertext links that send you to whatever sections you choose. They are great for helping people navigate big pages—and I have big pages. I just can't shut up when I get rolling.

 This tutorial is online at http://www.htmlgoodies.com/tutors/pagejump.html.

How You Do It

You need to place two items on each page:

- A basic link command pointing to another section of the page
- The point where the page jumps

Here's the basic link command:

```
<A HREF="#codeword">Blue Words, Blue Words</A>
```

This command then denotes where the link scrolls on the page:

```
<A NAME="codeword">
```

You place this command at what you want to represent the top of the browser screen. When the page jumps to this point, wherever the code word is placed in the code is what is at the top of the browser window. I usually put some space on the page before the code word by using <BR> flags so that I don't cut any words off, but that's just a suggestion.

These jumps offer a great look. Netscape Navigator just jumps right to the spot and Internet Explorer actually does a quick scroll.

Here's What's Happening

Take a look at this quick rundown:

- The A HREF command is the same as a basic link except the link is to a code word rather than to a URL.
- Please notice the # sign in front of the code word. You need that to denote it's an internal link. Without the # sign, the browser looks for something outside the page named after your code word, and it isn't going be there.
- Your "codeword" can be just about anything you want. I try my best to keep it short and make it represent what it is jumping to.

○ The point where the page jumps follows the same general format, except you replace the word HREF with the word NAME.

○ Please also notice no # sign in the NAME command.

○ Where you place the <A NAME="codeword"> page jump target is the section of the HTML page that appears at the top of the browser window after the page jump occurs.

For example, let's say I want to create a link that jumps me halfway down the page. I use the code word "halfway" to denote that it's jumping 50% of the page.

The link would look like this:

```
<A HREF="#halfway">Click To Go Half Way Down the Page</A>
```

Now you need to place "halfway" in the code so that the link has somewhere to jump. That point would be put into the code using this flag:

```
<A NAME="halfway">
```

Notice that "HREF" is replaced with "NAME" and that there is no # mark in front of the code word. That flag is simply placed on the page as a "point" for the link to jump the user to.

FAQs from the HTML Goodies Web Site

Q. Is there a limit to the number of letters a code word can have?

A. There might be a limit to the number of letters you can use, but I haven't found it yet.

Q. Can I have spaces in my code word?

A. No. Just run the text all together or use underscores (_) between words. No spaces allowed.

Q. Do I have to use a different code word for every page jump on my site?

A. You mean completely? No—just on the same page. You can use the same code word on different pages. I do it all the time.

Now, let's say you have a tutorial—much the same as this one but online—and that you jump from page to page. It would make things a lot easier if, when you jump between pages, you could have the jumped-to page load at a specific point rather than loading at the top each time. Well, you can.

Jumping to a Specific Page Section

Okay, let's say you want to jump to a page at a certain point. You do so using a basic A HREF command that denotes both the page and the NAME target. It's going to look a lot like what we used above.

For the sake of example, I am looking at a page with this URL:

```
http://www.htmlgoodies.com/joe.html
```

I want to jump from that page to a whole other page. The page I am going to is:

```
http://www.htmlgoodies.com/pagejump.html
```

Furthermore, when I click to jump from joe.html to pagejump.html, I want pagejump.html to load as a specific point rather than loading right at the top.

To do that, I have to add an <A NAME="—"> code word flag just as we did above. I will use the flag:

```
<A NAME="welcomeback">
```

That flag is placed halfway down the code on the page pagejump.html as that is the page I am jumping to.

The Link Form

Take a look at the following code:

```
<A HREF="http://www.htmlgoodies.com/tutors/
➥pagejump.html#welcomeback">Blue Words, Blue Words</A>
```

See what's happening? I did a simple A HREF link back to the page—but I added the # sign and then the code word! No slashes or dots; just run it all together.

When the user clicks that link she'll go to the page and right to that section.

Use page jumps often. I think they're great. Your visitors thank you, too.

 I have a page for you to try out these page jumps; see http://www.htmlgoodies. com/book/pagejump.html.

Active Images (Images That Act Like Links)

This is a topic covered in the Primers section of HTML Goodies, but it deserves its own short section here. As the new wave of HTML artists are trying their hands at the craft, this is the question they ask most: How do I make an image act as a link to another page?

 This tutorial is online at `http://www.htmlgoodies.com/tutors/imagelink.html.`

Remember the basic text link format:

```
<A HREF="http://www.htmlgoodies.com">Click here for HTML Goodies</A>
```

`Click Here for HTML Goodies` shows up on the Web page, and it shows up in blue. Figure 2.1 shows an image whose name is `cool_computer.gif`. I use it as a link to the HTML Goodies page.

Figure 2.1
Hello, my name is
`cool_computer.gif.`

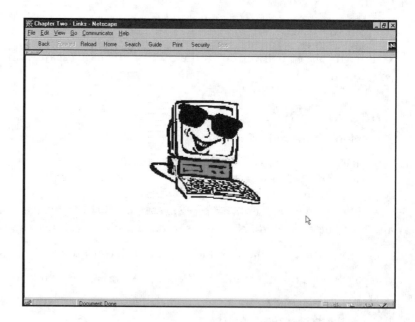

You can make an image a link by simply replacing the text that explains the link (in my example, it's `Click here for HTML Goodies`) and substitute the HTML code for an image.

```
<A HREF="http://www.htmlgoodies.com"><IMG SRC="cool_computer.gif"></A>
```

Figure 2.2 shows you what you get.

Figure 2.2
*The image is now a link.
Notice the mouse pointer
has turned into a hand,
which indicates a link.*

When you place your pointer over the image, you see it's active and points to the HTML Goodies home page. You're done. Almost.

FAQs from the HTML Goodies Web Site

Q. Can I use a JPEG image as a link?

A. Yes, just follow the same format I do with my GIF image.

Removing the Blue Border Around the Link Image

Look again at the image in Figure 2.2. See the border? That happens when you make an image active. Remember that linked text is blue? That's what happens here. If you like it, great. You're done. I think it looks unprofessional. I get rid of it. This is how:

```
<A HREF="http://www.htmlgoodies.com"><IMG BORDER="0" SRC="cool_computer.gif"></A>
```

Please be aware that that's BORDER equals 0, as in "zero;" not BORDER equals O as in the letter.

All I did was add the command BORDER="0" inside the image command, right between IMG and SRC. That sets the blue border around the active image to 0. You can see the borderless image in Figure 2.3. If you'd like, you can do the opposite and write in BORDER="50". That gives you a huge blue border.

Figure 2.3
The border around the link image is gone!

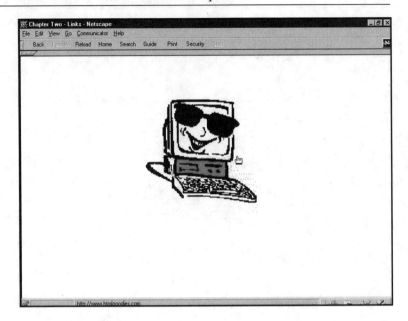

Lay your pointer on the image. It's still active, but no blue border. That looks much crisper.

FAQs from the HTML Goodies Web Site

Q. I found that I can set the link color to the same color as the background and the border disappears. That also allows me to make the border a lot bigger and gives the image some room.

A. Yup, that'll do it. You might want to think about also setting space apart for your image by using table commands to surround the image with a table cell and then using the cellpadding command to set space. (Read about tables in Chapter 5, "Tables.") By the way, make sure you set the VLINK color to the same shade as the background; otherwise the border shows up after someone has visited the linked page. You might also run into a few problems if the user has his or her own background colors set rather than using what you send them.

That's about it. However, remember that all images should have HEIGHT, WIDTH, and ALT commands attached to them to make the transfer of pages much faster and easier to understand. To learn more, go to Chapter 3, "Adding Images and Backgrounds."

 You can see a couple of active images demonstrating these sections at http://www.htmlgoodies.com/book/active.html.

Creating Links That Open a New Browser Window

I used to receive at least one letter a day asking for information on how to make a link open a new browser window, so I put this section together.

Opening a new browser window can help when navigating through frame pages, keeping one set open while you browse another. It is also good when you want to download out of frames pages. It also helps when you have a MIDI sound file on a page that you want to have continually playing through many pages, and this is a good way to show another page quickly and have your pages remain open. Remember, however, that the more pages you open through more browser windows, the more you are taxing the user's computer. You slow the process a bit and might crash computers that have less memory capacity.

 This tutorial is online at `http://www.htmlgoodies.com/tutors/new_win.html`.

You have two windows open at the same time when you use these commands. Keep this in mind:

- You can get back to the original browser screen by closing the top-level window. In Windows 3.*x*, choose Close under the File menu in the browser's top left. In Windows 95/98, select the button in the upper-right corner. Macintosh users can find the button in the upper-left corner. Of course, you can always toggle between the two new open windows.

- If you choose Exit, you close the browser altogether. You don't want to do that.

Here's the basic HTML code for creating a link that opens a new browser window:

```
<A HREF="http://www.site.com/page.html" TARGET="resource window">
➥Text Text Text</A>
```

See that `TARGET="resource window"`? That's what does it.

How Do I Stop It from Happening?

I also get letters stating that a client-side imagemap or a frames page is causing a new window to open. If you want to get rid of it try this:

```
<A HREF="http://www.site.com/page.html" TARGET=="_Top">
➥Text Text Text</A>
```

Notice that I targeted the link to the top of the page. This is the default in HTML. Not putting it in has always resulted in an `A HREF` link jumping to the top of the same browser window. You need to force the browser's hand to stop the new window from popping up to display the page the A HREF link is pointing to. Please notice the underline mark (under-score) before the word Top. Notice also that the "T" is capitalized.

FAQs from the HTML Goodies Web Site

Q. I have found that closing the browser and opening it again also solves the problem. Is this true?

A. I've heard that, too. I have also heard that holding the Shift key and selecting Reload often solves the problem.

Now go and use the commands for good, not evil. They are yours to exploit at your own will.

 See new windows galore at http://www.htmlgoodies.com/book/new_windows.html.

How to Create a Dynamic Page

If you see this tutorial online, you are treated to a slide show of sorts. Without you doing anything, the pages before you change every three seconds. That's the purpose of these commands, to perform a redirect with no user input.

 This tutorial is available online at http://www.htmlgoodies.com/tutors/dynamic1.html.

No, this tutorial has nothing to do with Dynamic HTML (DHTML). You find that in lucky Chapter 13, "Explorer-Specific Tutorials and DHTML." I use the term *dynamic* here because the process occurs without any input from the user. Plus, I was calling these commands dynamic long before DHTML was even a twinkle in the Internet's eye. I like to think of myself as progressive and ahead of the curve. My wife just says I'm lucky.

If you'd like to sound intelligent at your next cocktail party, the commands' actual name is *meta-refresh*.

Before you get started, wait—this page uses things called *meta commands*. What you learn here is a small part of what meta commands can do. See the section "Using Meta Commands with Search Engines" in Chapter 15, "Other Stuff You Should Really Know," for gobs more.

Getting a Page to Change

This is a great effect that offers your readers some surprises. I've seen this used to take people on guided tours, to tell jokes, and almost talk to the viewer, which is just what I do with this tutorial online. You should be able to find an equally good use.

Here are the commands I placed on my HTML document to get the page-changing effect:

```
<META HTTP-EQUIV="refresh"
CONTENT="5;URL=http://www.page.com/page.html">
```

I placed it right after the <HTML> (and <HEAD> if you're using one) command and just before the <TITLE> and </TITLE> commands.

Here's What You Are Telling the Computer To Do

Here's a list of the code broken down:

- META HTTP-EQUIV Tells the computer that after the page is loaded to find an HTTP equivalent item—another Web page in other words.

- REFRESH Tells the computer that it's supposed to refresh the page. It reloads the page, but because you are offering a different URL, it loads that new page rather than refreshing itself.

- CONTENT A strange word in this case. It denotes the number of seconds before the meta-refresh is to occur. I have this one set at five seconds. You can set it at whatever you want.

- URL The address it's supposed to load after the five seconds (or however many you denote).

FAQs from the HTML Goodies Web Site

Q. How can I make this change almost instantaneous?

A. Set the content to 0.

The CONTENT command includes the URL command, so no quotation mark after the 5 or before the URL. Make a point of copying exactly what is noted in the preceding code. It doesn't work otherwise.

How to Add Sound

Those of you who saw this tutorial online should have gotten a little "ta da" sound when you logged in. That's another thing you can do with this META format. I had it set up so that after the page loaded, your browser should have played a little .au file called tada.au (clever name, eh?).

Here's the command that did the job:

```
<META HTTP-EQUIV="refresh" CONTENT="1; URL=http://www.page.com/tada.au">
```

I simply replaced the URL with a sound file address.

There are a few assumptions you make using these dynamic commands:

- The viewer has a browser level 1.1 or higher. If your viewer is using 1.0 or a browser with text-only capabilities (yes, they do still exist, contrary to the growth of the World Wide Web), the dynamic page that is supposed to change just sits there. Then the viewer waits...and waits...and nothing happens. He swears at you and moves on.

- The viewer can play what you have offered because you use a sound file. That's a tough call because there are many different filenames. I suggest trying wav or .mid first (my opinion). Those are very common music formats and most browsers are able to run them.

- People care to see the little page change or hear that "ta da" every time they log on—a very big assumption.

You can read a great deal more about incorporating sounds into your Web pages in Chapter 10, "Sound and Video."

FAQs from the HTML Goodies Web Site

Q. Can I set it so that the sound only plays once?

A. I did that by creating only one page that has the sound on it. Past that, every link back to the page that has the sound goes to a copy of that page—the one without the sound file on it. The effect is that the page loads without playing the sound. Of course, it doesn't work if the user hits the Back button.

My suggestion is to use these pups sparingly and offer those less browserly-endowed a way around the effect. Put something on the page that is supposed to change but enables users to click and join in the merriment of your page.

 Go to `http://www.htmlgoodies.com/book/metarefresh.html` *to see this in action.*

So You Don't Want Links Underlined?

Please note that taking the underline away from links requires that your browser recognize style commands. That generally means Netscape Navigator browsers 3.0 or later or Internet Explorer–style browsers. Take a look at the links in Figure 2.4.

This tutorial is online at `http://www.htmlgoodies.com/tutors/nounderlineonlinks.html`.

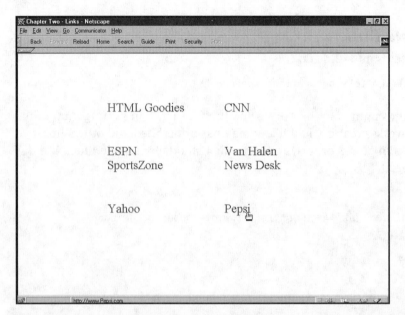

Figure 2.4
Links with no underlines.

Notice anything about them? They are not underlined, yet they're still active. Notice that the pointer is a hand over top of the Pepsi link?

By the way, if you followed this tutorial and your links are still underlined, you might not have a browser level high enough to run this command. You can still use the commands, though; others have the correct browser!

For a good while, people wrote to me and asked how to rid the links on their page of the awful underline. I always wrote back that you could always get rid of it—just go into your browser's preferences and set it, so the links are not underlined. Done.

But I knew what they wanted. They wanted the links to be without underlines on all browsers, not just theirs. Here's how you do it:

```
<STYLE>
<!--
A{text-decoration:none}
-->
</STYLE>
```

You place that STYLE block statement inside the HEAD commands on your HTML document. In that position, it affects all the links and makes them plain, like you see here. The links retain their coloring, but lose their underline.

Affecting Just One Link

To make just one link lose its underline do this:

```
<A HREF="wherever" STYLE="text-decoration: none">Huh</a>
```

I added the style commands right into the A HREF link itself rather than putting it up in the <HEAD> commands. This works great if you'd like some links underlined and others not. I've seen non-underlined links in blocks of text, and those that stood alone underlined. It did make the page easier to read.

Pretty slick.

 See a few links that aren't underlined at http://www.htmlgoodies.com/book/ nounderline.html.

Chapter 3

Adding Images and Backgrounds

Images are a big part of what makes the Web so great. Learning how to manipulate images on your Web page is key to building a great site.

Grabbing Images Off the Web

Let me state up front that just because you have the ability to grab an image does not mean that you always can…legally. Copyright laws, contrary to what some people believe, apply to the Internet. I have a whole slew of copyright questions and answers in Chapter 15, "Other Stuff You Should Really Know." For now, a good rule of thumb is to always ask permission to use the images you want unless the person is specifically offering the image for downloading. Just to be more of a party-pooper, if you know the image being offered is copyrighted, don't use it. You are just as guilty for posting the image as the person offering it.

As a fine Ohio State trooper once told me, "Ignorance of the law is no excuse, young man." Then he gave me a $70 ticket.

If you'd like to brush up on how copyright laws work in regard to the Internet before pushing on, see the copyright reference in Chapter 15.

 This tutorial is available online at `http://www.htmlgoodies.com/howto.html`.

Always make a point, when downloading images and placing them on your own server, to run them. Don't make an HREF link to other people's servers running the image. By doing that, you are unnecessarily taxing the other person's server and might be breaking a copyright law. Furthermore, if the image is on your server, you get it to load to your page much faster.

How It's Done

After you have determined whether or not you can legally use an image from another site, it's a fairly simple process to grab that image for your own use. Begin by simply going to the Web site with the image you want to use. After the image comes up on the screen, place your pointer on it. Figure 3.1 shows an image of a basketball for demonstration.

Figure 3.1
An image with a pointer on top.

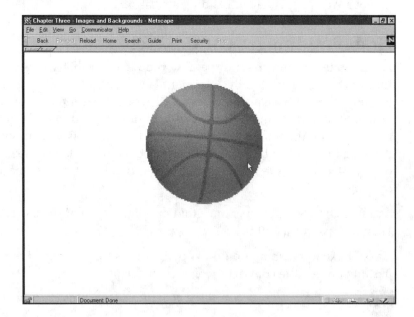

When your pointer is on the image, click the right mouse button. Macintosh users should push the mouse button and hold it. A menu appears, as shown in Figure 3.2.

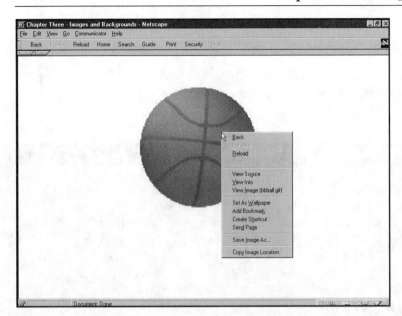

Figure 3.2
The menu that appears with a right-click.

Now choose to save the image, as shown in Figure 3.3.

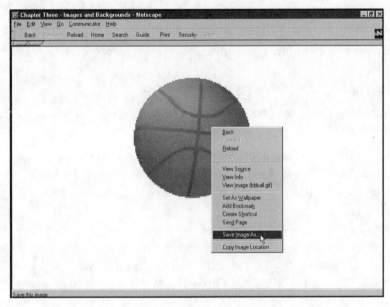

Figure 3.3
Choosing Save Image As from the right-click menu.

When you choose to save the image, your computer's Save As dialog box pops up. There you tell it where to save the image on your computer's hard drive or to floppy disk.

Enjoy!

 You can try to download an image (with the instructions printed right underneath) from `http://www.htmlgoodies.com/book/trydownload.html`.

FAQs from the HTML Goodies Web Site

Q. How do I get images right next to each other?

A. You mean so they look like one larger image? Just use two image commands and place them next to each other—on the same line. Placing one below the other might create a space between them. Also, if the images are active, make sure to use BORDER="0", or they'll never butt against each other.

Aligning Text with Images

People ask all the time how to get images onto pages. If you aren't sure how yet, take a look at Primer 5, "Placing an Image on Your Page." After people get those images onto a page, they start asking how to get text to align or wrap around the images they have placed there. That's the purpose of this tutorial—to tell you how to get the text to wrap.

 You can get to this tutorial online at `http://www.htmlgoodies.com/tutors/align.html`.

Getting Text to Wrap

One of the more popular questions I receive is how to get text to wrap around a left- or right-aligned image as in the example in Figure 3.4.

Notice that the two images, the hand and the book, are sitting far left and then far right and the text just wraps around them. This is done by adding one command to the image itself. This is the code for the pointing finger:

```
<IMG SRC="finger.gif" ALIGN="left">
```

Notice that all I did was add the ALIGN="left" command inside a basic image command and between the IMG and the SRC. "But wait!" you say, "The image was already aligned to the left before you added the ALIGN command." Yes, I know. The ALIGN command caused the wrap of the text. Without it, you wouldn't get the effect.

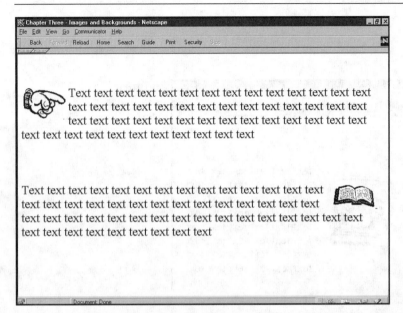

Figure 3.4
*Text wrapping around left-
and right-justified images.*

The image was to the left of the page because that is the browser's default placement of the image. Adding the ALIGN="left" forces the image to stay left while the text cascades down and around it.

As for how I got the image to move to the right and the text to wrap, this is the code:

```
<IMG SRC="book.gif" ALIGN="right">
```

This is the same format except I told the image to align to the right. In this instance, the image was moved and the text wrapped around it. I use these commands all the time; they are very useful. Now let's get a bit fancier.

Centering an Image in Text

Figure 3.5 shows an example of text wrapping on either side of an image. Isn't that a neat trick, getting the image in the middle of flowing text? It actually isn't much of a trick. It's a three-celled table with half the text in one side and half in the other.

To do it, I wrote the text I wanted and split it into the two parts. I made sure to write enough text so that the image height was equaled. I then put it all into this table format:

```
<TABLE BORDER="0" CELLPADDING="3" CELLSPACING="3">
<TR>
<TD> First Half of Text</TD>
<TD> Image</TD>
```

97

```
<TD> Second Half of Text</TD>
</TR>
</TABLE>
```

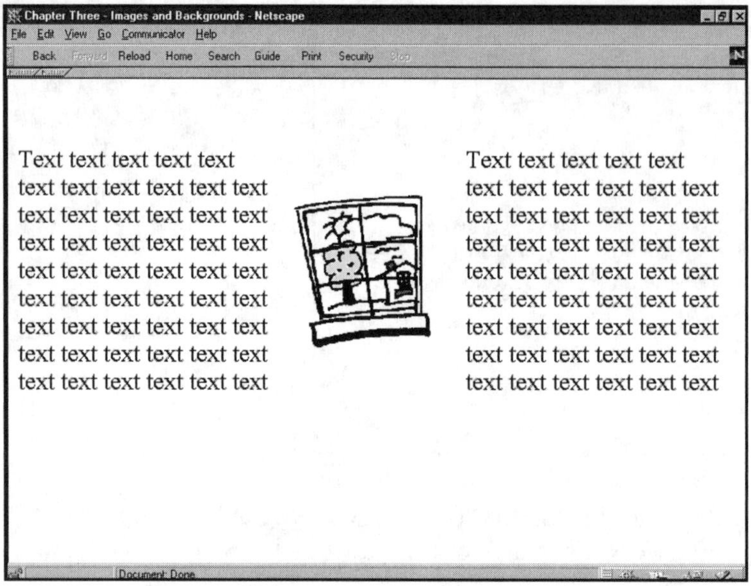

Figure 3.5
An image in the middle of text.

FAQs from the HTML Goodies Web Site

Q. Why can't I use `ALIGN="center"` **so that text wraps around both sides?**

A. Because the command doesn't work that way; that's the best reason I can give. Go with table cells.

If you're following through the book in order, you probably haven't gotten around to tables yet. I cover them in mind-numbing detail in Chapter 5, "Tables." For now, look over the format I offer here and understand what this does. It offers a jump-start.

Speaking of Tables...

Does the `ALIGN="###"` command work when you are using tables? Sure does. Just make a point of adding `ALIGN="left"` or `ALIGN="right"` inside the main `TABLE` command. Like so:

```
<TABLE BORDER="3" CELLPADDING="3" CELLSPACING="3" ALIGN="left">
<TR>
<TD>Table Cell</TD>
<TD>Table Cell</TD>
```

```
</TR><TR>
<TD>Table Cell</TD>
<TD>Table Cell</TD>
</TR>
</TABLE>
```

Figure 3.6 shows a table aligned to the left of the text.

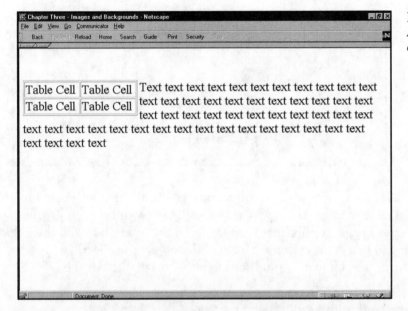

Figure 3.6
A table aligned to the left of text.

Of course, you can also align the table to the right of the screen by changing the command to `ALIGN="right"`, just like in the earlier image commands.

FAQs from the HTML Goodies Web Site

Q. Can I wrap a list around an image?

A. Yes. Just follow the `ALIGN="###"` format and put the UL or OL list where you would regular text. (If lists are also new to you, you can read about them in Chapter 1, "Playing with Text.")

Aligning One Line of Text

If you want to align one line of text (a title, for instance) with a picture, use one of three commands in the `ALIGN` flag: `top`, `middle`, or `bottom` (see Figure 3.7).

Figure 3.7

Lines of text top, middle, and bottom aligned with images.

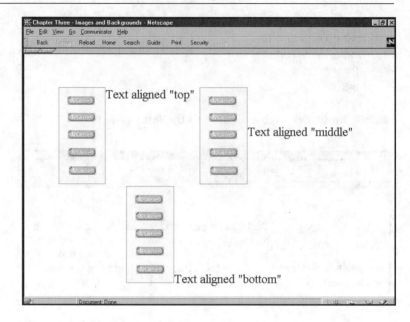

Remember that the top, middle, and bottom ALIGN commands refer to the text in relation to the image. They do not place the image. The only real downfall is that you cannot use two ALIGN commands in the same image. For instance, you can align the image left and then the text top just by putting in two ALIGN commands, but you can't get the effect. You need to align the text inside the image command, and then align the image through the <P> command.

These align commands also work with headings and HR flags. Give it a try.

Aligning Two Lines of Text Around an Image

If you've tried the top, middle, and bottom commands, you know that after you run out of browser screen and get more than one line of text, the second line jumps under the picture. The following code shows you how to get that one-line effect and denote exactly where the line breaks and jumps under the image, or how to get only a small amount of text to wrap around the image and then jump below the image:

```
<IMG ALIGN="left" SRC="image.gif">Text text text text text text
<BR CLEAR="all">
text text text text.
```

That little <BR CLEAR="all"> doodad clears the remainder of the picture wrap and starts you on the next line under the picture (see Figure 3.8).

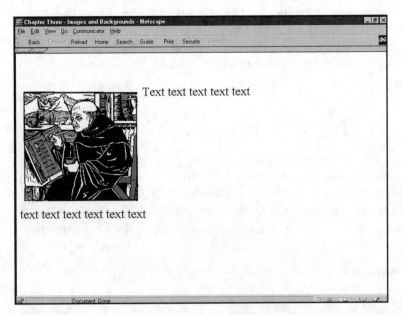

Figure 3.8
Text wrapping, and then jumping under an image.

Some may say they want the text to start down the picture a bit. What they want is the same effect as the ALIGN="middle" or ALIGN="bottom" commands. This is easy to do—add blank lines.

"But," you say, "I have tried adding 50 <P> commands and I never get more than one line." That's true. That's because you never put anything on the line after the <P> command. Try this:

```
<P> <P>
```

This little deal adds a couple blank lines. Why? Because the   is a space. You've put something on the line so the next <P> can act. The space is invisible, so no one sees it and you get two blank lines. Slick, huh? Use a few to "bump" your text down the image face.

Some programmer friends of mine tell me that I can get the same effect by simply adding a slew of <BR> flags. That's true, but I like this method. I just grew up on it. If you'd rather add multiple <BR> flags, go for it.

FAQs from the HTML Goodies Web Site

Q. Why do you add blank spaces to get text to the top? Why not use the VALIGN="top" command to do the trick?

A. Because VALIGN is a newer command and my method works across all browsers at all levels. If you want to use the VALIGN command, and the text being at the top isn't terribly needed, use it.

Using HEIGHT, WIDTH, and ALT Commands

Have you ever gone into someone's site and sat there waiting, looking at a blank page? You know the page is loading because the little numbers across the bottom are rolling, but you see nothing and the browser screen is blank. My pages don't do that. When you log onto HTML Goodies, the entire page's text loads right away. The images are not there yet, but little boxes that appear to be pressed into the page are just waiting for the image to arrive. Sometimes even text tells you what's going to go in the box. Neat trick, huh?

Actually, it's not all that tough to do. Make a point of denoting every image on the page with HEIGHT, WIDTH, and ALT commands.

HEIGHT *and* WIDTH *Commands*

This is an example of how to use the HEIGHT and WIDTH commands:

```
<IMG HEIGHT="45" WIDTH="22" SRC="image.gif">
```

The commands are denoting the image's height and width in pixels. *Pixels* are little colored dots. If you put enough of them close together, they form a picture.

The word pixels actually is a combination of two other words, *picture* and *element*.

Those of you with vivid imaginations know that the HEIGHT and WIDTH commands can be used to change an image's shape. If the image is really 50×50 and you put in HEIGHT and WIDTH commands of 150 and 10, you distort the picture pretty well. For an example, see Primer 6, "Manipulating Images."

A better way to use the commands is to denote an image's exact height and width. I know that seems a bit silly on the surface, but if you do it for all the images on your page, the page and its text load completely, leaving open spaces for the pictures to load later. The viewer is reading and surfing your site immediately, rather than waiting for the whole page to load.

FAQs from the HTML Goodies Web Site

Q. Should the HEIGHT and WIDTH numbers be exactly the same as the image, or maybe a little bigger?

A. No, go with the exact size.

Q. You talk about HEIGHT and WIDTH, but you never tell how I can make it so that one image loads before another one.

A. I don't talk about it because you can't do it. The images load in the order they are on the page, or at least try to come in that order (as long as Net congestion doesn't hinder their working).

ALT *Command*

I get letters from people saying they want the commands that place text in those little yellow boxes, or they want the commands that make the little yellow boxes pop up when a mouse pointer is placed on an image. Here you go: the ALT command.

FAQs from the HTML Goodies Web Site

Q. You should let your users know that they need to use the ALT command every time they place an image. That ALT command is read by computers used by the blind and tells them what the image is.

A. Good point. Thanks for writing. This user is correct. When you place text using the ALT command you are helping those using disabled-assistant browsers to "see" what your image represents. To that end, don't be too goofy with your ALT text. Make a point of having the text represent what the image looks like.

ALT is short for alternative. It's the text that pops up as an alternative to the actual image. It also sits inside the image box and pops up in the yellow box, officially known as a ToolTip. All that is from one little command. It's a great world, isn't it?

The text following the ALT commands is used to tell the viewer what's coming. Other text could be entered so that more information about a picture is given as the person lays the mouse pointer over it. Here's the format:

```
<IMG HEIGHT="45" WIDTH="22" ALT="Good Picture" SRC="image.gif">
```

Figure 3.9 is an example of the ToolTip box popping up.

103

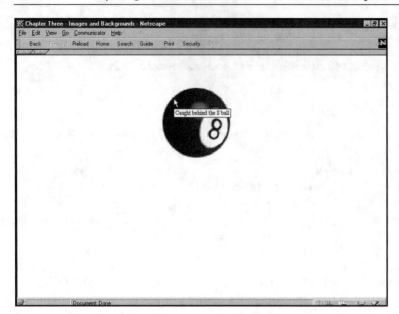

Figure 3.9
The ToolTip window that pops up when you place your cursor on an image.

And that's that. Use the HEIGHT, WIDTH, and ALT commands to help your viewers understand and move through your pages faster.

 To see an ALT *command in action, go to* http://www.htmlgoodies.com/book/alttest. html. *Watch it as the page loads; you see the text in the box.*

How Do I Find Each Image's Size?

The best way to determine an image's size is to grab a graphics editor either by buying one or by downloading one of the shareware versions off the Web. I'm partial to Paint Shop Pro for my shareware download. You can also get the height and width of an image using your browser.

In Netscape, right-click the image. Mac users click and hold. Choose the menu item, "Show Image." The height and width is in the title bar.

In Internet Explorer, right-click the image. MAC users should click and hold. Choose the menu item Properties. The height and width pops up in the box.

If your pages are already written, I would suggest that you take the time to go in, grab each image's height and width, and add it to the existing IMG flags. I believe it's that important.

 To try getting an image by itself on the screen to get the height and width, go to http://www.htmlgoodies.com/book/hw.html.

Making Lines with Images

Here is a great trick that helps you create nice, straight, colorful lines on your page without taxing or slowing your server. Look at the series of horizontal lines in Figure 3.10.

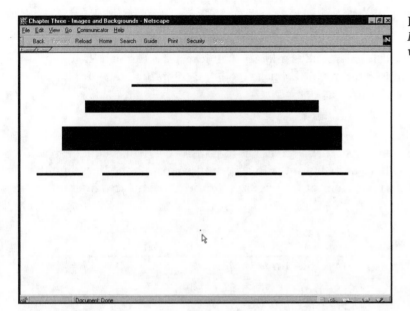

Figure 3.10
Horizontal lines created with images.

Every line you see was created using the same image. You can see the image if you look very hard: It's the dot right at the tip of the mouse pointer. That's what has become known as the 1×1 image. It's only one pixel tall and one pixel wide, but it can do some great things with the image's height and width.

 To see this tutorial online, go to `http://www.htmlgoodies.com/tutors/1x1.html`.

The Image

No way around it, you need to be able to make an image—a 1×1 pixel image. I use Paint Shop Pro; it's shareware and available at a number of different sites. At the time of this writing, `http://www.jasc.com` and `http://shareware.cnet.com` have it.

That done, use the image program to create a 1×1 image. Some programs don't enable you to make anything smaller than 2×2. That's fine; do it.

How to Use the Image

Easy as pie. When you have the little image, you can play around with its size through HEIGHT and WIDTH commands. See that thick black line in Figure 3.10? Here's the code I used to make it:

```
<IMG WIDTH="500" HEIGHT="25" SRC="1x1.gif">
```

It's just a little image named 1x1.gif made far larger than it really is through the use of HEIGHT and WIDTH commands. Since the little image is all one color, the line is a solid color the whole way across. It's a great effect.

Why on Earth Would I Do This?

Speed—pure and simple. Remember that a server has to transfer every image that is placed on a page. The smaller the image, the faster the image travels across phone lines, and the faster the image loads. Let's take a look at relative sizes for the different sized lines in Table 3.1.

Table 3.1   Image Sizes

Line Size	Bytes Required
300×2 (thin line)	256 bytes
500×25 (thick line)	3001 bytes
1×1 (small image)	8 bytes

You can see that the 8-byte image loads and displays far faster than creating the images in different sizes. In addition, one image creates all the lines rather than the server being asked for three different lines.

You can add some color into the deal if you go with a 2×2 or larger image. I once made a 6×6 image and changed the color of every pixel in my graphics editor. It made a very ugly line, but it was only 16 bytes.

If you make a multiple-pixel image, you can set different lines or columns of pixels to different colors and make some beautiful multicolored lines.

It's all about making your page come in faster. Try a few of these for yourself and see if you don't like them. They add crisp lines and blocks of color to your page without the need for large byte-filled images.

 You can download a few different 1x1 images from http://www.htmlgoodies.com/book/ 1x1images.html. *Don't worry, they're much larger than the dot, so they are easier to download.*

Creating Thumbnail Images

If you've ever gone into a page that loads a bunch of large pictures, you know that it can get annoying. The pictures often are loading way off the browser window and it's difficult to see it all at one time. Here's where thumbnail images come in handy (see Figure 3.11). You offer very small versions of the pictures for viewers to click, so they can see the larger version. It makes for smaller pages that are easier to view. Furthermore, it enables the viewer to be in charge of what she wants to see.

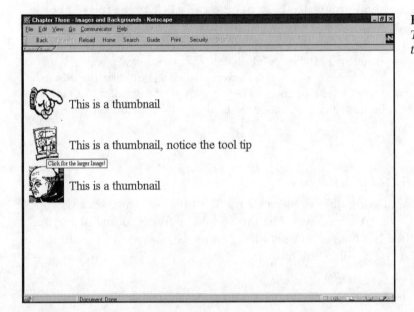

Figure 3.11
Three examples of thumbnail images.

To see this tutorial online, go to `http://www.htmlgoodies.com/tutors/thmbnail.html`.

If you have a photo gallery of favorite pictures you want people to see, I suggest you offer them one of three ways:

- Text links to images—Offer text descriptions of the pictures with a link directly to the image. This makes for the fastest load. I do this with my image pages. Most people don't like this suggestion because it doesn't create very fancy pages.

- Two images—Offer a smaller version of the picture, or a detail of the picture, for people to click to see the larger second image.

- One image—Have the image act as its own thumbnail.

FAQs from the HTML Goodies Web Site

Q. When should I use thumbnails?

A. A funny statement I like goes, nothing is less exciting to me than your kids or your vacation. Use that rule. If the image is needed for the page, use it. If it's something you're offering because you're being nice, use one of the thumbnail formats mentioned here so the user can decide whether he wants to sit through the load time.

Q. When I make thumbnail images so that people can click them to see the bigger picture, do I have to have that big picture on its own page?

A. No, your browser has the ability to display just a picture. It doesn't have to be on an HTML document; just make the HREF link point directly to the picture. However, I am a fan on consistency across pages. If you use a background image or color then do your users a favor and take the time to create a page for each of the images to maintain consistency. Plus, if a page for each image exists, that page can contain some BACK navigation (a link back).

Offering Text Links to Images

This is the first method of offering links to images. I think it's the way to go because you speed your pages along by only offering text. The text should be in the format of a hypertext link that points right at the image. Let's say I have an image of my last vacation to Las Vegas. I call it lv.gif. Here's a possible link format:

```
<A HREF="http://www.htmlgoodies.com/lv.gif">
See me and my wife in Vegas! We just lost it all!</A>
```

Notice it's a simple link format with the text pointing right at the image. The image shows up in the browser screen's top-left corner. If you want to place the image more specifically, point the link to an HTML document that contains the image and the coding to place it. I prefer that it only point to the image. That way only one item has to load the image, rather than two (the page and the image).

Offering Two Images

This is the way I see most thumbnail images set up. One smaller image acts as the thumbnail that is attached to the larger. Like so:

```
<A HREF="http://www.htmlgoodies.com/thumb.gif">
<IMG SRC="bigimage.gif"></A>
```

Notice this is a simple A HREF link with an IMG command in place of the link words. The smaller image just links to the larger. You can also get rid of the blue border that appears around the link image by entering BORDER="0" inside the IMG command and just before the SRC portion. See Primer 5 for more on making image links.

You may also want to think about making a page for each image. I hit on this in one of the FAQs earlier, but I wanted to hit it here again. If you have a page for each image, you can keep some consistency carrying a background image or color. In addition, you can align the image or possibly offer some extra text about the image. You can do so much more and it's really not that much more work.

This method's downfall is that it requires two images to load. The first is the thumbnail image and the second is the larger image. This takes time...and hard drive space. On the up side, you can offer a detail or a smaller section of the original image.

If I were to suggest choosing either a detail or a smaller version of the picture, I'd advise using the detail. If the image is a landscape, you could use just a section of the trees; if the image is a photo of a person, you could use just the eyes. It can be quite alluring. By offering a detail of the picture, not only do you give a good thumbnail, but you also keep some of the image hidden. This may draw the user to click.

By offering the full picture, oftentimes you've made it so small, maybe 50×100 pixels, that detail is lost and the image really doesn't give a good representation.

Offering the two images is my preferred method of setting up thumbnails. However, one more method remains.

Offering One Image

What you do here is offer the same image as both the thumbnail and the larger image. This is done via the same link format as described earlier, but here you make the link to the same image that is being offered as the thumbnail. The thumbnail version is created through the use of HEIGHT and WIDTH commands. It looks like this:

```
<A HREF="http://www.htmlgoodies.com/bigimage.gif">
<IMG HEIGHT=50 WIDTH=50 SRC="bigimage.gif"></A>
```

Remember that you are denoting pixels per inch, not a percentage, when resizing an image using the HEIGHT and WIDTH commands. No hard or fast rules exist for this; you may have to simply play around with numbers until you get the size you want.

Notice how much faster the one-image method loads when the user clicks the thumbnail. That's because the image that the viewer receives is already loaded into the browser's cache. The cache is a small section of the hard drive where browsers keep images and pages while they display them. The image appears much quicker because you are not opening a whole new picture—you're just offering the same picture at the normal size. It just pops up onto the screen.

The trade-off is that the page that contains the thumbnail does not load very fast. Even though the image is small due to the HEIGHT and WIDTH commands, it is still full size in terms of bytes to be downloaded.

FAQs from the HTML Goodies Web Site

Q. My thumbnails look bad, all out of shape. Why?

A. Remember that you need to keep the same general parameters if you are making a smaller version of the original. If the original is a rectangle and you make it a square in the thumbnail, you're going to get less-than-pleasing thumbnails. Keep the same general dimensions.

 This tutorial shows you some examples of using the thumbnail methods at http://www. htmlgoodies.com/book/thumbs.html.

Loading a Low-Res Version of an Image First

Figure 3.12 shows an example of a LOWSRC command at work. Actually, two images are working. One is a very low-byte version of the main color version. Notice the two images? One is black and white line art, just an outline of the other, and the other is color. The previous image is static. The online effect is that the image that is mostly line art pops up first, and then the more intricate color version is loaded over top. The images are the same, except the black and white line art takes up far fewer bytes. I tell the browser to load it first so that the viewer isn't looking at a blank box while waiting for the pretty color one to load.

 Okay, I'll level with you: This doesn't translate to book very well. You should see it online. Go to http://www.htmlgoodies.com/tutors/lowsrc.html. *Note: This tutorial only works with Netscape Navigator! Internet Explorer does not yet support the command.*

LOWSRC is a very helpful image command that moves your page along if you are determined to use large, byte-filled graphics. This is the command that made the image in Figure 3.12:

```
<IMG HEIGHT="212" WIDTH="300" ALT="Phydueaux the Cat" SRC="cat.gif"
  LOWSRC="bwcat.gif">
```

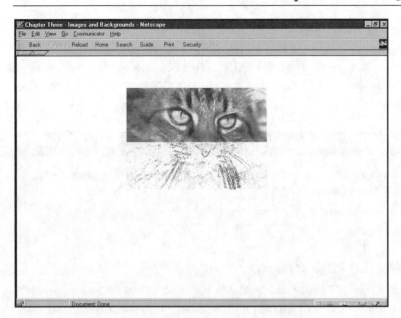

Figure 3.12
The LOWSRC *command loading an image.*

One image command produces the picture...or two pictures in this case. This is what's happening:

- IMG   Starts it all off like any other image command.
- HEIGHT and WIDTH   Denote the size of the image.
- ALT   Ditto always using this.
- SRC   The large color picture that came over the black and white image. The color image name is cat.gif.
- LOWSRC   The key to this tutorial. It is the black and white image of the cat's face that comes in first. The LOWSRC image name is bwcat.gif.

Why Would I Do This?

Because it helps your viewer a great deal. Plus it looks cool. You see, if you have a huge image that is going to come in, that takes time. The color image in Figure 3.12 is 56,000 bytes. However, the black and white line art image is only 3000 bytes and it loads in a heartbeat. The color image is just wiped over it. Using the HEIGHT and WIDTH commands creates a box where the picture goes, and the ALT command informs the viewer what is going in. By using this LOWSRC command, however, a smaller byte version of the picture zips right in, giving an example of what is to come. Neat, huh?

111

When Would I Use This?

No good reason exists why you couldn't use this all the time, but remember that it does make each picture two hits of the server. That slows the page a bit. I would reserve it for really large images. Smaller images do just fine with the HEIGHT, WIDTH, and ALT commands discussed earlier in this chapter.

FAQs from the HTML Goodies Web Site

Q. Can I use two different pictures in the LOWSRC command or must they be a different version of the same shot?

A. No, use two totally different shots if you'd like. Just make sure they are the same size.

How Do I Make the LOWSRC Picture?

If you haven't taken this from what I wrote earlier, the purpose of the LOWSRC command is to quickly put up a picture that underlies a larger picture. Make whatever picture you use for the LOWSRC as low on the bytes as possible. Otherwise, the whole process is loopy.

I made the black and white line art image by opening the original color picture in my Paint Shop Pro graphics program and reducing the color level to two colors, black and white. That immediately dropped the amount of bytes from 56K to 3K. Nice drop. I then used one of Paint Shop Pro's image filters to change it to line art. You can do the same.

 Go to the main tutorial to see the example in Figure 3.12, but head to http://www. htmlgoodies.com/book/lowsrc.html *if you'd like to see the example with two different images. Try reloading the page again and again to get the full effect.*

Transparent Images

I get letters all the time asking how to make parts of an image invisible or transparent. So many times someone puts an image on their page and it looks great until the background comes in—then the little icon reveals itself as square rather than round. Oh, the humanity!

On some pages, you can see right through the image to see the background. I used to think the person went in with an image program and simply cut holes with the crop command. Don't laugh; it seems plausible.

 This tutorial is online at http://www.htmlgoodies.com/tutors/transpar.html.

What Is Actually Happening

Not cropping. The person who provides a transparent image has simply run the GIF (yes, it has to be a GIF) through a transparency program, highlighted the color that she wanted made transparent, and saved the image again in a special format called GIF89a.

It's named *GIF89a* because the GIF format was standardized in 1989. The transparency was the second part of the list of standards, thus the *a*.

Where Do I Get a Transparency Program?

A good many of them are available for free on the Net. See the link for Yahoo!'s Transparent Image Page in the Net Notes section of the tutorial found at the end of this section. There you can surf for a program.

I'm sure all the programs that come up are good, and I can't attempt to explain here how they all work, so I'll only go over the one I use: LView Pro. Net Notes gives you links to get the program. Whatever program you choose, read over the instructions provided either on the downloading page or in the Help section of the program itself. The process is very close to what is explained here.

FAQs from the HTML Goodies Web Site

Q. I have an image that I want to give a transparent background, but I keep getting speckles of color when I run it through the LView Pro program. What's wrong?

A. For the background to be completely transparent, it must be one color, so it is acted upon equally. If your background has more than one color, not all is blanked out and you get those speckles.

Q. My friend says he uses totally transparent images. Why would he do that?

A. For spacing. He knows the image is *x* pixels wide so that it stretches everything around it (like text and table cells) to that width. The image does the work by setting the size, but doesn't show up on the page. It's pretty clever, actually.

Making Transparencies with LView Pro

To create a transparent GIF with LView Pro, follow these steps:

1. Open the program; you get something that looks like Figure 3.13.
2. Open the GIF. This is the GIF that you want to alter to make one part be transparent. When it opens, it looks something like Figure 3.14.

Figure 3.13
The LView Pro program.

Figure 3.14
*The LView Pro program
with an image open.*

3. Under the Retouch menu, choose Background Color to alter the background color. If your image is small such as the one in Figure 3.14, you find it under the R header (see Figure 3.15).

Figure 3.15
*The LView Pro Program
Retouch menu.*

4. Choose the color to make transparent. I'm choosing white. A color pallet pops up and now I only have three colors in this image. Your images can have many more. You have to choose the color you want. It can be confusing at times. See where it says to Mask selection using? You know you've chosen the correct color on the pallet because the part of the image you want transparent blackens (or whitens), as shown in Figure 3.16.

Figure 3.16
Choosing the color to be made transparent.

5. Save it correctly. Now that you've denoted a color to make transparent, choose Save—not Save As. You get the dialog box shown in Figure 3.17.

Figure 3.17
The Save this image to file dialog box.

6. Choose Yes. You're done. Now the image comes up with that portion of color you highlighted transparent. In the image I used, every part that was white is now transparent. Figure 3.18 shows the image placed on a gray background so that you can see that all the white parts are now transparent.

So go and make your own transparent GIFs...you have the power.

 To see a couple of before and after transparencies, go to `http://www.htmlgoodies.com/book/transparent.html`.

Figure 3.18
A transparent image.

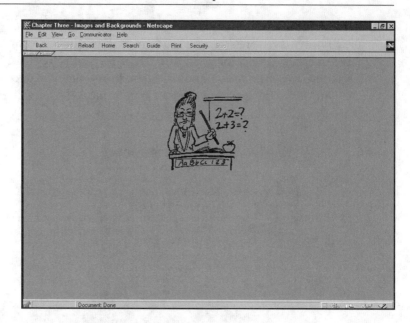

Creating Animated GIFs

Ah, the animated GIF, or as I call it, the "anti-java." The image in Figure 3.19 is an animated GIF. On this page it's obviously not moving. If this were on the HTML Goodies site, that little arrow would be whizzing around the dial at breakneck speed. Thank goodness you're here where it's safe.

 You really need to see the image online just spinning around and around. Go to `http://www.htmlgoodies.com/tutors/animate.html`.

My testing shows that animated GIFs run on all browsers. They can because of the way the animation is created. This is not something created by Java or a JavaScript. What is actually happening is that the browser is placing one GIF after another into that same space. A little series of counting numbers called a *SMPTE Code* (Society of Motion Picture and Television Engineers Code) is embedded in the image, sort of counting one-hundredths of seconds and telling the image when to post the next cell. Your eye just perceives it as a fluid movement, such as in a movie.

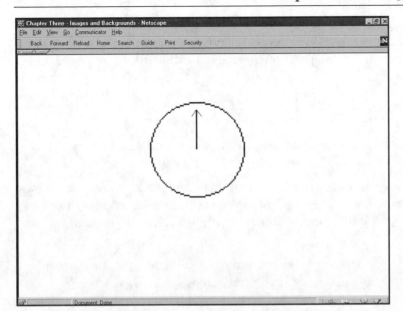

Figure 3.19
An animated GIF.

The problem with showing you how to create an animated image, be it here or online, is that the method I show isn't the only way of doing it. A great number of programs assist you in creating your animated GIFs. What I show here is only one method. However, I chose this particular program because it is easy to understand and gives a general idea of the process. In the "Net Notes" section links to pages offer other programs to animated GIFs. Whatever you choose, either follow the instructions included on the download page or those found in the program's Help section. No matter which program you choose, I can safely say that the process is very close to what I outline here.

FAQs from the HTML Goodies Web Site

Q. I often see animation on other sites that runs once and then stops. Why?

A. The author could have wanted it that way. It may also be that you're using an Explorer browser. For some strange reason they do that now and again. Having your cache set to 0 would also do it.

Before you go any further, you must first get a program. To follow this tutorial specifically, you need the GIF Construction Set for Windows and W95 and—if you can find it—Mac, by Alchemy Mindworks, Inc. It is at the time of this writing a shareware program. That means it's free, but if you like it, you are requested to send in a few bucks. Go get it and install it on your computer. You can download it from `http://www.mindworkshop.com/alchemy/gifcon.html`.

Please understand that programs change over time and the interfaces that are shown here may already be out of date. However, the process of creating an animation is basically the same from program to program. The major differences are how the images are placed and how much control you have over the animation itself.

Other programs are out there that animate. PC users can grab some different programs at `http://search.yahoo.com/bin/search?p=%2Bgif+%2Banimation+%2Bsoftware`.

Mac users can try at `http://www.graphicssoft.about.com/compute/graphicssoft/cs/ gifan-imationswmac/`.

The Paint Shop Pro program that I keep mentioning in this chapter now comes with something called Animation Shop. It is very easy to use and gives you a lot of control. It's a little different from the program shown in the tutorial mentioned earlier in this section, but the outcome is the same.

Use the tutorial simply as a springboard to understanding how your personal animation program works. I'm sure it's very close to what you read later.

FAQs from the HTML Goodies Web Site

Q. I got some shareware programs, but every time I use them this box keeps popping up asking me to pay $20 to the author. How do I get rid of that?

A. Pay the $20. It's only fair—you're using the program, aren't you?

Q. I found a program you can use to crack the code so the nagging shareware window asking for money doesn't pop up. Want it?

A. No. What you are doing is illegal.

Making the GIFs for Your Animation

Did you go and get the GIF Construction Set yet? If not, did you get one of the other ones? Did you install it on your computer? Okay, good. Now, on to the hard part. No, not the creation of the animation, but rather the pictures that you animate.

I know you've seen a flip book. It's one of the books that have a little picture up in the right corner of each page and if you flip the pages quickly enough it appears as if the little picture is moving. It's the same principle as a movie or video tape—a bunch of still pictures rolling past rather quickly and your eye perceiving it as movement.

Where do you get the pictures? You make them! You could go out into the world of cyberspace and find them, but what fun would that be?

You need to follow a few guidelines when you create the GIFs. These aren't my guidelines, either. These are the specs the GIF Construction program requires:

- You must save the images in GIF (CompuServe) format.
- You must save the image at the 256 color level.
- All the images you use must be the same size.

Why? The easy answer is that the GIF Construction program requires it. The actual reason is that you are literally creating a little movie frame by frame. All the frames must be the same size, they must all be in the same format, and all at the same color level.

These are a few tips:

- Create a template for your images. Remember the clock animation I did? I created a white square using my graphics program. I then drew a circle in the middle of the square and saved it, at the 256 color level, as `clock.gif`. I was then able to open that template, draw a line to 1:00, and save it under another name. Ditto for 2:00, 3:00, 4:00, and so on, until I went the whole way around the dial. That way I was sure the circle would remain stable through the complete animation. Still with me?
- Place each animation, and the images that make it up, on its own disk. Thank me for this later.
- Make your GIFs as small as you can without losing any detail or color.
- Make your GIFs with the fewest number of bits as possible yet still keeping the color and detail.

The reasoning for the last two tips is obvious. Remember that the browser loads one GIF panel after another, giving the impression of movement. If the GIFs are huge, it's slow. They load faster and look better if they are small.

If you don't have any GIF images to use in your animation, I can give you four from my collection. They are four arrows, all the same size, all saved at the 256 color level. You can make a four-panel animation of an arrow spinning to the right, round and round.

Download all four and place them in a directory. Do not change the names of the images. Also, don't worry that the numbers appear to be out of order. You can fix that when you make the animation. My suggestion is to place all the images in an empty directory on your hard drive or on a blank floppy disk. It makes your first one easier. Follow these four links to get your arrows:

Left Arrow: `http://www.htmlgoodies.com/images/arrow1.gif`

Right Arrow: `http://www.htmlgoodies.com/images/arrow2.gif`

Up Arrow: http://www.htmlgoodies.com/images/arrow3.gif

Down Arrow: http://www.htmlgoodies.com/images/arrow4.gif

When you follow the link, the image appears in the upper-left corner of the browser, all by its lonesome. After it's there, follow these steps:

1. Place your mouse pointer on the image.

2. PC users should right-click. Macintosh users hold the button down for three seconds; a menu pops up.

3. The name of the GIF and a menu item enabling you to save the image are on that menu. Choose to save the image.

4. A dialog box enables you to save the image on your computer.

5. You could change the names to anything you want at this point, but for this tutorial, keep them the same as I use.

6. After you have chosen where the image save to, click OK.

Making the Animated GIF

Now that you have some GIF images to work with, make the animation. Follow these instructions straightaway:

1. Close your browser. Open the GIF Construction program you downloaded and installed.

2. A box with some buttons along the top opens. The buttons read View, Insert, Edit, Delete, and so on. It looks like Figure 3.20. If what you have is close to this, you're ready to go.

Figure 3.20
The GIF Construction Set interface.

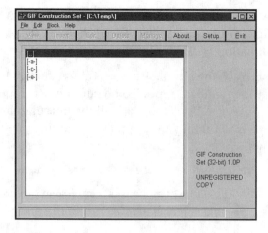

3. Go under the File menu at the top and choose New.

4. A highlighted line appears and states HEADER GIF89a SCREEN 640×480; 640×480 deals with the image's number of pixels high and wide. Remember that this is a computer image; it is made up of little dots of color.

5. 640×480 is not the correct size of the arrow images you downloaded. They are only 30×30 pixels. Click the highlighted HEADER GIF89a line twice.

6. A box should pop up, where you again see the numbers 640 and 480. It looks like Figure 3.21. Change those numbers to 30 and 30 and click OK.

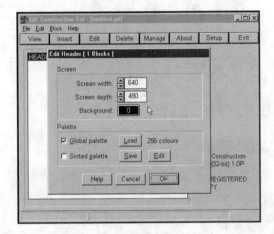

Figure 3.21
The Construction Set's Edit Header dialog box.

7. You're back to the original screen and the line should now read 30×30. Does it? If not, try again to change the numbers.

8. You must now tell the system what you want to happen regarding the movement of the GIFs. For now you are going to *loop* the animation, meaning the pictures continue to go one after the other at all times. Other formats are covered in the program's Help section.

9. Click the Insert button; a box that looks like Figure 3.22 pops up. Choose Loop. It should now say LOOP under the HEADER line.

10. Now it's time to start placing images. Remember this: All images must have a CONTROL command before them. Always. No exceptions. That code embeds the SMPTE command I told you about earlier.

11. Click Insert and choose CONTROL. CONTROL is now on the screen.

12. Click the highlighted CONTROL that just popped up. Another box appears, and it looks like Figure 3.23.

13. You can do more in this box, such as set transparent colors, but for now I am only concerned with speed. The other items are explained in the program's Help section.

See in the box where it says 1/100ths of a second? That's the time span between the current GIF and when the next one loads. More one-hundredths make it slower, fewer make it faster. For now, Insert 15 for 1/100ths of a second. Choose OK.

Figure 3.22
The Insert Object menu.

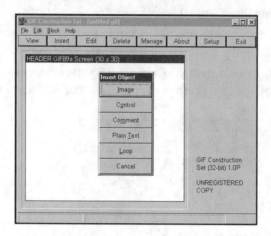

Figure 3.23
The Construction Set's Edit Control Block dialog box.

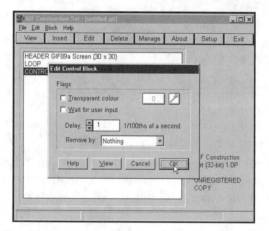

14. Click Insert again and choose IMAGE.

15. Another box pops up and enables you to find and choose the images you downloaded from me. Find arrow1.gif and choose it. It appears on the screen.

16. Choose Insert again and select CONTROL.

17. Double-click the line and again change the 100ths of a second to 15. Click OK.

18. Choose Insert again and choose IMAGE.

19. When the box pops up, find arrow3.gif and select it.

20. Follow the format again and place another CONTROL, changing it to 15 1/100ths of a second.

21. Again choose Insert and IMAGE and place arrow2.gif.

22. Place another CONTROL, changing the 1/100ths of a second to 15 again.

23. Place the last image—arrow4.gif. See how you're doing the same thing again and again: control, image, control, image, control, image, and so on?

24. After you place all four images, this is what is written in front of you:

```
HEADER GIF89a SCREEN 40x40
LOOP
CONTROL
IMAGE ARROW1.GIF 30X30,256
CONTROL
IMAGE ARROW3.GIF 30X30,256
CONTROL
IMAGE ARROW2.GIF 30X30,256
CONTROL
IMAGE ARROW4.GIF 30X30,256
```

25. You're not quite finished yet, but you can see it run at this point. Click View. The screen goes black and the arrow spins around.

26. To get back, press the Esc key.

27. Save the image animation by choosing Save As under the File menu.

28. If you have any problems, you now get a warning and are informed of what needs to be fixed. If you don't get a warning, good job. Save it under a name you can remember.

The program undergoes a long list of movements for your entertainment while it compiles your animation.

FAQs from the HTML Goodies Web Site

Q. I ran my animated GIF through the LView transparency program and now it doesn't work. Why?

A. Because you broke it. Remember that this animation is a series of images, not just the one. The best way is to make the cells transparent, and then build them into an animation. Many programs enable you to do that along the way of building your animation.

Q. I am using the GIF Construction Set and every time I put in an image it tells me that I need to pick a color pallet. What in the world is that?

A. You are not using the correct 256 color level—otherwise you wouldn't get that message. The program doesn't understand your image because you are using more than the expected 256 colors. Choose the option to use local pallet and go on.

Placing an Animated GIF on Your Page

Place the animation using the last name you gave it just as you would any image, via the image command format:

```
<IMG SRC="animation.gif">
```

Don't try changing the pixel size. Let it remain just as you saved it.

In case you're wondering, the animated GIF is totally self-contained. It runs on its own. The images you used to make up the animation are no longer needed.

FAQs from the HTML Goodies Web Site

Q. Do I have to upload the images that I used to create the animation along with the animation?

A. No, but if you do it doesn't hurt anything. In fact, if you have the space it's a good way to keep the images safe in case you need them later.

I hope this helps. It really is easier than it may seem at first. After you roll through your first one, you wonder what you thought was so hard. Make a point of reading the banner creation primers in Chapter 14, "Building Web Site Banners," for more information.

Creating Horizontal Lines with the HR Command

You probably already know that you can place a line simply by typing <HR> on the page. (*HR* stands for horizontal rule, by the way.) It makes a nice line, with a little bit of shading all the way across the screen, plus it needs no end command. And it's centered. Cool, but all those lines looking the same gets dull. Let's change it a bit.

I want to shake the hand of whomever came up with this <HR> line. It is a great and simple way to break up your page. I use them to death. Here I try to get into the more subtle sections of the <HR> line. This one is online at http://www.htmlgoodies.com/tutors/hr.html.

Changing the Rule's Width

You change the width of the line by adding a subcommand to <HR>. I do this with all my lines. The line going all the way across the page is a bit much, so I only have mine go 60% or 80% of the page. I just added different percentages to a series of HR commands. Here's the format:

```
<HR WIDTH="60%">
```

Figure 3.24 shows horizontal rules with widths set to 20%, 40%, 60%, 80%, and 100% (and back down again), respectively.

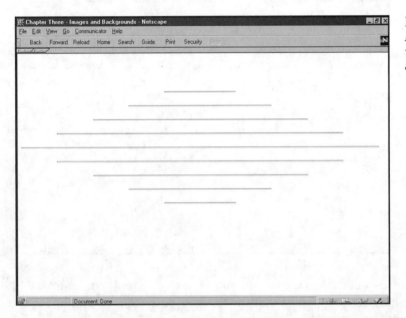

Figure 3.24
Horizontal rules set to widths of 20%, 40%, 60%, 80%, and 100%.

Notice it's done with an HR command with WIDTH="##%" added. You can set the width to any percentage you want. No need to stay with round numbers. If you really want a line that only goes 17%, that's fine. Just remember to include the percentage sign! You can, however, lose the percentage sign if you'd like and go with pixels. This enables you to be more precise.

FAQs from the HTML Goodies Web Site

Q. How do I get the HR line to appear like it's coming out of the page rather than going in?

A. You can't, though if you stare at it long enough it gives that appearance.

Changing the Rule's Height

Do you want a thicker horizontal rule? You can do that, too. Just look at Figure 3.25. Here's the format:

```
<HR SIZE="6">
```

Figure 3.25
HR lines showing thickness levels 1 through 6.

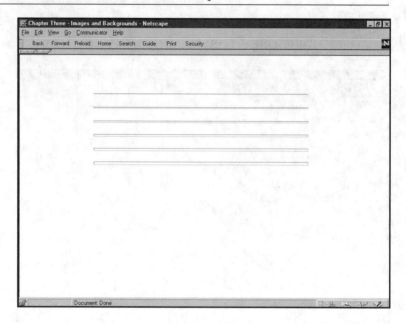

Think of the size command as an equal to the H# commands in that six of them, numbered 1 through 6—1 being the most narrow. Notice that the lines are only 60% width. I just used both commands inside the same <HR> command—nothing to it. Try some higher numbers. Some newer browsers can have just about any number of pixels.

Aligning Horizontal Rules

You can use your old friend, the ALIGN command on horizontal rules, too. It works just the way you think it would. I added ALIGN="###" inside the command. Here's what made the four lines shown in Figure 3.26:

```
<HR WIDTH="60%" ALIGN="LEFT">
<HR WIDTH="60%" ALIGN="RIGHT">
<HR WIDTH="60%" ALIGN="LEFT">
<HR WIDTH="60%" ALIGN="RIGHT">
```

You can also state ALIGN="CENTER", but that's a bit of overkill, as the line centers for you anyway. Notice also that I used the WIDTH command in there.

Horizontal Rules without Shading

You can also create horizontal rules that don't have any shading (see Figure 3.27). This is how you do it:

```
<HR WIDTH="60%" NOSHADE>
```

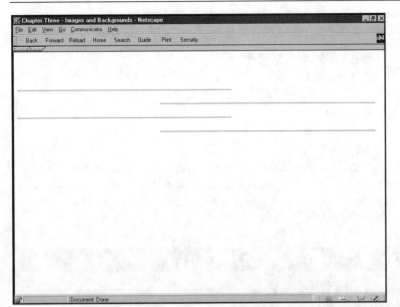

Figure 3.26
HR *lines aligned left and right.*

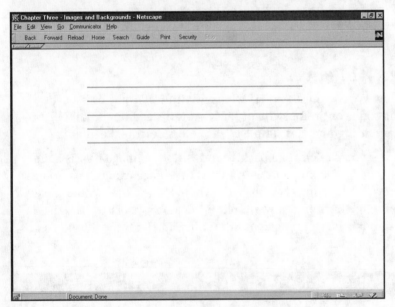

Figure 3.27
HR *lines with no shading.*

FAQs from the HTML Goodies Web Site

Q. I want to put an image in the HR line. Can I?

A. No, not yet at least. What you can do is open your image with a paint program and draw a horizontal rule in your image. This gives you the effect you're looking for.

Backgrounds

One of the staples to building a great looking Web page is a good background. Be it color (covered in Chapter 1, "Playing with Text") or an image, a background can really make a page stand out. I think a good background image makes the difference in a pretty good page and a great page.

FAQs from the HTML Goodies Web Site

Q. I want my background to become a rainbow of colors, dark to light. How do I put in the hex commands?

A. No dice. You need to use an image to do that. The backgrounds achieved through hex codes go for one color.

Background Image Wallpaper

The name is a bit misleading. When you see an HTML page with *wallpaper*, or backgrounds, it is most often not one continuous GIF or JPEG—it is instead one small GIF or JPEG repeated, or "tiled," and it is equally as simple as the colors described earlier.

Before someone tells me—yes, you can create a background with one image that is large enough to cover the entire screen. The problem with that is the image would have to be so large that it would take forever to load into the browser window. The viewer could have lunch before your page comes in. Try it if you want, but bring a newspaper to pass the time. First you need a background image. I make most of mine. I'll get to how to make a background in a second.

FAQs from the HTML Goodies Web Site

Q. This guy had a page where the background was one large sunset. How did he do that?

A. With one huge image. Did the page take a long time to load? I'll bet he also took great pains to make sure that the text on the page was not larger than the image or it would have started to double up and display again. You just weren't allowed to see it. Clever move, since it appears from your letter he pulled it off.

Because you need a scanner or an image program to make backgrounds, and I know not everyone has one of these at their fingertips, the best way to use a background is to grab one off the Internet. You can find a few good background repositories around. See "Net Notes" at the end of this tutorial for links.

Now that you have a GIF or JPEG for your background, you want to put it in the same directory in which you place all your other images. Again, all background commands are placed inside the <BODY> flag. The format is this:

```
<BODY BACKGROUND="image.gif">
```

Browsers also enable you to use the commands together. You offer a color and then an image. The background changes color and is then wiped over by the image. This is the format for your records:

```
<BODY BGCOLOR="#FFFFFF" BACKGROUND="image.gif">
```

Make Your Own Wallpaper

No hard or fast rules exist for this except that you need to have access to an image scanner or image creation program. Most copy places have them. A local college or university might be helpful, too. I'm going to describe the process using a scanner first.

Easy Wallpapers

Just follow these steps:

1. Find a piece of paper, other than white, that already has text on it. That way you know that when you use it as a background, your text shows up. Papers that work well for this include diplomas, citations, stationery, and fancy copy paper.

2. Simply scan a portion of the paper that does not contain any text and crop a perfect square in an image editor. Make it kind of small—30×30 is about as small as you can go and still keep enough detail from the scan.

3. Use it as a background. Most of the wallpapers offered in the links seen later in the chapter were made this way.

Harder, Geometric Wallpapers

Now it gets a little tougher:

1. Find a geometric image to scan. Bricks work well, as does lined paper.

2. Scan the picture.

3. Using a graphics program, crop the picture so that the items on the ends and top are cut exactly in half. That way they line up when posted as wallpaper.

4. This is tough. Try doing one on lined paper first, for practice. You are successful when the image tiles do not have seams when you crop. It simply looks like one large image. It's tough but the effect is well worth it.

If you have access to an image program, try the following:.

1. Scan any picture you want as a background and crop it small.

2. Use your image program to do an offset of 50%. This turns the picture in upon itself. The effect will be like folding over a paper so that what was in the middle is now on the edges.

3. Use the program to touch up any lines that don't come together at the midpoint of the graphic.

4. Save it. Doing the 50% change guarantees that the graphic you just created lines up perfectly as a background when it tiles. It works. Trust me. Have I steered you wrong yet?

FAQs from the HTML Goodies Web Site

Q. I went to a page and the background didn't scroll along with the text. Cool! How do I do that?

A. You must be using the Internet Explorer browser; the command only works with that browser. Add this BGPROPERTIES="fixed" to the BODY flag and that's that.

One More Thing...

These background commands are great, but let me warn you that any image you add to a page slows its completion. Keep your background images small or avoid using them at all. Load time is important. A page that doesn't load doesn't get read.

Just remember that anytime you choose to add a background, be it color or image, that background must not interfere with the text. The most important thing about a Web site is its content. If I cannot read the text, I cannot get the content.

Please be honest with yourself. Post your background and take a look. Can you read your text? If not, then lose the background.

You might think that changing the text to a different color is the best method, but it is not. The background is never more important than the text. If you cannot read your text because of your background, always change the background rather than changing the text.

I have a series of background examples and a bunch of backgrounds for you to download at http://www.htmlgoodies.com/book/background.html.

Net Notes

Yahoo!'s Background Image Page: http://dir.yahoo.com/Arts/Design_Arts/Graphic_
Design/Web_Page_Design_and_Layout/Graphics/Backgrounds/

You get more background images than you could possibly use from this site.

Sideline Backgrounds

Currently a very popular Web page design element, *sideline backgrounds*, are a stripe of color
or an image down the left side of the page. On that stripe you put icons and text that deal
with the larger section of the browser window. It's a solid, clean look. Figure 3.28 shows an
example from the HTML Goodies Web site.

Figure 3.28
*An example of a sideline
background on the HTML
Goodies Web site.*

 You can see this online at http://www.htmlgoodies.com/tutors/sideline.html.

How You Do It

First, you need a program that creates graphics for you. Create an image that is long and
thin; the thickness, or height of the image, is up to you. Keep it fairly small to cut down

on bytes and load time. The length is set. It has to be long enough to span the entire screen. Go with something at least 1600 pixels wide. When an image is defined as 650×10 (or something comparable), it fails to address 800×600 and 1024×768 monitor resolutions. A width of 1200 covers all resolutions. The image I'm using on this page is 25×1600 pixels. That's pretty long and thin.

Using the graphics program again, make the left side a different color. I made mine lime green with an extra little stripe of gold. That's an eye-catcher, don't you think? How much of the left side of the image you color determines the thickness of your sideline stripe. When you use the thin image as a background, the color lines up and you have a stripe.

You could try making a much taller image if you want a look other than straight up and down. Figure 3.29 is an example of a sideline background that uses a more textured stripe on the HTML Goodies Web site.

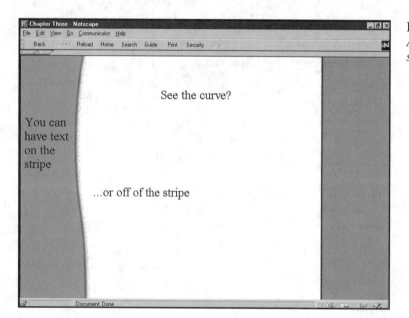

Figure 3.29
An HTML Goodies Web site background stripe.

The sideline stripe is done via a very tall image that completes one full curve. When the image doubles up, the ends meet perfectly. The stripe on the right is also part of the background image.

You have to be careful using this kind of background to get the text exactly where you want it—on or off the stripe. I'll tell you how in the section, "What About Text?" in a moment.

Do I Have to Use Just Color?

No. If you'd like to place an image on the side instead of using color, do it. Just remember that it's going to occur again and again. Some football sites use what appear to be yard markers, some sites make the side of the page look like a loose leaf notebook, and so on.

What About Text?

Yeah! What about text?! Oh, you're asking me. A couple of ways of dealing with this do exist. The easiest is if you own and use Microsoft Internet Explorer. Just add this command in your <BODY> command at the top of your page:

```
LEFTMARGIN="###"
```

The numbers are relative. One is bigger than two, two is bigger than three, and so on. You have to play with the numbers to get just the right indentation. That means one that does not cover your stripe. Remember, however, that not everyone uses Explorer.

But I Don't Have Explorer; I Use Netscape Navigator!

That's what I said. Here's how I indent. Please remember, this is only to get text off the stripe. I'll show you how to have items on the stripe in a moment in the section, "Placing Items on the Stripe." Now, someone is going to go bonkers about me saying this isn't right and that he knows a better way of doing it. All that aside, if all you want is the text off the stripe, this is how I do it—and it works. Add <OL> commands at the top. I don't add any <LI> commands, list items, or </OL>. You find that every <OL> pushes all the text in just a little bit. Just keep adding OL until the text bumps over far enough for you.

Let's remember I taught myself HTML. I use what works no matter how strange it seems. I think that's a good way of learning.

Placing Items on the Stripe

This is a bit extensive because it involves using a table. If you haven't already, you can read about tables in Chapter 5, "Tables." First you create the sideline stripe background, and then you create a large table with two cells that house everything that appears on the page. That table has one cell not wider than the stripe and another cell not wider than the open space. Imagine Figure 3.30 as the table's format.

Figure 3.30
A sideline background with table borders showing.

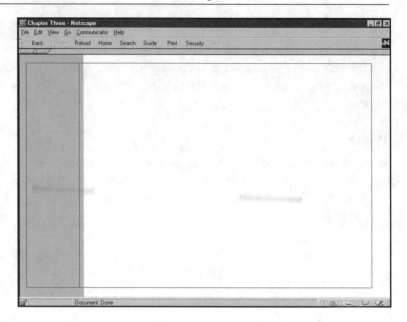

Constructing the table is not the hard part. As you can see, the table in Figure 3.30 is just two cells. Here's the code that made it:

```
<TABLE BORDER="0" CELLSPACING="5"
CELLPADDING="5">
<TD ALIGN="----" WIDTH="###">
<TD ALIGN="----" WIDTH="###">
</TABLE>
```

You place everything that goes in the left column (on the stripe) after the first <TD> and everything that goes on the other side under the second <TD>. The BORDER="0" command makes the table borders invisible.

Now the Trick

You need to play with this a bit. Notice in the code that the <TD> commands have a WIDTH="###" attribute—that's the key here. You need to make the width of the left cell a bit smaller than the width of the stripe and make the width of the right cell just a bit larger than the open space.

The CELLSPACING and CELLPADDING commands leave the gutter between the two. Make it a large number, 5 or larger. I always use pixels to do this; percentages aren't as precise. It seems like you should be able to find out the pixel width of the stripe, knock off a few, and make it work, but it has never yet worked for me. I always have to play with the numbers a little to get it straight.

I have also found that setting the BORDER to 1 helps find the pixel numbers. You can always go back in and set it to 0 after you're done.

Can I Get a Right-Side Border?

Yes. Just make your left sideline very wide. It appears to be a right sideline. Play with it until you get the look you want.

 You have to see this in action to fully appreciate what I'm saying here. Go to `http://www.htmlgoodies.com/book/sideline.html` *for a good look around.*

FAQs from the HTML Goodies Web Site

Q. I read your tutorial on sideline backgrounds. You suggest making a table that goes over the sideline. If that works, why not just make that table the background and color the one cell a different color?

A. Because it wouldn't look right. The table wouldn't conform to all screen settings nor would it go to the edges of the browser window. It would look like a large table instead of a background.

Q. I saw this page where the sideline stripe had links on it and when you clicked on the links, the right section changed. Is the page just reloading a new table every time?

A. Nope. You're seeing this same effect being done with frames. It's a bit more complicated (and is explained in Chapter 6, "Frames").

Image Formats On The Web

I added this tutorial to the second edition even though I do touch upon the topic in other places earlier in this chapter. This tutorial goes much more in depth than the mentions you find in other areas. This is a long tutorial that gets into a great deal of examples and discussion. Read slowly. It's pretty thick.

 This tutorial is best when viewed on the Web. Screen captures are later, but they might not show the effects as well as I had hoped. You can find this tutorial online at `http://htmlgoodies.earthweb.com/tutors/image_formats.html`.

As the tutorial goes on, I'll offer links to the examples described in the tutorial. Okay? Here you go.

I did something yesterday that was very unlike a computer professional. I actually took the time to read the back of the box that contained my new Paint Shop Pro version 5.0 graphics program. Toward the bottom, the box proclaimed the program supported 44 different image formats. Wow!

On the Net, luckily, you really only have to deal with three main types of images: GIF (actually named "CompuServe GIF" if you want to get picky), JPEG, and Bitmaps. At the moment, those are the only three that are roundly supported by the major browsers. But what's the difference between them? What does it mean if a GIF is interlaced or non-interlaced? Is a JPEG progressive because it enjoys art deco? Does a Bitmap actually offer directions somewhere? And the most often asked question: When do I use a specific image format?

I've been meaning to write this tutorial for a while. I offer it as a catch-all answer to the many questions I get about images and their use.

Image or Graphic?

Technically it's neither. If you really want to be strict, computer pictures are files, the same way Word documents or solitaire games are files. They're all a bunch of ones and zeros all in a row. But you and I do have to communicate with one another, so let's decide.

Image. I'll use "image." That seems to cover a wide enough topic range.

I went to my reference books and there I found that "graphic" is more of an adjective, as in "graphic format." Denote images on the Internet by their graphic format. GIF is not the name of the image. GIF is the compression factors used to create the raster format set up by CompuServe. (More on that in a moment.)

So, they're all images unless you're talking about something specific.

Forty-four Different Graphic Formats?

It does seem like a big number, doesn't it? In reality, 44 different graphic format names do not exist. Many of the 44 are different versions under the same compression umbrella, interlaced and non-interlaced GIF, for example.

Before getting into all 44, more than that exist even, let me back-pedal for a moment.

There actually are only two basic methods for a computer to render, or store and display, an image. When you save an image in a specific format you are creating either a raster or meta/vector graphic format.

Raster

Raster image formats (RIFs) should be the most familiar to Internet users. A Raster format breaks the image into a series of colored dots called pixels. The number of 1s and 0s (bits) used to create each pixel denotes the depth of color you can put into your images.

If your pixel is denoted with only 1 bit per pixel then that pixel must be black or white. Why? Because that pixel can only be a one or a zero, on or off, black or white.

Bump that up to 4 bits per pixel and you're able to set that colored dot to one of 16 colors. If you go even higher to 8 bits per pixel, you can save that colored dot at up to 256 different colors.

Does that number, 256, sound familiar to anyone? That's the upper color level of a GIF image. Sure, you can go with less than 256 colors, but you cannot have more than 256.

That's why a GIF image doesn't work well for photographs and larger images. A whole lot more than 256 colors are in the world. Images can carry millions, but if you want smaller icon images, GIFs are the way to go.

Raster image formats can also save at 16, 24, and 32 bits per pixel. At the two highest levels, the pixels themselves can carry up to 16,777,216 different colors. The image looks great! Bitmaps saved at 24 bits per pixel are great quality images, but of course they also run about a megabyte per picture. It's always a trade-off.

The three main Internet formats, GIF, JPEG, and Bitmap, are all Raster formats. Some other Raster formats include the following:

- CLP—Windows Clipart
- DCX—ZOFT Paintbrush
- DIB—OS/2 Warp format
- FPX—Kodak's FlashPic
- IMG—GEM Paint format
- JIF—JPEG Related Image format
- MAC—MacPaint
- MSP—MacPaint New Version
- PCT—Macintosh PICT format
- PCX—ZSoft Paintbrush
- PPM—Portable Pixel Map (UNIX)
- PSP—Paint Shop Pro format
- RAW—Unencoded Image format

- RLE—Run-Length Encoding (used to lower image bit rates)
- TIFF—Aldus Corporation format
- WPG—WordPerfect Image format

Because I brought up pixels, I thought now might be a pretty good time to talk about pixels and the Web. How much is too much? How many is too few?

A delicate balance exists between the crispness of a picture and the number of pixels needed to display it. Let's say you have two images, each is 5 inches across and 3 inches down. One uses 300 pixels to span that 5 inches, the other uses 1500. Obviously, the one with 1500 uses smaller pixels. It is also the one that offers a more crisp, detailed look. The more pixels, the more detailed the image is. Of course, the more pixels the more bytes the image takes up.

So, how much is enough? That depends on whom you are speaking to, and right now you're speaking to me. I always go with 100 pixels per inch. That creates a 10 thousand pixel square inch. I've found that allows for a pretty crisp image without going overboard on the bytes. It also allows some leeway to increase or decrease the size of the image and not mess it up too much.

The lowest I'd go is 72 pixels per inch, the agreed upon low end of the image scale. In terms of pixels per square inch, it's a whale of a drop to 5184. Try that. See if you like it, but I think you find that lower definition monitors really play havoc with the image.

Meta/Vector Image Formats

You may not have heard of this type of image formatting, not that you had heard of Raster, either. This formatting falls into a lot of proprietary formats, formats made for specific programs. CorelDRAW (CDR), Hewlett-Packard Graphics Language (HGL), and Windows Metafiles (EMF) are a few examples.

Where the Meta/Vector formats have it over Raster is that they are more than a simple grid of colored dots. They're actual vectors of data stored in mathematical formats rather than bits of colored dots. This allows for a strange shaping of colors and images that can be perfectly cropped on an arc. A squared-off map of dots cannot produce that arc as well. In addition, since the information is encoded in vectors, Meta/Vector image formats can be blown up or down (a property known as "scalability") without looking jagged or crowded (a property known as "pixelating").

So that I do not receive e-mail from those experts in computer images, know a difference exists between Meta and Vector formats. Vector formats can contain only vector data whereas Meta files, as is implied by the name, can contain multiple formats. This means there can be a lovely Bitmap plopped right in the middle of your Windows Meta file. You never know or see the difference but, there it is. I'm just trying to keep everybody happy.

The following sections offer examples of the image formats discussed here. The images are all from my wife's and my trip to Turkey in the summer of 1998. It was a wonderful time in a wonderful country.

What's A Bitmap?

I get that question a lot. Usually it's followed with "How come it only works on Microsoft Internet Explorer?" The second question's the easiest. Microsoft invented the Bitmap format. It would only make sense they would include it in their browser. Every time you boot up your PC, the majority of the images used in the process and on the desktop are Bitmaps.

If you're using an MSIE browser, you can view Figure 3.31. Netscape Navigator browsers still don't show the format. The image is St. Sophia in Istanbul taken from the city's hippodrome.

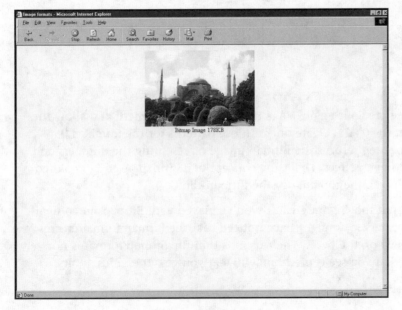

Figure 3.31
Bitmap image (300×203, 178K): http://www. htmlgoodies.com/book/ bitmap.html.

Against what I said earlier, Bitmaps display on all browsers, just not in the familiar `<IMG SRC="name">` format you're all used to. I see Bitmaps used mostly as return images from PERL Common Gateway Interfaces (CGIs). A counter is a perfect example. Page counters

139

that have that "odometer" effect () are Bitmap images created by the server, rather than as an inline image. Bitmaps are perfect for this process because they're a simple series of colored dots. Building them doesn't call for any fancy technique.

This is actually a fairly simple process. In the script that runs the counter, you "build" each number for the counter to display. Note the counter is black and white. That's only a 1 bit per pixel level image. To create the number 0 in the counter seen earlier, you would build a grid 7 pixels wide by 10 pixels high. The pixels you want to remain black, you would denote as 0. Those you wanted white, you'd denote as 1. Here's what it looks like:

0 0 0 0 0 0 0

0 0 **1 1 1** 0 0

0 **1 1 1 1 1** 0

0 **1 1** 0 **1 1** 0

0 **1 1** 0 **1 1** 0

0 **1 1** 0 **1 1** 0

0 **1 1** 0 **1 1** 0

0 **1 1 1 1 1** 0

0 0 **1 1 1** 0 0

0 0 0 0 0 0 0

See the number zero in the previous graph? Take the graph as one element and allow the bolded number 1s to form the 0. You create one of those patterns for the numbers 0 through 9. The PERL script then returns the Bitmap image representing the numbers and you get that neat little odometer effect. That's the concept of a Bitmap. A grid of colored points. The more bits per pixel, the more fancy the Bitmap can be.

Bitmaps are good images, but they're not great. If you've played with Bitmaps in comparison to any other image formats, you might have noticed that the Bitmap format creates images that are a little heavy on the bytes. The reason is that the Bitmap format is not very efficient at storing data. What you see is pretty much what you get, one series of bits stacked on top of another.

Compression

I said earlier that a Bitmap was a simple series of pixels all stacked up. But the same image saved in GIF or JPEG format uses fewer bytes to make up the file. How? Compression.

Compression is a computer term that represents a variety of mathematical formats used to compress an image's byte size. Let's say you have an image where the upper right corner has four pixels all the same color. Why not find a way to make those four pixels into one? That would cut down the number of bytes by three-fourths, at least in the one corner. That's a compression factor.

Bitmaps can be compressed to a point. The process is called "run-length encoding." Runs of pixels that are all the same color are all combined into one pixel. The longer the run of pixels, the more compression. Bitmaps with little detail or color variance really compress. Those with a great deal of detail don't offer much in the way of compression. Bitmaps that use the run-length encoding can carry either the common .bmp extension or .rle. Another difference between the two files is that the common Bitmap can accept 16 million different colors per pixel. Saving the same image in run-length encoding knocks the bits per pixel down to 8. That locks the level of color at no more than 256. That's even more compression of bytes to boot.

Figure 3.32 shows the same image of St. Sophia in common Bitmap and the run-length encoding format. Do *you* notice a difference?

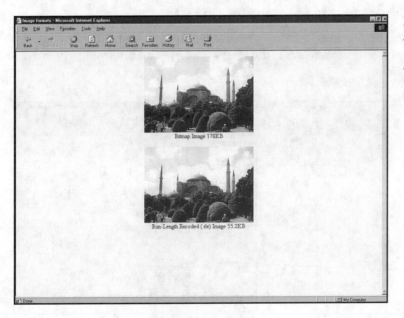

Figure 3.32
Bitmap image (300×203, 178K). RLE image (300× 203, 52.2K) http://www. htmlgoodies.com/book/ bitmaprle.html.

In case you're wondering, the image was saved in Windows version run-length encoding (a CompuServe version also exists) at 256 colors. It produced quite a drop in bytes, don't you think? And to be honest, I really don't see a whole lot of difference.

So, why not create a single pixel when all the colors are close? You could even lower the number of colors available so that you would have a better chance of the pixels being close in color. Good idea. The people at CompuServe felt the same way.

The GIF Image Formats

So, why wasn't the Bitmap chosen as the King of all Internet Images? Because Bill Gates hadn't yet gotten into the fold when the earliest browsers started running inline images. I don't mean to be flippant, either; I truly believe that.

GIF, which stands for Graphic Interchange Format, was first standardized in 1987 by CompuServe, although the patent for the algorithm (mathematical formula) used to create GIF compression actually belongs to Unisys. The first format of GIF used on the Web was called GIF87a, representing its year and version. It saved images at 8 pits-per-pixel, capping the color level at 256. That 8-bit level enabled the image to work across multiple server styles, including CompuServe, TCP/IP, and AOL. It was a graphic for all seasons, so to speak.

CompuServe updated the GIF format in 1989 to include animation, transparency, and interlacing. They called the new format, you guessed it: GIF89a.

No discernable difference exists between a basic (known as non-interlaced) GIF87a and GIF89a formats. See for yourself in Figure 3.33 (the image is of me and another gentleman playing a Turkish sitar).

Figure 3.33
GIF87a image (300×231, 61.4K). RLE image (300× 231, 61.4K) http://www.htmlgoodies.com/book/gif8789.html.

Even the bytes are the same. It's the animation, transparency, and non-interlacing additions to GIF89a that really set it apart. Animation and transparency are covered previously in this chapter. However, here's a brief look at interlaced versus non-interlaced frames.

Interlaced Versus Non-Interlaced GIF

The GIF images of me playing the Turkish sitar were non-interlaced format images. This is what is meant when someone refers to a "normal" GIF or just "GIF."

When you do *not* interlace an image, you fill it in from the top to the bottom, one line after another. Figure 3.34 shows two men coming onto a boat used to cross from the European to the Asian side of Turkey. The flowers they are carrying were sold in the manner of roses you might buy your wife here in the United States. I bought one. (What a guy.)

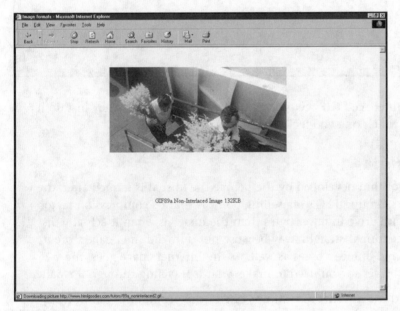

Figure 3.34

A GIF89a non-interlaced image (487×439, 132K) only in part of the way. See the effect for yourself at `http://www.htmlgoodies.com/book/gifnonlace.html`*. Watch quickly because once it's in, the effect doesn't happen so slowly the second time you try.*

Hopefully, you're on a slower connection computer so you got the full effect of waiting for the image to come in. It can be torture sometimes. That's where the brilliant Interlaced GIF89a idea came from.

Interlacing is the concept of filling in every other line of data, and then going back to the top and doing it all again, filling in the lines you skipped. Your television works that way. The effect on a computer monitor is that the graphic appears blurry at first and then sharpens up as the other lines fill in. That enables your viewer to at least get an idea of what's coming up rather than waiting for the entire image, line by line. Figure 3.35 is of a spice shop in the Grand Covered Bazaar, Istanbul.

Figure 3.35

A GIF89a interlaced image (191×300, 55.4K) only in part of the way. See the effect for yourself at http://www. htmlgoodies.com/ book/gifinterlace. html. *Watch quickly because after it's in, the effect doesn't happen so slowly the second time you try.*

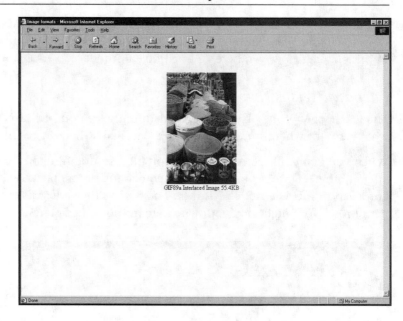

Both interlaced and non-interlaced GIFs get you to the same destination. They just do it differently. It's up to you which one you feel is better.

JPEG Image Formats

JPEG is a compression algorithm developed by the people the format is named after, the Joint Photographic Experts Group. JPEG's big selling point is that its compression factor stores the image on the hard drive in fewer bytes than the image is when it actually displays. The Web took to the format straightaway because not only did the image store in fewer bytes, but it transferred in fewer bytes as well. As the Internet adage goes, the pipeline isn't getting any bigger so you need to make what is traveling through it smaller.

For a long while, GIF ruled the Internet roost. I was one of the people who didn't really like this new JPEG format when it came out. It was less grainy than GIF, but caused computers without a decent amount of memory to crash the browser. (JPEGs have to be "blown up" to their full size. That takes some memory.) There was a time when people only had 4 or 8 megs of memory in their boxes. Really. It was way back in the Dark Ages.

JPEGs are "lossy." That's a term that means you trade off detail in the displayed picture for a smaller storage file. I always save my JPEGs at 50% or medium compression.

Figure 3.36 shows a single image saved in normal, or what's called "sequential" encoding. That's a top-to-bottom, single-line, equal to the GIF89a non-interlaced format. The image is of an open air market in Basra. The smell was amazing. If you like olives, go to Turkey. Cucumbers are big too, believe it or not.

Figure 3.36
Three JPEG images, each is 171×300 pixels, but notice the bytes that are required to make up the image. The bytes go down as the compression goes up...as does the image quality. See the effect for yourself at http://www.htmlgoodies.com/book/jpegcompression.html.

The difference between the 1% and 50% compression is not too bad, but the drop in bytes is impressive. The numbers I am showing are storage numbers, the amount of hard drive space the image takes up.

You've probably already surmised that 50% compression means that 50% of the image is included in the algorithm. If you don't put a 50% compressed image next to an exact duplicate image at 1% compression, it looks pretty good. But what about that 99% compression image? It looks horrible, but it's great for teaching. Look at it again. See how it appears to be made of blocks? That's what's meant by lossy. Bytes are lost at the expense of detail. You can see where the compression algorithm found groups of pixels that all appeared to be close in color and just grouped them all together as one. You might be hard pressed to figure out what the image was actually showing if I didn't tell you.

Progressive JPEGs

You can almost guess what this is all about. A progressive JPEG works a lot like the interlaced GIF89a by filling in every other line, and then returning to the top of the image to fill in the remainder. Figure 3.37 is presented three times at 1%, 50%, and 99% compression. The image is of the port at Istanbul from our hotel rooftop.

Figure 3.37

Three JPEG Progressive images, each is 300×160 pixels. Again, as the bytes go down, the compression goes up and the image quality drops. See the effect for yourself at `http://www.htmlgoodies.com/book/progressivejpeg.html`.

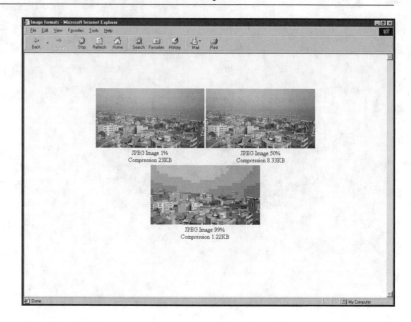

Obviously, here's where bumping up the compression does not pay off. Rule of thumb: If you're going to use progressive JPEG, keep the compression up high at 75% or better.

Which Image Should I Use Where?

I cannot give you just one good answer to this question. No matter what I say, someone else can give you just as compelling a reason why you should do the opposite. These are the rules I follow.

- Small images, such as icons and buttons: GIF (usually non-interlaced—my preference)
- Line art, grayscale (black and white), cartoons: GIF (usually non-interlaced—my preference)
- Scanned images and photographs: JPEG (I prefer progressive)
- Large images or images with a lot of detail: JPEG (I prefer progressive)

That said, ask yourself, "Do people really need to see this image?" Can I get away with text rather than an image link? Can I make links to images enabling the viewer to choose whether to look or not? The fewer images you have on a page, the faster it comes in. I would also attempt to have the same images across multiple pages, if possible. That way the viewer only has to wait once. After that, the images are in the cache and they pop right up.

How Do I Save in These Formats?

You have to have an image editor. I own three. Most of my graphic work for the Web is done in Paint Shop Pro. I do that because Paint Shop Pro is shareware and you can get your hands on the same copy I have. That way I know if I can do it, you can do it.

To get these formats, you need to make a point of saving in these formats. When your image editor is open and you have an image you wish to save, always choose Save As from the File menu. You get a dialog box that asks where you'd like to save the image. Better yet, somewhere on that dialog box is the opportunity for you to choose a different image format. Let's say you choose GIF. Keep looking. Somewhere on the same dialog box is an Options button (or something close). That's where you choose 87a or 89a and interlaced or non-interlaced, formats.

If you choose JPEG, you get the option of choosing the compression rate. You may not get to play with the sliding scale I get. You may only get a series of compression choices, high, medium, low, and so on. Go high.

Do You Edit and Create Images in GIF or JPEG?

Neither. I always edit in the Paint Shop Pro or Bitmap format. Those formats are best for editing and creating. I can always save in the format I choose after the image has been created. Others have told me that image creation and editing should only be done in a Vector format. Either way, make a point of editing with large images. The larger the image, the better chance you have of making that perfect crop.

Edit at the highest color level the image program offers. You can always resize and save to a low-byte format after you've finished creating the file.

Now you've got the lowdown on the images that work over the World Wide Web. If you haven't already, try your hand at creating your own graphics. I enjoy it. It's the adult version of finger painting.

Just remember, expect no right or wrong answers when creating images. Pretty much anything goes as long as your images help the user to understand what your page is all about.

Chapter 4

Imagemaps

You've seen how you can turn any image into a link. Imagemaps enable you to turn one image into many links. You can make different areas of the same image lead to different HTML pages, sounds, other images, or whatever you want.

This thing is called an *imagemap* because it is the map the computer uses, not the image. The image is simply there for the user to see and use as a guide. It's the map that the computer uses to make the links.

When you create an imagemap you've laid a point graph—a map—over an image. One is lying on top of the other. The image is just there for the visual. It is the map and its coordinates that are lying on top of it that the computer uses, thus the name imagemap.

The two types of imagemaps are server-side and client-side. Server-side imagemaps are older and more complex, but they work on virtually every browser, but client-side imagemaps are easier to create. I'll show you both in this chapter (as well as how to make fake imagemaps), but I suggest that you consider building client-side imagemaps.

Server-Side Imagemaps

This is the beauty of an imagemap. One image is divided into sections. Each is assigned a different URL. The success of an imagemap is how well the image leads the viewer. Unless the image is fairly blatant about what each link does, it's better to go with simple blue hypertext links.

The original version of this tutorial is on the HTML Goodies site at `http://www.htmlgoodies.com/tutors/imagemap.html`. *This was also the first of the HTML Goodies tutorials to win an award. You should head to this link, so you can try out an imagemap at* `http://www.htmlgoodies.com/book/imagemap.html`.

Note

This tutorial refers to the use of a CGI, a Common Gateway Interface. You need to attach to a CGI to make this work. Chances are your server has one, but you have to ask your server technician or ISP exactly where it is.

A CGI is a small program, usually in the Perl or C++ computer language that does some of the work for you.

Again, ask the people who take your money each month if they have one available to you. I assume they do if you're on a server of any size.

I have no doubt you can create the items needed for an imagemap. What I am concerned with is whether your server enables you to use this type of imagemap. You see, an imagemap in this format must be connected to a little ditty called a CGI.

"No problem!" you say. Imagemaps are all over the Web. "I'll just connect to one and use it." Hmmm. If only people were always that generous with their CGIs.

You may be searching for a long while before you find a public domain imagemap CGI.

The picture in Figure 4.1 is an imagemap. It's just one large image, even the text. You can click each cat's face to go to a different page devoted to that cat. One image sends you to three different pages.

Does that image do the trick? Is it blatant enough that someone knows what to do? I think so. You can see the three cats and you are instructed to click. I think it gets the job done.

The Imagemap Command

Following is the basic code to insert an imagemap. Please don't be thrown because the IMG command went to the next line. This all goes together. I just put the IMG on the next line because the entire command is just too long to fit across the page.

```
<A HREF="http://www.htmlgoodies.com/cgi-bin/imagemap/~jburns/imap.map">
<IMG SRC="imap.gif" ISMAP></A>
```

There are three parts to an imagemap: the CGI, a map, and a GIF. The map in the command is titled `imap.map`.

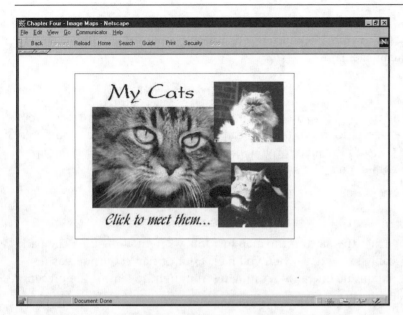

Figure 4.1
A CGI-driven imagemap.

All three of these items must be grouped together in the format of a hypertext link. Notice the <A HREF> and </A> at the front and back of the command, respectively. A link's format makes it active and clickable. Let's take the three items in order of appearance. Please remember that this command format works on my server. You must configure the command so it works on your server. I'll get into how in a moment.

The CGI

The very first thing the preceding command does is it tells the computer where to get the CGI. This is known as the *path* to the CGI. The path is as follows (remember it follows the A HREF):

```
http://www.htmlgoodies.com/cgi-bin/imagemap
```

The beginning portion tells the computer where to find the CGI. Sometimes the CGI is in a "bin" (bin) like it is here. Computer people tell you that *bin* stands for binary, which in turn has to do with the UNIX-type format the CGI is using, and on and on. Unless you're actually thinking of writing your own CGIs in UNIX, bin probably means nothing more than a place where a lot of stuff is, such as a trash bin. Get it? imagemap is the actual CGI name being used.

You notice that the CGI does not have an extension. Depending on how your server is configured, it may not. However, it may. .pl is a common extension for CGI programs if the CGI script is written in the Perl programming language.

Again, please don't try to connect to this CGI. It doesn't work. You have to be on this server for it to react favorably. Go to your Webmaster or technical people and ask for your own server's specific path to the imagemap CGI.

The Map

Now that you have told the computer where the CGI is, tell the computer where the map that the CGI is going to read is. Once again (shake head here), you have told the computer the CGI's location. That CGI reads the map for you, but it needs to know where the map is. The second part of the command is the *path to the map*. The preceding path is as follows:

```
~jburns/imap.map
```

Now, the tricky part. Notice that the path to the map just follows right along after the path to the CGI. Why? You probably know that when you have a/lot/of/names/ inside slashes—those are directories. They are inside one another moving from right to left. In the preceding path, `imap.map` is inside `~jburns`.

But is the path to the map inside the CGI? No. When you put them together you tell that specific CGI the path it should take to find the map it is supposed to read. You are giving it directions.

Notice that I only wrote the server's URL (`http://www.htmlgoodies.com`) once. It would seem the path to the map would need it again. You can write it all out again if you'd like, but it is not needed. The computer understands that the path to the map is on the same server as the path to the CGI. These plastic thinking boxes are so smart.

Making the Map

Hey! I need a map, right? Where do I get a map? Good question. You have to make it. You can't just go somewhere and download a map for your GIF. The map you use has to be custom made for your purposes. What does a map look like? It looks like this:

```
default http://www.htmlgoodies.com
circle http://www.htmlgoodies.com/fido.html 433,67 478,108
rect http://www. htmlgoodies.com/stimpy.html 107,18 372,75
poly http://www. htmlgoodies.com/chloe.html 3,108 103,63
103,76 123,78 33,126
```

Neat, huh? It's kind of a gri with points denoted for each URL—a grid of points that the CGI reads. A certain URL is sent for when the mouse is on a certain area on the map grid.

A ton of shareware programs enable you to make a map. I could not even begin to explain each one here. You must go out, find one you like, and use its instructions to make your map. That said, my favorite program for Windows is MapEdit. It is wonderfully easy. Others have told me that Map This is also good. The best program for Macintosh is MAC Image Map.

When you have created your map, you can place it in any directory you want as long as the path to the map is correct. I always place my map and the GIF that goes along with it in the same place. It makes things a little easier.

The Image

No matter what map creation software you choose, you are asked to create your map using an image. Of course, this image is the one that appears on the page as your imagemap. For instance, the preceding map was created over top of the GIF you see. It's just the way the programs work. They display the GIF you choose and then you section the GIF off and assign URLs. But I'm rambling.

This is the command for placing the image:

```
<IMG SRC="imap.gif" ISMAP>
```

Notice that it is just a normal image command with the addition of ISMAP. The computer displays this image for people to click. It is, for all purposes, your imagemap.

So pick a nice one.

You place the ISMAP inside the image command to alert the computer to avoid activating the image, and instead read the map that is lying on top of it.

Please note that I allowed the blue border to remain in the preceding example and in Figure 4.1. In an imagemap setting you should really lose it by adding the command BORDER="0" in the image command between IMG and SRC. The border is too distracting.

FAQs from the HTML Goodies Web Site

Q. How small can I make the section of an imagemap? I want to make the alphabet and each letter a different section.

A. It can be made as small as four pixels square. Just be nice to your users and don't go so small that they have a hard time getting it to run.

Putting It All Together

The following is the basic format of an imagemap:

```
<A HREF="PATH TO CGI / PATH TO MAP"><IMG SRC="image.gif" ISMAP></A>
```

Telling you exactly what the paths are for your server is difficult. I have no idea where on the server that your Webmaster has placed the imagemap CGI, if one exists at all. My guess is that one does. You just have to follow the instructions and path structure to connect them all.

FAQs from the HTML Goodies Web Site

Q. I can't get this map program thing to work. Can't I just guess at the points and make the map myself?

A. Sure, if the image is geometrical, you can probably take an educated guess as to where the points are. You need to know how many pixels across and how many down, and then guess away. You may even be able to pick out the point by opening the image in an image editor and rolling your pointer across the image and watching the pixels fly by. Just make sure you save the map with the .MAP extension.

Q. I copied exactly what you had on the page for my imagemap and it didn't work.

A. It didn't work because you are not on my server. You need to contact your own server people and ask them if they offer an imagemap CGI and if so, what the paths to attach to it are.

I want to make one more point about using an imagemap. Many people surf with their inline images turned off. That means they don't see any pictures when they surf, just text. It happens more often than you think. People get tired of waiting for a large imagemap image to load. They just want to get moving.

Because of all that, I suggest that you always offer links to the items linked to your imagemaps. You could also offer a link to a text-based version of your page. Try to be helpful to your users—all your users.

Hopefully this has helped a bit. I understand it all may seem a bit overwhelming at the moment, but try to muddle through it. After you do your first map, you may wonder what you thought was so hard.

Net Notes

Here are some URLs worth checking out:

Grab MapEdit: `http://www.boutell.com/mapedit` available for MAC now too!

Yahoo!'s imagemap links:`http://www.yahoo.com/Computers_and_Internet/Internet/World_Wide_Web/Imagemaps/`

Client-Side Imagemaps

The *client-side imagemap* is run by the browser rather than a CGI. What happens is that you provide all the information required to run the map in your HTML document. That's why it's called a client-side map. The map's functions are provided on the client's end of things rather than by a CGI on your server's side.

 This tutorial can be found online at `http://www.htmlgoodies.com/tutors/cs_imap.html`. *Go and see how it works.*

Figure 4.2 is a client-side imagemap. Do you like the graphic? I got it by scanning a clip art book. You should get one, or six. They're great. All the images are in crisp black and white and scan wonderfully. Better yet, none of the images are under copyright. You can use them to your heart's content.

The image is a drawing of a monk that I used to create links to some medieval sites for a friend's Web page. The image in Figure 4.2 is sitting alone. On this Web page it was surrounded by strange gothicimages. Oooooh, scary.

In the tutorial for this section I used the same image, but here the images have links to more popular pages. I'd like to point out that the image was allowed to keep its blue border for demonstration purposes only. When using an imagemap, you should really add `BORDER="0"` to the image command to lose the border altogether.

Remember the last time you ran your pointer over a basic CGI-run imagemap? Hopefully it was the previous online tutorial. The map's coordinates fly by in the online example. That's because the pointer was reading the map. Here, the pointer is still reading the coordinates; it's putting up the URL associated with the coordinates.

Let's Make a Map!

You can make a map by hand if you have a paint program that displays your images' coordinates. Otherwise, you need to go and get a map-making program. A million different programs are out there that can do the trick for you. I could not even begin to explain each one here. You must go out, find one you like, and use its instructions to make your map.

Figure 4.2

A client-side imagemap.

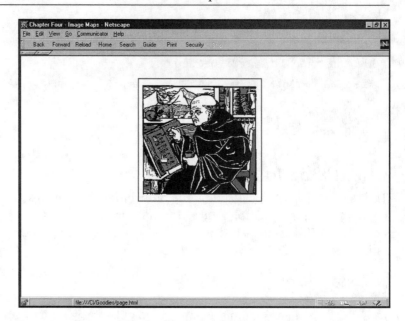

Tip

See the previous tutorial on CGI-driven imagemaps for more on how to make a map.

The difference between the last imagemap tutorial and this one is that with a CGI-driven imagemap, you actually use the map you make. In this tutorial, you are creating the map just so you can find the points on the grid. You then transfer those points right to the HTML document.

Putting the Image on the Page

After you have the map finished and know the points, you need to place them and the image they support on the page. Do the image first. The following is the command I used to place the monk image in Figure 4.2:

```
<A HREF="monk.map"><IMG SRC="monk.gif" ISMAP USEMAP="#monkareas"></A>
```

Neat, huh? Look at what's happening:

● A HREF=   Denotes the link to the map. You must place the name of the map you created after the HREF. This is the map you created using the map program you downloaded.

156

- ● IMG SRC=   Denotes your basic image command.

- ● ISMAP   Stands alone. It tells the browser that this is an imagemap. The browser is basically being told that the image is active, but to read the map instead of activating the image.

- ● USEMAP=   Tells the browser where to find the map coordinates. Notice that the format is that of a page jump. The browser is being told where on the page to look for the map coordinates. In this case the coordinates are on a section of the HTML document marked monkareas. Please notice the preceding # mark! You need that.

- ● </A>   Ends it all.

The Coordinates

Okay, okay, you have the image up there. Where do you put the map's coordinates? Glad you asked. You place them on your HTML page. "Are the coordinates showing up on the page?" you ask, perplexed. "No," I answer brazenly. You set them aside as commands rather than straight text.

These are the coordinates for the map. Remember what the map looked like? Well, here are those same coordinates in client-side imagemap format:

```
<map NAME="monkareas">
<area SHAPE=RECT COORDS="91,30 186,98" HREF="http://www.nfl.com"
 ALT="NFL Home Page">
<area SHAPE=CIRCLE COORDS="25,72 28,97" HREF="http://www.cnn.com"
 ALT="CNN Home Page">
<area SHAPE=CIRCLE COORDS="107,158 132,162" HREF="http://www.cbs.com"
 ALT="CBS Home Page">
<area SHAPE=POLY COORDS="9,115 86,79 98,116 69,131 86,175 48,206"
 HREF="http://www.cnn.com" ALT="USA TODAY Home Page">
<area SHAPE=default HREF="http://www.htmlgoodies.com">
</MAP>
```

FAQs from the HTML Goodies Web Site

Q. Where do I put the coordinate text on the HTML document?

A. Pretty much anywhere, but the rule of thumb is beneath the map image, which is usually way down at the bottom of the page. That's where I put it.

Here's How You Do It

You first denote that these are the coordinates for the map. You do that with MAP NAME=. See that? You place the name you used after the # mark—just don't use the # mark here. The browser jumps to this part of your page to read coordinates rather than going to a CGI.

Then it's a matter of following the format again and again.

- AREA   Denotes that this is a new section of the map.
- SHAPE   Denotes the shape you used. The map program tells you all this.
- HREF   Denotes the URL this section points to.
- ALT   Tells users who have their inline images turned off that this is an imagemap.
- DEFAULT   Follows the previous format. It denotes a URL for every part of the map not set aside by an imagemap set of coordinates.
- </MAP>   Wraps up the whole deal.

That's it. Follow all this and you should have a client-side imagemap. People are soon clicking like crazy.

Once again, not everyone surfs with their images turned on and many people surf with text-only browsers. If you offer an imagemap, it's always best to offer hypertext links too, or offer one link a text-based version of your page. Be nice to all your visitors.

 I made another map for you to look at. Make sure you view the source code. Go to http://www.htmlgoodies.com/book/anothermap.html.

Fake Imagemap

Figure 4.3 looks like all the other imagemaps you've seen so far, right? If you were to run your mouse over it and keep an eye on the status bar at the bottom of the browser window, you'd see it acts like an imagemap. If you click the section you want, it would work. Go to the page. The trick is that this thing isn't an imagemap. In fact, it isn't an image at all. It's six images. Stay with me here.

 This is another tutorial you have to see to believe. It's so easy, but looks great. Head to http://www.htmlgoodies.com/tutors/fakemap.html.

This is a fake imagemap. Figure 4.4 shows what that fake map looks like in what intellectuals call an *exploded view*.

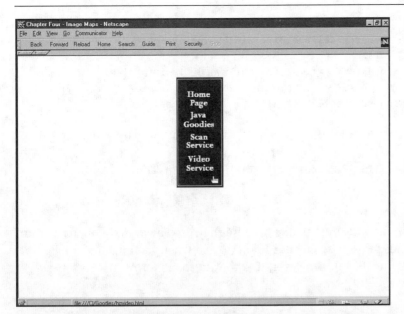

Figure 4.3
A fake imagemap.

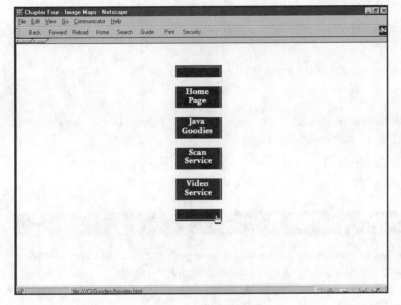

Figure 4.4
A fake imagemap exploded view.

See what I did? I took one image, cropped it into six and made each one active. The following is the code that I used to put the fake map together:

```
<center>
<A HREF="index.html"><img src="mapo2.gif" width="100" height="25"
```

```
  border="0"></A><BR>
 <A HREF="index.html"><img src="cellone.gif" width="100" height="45"
  border="0"></A><BR>
 <A HREF="/javagoodies/index.html"><img src="celltwo.gif" width="100"
  height="45" border="0"></A><BR>
 <A HREF="scan.html"><img src="cellthree.gif" width="100" height="45"
  border="0"></A><BR>
 <A HREF="hgvideo.html"><img src="cellfour.gif" width="100" height="45"
  border="0"></A><BR>
 <A HREF="hgvideo.html"><img src="mapo3.gif" width="100" height="25"
  border="0"></A><BR>
 </center>
```

I included the <CENTER> commands in the code because they do play a pretty big part. You can also add ALT commands to each image, but I don't do so when I am making a fake imagemap. I think it kills the illusion. However, if you want to, go for it—it's your page.

The Image(s)

You can do this one of two ways:

- Create one image and cut it up.

  or

- Create a template image. Add words to the image and keep saving in a different name.

I used the first method. Both methods work, but I thought it was easiest to cut the image up. You need an image editing program to do this.

When you have the images and are sure they line up correctly, simply build the map. Make sure the images load in order, top to bottom, left to right.

FAQs from the HTML Goodies Web Site

Q. You said that the fake imagemaps had to be one picture cut up. Well, I did it with five pictures lined up along the top of the page.

A. Wonderful. I'll bet it looks great. Good thinking. There are no rules to any of this. If it looks right, it probably is right.

Getting It All to Line Up

This is the tricky part. You know each image is active. That means you need to use the `BORDER="0"` command to eliminate the blue border that would normally form.

First, make sure all your images are of equal width and height, so they line up and form a perfect second image. It kills the entire effect without it.

FAQs from the HTML Goodies Web Site

Q. I made a fake map but it keeps getting messed up. There are five images left to right and the last one keeps jumping down to the next line. How do I stop that?

A. Make the images smaller. If five are going across the top, knock them down a bit. You can set it so that the page scrolls right by surrounding the images with `<NOBR>` and `</NOBR>`. That disallows the break. A page that scrolls to the right is not really a good idea. People want it all on their screen in one shot. Go with smaller graphics.

The use of a line or smaller image that moves through the multiple images gives a greater perception that the image is solid rather than a sum of parts. See the white box I have running through the image? This takes a little practice.

Keep all the commands tight together. If a space is between the image and `</A>`, that space shows up and kills the effect.

Run it all together. If you have two images that sit next to each other on the same line, do not skip the second image's commands to the next line. That works on some browsers, but on all. In earlier versions, in particular, you go to the next line as a space.

That space appears when the images line up and kill the effect. Run it all together in a long line or at least butt the `</A><A HREF...>` commands against each other.

Always use an alignment of some kind surrounding the multiple images. I am using `<CENTER>` in this example. If you don't want it centered, use `<P ALIGN="left"></P>` or `<P ALIGN="right"></P>`. It helps greatly.

This is a lot of common sense. If your image is 100×100 to start and the parts you create do not add up to 100×100, expect trouble. Just take your time with creating and cropping the images and you should have no trouble with this one after a few tries.

 I made you another fake map to work with at `http://www.htmlgoodies.com/book/` `anotherfakemap.html`.

Make sure to look at the source code.

Part III

Getting More Control Over the Layout of Your Web Pages

5 *Tables*

6 *Frames*

7 *Link Buttons and Forms*

8 *Cascading Style Sheets and Layers*

Chapter 5

Tables

You want a table? Okay. Figure 5.1 shows a table of the Brady family. Feel free to sing.

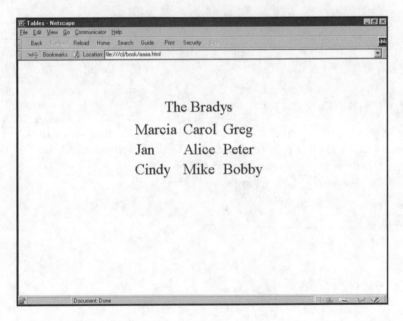

Figure 5.1
A simple table of the Brady clan.

Hey! That's not what I wanted!

Yes it is. You asked for a table. That thing was made using the <TABLE> </TABLE> commands. That's a table because... Oh, wait. I bet Figure 5.2 is the thing you were looking for.

Figure 5.2
A much better table of the Brady clan.

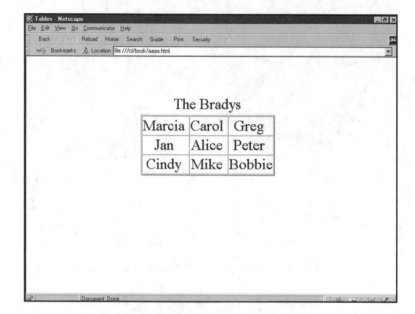

Am I right? You wanted those fancy frame lines so that it looks like a graph or, dare I say, a table?

The Simple Table Flags

First things first...let me explain the table I showed you in Figure 5.1—the one you didn't want. It makes explaining the framed table a whole lot easier. The following is the little program I wrote to give me the Brady family table shown in Figure 5.1:

```
<TABLE>
  <CAPTION>The Bradys</CAPTION>
  <TR>
    <TD>Marcia</TD>
    <TD>Carol</TD>
    <TD>Greg</TD>
  </TR>
  <TR>
```

```
        <TD>Jan</TD>
        <TD>Alice</TD>
        <TD>Peter</TD>
    </TR>
    <TR>
        <TD>Cindy</TD>
        <TD>Mike</TD>
        <TD>Bobby</TD>
    </TR>

    </TABLE>
```

Now, don't be put off by this little ditty. At first glance it looks rough, but look again. Only four commands are being used again and again. The following are those commands:

- <TABLE> and </TABLE>   Start and end the entire thing. I think that makes perfect sense. This is a table, after all.
- <CAPTION> and </CAPTION>   Place a caption over your table. In my example the caption is The Bradys. These flags also bold your caption text and center it across your table cells.
- <TD>   Denotes table data. You put this in front of every piece of information you want in a cell. You need a </TD> at the end of each data cell.
- <TR>   Used when you want a new table row to begin. Again, make sure you close each row with a </TR>.

Table flags create a series of cells. Each cell's data is denoted by the <TD> flag. Please note that even though the preceding program has each cell (or <TD>) flag on a new line, the cells keep going to the right until you tell the computer that a new row of cells starts; you do that by using the <TR>, or table row, command.

Think of it as constructing a tic-tac-toe board. You need nine cells for the board, right? Three across in three rows. Use the <TD> command to make three cells across and use <TR> to jump to the next row. Keep going until you have nine cells in three rows of three. Nothing to it.

Remember that whatever follows the <TD> command appears in the cell. The widest cell in each column determines the width of each column. One column could possibly be three times as wide as the other columns. Just because one column is a certain width doesn't mean the others are the same. The biggest wins, in other words; in life as well as in HTML.

FAQs from the HTML Goodies Web Site

Q. Where's my table? I copied everything from your page and it's not showing up!

A. I bet you forgot to get the end table flag: </TABLE>. If you miss that, nothing shows up.

Q. I made a table, but the first row isn't in cells. It's just text.

A. You may have missed an end quotation mark somewhere before the table started. I have done this a few times. The next quote the browser sees is after the first table row, so it ignored the first few <TD> flags until it got to an end quote. That finished the command before the table started. Check your code carefully.

Q. You say in your table tutorial that I need a </TD> and a </TR> for every <TD> and <TR> I write. I've been told that you really only need one </TD> and one </TR> at the very end of the table. Which way is right?

A. I have seen tables done both ways. In fact, I have seen many tables done without any end flags. I used to make my tables that way when I started, but the traditional format is an end flag for every flag you open. If you follow that format, you are not running into any trouble.

Really Fancy Table Stuff

Now let's move on to making the fancy lines between cells. Figure 5.3 is the same table you saw before.

Okay, so I changed the Bradys' names, but you get the idea. The following code is the program I used to create the tables in Figures 5.2 and 5.3. Please note that the flags are the same as the first table you looked at! I just added a few more commands inside the table flags, but you already know about them.

```
<TABLE BORDER="3" CELLSPACING="1" CELLPADDING="1">
<CAPTION>The Bradys</CAPTION>
<TR>
<TD ALIGN = "center"> Agnes</TD>
<TD ALIGN = "center"> Wilma </TD>
<TD ALIGN = "center"> George </TD>
</TR>
<TR>
<TD ALIGN = "center"> Gwen </TD>
<TD ALIGN = "center"> Skippy</TD>
<TD ALIGN = "center"> Alvin </TD>
```

```
</TR>
<TR>
<TD ALIGN = "center"> Melvin </TD>
<TD ALIGN = "center"> Harold </TD>
<TD ALIGN = "center"> Joe</TD>
</TR>
</TABLE>
```

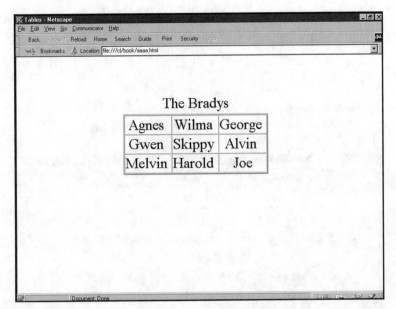

Figure 5.3
A simple table with borders.

If it looks to you like all the work is done in the <TABLE> flag, you're right. You are using the following three commands to do the work for you:

- BORDER   Tells the table how large the border should be. This is all relative. Three is larger than two, two is larger than one, and so on. Try different numbers. I happen to like the look of BORDER="3". BORDER="0" gets rid of the lines altogether.

- CELLSPACING   Tells how much space you'd like between cells. I'd keep this kind of small. Large spacing tends to defeat the purpose.

- CELLPADDING   Tells how much padding is required between the text and the walls of the cell. Note that the cell walls tend to fill out. A higher number fills out more. Try a few different numbers. Sometimes bigger is better.

How about that new ALIGN command in the <TD> flag? See it? I have told the <TD> flag that I want the data that follows centered within the cell walls outlined in the table command.

Remember that using an ALIGN command inside a <TD> only affects the data in that one cell. You need to add an ALIGN command to the other <TD> cells if you also want them affected. Can you do other ALIGN types? Sure. Try ALIGN=left and ALIGN=right. Use them in combination. Save them, trade them!

FAQs from the HTML Goodies Web Site

Q. Can I use <BR> and <TP> flags inside the <TD>, after the <TD> flag?

A. Yes. Create your text any way you'd like. It all manipulates inside the table cell.

Activating Cells for Links

Wouldn't it be great if you could make a table with words and the words in the table were active, so you could click them? You can do just that. Take a look at Figure 5.4.

Figure 5.4
A table showing four links in four cells.

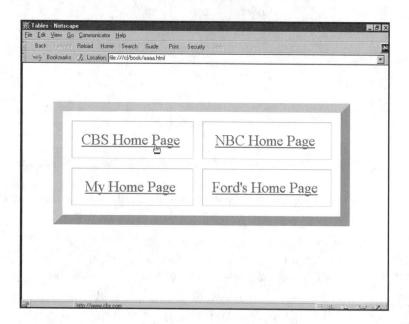

The flags are the same for this table except that you place a link command after the <TD> flag. The tag for the upper-left cell looks like this:

```
<TD align="center"><A HREF="http://www.cbs.com">CBS Home Page</A> </TD>
```

By the way, the BORDER, CELLSPACING, and CELLPADDING flags are all set at 20 in Figure 5.4, which gives you an example of some larger numbers.

FAQs from the HTML Goodies Web Site

Q. **You may want to add to your table tutorial that tables are great for creating your page's layout. You use the table cells to create the geometric look of the page and then set the border to 0 so that the table borders disappear, but the formatting remains.**

A. That's correct. In fact, I do that all the time. The entire HTML Goodies home page is one big table. Good thinking. Thanks for writing.

Images in Cells

Can you put images in each of the cells? You bet. Here you go—just take a look at Figure 5.5.

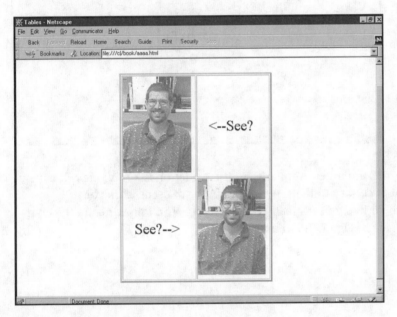

Figure 5.5
Images placed in a table cell.

All you have done is followed the <TD> flag with an image flag. This command creates the upper-left cell:

```
<TD ALIGN="center"><IMG SRC="joeburns.gif"></TD>
```

Framing Images

I am asked at least once a week how to frame an image. What you have done until now is framed two images. A frame around one image is nothing more than a one-celled table. Figure 5.6 shows a framed image.

Figure 5.6
A framed image.

The commands for doing this are much simpler than the earlier ones. Only one cell is here to deal with it, so it is not necessary to tell the table any type of CELLPADDING or CELLSPACING. You can if you'd like, but it's really not necessary. The following are the commands that placed the image in Figure 5.6 in a frame:

```
<TABLE BORDER="10">
<TR>
<TD ALIGN="center"><IMG SRC="joeburns.gif">
</TD>
</TR>
</TABLE>
```

Centering the Image

One more hint: See how the images in the cells are pushed into the upper-left corner (refer to Figure 5.5)? They're not quite in the center. Some space is on the right and bottom of the image. I know a quick trick to fix that. Check out Figure 5.7.

Figure 5.7
Centering an image inside a table cell.

Add a `<TR>` tag before the `<TD>` that holds the image, and then close both tags with `</TR>` and the `</TD>`. The trick is to make sure the `</TR>` and the `</TD>` are on the same line as the `<TD>` and `<TR>`, like so:

```
<TABLE BORDER="10">
<TR><TD ALIGN="center"><IMG SRC="joeburns.gif"> </TD></TR>
</TABLE>
```

Again, notice that the end flags are on the same line as the start commands. The effect is lost if you move the end commands to the next line. By the way, technically it isn't supposed to work like this—no matter what line an HTML flag is on, it should always work the same. I've found, however, that when it comes to centering things, where you put your flags often makes a big difference.

Finally...

Just about anything goes inside a table. The table flags just surround the items with a frame. Try putting a few of your page's items within a frame or a table; it looks professional. Just don't go overboard with it. If you do, it starts to take on the not-so-nice look of too many lawn ornaments.

 I have a couple of larger tables for you to look at online at `http://www.htmlgoodies.com/ book/bigtables.html`. *Make sure you look at the source code.*

173

Advanced Table Commands

This section only deals with three commands. Some advanced tutorial, huh? Actually, these three commands are great when you want more control over the spacing of your table cells. I strongly suggest that you read over the first part of this chapter before beginning. Otherwise, this stuff is way over your head. Then you call me a name. Then you bring my mother into it, and nobody wants that.

The COLSPAN *Command*

Figure 5.8 shows a simple table that uses the COLSPAN command to create a single table cell that spans the entire width of the table.

Figure 5.8

A table with the COLSPAN *command.*

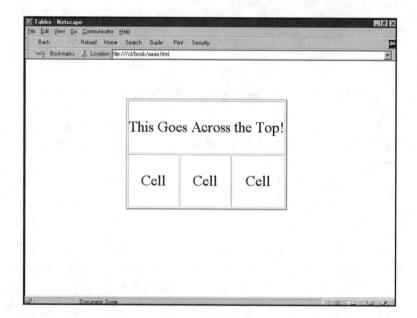

See how the top row spans across three columns? That's what the COLSPAN command does. It really isn't that tough to do. The problem comes in figuring out where the <TR> flag goes. If you place a <TR> in the wrong place, you can mess up the table's complete configuration. The following is the program that created the table:

```
<TABLE BORDER="3" CELLPSACING="3" CELLPADDING="3">
<TR>
<TD ALIGN="center" COLSPAN="3">This Goes Across the Top!</TD>
</TR>
<TR>
<TD ALIGN="center">Cell</TD>
```

```
<TD ALIGN="center">Cell</TD>
<TD ALIGN="center">Cell</TD>
</TR>
</TABLE>
```

Notice the first <TD> line. See how it contains the ALIGN command plus that COLSPAN thing I talked about? The deal is a table is a series of columns (the up and down sections) and rows (the left to right sections). I wanted the first <TD> cell to span across three columns, so I added the command COLSPAN and told the span to go across three columns. Note that three cells (columns) are being spanned by that command.

If I had written COLSPAN="2", the span would have been only two columns. Note where the first <TR> flag fell—it is immediately after the row that spanned three columns. If I had spanned only two, I would have had to place another <TD> cell before the first <TR> flag.

Drawing your table before writing your HTML code is best. That helps you see where the table rows must break to keep within the square that is the table.

FAQs from the HTML Goodies Web Site

Q. You may want to add the command VALIGN="top" **to your advanced table tutorial.**

A. I am. VALIGN stands for vertical align. Using the top command like you did sets all text right to the top of the cell.

The ROWSPAN *Command*

I would think that you can guess what is going to happen here—basically the same thing that just happened in the previous section, but this command spans rows rather than columns. Figure 5.9 shows an example.

The following is the HTML code that made the table in Figure 5.9:

```
<TABLE BORDER="3" CELLPSACING="3" CELLPADDING="3">
<TR>
<TD ROWSPAN="2" ALIGN="center" WIDTH="75">How about this?</TD>
<TD ALIGN="center" WIDTH="75">Cell</TD>
</TR>
<TR>
<TD ALIGN="center" WIDTH="75">Cell</TD>
</TR>
</TABLE>
```

Figure 5.9
A table with the ROWSPAN
command.

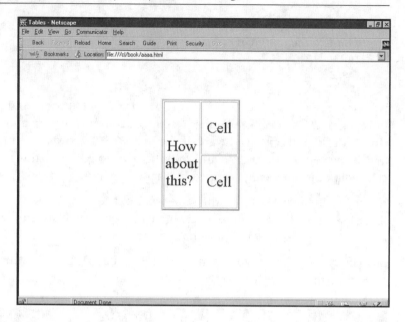

See what happened? I simply told the column to span more than two rows. I think it's a bit confusing too. You tell columns to span rows and you tell rows to span columns. It confuses me every so often.

Again, the best thing to do is draw out the table before you attempt to create it with HTML commands. Getting the span is never the difficult thing. The problem is where to place the <TR> command to keep this information inside the four corners.

FAQs from the HTML Goodies Web Site

Q. Can I set a separate CELLPADDING **for each cell?**

A. No. A table always stays four-sided. If you leave the <TD> blank, you don't get the cell (coming up in the next tutorial), but you still have to put those <TD> flags in there to stay four-sided. Setting an individual CELLPADDING affects all the other cells, anyway.

What's That WIDTH="*nn*" *Deal?*

Yeah, I did just pop that up out of nowhere, didn't I? That command denotes the width of the cell. When you use numbers, like I did earlier, it is defining the width in pixels. If you use percentages, such as WIDTH="20%", it denotes the width of the cell in relationship to the screen. The percentage sign is required.

This helps a lot in defining the space your tables take up on the page. Using percentages helps keep the cells somewhat equal between browsers and differing screen settings.

FAQs from the HTML Goodies Web Site

Q. Can I set a separate width for each cell?

A. To a point. You can make some cells wider than others by using the COLSPAN and ROWSPAN commands, but it must all stay within four sides. (No row can stick out farther than other rows, and no column can stick out farther than other columns.)

I have an example of a very intricate table created using the COLSPAN and ROWSPAN commands. Try to figure out the code yourself before you look. Go to http://www.htmlgoodies.com/book/fancytable.html.

Can I Use COLSPAN *and* ROWSPAN *Commands Together?*

Yes. As a matter of fact, the HTML Goodies master page (at http://www.htmlgoodies.com/tutors/master.html) is little more than a giant table using both ROWSPAN and COLSPAN commands. Bop over, take a look, and feel free to look at the view-source to see the commands.

Good luck with these two new commands. Take my word for it—these give you more headaches than you want. You may be sorry you saw this tutorial, so go look at another...

A Table Within a Table

I've pointed out many times that you can combine different HTML flags to create new effects. Figure 5.10 shows a good example of that—a table within a table.

Check out an online example of a table within a table within a table. Go to http://www.htmlgoodies.com/book/tableintableintable.html.

The following is the code that created the table in Figure 5.10. The outer table's commands are regular text and the inner table's commands are italicized so that you can quickly tell them apart.

```
<TABLE BORDER="3" CELLPADDING="10" CELLSPACING="10">
  <TR>
    <TD>
      <TABLE BORDER="3" CELLPADDING="3" CELLSPACING="3">
      <TR>
        <TD>2nd Table</TD>
        <TD>2nd Table</TD>
      <TR>
```

```
          <TD>2nd Table</TD>
          <TD>2nd Table</TD>
       </TR>
       </TABLE>
     </TD>
     <TD> The cell next to this one has a smaller table inside of it,
  a table inside a table.</TD>
     </TR>
  </TABLE>
```

Figure 5.10
A table within a table.

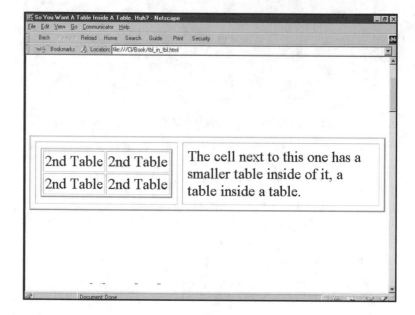

For those of you already up-to-speed on tables, you can probably pick up from the code how it's done. You make a point of ending every line with an end command. It can get confusing, but each <TD> and <TR> must be closed as soon as it ends.

> **Tip**
>
> When I do a table in a table, I tend to get a little confused about what goes with what. What I do is create all the tables separately, making sure every section has its own end command. I create the tables that go in the cells first. The last thing I make is the larger table. That way I can create the large table and when I need to fill in the <TD> with a smaller table, I just cut and paste it in. It also helps me remember to follow the smaller table with a </TD> for the larger table's benefit. It's super easy to forget one and doing so messes up the whole table scheme.

FAQs from the HTML Goodies Web Site

Q. I tried to create a table in a table, but all I get are the horizontal lines, no verticals. Why?

A. You are missing some </TD> and </TR> commands. Remember, every <TD> or <TR> you write needs an end command when doing any table.

Using Tables to Make an HTML Calendar

Why didn't I think of this sooner?! This is why I read the e-mail from viewers—you give the best ideas. I should have seen this coming, but I didn't. Instead, I received 50 requests to make an HTML calendar, so I made one. Take a look at Figure 5.11.

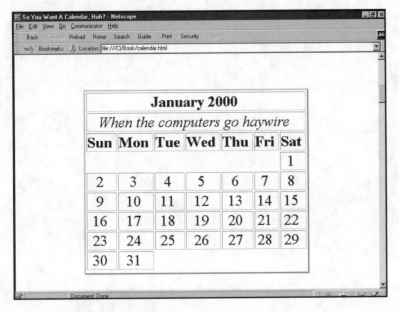

Figure 5.11
A calendar created with tables.

Isn't that neat? It's not that rough to do. It's actually just a simple table with a couple of additions. The following is the really long-winded code I used to create the calendar:

```
<TABLE BORDER="3" CELLSPACING="3" CELLPADDING="3">
<TR>
<TD COLSPAN="7" ALIGN=center><B>January 2000</B>
</TD>
<TR>
<TD COLSPAN="7" ALIGN=center><I>When the computers go haywire</I></TD>
```

```
</TR>
<TR>

<TD ALIGN=center>Sun</TD>
<TD ALIGN=center>Mon</TD>
<TD ALIGN=center>Tue</TD>
<TD ALIGN=center>Wed</TD>
<TD ALIGN=center>Thu</TD>
<TD ALIGN=center>Fru</TD>
<TD ALIGN=center>Sat</TD>
</TR>
<TR>

<TD ALIGN=center></TD>
<TD ALIGN=center></TD>
<TD ALIGN=center></TD>
<TD ALIGN=center></TD>
<TD ALIGN=center></TD>
<TD ALIGN=center></TD>
<TD ALIGN=center>1</TD>
</TR>
<TR>

<TD ALIGN=center>2</TD>
<TD ALIGN=center>3</TD>
<TD ALIGN=center>4</TD>
<TD ALIGN=center>5</TD>
<TD ALIGN=center>6</TD>
<TD ALIGN=center>7</TD>
<TD ALIGN=center>8</TD>
</TR>
<TR>

<TD ALIGN=center>9</TD>
<TD ALIGN=center>10</TD>
<TD ALIGN=center>11</TD>
<TD ALIGN=center>12</TD>
<TD ALIGN=center>13</TD>
<TD ALIGN=center>14</TD>
<TD ALIGN=center>15</TD>
</TR>
<TR>
```

```
<TD ALIGN=center>16</TD>
<TD ALIGN=center>17</TD>
<TD ALIGN=center>18</TD>
<TD ALIGN=center>19</TD>
<TD ALIGN=center>20</TD>
<TD ALIGN=center>21</TD>
<TD ALIGN=center>22</TD>
</TR>
<TR>

<TD ALIGN=center>23</TD>
<TD ALIGN=center>24</TD>
<TD ALIGN=center>25</TD>
<TD ALIGN=center>26</TD>
<TD ALIGN=center>27</TD>
<TD ALIGN=center>28</TD>
<TD ALIGN=center>29</TD>
</TR>
<TR>

<TD ALIGN=center>30</TD>
<TD ALIGN=center>31</TD>
<TD ALIGN=center></TD>
<TD ALIGN=center></TD>
<TD ALIGN=center></TD>
<TD ALIGN=center></TD>
<TD ALIGN=center></TD>
</TR>

</TABLE>
```

You can simply copy out this code, write it to your page, and get the calendar shown in Figure 5.11. Again, this is a lot easier if you understand tables. Entering a COLSPAN command that tells the top to span across all seven columns created the two headers.

Simply entering a number for the day created each cell. The trick is making sure each day gets the correct numbers. Notice that each little grouping is seven items that represent each day of the week.

You can activate each cell simply by putting an HREF command and activating the number to be clicked:

```
<TD ALIGN=center><A HREF="http://www.page.com">22</A>
```

Offering a <TD> command, but giving no data creates the raised look, where no days listed. You must offer the <TD> to keep the format square, just don't offer any information.

FAQs from the HTML Goodies Web Site

Q. You tell me how to make it so that no cells appear in a calendar. I would like cells like that on a regular calendar, but I want the cells to be empty. I have tried putting a ton of spaces after the <TD> because it has to be blank, but no luck. How do you do it?

A. You're on the right track. You do need a space, but the space needs to be a space other than one created by hitting the spacebar. Use the   command discussed in Chapter 1, "Playing with Text." Place the command right after the <TD> (without using the quotation marks), and you get your cell walls.

 Check out a full-year calendar online at http://www.htmlgoodies.com/book/fullyear. html. *I did it by creating 12 tables inside a larger table, but I made the outer table's border equal to 0, so it is only acting as a layout template. Think about how you would write the code for a full year before looking.*

Adding Color to Your Tables

I receive letters all the time asking me how to put different colors in table cells. I should point out that this section does not get into the creation of the table itself, only changing the background and text color.

 This stunning color table tutorial can be found online at http://www.htmlgoodies. com/tutors/colortbl.html.

Changing Cell Colors

Figure 5.12 shows a table with different colored cells.

The following is the HTML code that created the multicolored table in Figure 5.12:

```
<TABLE BORDER="4" CELLSPACING="4" CELLPADDING="4">
</TR>
<TD BGCOLOR="#ffff00">Yellow Stars</TD>
<TD BGCOLOR="#00ff00">Green Clovers</TD>
</TR>
<TR>
<TD BGCOLOR="#ff00ff">Purple...moons, I guess.</TD>
<TD BGCOLOR="#00ffff">Blue something or other... </TD>
</TR>
</TABLE>
```

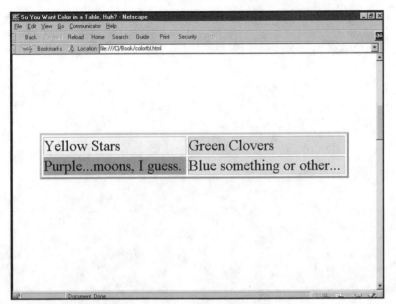

Figure 5.12
A table with multicolored cells.

Notice it's just a basic table with a BGCOLOR= command stuck in now and again for good measure. Insert either the hex code or the word code for the color you like and you're off and running. A long list of color words and hex codes are in Appendix B, "Useful Charts."

FAQs from the HTML Goodies Web Site

Q. Does it matter if I use hex codes or word codes for my tables' colors?

A. Nope. In fact, you can use them both, although I suggest that you use very basic colors that doesn't dither (see the non-dithering color chart in Appendix B). If your table, full of intricate color, shows up on a computer that can't handle it, it looks like a mess.

Changing Text Colors

You can also change the color of text in your tables. It's really easy—you just have to make sure you don't make some combination of text and cell colors that makes everything too hard to read. Figure 5.13 shows some interesting color combinations.

The HTML code for one of the cells in Figure 5.13's table follows. You can see how the cell and text color commands are combined:

```
<TD BGCOLOR="#ffff00"><FONT COLOR="#800517">Something Old</FONT> </TD>
```

Figure 5.13
A table with multicolored text and cells.

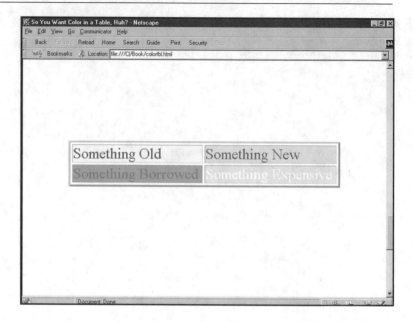

Notice that it's the same commands for the table. I just used the font color commands to change the text color. Put it all together and you can create some pretty awful-looking tables (and some gorgeous ones).

FAQs from the HTML Goodies Web Site

Q. Color is nice, but can I get an image as a background in a table cell?

A. Sure, but only in later browsers, versions 3 and 4. You would handle it the same way you handle a background image in the <BODY> flag. You add BACKGROUND="*image.jpg*" inside the <TD> and exchange *image.jpg* with the name of your image. It's a neat effect, but keep load time in mind. The more images you include, the slower your page loads.

I've created the Purina checkerboard pattern (nine red and white alternating cells) online at http://www.htmlgoodies.com/book/checkerboard.html. *Think about how you would do it, and then go see it.*

Changing Table Border Colors

Whoever decided that tables should have color capabilities shall be brought before me for a good lashing! As soon as people learn that they can put color in table cells, the next volley of questions includes how to put color into the table borders. Many people out there are creating color test patterns to make sure their new Trinitron monitor can actually handle 16 million colors. Wow!

But I digress. Let's try out a few different angles, for those using the newfangled browsers and those who still dig the earlier versions. I still surf with browser versions 1.1 every so often. I figure it's a good page if I can still see all the important parts using the earlier browsers.

But I digress again...

 Point your browser to `http://www.htmlgoodies.com/tutors/bordercl.html` *to see this tutorial in action.*

Take a look at Figure 5.14. (See the text in the second table? Can you tell me what song that's from?)

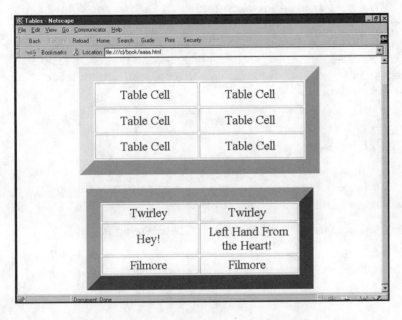

Figure 5.14
A table with multicolored borders.

You are using a higher-level browser if you go to the Web site (or type the following HTML code) and the two tables in Figure 5.14 are green and then purple. You can run some table border commands. If both of them are purple, stay with me and I explain that stuff later. First, the HTML commands:

```
<TABLE BORDER="30" CELLPADDING="10"
CELLSPACING="3" BORDERCOLOR="#00FF00">
```

185

I am only showing the main TABLE command because nothing is new with the rest of the table.

As you can see, I made a point of making the borders quite large (30 in fact). That's to see the colors more than anything. The border around the table is green because I entered this in the <TABLE> flag:

```
BORDERCOLOR="#00FF00"
```

Those of you who still use hex codes know that little ditty, 00FF00, as green. Those of you who are now using word color commands should type "green". You get the same effect.

FAQs from the HTML Goodies Web Site

Q. How can I make the borders around just one table cell a different color?

A. You are on a quest to make the ugliest table ever, huh? You can do it, but it only works on Explorer browsers. Use the command BORDERCOLOR= to get the effect. The command BORDERCOLOR="#00FF00" gives you a green border around the cell. In fact, Explorer offers a bunch of other commands to play with that Navigator doesn't. See Chapter 13, "Explorer-Specific Tutorials and DHTML," for the entire list.

Some Extra Play with Colors

Now I know what you're thinking: How do I get images into my table borders? Sorry, but you can't. But why, Joe, why?! Table borders don't accept images or patterns right now. That may all change soon, but at the moment it doesn't work.

(Oh, and by the way: The lyrics came from "Billy the Mountain" by Frank Zappa.)

I have a table online that uses absolutely every color command available to tables. It looks like a box of Crayolas exploded, so go take a look at http://www.htmlgoodies.com/book/uglytable.html.

Chapter 6

Frames

Frames were a massive hit when they first came out and they are in widespread use today. I'll tell you every trick to using them, but keep in mind that using frames means loading multiple pages into the same browser window. That can take a while and can bore your readers. Consider whether you really need them before using them. If you do decide to use them, make the pages mostly text and go easy on the big images. Be good to your readers and they'll be good to you. At least they won't send you nasty e-mail.

 This tutorial can be found online at http://www.htmlgoodies.com/tutors/frame1.html.

Advice on Using (or Not Using) Frames

Frames are a little different from anything you've done in HTML. Frame commands enable you to display more than one page at the same time in the same browser screen. What goes in the frame cells? I'm glad you asked. Other pages go in the frame cells. Those pages can contain anything a normal page does: text, graphics, images, and so on.

I went on a short surfing trip with my Internet Explorer browser to find a few good examples of sites using frames. I thought these were particularly nice. The page layout was attractive and it was pretty easy to navigate through the site.

Figure 6.1 shows the main page from Film.com (http://www.film.com/), a site all about current movies and the movie business.

Figure 6.1
Film.com makes good use of frames by putting a menu of links at the bottom of the middle frame.

Notice the links are along the bottom. They stay on the page, while the larger frame window at the top changes when you click. Figure 6.2 shows another good example of frames being used by the Internet Yellow Pages (`http://www.the-yellowpages.com/index.html`). This is the same basic idea in a slightly different layout.

Figure 6.2
Good use of frames on the Internet Yellow Pages.

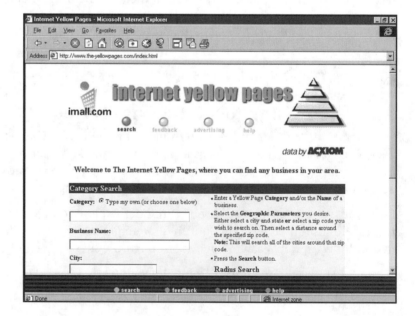

Finally, just to prove that not everyone loves using frames on their home page, the following is the Campaign Against Frames home page (see Figure 6.3). The page is called "So you like frames?" (`http://hem.passagen.se/ceel/frames/frames.htm`). The page is an example of using too many frames.

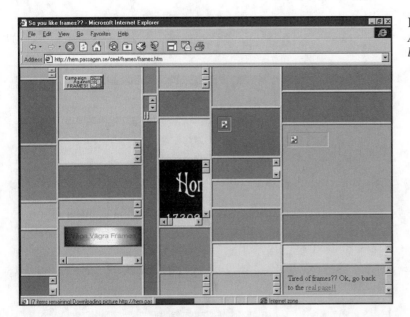

Figure 6.3
A reminder that it is possible to overuse frames.

Now let's get into how you make your own frames. Hopefully you do better than the layout in Figure 6.3.

Simple Frames

Figure 6.4 shows a rather involved frame page. The browser screen has been broken up into six different frames. Remember that each frame window is displaying a full HTML document, so this frame setup needs to load seven pages to work properly—the six pages that show up in the frame windows plus the page that has the frame commands.

In case you're wondering, this is the code that created those six frames:

```
<FRAMESET ROWS="20%,45%,35%">
  <FRAMESET COLS="100%">
    <FRAME  SCROLLING="no" SRC="page01.html">
  <FRAMESET COLS="50%,25%,25%">
    <FRAME SCROLLING="no" SRC="page02.html">
```

```
    <FRAME SRC="page03.html">
    <FRAME SRC="page04.html">
  </FRAMESET>
  <FRAMESET COLS="30%,70%">
    <FRAME NORESIZE="YES" SRC="page05.html">
    <FRAME SRC="page06.html">
  </FRAMESET>
</FRAMESET>
```

Figure 6.4
A Web page with six frames.

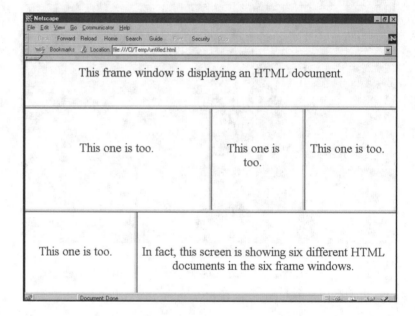

Don't be put off by it just yet. By the end of this tutorial you'll understand everything you see and be able to create frames with the best of them.

FAQs from the HTML Goodies Web Site

Q. Where do I put the text that appears in the two frame windows? After the `<BODY>` command?

A. Nowhere, actually. This is the question I get most often from people starting to work with frames. The text that appears in the frame window is actually a full HTML document in itself. Look again at the code in the first frame tutorial. See how the FRAME SRC command is calling for a whole other page? You need to create full documents to fit into those frame windows.

Q. Do I really need a `<BODY>` flag on the HTML page that holds the frame template?

A. No. My frame template pages contain only a `TITLE` and the frame commands. In fact, that's the way most browsers like it these days.

Q. Do I have to put a title on the pages that go into the frame windows? It doesn't appear anywhere.

A. Technically no, but I suggest you do it anyway. Many people want to break the pages out of their frame window and see them full-screen. In that case it is nice to have a title.

Creating Frame Columns

Figure 6.5 shows a very simplified version of a Web page with two frames. The frames break up the browser screen into two sections: `Page_A.htm` and `Page_B.htm`.

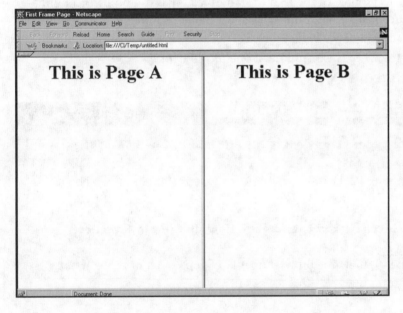

Figure 6.5
A Web page with two frames in columns.

The frame commands that create the Web page in Figure 6.5 look like this:

```
<HTML>
<TITLE>First Frame Page</TITLE>
<FRAMESET COLS="50%,50%">
```

```
<FRAME SRC="PAGE_A.htm">
<FRAME SRC="PAGE_B.htm">
</FRAMESET>
</HTML>
```

Neat, huh? I wanted to display two pages at the same time, so I simply split the screen into two parts and placed a different page in each part. Please note that a hypertext link on each page sends you back to the tutorial. Look again at the small HTML frames in the previous code. This is what the commands are doing:

- <FRAMESET> Starts any frame page. It alerts the browser that frames are going to be used.

- COLS Denotes that I want columns. In this case I want two, each 50% of the screen. You can do other percentages; go nuts if you want. Make sure you separate the percentages by commas and get it to add up to 99% or 100%. 99%?! Yes. You see, 33%, 33%, and 33% add up to 99% and split the screen three ways. The browser just distributes the final 1% over the three spaces.

- FRAME SRC Denotes the source of the frame. Frames read like you do, left to right. The first offered source is hard left. I only have two frame sections, so I need only two sources.

- </FRAMESET> Ends the whole deal. You need one of these for every <FRAMESET> you use.

FAQs from the HTML Goodies Web Site

Q. Do I have to write pages skinny enough to fit in only one half of the page frame?

A. Nope. The browser crams it all in there, but it tends to look smooshy. (How about that word?)

Q. What if my page is taller than the screen? How do I put in a vertical scrollbar?

A. Don't concern yourself with it. The browser does it for you. Write for content, not frames.

Adding Frame Rows to the Mix

Do you want two frames in rows (left to right) instead of columns? Simply use the command ROWS rather than COLS. In fact, if you take the previous example and replace the command COLS with ROWS, you get something that looks like Figure 6.6. The frame you define first goes on the top (PAGE_A.htm in this case).

```
<HTML>
<TITLE>First Frame Page</TITLE>
<FRAMESET ROWS="50%,50%">
<FRAME SRC="PAGE_A.htm">
<FRAME SRC="PAGE_B.htm">
</FRAMESET>
</HTML>
```

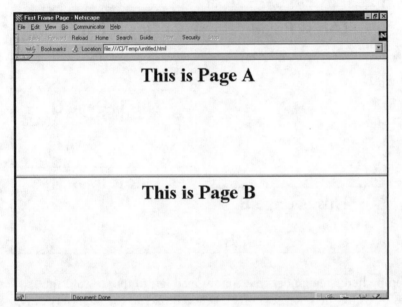

Figure 6.6
A Web page with two frames in rows.

Combining Frame Columns and Rows

Now it starts to get a little goofy. You can make really complex and creative Web pages by combining frame rows and columns. Just remember what I've already said: The more frames you have, the longer it takes to load your Web pages. Figure 6.7 shows a Web page with a combination of frame columns and rows.

The following are the frame commands I used to create the rows and tables shown in Figure 6.7:

```
<FRAMESET COLS="50%,50%">
  <FRAMESET ROWS="75%,25%">
    <FRAME SRC="PAGE_A.htm">
    <FRAME SRC="PAGE_B.htm">
```

```
  </FRAMESET>
  <FRAMESET ROWS="33%,33%,33%">
    <FRAME SRC="PAGE_C.htm">
    <FRAME SRC="PAGE_D.htm">
    <FRAME SRC="PAGE_E.htm">
  </FRAMESET>
</FRAMESET>
```

Figure 6.7

A combination of frame columns and rows.

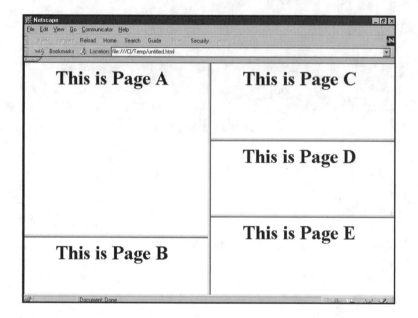

Let's look at what's happening here. Remember that frames read left to right. I told the computer I wanted frames by using the <FRAMESET> flag. I then broke up the page vertically, just as before.

This is where the rows come in. I added a new <FRAMESET> flag denoting ROWS. I asked for 75% and 25%. That breaks up the first column into two rows. I then offered two sources for the first column's two sections. The first frame that's offered a source is always the top one. I then put in a </FRAMESET> to denote I was done with breaking up the first column. Still with me? Good...let's go on.

Note that I did another <FRAMESET> flag denoting ROWS, but this time I set the rows at 33%, 33%, and 33%. I then denoted SOURCES for those three rows in column two. I then added a </FRAMESET> to end those rows and another </FRAMESET> still to end the whole deal. Please note that I am going to show five different pages on the same browser screen. Still with me? Good.

FAQs from the HTML Goodies Web Site

Q. I get nothing! My frame pages are blank and I'm ready to throw this computer down the stairs.

A. Make sure everyone's out of the house before you go crazy. If the page comes up blank, it is probably one of two things: You either have a piece of code other than the `<TITLE>` commands before the `<FRAMESET>` command, or you are missing a `</FRAMESET>` command or two. You need one for every `<FRAMESET>` you open. You could also have misspelled something, but at this point I would assume you have checked that fully.

Q. The exact frame code works perfectly in Internet Explorer, but loads a blank page in Navigator. Am I going nuts?

A. Yes, you are going nuts. Actually, you're getting caught in another of those wonderful differences between browsers. You find that Navigator is far less forgiving than Internet Explorer. You have missed a `</FRAMESET>` command. Explorer didn't mind; Netscape decided to punish you.

Why Use Frames?

Good question, because frames have a few downfalls. First, they take longer to load than single pages, and second they're a little hard to write. On the up side, they are fantastic for presenting information.

I'm not saying you need to use frames on every page, but if some of your pages are to show comparisons between items, frames are the way to go. They break the page up in attractive geometric patterns and offer nice page layouts. In addition, a frame page allows for some fun interaction between your viewer and your page. Imagine a list of links in a left frame that functions as a menu. Each time a user clicks an item in the left frame, what he or she requested comes up in the right frame. That's a good layout with good-looking interaction.

The next few sections show how to get that interaction on your page.

Dynamics of Frames, NAMEs, and TARGETs

The question now is how to control page changes in your frames. The following are the three basic methods of changing data within frames:

- Click a link in a frame—Just that frame changes pages.
- Click a link in a frame—Another frame on the screen receives the information.
- Click a link in a frame—The frames go away and you get a full page.

Click a Link in a Frame—Just That Frame Changes Pages

This is the default. It happens without you doing a darn thing. If that's all you want, do nothing more than what you already know. Browsers are programmed to handle frame clicks just that way. The other two methods require a little more work.

Click a Link in a Frame—Another Frame on the Screen Receives the Information

Now let's get into that useful effect I've already talked about: Your user clicks an item in a menu frame and the page she requested shows up in another frame. Not only does it look good, the effect is quite functional. The links are always visible and you're only loading one new page rather than several through a whole new frames page.

Setting this up is basically a two-step process. First you have to create and name each frame. Then you create the HTML pages that appear in the frames. The links between the frames that cause the menu effect are on those HTML pages.

See Figure 6.8. In this example, you place a link in the page in frame A. When you click that link it loads a new page into frame C. Now it's time to talk about two new commands: NAME and TARGET.

Figure 6.8

A three-frame page before clicking the link in frame A.

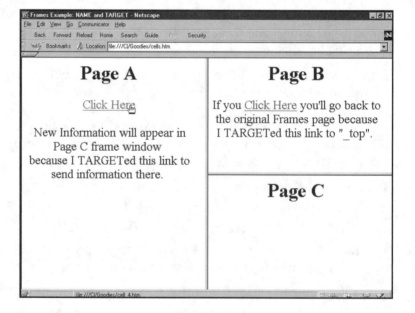

The following is the code that builds those three frames:

```
<FRAMESET COLS="50%, 50%">
  <FRAME NAME="A" SRC="PAGE_A.htm">
  <FRAMESET ROWS="50%, 50%">
    <FRAME NAME="B" SRC="PAGE_B.htm">
    <FRAME NAME="C" SRC="PAGE_C.htm">
  </FRAMESET>
</FRAMESET>
```

The frames must have names to send data from one frame to another. "Ah, ha!" you say, "That's the NAME deal." Bingo. Name them whatever you want, but I suggest you keep it simple with capital letters. (I named mine A, B, and C.)

The second step is inserting the link in frame A's HTML page that causes frame C to change. Here's the link code that must be inserted in cell_1.htm:

```
<A HREF="PAGE_D.htm" TARGET="C">Click Here</A>
```

See how the code is a normal hypertext link except the command TARGET is added to direct the output of the link? When you click this link on the page in frame A, it tells frame C to load PAGE_D.htm (see Figure 6.9).

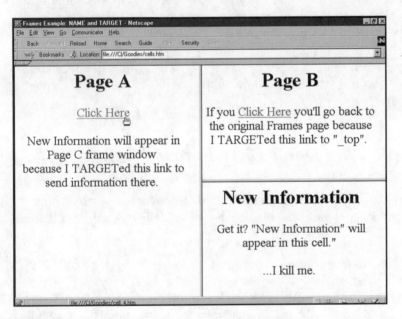

Figure 6.9
Clicking the page in frame A changes the page in frame C.

 If you'd like to try out target hypertext links and such firsthand, I've put together an extra tutorial for you at http://www.htmlgoodies.com/book/frames.html.

Completely Leaving a Frames Page

Now you can send information from one frame to another. One limitation to this approach is that you're ending up in a frame page—and some of the larger pages are squished inside a frame. Let's say you want to click a link in a frame and have it go to a page that pops up in a full browser window. You have to tell it to do that. Remember: The default has the information stay in the same frame.

You need to TARGET the hypertext link to be its own page. Just follow the format discussed in the previous section, but make the TARGET "_Top". Note the underscore before the word Top. The code looks like this:

```
<A HREF="http://www.cbs.com" TARGET="_Top">
```

FAQs from the HTML Goodies Web Site

Q. I can't get that "_Top" target to work.

A. Netscape Navigator version 4 (or later) is the picky one. Is that the browser you're using? Even though HTML is not case-sensitive, capitalizing the T in Top fixes the problem.

Q. I want people to be able to bookmark my page, but it has frames. How can I set it up so that even if the person goes three or four pages deep in the frames, it always goes to those pages?

A. You really can't because the page that is being bookmarked is the frame template page and it only calls for the pages that are on its code—the first two pages. It can be done, but you need to set it up so that a new frame template loads each time. It's not so bad, I've done it before.

What About People Who Don't Have Frame-Ready Browsers?

That's a problem. The browserly challenged get an error code if they attempt to log onto a page with frames; either that or they receive a blank page. A couple of ways around it are:

- Don't do frames. (You could have guessed that one, I know.)
- Use <NOFRAMES> and </NOFRAMES> commands.

Tell me more about the <NOFRAMES> flag, you say? Well, it's simple. You write a basic frame page like any of the three listed previously, but immediately following the first <FRAMESET> flag you put in a <NOFRAMES> command and write a message to the browserly challenged.

Like so:

```
<FRAMESET COLS="50%,50%">
<NOFRAMES>

Greetings Browserly Challenged. The page you are attempting to enter has frames,
and if you're reading this message--you don't have the ability to see it.
 I suggest you go <A HREF="page.html">To my non-Frame version</A> of this page.
</NOFRAMES>

<FRAME SRC="PAGE_A.htm">
<FRAME SRC="PAGE_B.htm">
</FRAMESET>
</HTML>
```

The person who can't see frames gets the message and the person who can read frames gets the frame page. I should say here that you might also want to put an entire page's text between the <NOFRAME> flags. That way the page displays and the user doesn't have to click to go to a page he can read. I do it as it's shown earlier because I also like to offer links to browser home pages, so people can download a frame-ready browser and get in on all the fun. Isn't technology wonderful?

You can use other commands when creating frames that create different margin sizes and such. I cover this in the next section, "Advanced Frame Commands." It contains a few more tricks and bits of knowledge. Plus it's sugar free and low in fat.

Advanced Frame Commands

So far I've only touched the surface of what you can accomplish with frames. This section tells you about some more sophisticated uses and shows you how to hide frames to make your Web page more visually appealing.

 For interactive examples of how frames work, check out http://www.htmlgoodies.com/ad_ frame.html. *I have the tutorial set up so that one page fills all the cells (see Figure 6.10). I explain it all here in this book, along with a bunch of advanced commands. Seeing it in action might be easier for you than reading it here.*

Let's get started. To demonstrate these commands, I wrote a very simple frames code that simply splits the browser screen in half. Figure 6.11 displays the results of the code.

```
<FRAMESET COLS="50%,50%">
<FRAME SRC="PAGE_ONE.html">
<FRAME SRC="PAGE_TWO.html">
</FRAMESET>
```

Figure 6.10
An interactive frames tutorial for this book.

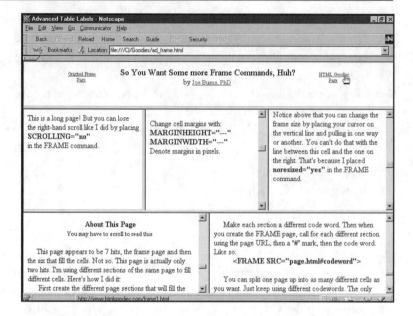

Figure 6.11
A simple page with two frames.

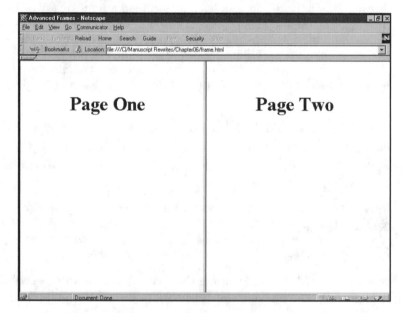

Resizing Frame Window Borders: BORDER="###"

Now play with the frame window border itself. The frame window border in Figure 6.11 is the gray stripe down the center that splits the page. you use the BORDER="###" command, which goes inside the <FRAMESET> command:

```
<FRAMESET COLS="50%,50%" BORDER="50">
```

It affects each of the borders denoted by that particular <FRAMESET> command. If you have more than one <FRAMESET>, you can set the borders to different sizes. The preceding code sets the border to 50—that's huge (see Figure 6.12).

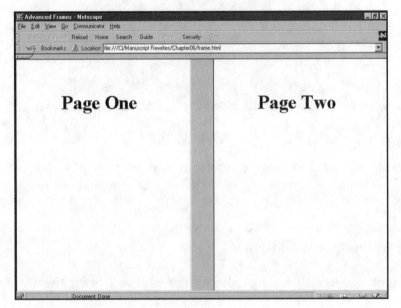

Figure 6.12
A frame border set to 50.

Changing the Space Between Frames

This command allows you to set a specific number of pixels between the frame windows. I find it acts a lot like the border command. Again, you can use it every time you use a new <FRAMESET> command.

```
FRAMESPACING="###"
```

Figure 6.13 has the FRAMESPACING set to 700 pixels. Why? Because I can, that's why! This is the code I used to get it:

```
<FRAMESET COLS="50%,50%" FRAMESPACING="700">
```

Figure 6.13
Using FRAMESPACING *to add space between frames.*

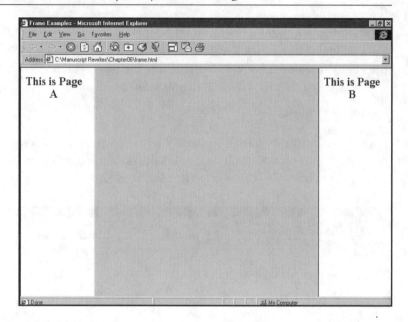

Changing Frame Window Margins

You can also change how much space surrounds the text on the top and bottom of your frames. It's a good way to add whitespace to the frames so that the text doesn't butt against the border. The following are the commands you use:

- ● MARGINHEIGHT="###"   Sets the space above and below the text.
- ● MARGINWIDTH="###"   Sets the space on either side.

Both commands go inside the <FRAMESET> flag. The following is a <FRAMESET> using the two commands:

```
<FRAMESET COLS="50%,50%" MARGINHEIGHT="200" MARGINWIDTH="200">
```

That sets some pretty wide margins around the text. Remember that the numbers are in pixels. Again, you can set new margins each time you use a new <FRAMESET> flag.

Keeping Your Frame Window Borders in Place

Anyone visiting your Web site can put her mouse cursor on one of your frame borders and adjust its size by dragging the frame one way or another (see Figure 6.14).

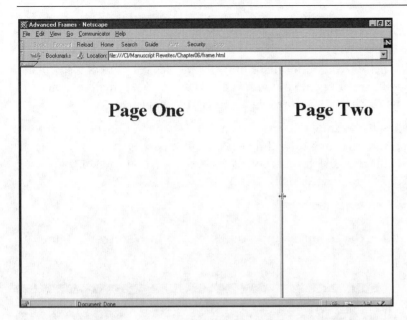

Figure 6.14
*Changing frame sizes by
dragging them.*

You can stop people from changing your frame sizes by placing a RESIZE="no" command in
your FRAME flag. The <FRAMESET> looks like this:

```
<FRAMESET COLS="50%,50%" RESIZE="no">
```

This prevents the user from pulling your frame window borders. You can use this command every time you use a new <FRAMESET> command. You can also use this command
inside the <FRAME SRC> command to keep certain frame window borders from being altered.

To Offer or Not to Offer...A Scrollbar

You probably already know that you get a scrollbar when your page is longer than the
browser screen is tall. It just happens without your asking for it. Browsers are nice that way.

Now you want to be in control. The layout of frames can be greatly disturbed if you have a
scrollbar popping up in every other frame window. The following is the command that
gives us the power:

```
SCROLLING="###"
```

This command can either be placed in the <FRAMESET> command where it affects everything under that command's umbrella, or in individual <FRAME SRC> commands where it
affects just that frame window.

The three settings for this command are : `"yes"`, `"no"`, and `"auto"`. You can guess what each one does.

`"yes"` provides a scrollbar whether you need one or not; `"no"` denies your use of a scrollbar whether you need one or not; `"auto"` gives you one when you need it. I actually see no need for the `"auto"` command. That's the same effect you get by using `"no"`.

I've slightly changed the familiar example I've been using in this chapter to show how this one works. I have made page A very long by adding `Blah...`. The page is longer than the screen, but as you can see in Figure 6.15 it does not have a scrollbar. I set the left frame window to `SCROLLING="no"`. The command looks like this:

```
<FRAME SRC="PAGE_A.html" SCROLLING="no">
```

Again, please note that I placed the command in `<FRAME SRC>`, not in `<FRAMESET>`. Figure 6.15 shows the result.

Figure 6.15
A page without scrollbars.

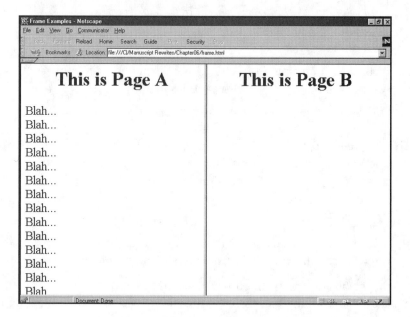

I often set my frames to disallow all scrollbars because I think a scrollbar popping up in the middle of a frames page looks bad. If you set the scroll to `"no"`, you have to be very careful. Avoid creating pages that scroll farther than the size of the screen, and remember that many people have smaller screens than you do.

A Tip for Filling Multiple Frame Windows with One Page

Take a look at Figure 6.16. It appears to be seven different pages—the page that contains the frame code, and then the six individual frames. Not so. It is actually only two pages. I'm using different sections of the same page to fill in the different frames.

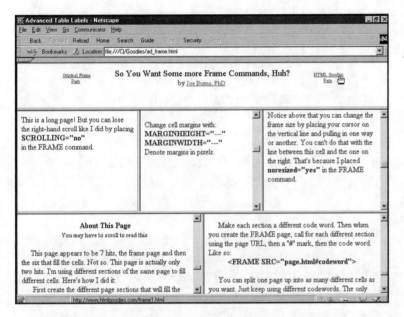

Figure 6.16
Only two different HTML pages are in this picture.

To do this, create the one single HTML page that contains all the text and graphics that you want inserted in the frames. Divide that page into the sections that you want displayed in the frames by marking each new section with this:

```
<A NAME="codeword">
```

Make each section a different *code word*. When you create the frame page, call for each different section using the page's URL, a pound sign (#), and then the code word. Like so:

```
<FRAME SRC="page.html#codeword">
```

You can split one page into as many different cells as you want; just keep using different code words. The only downfalls I've found are that you always get a scrollbar, and sometimes deleting the scrollbar eliminates the text. Try it for yourself and see what happens.

I put about 10 of these between each page section:

```
<P>
 
<P>
```

205

That little combination puts spaces between sections so that words don't bleed over from cell to cell.

FAQs from the HTML Goodies Web Site

Q. **I tried your trick of using one page to fill all the frame windows, but now none of the hypertext links work. They keep loading in other frames and look terrible.**

A. Remember that it's one page doing all the work, so you really can't change one frame window without changing all the others. My trick is best for displaying a lot of information in frames very quickly without loading seven different pages. I said it was cool, not the end all.

You can find an example of a frame page using all these commands here. Try it out at `http://www.htmlgoodies.com/book/advframes.html`.

Seamless Frames

People have been writing and asking me how this is done for a while now. These seamless frames give a great look to the page. In addition, they also make a great sideline background, left or right. I give examples of each use, but first let's look into how it's done. Figure 6.17 shows you what I'm talking about.

This tutorial is online at `http://www.htmlgoodies.com/tutors/seamless_frames.html`.

This is a nice clean look, with links on one side and the full screen on the other. The links in the left frame control the main window. This is a solid presentation.

You achieve it through frame commands, as you most likely gleaned from the title of the tutorial. You should make a point to first read and understand this chapter's first frame tutorial. I am not going into more than creating this effect. I am assuming you have some frame knowledge going in.

The only difference between this frame tutorial and the other is that with this one you add a few commands to hide the frame borders.

The Main Frame Command

I cover the remainder of the frame code in a moment. Right now I want to focus on the main <FRAMESET> flag. It looks like this:

```
<FRAMESET COLS="15%,*" FRAMEBORDER="0" FRAMESPACING="0" BORDER="0">
```

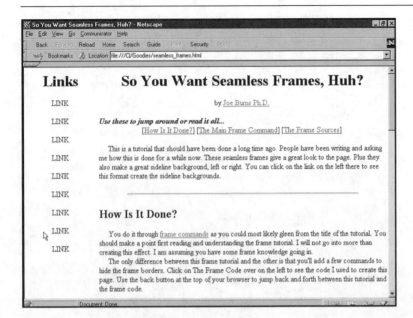

Figure 6.17
Two seamless frames.

Notice I have done little more than add three commands—FRAMEBORDER, FRAMESPACING, and BORDER—and set them all to 0. It goes the other way, too. You can set the command to 50 to get really wide borders. You want seamless frames here, however.

Two pages are being displayed in the preceding example. The seamless effect is achieved because I have set the background color of the two source pages to white [#FFFFFF]. If I set the colors otherwise, the effect would be more of a sideline background; the seam would then be visible. The following is the exact same frame code as was just used. The only change I made was setting the background color of the page that loads in the left frame to blue (see Figure 6.18).

The following is the main FRAMESET command from before:

```
<FRAMESET COLS="15%,*" FRAMEBORDER="0" FRAMESPACING="0" BORDER="0">
```

See the COLS="15%,*" in there, right after FRAMESET? That asterisk is a nice way to speed up your math skills. Put the asterisk in the second position and it does the 100% math for you. You can also use it for a right frame just by flipping it around: COLS="*,15%".

I have seen a great use of this format at the Van Halen News Desk (http://www.vhnd.com), where the colors appear to go from light to dark into the frame (see Figure 6.19).

Figure 6.18
Two seamless frames showing pages with different background colors.

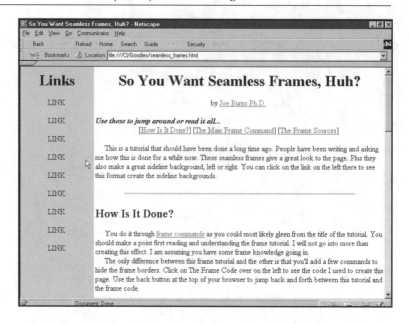

Figure 6.19
Great seamless frames with blended background colors.

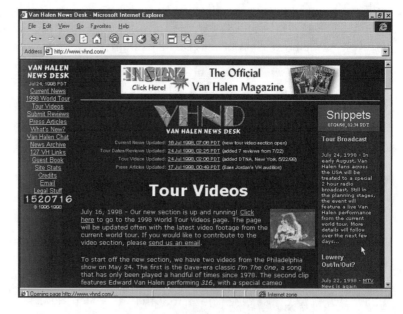

I liked the band better when David Lee Roth was the lead singer. Moving along…

The Frame Sources

These are the commands that fill the frame windows:

```
<FRAME NAME="left" SRC="left.html" MARGINWIDTH="3" MARGINHEIGHT="10"
SCROLLING="no">
<FRAME NAME="main" SRC="mainwindow.html" MARGINWIDTH="3" MARGINHEIGHT="10">
```

The frame sources are the same as you have used in the past. Each is given a target name so that the links in the left side target the information to the larger, right window. See the original frame tutorial at the beginning of this chapter for more on how to target frame HREF links. Just as a quick refresher, the format for targeting a link in this frame setup would be as follows:

```
<A HREF="newpage.html" TARGET="main">Click Here</A>
```

In the previous example, I set the MARGINHEIGHT and MARGINWIDTH to my liking. You can play with the sizes to get the text closer or further from the actual seam. Any text centering is done on the source page itself by surrounding text with <CENTER> </CENTER>.

Notice also that a SCROLLING="no" command was added to the left frame to eliminate the scrollbar, should a visitor have his screen settings lower than you had hoped. A scrollbar would kill the entire effect.

FAQs from the HTML Goodies Web Site

Q. You said to not have a scrollbar on the left frame window, but on some screens the links I have go off the bottom and people cannot get to them. What should I do?

A. I know you would like me to say to use the scrollbar, but I won't. That kills the effect and two scrollbars is not good page design. My suggestion is to lessen your links—either make them smaller or make fewer of them so that they do fit on the small-screen browsers.

As long as all your links are on your site you have control in terms of background color, text size, and image width, but if an outside page comes through one of your links and has a different background (or the like), the effect dies. I'd be rather picky about what links are used in this format. I would make the link to anything you don't have control over open a new browser window or target the output of the HREF link to "_top"; that way the page opens in a full browser screen with no frames.

That should do it. Adding more frames to the mix can compound the effect. You could create many seamless connections. The problem comes when you shift the pages or link to a new page—that pesky scrollbar shows up and it's all defeated. I would stick with the lowest number of frames you need in this format.

 Go to `http://www.htmlgoodies.com/book/seamless.html` *for a couple of examples of seamless frames in action.*

Changing Multiple Frame Cells

 You can see multiple frames in action by going to `http://www.htmlgoodies.com/tutors/` `2atonce.html`. *Go see it. Watching it happen is fun.*

What you're doing here is allowing your user to change the content in more than one frame window with one click. You already know how to use TARGET commands to get this effect in one frame window. Now set it up so that one click changes many windows. Figure 6.20 shows what you start with.

Figure 6.20

Before clicking the Change Three Frames at Once button.

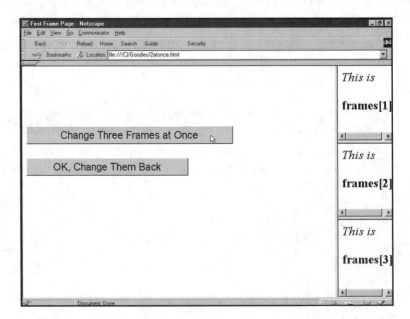

And now for my first trick: The pointer in Figure 6.21 is poised on the Change Three Frames At Once button (insert drum roll sound effect). When I click one I get the results shown in Figure 6.21.

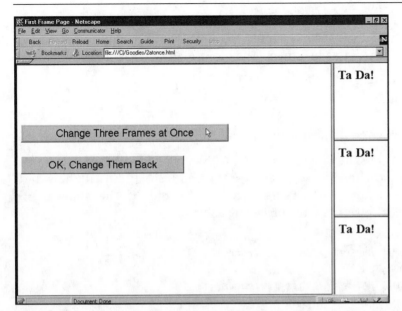

Figure 6.21
*The results after clicking
the Change Three Frames
at Once button.*

(Insert cymbal crash sound effect.) I click the OK, Change Them Back button and restore the original frames shown in Figure 6.20.

Good trick, huh? Unlike the true magicians, I reveal my tricks to you. I am using some simple JavaScript commands to change the three frames to the right. By the way, if JavaScript is new to you, keep reading. I'll get you through this tutorial, and then you can read more about JavaScript in Chapter 11, "Java Applets and JavaScript."

You need to start with the code I created to make the four little frame cells in Figure 6.21:

```
<FRAMESET cols="85%,15%">
    <FRAME SRC="zippy1.html" NAME="A">
    <FRAMESET rows="33%,33%,33%">
        <FRAME SRC="zippy2.html" NAME="B">
        <FRAME SRC="zippy3.html" NAME="C">
        <FRAME SRC="zippy4.html" NAME="D">
    </FRAMESET>
</FRAMESET>
```

Please note that the pages that appear in the three smaller windows are named zippy2, zippy3, and zippy4. But in Figure 6.20, I labeled them frames[1], frames[2], and frames[3]. I did that for a reason—keep reading.

Look at the code. See the four frame cells? I have given them the names "A" through "D", in case I want to target any of my HREF link outputs. What you may not already know is that the frames had names before I named them. The browser already has "ordered" them for you.

Frame Order

When displayed, frames are given number names in the order they appear in the code.

The numbers, however, do not start with 1. They start with 0. Look to the right side of Figure 6.20. See how they are named frames[1], frames[2], and frames[3]? That's how the browser sees them. Where's frames[0]? That's the large frame on the left. The following shows how the frames break down using the preceding code:

```
<FRAMESET cols="85%,15%">
<FRAME SRC="zippy1.html" NAME="A"> This is frames[0]
<FRAMESET rows="33%,33%,33%">
<FRAME SRC="zippy2.html" NAME="B"> This is frames[1]
<FRAME SRC="zippy3.html" NAME="C"> This is frames[2]
<FRAME SRC="zippy4.html" NAME="D"> This is frames[3]
</FRAMESET>
</FRAMESET>
```

See how the frame windows are numbered starting with 0? Please also note that the word used is *frames* with an *s*. That means more than one. Forgetting the s messes up the whole deal. Now that you know that, go on to use it to your advantage by changing multiple cells.

FAQs from the HTML Goodies Web Site

Q. Your tutorial on changing multiple frames at once is interesting, but why go to all that trouble when you can just load a new frame template page and get the same effect?

A. Mine's faster. It also requires only the new pages to load. Your method works just fine, but it takes longer and taxes the server more than it should. That said, yours makes it easier to bookmark specific pages in the frame windows.

The following is the command I used to change the three cells:

```
<FORM>
<INPUT TYPE="button" Value="Change Three Frames at Once"
onClick="parent.frames[1].location='zippy5.html';
```

```
parent.frames[2].location='zippy6.html';
parent.frames[3].location='zippy7.html';">
</FORM>
```

This is a breakdown of the code:

- `<FORM>` Tells the browser a form type is going here.
- `INPUT TYPE="button"` Does what its name implies.
- `VALUE=` Denotes what is written on the button itself.
- `onClick=` Denotes that what follows should happen when the button is clicked. Please keep the capitalization on the letter *C*.
- `parent.frames[1].location='zippy5.html';` The JavaScript command that does the trick for you.
- `"parent"` The main page, the frame page.
- `"frames[1]"` The frame that is affected.
- `"location='###'` Denotes what fills the frame when clicked. In this case it's pages called `zippy5`, `zippy6`, and `zippy7`.
- `(;)` semicolon Placed at the end of each frame command line. Without it, you get errors like crazy.
- `</FORM>` Ends the entire deal.

You can add as many or as few of the location commands as you want. If you have 20 frames, you can change them all with one click. Just make sure to add a new `parent.frames[#].location='###';` for each one. However, you only need one `onClick` command.

I caution you that the quotation marks surrounding the location page are single. Double quotation marks are surrounding the run of `parent.frames[#].location='###';` commands. Make sure you get the quote marks right, or you will have errors galore.

Well, there you go. As many frames as you can write—that's how many you can change with the click of a button. Good luck with this, but remember that when you are reloading multiple frames, you are loading multiple pages. The process may be very slow. If you use this function, do your best to offer low-byte pages for the shortest loading time.

 Go to `http://www.htmlgoodies.com/book/coupleframes.html` *to see another example and to also see how to lose the button and do it simply through a blue-letter hypertext link.*

Frames Border Color

Well, I guess the HTML Goodies Web readers really want to know how to do this. The number of letters lately has been huge; I guess colored frames are the "in" thing as of late.

Used correctly, adding color to frame window borders can look great. Better yet? They're super simple.

See the green frame in Figure 6.20? I made it by adding the command BORDERCOLOR="###" to the main <FRAMESET> command. I set the color to lime green. It looks awful, but makes the point.

You can get multiple colors across different frame windows, but you can only do it if you are using multiple <FRAMESET> commands. For instance, if you have your main <FRAMESET> breaking the page into two areas, you can change that border color by following the method outlined earlier.

You can use another color if you then add a second FRAMESET command to break one of the columns into smaller sections.

FAQs from the HTML Goodies Web Site

Q. Can I set only some frame window walls to color and leave the others without?

A. Yes—if you use multiple <FRAMESET> commands. That way you can set some of the frame borders to a specific color and the rest to "#c0c0c0", their default color. You are setting their color, but the computer thinks you've done nothing.

Frames Yes! Frames No!

Frames, frames, frames. You either love them or hate them. Either way, you have to deal with them. Maybe you won't write them to your pages, but others do.

One of the most popular formats of Web page design is that two-column, seamless-frame look. I have a tutorial on it in this chapter. Although I'm not a fan of frames myself, I do like this look when done correctly. You get a nice row of buttons down the left side that controls what comes up in the frame on the right. It looks good as long as the author only puts pages built for the format into that larger frame. But that doesn't always happen.

Often authors want people to be able to leave their site easily, so they "lock" in the user by making it so that all pages open in that right frame window unless the user makes a point of leaving the frame system altogether. You can imagine what that does to the look of some pages. They get scrunched into a smaller space than what they were built for and just look terrible.

On the other hand, I'm often asked how to keep pages in a frame format. Users are pretty knowledgeable now about looking at source code and isolating a page outside of the frame setting it was built for. That's just as bad as scrunching a page down to fit in a smaller space than it was built for.

Here I'm going to give you the code for preventing your pages to appear in frame windows and preventing your pages to appear without being set into a frame window.

First, getting out...

No Frames!

This one's pretty simple. One line of JavaScript in the BODY flag does the trick. Here's the format:

```
onLoad="if(parent.frames.length!=0)top.location='pagename.html';"
```

This is what's happening:

This is a conditional statement (note the "if") that checks for a frame format.

The line `parent.frames.length!=0` checks to see if frames are there.

- `parent` The top level window, the one you're looking at.
- `frames` Denotes that frames are involved.
- `length` A count of the number of frames.
- `!=0` JavaScript for "not equal to zero".
- `top.location` Sets up a hypertext link to refill the top location, the browser screen you're looking at.
- `pagename.html` The name of the page this JavaScript is sitting on. Thus, the line of code reloads itself into the top level window.

Put that code into your HTML document's <BODY> flag, and as long as the browser understands JavaScript 1.0, which almost all browsers do, the page is not letting itself to sit within a frame format.

Yes Frames!

So you've got a page that you want to be sitting in frames. Maybe some code doesn't work without a frame to target, or you just simply like the look. The following is the code you need to stop people from taking your page out of a frames format:

```
<SCRIPT LANGUAGE="javascript">

if (self==parent)
{
```

```
document.write('<b>THIS IS A FRAME ELEMENT</B>')
document.write('You will be transported to frames in a second')
document.write('<META HTTP-EQUIV="refresh" CONTENT="1; URL=framepage.html">')
}
</SCRIPT>
```

This code sits after the <BODY> flag before any other text.

The code is, again, a conditional statement. The first line asks if the page, self, is equal to, ==, the top level page, parent.

If it isn't, meaning it is opening in a frame window, nothing happens and the page loads as it normally would. But if it is the top level window, three lines of code are written to the page using document.write() statements.

The first line simply alerts the user that the page is a frame element. The second tells the user he is being taken to a frame page in a second. The third line is a basic META REFRESH that loads the frame window.

I have this written in a very basic format. The following are a couple of ways to jazz up the text any way you want:

- Set the META REFRESH to 0 rather than 1, the change is almost instantaneous and the user might never see the text.
- Put a link to the frame page in one of the lines of text in case the user's browser doesn't understand the META command.

Yes, I could have gotten this effect by using the same JavaScript linking method as was used in the previous "No Frames!" example, but I thought this was a little more efficient.

Examples

Okay! I have a two-window frame page set up. The page that appears in the top frame offers a link to a page that does not enable itself to appear in a frame setting.

The page that appears in the bottom frame window has a link to a page that does not enable itself to appear outside of a frame setting.

No tricks. Feel free to look at the code—no targets. You just see the JavaScript that I showed you here.

Tip

You may want to do the one on the bottom first. When a page opens in a window by itself using this code, your BACK button doesn't work real well. The page just keeps opening itself up. You need to right click the BACK button to get your history list, and then choose the tutorial. It'll be clearly marked.

 Would you like to see these at work? Go to the online example at `http://www. htmlgoodies.com/book/no_go_frame_page.html`*. I have them both working out of the same example.*

Okay, you decide. Do you stay in a frames setting or do you get out? It's your choice. Now no one can force you.

Chapter 7

Link Buttons
and Forms

You know that the World Wide Web is held together through a series of hypertext links, or, as a student of mine called it, "A web of blue words." Actually, that's not a bad way of putting it.

Now it's possible for you to use hex codes to change the color of the links and visited links (see Chapter 1, "Playing with Text," for more on that). You can also make an image active by placing it in the hypertext anchor command (see Chapter 3, "Adding Images and Backgrounds"). You can also make an imagemap (see Chapter 4, "Imagemaps").

Click Here *This tutorial is online at* http//www.htmlgoodies.com/tutors/formbutt.html.

In this chapter I show you an easy way to make your own link button, with your own wording—a nice, classy departure from all the blue words.

Figure 7.1 shows a typical link button.

If you click that thing it jumps you to a new page. Plus, the button moves when you click it. Movement! Cool!

I really think these buttons look professional and they're not all that tough to make. Contrary to what some of you who are new to HTML might think, the button shown in the figure is not an image (such as a .gif or a .jpeg). It is made through FORM commands.

Figure 7.1
A clickable button.

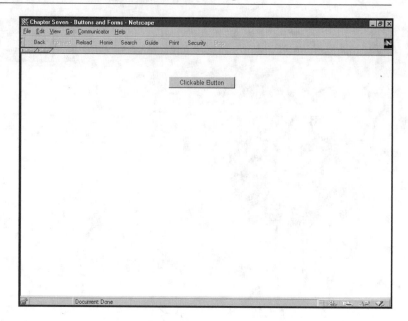

How to Make a Link Button

The following are the commands I used to place the button in Figure 7.1:

```
<FORM METHOD="link" ACTION="http://www.htmlgoodies.com/page1.htm">
<INPUT TYPE="submit" VALUE="Clickable Button">
</FORM>
```

The first command, FORM, has three parts. The following is what each means:

- FORM   Tells the computer a form item is going here.
- METHOD   Tells the computer how to handle the FORM command. In this case, you are making a link.
- ACTION   Denotes what connection you want to make. In this case, I made a connection to something called page1.htm at http://www.htmlgoodies.com.

The second command, INPUT, places the button. It has two parts:

- INPUT TYPE   Tells what type of input occurs (duh!).
- submit   Indicates just what it implies. In this case you want to "submit" something. You see, the FORM command is looking for a link—you are "submitting" a link. Get it?
- VALUE   The wording that appears on the button.

And finally, end the whole deal with this:

```
</FORM>
```

What About That "?" Mark?

Yes, that can be a bit of a problem. However, since the first edition of this book I've found a method for losing that question mark. You simply make the same link button previously mentioned in JavaScript. This is easy. Just copy the following code and then change out the page that you'd like to link to.

```
<FORM>
<INPUT TYPE="button" onClick="parent.location='page.html'">
</FORM>
```

How's that for an easy fix to that question mark problem?

 Try out a few link buttons at http//www.htmlgoodies.com/book/linkbuttons.html.

Lining Up Link Buttons

You need to separate the link buttons to get them to line up and point at different places. You have to make it, so the other buttons don't know that other buttons are on the same page. Sounds covert, huh? This is a rather simple idea, but it does get a bit involved. You separate the buttons using table commands. You can read all about tables in Chapter 5, "Tables."

Some of the newer browsers (version 4 and later) enable you to separate the buttons with a simple <P> command. However, keep in mind that not everyone on the World Wide Web is using the highest browser. You do a little more work if you follow the table format I am about to describe, but you are more certain the buttons work on all browser levels.

 This tutorial in online at http//www.htmlgoodies.com/tutors/linebutt.html.

Using tables also allows you greater control over page layout.

Figure 7.2 shows several link buttons all lined up in a neat row. They all work and they all go to different pages.

The following is the code that lines up the buttons:

```
<TABLE BORDER="0">
<TR>
<TD><FORM METHOD="LINK" ACTION="http://www.htmlgoodies.com/">
<INPUT TYPE="submit" VALUE="HTML Goodies">
```

```
</FORM></TD>
<TD><FORM METHOD="LINK" ACTION="http://espnet.sportszone.com/">
<INPUT TYPE="submit" VALUE="ESPN SportsZone">
</FORM></TD>
<TD><FORM METHOD="LINK" ACTION="http://www.perrier.com/">
<INPUT TYPE="submit" VALUE="Perrier Home Page">
</FORM></TD>
</TR>
</TABLE>
```

Figure 7.2
Clickable buttons all lined up.

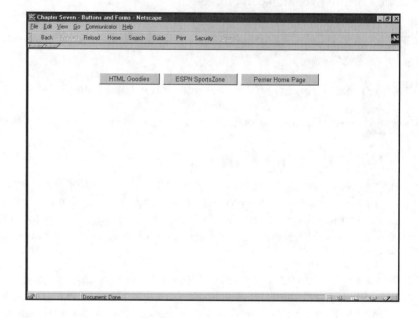

The following is a play-by-play:

- ⬤ `TABLE BORDER="0"`   Tells the browser a table format goes here. The `BORDER="0"` part just tells the browser not to place any defining lines around the cells you create.
- ⬤ `TD`   Stands for table data. It denotes the information that goes in the individual table cell. In this case, the data is a form button.
- ⬤ `TR`   Stands for table row. It denotes the beginning of a new row of table cells.
- ⬤ `<FORM>` through `</FORM>`   The form button format explained in the form button.
- ⬤ `</TABLE>`   Wraps up the whole deal.

If you want to line up your link buttons vertically, as is done in Figure 7.3, you only have to make a couple of additions to the code already discussed.

Figure 7.3
Stacked, clickable buttons.

The following is the code that aligns the buttons vertically:

```
<TABLE BORDER="0">
<TR>
<TD ALIGN="center"><FORM METHOD="LINK" ACTION="http://www.htmlgoodies.com/">
<INPUT TYPE="submit" VALUE="HTML Goodies">
</FORM></TD>
</TR>
<TR>
<TD ALIGN="center"><FORM METHOD="LINK" ACTION="http://espnet.sportszone.com/">
<INPUT TYPE="submit" VALUE="ESPN SportsZone">
</FORM></TD>
</TR>
<TR>
<TD ALIGN="center"><FORM METHOD="LINK" ACTION="http://www.perrier.com/">
<INPUT TYPE="submit" VALUE="Perrier Home Page">
</FORM></TD>
</TR>
</TABLE>
```

Notice that I just added a couple of <TR> and ALIGN="center" commands. The
ALIGN="center" command is my preference. You don't need it for them to be up and down.
If you leave it out, the buttons are left aligned.

You can align the buttons in just about any order. How they line up is not the table cells' real use, although it helps a good deal. Their real use is to separate the buttons, so they work apart from each other. Just enter the button's commands as table data.

Again, later browser versions allow for easier separation, but I suggest following this format. This ensures that the buttons work across different browser versions. In addition, the tables give you a lot more control over page layout.

May you have many buttons.

 Try out a few stacked buttons at `http://www.htmlgoodies.com/book/stackbuttons.html`.

Simple Forms

Forms are a good idea. A form does basically what e-mail does—it sends information. Forms also look professional when Net surfers can enter information right to your page, rather than using a `mailto:` command.

Please be advised that at the moment, only MS Explorer browser version 4.0 supports the `mailto:` command in terms of forms. Although the form commands work in Internet Explorer,(that is, the elements appear on the page), Internet Explorer does not recognize all the form commands as one item the way Netscape Navigator does. A Guestbook is an example of this.

The First Step to Building a Form

The following section simply introduces you to the elements of a form. The section on Guestbooks that immediately follows explains the concept of putting the elements together. Read it all before attacking forms.

 This tutorial in online at `http://www.htmlgoodies.com/tutors/forms.html`.

The first thing you must tell the computer is that you are starting a form and what you want done with the form data. The command is as follows:

```
<FORM METHOD="POST" ACTION="mailto:your email address">
```

The command did three things:

- Told the computer a FORM was starting.
- Stated that the METHOD of dealing with the form data is to POST it.
- Posted to your e-mail address through the `ACTION="mailto:your email address"` command.

Remember that you need to put your e-mail address immediately after the mailto: without a space. This is where the results of the form are sent.

That's nice and simple. Now that the computer knows a form has begun, it's looking for any number of form styles to deal with. I go over five here: TEXT, TEXT AREA, RADIO BUTTON, CHECKBOX, and POP-UP BOX. These are, by far, the most used on the World Wide Web.

The Text Box Form

This is a basic, long box that allows for one line of text (see Figure 7.4). When placed on a page, your reader is able to type information such as her name or e-mail address.

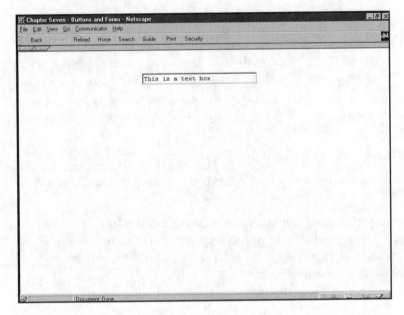

Figure 7.4
A text box.

You may have to click the box to activate it, but it works. If this is your first time making forms, you might think that the box is a .gif or a .jpeg. Not so. The box is placed on the page via HTML, not as an image. This is the command that places it on the page:

```
<FORM METHOD="POST" ACTION="mailto:your email address">
<INPUT TYPE="text" NAME="name" SIZE="30">
</FORM>
```

You already know what the <FORM> and </FORM> commands do. The following are three parts to the text box command:

- INPUT TYPE   Tells the computer that a form item is going to be placed here. Remember when you placed the command to alert the computer that form items are placed on this page? Well, this is your first form item. This form type is text.

- NAME=   Where you define the name you assign to the box. Remember that this is a form that is sent to you through the mail. When you receive the mail, it won't be just like the page. Only the text arrives, so you have to denote what each piece of text is. When the mail arrives from this text box, it says NAME=*(whatever is written in the box)*.

  That way you know this information was written in the box marked *name*. Also remember that you don't have to call the box *name*—call it whatever you want. It comes to you with that name. If you're using the box to get the reader's name, call it name. If you're using the box to get the reader's e-mail address, call it email.

  You can extend what text you use in the NAME="###" section by separating words by an underscore (_). For example, if you wanted to write something more specific than "*name*" in the preceding example, you could use the following:

  NAME="name_of_person_writing_from_my_web_page"

It works just fine. Just make sure you use an underscore between each word. Underscores are good! Spaces are bad.

- SIZE   Denotes how many characters long this box is. Make it 60 or 100 if you'd like. I've found that 30 is usually a good size for people entering text. You should understand that you can also "force" an answer this way. Let's say you are asking for a ZIP code. You could reinforce that by only making the text box seven spaces wide. If you are interested in a state, but only want the two-letter code, only offer two spaces. It won't always work, but it does help.

The Text Area Box Form

This is a larger box, such as the one before, that allows your reader to enter text. The difference between the text box (earlier) and the text area (this example) is that the text box only gives you one line. The text area, however, is much larger and you can use as many words as you want. Take a gander at Figure 7.5.

Figure 7.5
A text area box.

Neat, huh? Go ahead and write in it. It'll work. You may have to click the box to activate it. The following is the command that made it appear:

```
<FORM METHOD="POST" ACTION="mailto:your email address">
<TEXTAREA NAME="comment" ROWS=6 COLS=40>
</TEXTAREA></FORM>
```

Please note that <TEXTAREA> requires a </TEXTAREA> flag, whereas the <TEXT BOX> flag does not. The following are its parts and what they mean:

- TEXTAREA   Yells to the FORM command that here sits another form item. This one is a text area box.

- NAME   The same as before. The reader information in this box arrives in your e-mail box denoted by the name you use. In this case, what is written in this box arrives in your e-mail box with the word comment. Again, this can be as involved as you like, just separate the words with underscores.

- ROWS   Tells the computer how many rows of text it accepts.

- COLS   Tells the computer how many characters are in each row. This text box accepts 6 rows of text, 40 characters each. Go ahead and make the box bigger or smaller. You're in charge here.

227

The Radio Button Form

This is a neat little deal that places a circle on the page. That circle is active and a reader can use the mouse to click it. When the radio button is chosen, it darkens. Figure 7.6 shows three radio buttons.

Figure 7.6
Three radio buttons.

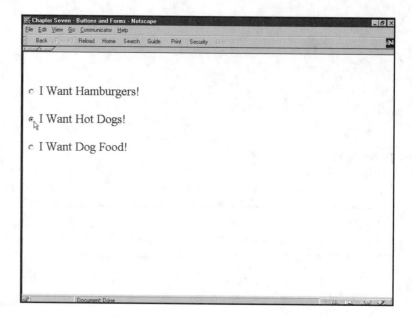

I have three of them there to prove a point, and it's not that I prefer hamburgers! The point is that radio buttons are a one-choice deal only. Only one button can be selected when you use radio buttons. When another is selected, the first one becomes unselected. Go ahead. Try it.

Why are they called radio buttons? They act as the radio buttons used in older car radios. When you pushed one, the dial moved. When you pushed another, the first button popped out and the dial moved to your new choice. You're probably too young to remember. It was back when only AM was a big selling radio, back before dirt. The following is the command for placing radio buttons on your page:

```
<FORM METHOD="POST" ACTION="mailto:your email address">
<INPUT TYPE="radio" NAME="I_want_to_eat" VALUE="hamburgers"> I Want
➥Hamburgers!<p>
<INPUT TYPE="radio" NAME=" I_want_to_eat " VALUE="hot_dogs"> I Want Hot Dogs!<P>
<INPUT TYPE="radio" NAME=" I_want_to_eat " VALUE="dog_food"> I Want Dog Food!
</FORM>
```

The radio button form command is long, but it's not that difficult to understand. The following are its four parts and what they mean:

- TYPE   Tells the computer what type of form item it is. In this case, it's a radio button.

- NAME   Indicates the category the button is in on your form page. The example asks people to choose one of three foods. All the foods fall under the NAME of "I_want_to_eat". That's the radio buttons' group heading.

- VALUE   The name assigned to the button. Notice the choice of hamburgers has a value of "hamburgers" and so on.

Why on earth would I want to label all those buttons with different names?

Remember that this is going to be sent to you through e-mail. You have to be able to read what the person chooses. Say you had a Guestbook with a section of radio buttons asking which page the user is signing in from. Your NAME in the command might be "signing_in_from". Each of the radio buttons is assigned the VALUE of each of your pages. Say a person chooses the radio button assigned to your home page. That button's VALUE might be "home_page".

Thus, when the form arrives to you, the e-mail would read "signing_in_from_home_page".

If the hamburger button in the food example is chosen, the text that arrives in your e-mail box would read "I_want_to_eat hamburgers."

Pretty darn slick, huh?

The Check Box Form

The check box is pretty much a clone of the radio button except for two features (see Figure 7.7):

- The item it places on the page is square and is marked with an X when chosen.

- You can check as many as you'd like.

Note that you can choose one, several, or all the check boxes. I've chosen two in this example. This check box is basically a fancy radio button. The following is what placed the check boxes on the page:

```
<FORM METHOD="POST" ACTION="mailto:your email address">
<INPUT TYPE="checkbox" NAME="I_want_to_drink" VALUE="soda">
I Want To Drink Soda!<P>
<INPUT TYPE="checkbox" NAME="I_want_to_drink" VALUE="apple_juice">
I Want To Drink Apple Juice!<P>
```

```
<INPUT TYPE="checkbox" NAME="I_want_to_drink" VALUE="water">
I Want To Drink Water!
</FORM>
```

Figure 7.7
A few check boxes.

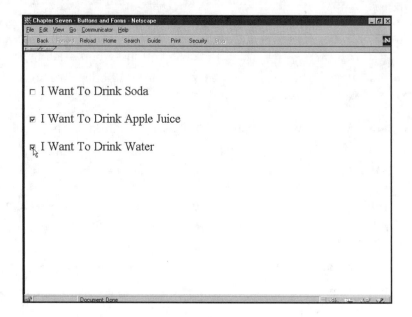

Each of the items means the same as they did for the radio button form, so I do not need to go over them again. Please note, however, the TYPE is now checkbox instead of radio.

Remember that when the text from a check box arrives at your e-mail box, the output from every box the user checks shows up. It can fill up your e-mail pretty quickly. With radio buttons, only one item under each NAME heading arrives. With check boxes, every item can be checked, thus, every item can arrive.

I like radio buttons much more than check boxes because radio buttons force a choice. Check boxes invite people to check everything every time. That can waste your time reading through it all. I like to make a one-choice deal. This is easier on you and if people want to leave more information or ask questions, they always have the TEXT AREA box for that purpose.

The Drop-Down Box Form

I love these drop-down boxes, but I don't use them too often. I like to have all the items people can choose out in the open. The drop-down box, unless clicked, only shows one item. But this is your form and you can do anything you want. Figure 7.8 shows a drop-down box. You have to click it to see all the choices. This one is for people to choose their favorite color.

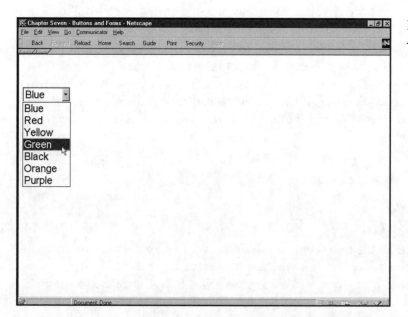

Figure 7.8
A drop-down box.

The following are the commands that placed the drop-down box on the page:

```
<FORM METHOD="POST" ACTION="mailto:your email address">
My favorite color is: <SELECT NAME="Favorite_Color" SIZE="1">
<OPTION SELECTED>Blue
<OPTION>Red
<OPTION>Yellow
<OPTION>Green
<OPTION>Black
<OPTION>Orange
<OPTION>Purple
</SELECT>
</FORM>
```

Although this looks a little bit more involved, it really isn't. This is the same thing again and again. The following are the parts and what they mean:

- SELECT   Tells the computer another form is going here. This time it's a selection, or drop-down form.

231

- NAME   Means the same thing it always means. This is the heading of the form item. It denotes how the results of the reader arrives at your e-mail box. In this case it says Favorite_Color= and then the reader's choice.

- SIZE   Denotes the size of the box. Here, 1 means one line or item is shown. Try putting 2 there if you'd like to see what it does. I prefer 1. More than one item tends to defeat the purpose of the drop-down box.

- OPTION SELECTED   Denotes which option appears in the box. Note in the figure that Blue is the first item in the list. Blue would be visible before you click the drop-down box. You may want to avoid using an item someone can choose in this position, but rather something that reads Click to Choose, or words to that effect, to provide the user more instruction.

- OPTION   Denotes another choice that is visible when you click the item.

- </SELECT>   Finishes the entire deal.

Send and Reset Buttons for Your Forms

Now that you have placed all the form items you want on your page, you need a way to have the results sent to your e-mail box (or wherever you said this would go in the original form statement). You should also give your Web visitors a way to quickly erase the information they've entered in your forms. To do these two things, you'll create Send and Reset buttons for your forms (see Figure 7.9).

Figure 7.9
Submit Query and Reset buttons.

The following are the commands that put the buttons on the page:

```
<FORM METHOD="POST" ACTION="mailto:your email address">
<INPUT TYPE="submit"><INPUT TYPE="reset">
</FORM>
```

Easy, huh? Now when you click the buttons, the form enacts the ACTION you noted in the original FORM command. In this case it would have been mailed to your e-mail box.

If you would like to put your own words on the Submit and Reset buttons, add VALUE="####" to the previous commands:

```
<INPUT TYPE="submit" VALUE="Click to Send It!">
<INPUT TYPE="reset" VALUE="Wait! Start over.">
```

Finally!

Make sure you end your form with this:

```
</FORM>
```

That's a start on forms, but you can do much more than what I have described here. You can connect to Common Gateway Interfaces (CGIs), databases, or other data-collection devices with forms. All I wanted to do here is give you a very basic, very easy form for you to use on your Web pages. I believe I have. Now off to help others. Thank you, citizen.

 See some of these commands in action at http://www.htmlgoodies.com/book/form.html.

Creating a Guestbook

I get a great many e-mails asking me to put up a tutorial on making a Guestbook. Here it is! I go over three different types of Guestbooks: Simple mailto: Guestbooks, Guestbooks that offer a page thanking the person for writing, and Guestbooks that post what your visitors write to a separate page.

 This tutorial in online at http://www.htmlgoodies.com/tutors/g_book.html.

A Basic Guestbook

Let's start at the beginning. Figure 7.10 shows a simple Guestbook.

Figure 7.10

A simple Guestbook.

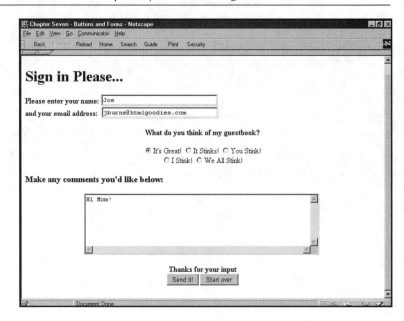

This is the program that created the Guestbook. Just copy it from here:

```
<H1> Sign in Please...</H1>
<FORM METHOD="POST" ACTION="mailto:user@writemehere.com">
<B>Please enter your name: </B><INPUT NAME="username" size="30"> <BR>
<B>and your email address: </B><INPUT Name="usermail" size="30">
<p>
<CENTER>
<B>what do you think of my Guestbook?</B>
<P>
<INPUT TYPE="radio" NAME=I_think_that VALUE="It's_Great">It's Great!
<INPUT TYPE="radio" NAME=I_think_that VALUE="It_stinks">It Stinks!
<INPUT TYPE="radio" NAME=I_think_that VALUE="You_stink">You Stink!
<BR>
<INPUT TYPE="radio" NAME=I_think_that VALUE="I_stink">I Stink!
<INPUT TYPE="radio" NAME=I_think_that VALUE="We_all_stink">We All Stink!
<P>
</CENTER>
<H3>Make any comments you'd like below:</H3>
<CENTER>
<TEXTAREA NAME="comment" ROWS=6 COLS=60></TEXTAREA>
<P>
<B>Thanks for your input</B>
<BR>
```

```
<INPUT TYPE=submit VALUE="Send it!">
<INPUT TYPE=reset VALUE="Start over">
</CENTER>
</FORM>
```

Simple `Mailto:` *Guestbooks*

What you have in the preceding code is a very simple Guestbook set up using two text boxes, five radio buttons, and a text area.

If all you want is a simple Guestbook that sends mail to you, boom—you're done. Just cut and paste the Guestbook to a page, place your e-mail address where it says *user@ writemehere.com* and put it up for the world to use.

However, this approach only works with Netscape-style browsers and Explorer 4.0. Earlier Explorer browsers do not recognize this as a form working with a `mailto:` command. It simply puts up the e-mail box as if it was a regular `mailto:` `HREF` command.

- No confirmation of sent mail is received.
- The text arrives as one long line, like so: `Hello+I'm/+very=glad/=to=meet+you. +/I+like+/your+%Guestbook.$`. You can read it, but it's tough.
- The mail arrives as an attachment labeled a `.dat` file.

The `.dat` file suffix stands for data. It has to be opened in a text editor or after changing the suffix to `.txt`. You may be able to alter this in your e-mail program. Often, a configuration you can alter puts an attachment right into the e-mail body. Look through your configuration settings for that.

Augmenting Your Guestbook Output

These are a couple of commands you might want to play around with. The first helps you read the e-mail that arrives in your box. Add `enctype="text/plain"` to your `FORM` command. It looks like this:

```
<FORM METHOD="post" ACTION="mailto:your email address" enctype="text/plain">
```

In most cases, that delineates the mail and sets it to plain text. The output of the Guestbook should then look something like this:

```
NAME = Joe Burns
EMAIL = jburns@htmlgoodies.com
COMMENT = Hi Mom!
```

Wouldn't it be great if you could set up your Guestbook so that the subject line was filled out automatically? That way you would immediately know where the mail came from. If you had multiple Guestbooks, you could keep better track of where people were writing you from. Well, the following is how you do it:

```
<FORM METHOD="post" ACTION="mailto:jburns@htmlgoodies.com?subject=
This appears in your email's subject line" enctype="text/plain">
```

I used my personal e-mail address for this example. You would put your e-mail address in place of mine. After the e-mail address, I just added a question mark, the word `subject`, the equal sign, and the text I wanted to appear in the subject line of the e-mail.

Having underscores in the text is not necessary for the subject line. Also notice the patter of quotation marks. No quotation mark is before the subject line text. Just make sure you follow the pattern given here.

FAQs from the HTML Goodies Web Site

Q. Can I make it so that the Guestbook sends mail to two different addresses?

A. You mean like a CC? Yes, in some cases. Many later browsers enable you to post as many e-mail addresses as you'd like, as long as you separate them by commas (with no spaces).

Guestbooks with Virtual Pages

This is a Guestbook that allows the viewer to fill in information. When the viewer sends the form data, another page pops up, thanking the viewer for the input. The viewer must then select Back to return to the main page.

 My current Guestbook is this kind. You can see it in action online at `http://www.htmlgoodies.com/feedback.html`.

Sending the user to a virtual page is done by attaching a Guestbook form's e-mail output to a CGI. A CGI is a small program, usually written in Perl, Java, or C++ computer languages, that does little tricks.

It gets a little involved, but fear not. I have full instructions, just not right here.

For instructions on how to attach your Guestbook to a CGI, see Chapter 12, "Common Gateway Interface (CGI)." It has a tutorial that gives you the HTML document, the CGI, and instructions on how to get them both up and running on your server.

Image Submit Buttons

An example of what I'm talking about is shown in Figure 7.11 in a simple form. However, instead of a link button starting it off, the user clicks an image.

Figure 7.11
A Guestbook with an image submit button.

I do not need to show you how the form is made. I go over that in the forms and the Guestbook tutorials. What I am concerned with here is the input button. The following is the format I used to make the button:

```
<INPUT TYPE="image" SRC="hgbutt.gif" HEIGHT="24" WIDTH="129"
  BORDER=0 ALT="picture button">
```

Notice it's the same format at the normal link button, except the type is now IMAGE instead of SUBMIT. The SRC has to be added to call for the image. The HEIGHT, WIDTH, BORDER, and ALT commands define the image for the browser and lose the blue border that comes with an active image link.

I hope you can use this in your own pages.

 I have a fully functioning Guestbook for you to try and use if you'd like at http://www. htmlgoodies.com/book/form.html.

So You Want a Searchable Database, Huh?

I am asked time and time again: "How do I set up a searchable database?" The answer is a few different ways, but some are harder than others.

 This tutorial in online at `http://www.htmlgoodies.com/tutors/database.html`. *Let's take a quick look at the three main methods.*

Search Someone Else's Database

Ever been at a page and the author invites you to search Yahoo! or Webcrawler right from his own page? You think this person must be pretty high up the ladder to be able to pull off this kind of deal. Not really—anyone can do it. Figure 7.12 shows an example of a page on my site that allows you to search three different search engine databases.

Figure 7.12
Various search engines.

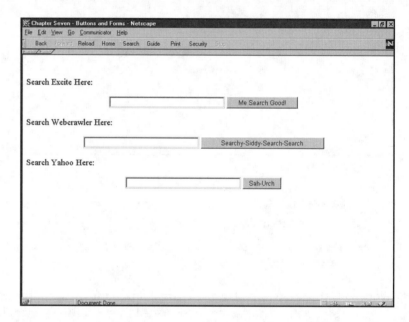

Actually, I lied (and I may lie later). Even if you were to use the items and search Yahoo!, my site didn't actually perform the searches. The search was done by Yahoo!. I just allowed you to initiate the search from my home page. When you get your results, you're no longer in Kansas Goodies anymore—you're transported to the Yahoo! site. If this seems a bit confusing, hang in there. All I am doing is allowing you to search Yahoo! from my page.

Let's look at the code I used to create the Yahoo! search:

```
<FORM ACTION="http://search.yahoo.com/bin/search">
<INPUT SIZE=30 name=p>
<INPUT TYPE=submit value="Search">
</FORM>
```

This is a simple set of FORM commands, set up much like you would to create a link button or a simple mailto: Guestbook. However, in this case you are using the form to send the information contained within the text box to a search engine. That's what you call the actual program that searches the Yahoo! database, a *search engine*. In the previous example you are sending the info to Yahoo!'s CGI bin to be worked on by something called *search*.

The following are the Webcrawler and Excite lines:

```
<FORM NAME="wcsearchform" ACTION="http://webcrawler.com/cgi-bin/WebQuery"
  METHOD="GET">
<FORM NAME="search" ACTION="http://www.excite.com/search.gw" METHOD="get">
```

Notice they also sent the text box's output to a search engine. One goes to something called WebQuery and the other goes to search.gw. After the data is sent to the search engine, the site's database is rummaged through and you get your results.

Note again, however, that you do not use my site to search—you only send the information from my site. After that's done, I'm totally out of the picture and you're at the search engine's site.

One more thing: Notice the METHOD and name="p" in the Yahoo! search? Those are little items that each search engine uses to denote how to manipulate the data it receives and what to name the output sent through the text box. Each search engine works differently and you must make sure to use the search engine's format, exactly, on your page.

Where do you get the format for all this? Directly from the search engine itself. This is not that tough. Go to the search engine site and look at the source code. Just grab the part that goes from <FORM> through </FORM>. You may need to knock out some stuff in the middle, such as extra text or table commands, but it's all right there. Put it on your page.

One thing, though. You may notice when you get the code that the ACTION section does not include the search engine's entire address. That's because the full address wasn't needed when the code was on the original site.

Because the domain is added as the default, you know that you don't need to put the full address on links to pages within your own site. Now the code you took from their site is on your site and it needs the full address.

For instance, let's say you took some code from a search engine at `http://www.joe.com`. The code you take from the site may read like this:

```
ACTION="/search/findit/"
```

Notice the slash before the first directory? That tells the computer to add the domain before the slash as a default. The code is on your site and you need to add the full address right into the code. The code should be altered to look like this:

```
ACTION="http://www.joe.com/search/findit/"
```

Remember, the code now requires the full address because it is going from your site to perform the search. Without it, the code looks for something on your site called `/search/findit/` to perform the search. The server doesn't find it and you get errors.

But I Want to Search My Site!

This is a tough call. I have gone through the process and can tell you that it is rough and outside the scope of this book. The process occurs in two steps:

1. Creating a database and placing it on your site.

   This database has to be in a format the server understands. Excel often works, as does Lotus.

2. Writing a CGI to do the searching.

   Maybe you are one of those people who has access to someone who writes one of these for a small amount of money.

Another solution exists, but it isn't cheap. You can use the Excite search engine. It is a self-contained package that your Webmaster may already have. Mine did: $275.

The search engine was wonderfully easy. It installed quickly and made an entire directory searchable. All I did was point it in the right direction. It compiled the data and was up and running in a matter of minutes. After a month, I had to take it down. So many people were using it that the search engine was taking up three out of every five cycles of the computer's brain. In layman's terms, it was about to crash the whole system by overworking it. I still have it and I still use it to search, but I don't make it available to others. It slowed the site tremendously.

I do not have a whole lot more to tell you. You know how to search other databases from your site, and have a couple of ideas about how to set up Excite and other CGI-driven searches. You may want to contact your site administrator to look into those paths.

But I Want to Search My Site! (Take Two)

 If the Excite database is unavailable to you or you'd rather not spend the money, I have another suggestion. Use a JavaScript-based search engine. I have one you can have for free on the HTML Goodies site. Point your browsers to `http://www.htmlgoodies.com/db.html`.

You can search my site using the JavaScript database. Afterwards, select the link on the page that sends you to a tutorial on how to alter the database for use on your own site.

The process is simple. The JavaScript doesn't search your site, but instead searches itself. You enter all your page names, their addresses, and keywords that denote each page into the JavaScript itself. Then when someone puts in a keyword, the JavaScript searches what you have put into it and returns the results. This is a self-contained process that works very well.

Go see my JavaScript database in action. If you like it, it's yours. Just follow the instructions online for altering the Script to search your own pages.

But I Want to Search My Site! (Take Three)

Okay, I have one more way you can go about searching your own site. I was given this tip by a technical editor of this book, Bill Bruns. (Thanks Bill, great tip!)

This is what you do. First submit all your pages to a search engine that allows you to use a *hidden value*. I explain what that means in a moment. I don't know that this works with all search engines, but I know HotBot (`http://www.hotbot.com`) and AltaVista (`http://www.altavista.com`) enable it. What you do then is create the same basic search format I talked about earlier, which allows people to use search engines from your site. This differs in that you are going to add to your code a hidden field that denotes your domain.

Let's say I do this with my HTML Goodies site. The domain is htmlgoodies.com. I would submit all my pages to HotBot. Then I would create the code that allows people to search HotBot from my site. The search, however, would be altered in the code because I would have added a hidden field. That hidden field tells HotBot to search only for files that are on the domain htmlgoodies.com.

By limiting the search to that domain, I am in a sense setting up a search of my site only. Very clever.

The following is the code I would use to set up a search of HTML Goodies on HotBot:

```
<FORM action="http://www.hotbot.com/" method="GET">
        <INPUT type="hidden" name="SPID" value="2904">
        <INPUT type="hidden" name="_v" value="2">
        <INPUT type="hidden" name="domain"
```

```
value="www.htmlgoodies.com htmlgoodies.com">
        <INPUT type="hidden" name="SM" value="phrase">
        <INPUT type="hidden" name="RD" value="DM">
        <INPUT type="hidden" name="OPs" value="R">
<B>Search </B>our site with <a href="http://www.hotbot.com/">Hotbot</a>:
        <INPUT type="text" size="15" maxlength="25" name="MT">
        <INPUT type="submit" value="Search">
</FORM>
```

Most of the code was taken right from the site. The extra code that creates the hidden field was entered to limit the site to my pages only.

Remember that you are sent to HotBot (or whatever search engine you're using) when you use this method. With the Excite and JavaScript method, you can remain at your site for the search.

You need to play around a bit to get the correct format, but you'll find it. This is usually pretty clear from the remainder of the code.

Somehow, some way, you'll get a search on your page.

TABINDEX **and a Few Other Neat Tricks…**

There have been some great advancements in using forms since the first edition of this book. However, most of them are rather complicated and hard to implement. I wanted to wrap up this chapter with a few of the easier tricks that have come out since the original printing of this book.

Today I'm staying on the easy side of things. This is just about as simple as a tutorial gets. Yet, even though the commands you're going to learn are easy to use, they make such a nice effect.

I speak first of TABINDEX.

The Command In Action

 Okay then! Let's see this pup in action. Take a look at Figures 7.13, and also visit the following example at http://www.htmlgoodies.com/book/tabindex.html.

Don't lie to me. You thought that was cool. I showed the effect to a couple of programming friends of mine, as well as a couple of students, and they all immediately saw the benefits. Too often you fill out forms and the elements are nicely displayed, but they're not in order, at least not in order of how they appear in the code.

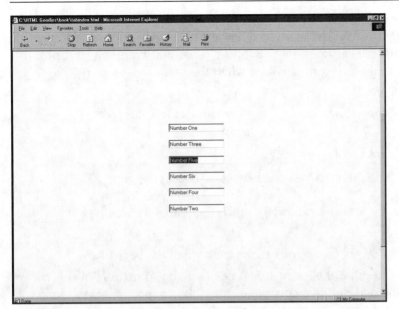

Figure 7.13
The Tab key jumps from text box to text box in whatever order you decide.

Using the TABINDEX attribute, you can "force" the tab to jump to the next logical form element. How cool.

The following is how I got the effect:

```
<FORM NAME="joe">
<INPUT TYPE="TEXT" TABINDEX="1" VALUE="Number One" NAME="burns">
<INPUT TYPE="TEXT" TABINDEX="3" VALUE="Number Three">
<INPUT TYPE="TEXT" TABINDEX="5" VALUE="Number Five">
<INPUT TYPE="TEXT" TABINDEX="6" VALUE="Number Six">
<INPUT TYPE="TEXT" TABINDEX="4" VALUE="Number Four">
<INPUT TYPE="TEXT" TABINDEX="2" VALUE="Number Two">
</FORM>
```

The attribute TABINDEX is added into each of the form elements, in this case the text boxes. I then set the attributes to the numeric order I wanted the tab to follow. It works on any form element and it's easy, easy, easy.

Focus onLoad

Well, I can't leave it at that. The TABINDEX is a great attribute, but this is an HTML Goodies tutorial. It has to get a little more difficult before you can finish.

243

As you know, when someone logs into a page that contains a form, the cursor does not jump to a form element right away. The user has to click the first element to start filling out the form. After that, the tab key does the bulk of the work. But! Wouldn't it be nice if you could force the focus to the first form element when the user logged into the page? Why, yes. Of course it would.

 If you'd like to see it happen, go to `http://www.htmlgoodies.com/book/onfocus.html`.

Now let's find out how it works. This goes in the BODY tag:

```
onLoad="self.focus();document.FORM_NAME.ELEMENT_NAME.focus()"
```

Even if you don't know JavaScript, you can pretty much figure this one out just by reading left to right.

- ● `onLoad`   Means the following commands are enacted when the page loads.
- ● `self.focus();`   Indicates that the focus should be placed on something in this current page. This is a method, so the empty parentheses, (), are required. Don't forget them.
- ● `document.FORM_NAME.ELEMENT_NAME.focus()`   A hierarchy statement that forces the focus to the document to a specific form inside the document, and then to a specific item inside the form. That focus comes in the guise of the cursor.

  To be more specific, look at the previous form code, the code I used to show the TABINDEX. I named the form itself "joe" and the first form element "burns". Thus, the actual line I put into the page BODY command looks like this:

  ```
  onLoad="self.focus();document.joe.burns.focus()"
  ```

Change the form and element names when you post this to your own page.

Losing the VALUE Text

Note from the previous section that I have placed text inside the text boxes in the example form. I see this done a lot. You get that text by adding the attribute VALUE="text text text text" to the text box tag.

Have you ever been to a form that had text in a box you were supposed to write in? The problem is that you click the text box and the text remains. You need to highlight and erase all that text before you can put in your own text.

Well, erase no more. Dig this.

 See this effect for yourself at `http://www.htmlgoodies.com/book/erase.html`.

Ta da! No text. The following is what the code looks like:

```
<FORM>
<INPUT TYPE="text" VALUE="This is text in a text box" SIZE="45"
onFocus="this.value=''">
</FORM>
```

This is that little blip of JavaScript that does the trick. I have it in the following code:

```
onFocus="this.value=''"
```

When focus is brought on the box (onFocus), the value of the box (this.value) is set to nothing. Note the empty quotes at the end of the code. Make a point of having the quotation marks right up next to one another such as I do. If you have space between them, that space appears in the form element.

So, there you go. You've got a few new form tricks to add to your bag. These are solid tricks that actually add usability to your pages. How often can you say that?

Working with Internet Explorer's AutoComplete

If you're reading this section, you most likely know what I mean by Microsoft Internet Explorer's AutoComplete. This is a rather nice function that Microsoft has put in its browsers 5.0 and higher to help you out when you're filling out forms. I love the silly thing. I only need to write in a couple of letters and down drops a list of suggestions I might want to choose. It stops me from having to write everything, every time. I use it a great deal, but I've always wondered how it worked.

 See this tutorial online at http://www.htmlgoodies.com/autocomplete.html.

After reading up on it, I found not only how it worked, but also how I could use it to my advantage. These are the basics. Most of it is actual information from the Microsoft company pages.

How It Works

When you enter information into a form and submit it, Internet Explorer sets up what's known as a vCard. The reason the function is so successful is that Web authors tend to use the same NAME attributes for many form elements across pages.

For instance, I bet you've filled out a ton of forms that ask for your name. Allow me to demonstrate. I offer you the ability to try each of these elements on one page here: http://www.htmlgoodies.com/book/autocomplete.html.

In the first section, type the first few letters of your name in the text box just below. If you're using IE 5.0 or higher, I bet your name appears as a choice you can make. Try it in the e-mail box, too. I bet you get your e-mail address as a choice. It won't work for everyone, but I bet it works for the majority of you. It looks something like Figure 7.14.

Figure 7.14

The AutoComplete box drops down.

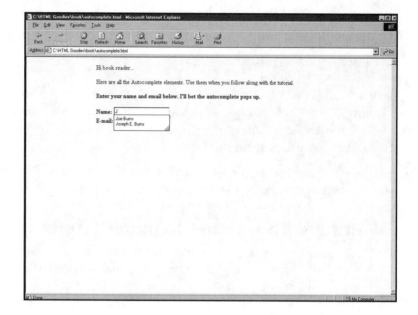

If it worked for you—and I bet it did—you're probably wondering how I knew each item would come up. First, the following is the code from the previous form:

```
<FORM>
Name: <INPUT TYPE="text" NAME="name">
E-mail: <INPUT TYPE="text" NAME="email">
</FORM>
```

This is the NAME attribute that does the trick. I'm basically making a guess that sometime, somewhere, you filled out a form that asked for your name and e-mail address. In addition, I am guessing that the form used the NAME attributes "name" and "email". They are very common.

If it worked you have a couple of vCards on your system named "VCARD_NAME" and "VCARD_EMAIL." When you filled out the other form and submitted it, the card was created. Now, from that point on, whenever you run into a form that has an element with a NAME attribute set to "name" or "email", the text from that vCard is suggested to you.

Let me attempt to prove that point again. The next form on the example page looks exactly like the previous one, except the first text box has its NAME attribute set to "griswald" and the second set to "ookook". Go ahead, try to put your name and e-mail in. You'll most likely get no help from AutoComplete.

You didn't get any help because you don't have VCARD_GRISWALD or VCARD_OOKOOK on your computer. Luckily, I didn't give you the opportunity to submit the form, or you would have.

Using AutoComplete on Your Forms (Or Not)

Just with what you've read so far, you can probably guess how to use the AutoComplete to your advantage when you design your own Web page. Maybe you'd prefer that your visitors only be given the opportunity to choose from responses they've put into forms that you've created. This would be useful if you have a form page where people need to put in shipping numbers or part numbers, and all those other AutoComplete responses might clutter things up. Maybe you would just like to be an island unto yourself.

In any case, make a point of giving each of your form elements an extremely odd NAME attribute, maybe even a random set of letters. That way, only responses given to your own form are offered as choices.

I Want the Silly Thing Turned Off Altogether

If that's the case you need to start playing around with the AUTOCOMPLETE attribute. If you'd like to shut off AutoComplete for the entire form, put the attribute in the main FORM tag, set to "off".

```
<FORM METHOD="post" ACTION="/cgi-bin/joe.cgi" AUTOCOMPLETE="off">
```

You can also set individual form elements to "on" if you want to override the attribute in the main FORM tag. That way each of the form elements can be turned off except that one you set to "on".

Of course, you can also set individual form elements to "off".

How Do I Erase My AutoComplete Responses?

From the menu bar at the top of your browser, choose Tools, Internet Options, Content Tab, AutoComplete Button, Clear Forms.

How Do I Clear Just One AutoComplete Response?

In a form element, put in at least one letter so that the AutoComplete responses are made visible. Using your arrow keys, scroll down to highlight the response you want to erase. Push the Delete key on your keyboard. The response erases itself from the list.

I love AutoComplete, and now that I have a fairly good handle on how it works and how I can manipulate it for my own purposes, I like it even more. I hope you get to use the previous code I've shown. I've already found a couple of uses for it myself.

Chapter 8

Cascading Style Sheets and Layers

Wouldn't it be nice if you could say to all browsers that enter your page, "This is how I want you to handle my text?" You could make all <H3> commands Arial font. You could make all paragraph commands indent a half inch. You could specify a distance between your lines! You could ask for the world on a string! You wouldn't get it, but you could ask. I'm talking about the other stuff.

 This tutorial is online at http://www.htmlgoodies.com/tutors/ie_style.html.

Explorer 3 and above and Netscape 4.0 and above (and those to come) offer you more control through the use of what are called *style sheets*. This is actually a novel concept. Instead of writing font size, weight, margin commands, and so on again and again, you write them once and the whole page feeds off that one master list—that one style sheet.

In fact, the 4.0 version of HTML (see Appendix A, "Everything You Need to Know About HTML 4.0") expects that you depend on these style sheets for a great deal of your writing. That's not to say you have to—the more traditional method of tagging every item still works just fine—but if you read my synopses on HTML 4.0, notice that a few commands are going to the trash heap in favor of using style sheets for the effect. This is not a bad idea, but don't think that the methods you already know are going to be out of date any time soon. Read this over and if you think this is a better method, great. If not, feel free to tag everything individually. That works just fine.

FAQs from the HTML Goodies Web Site

Q. **I went through your style sheets tutorial and put some on the page. It worked in Internet Explorer, but Navigator gave me some problems. It didn't do some of the commands and didn't understand others. Some it produced just fine. What's with that?**

A. You probably had problems because the style sheet commands used were not standard code. Microsoft's version of style sheets was the one adopted by the W3C (they're the people that decide what is and is not standard HTML code). Netscape implemented the standard code into its browser Navigator so all standard codes should run just fine. You must have run into code not in the W3C standard, thus not understood by the Netscape Navigator.

So are these things called style sheets, cascading style sheets, or CSS? Choose any one—they all mean the same thing. I tell you what I really find funny: I had the original style sheets (sometimes called Explorer style sheets when referenced on other pages) up for six months when Netscape 4.0 came out. All of a sudden I was overrun with letters asking me when I was going to put up a tutorial on cascading style sheets and CSS, even though they mean the same thing. Yet this pup had been sitting and waiting all along. The name had just changed a bit, so it was thought of as a new thing.

The term *cascading style sheets* is used because more than one style sheet can affect the same page. For instance, assume you are using a style sheet on the actual document—called an *inline*—and a style sheet that is being referenced by multiple pages—called a *span*. Both can have an effect on the items in the page. If both the inline and the span style sheet attempt to affect the same item, an <H1> command for instance, the closest to the <H1> command wins. In this case it's the inline.

In case you're wondering, if two inline style sheets attempt to affect the same <H1> command, the one listed second in the actual HTML document wins. Going from the top of the document it's closest to the command.

The following are three ways to implement a style sheet:

1. Putting a separate style sheet on each page.
2. Placing a style sheet command inside an HTML flag.
3. Creating one style sheet and linking all your pages to it.

 Point your browser to http://www.htmlgoodies.com/book/stylesheet.html *to see a page with a rather large style sheet. Make sure to look at the source code.*

One Style Sheet—One Page

This is the way I see style sheets being used most often: the style sheet commands are directly in the HTML document. If you look at the source code of some popular pages, such as CNN.com or ESPN's SportsZone, notice that this type of style sheet is being used.

I also use this method on the HTML Goodies site. The style sheet commands are placed between the <HEAD> and </HEAD> flags and it looks like this:

```
<HEAD>
<STYLE="text/css">
<!--
BODY {background: #FFFFFF}
A:link {color: #80FF00}
A:visited {color: #FF00FF}
H1 {font-size: 24pt; font-family: arial}
H2 {font-size: 18pt; font-family: braggadocio}
H3 {font size:14pt; font-family: desdemona}
-->
</STYLE>
</HEAD>
```

In all fairness, I should mention that when used like this, it technically isn't a style sheet, it's an inline style *block*. But another term just pushes something useful out of your brain, so if I continue to call it a sheet, it's habit more than anything.

Follow these rules to place a style sheet (block) on your page:

- It must be within the <HEAD> and </HEAD> commands.
- The text must be surrounded by <STYLE TEXT="text/css"> and </STYLE>.
- Remember that CSS from earlier? It stands for cascading style sheets. The style sheet is text, so if you type it on the page, it shows up and you can't have that. In addition to the style commands, surround the text with <!-- and -->. Those happy little commands make the text invisible. Just like Wonder Woman's jet. Man, I loved that show. I think it was called *Superfriends*…

Hey! Make with the Style Sheet Already, Bub!

This gets a little confusing, but this madness has a method. Now that you know the big picture, let's look at the format for individual style commands:

```
TAG {definition; definition; definition}
```

This is a sample line from a style sheet:

```
H2 {font-size: 16pt; font-style: italic; font-family: arial}
```

These are a few things I want to point out about the individual style command:

- The thing surrounding the definition is a curly bracket ({), not a parenthesis or a square bracket.

- The spaces! You don't have to leave them, but it helps when you read your style sheets later. Just don't forget the semicolons.

- Each definition is separated by a semicolon, but the definition contains a colon! Confusing, I know, but that's the way it goes in Internetland.

You're not limited, either. If you can somehow find a way to use 30 style sheet commands to affect the same <H2> flag, good for you! Just remember to separate them all by semicolon.

What HTML Tags Can I Define?

As far as I can tell, you can define any HTML tag.

Now, some definitions are silly with some tags. I mean, a font definition with an <HR> tag seems a bit goofy, don't you think? I see style sheets using the following flags the most:

- <H1> through <H6>
- <P>
- <BODY>
- A:link   Denotes the unvisited link
- A:visited   Denotes the visited link
- <DIV>   Denotes a division of the page

Twenty-Eight Style Sheet Command Definitions

These are 28 very common style sheet commands. You can put together myriad looks with these. However, this list is less than half of those available. At the end, I give a couple of links to full commands' lists—but I bet these become your work horses. Most of the other commands are overly specific.

The FONT/TEXT definitions:

- font-family   Denotes typeface.
  ```
  H2 {font-family: arial}
  ```

- font-style   Denotes the style of the text. Use normal, italic, small caps, or oblique for commands.

    H3 {font-style: small caps}

- font-size   Denotes the size of the text. Specify in points (pt), inches (in), centimeters (cm), pixels (px), or percentages (%).

    H4 {font-size: 20pt}

- font-weight   Denotes text presence. Specify in extra-light, light, demi-light, medium, bold, demi-bold, or extra-bold.

    A:link {font-weight: demi-light}

- font-variant   Denotes a variant from the norm. Specify normal or small-caps.

    H2: {font-variant: small-caps}

- text-align   Justifies the alignment of text. Specify as left, center, or right.

    H1 {text-align: center}

- text-decoration   Lets you decorate the text. Specify as italic, blink, underline, line-through, overline, or none.

    A:visited {text-decoration: blink}

- text-indent   Denotes margins. Most often used with the <P> flag. Make sure you use </P> also. Specify in inches (in), centimeters (cm), or pixels (px).

    P {text-indent: 1in}

- word-spacing   Denotes the amount of spaces between words. Specify in points (pt), inches (in), centimeters (cm), pixels (px), or percentages (%).

    P {word-spacing: 10px}

- letter-spacing   Denotes space between letters. Specify in points (pt), inches (in), centimeters (cm), pixels (px), or percentages (%).

    P {letter-spacing: 2pt}

- text-transform   Denotes a transformation of the text. Specify capitalize, uppercase, or lowercase.

    B {text-transform: uppercase}

- color   Denotes color of text. See Appendix B, "Useful Charts," for a few color codes. If you use the six-digit hex codes, make sure you place a pound sign (#) in front.

    H3 {color: #FFFFFF}

The MARGIN/BACKGROUND commands:

> ### Note
>
> When used with the <BODY> flag, these commands affect the entire page!

- ● margin-left   See margin-top.

- ● margin-right   See margin-top.

- ● margin-top   Denotes space around the page. Specify in points (pt), inches (in), centimeters (cm), or pixels (px).

  ```
  BODY {margin-left: 2in}
  P {margin-right: 12cm}
  BODY {margin-top: 45px}
  ```

- ● margin   Denotes all three margin commands in one command. The pattern follows top, right, and then left.

  ```
  P {margin: 3in 4cm 12px} (note no commas or semi-colons)
  ```

- ● line-height   Denotes space between lines of text. Specify in points (pt), inches (in), centimeters (cm), pixels (px), or percentages (%).

  ```
  TEXT {line-height: 10px}
  ```

- ● background-color   Denotes page's background color. Specify the color in hex or word codes, or use transparent.

  ```
  BODY {background-color: #ffffff}
  ```

- ● background-image   Denotes the background image for pages. Specify the image you want through that image's URL.

  ```
  BODY {background-image: http://www.page.com/dog.jpg}
  ```

- ● background-repeat   Denotes how the image tiles. Specify repeat-x, repeat-y, or no-repeat.

  ```
  BODY {background-repeat: repeat-y}
  ```

- ● background-attachment   Denotes how the image reacts to a scroll. Specify scroll or fixed.

  ```
  BODY{background-attachment: fixed}
  ```

The positioning/division definitions come into play when you begin working with text and image positioning. Note that these examples are given using a specific item:

- ● `position` Denotes the placement of an image or a division of the page. Specify either `absolute` for specific placement or `relative` for placement relative to other images.

  ```
  <IMG STYLE="position:absolute" SRC="joe.jpg">
  ```

- ● `left` Denotes amount of space allowed from the left of the browser screen when positioning an item. Specify in points (`pt`), inches (`in`), centimeters (`cm`), pixels (`px`), or percentages (`%`).

  ```
  <IMG STYLE="position:absolute; LEFT: 20px;" SRC="joe.jpg">
  ```

- ● `top` Denotes amount of space allowed from the top of the browser screen when positioning an item. Specify in points (`pt`), inches (`in`), centimeters (`cm`), pixels (`px`), or percentages (`%`).

  ```
  <IMG STYLE="position:absolute; LEFT: 20px; TOP: 200pt"
    SRC="joe.jpg">
  ```

- ● `width` Denotes width of image or page division. Specify in points (`pt`), inches (`in`), centimeters (`cm`), pixels (`px`), or percentages (`%`).

  ```
  <IMG STYLE="position:absolute; WIDTH: 80px; LEFT: 20px;
    TOP: 200pt" SRC="joe.jpg">
  ```

- ● `height` Denotes height of image or page division. Specify in points (`pt`), inches (`in`), centimeters (`cm`), pixels (`px`), or percentages (`%`).

  ```
  <IMG STYLE="position:absolute; HEIGHT: 55px WIDTH:80px;
    LEFT: 20px; TOP: 200pt" SRC="joe.jpg">
  ```

- ● `overflow` If the item is too large for the specified height and width, this tells the page what to do with the overflow. Specify `visible`, `hidden`, or `scroll`.

  ```
  <IMG STYLE="position:absolute; overflow: hidden;
  WIDTH: 80px; LEFT: 20px; TOP: 200pt" SRC="joe.jpg">
  ```

- ● `z-index` Denotes an item's position in the layering structure. The lower the number, the lower the layer. An image marker with `20` goes over the top of an image marked with `10`. Specify by number.

  ```
  <IMG STYLE="position:absolute; Z-INDEX: 10; overflow: hidden;
    WIDTH: 80px; LEFT: 20px; TOP: 200pt" SRC="joe.jpg">
  ```

What It All Looks Like

Here again is the style sheet from the online version of this tutorial:

```
<STYLE TYPE-"type/css">
<!-- BODY {background: #FFFFFF}
A:link {color: #80FF00}
A:visited {color: #FF00FF}
H1 {font-size: 24pt; font-family: arial}
H2 {font-size: 18pt; font-family: braggadocio}
H3 {font size:14pt; font-family: desdemona} -->
</STYLE>
```

Now remember, this is all you have to do. No commands exist to put in the text itself, no extra items to place. This style sheet is enacted automatically when one of the listed items appears. Just sit back and watch the show unless you want the same command handled differently in two different parts of the page.

What if I Want the Same Tag Handled Different Ways?

What you do is assign different "classes" of tags. Real simple. Look here:

```
H3.first {font-size: 20pt; color: #FF00FF}
H3.scnd {font size: 18pt; color #DD00FF}
```

See what I did? I labeled the <H3> flags separately by adding a period and then a suffix. I used first for the first type and scnd for the second type. You can use whatever you want. I like these determinants. When you place them on your page, do this in the text:

```
<H3 CLASS="first">This will be affected as outlined in"H3.first"</H3>
<H3 CLASS="scnd">This will be affected as outlined in "H3.scnd"</H3>
```

One Style Sheet—Many Pages

First, create a style sheet following the format given earlier. This is the only thing on the page. Do not make this an HTML document, just the style sheet commands! Make the file so that if I wanted, I could just copy and paste what you have right into my own <HEAD> flags. Which is just about what you are asking the computer to do. The style sheet is a simple text file with a .css suffix.

Let's say you name your style sheet fred. Its name would become fred.css. The suffix is required for browsers to recognize it as a style sheet rather than a simple mesh of letters. Place this command on your page to call for the style sheet:

```
<LINK REL=stylesheet HREF="http://www.yourserver.com/fred.css"
  TYPE="text/css">
```

This is what's happening:

- ● LINK   Tells the browser something must be linked to the page.
- ● REL=stylesheet   Tells the browser that this linked thing is relative to this page as a style sheet.
- ● HREF="*www.yourserver.com/fred.css*"   Denotes where the browser finds the style sheet.
- ● TYPE="text/css"   Tells the browser that what it is reading is text that acts as a cascading style sheet. If the document isn't text with a .css suffix, no dice.

Every page that contains this command is affected by the one style sheet you created and placed in your directory. One sheet, many pages.

FAQs from the HTML Goodies Web Site

Q. I have followed your style sheet tutorial but I'm not getting the effect.

A. The most common reasons include misspelling or miscoding the commands themselves. Check that carefully. If you're positive they are correct, it might be that your browser does not support the commands you are calling for. I'm sorry to say that not all style sheet commands are universal. If you're sure your version does support that specific style sheet command, it might be that the browser has "turned off" the use of style sheets. In Internet Explorer, look under Options or Internet Options, depending on your browser version. In Netscape Navigator, look under Preferences. There you find a box that allows you to "turn on" style sheet capabilities. If it's already clicked to enable style sheets, it has to be your coding.

Can I Use These Style Elements on Individual Items?

Yes, you can. They simply sit inside the flag you are working with. Just make sure to denote them using the STYLE command inside the command. Because they sit inside another command as just a defining command, they don't require a </STYLE> flag. In that position, they affect only what you say they will, rather than the entire page. Like so:

```
<FONT STYLE="font-weight: extra light; font-family: courier">
affected text</FONT>
```

Follow this format and you can define a style for just about any HTML flag. Also, a method of setting up classes of items works pretty much the same way. But that's another chapter.

See these sites for a full list of CSS commands:

- C-Net's Table of Style Sheet Commands:
  http://www.builder.com/Authoring/CSS/table.html?tag=st.bl.7258.dir2.bl_table

- The World Wide Web Consortium's Style Site: http://www.w3.org/Style/

 Point your browser to http://www.htmlgoodies.com/book/stylesheet.html *to see a page with a rather large style sheet. Make sure to look at the source code.*

Positioning Things Precisely on Your Web Page

Wouldn't it be great if you could make a point of placing every item on your page exactly where you want it? Even better, make that placement exactly the same on every browser your page is viewed in? It looks like the answer is a series of cascading style sheet commands that enable you to denote—to the pixel—where you want an item to be pinned up.

You should know that style sheets are not universal at the time of this writing. Netscape Navigator version 4.0 and Explorer 3- and 4-level browsers understand the style commands, but not always exactly the same way. At the moment it's still a bit buggy. In fact, it's quite buggy. Netscape Navigator understands the "standard" style sheet code, but not all the code available through Internet Explorer is standard. You need to make sure those viewing your page are using one of the listed browsers for this to work. I stress the word *need*. If the browser doesn't get these positioning commands, the page looks either like crud or just straight text.

FAQs from the HTML Goodies Web Site

Q. Because style sheets are not universal yet, how do I make it so that people see the pages the way I want them to look on any browser?

A. For one, don't make overly intricate pages, but that's not always possible. The next best step is to not make the style sheet effects vital to the page. Those effects that are vital should be done the traditional way—by placing the tags individually. You could also set up a JavaScript browser choice that first recognizes the type of browser the user is working with and in turn send them to a page made just for that browser. See Chapter 11, "Java Applets and JavaScript."

 I have a few positioning examples for you at http://www.htmlgoodies.com/book/position.html.

Positioning an Image

You may notice soon that I am doing this by including all the style sheet commands inside the items that I am positioning. You might wonder that if these are style sheets, why not put these in a text/.css file or in the HEAD commands inside a <STYLE> flag. You can do that, but to teach this, it is easier to include the commands with the item that I am positioning. In addition, I like doing it this way. To each his own...

You are going to state to the browser that it should position the upper-left corner of an image in a specific plot point on the page. The image in Figure 8.1 is positioned exactly 25 pixels from the top of the page and 170 pixels from the left.

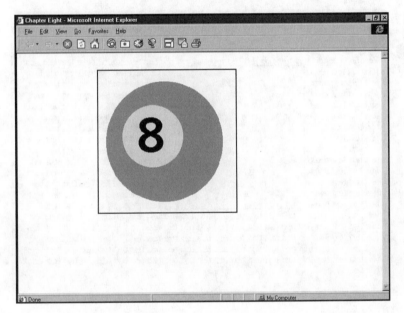

Figure 8.1
Precisely positioning an image with the <STYLE> command.

This is the code I used to place the image at that specific plot point:

```
<IMG STYLE="position:absolute; TOP:35px; LEFT:170px; WIDTH:50px;
HEIGHT:50px" SRC="circle.gif">
```

This is how it works:

- **IMG**   Denotes that this is an image.

- **STYLE=**   Proclaims that what follows are style commands.

- **position:absolute;**   States that the image goes exactly where indicated. If text or another picture is already there, tough—this goes right over the top of it. That is one of the drawbacks to this positioning stuff.

- ○ `TOP:35px; LEFT:170px;` The plot points for the image: 35 pixels down from the top and 170 pixels in from the left.

- ○ `WIDTH:50px; HEIGHT:50px` The height and width of the image itself in pixels.

Notice the semicolon between each section.

Now, when the style sheet commands proclaim that the position is absolute, they're not kidding. Here's the same example with some text on the page. Notice the image didn't care that there was text around (see Figure 8.2). It was put into position and that's that. Keep that in mind when positioning items.

Figure 8.2

A positioned image sitting on top of text.

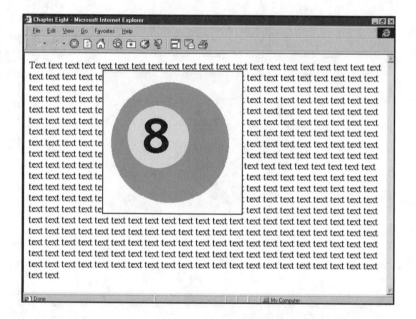

FAQs from the HTML Goodies Web Site

Q. Can I set the position with percentages? That way I could say 20% from the left and the screen size wouldn't be such a problem.

A. I have never seen it done with percentages. My quick experiment with them failed. I would say that pixels are your friends for now.

Positioning Text

You can position text in the same way you positioned an image. Figure 8.3 shows an example where a block of text is positioned 80 pixels from the top of the window and 400 pixels from the left of the browser window.

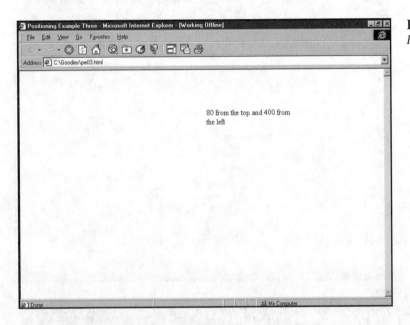

Figure 8.3
Positioned text.

This is the command I used to position the text:

```
<DIV STYLE="position: absolute; TOP:80px; LEFT:400px; WIDTH:200px;
HEIGHT:25px">80 from the top and 400 from the left</DIV>
```

This is what's happening in the code:

- ◗ DIV   Denotes that this is a "division" of the page. A section, if you will.
- ◗ STYLE=   Denotes that some style commands are put to work.
- ◗ position: absolute;   Denotes that this division is placed exactly where you want it placed.
- ◗ TOP:80px; LEFT:400px;   Denotes the positioning of the division.
- ◗ WIDTH:200px; HEIGHT:25px   Denotes the height and width of the division.
- ◗ /DIV   Ends the division section.

The text in Figure 8.3 wrapped to the next line because I made the width of the division too small for the text in it. Figure 8.4 shows the same example with the division width set to 300px.

Figure 8.4

Text does not wrap with the DIV width set higher.

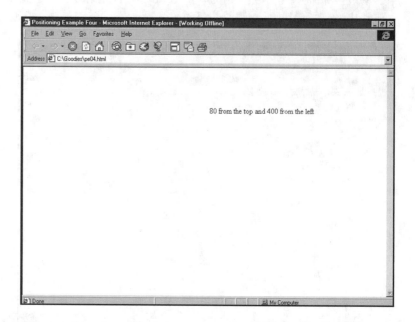

FAQs from the HTML Goodies Web Site

Q. It looks like I could use this to place an image and then place text. If I do it correctly, it appears I could put text across the picture, sort of like a label.

A. Yup. That's true, but I would suggest doing it through layering commands, or through a table cell so that you can ensure that the text is laid on top.

You can add color to the text by adding the following command to the mix. Now the division you set up is filled in with the chosen color (see Figure 8.5).

```
background-color: yellow
```

This works with either word or hex color codes. However, if you use a hex color code, make sure to place a pound sign (#) in front of the six characters, like so: `background-color: #FFFFFF`. This style sheet format is required, unlike basic HTML code.

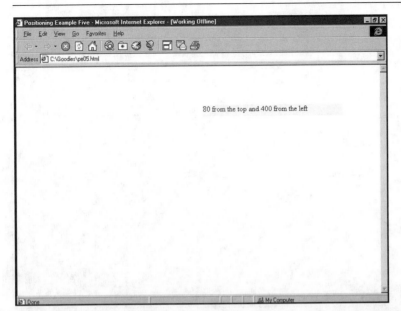

Figure 8.5
Background color added to the text.

FAQs from the HTML Goodies Web Site

Q. How do I set the positioning so I am sure it fits all browser screens from lowest to highest resolution?

A. You really can't make an exact science out of this, but the best answer I have is not to avoid using these commands on just one item. The purpose is more to create the full layout of the page by sectioning it off through divisions. Using it on one item creates problems.

Can I Set Other Styles?

Sure! You can set just about any style command that works on text. Just make sure that you give the division enough space to house the text if you set the font size higher. Figure 8.6 shows an example where I've used as many text-based style commands as I could find before it got boring. The code looked like this:

```
<DIV style="position: absolute; font-family: arial; font-style: italic;
  font-variant:small-caps; font-weight:bold; text-decoration:underline;
  letter-spacing: 2px; top: 80px; width: 400px; left: 400px;
  height: 25px; background-color: yellow">
80 from the top and 400 from the left</DIV>
```

Figure 8.6
Multiple style sheet commands positioned.

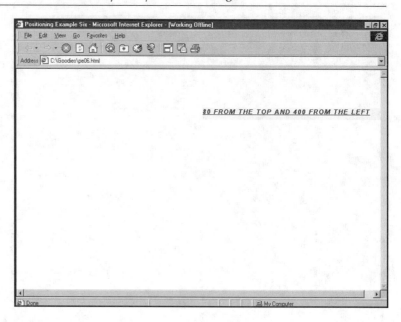

Using Classes and IDs

You can quickly use CSS commands in a great couple of ways. When I speak to people about CSS, the main thing I hear about is the time the sheets save them. They've set up a series of formats for certain commands and the sheet takes care of the styles without any extra work.

The reason I like these two commands in particular is that they're quick, even for those who do not regularly use style sheets. They're easy to understand and save on the fingers by cutting down on the typing. I swear my finger used to be longer.

I had a student call these commands "style sheets lite." That's a good way of thinking about it. People who understand HTML can understand the class and ID format much easier than learning how to create a full style sheet block. I offer this tutorial at the end of this section if for no other reason than the ease of learning.

It should be said that style sheets are not universal as of the writing of this book. I know I've said this before, but here I go again. Your viewer needs to be using Netscape 4.*x* or any version of Explorer. Even then, the commands are very buggy. You do not need to be overly concerned that a browser that doesn't read style sheets is baffled by this. Earlier browsers are great at ignoring commands they do not understand. The text just appears as normal. You could also make a point of using a JavaScript meant to "see" the user's browser and send them to a page that is suited to their system. I have one in the JavaScript section of this book—use classes and IDs, but don't rely heavily on them.

First, you need to have a general understanding of style sheet commands. Don't be put off at this point. They are very easy to grasp. At the end of this tutorial, you will have no trouble implementing them on your page.

This is a style sheet model, so you need to do two things to get started:

1. Set up the style section within the <HEAD> flags.

2. Set up the classes.

FAQs from the HTML Goodies Web Site

Q. Do my inline style sheet commands have to go in the <HEAD> flags?

A. Technically, no. Just make sure they are above the actual item that is calling for them, so that the commands are already in the browser's memory before you call on the effect. That's why I suggest putting them in between the <HEAD> commands; that way they load first and are out of the way without jumbling up your page.

Setting Up the STYLE Section

To get started, you need to insert the following code between your HTML document's <HEAD> flags:

```
<STYLE type="text/css">
<!-- Classes and IDs will go in here... -->
</STYLE>
```

Setting Up the Classes

Now here's the fun part. Let's set up a class. For the sake of argument, let's say I want to set up a class of text that is Arial font, 20pt size, bold, and orange. You could do it this way:

```
<FONT FACE="arial" COLOR="orange" SIZE="+2"><B>text in here</B></FONT>
```

That's a good bit of text, plus I'd have to type it every time I wanted that class of text to come up. If I did a Netscape table where I wanted every cell to have that type of text, I'd have to write it every time for every cell. Yeah, I could copy and paste it again and again, but I'd rather write it out once, assign a class to it, and refer to that class when I want it.

This is the class structure that equals the text:

```
.pumpkin { font-family: arial; font-size: 20; font-style: bold;
color: orange }
```

The class is identified through a period and then a code name. I chose "pumpkin" for this example, mainly because I am setting the text to orange.

What follows are the style sheet commands, separated by semicolons and encased within those fancy braces. See that in the class statement? Place that class statement inside the <STYLE> flags from earlier. It should look like this between your <HEAD> flags:

```
<STYLE type="text/css">
<!-- .pumpkin { font-family: arial; font-size: 20;
  font-style: bold; color: orange }-->
</STYLE>
```

Putting the Classes to Work

Okay, you're ready to go. The class is in place and you can call on it any time you want within the same document. Obviously, if you follow the steps to use an external style sheet, you can use this across pages, but this tutorial is set up to work within the same page.

You can call for this as part of any command that is used to alter text. Figure 8.7 shows a few examples.

Figure 8.7
Showing classes.

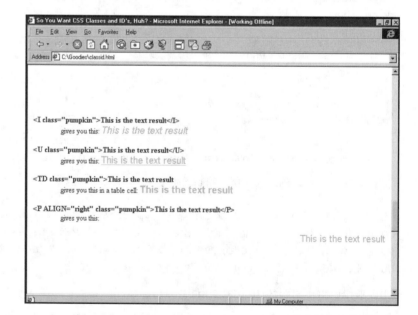

Can I Have More Than One Class?

You also can have as many classes as you'd like, as long as you keep using different code words to denote the many classes. Just keep lining them up, one after the other in the style sheet section up in the <HEAD> flags.

What About Those IDs?

The ID command works exactly the same way as the class command. It exists to enable you to incorporate these style sheet models into JavaScript or DHTML. I wouldn't get too worried just yet; that's still a bit into your HTML future. Unless you are attempting to use these with JavaScript, stick with the class command. You can use the ID command, but it doesn't do anything different or better than the class command. In case you want to give it a whirl, this is how to use it.

In the style section of your <HEAD> flag, denote the ID by a pound sign (#) and a code word. Like so:

```
#pumpkin { font-family: arial; font-size: 20; font-style: bold; color: orange }
```

From that point on, it's the same format as the class commands (see Figure 8.8). Like so:

```
<P ID="pumpkin">This is the text result</P>
```

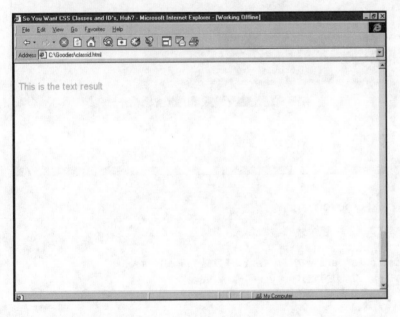

Figure 8.8
Orange text!

The ID and the class formats can be used on the same page. I'm using both on this page, with the same code word. I think these are great. You could put together your entire style sheet system using only these class models. Here's to good pages.

 I have a few more examples of classes and IDs at `http://www.htmlgoodies.com/book/` `classid.html`. *Make sure you look at the source code to see the style sheet commands.*

CSS and Forms

Please note that these commands only work with Microsoft's Explorer browser version 4.0. If you haven't already, you may want to read through my tutorial on cascading style sheets and forms before you attack this one. It helps a great deal. That said, let's get started. Dig the fancy guestbook shown in Figure 8.9 (notice the ToolTip, the thing that looks like a pop-up text box where the mouse cursor is).

Figure 8.9
A multicolored form.

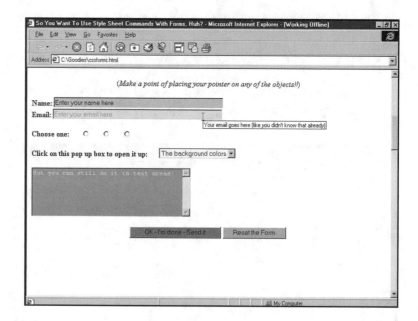

This is the code I used to create the form:

```
<FORM method="post" ACTION="####@######.###">
<b>Name:</b>:
<INPUT TITLE="Your name goes here" TYPE="text" SIZE="50"
 STYLE="background:00BFFF" VALUE="Enter your name here">
<BR>
<b>Email:</b>:
<INPUT TITLE="Your email goes here (like you didn't know that already)"
```

```
   TYPE="text" SIZE="50" STYLE="color:ff0000" STYLE="background:00ff00"
   VALUE="Enter your email here">
<p>
<b>Choose one:</b>
<INPUT TITLE="You can't change the color of checkboxes or radio buttons,
but you can add this text" TYPE="radio" STYLE="background:00BFFF">
<INPUT title="ditto" TYPE="radio" STYLE="background:00BFFF">
<INPUT title="ditto, ditto" TYPE="radio" STYLE="background:00BFFF">
<P>
<b>Click on this pop-up box to open it up:</b>
<SELECT SIZE="1" STYLE="background:ffff00">
<OPTION SELECTED>The background colors
<OPTION>even work with
<OPTION>pop-up boxes.
<OPTION>Cool,Huh?
</SELECT>
<P>
<TEXTAREA TITLE="another yellow box" ROWS="6" COLS="40"
   STYLE="color:00ff00" STYLE="background:ff0000">
But you can still do it in text areas!</TEXTAREA>
<P>
<INPUT TITLE="Send it off to me" TYPE="button" STYLE="background:871eb0"
   VALUE="OK - I'm done - Send it">
<INPUT TITLE="No Wait! Stop!" TYPE="button" STYLE="background:87b4b0"
   VALUE="Reset the Form">
</FORM>
```

Eeeeew! That's gross!

Agreed. You are seeing this in shades of black and white. If you'd like to see this in full living color go to the HTML Goodies site (`http://www.htmlgoodies.com/beyond/cssforms.html`). Wear sunglasses. It's quite bright, but it does the trick for this tutorial. Without looking directly into the awful colors, direct your attention there one more time. The following are four new things you can add to your MSIE guestbook forms:

- Background color
- Separate text color
- ToolTip (pop-up text box) on mouse-over
- Colored buttons

Each of these is created via style sheet commands added right into the form element.

FAQs from the HTML Goodies Web Site

Q. If I use these commands and a person running Netscape uses the forms, will it still work?

A. Yes. The browser just ignores the commands and produces a normal-looking Guestbook form.

Now let's take a look at each of the four new things you've added.

Adding a Background Color

The background color is added to all the items through the background STYLE command. This is a basic text box with the command added to it:

```
<INPUT TYPE="text" SIZE="50" STYLE="background:#00BFFF">
```

That STYLE="background:#00BFFF" is the command that does the trick. Simply add that to any of the form elements, except radio buttons and check boxes, and you get the color denoted by the hex code. For a whole lot of hex codes, see the Goodies color chart in Appendix B.

The reason you can't get color in the radio buttons or check boxes is quite scientific and difficult to understand: They don't have backgrounds to color in. So far, so good? Stunning. Let's move along...

Adding a Separate Text Color

Notice again that text is in the preceding boxes. That's fairly easy to do, as is changing the color of said text. Let's use the previous example, but add some green text. It looks like this:

```
<INPUT TYPE="text" SIZE="50" STYLE="background:#00BFFF"

STYLE="color:#00ff00" VALUE="This text appears in the box">
```

See the two new commands? I added them right after the background commands. They look like this:

```
STYLE="color:###ff00" VALUE="This text appears in the box"
```

The VALUE= command denotes the text and STYLE="color:###" denotes the color of the text. Use it for any form item that accepts text, and you're good to go. Is that stuck on a brain cell? Going forward...

FAQs from the HTML Goodies Web Site

Q. Can I use word color codes in style sheets?

A. Yes.

Adding a ToolTip on Mouse-Over

I think the coolest thing in this tutorial is a little text box popping up if you place your pointer on top of almost any of the items. That box is called a ToolTip. It works the same way the ALT command does with images.

The little yellow box you see is created via a TITLE command. Here's the code that produced the text box in the preceding image. See how the pointer is sitting on it and it's producing a yellow ALT-type box?

```
<INPUT TITLE="Your email goes here (like you didn't know that already)
" TYPE="text" SIZE="50" STYLE="color:#ff0000" STYLE="background:#00ff00"
 VALUE="Enter your email here">
```

That's not so tough, huh? This is a simple trade. You add the TITLE="###" deal and the computer gives you the box. Supply and demand.

FAQs from the HTML Goodies Web Site

Q. Why can't I get a yellow box to pop up on the Select drop-down box?

A. Because the code doesn't enable it. I assume that's because the box itself requires being clicked to work—but that's a guess.

Adding Colored Buttons

There was a time when my e-mail was full of requests for colored form buttons. There was no such thing at the time, so I created one through images and onClick JavaScripts. This is really involved and might not be worth the trouble. This, however, is so super simple I can't believe it. Plus, I've already shown you how to do it. Here's the code for the Send button discussed earlier:

```
<INPUT TITLE="Send it off to me" TYPE="button"
 STYLE="background:#ff00ff" VALUE="OK - I'm done - Send it">
```

There you go. A simple submit button with many of the commands from earlier in this chapter stuck in for good measure.

FAQs from the HTML Goodies Web Site

Q. Is there a way to change the framing around these images to a different color?

A. I don't understand why people want to create items with so much color it would be blinding. Luckily, no.

Now, please. I made the color scheme to prove a point. This is not a contest. Do not attempt to create a form with the worst grouping of hues. I cannot be held responsible if you do. They're your eyes.

CSS and Cursors?

Ah, the cursor. Some like the pointing finger, some like that I-beam-looking thing, and others try to lose the cursor altogether. Whatever your cup of tea, CSS version 2.0 is trying to help. Internet Explorer 4.0 has supported these commands as of January 1998. Netscape Navigator can't be too far behind. Still, I would suggest you use these commands if you find them useful. Navigator browsers are great at simply ignoring commands they don't understand.

Seventeen different cursor properties have been incorporated into standard CSS, so you can be pretty sure some of these work. I say "some of these" because the cursor look depends a lot more on the operating system and settings your user has set. If you didn't know it, you can set your cursor to a whole bunch of different standard settings and even install new cursors that animate. At one time, my cursor was Snoopy on his Sopwith Camel. When I clicked on something it became a TV set with snow on the screen. I'm just a fun guy, I guess.

 You can test out all 17 cursor settings online at `http://www.htmlgoodies.com/beyond/css_cursors.html`. *Make sure you look at the source code to see the style sheet commands.*

The Style Sheet command is incorporated by adding the STYLE="--" format into the anchor command like so:

```
<A HREF="goodies.html STYLE="cursor: auto">Text</A>
```

Of course, you can also put these into a Style Block and alter the cursor for all your links simultaneously (see Figure 8.10):

```
<STYLE>
    link {cursor: crosshair}
</STYLE>
```

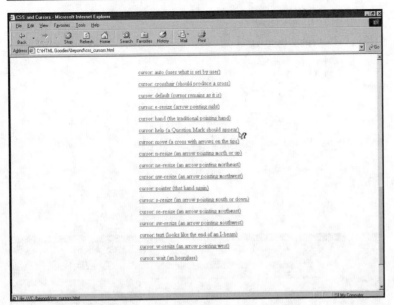

So, here you go. These are the chosen 17. Depending on a lot of factors, you may get it or you may not. Try incorporating a few into your pages. One of the funniest methods I've seen of using these commands was a page where the author set up a list of links and put a different arrow on each link. When you ran your pointer over the links one after the other, the arrow spun around. This is a little thing, but interesting nonetheless:

- cursor: auto (uses what is set by user)
- cursor: crosshair (should produce a cross)
- cursor: default (cursor remains as it is)
- cursor: e-resize (arrow pointing right or *east*)
- cursor: hand (the traditional pointing hand)
- cursor: help (a question mark should appear)
- cursor: move (a cross with arrows on the tips)
- cursor: n-resize (an arrow pointing up or *north*)
- cursor: ne-resize (an arrow pointing *north*east)
- cursor: nw-resize (an arrow pointing *north*west)
- cursor: pointer (that hand again)
- cursor: s-resize (an arrow pointing down or *south*)
- cursor: se-resize (an arrow pointing *south*east)

- cursor: sw-resize (an arrow pointing southwest)
- cursor: text (looks like the end of an I-beam)
- cursor: w-resize (an arrow pointing left or west)
- cursor: wait (an hourglass)

There you go. Use them wisely.

 Try the 17 out at http://www.htmlgoodies.com/book/cursor.html.

CSS and the Scrollbar

Do you like my scrollbar hown in Figure 8.11?

Figure 8.11
The scrollbar is the same orange as the background.

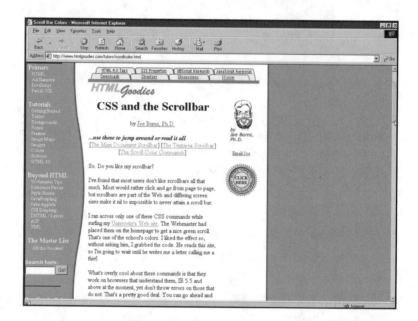

I've found that most users don't like scrollbars all that much. Most would rather click and go from page to page, but scrollbars are part of the Web and differing screen sizes make it nil to impossible to never attain a scrollbar.

 This tutorial is online at http://www.htmlgoodies.com/tutors/scrollcolor.html.

I ran across only one of these CSS commands while surfing my university's Web site. The Webmaster had placed them on the homepage to get a nice green scroll. That's one of the school's colors. I liked the effect, so without asking him, I grabbed the code. He reads this site, so I'm going to wait until he writes me a letter calling me a thief.

What's overly cool about these commands is that they work on browsers that understand them, IE 5.5 and above at the moment, yet don't throw errors on those that do not. That's a pretty good deal. You can go ahead and plop these on your page and not worry about any cross-browser concerns.

Furthermore, the cool thing about these commands is that they not only affect the main browser scroll, but any scroll that appears through form elements or iframe flags, discussed in Chapter 13, "Explorer-Specific Tutorials and DHTML."

Moreover, what's cool is that you can affect each scrollbar separately.

The last cool thing is setting the main command to the same color as the background of the page so that the scroll basically disappears except for the little button the user moves up and down.

End of statements involving the word "cool".

The Main Document Scrollbar

I got the effect on the document's main scrollbar, the one on the far right, using a style block in the <HEAD> flags of the document. It looks like this:

```
<STYLE TYPE="text/css">
BODY
{
scrollbar-base-color: orange;
scrollbar-arrow-color: green;
scrollbar-DarkShadow-Color: blue;
}
</STYLE>
```

Now that you see the code, look to the right and pick out what each element does. You may need to look rather closely to find the effect of the scrollbar-base-color command. Hint: Look closely at the border around the arrow and moveable button.

Hey! That was a lousy hint. It basically told you the answer.

The Textarea Scrollbar

Before I explain any further, I wanted to show you a textarea box with a colorful scrollbar. I made it using inline STYLE attributes.

I am putting this text in to make a scrollbar appear in the textarea box. Try it out for yourself.

This is the code:

```
<FORM>
<TEXTAREA COLS="10" ROWS="10"
STYLE="scrollbar-base-color:pink;scrollbar-arrow-color:purple;">
Text in the box
</TEXTAREA>
</FORM>
```

I changed the colors a little to show that, as with all CSS commands, the commands closest to the element win. The inline commands in the textarea box override the commands that altered the main scroll on the far right. If I didn't override the main commands, the colors would have simply been transferred to the textarea box.

The Scrollbar Color Commands

You can take the format for using the commands from here also. Here I'd like to simply show you each of the commands and what they do. You can use these commands in tandem as you've seen previously.

You need to go online to a new page so that I can isolate the effect from the style sheet commands that already appear on this page. Plus, the color changes don't show up very well in this black-and-white book.

 See the different textarea boxes and their colors, online at `http://www.htmlgoodies.com/tutors/scrollcolor02.html`*. Each of the textarea boxes display a command and what it does.*

This is the list just for your reference:

- `scrollbar-arrow-color` Changes the small arrow at the very top and bottom of the scrollbar.
- `scrollbar-base-color` Colors the overall scrollbar.
- `scrollbar-DarkShadow-Color` Alters the color of the bottom and right-side "sides."
- `scrollbar-Face-Color` Adds color to the top of the buttons, scroll, and track.
- `scrollbar-Highlight-Color` Adds color to the track and the left and top "sides."
- `scrollbar-Shadow-Color` This acts such as the previous `scrollbar-DarkShadow-color` command, but with not as much depth to the color.
- `scrollbar-Track-Color` Just as it says. It adds a flat color to the track of the scrollbar.

Use them all and make some really terrible scrollbars, or use them wisely and you can make a scrollbar that actually compliments the work that you do.

As always, these are style sheet commands so be very careful of the capitalization. It matters.

 See the style sheets in action for yourself. Remember that you must be using IE 5.0 or higher. Go to http://www.htmlgoodies.com/book/scrollbarcolor.html.

Using Layer Commands

You can almost guess from the title of this section what these commands do. If you have already read the cascading style sheet tutorials in this chapter, you know it is possible to position an image on a page down to the pixel. You should also know that if there happens to be text where you position the image, tough. The image lays over the text. You have, in effect, created two layers, one over the other.

To this point, when I talked about a command only working in one browser or another, I said the command worked only in IE. Well, the tables have turned. Layers only work in Netscape Navigator browsers.

In this tutorial you learn how to use what might be considered a mistake in position of images to your advantage. You can place items on top of each other via the layer commands. You can place text over an image, place an image in the corner of another image, or lay three images on top of a background image. I've found these layer commands quite helpful. I bet you do, too. So let's get started.

Let us imagine I have these three images, as shown in Figure 8.12.

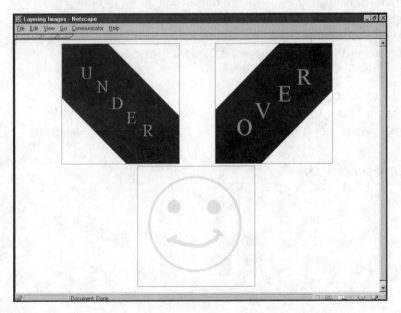

Figure 8.12
Three separate images.

All three images are wonderful by themselves, but I would really like to lay one on top of another, sort of build an "X" with the first two layers and put the smiley face over both of them as shown in Figure 8.13.

Figure 8.13
Three layered images.

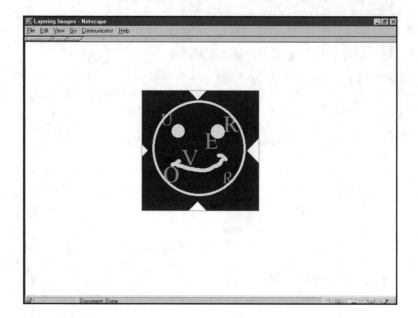

Neat, huh? Let me state right up front that I am able to make such an "X" because I made the images that lay on top transparent, so you could see through the top images. If the top image, the smiley face, weren't transparent, it would simply cover the bottom two images. See the information on transparent images in Chapter 3, "Adding Images and Backgrounds," if you don't already know how this is done.

What you see in Figure 8.13 are three images, all the same size. I did that on purpose. They are all 250×250 pixels. I then denoted that each image be placed in the same space. I then denoted that each image is a layer section in and of itself. Here's the code that makes the layered image:

```
<LAYER NAME="under" LEFT=250 TOP=100>
<IMG SRC=x1.gif>
</LAYER>
<LAYER NAME="over" LEFT=250 TOP=100>
<IMG SRC=x2.gif>
</LAYER>
<LAYER NAME="overagain" LEFT=250 TOP=100>
<IMG SRC=x3.gif>
</LAYER>
```

This is what's happening in the code:

- LAYER Denotes to the browser that this is a layer. Please note that the first layer you place is the bottom layer. They continue to go over top as you add layers.

- NAME Names the layer, obviously. This doesn't come into much play in this tutorial, but is important in later layer get-togethers.

- LEFT and TOP Denote the image placement *on the browser window.* Maybe I should state that again...*on the browser window!*

  LEFT is from the left of the screen to the upper-left corner of the image. TOP is from the top of the screen to the upper-left corner of the image. The numbers are pixels. You play with numbers a lot to get the image exactly where you want it. Think of the browser screen width as around 600 pixels and the height as around 500 pixels.

- IMG SRC Acts such as any old image command. You can add HEIGHT and WIDTH if you'd like.

- </LAYER> Ends each layer.

As shown, it is necessary to do one of these LAYER commands for each layer you want.

FAQs from the HTML Goodies Web Site

Q. Is layering the same as absolute positioning?

A. Very close. The difference is that in layering, the items can be given a pecking order, sometimes called a "Z" axis. This one goes on top of this one, on top of this one, on top of this one, and so on. Positioning sets it, so the last one listed goes on top. These layers enable you to have an image move horizontally through multiple images. You can then denote which goes on top and which goes underneath the horizontal image.

Q. Can I use the layer commands to set up an imagemap like your fake image?

A. Yes, it's necessary to just surround the image command with the hypertext commands to activate the image.

 I have a few examples of layering that incorporate JavaScript at http://www.htmlgoodies. com/book/layering.html. *It knocks your socks off, so don't wear your shoes while looking.*

Layering in General

The process of creating a layered image is not difficult. However, a few items might trip you up. I learned most of this from a lot of trial and error, so the following are a few items you should know before you waste time messing around.

Layered images do not react to ALIGN or CENTER commands. They do not care if text is in the way, they place things right where you say to place them without any regard for what's around.

See the three-layered image in Figure 8.13? All three images are placed 250 pixels from the left of the screen and 100 from the top. That's why they layer. I have them all in the same place. The thing is that the layered image is at 250 in and 100 down no matter what. You must write the rest of your page accordingly, leaving a big enough text space so that the image has a place to sit. If not, it layers directly over what is sitting in its space. Which itself might be a neat effect.

If you want it to sit in the open such as mine, you need to leave a big space right where you want it to sit. I do it by adding these:

```
<P>   <P>
```

Each one of those adds two open lines. You need the   to add a space on a line. You see, just putting in a lot of <P> commands doesn't do it. There has to be something on a line for the next <P> command to work. You can't use any characters because you need the blank line; use a space. That space is created by . And no, just putting a space by hitting the spacebar doesn't do it.

The layers do not have to be in the exact same space. I have them that way for demonstration purposes. If you have two oddly shaped images and you only want part of one overlapping the other, it works. The best method I have found for placing through layering? Creating a deck of cards fanning out in a hand. Clever. You have to play with the LEFT and TOP pixel numbers a bit to find the correct placement.

Don't go crazy layering things because it currently only works with Netscape 4.0 or later. If you have a chance to see a layered page in a browser window that doesn't support the commands, do it. You'll see how bad it looks when the commands aren't supported. All the images show up, they just aren't where you want them to be. Bummer.

Part IV

Beyond HTML

9   *Behind the Scenes on Your Web Site*

10   *Sound and Video*

11   *Java Applets and JavaScript*

12   *Common Gateway Interface (CGI)*

13   *Explorer-Specific Tutorials and DHTML*

14   *Building Web Site Banners*

15   *Other Stuff You Should Really Know*

Chapter 9

Behind the Scenes on Your Web Site

Try this for fun. Without telling them what you are doing, ask a few of your friends what the <HEAD> commands on an HTML document are for. I bet you get a variety of answers. I received a letter from a person who really chewed me out for not involving the HEAD commands in the HTML Goodies primers. I asked why this struck such a chord with her and she answered that the commands have to be in the document for it to work correctly. "No they don't," I replied. "Yes they do," she replied back. "No they don't," I wrote back. "Do too," she replied. The conversation went downhill from there.

Actually we're both right. This is a very basic HTML document format. You've seen this example a hundred times I'm sure:

```
<HTML>
<HEAD>
<TITLE></TITLE>
</HEAD>
<BODY>
Displays in browser window
</BODY>
</HTML>
```

When I was learning to use HTML, I saw that same example over and over again. I thought the HEAD commands made things pop up in the blue bar at the top. You see, the <TITLE> commands were all I ever saw inside. Because I was left to my wits to learn this language, I figured I didn't need those commands. I wrote without them for a good long time. None of the pages ever seemed incorrect or flawed, so I never felt I needed them.

It wasn't until I started playing with JavaScript and META commands that I even cared what they did. This is all true. When I teach HTML in a classroom, I do not incorporate the HEAD commands until after the students learn to manipulate text with bold, italic, and other types of commands, and that's usually well into the semester.

I'm sure that statement is right now driving someone out of his skull. Again, I say what would you tell students who are just being introduced to the language about what those commands do? Header commands are a great part of HTML. I know that now. I still think they should be taught separately as something that can be incorporated rather than something that is required.

I don't know why I told you that…I guess I just love sharing with you people. So let's get started.

What the <HEAD> *Commands Actually Do*

The HEAD commands do three things:

- Contain information regarding the document. This data does not appear in the browser window when the page is loaded. The data is mainly used for helping search engines with page descriptions, browsers with base domains, and other data not generally regarded as display content.

- Separate the page into two distinct sections. Ever go into a page that doesn't load, but somehow the title is up there? This is inside the HEAD commands.

- Load first and the stuff included between them is run first by the browser.

FAQs from the HTML Goodies Web Site

Q. A friend told me she uses the HEAD command because it helps the page load faster. Any truth to that?

A. If she means that she incorporates in the HEAD commands items the page will need later so that the page doesn't load each event separately, yes. What she says has a ring of truth.

Q. I am using an HTML helper program that puts the HEAD commands in for me every time I write a page. Because I don't put anything other than the <TITLE> commands in there, should I take the HEAD commands out?

A. Nah. The effort isn't worth the benefit. The HEAD commands are only 12 extra characters. They're not slowing the page. Let them go. You may update the pages later and need them.

Information Regarding the Document

The following commands are used to describe information contained within the HTML document.

TITLE *Commands*

This is the command that appears most often between the HEAD commands. It places text within the color bar at the very top of the browser.

I must say I liked it before the newer-version browsers placed their names after the TITLE text. That wasn't always the case. It was just text you wrote. In addition, if you wrote a lot of TITLE commands, they were all compiled, one after the other. You could have animation in the blue bar at the top—it was great. The newer browsers don't go for more than one TITLE command these days.

Man, I'm starting to sound like Dana Carvey's Grumpy Old Man. There were lots of TITLE commands. And that's the way I like it!

At this point in time you begin constructing the fully functioning HEAD command extraordinaire:

```
<HEAD>
<TITLE>Big Fat Head Commands</TITLE>
</HEAD>
```

META *Commands*

I have a full tutorial on META commands and what they do later on. You should check it out for gobs of META commands information. Here, I quickly outline some of the more popular ones:

- `<META NAME="keywords" CONTENT="key,word,key,word">` Offers key words to the search engines that use them in their searches.

- `<META NAME="description" CONTENT="Great page! Come see!">` Offers a description of the page for search engines that use them.

- `<META NAME="generator" CONTENT="Notepad">` Tells search engines what program was used to create the document.

- `<META NAME="author" CONTENT="Some Body">` Tells search engines who wrote the document.

- `<META NAME="copyright" CONTENT="Copyright © 1997 Me">` Tells search engines...blah, blah, blah.

● `<META NAME="expires" CONTENT="15 September 2000">` Automatically expires the document in the search engine's database. This is equal to a delete in those search engines that support the command.

Our super duper HEAD command section grows to this when you add those commands:

```
<HEAD>
<TITLE>Big Fat Head Commands</TITLE>
<META NAME="keywords" CONTENT="key,word,key,word">
<META NAME="description" CONTENT="Great page! Come see!">
<META NAME="generator" CONTENT="Notepad">
<META NAME="author" CONTENT="Some Body">
<META NAME="copyright" CONTENT="Copyright © 1997 Me">
<META NAME="expires" CONTENT="15 September 2000">
</HEAD>
```

The BASE HREF *Command*

The BASE HREF command is one of those commands some tell me has to be used, while others can't see a reason for it. You decide for yourself. This is the format:

```
<BASE HREF="HTTP://www.htmlgoodies.com/>
```

The command acts as a reference for the remainder of the page. When you use BASE HREF, whatever you place between its quotation marks is added in front of any links you write. For example, I wrote this link:

```
<A HREF="page.html">
```

Because my document employs the BASE HREF command, the link now becomes http://www.htmlgoodies.com/page.html.

"So what?" you say. "It already does that on my machine." That's true and it will continue to do that as long as the document remains on the site that possesses the correct BASE HREF. What if someone downloads the page and runs it off of her hard drive? The link would be dead without the BASE HREF command. With it, the domain is added and the link works from anywhere.

I have yet to adopt the BASE HREF command because of the setup of my pages; I include page jumps a lot. If I use a BASE HREF, the page jump only works on the server. If the document is on the hard drive, it doesn't jump because the BASE HREF command doesn't stop adding the domain to it. However, when the page is posted to the Net it tends to reload the page with the entire domain attached, rather than jumping to the page section I want. This is way too much of a hassle.

Let's continue making our super duper HEAD command section:

```
<HEAD>
<TITLE>Big Fat Head Commands</TITLE>
<META NAME="keywords" CONTENT="key,word,key,word">
<META NAME="description" CONTENT="Great page! Come see!">
<META NAME="generator" CONTENT="Notepad">
<META NAME="author" CONTENT="Some Body">
<META NAME="copyright" CONTENT="Copyright © 1997 Me">
<META NAME="expires" CONTENT="15 September 2000">
<BASE HREF="HTTP://www.htmlgoodies.com/>
</HEAD>
```

FAQs from the HTML Goodies Web Site

Q. Can I put any HTML code, such as an image, into the HEAD commands?

A. Yeah. It runs first and appears first on the page. This is not a good idea though. Keep what is in the head commands simply for description and assistance to the visible text that appears between the BODY flags. If for no other reason, to keep it all straight in your own mind.

Parts Two and Three

Earlier I said that the HEAD commands break the page into two distinct sections and also are loaded and run first. That comes into play when you have a script of some sort. Let's take JavaScript, for example.

If you place your JavaScripts in the HEAD commands, they are run first. The JavaScript usually has two parts: a script and something that calls for that script to place an object on the page.

Separating the script from the element that calls for it speeds the use. The script is already running by the time the call is made for its services.

As for separating the document into two parts, it is often possible that two entities don't run together. Again, I use two JavaScripts for an example. Placing one inside the HEAD commands and the other inside the BODY commands tends to separate them enough to calm the fight. They often then both run.

What about style sheet commands? If you are running any on your page, you need to denote to the browsers where to find the CSS files or what each class means.

Adding a JavaScript and some style sheet commands to our super duper HEAD command section, you get the finished product:

```
<HEAD>
<TITLE>Big Fat Head Commands</TITLE>
<META NAME="keywords" CONTENT="key,word,key,word">
<META NAME="description" CONTENT="Great page! Come see!">
<META NAME="generator" CONTENT="Notepad">
<META NAME="author" CONTENT="Some Body">
<META NAME="copyright" CONTENT="Copyright © 1997 Me">
<META NAME="expires" CONTENT="15 September 2000">
<BASE HREF="HTTP://www.htmlgoodies.com/>
<SCRIPT LANGUAGE="JavaScript">
</SCRIPT>
<STYLE="text/css">
</STYLE>
</HEAD>
```

Well, there it is. The ultimate HTML document HEAD section. Of course, all that is not needed, but it can't hurt to add it. This helps search engines and some of your site users. I've altered the program I sometimes use to write HTML to include the six META commands already. I'm not so sure about the BASE HREF command, though...

 I have an HTML document that uses multiple commands between the HEAD commands at http://www.htmlgoodies.com/book/headcommands.html. Make sure you look at the source code.

Declaring Your Version of HTML

If you've made your way through the HTML Goodies site, you probably have looked at the source of some of my documents. I know some of you are looking because every now and again, I get a letter asking what that strange, cryptic command at the top stands for. If you don't know what I'm talking about, this is the command:

```
<!DOCTYPE HTML PUBLIC "-//W3C//DTD HTML 4.0//EN">
```

That's a strange looking thing, huh? This is called an *HTML Declaration*. Basically it's declaring what version of HTML the browser is to use when reading this document. It also tells the viewer, if they care to look. This is long, but rather easy to understand. This is what it means:

- !DOCTYPE HTML PUBLIC Proclaims this is an HTML document type that can be read by public browsers.

- ⊙ -//W3C   Represents the HTML organization that proclaims what HTML flags are to be considered standard. You can visit the World Wide Web Consortium's (hence, W3C) page at http://www.w3.org and read about HTML until your brain is full.

- ⊙ //DTD HTML 4.0   Stands for Document Type Description Hypertext Mark-Up Language (version) 4.0.

- ⊙ //EN   Means the document will be written in English.

FAQs from the HTML Goodies Web Site

Q. Must I use an HTML declaration? What if I don't?

A. This is up to you. I've been told by those in my school's computer science department that if you fail to use a declaration, the default HTML version, usually the highest version out, is enacted. At the moment, that's 4.0.

Q. Do I put the declaration between the HEAD commands?

A. No. It goes on the page first thing—even before the HTML command.

My assumption is that once you read this, you will right away ask if you need to hurry and go put the command on your pages. I can tell you that I use it on every page now. I started putting it on when I first learned about it. Some of my very early pages do not have the command and I'm in no real hurry to get it on them, mainly because the pages use very early (and very basic) commands that do not belong to a higher version of HTML. Besides, I've been told the default is the highest HTML version. I would not be doing myself any good by altering the page.

I would suggest using the declarations if you are trying to write in HTML 4.0, specifically XML (extensible mark-up language). I have tutorials on both with sample declarations in the book. See Appendix A, "Everything You Need to Know About HTML 4.0," and Chapter 15, "Other Stuff You Should Really Know," respectively.

These are the two rules of thumb that one of the HTML big-heads told me: Use the declaration if you're using META commands or plan to use HTML validators.

 For an example of a page using an HTML declaration intended to enable the page to run HTML 4.0 go to http://www.htmlgoodies.com/book/declair.html.

Web Pages Without the .html Extension

After I put up HTML Goodies I began getting letters asking how I post pages that do not require the .html extension. To some it may seem simple enough, but to those new to the HTML game, it isn't. So this is the trick.

This tutorial is online at http://www.htmlgoodies.com/directory/. *Please note the* .html *extension is not on* directory—*just the slash afterward.*

My assumption is that you have a WWW site right now, correct? That means that you have a general idea that you need to place files from your computer to a server, so the whole world can see them.

When you upload, you are uploading to a directory. That directory is a little section of the server's hard drive set aside and given a name. Let's say your home page address is as follows:

```
http://www.fred.com/~wwwuser
```

The name of the directory that you upload or FTP all your files to is named wwwuser. See that? What you may not know is that the directory has a certain set of rules that it follows. The main rule is that it enables any and everybody to look at its contents. This is a WWW directory and people can access it, right? Another rule is that you are given personal access, with the use of a login and password, to place and remove files.

The rule you may not be aware of—and the one that will be of the utmost importance to this tutorial—is that the directory has been told to look for a specific filename when someone logs on. Notice the address again. It doesn't call for any specific page. It could, of course, just by adding a slash and then the page name, such as:

```
http://www.fred.com/~wwwuser/joe.html
```

But that's not what happened. The directory's name is all that was listed. Again, look at the online example. This is the URL:

```
http://www.htmlgoodies.com/directory/
```

None of these addresses calls for a certain page, but one comes up. That's because of the third rule I spoke of earlier. I hope you were paying attention...and spit out that gum.

The Index Page

When you got your WWW site, you were told to give the home page a certain name. The vast majority of the time that name is index.html. Why? Because the directory that holds your WWW files has been told when someone tries to get access to the directory, by default, display the index.html page. Get it?

Don't get flustered if your default page isn't index.html. I have been on many different servers. One wanted www.html, the other wanted HomePage.html (note the capitalization), and a third wanted default.html. My Webmaster wizards here at HTML Goodies tell me that you can configure a server to search for `booger.html` if you really want. But that would lead to a sticky situation. Rim-shot. (Thank you folks, good night! Try the veal.)

How to Do It

It took me a while to get to this, didn't it? I tend to ramble. The rule of thumb here is to remember that any *subdirectory* (a directory inside a directory) retains all the properties of the parent directory. Any directory inside a bigger directory will do what the big directory does just because. That's my best "Gen-X" speak.

If you make a directory inside of `wwwuser`, that directory will also display its own `index.html`. If you make a smaller directory inside that directory, it will display its own `index.html`. Get it?

FAQs from the HTML Goodies Web Site

Q. I am following your tutorial on losing the `.html`. The problem is that now I have two different index.html pages. I have already erased my original by saving the new one right over it. How do I solve this?

A. I have done that at least 10 times. The best way to keep it straight is to create the same directory structure on your computer's hard drive as is on your server. If your WWW address uploads to a directory called wwwuser, create a directory on your hard drive named the same. Then create the subdirectories so that your computer reflects the server. Now you lessen your problems. My hard drive is set up as an exact duplicate of HTML Goodies. Of course, always make backups. You don't know this, but HTML Goodies is fully posted on three servers. You only get to see one. If that one crashes, the next one can be used immediately.

Creating a Directory

I have received so many letters telling me that I go the long way in making a directory. True, software programs are out there that will do all this with the click of a button, but in case you don't have such an animal, try this. If you do have a program that will do all this on-the-fly, go nuts. You may save yourself a few hours by first calling to ask your server people how they want you to create subdirectories, or if they want you to create them at all.

I know this listed just a minute ago, but so you can avoid flipping back and forth, this is the process again:

1. Telnet in to your site.
2. Get to your directory. Usually when you Telnet into your site, you are either in your WWW directory (where you keep all your files) or in a previous directory.

3. Try typing : `cd` *[name of your www directory]* at the prompt.

4. If that doesn't work, type `cd` `..` (two periods) and then try Step 3 again. If you don't get any errors, you're there.

5. If you like, you can type `ls` at the prompt; that gives you a listing of all your files.

6. To create the directory, type `mkdir` *[directory name]*.

7. Do another `ls` command; you should see that directory sitting there.

8. Some servers need for that directory to be "turned on" before anyone can use it. Just to be safe, type `chmod` *[directory name]* `a+rx` now. If the server doesn't take that command, try substituting `a+rx` with `777`.

9. Log out. You're done.

Now you have a second directory sitting inside your `wwwuser` directory. That directory responds to its own `index.html`. Let's say you named the directory *skippy*. Now you can tell people to go to the following URL and they'll get the main page with no html. Now, how easy it that?

    http://www.fred.com/~wwwuser/skippy

 For an example of losing the `.html` *across many pages go to* `http://www.htmlgoodies.com/book/.`

Chapter 10

Sound and Video

Sounds on the Net are a great thing. If you have a computer equipped with a sound card and a few shareware programs, you can hear as much as you care to download. Van Halen is my favorite music group. I was able to download the sound files of two new songs before their Greatest Hits album came out. I still bought the CD, of course. The sounds are neat, but are not quite the quality of my Sony home sound system. I can rattle pictures off the walls with that pup.

This is not to say that only music can be played over the Net. Any sound—from a dog barking to full orchestras—can be turned into a computer file and played over the Web. This chapter covers two ways of offering sounds over the Internet: using Helper applications and embedding the sounds.

FAQs from the HTML Goodies Web Site

Q. Before I ask about putting a sound on my page, I have to ask...is it legal to do that?

A. If you wrote and performed the song, yes. If you didn't, you get into a gray area. Permission conquers all in discussions of copyright. If you have permission to play the music, you're good to go. BMI and ASCAP (the two big music licensing firms) are now selling site licenses. Your server may have one. If so, all you need to do is report to them you're playing the song. In turn, they report it back to the firm. Past that, just grabbing a portion of your favorite group's music and playing it is treading on thin ice. They might care, they might not. Even if you don't play the entire song, they might still get upset. Be prepared to take the sound down if you are asked to.

When I posted the first version of this tutorial, it was the most popular one on the HTML Goodies site. The tutorial is still visited often. Go to `http://www.htmlgoodies.com/tutors/` `embed.html` *to see it yourself.*

Helper Applications

This discussion is a bit out of date as plug-ins are used a great more than helper applications are now. Read it if you'd like. It'll give a quick sense of history.

When the World Wide Web got started, back when Mosaic was the browser and this new thing called Netscape Navigator 1.0 had just come out, sounds were available. They were played with the use of a helper application.

Helper applications are programs that were called upon by the Netscape Navigator browser, but were not part of the Navigator itself. (You can still do it all this way, don't get me wrong. Plug-ins, covered later, are making helper applications a bit of an endangered species.) You're using helper applications right now. Every browser has a different way of displaying the helper applications it's currently using. In some versions of Navigator, for instance, just click the Options menu, choose Preferences, and then choose Helper Applications—there they are. Roll down the list and you see a lot of extra applications and Ask User statements. To play a sound file (.wav, .au, or .aiff), you need to attach an application that the browser can use to play the sound.

I used (and still do) a program called WHAM. This is great and plays all types of sound files.

The following is how helper applications work:

- ○ The browser goes and gets the sound file, downloading the entire thing into a temporary directory.
- ○ The helper application is launched after the file is complete. Some helper applications, such as RealPlayer, actually launch and begin playing the file before it is completely downloaded.
- ○ The operating system (Windows 3*x*, Windows 95, MacOS, and the like) loads the sound file into the application.
- ○ The application plays the sound.

I always thought it was a pretty good system. Yeah, it took a bit of time, especially using a 14.4 or 28.8 modem, but it always worked.

Figure 10.1 shows a helper application playing a sound file on the HTML Goodies site. The helper application is one you find on most computers running Windows, the Media Player. All I did was go into Helper Applications mentioned earlier and assigned it to play certain types of sound files.

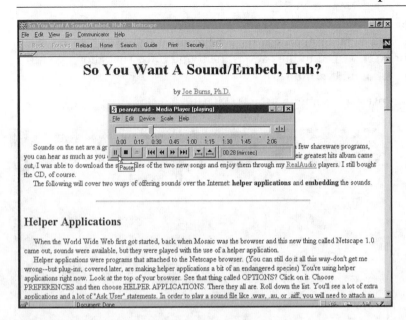

Figure 10.1
Helper application playing a sound file.

Putting Sound on the Page

Follow this format if you have a sound you'd like to offer. This makes your Web visitors use a helper application.

```
<A HREF="http://www.yoursite.com/filename.wav">Click Here</A>
```

Of course, sound formats other than .wav exist. Keep reading for information on a few more you can use.

Notice that the preceding code is nothing more than a simple link format pointed right at the sound file. All you need to do is offer the sound file. Place it in the same directory as the page that calls for it; the browsers take it from there. You just sit back and watch it happen. Just be sure to FTP-transfer the sound file to your site as binary or raw data; any other way can corrupt it. You can read more about FTP transfers in Primer 7, "Graduation Day."

Embedding Sound on a Page

Embedding a sound means that you include the sound commands in your HTML document and use a plug-in to run it.

Plug-ins are programs that help your browser perform at a higher level. They are called *plug-ins* because they must have the browser open to work. Helper applications are independent of the browser. Plug-ins are not.

A sound plug-in does the same thing the helper application does, but the sound plug-in works inside the browser window rather than starting up another program or having WHAM pop up and the browser pushed to the back as the sound runs. That allows you to play with the page while the sound is running.

Figure 10.2 shows a plug-in playing a sound on the HTML Goodies site.

Figure 10.2

Plug-in application playing a sound file.

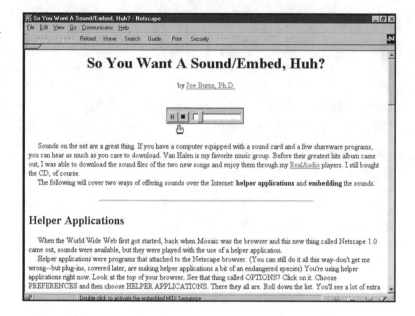

Notice the hand on the player that pops up? It is pointing with two fingers. I set up this embed so that the user has to click to start it, but it can start all by itself.

If you head to the Netscape home page or to Yahoo! and enter plug-ins, you are able to scan a ton of little programs that cover everything from sound to video to 3D VRML (Three-dimensional Virtual Reality Modeling Language). They all have specific requirements for browser types and platforms. Be sure to read the instructions before downloading. Not all four plug-ins that I installed dealt with sounds, but they have all worked right away.

If you're using a later version of Netscape Navigator, you might have run into something odd: a page that requires a plug-in and a pop up in your browser window asking if you'd like to get the appropriate plug-in. If you answer yes, it takes you to the Netscape plug-in page and you then download what you need.

FAQs from the HTML Goodies Web Site

Q. The tutorial about embedding sound is fine, but how do I make my sounds?

A. Look for a utility called Sound Recorder (or something similar). Open it. It usually looks a lot like the controls on a cassette machine If you have a sound card, you most likely have a microphone and CD player too. That recording device simply starts recording what is coming through the speakers when you hit the red button. When you have the piece you want, save it as one of three formats: .wav (a PC format), .au (a Sun format), MP3 (a CD quality format), or .mid (the MIDI format). Although other formats exist, these are the most popular on the Net.

An example of a Sound Recorder is shown in Figure 10.3.

Figure 10.3
Sound recorder tool panel (Windows 95).

Note

What is MIDI?

This is an acronym that stands for Musical Instrument Digital Interface. That's a program that acts as a go-between for an instrument and something that creates the sound. Sort of like running a guitar through a computer and out a speaker.

MIDI files work over the Net like a little program that runs the sound card. The MIDI file is not simply read like a .wav or a .au file. The MIDI file sort of "plays" the sound card. It tells the sound card what note to produce and for what duration. Put enough of them together and it sounds like music.

The Format for an EMBED *Command*

I'm going to show how to embed a sound file on your Web page. In this example I'll use a MIDI file, but this works with just about any sound format. In fact, if you have the ability to play MIDI files, and have already visited this tutorial online, you probably clicked and have listened to a MIDI of the Peanuts theme. I like it. This is the code you need:

```
<EMBED SRC="sound.mid" AUTOSTART=FALSE LOOP=
WIDTH=145 HEIGHT=55 ALIGN="CENTER">
</EMBED>
```

I should probably make it clear that EMBED is not an HTML standard command. At the time of this writing, it only works with the Netscape Navigator browser. If you use an EMBED command on your page, you should follow it immediately with this command:

```
<BGSOUND="###">
```

That basic command allows those running Internet Explorer to hear the sound you've embedded on your page. If you add one, add the other. Be good to all your viewers. The following is how EMBED works:

- **EMBED**   Tells the browser an embedded sound is here—go get the plug-in. Embed commands are associated with plug-ins.

- **HEIGHT/WIDTH**   Deal with the embedded object's size on the page. That little control panel at the top of the page in Figure 10.2 was created with a size of 145×55 high. You can read more about HEIGHT and WIDTH commands in Chapter 3, "Adding Images and Backgrounds." The embedded object is offered almost as if it were an image; that way the browser understands what the embedded thing is.

- **SRC**   Stands for *source*. It tells the browser where to go to get the audio file.

- **AUTOSTART**   Deals with whether you want the sound to play by itself or by the viewer starting the file after the plug-in box pops up. TRUE starts the file straightaway; FALSE prompts the viewer to play it.

- **LOOP**   Works basically the same way as AUTOSTART. TRUE loops the sound so that it plays forever. Make the loop FALSE if you only want it played once.

- **HIDDEN**   Works to enable you to hide the controls. Use YES and NO. By the way: If you hide the control, it might be a good idea to AUTOSTART the sound.

Note

The browser does one of three things if no plug-ins are available

1. Nothing. Very early level browsers use this tactic.
2. Puts up a dialog box asking you how you want to handle the file. Earlier versions of Navigator might do this.
3. Tells you a plug-in is needed and asks if you'd like to go get it.

FAQs from the HTML Goodies Web Site

Q. How do I make it so that the EMBED plays multiple audio files, one right after the other?

A. You need to take the files you want to play and edit them all together into one big file. I know of no other way.

Q. When I have an EMBED on my site, it plays great. When the person leaves the page, however, it stops. How do I keep it playing?

A. You must keep the window that contains the EMBED commands open. Either make all links on the page open new windows, or use the new window JavaScript to open a small window that contains the EMBED. (That window keeps it playing, unless the person closes it.)

Q. Isn't there a way to set the loudness of the EMBED?

A. Nope.

For more information on the new JavaScript window, see Chapter 11, "Java Applets and JavaScript."

More About EMBED

You can EMBED just about any type of sound file as long as the person using your page has the ability to read it. My plug-in plays just about any file except RealAudio. You can read more about RealAudio in the section "RealAudio: A Special Format" later in this chapter. What's great about RealAudio is that it plays the sound as it is being downloaded. This is called *streaming*. The play is almost instantaneous. Great invention.

Download time with an EMBED is not sped up or slowed down. The entire file must download before the plug-in plays it. What is different (and better) about this is that an EMBED starts the download process without anyone clicking blue words. You can also play with the page while the download is occurring, rather than just sitting and waiting, like you had to do with helper applications.

FAQs from the HTML Goodies Web Site

Q. What format would you suggest using to play sounds on the Net?

A. I suggest .wav first and MIDI second. If you're offering the files for download, try MP3. All are pretty popular. Of course, you can always offer an array of formats. Just

> find a shareware sound program that has the capability to save in multiple formats and then offer three or four—or offer any one you want. If someone wants the sounds badly enough, he can get the plug-in.

That's about it. Try embedding a few MIDI files and see what kind of response you get. I have one here and there. No one has complained yet.

 You can listen to me speak via an embedded sound file. I have a soft, yet soothing voice. Go to http://www.htmlgoodies.com/book/voiceembed.html.

RealAudio: A Special Format

I have stayed away from RealAudio mainly because in the past it couldn't be performed straight off a WWW server. You needed a RealAudio server to run the format.

 You can, however, hear me speak in RealAudio! Point your browser to this tutorial online at http://www.htmlgoodies.com/tutors/ra.html.

The process of RealAudio was explained to me by two different Internet server tech people. (These guys know words that don't exist in any language.) After they explained for a good 15 minutes, they stopped, noticed that my eyes had completely glazed over, and decided to give it to me in simple terms. Note that the process is much more involved than this, but this is the general idea:

> You put a sound on your WWW page, say a .wav or a MIDI. You are using what is known as a helper application or a plug-in. Either way, you are calling on a piece of software other than the browser itself to play the sound. The problem with that is that it takes some time because the entire file has to download, and then be loaded into the application before it can play. Depending on download speeds, Net congestion, file size, and your modem speed, this could take a long, long time.

> RealAudio beats them all by playing the sounds almost instantaneously. It amazed me the first time I heard and saw it work. If you did what I did, you went to the RealAudio site, didn't bother to read any of the documentation, grabbed the RealAudio converter, and placed a few files on your server.

Mine didn't work either.

It didn't work because of downloading time and pace. For example, if you download an image file and sit there watching the numbers tick by in the status bar, notice that the numbers are by no means consistent. You get a burst of data here and there, but you also have downtimes. You have to remember that you are not the only person being serviced by the system and that other people need the file too. That's the *downtime*—while others are being helped, or while the telephone line path to your house is very busy.

FAQs from the HTML Goodies Web Site

Q. I got RealAudio files to work by downloading them and then playing them off my hard drive.

A. Yup, that works. But it defeats the purpose of the files. You might as well have used .wav.

RealAudio works by creating a *buffer*, or specific connection, between your computer and a RealAudio server. After the connection is established, the transfer of data is consistent and at a set pace, usually the pace of your modem. It's a process known as *streaming*. That way the file can be played as it is being downloaded. The pace is the key here. HTTP servers don't offer the pace the RealAudio server does.

"But there has to be a way to play these things off of my site," you say.

"There is now!" I reply.

FAQs from the HTML Goodies Web Site

Q. I want a RealAudio server. How much do they cost?

A. The last time I checked into buying one (I really did this) the costs were up around 10 grand to get it running. That's before even attempting to find a server that would enable me to place the machine and hook up to the Internet. You see, RealAudio servers are *bandwidth* (the width of the pipe coming out of the Internet server) monsters. They use a ton of it. It can shut the place down. You need a very large investment in not only space, but in a number of connections.

RealAudio from Your Site

To run RealAudio sound files from your HTTP server, you're going to need a few things. Luckily they're all free for the downloading. You need the following:

- The RealAudio player version 3.0 or higher. Version 8 was out at the time of the writing.
- The RealAudio sound encoder.
- A RealAudio meta file.

These items and more are available at the RealAudio Web site `http://www.real.com`. I show you how to make one of those meta deals yourself.

First things first. If you're going to do this, your server must have two MIME type settings:

- `audio/x-pn-realaudio` Files with an .ra or .ram file extension.
- `audio/x-pn-realaudio-plugin` Files with an .rpm file extension.

These settings are nothing that you can do yourself. You need to contact your system administrator and ask for the settings to be made. Most servers already have these settings, but it's best to check.

Those settings tell the HTTP server to load the RealAudio server when it sees a file with the .ra or .ram extension.

FAQs from the HTML Goodies Web Site

Q. You tell us all the time to contact our system people. I don't know who they are. I am on Geocities (or Anglefire, or the like) and they tell me they can't enable me to do these things.

A. Well, those are free home page sites. What you are getting is free, so the system people can claim far more control over what you can and cannot do. Allowing someone to do a lot of this stuff can mess up a server. If you are very serious about doing the things in this book, you need to perhaps buy space on a server that allows more freedom. I like Geocities. They are smart not to enable every user to place CGIs, set MIME files, or create directories. It can cause many problems.

Creating the RealAudio Sound File

Use the RealAudio encoder to do this. If you haven't installed it on your computer yet, do it. It's rather simple to use. The hardest part is getting the .wav file to convert to RealAudio. That's the catch of this tutorial. You have to be able to make a sound file. Most newer computers have a mic or a sound recorder program on them. Use it to make a file and then open that file in the RealAudio encoder and encode it. You should now have a file with the same name as the original, but with a .ra extension. It stands for RealAudio.

Creating the RealAudio Meta File

Now it gets a little tricky. If this were a simple .wav or MIDI file, you could just transfer it to your server and make an HREF link to it to get it to play. Not so here. You need a buffer between the page and the RealAudio sound file. That buffer is the meta file. This is what you do:

1. Create a simple text file with a text editor. The file should only have the path to the RealAudio file on your server.

   For example, your file is called `joe.ra`. You place it on your server named `http://www.server.com/~fred`. Your meta file contains only this line of text:

   `http://www.server.com/~fred/joe.ra`

   Don't use any HTML commands. Don't use any quotation marks. Don't put anything else in the file other than the path to your RealAudio file. Just that.

2. Now save the small text document with the extension .ram. If you want to name the meta file *joe*, save it as `joe.ram`. Get it? Now you have your meta file ready to go.

3. Transfer the sound and the meta file to your server. Make sure the sound file goes as binary or you mess it up. You can read more about FTP transfers in Primer 7.

RealAudio in the HTML Document

Now it's time to call for the RealAudio file in a document. It would make sense to make a link straight to the sound file. Not so. In this case you make a link to the meta file. Note that the meta file only has the path to the RealAudio file inside it.

- The HTML document calls on the meta file.
- The call on the meta file denotes to the server that a RealAudio file is used here.
- The RealAudio file begins a download.
- The file starts playing after enough has downloaded to be read and understood.

...and off it goes.

So What's the Downside?

The following are a few downsides to serving RealAudio on your Web site:

- The viewer must have the RealAudio player installed. The players are a free download from the Real site, so you're pretty safe.
- The meta file text displays if the MIME settings are incorrect.
- The Net may be congested. The download is so sporadic that it doesn't work.

But it's better than nothing.

FAQs from the HTML Goodies Web Site

Q. I went to the RealAudio site and it now has RealVideo and an encoder, too. Will the video work like the audio in your tutorial?

A. People have told me it does. I have never tried it, but videos are usually so huge that I suspect Net congestion gets you. Go ahead and try it.

I have an example of a RealAudio file running off a Web server. You can find the example at http://www.htmlgoodies.com/book/realaudio.html.

Video on the Net

A video? On your home page? Yes. Videos have been on the Internet for a while now, and if you don't mind spending a healthy chunk of change for the required hardware and software, they're pretty simple to create.

This tutorial can be found online at http://www.htmlgoodies.com/tutors/video.html.

Many different video formats play on one type of computer or another, depending on the software the user has installed. However, three formats are used almost exclusively over the Internet.

I am not including the streaming videos such as RealVideo, Vivo, or NetShow. Remember that streaming means that the video is played in what's known as *real time*—it is played as it is being downloaded. I'm talking simple video formats.

- AVI—Stands for audio/video interleaved. It's a video format created by Microsoft that allows for video and audio to be saved together. This is the premier video format on the PC because it allows for many different compression schemes and reproduces a good picture. It also requires a lot of space. The extension for a file in this format is .avi.

- QuickTime—Apple computer's Macintosh-based format for playing movies. Apple has made the format quite popular on the Internet by creating players that enable the format to be run on an IBM. The QuickTime format is also popular because of its compression scheme. Files in QuickTime are usually less than half the size of their AVI equivalent, but do lose quality. The extension for a file in this format is .mov.

- MPEG—A video format created by the Motion Picture Experts Group, thus the name. The format runs on both Macintosh and IBM platforms and is valued for its compression rate. A large file can be transferred to MPEG and lose little quality while dropping the bit rate a great deal. The extension for a file in the format is .mpg.

I own PCs, so I capture in AVI format. After I have the video in AVI, I use two separate pieces of software to change the video from AVI into one of the other two formats. AVI can be turned into MPEG straightaway. The encoding process takes around two minutes for every one second of AVI video. QuickTime is a different story. The entire AVI file must be saved again with a different compression rate, known as *Intel Indeo*. The AVI can then be run through a QuickTime converter. That process is very fast.

Figure 10.4 shows three file formats with the same four-second video of me saying "Hi Mom. Look, I'm on the Internet." Then I wave. It's pure movie magic.

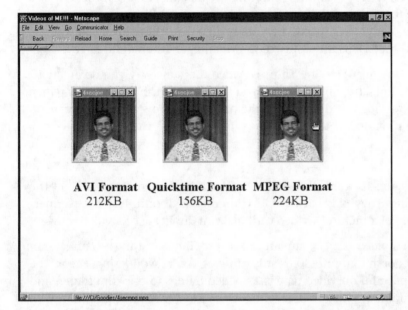

Figure 10.4
Three video formats and their sizes.

Let's note the differences in file size between format. Forget that. Note the file size, period. No doubt about it, people—these things take up a lot of space. How are they produced? First, let's look at how a real video is put together. It helps later.

Film and Video

I have no doubt that you all have seen a piece of film. A film is put together through one little picture replacing the one before it. As the filmstrip passes over the light, each frame (the frame is the little picture) is displayed. The frames roll past fast enough that your eyeballs perceive some sort of motion. The pictures on a filmstrip do not carry motion; your eye just perceives the quick passing of static frames as motion. It's a neat little trick that helps us later.

In case you're wondering, 24 frames pass over a film projector's light every second.

Video

Ah, video. A big fat cassette tape that carries pictures and sound. And it's not a whole lot more than that.

It would seem that if film used 24 frames per second, video would just follow through and do the same. Not so. You see, video is used mostly on television. Television uses a 30 frame per second speed, so video does too.

What about those slower video speeds like SLP and LP? They do run the tape more slowly, but still produce the 30 frames per second. By running the tape more slowly, the VCR is asking more and more information to be saved in a smaller and smaller space. This makes for a less pleasing picture. The slower speeds are a trade-off between picture quality and amount of data on a VCR tape. This little ditty of information is also helpful later.

Video is easy to serve up on your Web site. Think of video the same way you do an audio file. You can use the same link and embed format you would to run the audio. Just remember that when you embed a video, it shows up in the browser window as a gray square until it fully loads. Make room for it. The real trick is in making the videos.

Digital Video

The three video files in Figure 10.4 are all digital video. Each is a different format, but they basically do the same thing. They play back a "video" in digitized form. Just as a scanner makes a digital photocopy of a picture, a video card makes a duplicate of a video movie.

It makes a digital copy of a video rather than a film because film is not in the correct frame rate format. Twenty-four doesn't go into 30 cleanly. (In case you're wondering, the mathematical method used to put film on video tape is 1.5 video frames to one film frame. Add it up. It equals out.) In addition, video is already movement in a mechanical format. Video is captured motion played back through electronic *transducing* (change of one form of energy into another) of metal particles into color and motion.

Huh? Every time one of the 30 frames rolls past, the information saved on the VCR tape is read by a video reader or *head*. That head is electrified and the magnetic particles on the tape disrupt the electrical field the head is producing. That disruption is displayed to you as a picture. That's as un-technical as I could explain it without resorting to hand puppets.

Because the magnetic field is already there, why can't you just send that disrupted signal to a computer rather than another VCR or TV? You can. That's how those three pups in Figure 10.4 were produced.

FAQs from the HTML Goodies Web Site

Q. You've mentioned compression in a few different tutorials. What is that?

A. In layman's terms, *compression* is the capability to make an image or a video smaller by combining multiple pixels into one. Imagine an image with four dots all a slightly different shade of brown. By using compression, you can make it so that the four are combined into one—all the same color brown. That takes fewer bytes. You could store the image as only one pixel, but display all four pixels when the image is shown. Video is the same. If you can borrow from the frame before without loading a brand new frame each time (or combine pixels), you are using fewer bytes and compressing the file size.

The Trick Is Compression

In my opinion the future of TV and video is all in the compression rate. What if you could purchase a TV show to watch whenever you wanted? Say you want to watch the evening news right now. It may not be on right now. But what if you could put your credit card into a computer and order the show over the Internet? Would you? I would. I'd even pay a little more to get a copy without commercials. Video on demand—if it can ever be perfected, it puts a serious dent in video stores and movie houses.

At today's compression rates, a half-hour show would take up more than 75MB. That's where the future is: Compressing a show so that it downloads in a minute. It's coming, I can feel it in my bad knee.

FAQs from the HTML Goodies Web Site

Q. I'm working with a piece of video. You're right—these things are huge. Any suggestions on how to make my video smaller in terms of bytes?

A. I have a couple: Go with QuickTime format. It usually produces the smallest amount of bytes. Use compression to create the video. I usually set mine at 50%, capture 15 frames per second rather than 30, go in black and white if you can, make the screen smaller, and lose the sound. Those help.

Getting the Hardware

The equipment you need to capture video is quite simple: Something that plays the video, such as a VCR, and a video capture card that slides into your computer.

At the time of writing this second edition, I found yet one more rather interesting method of video capture. I was able to buy a cord that had the "card" inside the cord itself. You plug one end into your VCR and the other into a USB port on your computer, install some software, and the system was ready to go.

There are many companies selling the same format of cord. Search your favorite online computer hardware site to find a bunch to choose from.

In addition, you need a fairly strong computer with memory...lots and lots of memory. A big hard drive doesn't hurt either. You hook the VCR's out ports to the video capture card's in ports, install some software, and you're pretty much good to go. I'm sure the software comes with the card. Barring any unforeseen problems, you should be able to grab video with the best of them.

Cost is a factor, I'm sure. As with anything else, the better you buy, the more you pay. The more options you want, the more you pay. My video card has the ability to capture a full 30 frames per second in two different formats using a few different types of compression rations. I paid $600 for the card and the software to be able to capture and then edit video on my desktop.

I only paid $75 for the VCR to USB cord. Go figure.

 Head to `http://www.htmlgoodies.com/book/videos.html` *to play a couple of videos. You also get a full explanation of the exact equipment I use to capture, create, and edit my own digital video. It's the exact setup I use to teach to my university classes.*

Video Player Software

If you have attempted to play the three videos via the online version of this tutorial and couldn't, it's not because I don't like you—it's because you don't have the correct video player. You should have them. They're free. Some may have even come with your computer.

Try to grab a plug-in version of your player. It works much better than the older, helper application model. If one is not available, don't worry about it. Just get one that plays the video on my site so that you can see my smiling face. That's what's really important.

Net Notes

Most computers are already configured to play AVI and QuickTime formats. Some also have MPEG capabilities. If you are having trouble, try these sites for movie-playing helper applications:

AVI format: `http://www.microsoft.com/ms.htm`. You most likely use the Windows Media Player, now standard on all PCs. If you don't have it, go to the Microsoft site to download it.

QuickTime format: `http://www.apple.com/quicktime/`

MPEG format: `http://www.geom.umn.edu/docs/mpeg_play/mpeg_play.html`

MPEG format for UNIX: `http://www.mpegtv.com/`

These sites offer multiple-format movie-playing applications:

MacZilla, Movie Player for Macintosh: `http://maczilla.com/`

CineWeb: `http://www.digigami.com/cineweb/`

Chapter 11

Java Applets and JavaScript

So what is the difference between Java and JavaScript? Java is an object-oriented programming (OOP) language created by James Gosling of Sun Microsystems. JavaScript was created by the fine people at Netscape and is also an OOP language. Many of their programming structures are similar, but JavaScript contains a much smaller and simpler set of commands, which make it easier for the average weekend warrior to understand. JavaScript is also much easier to work with because you embed JavaScript directly into your HTML documents.

Java is a much larger and more complicated language that creates standalone applications. A Java *applet* (so called because it is a little application) is a fully contained program. With Java you have to create separate files, compile them, and go through all kinds of other black magic to make your work usable.

Java applets run independent of the HTML document that is calling for them. Sure, they appear on the page, but the HTML document did little more than call for the application and place it. If the programmer allows it, oftentimes parameters can be set by the HTML document. The delivery of the applet is done through a download. The HTML document calls for the application, downloads to the user's cache, and waits to run. JavaScript is wholly reliant on the browser to understand it and make it come to life.

What's the benefit of using one over the other? Several exist. If you can understand Java, it is amazingly versatile. Because of the size and structure of the language, it can be used to create anything from small Web page events, to entire databases, to full browsers. Java is the program I use to track my advertising banners.

In my opinion, JavaScript's main benefit is that it can be understood by the common human. It is much easier and robust than Java and allows for fast creation of Web page events. Many JavaScript commands are known as *event handlers*. They can be embedded into existing HTML commands. JavaScript is a little more forgiving than Java. It enables more freedom in the creation of objects. Java is very rigid and requires all items to be denoted and spelled out. JavaScript allows you to call on items that already exist, such as the status bar or the browser itself, and play with just that part. JavaScript is geared toward Web pages. Java is geared toward where it is needed most at the time.

Both create great Web page events and can offer interaction between the user and your Web page. But they are not created equally.

Which one should you use? Use the one that fits your needs. That sounds like a cop-out, but remember that the applets and JavaScript are most often offered on the Net as fully functioning items. You simply grab them and use them on your page (provided you are given permission). Many sites out there do nothing more than hand out applets or JavaScript. I have a list of them in Appendix C, "Valuable Links." The following tutorials teach you to implement these items on your pages. They do not teach you to write the languages, but rather instruct you on placing functioning applets and JavaScript on your Web pages. It is a good introduction to the formats. When you know how to get these pups on your pages, you understand more about their structures and can then more easily attempt to learn the language and create functioning JavaScripts or applets yourself.

FAQs from the HTML Goodies Web Site

Q. Where do I learn to write Java or JavaScript?

A. Since the first edition of this book I've posted a 30-Step JavaScript Primer series located at `http://www.htmlgoodies.com/primers/jsp/`. This has also been made into a book titled *JavaScript Goodies*. As for Java, your best bet is to grab a good book and start reading. This is a rough language, to say the very least.

Java Applets

This section deals with installing existing Java applets on your Web site.

A great number of people have mastered the Java language and have created numerous applets for you to use on Web pages. Really. I have a long list of sites in Appendix C whose entire reason for being around is to hand out functioning Java applets. Cool, huh?

I see applets handed out one of two ways. Either the applet sits on the creator's server and you attach to it or the applet is given right to you and you place it on your own server. I go over attaching to an applet on another server here and how to place the applet on your own server in the advanced applets tutorial coming up next in this chapter.

How Does Your Browser Know It's a Java Applet?

If you've read over my primers or have been working with the World Wide Web for a while, you know the Internet works by giving everything a filename and a suffix. In computer terms it's called *association*. The name image.gif is an example: image is the name of the item and .gif is its form. A page on the Web is done the same way. The title of this tutorial's online version is bookapplet.html. The name of the page is bookapplet and the type of page is .html.

By doing this, the computer can tell all these different file types apart. It associates an application with the item's format. Images are displayed using an image viewer, .html pages are displayed using the browser, and so on. When the computer sees the item's format by its suffix, it knows what application to associate it with, so it can open and use the item.

These applets work the same way, yet they run on their own, inside the browser window, without opening another program. The computer sees the applet as a name and then a suffix. In terms of an applet, the suffix is .class. Remember that applets are models made up of many little parts—a class of parts. Just as species are broken up into classes, so are applet parts. An applet is a class of like parts. Thus, you name the applet you are using in this fashion: applet.class. Still with me?

I said earlier that numerous sites hand out applets through the grace of the authors' hearts. Those are great sites and I show you how to use some of those applets. After you learn this, you are able to go to any site running a Java applet and—just by looking at the page's source code—see the text required to make the applet run and maybe even grab the applet itself.

I'm asking you nicely not to do that. Enough free applets are out there that you do not need to take them without permission.

If you do find an applet you like and it's not being offered for download, ask the author if you can use it. Most people on the Net are quite accommodating. If the author says no, respect that.

You see, it's really tough to use an applet and take the author's name off. Usually the copyright and author's name are in the compiled code. You might not know yet that applets are not text—they are compiled machine language. You can't get into it and that makes it super simple to show who actually wrote it and that you're using it without permission. Think of compiled code as many text elements being melded into one item—not to be broken apart.

The Dancing Text Applet

Here you go! People believe this Java stuff must be hard. Actually, Java is pretty easy to implement after the applet is compiled. Java is just reeeeeeeaaaaal testy. It likes everything to be just right. If it isn't, tough—no Java for you!

Figure 11.1 gives you a look at what you're going to install. What this little gem does is a little tough to grasp in the book, so I'll try to explain a little bit more. The text inside the black box is multicolored. Every letter is a different shade. The text is rolling up and down such as waves.

 All the parts you need to create this applet are available at http://www.htmlgoodies.com/ book/dancingtext.html.

Figure 11.1
Dancing text applet.

Sohail Nasim wrote the applet. He was nice enough to make the applet available to a download site called Gamelan (http://www.gamelan.com). Pronounce that gah-meh-lan. The Gamelan people were then nice enough to let me use the applet in the HTML Goodies book.

This is eye-catching and a great example for your first applet installation. This is what you need:

- The applet. Its name is SNSineText.class and I give you a link in a moment, so you can download it straightaway from the HTML Goodies Web site.
- The code that calls for the applet.

Let's take them in order...

The Applet

First, I want to quickly explain what this thing is again. An applet starts as a text document written in the Java programming language. After the author has finished the work, she runs the text document through another program called a *compiler*. That compiler changes the text into what's known as *machine language*. Now the applet is a fully-enclosed function program.

Compilation is not new. Most any program you receive on disk or CD-ROM is compiled into this, or another type of machine language. Ever wonder why you can't look at your Windows operating system code? Because it's in machine language, that's why.

Now that the applet is an application unto itself, you need to be a little more careful with how you handle it. Remember that it is no longer text, so it cannot be treated as such. When you FTP the applet either from my site to your hard drive or from your hard drive to your server, you must make sure the applet is sent as binary or raw text.

The easiest way to keep it all straight is to think of an applet as an image. It isn't, of course, but if you apply all the FTP concerns to it that you do an image, you have little problem.

If you'd like to read more about FTP concerns, I have a piece on just that in Primer 7, "Graduation Day."

 Let's go get the applet. If you point your browser to http://www.htmlgoodies.com/ book/SNSineText.class *(note the capitalization pattern), you have it. You can also find a link from the online version of this tutorial.*

When you arrive, one of two things happen. You may think I've tricked you because all that is on the screen are some squiggly lines in the upper-right corner. Stop! That's it! Now you can download it by choosing Save As from the File menu and saving it directly to your hard drive. Just make sure that when you save it you do so as All Files.

The second event might be that your browser just goes ahead and attempts to download the applet for you. You get a dialog box that asks what you want to do with the file. Save it. Just make sure you get it as All Files.

You know, I say to save it as "All Files," but in reality some version 5.0 browsers actually give you the opportunity to save in class format. If you're given that opportunity, use it.

I have found that Windows 95/98 sometimes wants to put the extension .exe on the end of the name. Don't let it. Erase the .exe and save it just as SNSineText.class. Do not change the name. Save it just as I show it.

FAQs from the HTML Goodies Web Site

Q. When I download an applet, can I change the name?

A. I wouldn't. Some of you can and some of you can't, and you have no real way to tell which is which. I would go with the name the author chose.

The Applet Code

All right, you're halfway there. Now for the code that calls for the applet:

```
<APPLET CODE="SNSineText.class" WIDTH=592 HEIGHT=80>
<PARAM name = text        value = "Welcome To My Page  Enjoy it!">
<PARAM name = TextColor value = "rycwopg rB cy rcwr ycwrBc op">
<PARAM name = BackColor value = "b">
<PARAM name = FontName  value = "TimesRoman">
<PARAM name = FontStyle value = "Bold">
<PARAM name = FontSize  value = "30">
<PARAM name = Amplitude value = "20">
<PARAM name = GapSize   value = "5">
<PARAM name = Offset    value = "15">
</APPLET>
```

You can transcribe it from here or go to the online version of this tutorial and copy and paste it from there. Either way, look at the main APPLET command:

```
<APPLET CODE="SNSineText.class" WIDTH=592 HEIGHT=80>
```

You can pretty much pick out what each part means:

- APPLET Alerts the browser that an applet goes here.
- CODE Tells the browser the name of the applet.

● WIDTH and HEIGHT   Set the window in which the applet runs. By the way, the applet allows you to change the WIDTH and HEIGHT commands to fit the text you put in the box.

If you just finished reading the applet tutorial before this, you might be asking where the CODEBASE command is. You don't need it. Remember that CODEBASE denotes the name of the directory where the applets sit. Because the applet and the HTML document that is calling for it sit inside the same directory, you have no need to look anywhere else. The CODE command alone does it.

The Parameter Commands

This is where this little gem shines. You have the ability, thanks to the author, to change this to your heart's content. The following are the parameters and what they do:

```
<PARAM name = text      value = "Welcome To My Page  Enjoy it!">
```

This sets the text that appears on the applet. Remember that you need to resize the box in the HEIGHT and WIDTH commands if you change the text. That way a lot of extra space is not around the items.

```
<PARAM name = TextColor value = "rycwopg rB cy rcwr ycwrBc op">
```

No, this isn't written in Klingon. The line allows you to denote a separate color for each letter. Notice the equal number of codes as letters? Welcome has a code of rycwopg. I have a letter code for color for every letter in the word Welcome. See how I have a letter color code for each letter and a space where the spaces fall in the text that appears on the applet? That's how you set the colors.

Why is it done this way? Because the author wants it done this way. No better reason for it.

The following is the color chart:

Black = b	Magenta = m
Blue = B	Orange = o
Cyan = c	Pink = p
Dark Gray = d	Red = r
Gray = G	White = w
Green = g	Yellow = y
Light Gray = l	

You need to set all the letters to the same color if you want an entire word to be the same color.

By the way, you must have a color code for each letter. If you don't, you get an error and the applet does not run.

The following command sets the background color. Notice I have it set to black. I did that to show the shape of the applet. If I were using this on the page, I'd set the background to the same color as the background of the page. The letters would then appear to be floating. Of course, this effect dies if you use a background image or the user has his own colors set. I'd still do it, though.

```
<PARAM name = BackColor value = "b">
```

The following sets the text font. You have your choice of TimesRoman, San Serif, or Helvetica.

```
<PARAM name = FontName   value = "TimesRoman">
```

The following is pretty self-explanatory as well. You can set the text to Plain, Bold, or Italic. If you want a combination of two or all three, separate them with plus signs (+); bold+italic is an example.

```
<PARAM name = FontStyle value = "Bold">
```

If you use a large font, make sure you make the HEIGHT and WIDTH larger to accommodate it.

```
<PARAM name = FontSize   value = "30">
```

The following is the height of the wave.

```
<PARAM name = Amplitude value = "20">
```

The following is the amount of space between the letters.

```
<PARAM name = GapSize    value = "5">
```

This is how far from the left edge the letters begin.

```
<PARAM name = Offset     value = "15">
```

Finally, the </APPLET> command ends the entire deal.

FAQs from the HTML Goodies Web Site

Q. Do I have to fill in every <PARAM> when I put an applet on my page? Sometimes I don't know what they are asking for.

A. Yeah, lots of times the author uses some cryptic message to denote something simple. Often an author creates a default so that if a parameter is not denoted, one is put in by the applet. I suggest you simply try running the applet without the parameter set; just leave empty quotation marks. If you get an error, you know you need to put in something. You might have to ask around or play the guessing game.

Q. Can I run more than one applet on a page?

A. As long as you install each applet correctly, you can install as many as you'd like.

Now Put Them On Your Server

When you have all the parameters where you'd like them, try it. The applet runs right off your hard drive. If it doesn't, you may have corrupted it in the download from my site.

If it works, FTP the applet and the HTML document to your server. Make darn sure the applet goes as either binary or raw data. If you send it as text, you corrupt it and the whole process comes to a stop.

FAQs from the HTML Goodies Web Site

Q. I keep getting the "Java class error" and "applet not found" errors.

A. First check to make sure the applet made it to your site in the upload. That is very seldom the reason, but it's good to check anyway. The most common reason for those types of errors is that you have corrupted the applet in one or more of the transfers. Let's work backward. The applet worked on the site you got it from, right? Did it work on your hard drive? If so, the upload to your server is the problem. If not, you corrupted it when getting it from the site yourself. Remember: Always treat these applets as if they were an image. You may need to ensure this because relying on an FTP program is not wise. They often see applets as text and upload them in ASCII format. That kills it. Force the FTP program's hand to send the applet as binary.

If you've sent everything correctly, open your browser, load the page, and watch the fun. Applets are not hard to install, they just need you to pay attention to what you're doing.

Hopefully you have gotten this one to work. If so, you can get just about any applet to work because they all work the same way. You get the applet (or applets—many effects are accomplished using three, four, or more!), get the code, set the parameters to your liking, upload the applet as binary, and upload the HTML document as text. Now you should be good to go.

As I said before, I grabbed this applet from Gamelan, but many other sites are just as helpful. You find a long list of them in Appendix C. Have fun—these things are a blast.

JavaScript

JavaScript is a programming language and I love it! I really enjoy writing and posting JavaScript to my own Web pages. You can make myriad events that spice up what otherwise would be pretty static pages. As you delve deeper, you begin to understand why the WWW—and I—have taken so strongly to JavaScript. JavaScript basics are discussed in this tutorial and you receive a JavaScript that posts this text:

You arrived at the page on [*the date*] at exactly [*current time*].

This appears where it usually reads Document Done. This is a neat little script that lets your user know you're thinking about them.

This is an important disclaimer, however: I wrote this JavaScript. Because I wrote it, I get to put a copyright on it. When I send you to go get the code, or when you read the code shown here in a second, you see where I put it. I entered it right into the code.

This is very common in the world of people who write JavaScript. People all over the Net write JavaScripts and then hand them out for free. I'm one of them. I don't ask for money, but I do ask that you keep our copyright statements intact.

Follow this tutorial straightaway and you see what I mean.

Let's Get Started

 First you need the script to place on your HTML page. I have it printed here. You can transcribe it from here, or better yet, you can get it online at http://www.htmlgoodies.com/ jstext.html. *I refer to the script often, so take a quick look at it. If you go for it online, you may want to download the page into your own computer. While you're online, see the script in action at* http://www.htmlgoodies.com/javabook.html *so you know the look you're going for. Now go!*

Welcome back. That was fast. Here it is:

```
<SCRIPT LANGAUGE="javascript">
<!-- Hide from browsers that do not understand JavaScript
//This script Copyright 1998 by Joe Burns, Ph.D.
```

```
//Keep this and the line above intact if you use this script.
//Thanks - Joe
    function dateinbar()
      {
      var date = new Date();
      var m = date.getMonth() + 1;
      var d = date.getDate();
      var y = date.getYear();
      var h = date.getHours();
      var mn = date.getMinutes();
      var sc = date.getSeconds();
      var t = m + '/' + d + '/' + y + ' at
➥exactly ' + h + ':' + mn + ':' + sc + ' ';
      defaultStatus = "You arrived at the page on " + t + ".";
      }
// end hiding -->
</SCRIPT>
<BODY BGCOLOR="#ffff00" onLoad="dateinbar()">
```

The JavaScript looks like chicken scratch, doesn't it? Yeah, it did to me too when I got started. Now let's get it up and running:

1. Open the text editor you use to write your HTML documents. Mark the page with <HTML>, <HEAD>, and <TITLE> commands like you would to start any other document. This JavaScript must be put into an HTML document to run. It is not a small application (as is a Java applet).

   Keep in mind that not all JavaScripts work this way. In fact, many are self-contained and you just plop them on the page where they run. That wouldn't make much of a tutorial. This is somewhat involved, but a very common style of JavaScript.

   When you are editing pages that contain JavaScript, you need to use an editor that does not have any margins. NotePad and Macintosh's SimpleText are great for this. I don't mean margins set to their widest point—I mean no margins, period. Using margins might corrupt the shape of the JavaScript, causing longer lines to break into two smaller lines. That halts the process completely.

2. Now copy and paste the entire jstext.html file you just looked at—the whole thing. Copy it from the browser screen. Don't download the page and take it from there. I wrote the script so it would display on the browser screen rather than running as the script that it is. Just copy it directly from the screen. Of course, you can transcribe it from here, too.

3. Place the script immediately following the <TITLE> commands, but still inside the </HEAD> you just wrote in the text editor. Please make a point of copying it exactly. Remember, not only must the script retain the same lettering, but also it must retain the same shape.

FAQs from the HTML Goodies Web Site

Q. I did exactly what you said and my JavaScript keeps giving me errors.

A. The most common reason for getting errors on a JavaScript from my site is that you are attempting to edit it in an editor that has margins that are corrupting it by changing the shape of the script. If in the script a line is very long, do not break it into two lines. Using margins does that, so edit without margins and don't try altering the format of the script. You only cause problems...and errors.

---

4. Look again at the script. I have allowed you permission to use it as long as you leave in my name. That's already done for you if you copy the whole deal.

5. Now look toward the bottom of the JavaScript. The very last line reads like this:

```
<BODY BGCOLOR="#ffff00" onLoad="dateinbar()">
```

This is not actually part of the JavaScript. This is going to act as the BODY command for the HTML document you're writing the script into. If you want to use BGCOLOR, LINK, VLINK, ALINK, or BACKGROUND commands in this document, put them in the BODY command just like you would in any other BODY command. Get them in the front part of the command before the onLoad command starts.

Note that the second half of the BODY command has an onLoad= command and then some attributes immediately after. That command is JavaScript and it tells the browser that when the page is loaded (the command is onLoad, get it?), start the JavaScript section in the HEAD commands titled dateinbar().You find that dateinbar() function in the script you pasted between the HEAD commands.

This is an explanation of the process of this tutorial. It helps you understand why you need all these little parts and what they all do.

First the browser loads the page. That means the JavaScript you pasted into the HEAD command is placed into your computer's brain. But it doesn't go to work. It just sits there waiting to be called upon.

Next, the BODY command loads and the onLoad="dateinbar" command is seen by the browser. That onLoad command triggers the browser to start running the JavaScript.

The JavaScript itself reads part of your browser. It gathers the day, the month, the year, the hour, the minute, and the second. After it has all the parts, it puts them all together in a nice sentence and displays it in the browser status bar for all the world to see.

Is That It?

Yes! Think of this JavaScript as just another piece of the puzzle. Implementing JavaScript has rules just as altering text with HTML has rules. You should be able to save and run it as long as you have followed the instructions, placed the script within the HEAD commands and after the TITLE commands, and made sure to add the onLoad command to your BODY commands.

JavaScript is a lot less scary than you'd think. Most people run into trouble in the script itself.

JavaScript Requirements

The following are a few items to keep in mind when posting a JavaScript to one of your HTML documents:

- Hide the script from less-powerful browsers—JavaScript is text. If the browser viewing your page does not have Java capabilities, the text is displayed. You can hide the text from earlier-version browsers by adding <!-- at the beginning and //--> at the end of your script. This does not affect the script's performance.

  If you look at the script I just gave you previously, you see where I used those commands. I also added some text; that's allowed. The text is not for the JavaScript, but to enable me to keep things straight.

- Keep the shape—JavaScripts like to retain their shape. You should make a point of editing your JavaScript/HTML documents in a text editor that does not have margins. Suggestions for editing JavaScript/HTML documents include Notepad (PC), Simple Text (Macintosh), or turning off the word wrap in your current HTML editor.

JavaScript Troubleshooting

The following are some suggestions of what to do if you can't get a script to work properly on your Web site:

- The script doesn't work—The quick answer is that it does. All scripts in this book and on the HTML Goodies site have worked for me before I handed them off to you. You can be sure that the script does work; just a problem is elsewhere.

● Nothing happens—Nothing? Then you might not have a browser late enough to run JavaScript, but that is seldom the case anymore. It may also be that you don't have the entire script. Many scripts have two parts, one on the HEAD command and one on the BODY command. It doesn't display if you do not have the command in the BODY that calls for the script. For instance, nothing would happen in the status bar if you forgot the onLoad command. If the script is functional and you have installed every part, you should either get the script's effect or an error code.

● I get an error code—You saw that coming, didn't you? Make note of the line the error code is coming from. That is the line from the *top of the page*, not from the top of the JavaScript. Count your <HTML> as line one. Remember to count the blank lines, too.

Fix the error code—Remember, form is key here. Most times, error codes can be fixed by making sure the script is in the exact form it was in when you took it from me. Make sure none of the lines haven't been chopped off early or jumped to the next line before it should have been. This solves most error codes. I know the code worked when you grabbed it from me. The error occurred somewhere in the transfer.

Careful now. If you get into these JavaScripts, you get hooked. I did.

 Just to show you that JavaScript is very versatile, I have posted another JavaScript that acts much the same as the one in this tutorial, except the text scrolls along the status bar. Woohoo! See http://www.htmlgoodies.com/book/scrolljs.html *for all the parts.*

Advanced JavaScript Commands

In the original JavaScript tutorial, the one just before this one, you implemented what one might call a "well-formed" JavaScript. The script was a huge scary thing that sat in the HTML document's HEAD commands. The script started with the traditional <SCRIPT LANGUAGE="javascript"> and ended with </SCRIPT>. It was then triggered to begin running by an onLoad command stuck in <BODY>. That format is very common and you see it a great deal as you write your own Web pages.

One of the great things about JavaScript is that it can be as complicated as the tutorial you just got through or as simple as the many examples in this tutorial.

Here you're going to go over a certain class of JavaScript commands called *event handlers*, which are commands that work directly with existing HTML commands. They work so closely, in fact, that they work by being embedded right into the HTML command itself.

They're called event handlers because they create events. They do things when your users do things. That's a terrible description, but I'm on a tight schedule here. Read on...

 To see these scripts in action, point your browser to http://www.htmlgoodies.com/ beyond/adv_js.html.

You're going to go over a few different JavaScript event handler commands here. I list them up front. I want you to keep an eye on their capitalization patterns—you must keep that pattern every time you use the command. If you don't, the commands don't work.

- `onMouseOver`   Creates the event when the mouse is passed over active text or an image.
- `onMouseOut`   Creates the event when the mouse is taken off an active text image.
- `onClick`   Creates an event when active text or images are clicked.
- `alert`   Opens up a dialog box that contains text and an OK button.

The `onMouseOver` *Event Handler*

I'm going to show you the format for using this command in a hypertext link first, explain what the parts mean, and then show you what it does. The following is the code:

```
<A HREF="http://www.htmlgoodies.com" onMouseOver="window.status=
➥'Click here to go to HTML Goodies'; return true">HTML Goodies</A>
```

Please keep in mind that the previous full line of code should all go onto one line. (It can't be shown here that way because of margin constraints.)

Now let's break it down. You should notice right off that the format is a hypertext link with some text stuck in right after the `htmlgoodies.com` URL. That's how these event handlers work. They are embedded right into an HTML command. You don't need the traditional `<SCRIPT>` and `</SRCIPT>` commands. The code just runs inside the HTML when your user passes his mouse over.

This line of JavaScript code does the work:

```
onMouseOver="window.status='Click here to go to HTML Goodies';
  return true"
```

Let's break it down:

- `onMouseOver`   The event handler. It denotes that something happens when the mouse passes over the active text.
- `window.status`   JavaScript code for the browser window status bar. That's the bar at the bottom of the screen where it reads `Document Done` after a page has loaded.

  The words that follow in single quotation marks are the words that appear in the status bar when the mouse passes over the active text. Please also notice the semicolon.

⬤ `return true` JavaScript that also checks to see if a status bar is there. If it finds one it reports back that the text can be placed. I know it seems strange, but you have to play by JavaScript rules to get this effect.

Finally, please take a long, slow look at the pattern of equal signs and single and double quotation marks. It can get confusing, but it has to be just so to get the effect.

Now, after all that mind-numbing detail, you get the results shown in Figure 11.2.

Figure 11.2
The `onMouseOver` *effect.*

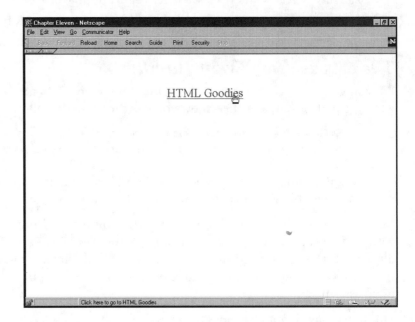

Look at the bottom line on the browser in Figure 11.2. The text `Click here to go to HTML Goodies` popped up in the status bar when the mouse passed over.

Let's go a little further, keeping the exact same format, but adding another event handler. Oh yes, these little puppies can be used in combination. What you're going to do is add the `onMouseOut` event handler so that when your users pass their mouse over the link, they get words in the status bar. When the mouse moves off the link, they get different words.

It gets very long and a little confusing. It also all has to go on one line. Here it is:

```
<A HREF="http://www.htmlgoodies.com" onMouseOver="window.status=
➥'Click here to go to HTML Goodies'; return true" onMouseOut=
➥"window.status='I said click!'; return true">HTML Goodies</A>
```

With this you get two messages every time your mouse moves on or off of the text.

onMouseOver *and Background Colors*

onMouseOver is good for more than just posting text. The following code allows your users to pass their mouse over text and change the actual background color of the page:

```
<A HREF=""onMouseOver="document.bgColor='black'">Black</a>
<A HREF=""onMouseOver="document.bgColor='green'">Green</a>
<A HREF=""onMouseOver="document.bgColor='yellow'">Yellow</a>
<A HREF=""onMouseOver="document.bgColor='red'">Red</a>
<A HREF=""onMouseOver="document.bgColor='brown'">Brown</a>
<A HREF=""onMouseOver="document.bgColor='white'">White</a>
```

Once again, notice the hypertext link format—except this time the onMouseOver is not pointed toward the window.status, but document.bgColor (note the capitalization pattern).

bgColor is JavaScript for the HTML document's background color. The background changes every time your users pass their mouse over a new color.

Figure 11.3 gives you a general idea of what it looks like in the browser.

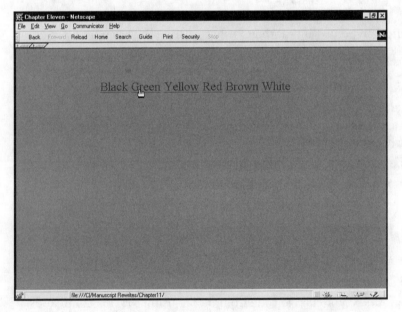

Figure 11.3
The onMouseOver *background color changer.*

You can set this up with any hex or word color code. A long list of them is in Appendix B, "Useful Charts."

You can make as many or as few choices as you want by adding or subtracting A HREF commands. What does not work are TEXT, LINK, or VLINK commands. They are a bit more stable.

327

Just for kicks, I give you one more little piece of code using the `onMouseOver` event handler. This is a fun little piece that can keep your users guessing. Look at this:

```
<A HREF="http://www.htmlgoodies.com" onMouseOver="parent.location=
➥'dude.html'";>HTML Goodies</A>
```

It all should look familiar by now. The only new item is the `parent.location` command. That is JavaScript for a new page.

This script basically loads the `dude.html` page (or whatever page you denote) when the mouse passes over.

This is a hypertext link that doesn't need to be clicked. Use it in good health.

The `Alert` Event Handler

I'm going to show you the `alert` event handler using the `onMouseOver`, because you're already familiar with it. The following is the basic format:

```
<A HREF="http://www.htmlgoodies.com" onMouseOver="alert
➥('Hello out there!')";>HTML Goodies</A>
```

Notice again that it's a simple hypertext link format, only this time the `onMouseOver` is going to enact this line of code:

```
"alert('Hello out there!')";
```

That code opens up an alert box with the text `Hello out there!` when the user passes the mouse over the link. The user has to click the OK button on the alert box to make it go away. Figure 11.4 shows what this looks like.

Just change the text inside the parentheses and single quotation marks to configure this for your own use. Whatever you write shows up on the alert box. Yes, you can type long sentences. The text just wraps right on the box.

The `onClick` Event Handler

You may be well ahead of me here, but I'll say it anyway. `OnClick` works exactly as `onMouseOver`, except `onClick` creates the effect when you click the active text or image.

The following is the background color change code from before using `onClick` commands:

```
<A HREF=""onClick="document.bgColor='black'">Black</a>
<A HREF=""onClick="document.bgColor='green'">Green</a>
<A HREF=""onClick="document.bgColor='yellow'">Yellow</a>
<A HREF=""onClick="document.bgColor='red'">Red</a>
<A HREF=""onClick="document.bgColor='brown'">Brown</a>
<A HREF=""onClick="document.bgColor='white'">White</a>
```

Figure 11.4
onMouseOver *calling on an* alert *event handler.*

This creates the same effect, only now the user must click to get the background color to change. The following is the alert event handler example using onClick:

```
<A HREF="http://www.htmlgoodies.com" onClick="alert
➥('Hello out there!')";>HTML Goodies</A>
```

Same effect, but you have to click it first.

Now, you may be thinking that onClick is just another version of onMouseOver and can only be used in hypertext links. Not so. Where onClick really shines is when you use it with form buttons. If you need to read about form buttons you can find them in Chapter 7, "Link Buttons and Forms." Let's get into a few examples, shall we?

Back and Forward Buttons

Why make your users click the Back and Forward buttons way at the top of the browser screen when you can plop them right on the page? Take a gander at Figure 11.5.

The following is the code that placed them:

```
<FORM>
<INPUT TYPE="button" VALUE="BACK" onClick="history.go(-1)">
<INPUT TYPE="button" VALUE="FORWARD" onCLick="history.go(1)">
</FORM>
```

Figure 11.5
Back and Forward buttons.

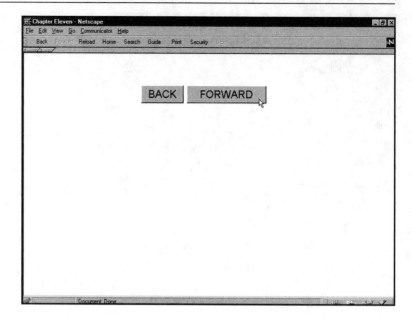

This is what's happening:

- ⬤ <FORM>   Starts the button.
- ⬤ INPUT TYPE="button"   Is pretty self-explanatory.
- ⬤ VALUE="###"   Denotes what is written on the button.
- ⬤ onClick=   Denotes that the event activates when clicked.
- ⬤ "history.go"   JavaScript that denotes movement through your history file. That's the file that keeps a record of everywhere you've been during that particular surfing jaunt; (1) sends it forward one step, (-1) sends you backward one step.

  If you'd like you can raise or lower those numbers. Setting it to (-4) takes your user back four pages if he has that many pages in his history file. If not, the button does not function.

- ⬤ </FORM>   Ends the button.

You should also know that you can separate these two, employing only one button. Just make sure you keep the beginning and end FORM commands in place.

Links Within Pages

People ask me all the time how to get link buttons to do jumps within pages. The quick answer is that you can't. The link button places a ? on the end of its links—that messes it up. Through the magic of an onClick event handler, however, you can create a button such as the one shown in Figure 11.6.

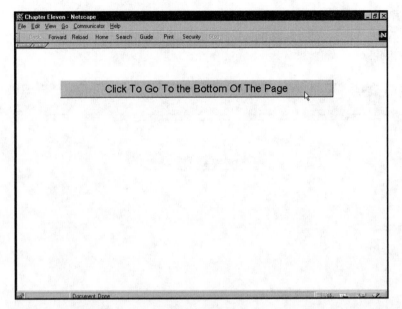

Figure 11.6
Internal link script.

This is what made it. Copy the code and place it on your page where you want the button to appear.

```
<FORM>
        <INPUT TYPE="button" VALUE="Click To Go To the Bottom Of The Page"
onClick="parent.location='#code'">
</FORM>
```

Please note that the full INPUT TYPE line of text should all be on the same line.

This is what's happening. The button is created the same as earlier, except for these things:

- onClick="parent.location='#code'"   Loads a page into the browser window. You saw parent.location earlier.
- '#code'   Denotes the point where this script jumps to. You're not offering a new page, so the script must look to the current page. On that page you see a place called #code. If you haven't already, read all about page jumps in Chapter 2, "Creating Links." It helps you understand this a little better.

This code denotes the point on the page where the button jumps:

```
<A NAME="code">
```

This is the same format as the page jump link. You need to choose a new "code" for every point you denote on the page.

Making an E-mail Button

If you could click the button in Figure 11.7, you'd send me a piece of mail. It works. Go ahead, click. I said click! Click! Oh, wait. This is a book. Right.

Figure 11.7
An e-mail button script.

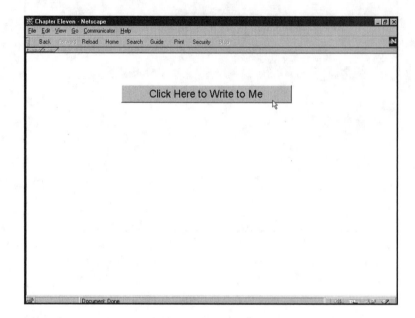

This is how to make the e-mail button:

```
<FORM>
<INPUT TYPE="button" VALUE="Click Here to Write to Me"
onClick="parent.location='mailto:jburns@htmlgoodies.com'">
</FORM>
```

Please note that the full INPUT TYPE line of text should all be on the same line.

The button works the same way as the link button, but this time it is enacting a simple mailto: (like you would use to create an e-mail hypertext link). See Primer 4, "Making a Link to Someone Else," if you don't know what I mean.

If you use this button, be sure to change out your e-mail address where mine sits now. Remember, no space between mailto: and the address.

FAQs from the HTML Goodies Web Site

Q. Can I set the button up to write to more than one person?

A. On later browsers you can add as many e-mail addresses as you want as long as you separate each with a comma and no spaces.

Well, that's a quick look at some JavaScript event handlers. They are great items because they're quick, they sit inside the HTML, and they do great tricks.

By the way, in case you're wondering, the onLoad command you used in the first JavaScript tutorial is also an event handler and works just like the others did. It just enacts the event when the page loads. If you'd like an alert box to pop up when the page loads, change the onMouseOver to onLoad.

If you haven't taken it from the tutorial, these event handlers are quite interchangeable. Try swapping one for another. You find great new events just from playing around. Just be very careful to keep the double and single quotation mark patterns the same or you get errors.

Enjoy!

 I have a few more intricate JavaScripts that employ onClick *and* onMouseover *commands at* http://www.htmlgoodies.com/book/morejs.html.

Opening New Windows

I can always tell when a new command is in vogue. I start getting all kinds of e-mail asking how to do it. Well, this is the new thing. I don't know why, but everyone wants to know how to create these little windows that pop up. All the Geocities.yahoo.com pages have them. Other pages use them as control panels operating the main window.

Figure 11.8 shows an example of what you are creating through this tutorial.

If you decide to go with this kind of pop-up window, use it sparingly. I think they become an annoyance after a while. You start yelling at the screen every time another one pops up. I do, at least. It really scares the cat.

If you insist on doing one, let's do it right! Let's start at the beginning.

Figure 11.8
A new Window script.

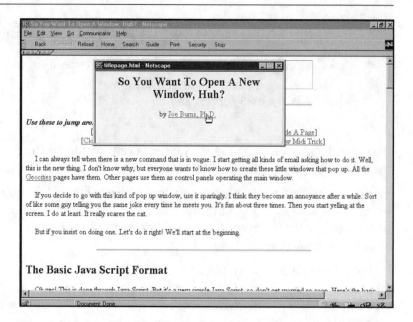

FAQs from the HTML Goodies Web Site

Q. What's the command that makes it so that someone cannot close the extra windows I make pop up?

A. Such a thing does not exist. You always run the risk of users closing windows as soon as they pop up.

The Basic JavaScript Format

Oh, yes! This is done through JavaScript. But it's a very simple JavaScript, so don't get worried so soon. The following is the basic format:

```
<SCRIPT LANGUAGE="javascript">
<!--
window.open ('page.html')
-->
</SCRIPT>
```

Heck, you're already familiar with most of this stuff. Because this is a script, you need the opening `<SCRIPT LANGUAGE="javascript">` statement, and the `</SCRIPT>` statement at the end. The `<!--` and the `-->` are used to hide the text from older version browsers (under 2.0) and text-only browsers that don't read JavaScript. You see, if you didn't have those in there, the text would display.

But it's the stuff in the middle that makes the magic.

`window.open ('page.html')` does just what it says—it opens a window (a new browser screen, actually) and fills it with the page within the parentheses and single quotation marks. The HTML document in the example that fills the window is called `page.html`.

That little script opens a new browser window and you get the effect. Wouldn't it be great if you actually had the ability to configure the window any way you wanted? You bet. This is how.

Configuring the Window

Now you get to the commands I used to get the little window effect. You can place this JavaScript anywhere on the page, but putting it toward the top or in between the HEAD commands ensures that it runs sooner in the process than if you put it at the end. This is a pretty robust script that doesn't need a special placement. This is exactly what I have:

```
<SCRIPT LANGUAGE="javascript">
<!--
window.open ('titlepage.html', 'newwindow', config='HEIGHT=100,
➥ WIDTH=400, toolbar=no, menubar=no, scrollbars=no,
➥ resizable=no, location=no, directories=no, status=no')
-->
</SCRIPT>
```

Please make a point of getting everything from `window.open` to `status=no')` on one line.

This is what's happening:

- `<SCRIPT LANGUAGE="javascript">` Starts the JavaScript.
- `window.open` JavaScript command that opens a new browser window.
- `'titlepage.html'` Name of the page that fills the window.
- `'newwindow'` Name of the window. This you need. You are going to use commands intended to alter the window that the script is opening. The item has to have a name so that the JavaScript knows what item it is dealing with. I went with `newwindow`, but it could have just as easily been zork, or woohaa, or raspberry.
- `config=` Denotes that what follows configures the window. (This command really isn't required, but it's a good idea to use just to keep things straight.)
- `HEIGHT=100` Denotes the height of the window in pixels.
- `WIDTH=400` Denotes the width of the window in pixels.

- `toolbar=no` Denotes if there is a toolbar on the newly opened window. Set this to yes if you want one, to no if you don't. The *toolbar* is the line of buttons at the top of the browser window that contains Back, Forward, Stop, Reload, and so on.

- `menubar=no=` Denotes whether there is a menu bar. Set this to yes if you want one and to no if you don't. The *menu bar* is the line of items labeled File, Edit, View, Go, and so on.

- `scrollbars=no` Denotes whether there are scrollbars. Ditto with the yes or no deal. I wouldn't make a new window that would need scrollbars, anyway. I think it kills the effect.

- `resizable=no` Denotes whether the user can change the size of the window by dragging.

- `location=no` Denotes whether there is a location bar on the newly opened window. Use yes or no again. The *location bar* is the space at the top of the browser window where the page URL is displayed.

- `directories=no` Denotes whether there is a *directories bar* on the new window. Use yes or no. This is the bar at the top of the browser window that has the bookmarks and such.

- `status=no` Denotes whether there is a status bar. Use yes or no. The *status bar* is the area at the very bottom of the browser screen that says Document Done.

- `</SCRIPT>` Ends the whole deal.

FAQs from the HTML Goodies Web Site

Q. I want two windows to pop up.

A. Then create two JavaScript commands that open a new window and list one right after the other. You get two windows.

Page Inside a Page

The example I gave relies on two pages: The first is the main HTML document that carries the JavaScript. The second is the HTML document that is displayed inside the new window.

Here I get a little fancier with the JavaScript code. I show you how to set it up so that the new window is included inside the main HTML document completely. One page. Two windows.

```
<SCRIPT LANGUAGE="JavaScript">
function openindex()
     {
OpenWindow=window.open("", "newwin", "height=250,width=250,toolbar=no,
➥scrollbars="+scroll+",menubar=no");
```

```
OpenWindow.document.write("<TITLE>Title Goes Here</TITLE>")
OpenWindow.document.write("<BODY BGCOLOR=pink>")
OpenWindow.document.write("<h1>Hello!</h1>")
OpenWindow.document.write("This text will appear in the window!")
OpenWindow.document.write("</BODY>")
OpenWindow.document.write("</HTML>")

OpenWindow.document.close()
self.name="main"
        }
    </SCRIPT>
```

The previous is a very basic script written by Andree Growney and myself. This JavaScript creates a "function" that opens a new window. Look at the top line of the script after the `<SCRIPT LANGUAGE="javascript">` line.

The function starts with the line: `function openindex()`. What that does in JavaScript speak is create a function called `openindex`. Then whatever is inside the curly braces following that statement is what the function is supposed to do. With me so far? In the case of this function, a new window is opened. The next lines of the script are quite similar to what you've seen so far:

```
OpenWindow=window.open("", "newwin", "height=250,width=250,toolbar=no,
➥scrollbars="+scroll+",menubar=no");
```

The line calls for the creation of a new window. As you can see, no external page is called for. You see just the empty quotation marks. This forces the JavaScript to look at itself for the information.

The name of the new window is `newwin`, and the statements following define what the window looks like.

Now let's get to the meat of this little ditty. Each of the lines start with this:

```
OpenWindow.document.write()
```

These lines denote a new line of text that is written onto the window that is being opened. Now look down the code. Note that the text inside the quotation marks of each new line is HTML code. Thus, the text written to this window is going to be read as HTML code. I only have a few lines here, but you can add as many as you'd like. Just be sure to preface each line with the `OpenWindow.document.write` command. Follow the format closely. One missing quote or parenthesis can kill the entire script.

Be sure to end the script that same way I have: `OpenWindow.document.close()`.

Calling for the Function

No, you're not done yet. When you create a function such as this, something must be used to "trigger" the function to work. Usually, as is the case here, you use a command in the BODY portion of the main HTML document. This is the deal:

- Configure the script and place it in the <HEAD> section of your main HTML document.
- To trigger the function, place onLoad="openindex()" in the <BODY> command of the main HTML document. That tells the browser to initiate the openindex function when the page is loaded.

Closing the Window

This seems like the next logical step in the process. You made it open, now make it close. The following are two ways of doing it:

- Every window carries what I call the "goodbye box" on the upper-right corner. This is the gray square that has a little X on it. Click that and away it goes.
- You could offer a button on the page that closes it when the user clicks the button.

I'm starting here because I don't think I need to go over the little goodbye box. The following is the code for the button:

```
<FORM>
<INPUT TYPE='BUTTON' VALUE='Close Window' onClick='self.close()'>
</FORM>
```

Either place that pup on the page that goes into the new window or place it in the code in the previous JavaScript format. You get a little button that closes the window when clicked.

A New Window MIDI Trick

I am asked at least once a day how to keep a MIDI playing in the background while a person surfs your site. This is a little rough because the page that has the MIDI embedded stops playing the file after you leave it. I suggest this: Place the EMBED commands on the page that fills the new window. That way people can surf all over the place on the main browser window and the MIDI plays away. The only real downfall is that the MIDI party stops cold if the person closes the little window.

I said it was a suggestion, not the end all.

Exciting, huh? Now you can make little windows pop up all over town. Again, I suggest that one new window might be a welcome help to your pages' users. However, a new window every other page would bring you to the level of telemarketers in some people's minds. Use this only when they are really needed.

 I have an example of a window opening and then closing by itself! Go to http://www.htmlgoodies.com/book/openclose.html.

Image Flip

This is one of the most asked-for items on the HTML Goodies site: an image flip. The image-flip script shown here works cross browser with no trouble. Plus, it's a snap to configure for your own use. Even better? This is an active image, so it can be clicked and take you to another page! This is the effect: First, Figure 11.9 shows the mouse pointer on the image. Figure 11.10 shows the mouse cursor off the image.

 You can see the tutorial and get all the parts you need online at http://www.htmlgoodies.com/tutors/imageflip.html.

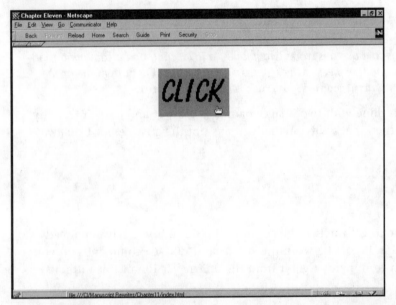

Figure 11.09
An image flip with mouse cursor on the image.

FAQs from the HTML Goodies Web Site

Q. How do I make it so that text highlights when my mouse pointer moves over it?

A. You could use an image flip to highlight one image and not the other. That would give the effect.

Figure 11.10

An image flip with mouse cursor off the image.

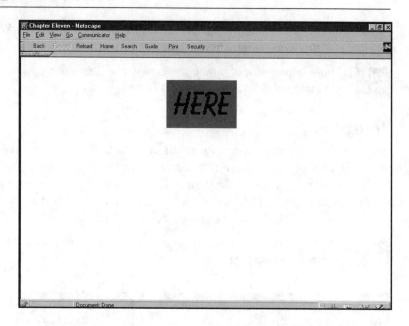

 You need four things to make this work: two images, a JavaScript, and a command that calls for the images and the effect of the script. You can get them right from the online tutorial at http://www.htmlgoodies.com/tutors/imageflip.html.

The effect I put together is done with two images named goof3.gif and goof4.gif. Why goof? Because I'm your father, that's why! Actually, that's not the answer, but I've always wanted to say that.

There. Now that that's settled...

The Script

You should have been able to get the two images from the links. If you haven't already, do so. Now you need the script. It goes between the <HEAD> and </HEAD> commands on your page. You can transcribe it from here or get it from the online version of this tutorial.

```
<SCRIPT LANGUAGE="JavaScript">
<!-- hide from none JavaScript Browsers
Image1= new Image(75,50)
Image1.src = "goof3.gif"
Image2 = new Image(75,50)
Image2.src = "goof4.gif"
function SwapOut() {
document.imageflip.src = Image2.src; return true;
}
```

```
function SwapBack() {
document.imageflip.src = Image1.src; return true;
}
// - stop hiding -->
</SCRIPT>
```

Denoting the Graphics

Now that you have placed that script into your document between the HEAD commands, you need to denote what graphics are used. You do that in this section of the script:

```
Image1= new Image(75,50)
Image1.src = "goof3.gif"
Image2 = new Image(75,50)
Image2.src = "goof4.gif"
```

When you start editing, remember that the image that appears first (without any mouseover) is the one listed second. Remember, this is a flip. When this script is made functional, the second graphic is the first to display, and then the original image comes back again. Are you with me?

Put in the names of your images in reverse order. Next, be sure to denote the images' width and height. The images I am using are 75 pixels wide by 50 pixels high. See that in the code? Put your height and width numbers in where I have (75,50). Width is listed first.

Before you ask, no, the images do not have to be the same size. But it does enhance the effect if they are.

Also keep in mind that these images need to load quickly. You see, the second image is not loaded when the mouse first goes over the area. When the mouse passes over, the script is activated and the second image is called for. Then you have a slight loading time span. With that in mind, go with small graphics.

Call for the Script

Now let's set up the magic. This is the command you place in the <BODY> section of your document where you want this image to appear:

```
<A HREF="index.html" onMouseOver="SwapOut()" onMouseOut="SwapBack()">
<IMG NAME="imageflip" SRC="goof4.gif" WIDTH="75" HEIGHT="50"
➥BORDER=0></A>
```

You know this format well. This is a simple HREF link command with some JavaScript event handlers. You can read about event handlers in the advanced JavaScript tutorial in this very chapter. Notice that the hypertext link is constructed so that the image is what is active. The height and width of the image are denoted and the image's border is set to 0.

The image that is being called for is the image you listed second in the script. Again, the script hasn't been called into play yet. The command is just displaying the image you tell it to—in this case, goof4.gif.

FAQs from the HTML Goodies Web Site

Q. Can I make an imagemap that works like an image flip, like in sections?

A. Sure! Make a fake imagemap and then make each image an image flip. This is involved, but what a great effect! (See the fake map tutorial in Chapter 4, "Imagemaps.")

I have built a fully functioning fake imagemap out of image flips. See it work at http://www.htmlgoodies.com/book/fakeflipmap.html. Be sure to look at the source code!

Creating More Than One Image Flip on a Page

I'm sure you can do this another way, but I add more image flips to the page by choosing a new word that goes in place of imageflip in the previous example. Let's say the new word is just *image*. I would then change out the word *imageflip* with the word *image* three times—once in the command and twice in the script. See that?

I would then change out the script with two new images and redo the entire process—a new script for each image flip I wanted, each with a different name used so that the browser can keep them separate.

Again, other methods probably exist, but the script is so small that I can copy and paste faster than by creating new JavaScript lines.

And that's that. Now go start flippin'.

Using External JavaScripts

People ask me all the time how they can set it up so that one page is inserted into a whole slew of HTML documents. Others want to only post a JavaScript once and have it appear in multiple HTML pages without copying and pasting on every page. Well, this is how you do it: Use an external JavaScript.

For the most part, I always tell you to place the JavaScript you want to run directly on the page it affects. That rule holds true for more involved JavaScript, but what if you could place a single JavaScript file into your site and run it off of every page, similar to what happens in a cascading style sheets model?

For instance, say you want a current date on every page. You could either copy and paste a date JavaScript into every page or you could place it once as its own page and link all the other pages to it. One script, many date stamps. This is how you can do it.

The Date Stamp

The JavaScript that posted the date in the online version of this tutorial does not appear on that HTML page. Feel free to go and look at the source code on the tutorial if you want, but it really doesn't. The script is written somewhere else. I know it's killing you. You want to look at the source code. Don't do it! Don't give in to the pressure! Be your own person!

Or go, "Look...I don't care."

To get that date on the page, I created what is known as a *JS* file, or a *JavaScript* file. The JavaScript file is nothing more than a JavaScript saved as a text file and given the extension .js.

Let's say you have a JavaScript like the one that placed the date shown just before. In fact, let's say you have exactly that script. This is what it looked like when I started:

```
<SCRIPT LANGUAGE="JavaScript">
<!-- hide script from old browsers
test = new Date()
month = test.getMonth()
month = (month * 1) + 1
day = test.getDate()
year = test.getYear()
document.write(" ",month,"/",day,"/19",year," ")
// end hiding script from old browsers -->
</SCRIPT>
```

There you go. This is a very short, simple script. Even if you are not overly schooled in JavaScript, you can pretty much pick out how it works. It gets the day, the month, and the year from your computer and posts them all in a row with slashes between the numbers. Ta da! You have a date.

Creating the JS File

Take the script and write it, all by itself, into a text editor. It should be the only thing on the page. Now, knock off the beginning and end SCRIPT commands. These things:

```
<SCRIPT LANGUAGE="JavaScript">
</SCRIPT>
```

Get rid of them. Erase them. You pick them up again later. Now the page should look like this:

```
<!-- hide script from old browsers
test = new Date()
month = test.getMonth()
month = (month * 1) + 1
day = test.getDate()
year = test.getYear()
document.write(" ",month,"/",day,"/19",year," ")
// end hiding script from old browsers -->
```

Now do a Save As command and save the file as text only, just the same way you would an HTML file. Give it a name of eight letters or less and add the extension .js.

Let's say you want to name this file george. Do a Save As, making sure you are saving as text alone, and give the file the name george.js. Again, make sure you give the file a name of eight letters or less. I have found that more than eight letters messes up the process. Why? My guess is that it's a leftover DOS concern. But that's a guess. You're now done with that.

Moving along...

Calling for the JavaScript File

You have the JavaScript file saved. Now you need to call for it in another document. Let's get back to the JavaScript that produced the date. I followed the same instructions I just gave you and created a file called datestmp.js.

I placed these commands to get the effect on my page:

```
<SCRIPT SRC="datestmp.js">
</SCRIPT>
```

See, I told you you'd pick up those two commands again—that's all you need. The JavaScript denoted by the .js extension appears any time you place those commands on your page. Just remember to lose the beginning and ending SCRIPT commands in the JavaScript file or you get an error.

This is how I tell people to set it so that they can change one page and content in multiple pages change. You set up this same format of a JS file, except the JS file is made up of document.write("") statements. Remember them from the new window tutorial?

Whatever you write in the quotation marks shows up on the page as text. Use enough of them and you can enter full paragraphs. That way, you change the text in the JS file and the text on all the pages that use the file update. Simple.

FAQs from the HTML Goodies Web Site

Q. **I want to use the external JavaScript using a script that is called for using an onLoad command. You only show it with a self-contained script. Can it be done?**

A. You have to write the onLoad command on each page. That's not going to come along with the script because it has to be placed in the BODY command on the page.

A Few Things to Keep in Mind

I found a couple of concerns through my experience:

- External JavaScripts work best with self-contained JavaScripts. Scripts that have multiple parts throw a lot of errors. This is better to just paste the script onto the document in those cases.

- External JavaScripts do not work with multiple scripts in the same .js file. You often find that an effect is created by two JavaScripts, one following right after the other. No dice here. To get the effect, you either need to have a <SCRIPT> command in the .js file or call for two JS files. Either kills the effect. In cases such as that it's best to just paste the scripts onto the page.

Remember the <!-- and //-->?

That's the general idea. Now go and JavaScript your viewers to death. Just remember to surround your JavaScripts with these two commands: <!-- and //-->.

I did that earlier, see? Those commands hide the text from viewers that cannot read JavaScript. It doesn't make the browser run the script, but it stops JavaScript-impaired surfers from getting any error codes when they access your page.

 See an online example of an external JavaScript at http://www.htmlgoodies.com/book/ externaljs.html.

Browser Choice Script

This effect is tough to show in book form, so I explain what happens here. This script sits on a page that your user logs onto. The script looks at the user's browser and loads the page you specify, depending on what browser the user is running.

You can see this tutorial online at `http://www.htmlgoodies.com/beyond/browserpage.html`.

This JavaScript is great for pages that have Internet Explorer- or Netscape Navigator-specific commands or Netscape-specific JavaScripts. You can create two different versions of each of your pages, one for Internet Explorer and one for Netscape Navigator, so that your user gets far fewer errors from your site. This is more work for you, and of course you don't have to double every page, but it's a great effect if you take the time.

Why Would I Want This?

I do and I do for you, and this is the thanks I get.

The two browser powers that be, Netscape and Microsoft, are having a bit of a tiff. They are in a fun game of one-upmanship. Each is trying to create a bigger and better mousetrap to squash the other. In doing so, the browsers are moving further apart in terms of *events* (things they do). That means that you get an error code, or a nasty message, or nothing if you are using one browser and the page you're visiting has stuff intended for the other browser. You can read a whole bunch of tips on how to get around some of these differences in Chapter 15, "Other Stuff You Should Really Know."

This little beauty of a JavaScript saves a lot of surfing headaches by solving the major problem of browser type right off the bat. If you wrote a page intended for Internet Explorer use alone—bingo—Internet Explorer users go to the page you set up for that browser. Netscape Navigator users go to another page you created for them.

This is a very simple script that assumes your users are running either Navigator or Explorer. I don't know that that's such a big assumption. The two browsers do own the majority of the market. However, the script is written in such a way that other browser types are supported and browsers that do not support JavaScript also get a page.

Let's Look at the Script

The script is rather small. It looks like this:

```
<SCRIPT LANGUAGE="JavaScript">

if (navigator.appName == "Microsoft Internet Explorer")
{location.href ="msiepage.html"}

else

if (navigator.appName == "Netscape")
{location.href ="nspage.html"}
```

```
else

if (navigator.appName != "Microsoft Internet Explorer")
{location.href="textpage.html"}


</script>
```

The script is very simple. The first section makes the statement, If this browser is Microsoft Internet Explorer, go to msiepage.html. That's the part that reads as follows:

```
if (navigator.appName == "Microsoft Internet Explorer")
{location.href ="msiepage.html"}
```

The second section is an else statement, which performs another test if the first wasn't correct. This section asks if the browser is Netscape. If it is then the page nspage.html is served up. Finally, let's set up a catch-all. It asks if the browser isn't Microsoft Internet Explorer. Well, you already know it isn't so if the browser didn't match the top two conditions it must be something other than Navigator or Explorer, right? Yes. You serve it up the text page.

This is a pretty simple and effective system.

How Do I Do It?

You need at least three pages:

- The page with the JavaScript and the simple version of the pages
- A page intended for Netscape Navigator users
- A page intended for Internet Explorer users

 When you have all three pages ready, FTP them all to your server. Remember that all hypertext links to this system need to go to the page containing the JavaScript, or no one gets the effect. See this JavaScript in action online at http://www.htmlgoodies.com/book/ choosebrowser.html.

Watch carefully. The effect happens mighty fast. When you get the page declaring your browser type, look at the location bar. You see you've been sent to one of the three pages listed in the previous script.

Shopping Cart

This is easily one of the most requested items at HTML Goodies, and with good reason. The shopping cart is becoming a large part of Internet commerce. Anyone with a number of items to sell would want to display their products in this across-page format.

 This is a very involved tutorial. Seeing it online helps a great deal. Go to http://www. htmlgoodies.com/beyond/shoppingcart.html.

As you go through this tutorial, you see why I have had to wait a while to get one of these carts to hand out. They are huge undertakings that require a great deal of talent and knowledge to write. When I went out looking for a cart to use in a tutorial, I ran across a lot of free, but cheaply built items. The good ones were all a pay-for deal. Until this one showed up on my doorstep.

This shopping cart was written by Gordon Smith for his Scottish Gifts Online World Wide Web Page. He used this shopping cart program to run the site.

I'm a big fan of Gordon's site for a couple of reasons. One, I'm Scottish. The Burns' have their own tartan and everything. Second, he allowed me to use this shopping cart programming to help you.

I'm a fan of Gordon himself because he's a heck of a JavaScript programmer.

What's a Shopping Cart?

A *shopping cart* is a series of pages linked through some sort of programming (usually Perl or JavaScript) that allows data to be transferred along with the viewer as she moves from page to page. This is an example:

A woman enters a site. That site sells clothing. One page displays the dresses the site has for sale, another displays the shoes, and yet another displays the accessories. The woman clicks to purchase a dress. The purchase is then added to her shopping cart. She then moves to the shoes page and clicks to purchase a pair. That item too is added to her shopping cart. Finally, she moves to the accessories page and adds a scarf. After choosing the items she wanted to purchase, she clicks the order link and a page pops up, listing all her purchases with a final price. That's the concept of a shopping cart.

It seems like a rather simple process on this side of the curtain, but behind the scenes it's quite a difficult task to get that purchase data to move along from page to page as the viewer shops around.

Note

Put quite bluntly, this shopping cart is very nice, however, it works in an insecure environment. That means none of the information being placed into it is secure.

If you intend to use this shopping cart for a purpose where money is involved, I suggest you don't. I have started numerous e-commerce sites and the one thing that I have found over the years is that people require that their monetary transactions happen within a secure, encrypted environment. That's something that is truly nothing to play around with.

If you are going to start an e-commerce site, I suggest you find a professional who can create your shopping cart within a secure environment. This tutorial just helps you understand how the cart functions. If you want to use it simply to enable your users to create a shopping list and then use a different, more secure method of payment, such as PayPal, this is a fine cart to use.

However, if you intend to use the cart and have the user put in a credit card number at the end, you're inviting trouble.

How Does This Shopping Cart Work?

I should state it right up front so that no mistake are made: This shopping cart uses cookies.

FAQs from the HTML Goodies Web Site

Q. I hate cookies. Is there any way to do a shopping cart without them?

A. Yes. You could carry the cookie information across from page to page by holding it in the location line of the browser. My art site `http://www.streetartist.com` does this. It was done that way so you could specifically avoid using cookies. Go to the site and try a search. Notice the location text becomes extremely long. That's the cookie information being carried across pages.

I want to give you the information regarding how to do it, but I don't really know. I paid a person to build the system for me in a language called PHP.

If you intend to use a shopping cart for e-commerce, I suggest you do the same. Hire a professional to do the job for you.

If cookies are a new concept to you, please read the cookie tutorial in Chapter 15 for a lot of important information. I make that statement because many people believe cookies are the scourge of the Internet high seas. I see them the same way.

Plus, if you want this shopping cart effect, you need to store the information somewhere as the viewer moves from page to page. The user's cookie is the easiest way to do it without inventing some new method of writing to the user's hard drive or to a file online.

Cookies are in wide use today and as long as your user knows you are using them, I don't see the problem. Be honest.

This is the great thing about this shopping cart: It is already fully self-contained and requires little assembly. In fact, the entire set of pages and programming were sent to me and I went in and cut away anything that wasn't specifically needed for the cart to work. I then entered a lot of comment lines into the code. Every time you need to alter or enter a piece of information to make this script work for your needs, it is denoted right in the page's code.

What you get here is a bare-bones template that enables you to add your own images, text, and prices. As long as you do not alter the JavaScript programming, the cart should work straightaway.

Let's See It

Go and play with the shopping cart program online, so you can get a feel for it; then come back to the book and I tell you how to alter it. Figure 11.11 shows a picture of the shopping cart template. You can probably figure all this out just by looking at the source codes of each page, but I go through it all anyway.

 You can view the shopping cart in action at `http://www.htmlgoodies.com/beyond/` `shopcartindex.html`.

This is what you are looking at: The shopping cart is in a frames format and it must stay that way or you get a warning and errors. The following are three pages of items you can buy.

- Page 1 has only one item on it, valued at $1.11.
- Page 2 has three items on it, valued at $2.22, $3.33, and $4.44.
- Page 3 also has three items on it, valued at $5.55, $6.66, and $7.77.

You add an item to the cart by clicking the button that reads Add This Item to My Total. Take a choice away by clicking the button that reads Subtract This Item from My Total. You can click to review your order at any time; you see the total of what you've chosen.

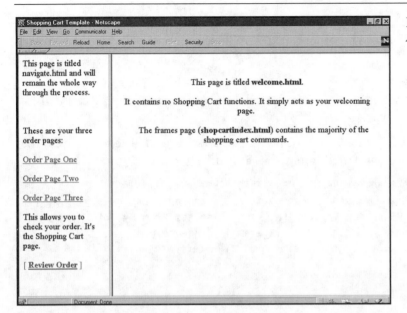

Figure 11.11
A shopping cart template.

The Pages

You need a series of seven items to get this to work on your server. You can download them one at a time or grab them all in a little zip file from the online version of this tutorial. Please remember that you need all the pages in order for this to work. The effect does not display outside the frames format and you get a bunch of errors. In short, get them all and put them in the same directory. The following are the pages you need to grab:

- shopcartindex.html The main frames page.
- navigate.html The page that appears in the left frame.
- welcome.html The page that appears in the right frame.
- pageone.html The first page of items.
- pagetwo.html The second page of items.
- pagethree.html The third page of items.
- order.html The page that appears when you ask to review your order.

You can go into these template pages and add text and images to your heart's delight. I am not going into that here. What I am going to do here is explain how to alter the shopping cart functions so that you can set prices and get the information sent to you.

You really only need to alter four pages: the three pages with shopping cart items (pageone.html, pagetwo.html, and pagethree.html) and the order.html page.

Altering pageone.html

If you understand how to alter this page, you can alter the other two shopping cart item pages. They all work the same.

Again, these instructions are printed right in the code of pageone.html. The following is the basic shopping cart item format pasted from pageone.html:

```
<INPUT TYPE=button NAME=addbox VALUE= "Add This Item To My Total"
➥onclick=Loc_additem('p1i1','1.11','Page_1_item_1','pageone.html')>
<INPUT TYPE=button NAME=subbox VALUE= "Subtract This Item From My Total"
➥onclick=Loc_subitem('p1i1','1.11','page_1_item_1','pageone.html')>
You Have Ordered This Many Of This Item:<INPUT TYPE=text NAME=p1i1
➥ SIZE=2>
```

This is what's happening:

- ● INPUT   Denotes a data input item.
- ● TYPE=button   Denotes that is a button.
- ● NAME=   Denotes a name for this item so that it can be recognized across pages. This is the addbox.
- ● VALUE=   Denotes what is written on the button.
- ● onclick=Loc_additem   Denotes that when this button is clicked, the item in the parentheses needs to be added.
- ● ('p1i1','1.11','Page_1_item_1','pageone.html')   Denotes the parameters of the item represented by this button.
- ● 'p1i1'   The item's identifier. p1i1 stand for page 1, item 1.
- ● '1.11'   The item's price. At the moment it's a dollar and eleven.
- ● 'Page_1_Item_1'   The page and item identifier that accompany this information when it moves to the order page.
- ● 'pageone.html'   Dittos. You see these items listed when you run the order form. The second button works the same way, except it subtracts the item.
- ● INPUT TYPE=text NAME=p1i1 SIZE=2   Denotes the little box that keeps a running total of how many of this item were ordered. Note the NAME= command—it is p1i1, thus linking this box to the buttons.

Actually, ('p1i1','1.11','Page_1_item_1','pageone.html') is the only section you should really be concerned about. It denotes the item identifier and price. If you alter it, as you have to change the price, you must change each item in two or three places. See that earlier? If you change the price, it must be changed twice. If you change the identifier, it has to be changed three times. With me so far?

You could have 20 or more items on each page. You just have to come up with new identifiers for each of the items so that the JavaScript shopping cart can distinguish one from another. The easiest way to do it is to simply copy and paste what is there earlier in this chapter and change out the little section within the parentheses.

FAQs from the HTML Goodies Web Site

Q. You say I can add items to the shopping cart program. Can I take them away? I only want two on each page.

A. Yes, just be sure to remove the entire block of code or you get errors.

Altering order.html

This page requires a great deal of information, so it can send the results of the shopping cart to your e-mail box. Slowly go through the page looking for sections written in all capital letters. I put them there, along with some comment statements pointing out some very important parts. (Note that all items that must be changed are not commented out. Look for CAPS.)

The biggest concern is that you make sure to change out the main FORM command that contains the mailto: section. This is set up to work just like a basic mailto: guestbook, that must be changed out with your e-mail address.

Using a CGI with the Order Form

The author of this shopping cart, Gordon Smith, has also included a CGI that works with this order form. The CGI is a Perl script and is named formmail.pl. The CGI is only available in the zip packet shown earlier. You also notice that a thanku.html page is included in the zip packet. That is the page that the CGI displays after someone has filled out and sent the form information to you.

Installing the CGI is a chore unto itself. I have three tutorials that walk you through the process of installing a very similar type of CGI in Chapter 12, "Common Gateway Interface (CGI)." If you follow the format I have laid out in my CGI tutorials, you are able to get this one up and running. Again, the CGI is only available in the zip packet download, but it is not required to make this work. The order form acts as its own simple `mailto:` form, so the information gets to your e-mail box.

FAQs from the HTML Goodies Web Site

Q. You say not to ask for credit cards with the shopping cart program. Then what do I need to do to be able to accept cards over the Net?

A. The first place I would go is your local bank. You need an affiliation with a financial institution to accept cards. You have to get what is known as a merchant account. The bank gives you the tools you need to process card numbers.

Q. How much does it cost to be able to accept credit cards over the Internet?

A. Prices vary but the pay structure is similar. You always have a setup fee and a monthly fee after that. It also costs a few cents every time someone "swipes" his card. Usually it's a small percentage (such as 1% or 2%).

Print with JavaScript

You know what I hate? I mean other than bad Christmas presents and the blink command. I hate it when I'm happily answering questions and, right out from under me, the variables change.

There I was, happily answering questions when a fellow asks if he can initiate a print using JavaScript. I happily answered that he cannot, but he can set where the page breaks when printing via CSS print commands. I also gave him the URL because I'm a nice guy. Here it is: `http://htmlgoodies.earthweb.com/beyond/css_print.html`.

Why am I "happily" answering that he cannot get a print, you ask? Well, it's certainly not because of the nice people who want to offer a link or button that allows a print at the user's request; it's because of those who would flood their pages with print commands so that when you visit their pages everything you look at prints. How fun is that?!

Well, as soon as I hit enter, posting the message, a bunch of email came in telling me that with IE5 you can use a JavaScript function to get the print to fire on its own. After gulping, I asked a few people about the actual command. It is:

```
window.print()
```

Print is a method of the object "window." At first I thought that the command was simply capturing the buttons along the top of the browser window, so all I had to do was substitute "print" with one of the other items, such as "mail" or "home". No dice. I also tried setting up the same type of format with items found in the menus such as "properties" and "Options." Error after error. This is apparently put into the DTD as a method unto itself.

Saving Grace!

The good thing about the command, the way the authors set it up, is that it does not immediately fire a print. It actually only fires the print window (see Figure 11.12).

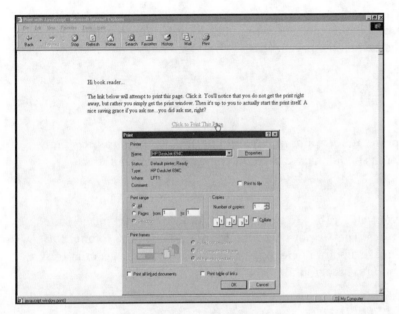

Figure 11.12
The print window.

Then it is up to the person who triggered the method whether to continue with the print or not. That's good because I can see a ton of problems with printers not being turned on and huge, huge files being set to print.

 You can try out the JavaScript print function online at http://www.htmlgoodies.com/ book/printjs.html.

This is the code:

```
<A HREF="javascript:window.print()">Click to Print This Page</A>
```

Using the command "javascript:" in place of a URL triggers the JavaScript. That enables a hypertext link to fire off the JavaScript.

And before you ask, yep, this works with almost any JavaScript event handler as long as the format enables you to write it as a specific line or trigger a function.

You can set it to print off an image:

```
<A HREF="javascript:window.print()"><IMG SRC="print_image.gif" BORDER="0"></A>
```

You can set it to trigger off a button:

```
<FORM>
<INPUT TYPE="button" onClick="window.print()">
</FORM>
```

And, if you really want to be annoying, off just about any event handler like this, adding onLoad forces a print request when the page loads:

```
onLoad="window.print()"
```

Some Suggestions

Okay, now you have the power to force a print request, but that doesn't mean to simply offer a print on any page. You should make a point of being helpful to your users.

Make a Page for Printing

The Goodies tutorials, as you can see, have a wavy background, a bunch of images, and stuff stuck in all over the place. They're not very good for printing. If I was to offer this page for printing, I would make a point of creating basically a text-only page, or at least a page with limited images and no background.

Make the Page Printer-Friendly

I would lose all text colors and make sure the width of the page was no more than 500px, left justified so that what was shown on the screen would print on the printed page in the same way.

Enable the User to Choose to Print

My print offering would be text at the bottom or an icon that doesn't intrude. Everyone knows they can already print your pages without any help from your coding. So, make this something you offer as a help rather than putting it into people's faces.

Never Attach This to a User Event

Don't set this to an onLoad, or an onMouseOver, or some other user event. It only tends to upset those who have visited your page and probably stops them from coming back.

There you go. Now you can set up a print request through JavaScript. If used correctly, this is a very nice addition to a page and a help to the user, so use it wisely and well.

Pre-Loading Images with JavaScript

When I get my brain wrapped around a topic for a tutorial, I usually do a great deal of researching around the Net, interviewing people I think might know the answer, and just generally playing around with trial and error. The primary purpose is to put together a good, all-encompassing tutorial. The secondary purpose is so I don't look like an idiot by writing something that's incorrect for the entire world to see.

That said, I bring you this tutorial on pre-loading images. This one was a bit of a struggle. Those with whom I spoke had never given this topic much thought. So I played around with it. This is what I found.

Why Pre-Load Anything?

Speed, man, speed! Fast, fast, fast!

Have you ever noticed that pages you've visited in the past always load faster than a page you're visiting for the first time? It seems like you only have to go through all that item-by-item downloading once and from that point on, you're good to go.

Well, the reason that page, and all those images, came so fast the second time was that they had been cached (pronounced "cashed"). If you go into the guts of your computer, you find the folders that house the Netscape Navigator program files. You most likely find them under the "Program Files" folder.

If you delve deep enough into the "Netscape" folder, you see a subfolder actually called "cache."

The cache for Internet Explorer is a little harder to find as it's located under the "Windows" folder and has the name "Temporary Internet Files." Whatever it's called, that folder represents a section of the hard drive set aside for the sole purpose of housing the HTML documents, images, and other types of files you view in your browser window.

The first time you entered into a page, that HTML document and the images it called for were all written to the cache for later use. The next time you enter into that page, the browser knows it can load the page and images off its own hard drive rather than waiting for the server to offer the files. As you've seen, it's a much faster process. So, this is the thinking to pre-loading:

> Why not cache all the images a user requires to move through your site when they first arrive? That way, the user moves through the remainder of your pages lickety-split. Great idea, huh?

Just remember that caching everything up front certainly takes longer than just download-ing the current page images and such. You can try to get around that by only caching what is needed for the next few pages rather than trying to throw everything down the Internet pipe at once.

Load 'em

Now that the teacher in me has babbled on, I'll get into how it's done. Please make a point of putting these commands in the HEAD section of your HTML document. Putting these commands within the BODY section slows the page a great deal. A student of mine found that out the hard way when a 40K image just took forever to come in. The misplaced pre-load commands were the reason. The following is the basic format:

```
<SCRIPT LANGUAGE="JavaScript">
Image1= new Image(175,50)
Image1.src = "image1.gif"

Image2 = new Image(25,30)
Image2.src = "image2.gif"

Image3 = new Image(125,80)
Image3.src = "image3.gif"

Image4 = new Image(65,224)
Image4.src = "image4.gif"

Image5 = new Image(89,201)
Image5.src = "image5.gif"
</SCRIPT>
```

The previous example is pre-loading five images I have named image1.gif, through image5.gif. The format is not new to you if you've ever tried to install almost any image flip JavaScript. Most of them use this method to pre-load the image that is "flipped-to."

Let's take a look at the format:

- Image1=new Image JavaScript that names an image that is to be captured.
- (175,50) The width and then height of the image to be cached.
- Image1.src= JavaScript for the location (source) of the image to be cached.
- image1.gif The actual name of the image.

The name of your images do not have to be `image1.gif`, `image2.gif`, and so on. You can use any names for the images. But the JavaScript `Image1=new Image` should follow the counting format I show previously.

If your images are in subdirectories or are on other servers, make a point of placing the entire path to the image where I only have the name so that the browser can find the image to cache it.

This JavaScript can go anywhere on the document, but I would suggest getting it up high. In the HEAD commands is best.

That's the trick. Just continue to follow this pattern again and again until you have cached (pre-loaded) all the images your users require.

So, go and try to pre-load a few images. You may just make it better for those who come around to see your pages.

Post by Screen Size

 I want to tell you a little about your computer. Travel to `http://www.htmlgoodies.com/` `book/screensize.html` *and I display your current screen settings.*

I posted the info on the page with a simple little JavaScript. It looks like this:

```
<SCRIPT LANGUAGE="javascript">
var width = screen.width
var height = screen.height
document.write("<B>You're set to "+width+ "X" +height+"</B>")
</SCRIPT>
```

Cool, huh? But knowing a user's screen setting goes well beyond simply making paranoid people believe you're watching them through their computer screens. If you know the size of a user's monitor, you can use that information to your advantage.

I get letters all the time asking me how to make pages look good on all sizes of computer screens. I've offered some tips in the past, but it's still been a problem.

In this tutorial, I offer two scripts. One acts as a general, overall direction script. The user is sent to a page designed for his or her screen. The second script is an internal script that writes items to the page depending on the user's screen settings. Let's start with the Big One.

Redirection Choice

This little script works just like the traditional Browser Choice script discussed earlier in this chapter. The script sits on a page by itself. The user logs into the page and, depending on their screen settings, the user is sent to a specific page made for their screen settings.

The script only checks the user's monitor width settings to make the choice. Because scrolling is common on the Net, I don't see a need to check the height of the page.

The JavaScript code that returns the user's screen settings width is screen.width. So, using that info, come up with the script that redirects the user. Remember, this script has probably never be seen by the user. You point your readers at a page that contains this script simply to get the redirecting effect. Thus, no need for images, extra text, or a lot of other fancy things.

The script looks like this:

```
<SCRIPT LANGUAGE="javascript">

if (screen.width == 1600)
{parent.location.href='1600page.html'}

if (screen.width == 1280)
{parent.location.href='1280page.html'}

if (screen.width == 1152)
{parent.location.href='1152page.html'}

if (screen.width == 1024)
{parent.location.href='1024page.html'}

if (screen.width == 800)
{parent.location.href='800page.html'}

if (screen.width == 640)
{parent.location.href='640page.html'}

if (screen.width <= 639)
{parent.location.href='text.html'}

</SCRIPT>
```

Now go see the script in action at http://htmlgoodies.earthweb.com/book/post_by_ screen_tester.html. *Remember, you don't see the script. It simply takes you to a new page created for your own screen setting.*

The script is set to test for the most common screen width settings: 1600, 1280, 1152, 1024, 800, 640, and those below 640. I talked to a few of my computer friends and they informed me that the chances of running into a screen width setting that differs from this is quite unlikely if at all possible.

This is the basic concept of the script.

```
if (screen.width == 1600)
      {parent.location.href='1600page.html'}
```

The script is set up as a series of IF statements. The browser checks one after the other down the line until the settings match. Notice the double equal sign. That's JavaScript for "is equal to."

When equality is found, the line of code within the curly brackets is triggered. In all cases, that code created a link in the parent window (the top level window) and the hypertext link is enacted. The script is written so that at least one of the IF statements is true.

Internal Page Choice

Okay, the page redirection is usually enough to solve the situation, but it also means that you have to create multiple pages. That's a bit of work, and for some things it might be overkill.

Let's say you have an image that is 850 pixels wide. On 800 and 640 and below screen settings, that banner rolls off the screen and creates a horizontal scrollbar. Not good. The easiest way to solve the problem is to create a 750px and a 630px version of the image for 800px and 640px browsers. All you need is a script that reads the browser width settings and writes the image code to the page, so the correct image is posted. I happen to have such a script right here.

Remember that this gets written right to the document, not on a page by itself such as the previous script. The script writes to the page depending on the screen setting rather than performing a full redirect.

```
<SCRIPT LANGUAGE="javascript">

if (screen.width < 639)
{document.write("Hello there")}

if (screen.width == 640)
{document.write("<IMG SRC=630px.gif>")}

if (screen.width == 800){
document.write("<IMG SRC=750px.gif>")}
```

```
if (screen.width >= 1024)
{document.write("<IMG SRC=850px.gif>")}


</SCRIPT>
```

 Now go see the script in action at http://htmlgoodies.earthweb.com/beyond/post_by_ screen_tester2.html. *See if the image posted doesn't fit nicely into your screen setting.*

This script works on much the same format at the script you just played with, but I make a couple more assumptions. Notice the same general IF statement setup.

```
if (screen.width < 639)
{document.write("Hello there")}

if (screen.width == 640)
{document.write("<IMG SRC=630px.gif>")}

if (screen.width == 800)
{document.write("<IMG SRC=750px.gif>")}

if (screen.width >= 1024)
{document.write("<IMG SRC=850px.gif>")}
```

It starts with the monitor tests. If the monitor setting is less than 639, the text "Hello there" is posted. My assumption is that a large image can only be shrunk so much, so there comes a point where you post text rather than a smaller image.

Next, the text looks for 640, 800, and anything 1024 and higher. Note the >=. That means "greater than or equal to." If you want you can continue the "equal to" format for all the screen sizes and create images for all. I just figured that after the screen was wide enough why keep making images?

Finally, notice that I get the image flag text to the page using a document.write statement. document.write does what it says. It writes text to the page. In this case, it writes the flag for a specific image to the page. Just remember to have any text you want written to the page in double quotes, so the JavaScript understands it is a text string and not a command to be followed.

The real beauty of this kind of scripting is that you only need one page. On that page is a script that posts differing items due to conditions.

What more can I say? You've got the tools so that your pages fit the user's screen settings. Use it to make better, and better displaying, pages.

Chapter 12

Common Gateway Interface (CGI)

What is this thing I'm calling CGI? This is an acronym for Common Gateway Interface. When I first started hearing about CGIs, I thought it was a programming language. Not so. CGI is pretty much an all-encompassing term that refers to an application that acts upon data that is offered to it. A CGI can be written in a great many programming languages, but the most popular are Perl, C++, and lately, Java.

Note

Since I first wrote this book, I have posted a series of Perl CGI primers. If you get the urge to delve further into the actual construction of these scripts, take a look:

```
http://www.htmlgoodies.com/primers/perl/
```

The three CGIs that are being offered to you in this chapter are all in written in Perl.

This chapter walks you through attaching to already existing CGIs and adding three very popular CGIs—a hit counter, a guestbook CGI, and a bulletin board server—to your own site.

Using a Hit Counter

This is without a doubt the number one item people ask me about. Everyone wants a counter. Why? I don't know. My guess is because someone else has one. I don't have a lot of room to talk. I have one.

Actually, some valid reasons to have a counter exist. The best I can think of is to track your site's traffic. If you have a counter on every page, you can get a general idea of what people find most interesting on your site and start gearing your content more toward your audience's interests.

If you get into selling advertising space on your site, a counter is quite helpful when the person paying for the banner ad wants to know how many people actually came to see it.

Having one is a pretty good thing...and it does look cool.

 This was one of the original HTML Goodies tutorials! This is online at `http://www.htmlgoodies.com/beyond/counter.html`.

If you have already attempted to surf the Net to find a nice, easy page telling you how to put up a counter, you have probably encountered something that uses words such as bitmap, standalone daemon, config file, and inetd. Right? Not exactly an easy "how to." The reason the pages are so darn technical is because counters are technical. This is a fact of Internet life.

This is the information you didn't want to read: I cannot give you a set command that plops a counter in place. What I can do is tell you how to go about finding the command that plops the counter on your page. Stay with me here, so I can get you a little closer to having a counter.

Granted, counters look great. They do, however, have several drawbacks:

- Slow page completion.
- Page transfer completely stopping if the counter CGI is down.
- Faulty counters that count incorrectly.
- The viewer never seeing your count if his inline images are turned off.
- Honestly, how good does a counter that only reads 15 look?

FAQs from the HTML Goodies Web Site

Q. I want my counter to start at 50,000, so it looks like I have a lot of visitors. How do I do that?

A. It depends on the counter in general. Some enable you to do that, some don't. You need to check out your counter's properties with the owner to find out.

If I haven't talked you out of a counter, let's go on...

Formatting a Counter

A counter is an image. In most cases, it's a bitmap. Remember that word from before? Don't let it throw you. An image is an image is an image. It shows up on your page. This little image, however, comes from the CGI that you attach to. The following is the command I used to get a counter on my page:

```
<IMG SRC="http://www.htmlgoodies.com/cgi-bin/counter?width=5&link=
{http://www.htmlgoodies.com/} {counter.html}">
```

Looks pretty scary, huh? It isn't really. The command is doing four things:

- `IMG SRC=` Tells the computer that what is returned from the CGI is an image. Where you place the counter command on the page denotes where the image falls.
- `"http://www.htmlgoodies.com/cgi-bin/counter?` The path (the URL, if you will) to the counter CGI.
- `width=5` Tells the CGI how large a counter to return.
- `{http://www.htmlgoodies.com/}{counter.html}"` The path back to the page that should receive the counter.

I liked this, too. The following is the very basic format almost all counters follow:

```
<IMG SRC="PATH TO THE COUNTER CGI/width=#&link=PATH TO THE PAGE">
```

Because counter CGIs can be written in many different ways, the actual format that works for you may differ slightly from this one, but not too much. The concept is that it's an image.

I have seen some counter formats that do not have the WIDTH command and others that do not enclose the path to the page in the brackets, but this is the format for the most part.

I told you this gets technical.

Finding a CGI Counter on the Net

The format works for my server and my server alone. You might think (spoken with evil British accent) "Hah! The fool! He has given us the path to his counter CGI! I shall change the information in the command with my page's address, so the counter returns a bitmap to me!!! Ha ha ha ha ha ha!" No dice.

You see, people who write these little counter CGIs know they are very popular. In turn—as is the case here—the CGI is written so that unless you are on the same server as the CGI, you get a nasty message in return. This is what you get if you attach to the CGI noted here:

```
Counter Only Counts Our Pages OK, Joe. You're beginning to anger me! Can I get a
counter or not?
```

Sure. You can in three ways. All three work, but one is just better than another.

From Your Internet Service Provider (ISP)

Always an easy answer, huh Joe? Well, yes. It could very well be that the people in charge of your server have a little CGI waiting just for you. All you have to do is attach to it. Contact her and ask. Either that, or you can surf to other pages on your own server and see how they got their counters to work. My guess is that a counter CGI is just waiting for you if you're on a server of any size or that allows imagemaps.

From the Public Domain

They have those things?! Yeah, you find a few on the Web. They are very overtaxed and can slow your page considerably, but they're out there. I have a few listed in "Net Notes" later in this chapter.

These are nice sites that enable you to choose the type of counter you want and then enable you to fill out a form that hands you the IMG format to place on your page. Read it over carefully before attaching! There might be costs if your site gets more than a set number of hits in a day and they make no commitment that the counters work every time. Some are done through a CGI as I explained earlier, others are done through Java, and others take a different tilt. Read the pages and make sure you understand and can handle how the counter is placed on your page.

A Counter CGI from a Private Site

Remember a little while back in this chapter where I have you talk in the sinister British voice and say that you just attach to my counter by just changing the command line from my page? Well, that's not too far from what you can do. But you should do this one thing:

Ask permission!

If you see a page that has a counter on it, look at the page's source. (You can see its source by opening Source under the View menu at the top of the page.) Look for the IMG command that put the counter on the page. The path to the counter CGI is going to be an URL. Take just the main URL (before all the directories) and log on. The main page more than likely has a hypertext link that allows you to write to the Webmaster of that specific site or to the people who run the server itself.

Write and ask for permission to make an attachment to the counter.

Disclaimer: I *did not* tell you to go and attach to counters at will until you find one that works! Doing that can really tee off people who put a great deal of work into assisting their own server's patrons.

Although you might get a counter for a short while, if you perturb the people who run the server, you can be locked out just that quickly. Be nice—ask. I bet you get a nicer note than if you're found using a counter CGI without permission.

FAQs from the HTML Goodies Web Site

Q. How can I get a counter that only I can see?

A. You probably already have it. Ask for permission to read your access file log. That keeps a running count of how many times you have been accessed.

Q. I can't get access to my log files. Now how do I get a counter only I can see?

A. Set a counter on the page and then set the counter's height and width to 0, so it disappears. Create an entirely new page with the exact counter commands on it. Look at the new page—it tells you the count of the other page.

Well, that's about all I can tell you. I know it's not a direct answer, but it at least sends you in the right direction. First ask yourself if you really want this counter thing. If so, do the legwork! It pays off. You get a nice counter sitting right where you want it.

Net Notes

The following are a few links to public domain sites that offer you the ability to attach to their counter CGI:

WebCounter Home page: `http://www.digits.com/`

The Counter Home page: `http://www.thecounter.com/`

WUSAGE Home page: `http://www.boutell.com/wusage/`

Of course others exist. Check out Yahoo!'s counter page: `http://dir.yahoo.com/Computers_and_Internet/Internet/World_Wide_Web/Programming/Access_Counters/`

Just for fun:

The Fake Counter Home page: `http://www.geocities.com/SiliconValley/Heights/5910/counter.html`

I have installed a counter from one of the public domain counter sites listed here at: `http://www.htmlgoodies.com/book/counters.html`.

Putting a Counter on Your Site

The previous section discusses attaching to a counter CGI located somewhere outside your personal site. Now I get into how you can install a counter CGI on your own site.

 This tutorial is online at `http://www.htmlgoodies.com/beyond/countcgi.html`. *The script for this section in both text and downloadable form can also be found at this URL.*

Please note that this section uses UNIX commands. The majority of servers on the Net are UNIX. If yours runs a different system, contact your Web server's technician to ask what additional steps you need to take.

It seems like everyone wants a counter on his page. I can understand. I love the look of a counter proclaiming to all that my page is cool enough for a couple hundred thousand to roll through. The problem is that counters are not all that easy to come by if you don't own the CGI. I do own the CGI and now I'm going to give it to you. You get a counter if you follow this section straight away. The counter looks such as the one in Figure 12.1.

Figure 12.1
Hit counter style on the HTML Goodies site.

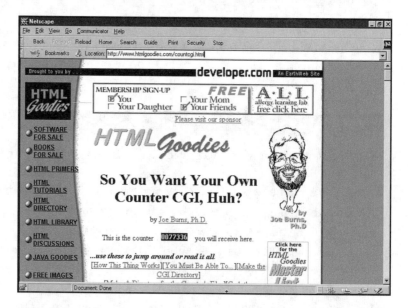

Be careful. Many not-so-nice people out there attach to your counter without your knowing it. Later I tell you how to lock those people out of this counter. I should say that this section does get tricky. CGIs are tough sometimes.

How This Thing Works

This is a very simple counter CGI. It returns a bitmap image counter such as the one shown in Figure 12.1. This is the process:

1. A server requests the page.
2. A code word is on on the page that is used when contacting the CGI.
3. The CGI checks in a counts directory for a file named after that code word.
4. If the file exists, the CGI adds one to the count in the file and returns the bitmap image of the count.
5. The CGI creates the file if it doesn't exist. The count starts at 1.

You need to create two things: the cgi-bin directory (if you don't already have one) and a directory where this CGI can keep record of all your counts.

To do this, you must be able to do the following few things with your Internet account:

- Gain access through Telnet or FTP (discussed in the next section)
- Create directories
- Change directory modification

If you don't know if you have these permissions, contact your server's technician or just start following along. You are told soon enough if something doesn't jive with the server.

Here you go...

FAQs from the HTML Goodies Web Site

Q. I don't have access through Telnet. What do I do?

A. Contact your server people and ask if you have access at all. You must be able to create and configure directories and place CGIs. Ask if you can do all that. If you can't, you may want to look for another server that allows you those privileges.

Creating Directories with FTP

Creating a directory on an FTP site is as easy as creating a directory on your own hard drive. You need some FTP software, though. If you don't know how to FTP, read Primer 7, "Graduation Day," for details.

Creating Directories with Telnet

For those of you who don't know, Telnet is another way to attach to your Internet server. With Telnet you are attaching directly to the server *shell*. This is where you can enter commands that directly affect the UNIX settings.

You should have received a Telnet program when you signed up with your Internet service provider (ISP). If not, read the section on Telnet in Chapter 15, "Other Stuff You Should Really Know."

All Telnets work the same way. Open the program, choose to connect, and type your WWW address without the `http://`.

You're good to go. Keep following along...

First, you need to Telnet into your server. Upon connecting, you are asked for your username and password. Put them in. Usually you get a few welcome greeting messages and then a prompt of some sort. I have worked with seven different servers and the prompt has been different on all seven. It should look something like this: `telnet%`.

Does that look familiar? If not, don't worry, you see the blinking cursor, which is where you enter information.

Why is this done? When you send files to your server, you send the files to a directory for them to be seen by the entire Internet community. It has a name. You need to find that name. Most of the time it is something such as `public-html`, `www`, or `default`.

For the sake of demonstration, let's say the directory's name is `www`. (That's the shortest name and thus easiest to write a couple hundred more times.) Depending on your system setup, you are either in that directory when you Telnet in, or in one above it. The smart money is that you are one above it. Type this at the prompt: `telnet% ls`.

Please note that I am using `telnet%` to represent the prompt. Your prompt may look different.

Press Return and you get a listing (that's what `ls` means) of everything in that directory. If you see the names all your HTML documents that Internet viewers can access, you are already in the correct directory. Skip the next part.

If you see your Internet directory's name (I called it `www` earlier), you are one above the directory. This is probably where most of you are.

You need to get into your `www` directory. Do that by typing this at the prompt: `telnet% cd www` (or whatever your directory's name is).

`cd` stands for change directory. That's what you just did. Put in the `ls` command again and you should see all your HTML documents.

Making the CGI Directories

CGI directories may already have been done for you. However, you should check that first. If when you typed one of the `ls` commands you saw a `cgi-bin`, you need not do this. You need to create a special directory for your CGIs. No, they cannot sit where all the other files are located—why becomes clear in a moment. I suggest you name the directory you are about to create `cgi-bin`, as that is what I am going to call it the rest of the way through this chapter. Please notice that is a hyphen between the `cgi` and the `bin`. You make the directory by typing this: `telnet% mkdir cgi-bin`.

If you get another prompt and no error messages, you did it. This is the first point at which you may be told you do not have the ability to place a CGI. If you do get an access denied type of error, you may not have been granted permission to create directories within your site. You can try contacting your service provider to ask for permission. If the answer is still no, you need to think about how badly you want to be able to do this. It may mean moving to a totally different server to gain access.

If you'd like to see your work, follow these steps:

1. Type this: `telnet% cd ..` (those are two periods).
2. Then type this: `telnet% ls`. You should see the new directory `cgi-bin`.
3. Now you need to make a directory for the counter files. Follow the same steps as described earlier, but this time create a directory called `count`. This is where the CGI stores the count it is keeping of visitors to each of your pages. Again, do an `ls`. You should see the two new directories, `cgi-bin` and `count` sitting before you.
4. Log out by typing `logout` at the prompt.

Grabbing the CGI Script and Modifying It

The CGI I am giving you is the exact CGI I use on my system. You need to copy it and save it to your hard drive as `count.pl` or `count.cgi`, depending on what format your server wants. You need to find out from your server's technician which one is preferred.

You can view and download the CGI counter script in text form at `http://www.htmlgoodies.com/countcgi.txt`.

The script may not be ready to go as is. You need to check a few things first:

◯ Look at the first line: `#!/usr/bin/perl`

That is the path to the Perl program in your server. It must be correct for this to work. The CGI does not do most of the work, the Perl program on your server does. This little CGI just sort of "brings" the information to Perl for manipulation. Find out if this path is correct by asking your server's technician. If it isn't correct, change it. Just be sure to open and configure the CGI in Notepad, Simple Text, or another text editor that does not have margins. Altering this CGI's shape by allowing word-wrapping stops it from working.

● Look at the third line down: $counterdir="/directory/sub/sub/counts

That's the absolute path to the directory, which contains the counts for the CGI. You made it when you created the count directory.

Why is this eliminated? Absolute path is a tough concept to grasp at first. Let's say your home page has this URL:

```
http://www.server.com/~joe
```

That little squiggly line before joe is called a *tilde*. This is a neat little space-saving trick. It says to the computer, "One directory is on this entire server called joe. Find it!" There might be five directories between the server name and joe, but you'd never know because of the tilde. The actual path to joe might be this:

```
http://www.server.com/names/men/tall/joe
```

This is the absolute path to joe. Get it?

Finding the Absolute Path

You have to log back into Telnet.

Follow the commands outlined earlier to get into the directory that contains your WWW files for all the world to see. Perform an ls command. You should see the cgi-bin and count directory sitting there.

1. Open the count directory by typing cd count.
2. When the prompt comes back up, type pwd and press Enter.
3. What is sitting before you is that directory's absolute path.
4. Copy it and enter it in the CGI.
5. Log out of Telnet.
6. FTP the CGI.

   Use whatever method you use for placing files on your server to now transfer the count CGI to the cgi-bin directory. Do not put the CGI in the count directory; it does not work there.

7. Transfer the file as ASCII. Yes, I said ASCII.

   You're getting close. Stay with me here. Log back on with Telnet and get to the directory where you keep your WWW files. You should see the cgi-bin and count directories using an ls command. Now "turn on" both directories. You are basically setting the file's modification instructions so that the server knows that this directory can be written to and read by other servers. Type this at the prompt:

```
telnet% chmod a+rx cgi-bin
```

If you get no error codes, success. If you did get an error code, try this instead:

```
telnet% chmod 775 cgi-bin
```

Sometimes that's allowed and the other isn't. If neither works, you don't have the correct permissions. Talk to your server technician to see if you can get them.

8. Now go ahead and "turn on" the count directory by following the same steps as detailed earlier—use count instead of cgi-bin.

9. That done, you need to "turn on" the counter CGI itself. Type the following at the prompt:

```
telnet% cd cgi-bin
```

You just opened the directory. Now type this:

```
telnet% chmod a+rx [cgi name]
```

10. Put in the name you gave to the CGI. Again, if a+rx doesn't work, try 775.

11. Log out. You're ready to count.

FAQs from the HTML Goodies Web Site

Q. My server people tell me that they don't want me using Perl. What else can I attach to to make your script run?

A. Nothing. This script is created to run Perl.

Q. Don't I need images 1 through 0 for this?

A. No. The CGI creates the images as bitmaps for you.

Getting the Counter on the HTML Page

This is the command you need to place on your page to receive a count:

```
<IMG SRC="/cgi-bin/count.cgi?codeword">
```

This is what's happening:

- IMG   Denotes that it's an image that is returned.

- SRC   The source path. Notice it's pointing toward the cgi-bin you created and then to the CGI inside the directory. Make sure to put in the exact name you used for the CGI. It may differ from what's shown here.

- ?codeword   The way you denote each page that receives a count. The code word can be up to 40 characters. Make up a different one for each page.

That's the general idea. If you have all the paths correct, and the permissions turned on correctly, you should receive a count straight away.

You Shouldn't Do This, but I'll Tell You Anyway

If you want your count to start at a certain level—10,000 for instance—you can do so by adding this to the end of the previous command:

```
&count=####
```

Just replace #### with the number you want to start with. Keep in mind that this only works the first time you access the page. If the counter already has a count of 1, no dice.

The only legitimate reason for doing this is if you're already using a counter, switching to a new one, and want to carry over your current numbers.

Keeping Others from Using Your Counter

You put this counter on your site to count your pages. If someone is nice enough to ask to use the counter CGI, it's up to you to decide whether to enable him. Some swarthy individuals out there just muscle right on in. This one is not tough to steal. You just copy the command and—poof!—you're counting. This CGI is not advanced and doesn't have a lock-out function. You need to do that by hand.

First log onto the Telnet again. Get to your count directory (where all the counter's numbers are kept) and do an ls to see all the files inside. The files are named after the code words you used. If you see one you didn't put there, someone is stealing from you. Lock them out. Now this is how to do just that.

For the sake of demonstration, say a file is there named fred. This is not your file, so some person is getting free counts from you without asking. Type these commands at the Telnet prompt press Enter after each:

- telnet% touch fred.LOCK
- telnet% rm fred

The touch command creates the file you write. In this case, you created a file named after the bad file with the .LOCK suffix. You then removed (that's what rm indicates) the file fred. You switched fred for fred.LOCK. Now the file fred is locked at 0—it cannot be written to.

The thief might change his code word. Lock him out again. He gets the message soon.

I do this once a week for the fun on of it. I kind of feel like Matlock.

FAQs from the HTML Goodies Web Site

Q. I cannot get this counter of yours to work! This is driving me nuts. What am I missing?

A. Make sure your paths are correct. Don't guess—check it carefully. That is what usually messes me up.

This is a tough one, no doubt about it. If you get it to work, you are very pleased with your own counter. It works very quickly and it runs right off your own server. This is a great upgrade to your site.

Putting a Guestbook on Your Site

This section covers placing a Guestbook CGI on your site (see Figure 12.2). HTML Goodies' online readers requested this topic for a long time. If you follow it, you are guided through the steps for placing a Guestbook CGI on your server. The CGI hopefully works the same as my Guestbook CGI, mainly because it's the same one. You can see it work at http://www. htmlgoodies.com/feedback.html.

This same script is described in great detail as part of my PERL primers at: http://www. htmlgoodies.com/primers/perl/perl03.html. It gets a little heavy but give it a look.

When you use this CGI, it returns a page thanking the user for writing (see Figure 12.3).

I assume here that you have already read the previous section on setting up a cgi-bin directory on your site. That is where you store the Guestbook CGI you get in this section. Just think of that cgi-bin you made as the future home of all the CGIs you get through the rest of your Internet life.

Getting the Guestbook on the HTML Page

Sounds like a new movie, doesn't it? I have links to the script; its HTML buddy is at the end of this section.

Figure 12.2
*The Guestbook from the
HTML Goodies Web site.*

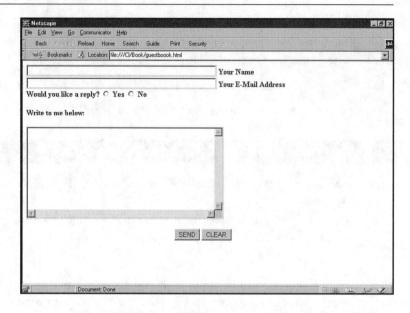

Figure 12.3
*The Guestbook
Confirmation page from
HTML Goodies.*

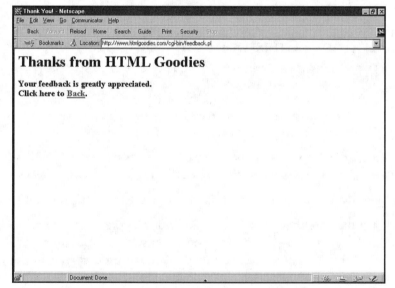

You need to copy the script and its HTML buddy from the HTML Goodies online site as
two files.

You can view and download the CGI Guestbook script in text form at http://www.
htmlgoodies.com/primers/perl/guestbookcgi_text.html. *You can view and download
the Guestbook HTML document in text form at* http://www.htmlgoodies.com/primers/
perl/guestbook_text.html.

Save the CGI script as gb.cgi (or with whatever suffix your server requires). (Some servers use .pl. Ask your server technician what suffix you should use.) You need to save the HTML document as gb.html. Save them both as source so that they keep their shape. Is this getting loopy enough for you yet?

You need to make a few changes to the HTML document so that it knows where the CGI is located. Look at this line in the script:

```
<FORM method="post" Action="/cgi-bin/gb.cgi">
```

This attaches this form's output to the CGI. Change that line so that the output is directed at the cgi-bin you created in the previous section. This is fairly easy. Take your full URL and add cgi-bin, a slash, and the name of the CGI file. For instance, your address is http://www.server.com/~fred.

The preceding Action statement would read as follows:

```
http://www.server.com/~fred/cgi-bin/gb.cgi
```

Get it?

You are now done altering the HTML document. Remember that these two documents were written for each other. They work together. You can change the text or add graphics to the HTML document, but you cannot change the FORM commands at all. If you attempt to add a third text box or another radio button, it doesn't work.

Modifying the CGI Script

You are concerned about two things here: the path to Perl and the path to Sendmail.

What happens is that the Guestbook information is sent to the CGI. The CGI and the information are loaded into the Perl program, or *shell*. The data is manipulated and then returned to your mailbox.

How the mail gets to your mailbox is the Sendmail question. Look at the CGI script:

```
open(MESSAGE,"| /usr/lib/sendmail -t");
```

That is the path that the server uses to find a little program that sends the mail. It needs to be correct for your server.

These paths are correct for the most part. Most servers are set up the same way, so you may not need to change anything. Then again, you may need to change them both. Talk to the tech people where your pages are located.

FAQs from the HTML Goodies Web Site

Q. How do I change it so that my return pages don't say what yours say?

A. The return page comes from the CGI, it is not another page. Look at the CGI's text in a text editor. Toward the end, you see the text thanking the person for writing. Alter that so that it says what you want. This Perl primer might help you a bit: `http://www.htmlgoodies.com/primers/perl/perl04.html`.

Activating the Guestbook

You now need to use your FTP program. Attach to your site like you would any other time you were going to transfer files. Send the HTML document to where the other HTML documents are. Do not put the HTML document and the CGI in the same directory; they do not work that way. Remember making a path to the CGI? That's because you place the CGI in the `cgi-bin` directory.

Depending on how your FTP is set up, you should see the `cgi-bin` directory in your window as you transfer the HTML document. Click the `cgi-bin` directory to open it and then send the CGI.

Send the CGI script as ASCII!

Yes, that's correct. Send it as ASCII text. Do not send it as binary. It is written to be sent as ASCII text. There. I said it three times, so you know it's not a typo. Log out of the FTP program.

Now log onto your `cgi-bin` and "turn on" the Guestbook CGI in the same manner you used to "turn on" the counter CGI earlier.

If all the paths are correct and you have turned on all the correct files, you should be able to open your browser, log on to the Guestbook HTML document, and run the CGI.

FAQs from the HTML Goodies Web Site

Q. This thing just does not work!

A. Almost every time I get to the bottom of this Guestbook CGI not working, it winds up being one of the paths. Check them carefully.

You might get a service error first time through. Read it. It tells you what the problem is. The most common problems are that it cannot find Perl, it cannot find a file due to incorrect paths or filenames, or your server doesn't support post capabilities. The first two can be repaired. The third cannot without first contacting your server technician.

Good luck. Please understand that placing a CGI is very difficult and only about a million little things can go wrong along the way. Take your time and make sure the paths and file-names are correct. It took me three hours to get this working on my first try. See if you can beat my record.

Billboard Server (BBS) CGI

People have been writing to me through the online site for a while now asking how they can get a billboard server (BBS) or a newsgroup-type effect. Others want to post the results of their e-mail guestbook without all the hassle. The answer is my BBS CGI. You can see at: `http://www.htmlgoodies.com/primers/perl/gb_post.html`. If you decide to post a message using the CGI on my site, please keep your comments clean. They are posted to another page for all to see.

If you're following this chapter in order, you should have already been introduced to creating a `cgi-bin` directory, placing CGIs in the directory, and turning them on, so they run as the CGIs they are meant to be. If not, start reading from the beginning—it does you a world of good.

Grab the CGI

The CGI I give you here is the CGI I use on my server. The file is in text format. You need to save it to your hard drive from HTML Goodies online as `bbs.pl` or `bbs.cgi`, depending on what format your server wants. You must find out from your server's technician which one is preferred. The script is available to you in text form at `http://www.htmlgoodies.com/bbscgi.txt`.

Altering the Script for Your Server

Creating this BBS page of e-mails is done almost totally in the CGI itself. Open this CGI in a text editor and configure it for your server and your site. Again, make sure you only edit the CGI in a text editor that does not have margins! Use Notepad on an IBM and Simple Text on a Macintosh. If you want to use any other text editor, turn off the word wrap. Just moving margins to their widest setting is not enough—lose them totally. If you alter the shape of this CGI script through word wrapping it does not work.

Let's make some changes:

1. Look at the first line: `#!/usr/bin/perl`.

   This is the path to Perl on your server. Make sure the path is typed correctly.

2. Look at the third line: `$guestbook="/directory/sub/sub/page.html";`.

   This is the absolute path of the page that this CGI creates to post the e-mail messages. You need to offer the absolute path. A straight URL address doesn't do.

3. Look at the fourth line of text. It should look like this: `$entriespage="http://`
   `www.server.com/~joe/bbs.html";`.

   This should be your home page address, followed by a slash and the name of the page you want the e-mails posted to. See that?

   "But why do I need to enter the same thing in two different formats?!" Because that's the way the CGI is set up. One posts the message, the other creates a link. They do different things, you see.

4. Look at line seven: `$maintainer="user\@emailaddress.com";`.

   This is where you put your e-mail address. Please make a point of keeping the back-slash before the @ sign. If you remove that backslash, the whole process stops.

   If you want, you can also go into other parts of the script and alter what is posted to the browser window.

5. Look at the script under where it reads: `sub thank_you{`.

   That's the text that pops up when someone sends a message. Change it to whatever you want. I suggest you keep a clean copy of this CGI before messing with it too much. Losing just one little character kills the whole deal real quick.

Use whatever method you use for placing files on your server to now transfer the BBS CGI to the `cgi-bin` directory. Do not put the CGI in just any directory. It does not work anywhere but in the `cgi-bin`. Do the following:

1. Transfer the file as ASCII. Yes, I said ASCII.

2. Go back in using Telnet and turn on the BBS CGI.

The HTML Document

 Remember when you saw my BBS work? You entered the data into a guestbook type file. You need to have that for this CGI to work. The HTML document is available in text form at `http://www.htmlgoodies.com/bbsform.txt`.

Now that you have the document, you can gussy it up to your heart's content, but you cannot change, alter, or add to the form items. This document was written for this specific CGI and vice-versa. Altering it stops the process cold. Wham!

See this line:

```
<FORM ACTION="/cgi-bin/bbs.cgi" method=post>
```

That's the line that attaches this document to this CGI. If you followed the instructions to the letter, the path is already correct. However, if you changed any of the names or altered any of the paths, you need to make sure this is pointed at the right place to find the CGI.

Transfer the file into your regular www directory (where your home page sits).

The BBS.html *Page*

You're basically done. If everything is set correctly, you can log onto your new page, fill out the elements, and get a bbs.html page created for all the world to see.

The problem is that this page fills quickly. It quickly becomes huge—and it also happens that some idiot posts an obscenity or some other numbskull comment thinking he is really cute. You want to either get rid of that or empty the page now and again. This is how:

1. Log into Telnet. Use the preceding commands to get into your www pages directory. That's where this bbs.html page is sitting.

2. Type rm bbs.html and press Enter.

3. Type touch bbs.html and press Enter.

4. Type chmod a+rx bbs.html and press Enter. (Use 775 in place of a+rx if it doesn't work.)

You just removed the bbs.html page and replaced it with a page of the same name, but blank. You then "turned it on" again. Easy, easy.

FAQs from the HTML Goodies Web Site

Q. How can I make your BBS post the newest messages at the top of the page rather than the bottom?

A. You can't do that without changing around the entire CGI.

Q. How can I block out those people I don't want from coming in and posting? You know, people who are writing nasty things.

A. That's something you need to work out with your server people. They can block that person completely. That's what I'd do, anyway.

Q. Can I limit the amount someone writes?

A. No. The CGI simply re-posts what is written. Another downfall of the process is that people can write HTML code to the page. If you install this, you need to keep a steady eye on it.

That's It!

Have fun. Now you can create BBS pages to your heart's content. Just remember that these pages fill very quickly and must be kept up. I just hope mine doesn't get too big that I have to take it down for sanity and space sake.

Chapter 13

Explorer-Specific Tutorials and DHTML

Doesn't Microsoft's Internet Explorer Web browser do everything Netscape Navigator does? Just about, but Netscape and Microsoft are in a fight for browser supremacy. Each is doing its best to offer features that the other does not handle. Some feel that's good, others feel it is making the World Wide Web a hard place to write for. As long as some commands are supported by both browsers and some aren't you have no conflict. Expect some errors and some strange-looking mistakes, however.

FAQs from the HTML Goodies Web Site

Q. Because you're talking about browsers specifically, I would like to know how people who make browsers make any money. Internet Explorer and Netscape Navigator are free over the Net. You can buy them, but why would you when they're free? Where do Microsoft and Netscape make their money?

A. Advertising. Netscape's home page and Microsoft's Internet Explorer page are two of the most visited sites on the Net. Every time you log on, you see advertising banners. Geocities, which gives away free home page space, has the same thing. An ad banner is always popping up. You create a product and give it away so people see the ad banners. HTML Goodies works the same way—it's free because I can sell enough advertising to keep it that way.

Here I attempt to provide a quick reference to what features and commands Explorer supports that Netscape does not. Please note that a lot of these are add-on commands to many existing tutorials that I have already posted. When possible, I make reference to the main topic tutorial.

Explorer supports three major features that Navigator has some trouble with: scrolling marquees, active channels, and inline frames.

Each of these features are covered later in this chapter.

Setting Static Backgrounds

This is a great effect. Add BGPROPERTIES="fixed" to your BODY command and the background images remain stationary while the text scrolls over them.

Specifying Page Margins

These go inside <BODY> and affect the entire page in that position:

- LEFTMARGIN="###" Denotes left margin in inches.
- TOPMARGIN="###" Denotes top margin in inches.

Loading a Background Sound

If you've read Chapter 10, "Sound and Video," for how to embed sounds, you have a general idea of what these commands do. They offer, as suggested, a background sound for the page.

Follow this format:

```
<BGSOUND SRC="sound.wav" LOOP="###">
```

- BGSOUND Denotes a sound is placed here.
- SRC Denotes the source of the sound. Sound can be in most any sound format, including MIDI; Explorer supports them all. Use this command in addition to the EMBED commands to make sure your sounds plays across platforms.
- LOOP Denotes the number of times the sound plays. Using infinite plays it forever and ever...until you go crazy.

Setting Table Properties

I get at least a letter a day asking how the background color of a table or table cell can be changed. Well, this is how you do it with Explorer. All commands are placed within the <TABLE> command, except where noted.

- BORDERCOLOR="###"   Refers to the color of the border. See the chart in Appendix B, "Useful Charts," for a few color commands.

- BORDERCOLORLIGHT="###"   Offers a softer version of the color requested.

- BORDERCOLORDARK="###"   Works inside the TH and TD commands, as does the preceding two commands.

- FRAME="###"   Tells the browser to display certain outside borders on the 3D table cell frame. Use these attributes:

    ABOVE   Border on top only

    BELOW   Border on bottom only

    LHS   Left border

    RHS   Right border

    HSIDES   Top and bottom borders

    VSIDES   Left and right borders

    BOX   All sides get a border

    VOID   No sides get a border (so there!)

- RULES="###"   Tells the browser to display certain inside borders on the 3D table cell frame. Try these:

    ROWS   Shows borders between rows

    COLS   Shows borders across columns

    ALL   Gives them all borders

    NONE   No borders

FAQs from the HTML Goodies Web Site

Q. Why doesn't Internet Explorer support the simply mailto Guestbook format?

A. It does with the release of Internet Explorer 4.0, but I don't know otherwise. They knew about using forms as a Guestbook and a few versions still came out that didn't support it. I thought that was a big oversight and based on the mail from my users, others did too. All's well that ends well.

Whether you make Internet Explorer your main browser or not is up to you. I still use Netscape Navigator for the majority of my HTML work. I usually use Internet Explorer to surf.

I do this because Netscape Navigator is very picky about its coding. You must have well-formed code for everything to show up correctly in Netscape Navigator. Internet Explorer is much more forgiving.

For example, if you forget the </TABLE> flag when creating a table, Internet Explorer displays the table just fine. Netscape Navigator does not.

Get both browsers. Check your Web pages in both browsers.

You can install both browsers on your hard drive at the same time. I've even had them both open at the same time—no problems.

 See a few of these commands in action at http://www.htmlgoodies.com/book/ iecommands.html.

Using IE Marquees

If you go to http://www.htmlgoodies.com/tutors/marquee.html with Netscape Navigator, you see the hilariously funny joke in text form at the top of the screen as shown in Figure 13.1. If you were using Microsoft Internet Explorer, that text would be scrolling, allowing you to read the joke again and again and again. As you all know, jokes get funnier the more you tell them.

Figure 13.1
Scrolling marquee with Internet Explorer.

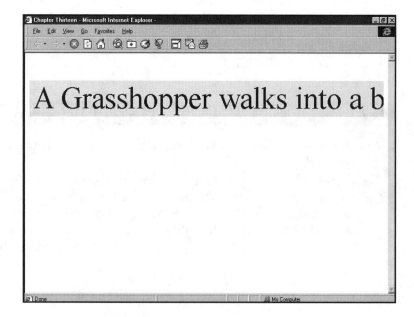

Marquee? It looks like a scroll. It is a scroll, but <MARQUEE> is the flag that makes it happen. This is a throwback to the marquees that used to scroll, announcing a movie or show at a theater. That said, this is what posts the fancy scrolling text in Figure 13.1 to your Internet Explorer Web page:

```
<MARQUEE BGCOLOR="#80FF00" LOOP="infinite" >text text text</MARQUEE>
```

This is what's happening:

- MARQUEE   Tells Internet Explorer that a scrolling marquee is going here.
- BGCOLOR   Tells the marquee what color to put behind the text. This color is in hex code, but you can also use word color codes. I have a whole list of them in Appendix B.
- LOOP="infinite"   Tells the marquee to roll that text forever. Put a number in place of infinite to tell it how many times it should roll.
- /MARQUEE   Ends the whole deal.

Can you do other things? You bet. I only used a few of the available commands. These are a few more. You place them inside the first MARQUEE command, just like the BGCOLOR and LOOP command in the preceding code.

- HEIGHT="###"   Specifies the marquee's height. Do it in percentage of the screen height or pixels.
- WIDTH="###"   Denotes the marquee's width. Do it in percentage of the screen width or pixels.
- ALIGN="###"   Uses top, left, or middle in the marquee banner.
- DIRECTION="###"   Uses left or right. That's where the text comes from. right is default.
- BEHAVIOR="###"   Has scroll as default. slide has the text come in and stop and alternate makes the text come from both sides every other time.
- HSPACE="###"   Tells the marquee how much space to leave on each side of the text. Write this in pixels.
- SCROLLAMOUNT="###"   Tells the browser how much space between successive scrolls. Do this in pixels.
- SCROLLDELAY="###"   Denotes the number of milliseconds (thousands) between each scroll.
- VSPACE="###"   Denotes the top and bottom space before the text. Do this in pixels.

FAQs from the HTML Goodies Web Site

Q. What happens if you use these commands in a page displayed by Netscape Navigator?

A. The text between the marquee commands displays normally—no scroll.

Q. What's up with the marquee tutorial? I can get that on Netscape Navigator using a scrolling JavaScript.

A. Yeah, I know, but this scroll is done using simple MARQUEE commands and it is an Explorer-only deal. Microsoft is selling ease here, not anything new.

I have this same marquee scrolling at http://www.htmlgoodies.com/book/marquee.html. *You get to see the entire joke. Make sure you look at the source code.*

Using IE Active Channels

Have you seen the icons shown in Figure 13.2 floating around lately?

Figure 13.2
Internet Explorer's Add Active Channel icon.

They're pretty popular little pups with the Internet in crowd. In fact, requests to put together a tutorial on the subject of active channels have been filling the Goodies mailbox. Here you go. This is a basic instructional look at what an active channel is and how you can get one on your site.

FAQs from the HTML Goodies Web Site

Q. Is there a way to use JavaScript to make it so that when someone logs onto your site they are automatically given an active channel?

A. I'm sure you can using an onLoad command (see the Advanced JavaScript section of Chapter 11, "Java Applets and JavaScript") with a function that forces the browser to look at the active channel .CDF file. Despite this, don't use it. I would be pretty cheesed if you did that without my permission.

An active channel is another idea from the laboratories of Microsoft. As such, you require the use of the Microsoft Explorer browser, version 4.0 or higher, to get in on all the actively channeled fun. I have no doubt that Netscape will include it very soon.

Think of it this way: the people who come to your site have the ability to set up a pathway in which you can *push* information (give information to the viewer) other than what is on the page. In activating this *pathway*, or channel, the user allows you a bit more leeway in bombarding them with information. Depending on what side of the argument you prefer, you can push or *pull* (take information from a site) just about anything; for example, a monthly newsletter, new site info, or a listing of new tutorials.

FAQs from the HTML Goodies Web Site

Q. If I set it up so that I push a newsletter to people through my active channel, where does it end up? I mean, where is it on the computer?

A. I found the few that I signed up for in my browser's cache (Temporary Internet File folder in Windows). I see that part as a bit of a downfall. If the items you push aren't pushed to the desktop, they are kind of hard to find.

Furthermore, the user who clicked to create an active channel with you now has an additional bookmark to your site. In fact, that's how people started referring to these little gems in the first HTML Goodies e-mails. Users wanted to know how to create the fancy bookmark. If you haven't already clicked a page to set up a channel, use your Explorer 4.*x* browser, head to my tutorial, and click the Active Channel logo. You get a box that looks a lot like Figure 13.3.

For now, just choose to add the site to your channel bar as I have it earmarked in Figure 13.3. Go ahead. You can always delete it later.

Figure 13.3

Internet Explorer Add Active Channel™ content dialog box.

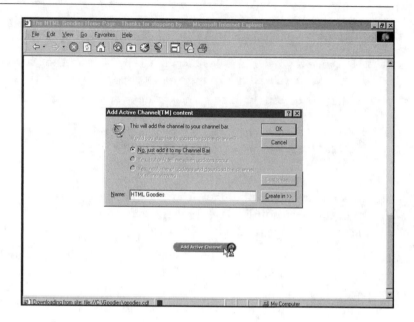

Now you should have an active channel set up with my site. To see the fruits of your labor, look at the very top of your browser window. There should be a button there marked Channels. A little satellite receiver image is near it. Go ahead and click that. The screen should split and you should see a little HTML Goodies logo next to the same satellite dish image. If you do not see an image, you may need to run your mouse over the text.

FAQs from the HTML Goodies Web Site

Q. I hate how the screen looks when I open the Active Channels menu. It's all pushed together.

A. That happens. Close the Channels menu and it returns to normal.

Creating an Active Channel Link on Your Page

Now that you have a channel that links you to my page, I want to show you how to get one on your page so that others can begin channeling through you. Hopefully someone begins channeling Elvis soon. (Uh, thank you very much.)

This is the format:

```
<A HREF="http://www.htmlgoodies.com/goodies.cdf"><IMG SRC="add_chan.gif"></A>
```

Notice it's little more than a basic A HREF link command. The only real difference is that this link is headed toward a file with a .cdf extension. add_chan.gif is the image I am using as the link, but you don't need an image for it to work. You can put in straight text if you want. That little image is just how I usually see these things identified on other Web pages, so I'm using it here.

Using the Channel Definition Format (.cdf)

.cdf stands for Channel Definition Format. This is a text file that denotes what you have available on your site, and it's what sets up your active channel. This is what my .cdf file, named goodies.cdf, looks like:

```
<?XML VERSION="1.0" ENCODING="UTF-8"?>
<CHANNEL HREF="http://www.htmlgoodies.com" BASE="http://www.
htmlgoodies.com">
<TITLE>HTML Goodies</TITLE>
<ABSTRACT>HTML/DHTML Tutorials and Java Script</ABSTRACT>
<LOGO HREF="http://www.htmlgoodies.com/goodieschannel.gif"
  STYLE="IMAGE" />
</CHANNEL>
```

This .cdf, and all .cdf files for that matter, are simple text such as any HTML document you've ever made. That text is then saved to a file and the file is given the extension .cdf. Again, think of it as creating an HTML file, except you use the .cdf extension instead of .html.

It may look like I have a basic HTML file here with a few mistakes. Not so. You see, the .cdf file is not written in HTML per se, but rather a cousin of HTML called XML (Extensible Mark-up Language). See Chapter 15, "Other Stuff You Should Really Know" for more on XML.

Creating the .cdf File

Let's make a file the old-fashioned way. Steal it...from Joe.

Go ahead and copy the .cdf file from earlier and paste it into whatever text editor you use to edit your HTML documents, such as Notepad, SimpleText, or WordPad.

This .cdf is about as basic as you can get. It does one thing: It sets up a channel. Many more events are available, and I get to them, but let's start with this.

You can see where to change out the text to suit your needs, but just so you know what you're doing, this is the .cdf again, and what each part means:

```
<?XML VERSION="1.0" ENCODING="UTF-8"?>
```

This is the XML declaration statement. It tells the browser that the following document is in XML format version 1.0. The question marks at the beginning and end are a nice touch, don't you think? The encoding statement tells the browser what format is being used to build this .cdf file.

```
<CHANNEL HREF="http://www.htmlgoodies.com" BASE="http://www.
htmlgoodies.com">
```

This is the encompassing channel statement. Everything that sits within the <CHANNEL> and </CHANNEL> commands refers to the channel's traits. The HREF and BASE commands denote the base URL of each of the filenames that follows. These are the same because my channel is on the main page, which is also the base address. Make your BASE your site's main URL.

For example, if your site is http://www.server.com/~bob/, that's the base you put in this command. All other pages sit inside that base address. Get it?

```
<TITLE>HTML Goodies</TITLE>
```

This is the title that appears in the channel. (Remember when you clicked the channels icon at the top? That's where this pops up.)

```
<ABSTRACT>HTML/DHTML Tutorials and Java Script</ABSTRACT>
```

This acts as a small description of the site.

```
<LOGO HREF="http://www.htmlgoodies.com/goodieschannel.gif" STYLE="IMAGE"/>
```

This is the icon that appears in the channel list. The format is XML. Follow it; you must remember that this is not HTML. The image cannot be animated and cannot be any larger than 30×80. If it is, it just gets scrunched down to size and looks pretty bad.

FAQs from the HTML Goodies Web Site

Q. What happens if I use an animated image for my channel?

A. Nothing, really. It doesn't animate and you get just the top-level image. The entire thing still loads, so you're wasting bytes.

You can incorporate a slew of other commands when you create your active channel. Use these few commands to get off the ground. They are listed in order by usefulness.

<ITEM>

This is an item that you can push to the user, such as an HTML file. It goes inside the CHANNEL commands. For example:

```
<CHANNEL>
<ITEM HREF="http://www.page.com/newsletter.html" PRECACHE="yes">
<CHANNEL>
```

Here an HTML page titled newsletter.html is pushed to the user. Notice the PRECACHE="yes" command. That addition to the ITEM command makes the browser go get the item and stick it in the cache. When you click the channel to read newsletter.html, it pops up straight away because it was precached.

<USAGE VALUE="###" />

This too goes inside the CHANNEL command. It tells how the browser is to use the thing within the <ITEM> command. The available values include desktop component, channel, and screen saver. This is an example:

```
<CHANNEL>
<ITEM HREF="http://www.page.com/newsletter.html" PRECACHE="yes">
<USAGE VALUE="channel" />
<CHANNEL>
```

This HTML document appears in the channel.

<SCHEDULE>

This displays the schedule for the active channel content. If you are pushing information that has an end date, you can use the command to have the channel end on its own, rather than going in and changing out the information yourself. This is an example:

```
<CHANNEL>
<ITEM HREF="newsletter.html" PRECACHE="yes">
<SCHEDULE STARTDATE="1998.02.28" ENDDATE="1999.09.31">
<INTERVALTIME DAY="5" />
<EARLIESTTIME HOUR="5" />
<LATESTTIME HOUR="12" />
</SCHEDULE>
<CHANNEL>
```

- INTERVALTIME   Denotes the update frequency. You can use DAY, HOUR, or MIN.

- EARLIESTTIME   Denotes the earliest time during the schedule when an update can occur. You can use DAY, HOUR, or MIN to set parameters.

- LATESTTIME   Denotes the latest time during the interval that an update can occur. You can use DAY, HOUR, or MIN.

That's about all you need to put together your own active channel. All those fancy commands aside, the bulk of your work is done by the short .cdf format I showed earlier. Add an item to distribute, and you are pretty much good to go. The rest of the commands do a good deal of fine-tuning, but are not needed to create a solid channel for your viewers.

Using Inline Frames with IE

Inline frames appear within the page (see Figure 13.4). They resemble table cells, yet what appears in the frame is not text on the page, but rather a whole other page, such as regular frames.

Figure 13.4
An inline frame in Internet Explorer.

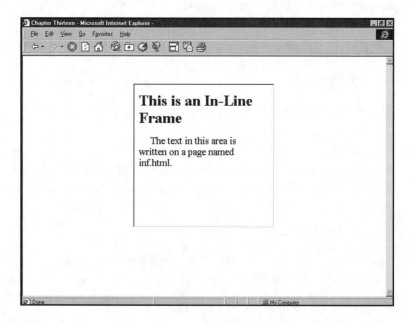

I know Figure 13.4 looks like a table cell, but it's really a frame with the text from another page displayed inside it. It has a page in a page—two, two, two pages in one. Let me stop now before I begin quoting Doublemint gum commercials.

FAQs from the HTML Goodies Web Site

Q. Can't I get the same look using table cells as I do with inline frames?

A. Yes, but you can't get that look of loading new pages into the frames unless you reload the entire page again and again.

Adding the IFRAME *Command*

The command for adding inline frames for IE browsers is as follows:

```
<IFRAME SRC="inf1.html"></IFRAME>
```

- **IFRAME**   Denotes the command that states an inline frame goes here.
- **SRC**   Denotes the source for the page, just like an image command.
- **/IFRAME**   Ends the entire command. You must have this for each IFRAME you post.

How's that for easy?

Adding Multiple Frames

If you can have one, you can probably have two. Dig Figure 13.5 and Figure 13.6.

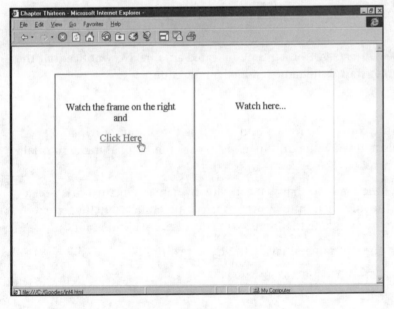

Figure 13.5
Multiple inline frames before clicking the Click Here link.

Figure 13.6
Results of clicking the Click Here link.

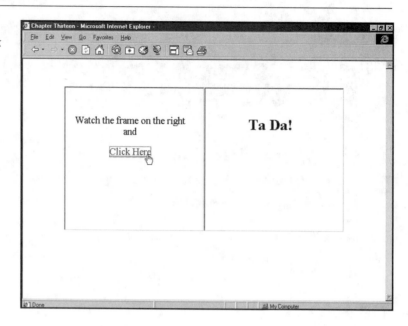

This is the code that made the frames in Figures 13.5 and 13.6:

```
<IFRAME SRC="inf2.html" NAME="left"></IFRAME>
<IFRAME SRC="inf3.html" NAME="right"></IFRAME>
```

Now I get into the beauty of inline frames—you can have movement between them. First, let's look at the code.

I need you to see that I used an </IFRAME> each time I created a frame. Now notice that the format for creating the frames stayed the same. I added a new command:

```
NAME="--"
```

If you already understand the concept of frames and targeting the output of hypertext links within frames, you already know the drill here. If not, see the original frame tutorial's section on targeting in Chapter 6, "Frames."

That NAME command names the frame so that you can target where a hypertext link's page appears. The default is for the information to appear in the same frame as the hypertext link. What I did here, though, was name the frames—in this case, left and right.

This is the format I used in the left frame to create the hypertext link:

```
<A HREF="inf4.html" TARGET="right">Click Here</a>
```

See? The right frame was named right, thus, the output of the click landed in the right frame. That's easy enough.

I Want a Button!

Calm down! You can have your button and click it too. Check out Figures 13.7 and 13.8.

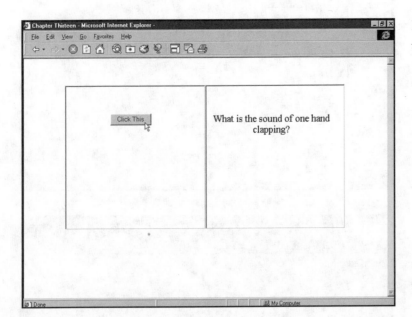

Figure 13.7
Before clicking the button.

This is the button's code:

```
<FORM ACTION="inf7.html" TARGET="right">
<INPUT TYPE="submit" VALUE="Click This">
</FORM>
```

Adding Invisible Frame Borders

Watch the browser screen shown in Figures 13.9 and 13.10.

Figure 13.8
Results of clicking the button.

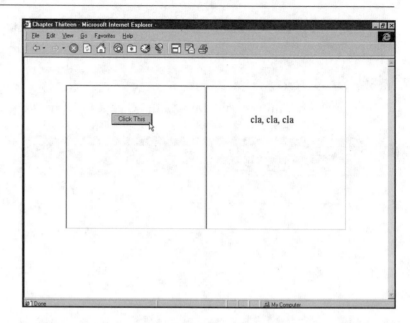

Figure 13.9
Before clicking the invisible inline frame border link.

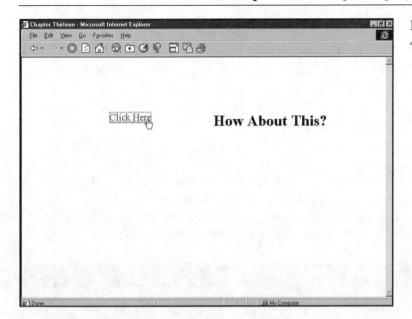

Figure 13.10
After clicking the link.

I think that's the neatest effect these frames offer. This is the code I used to make the frames:

```
<IFRAME SRC="inf8.html" FRAMEBORDER="0" NAME="left"></IFRAME>
<IFRAME SRC="inf9.html" FRAMEBORDER="0" NAME="right"></IFRAME>
```

See the FRAMEBORDER="0" command I added? That's what does the trick. You have two settings to choose from—1 and 0, 1 being the default. That gives you the slightly indented frame look I have. Choosing 0 causes you to lose the frame altogether. That's what I did in this case. Because I made the two source pages the same color as the main page without the borders. It looks like the frame is simply part of the same page. I got the blank look on the right by creating a page that was the same color as the main page, but without text. I think it's a great effect.

Altering Inline Frames

These are a few more commands that you can use to alter the frames on your page. I've used them all just to make sure they work. Just stick the command, with whatever setting you want, into the <IFRAME> flag to see it work.

- HEIGHT="###"   Acts just like the HEIGHT command in terms of an image. It defines the frame's height in pixels or percentage.

- WIDTH="###"   Acts just like the WIDTH command in terms of an image. It defines a frame's width in pixels or percentage.

- `MARGINWIDTH="###"`   Sets the margin width in either pixels or percentage.
- `MARGINHEIGHT="###"`   Sets the margin height in pixels or percentage.
- `SCROLLING="###"`   When set to `no`, this command stops the scrollbar from appearing if the information inside the frame is too long to display.
- `ALIGN="###"`   Works like the `ALIGN` command in terms of images. It denotes where text appears when surrounding the frame.
- `NORESIZE`   Prevents the user from being able to resize your frame.

These are great, but keep in mind that these are Internet Explorer-only deals. They do not display in Netscape Navigator browsers. Make a point of using these when you are sure a user is running Explorer or use a JavaScript to send users to certain pages depending on their type of browser. I have one in Chapter 11, "Java Applets and JavaScript."

FAQs from the HTML Goodies Web Site

Q. What happens if I use inline frames in a Netscape Navigator browser?

A. Nothing—literally nothing. The commands are ignored and no frames show up.

 Stop by `http://www.htmlgoodies.com/book/inlineframes.html` *to try out the examples in the tutorial.*

Using Dynamic HTML

What is Dynamic HTML? This is actually a little tough to get a handle on because it's beginning to mean different things to different people. The actual term stands for Dynamic Hypertext Markup Language.

The essence of the term stands for almost any coding that creates movement or interactivity by employing the standards of the 4.0-level Netscape Navigator and MSIE browsers. I've also heard DHTML discussed as being PowerPoint for the Web, but there was movement before with animation and interactivity with forms.

Yeah, see, that's the rub. For something to be considered DHTML it has to employ version 4.0 browsers. Again, I've heard an argument that DHTML is only viable if it occurs within the Explorer 4.0 browser.

On the other hand, some people have stated that DHTML includes Netscape's layering commands. Does it? It depends on whom you speak to.

FAQs from the HTML Goodies Web Site

Q. What do you think about DHTML?

A. This is actually the first new thing in a while that I'm really excited about. And what's better is these DHTML examples are starting to come out as fully functioning packages. You just drop the files in a directory and it works. I believe that in a year or so there will be so many applications of DHTML that you will be able to find what you need. Plus, if I can run this game (the example used in this section) with a few simple steps, imagine what you can do if you really took the time. These are great applications here. This could be really big.

The best description I can offer is that DHTML is any combination of style sheets, JavaScript, layering, positioning, and page division, at the 4.0 browser level, intended to create movement or user interactivity. (See the positioning tutorial in Chapter 8, "Cascading Style Sheets and Layers," for more on this.)

You find many examples of DHTML if you go to HTML Goodies online. I chose only two for this book that are a good introduction to the formatting. The first example is a very large, very involved DHTML game. The second is about as simple as you can get without someone else doing it for you.

 I wanted to show both ends of the scale in terms of DHTML. After you go through these two sections, try the others online at HTML Goodies. You can quickly browse the examples at http://www.htmlgoodies.com/beyond/layers.html. *If you get these to work, you can get any DHTML packages to work. This tutorial can be found online at* http://www.htmlgoodies.com/beyond/dhtml2.html.

Is Dynamic HTML Really Being Used?

At the beginning of this year, I went to my handy dandy little Internet counting program to see how many people had stopped by my site. I rolled through the numbers until I got to the last block of statistics. Those are the percentages of browsers coming to the site. Netscape Navigator had ruled the roost for the entire run of HTML Goodies until that day—Microsoft Internet Explorer: 82%.

FAQs from the HTML Goodies Web Site

Q. What happens if I run a DHTML program and the user pops in with Netscape?

A. I have found nothing but problems. The images usually display but not in their assigned positions. Ditto for any divisions you have set up. Usually, a JavaScript error results because certain items aren't denoted or given correct properties. This truly is a one-browser deal.

Shortly after being posted, my original online DHTML tutorial quickly became one of the most popular pages on this site. Soon after, I received this letter:

Dr. Burns,

We are developing DHTML authoring software that utilizes inverse mechanic and artificial behavior. Our Web site has numerous examples of interactive DHTML with JavaScript. We would be pleased if you could have a look and send us your comments.

Thank you,

Francoise White

So I went and looked. The SFAN Experimental Multimedia Page (http://www.dhtmlmagic.com/) is a great site that only gets better, I'm sure. Visually, it's stunning—images fly everywhere. In my most humble tone, I wrote back asking if I could use one of the site's examples as a DHTML tutorial. This is what I got back:

Dr. Burns,

Yes you have our permission to use our site and our demos for your tutorials. We would reciprocate. Let us know. We will contact you when our beta version [of a program to help you create your own DHTML events] is available for downloading.

Sincerely,

Francoise White

That said, the following sections are what I have for you.

Using DHTML for an Interactive Game

This is a great, visually pleasing video game (see Figure 13.11). The concept is you are flying an F-14 in space. (I know it's impossible, but go with me here.) A spaceship wants to blow you up. You want to do the same to it. Your fighter jet is given missiles and cannon shots. The spaceship has lasers.

Avoid the lasers and shoot the spaceship. What's even better about this is that when you shoot the spaceship, it blows up!

- M fires the missiles. You get 5.
- C fires the cannons. You get 15.
- The mouse moves the fighter jet up and down.

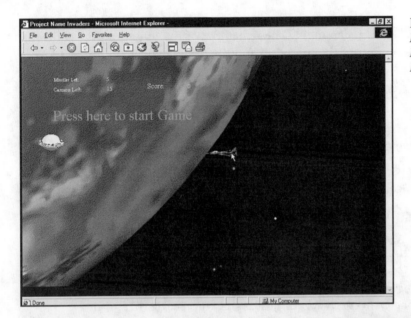

Figure 13.11
Interactive game using DHTML in Internet Explorer.

FAQs from the HTML Goodies Web Site

Q. The DHTML game you offer is amazing. How can I learn to build something like that?

A. Get into programming. You need to have a solid understanding of JavaScript to begin with and a good knowledge of layers, page divisions, and style sheets next. I probably never delve deep enough to learn to program this stuff myself because great people like Francoise White do it for me. Soon you are able to buy hundreds of DHTML applications on a CD-ROM. Mark my words. You can buy JavaScripts, applets, and animator GIFs now—DHTML isn't far behind.

Putting the DHTML on Your Page

The news gets even better. This game is fully self-contained. Simply take all the parts and place them in the same directory. Run the invaders.htm file and you're good to go.

This is an example, so it would help for you to open and look at the codes. You see that two pages are actually at work here. The main page (invaders.htm) and an external JavaScript work on the images. You can learn more about external JavaScripts in Chapter 11.

Each image is placed in a specific place through an absolute position style sheet command, and then given a span in which it can move. The remainder of the scripts outline paths for that image. Note the randomness of the spaceship and the rather deliberate vertical movement of the F-14 jet.

In addition, commands exist that inform the computer to run a third image when two specific images intersect. For instance, if the missile.gif and ufo.gif images occupy the same space, a third image, firea.gif, runs at that spot. The effect gives the impression that a missile hit the spaceship and the spaceship blew up.

The same thing happens with the spaceship, the lasers, and the F-14. If they intersect, the game is over and you're dead. R.I.P.

This is very clever and very involved. Be thankful that it comes to you ready to go.

Setting Up the DHTML

 You need 10 items for this to work. Forget one and you're out of luck. You can either grab each one by itself or grab them all in a big zip file. The items are available from the online version of this tutorial at http://www.htmlgoodies.com/beyond/dhtml2.html.

The following are the text documents:

- invaders.htm   The main page. It is still in .html format. Right-click to download. Macintosh users should hold the mouse down to perform a straight download. (30.9KB)
- getpos.js   The external JavaScript. (29.9KB)

The following are images:

- cannon.gif   The cannon shot. (2.24KB)
- earth.gif   The page background. (64.6KB)
- f14.gif   The plane. (4KB)
- firea.gif   The explosion. (27.6KB)
- laser.gif   The UFO's laser shot. (.15KB)

- ◉ `missileh.gif` The missile shot. (.6KB)
- ◉ `ufo.gif` The bad guy. (4KB)

The following is sound:

- ◉ `thrush.mid` The background music. (17KB)

The following is a file:

- ◉ `invaders.zip` Everything in a big zip file. (116KB)

FAQs from the HTML Goodies Web Site

Q. I keep getting errors when I play.

A. You must not have downloaded the items or not placed them on your pages correctly. You have to follow the same rules using this stuff as you do using JavaScript. The text editors cannot have margins. If they do, you corrupt the scripts and you get errors. Use Notepad or SimpleText when you open the files to see the coding.

Thanks again to Francoise White at the *SFAN Experimental Multimedia Page* for allowing me to post this DHTML example. Good luck putting it on your site. It really is a clever piece.

 Head to `http://www.htmlgoodies.com/book/dhtml2.html` *to play the game and get the parts you need to offer it from your site.*

Net Notes

Try these links for more DHTML fun:

Microsoft's DHTML Pages:
`http://msdn.microsoft.com/library/default.asp?url=/`
`workshop/author/dhtml/dhtml.asp`

Macromedia's DHTML Zone:
`http://www.dhtmlzone.com/index.html`

Yahoo!'s HTML Formats:
`http://dir.yahoo.com/Computers_and_Internet/Data_Formats/HTML/Dynamic_HTML/`

Yahoo!'s DHTML Games:
`http://dir.yahoo.com/Computers_and_Internet/Data_Formats/HTML/Dynamic_HTML/`
`Games/`

Using DHTML for Page Transitions

This is one of the latest and easiest DHTML items that allows you to create PowerPoint–type transitions when someone enters and exits your page. The effect is that one page is "wiped" over the last one. The only real downfall I have found so far is that the effect isn't rendered when the page is reloaded. You actually have to be coming or going for the first time.

Say I posted two pages, both containing the code. Then, using my Internet Explorer 4.0 browser, I jumped from one to the other. The transitions were set to random. Keep in mind that this image is a static picture. The circle continued outwards until the page had completely changed over (see Figure 13.12).

Figure 13.12
Using DHTML for a page transition.

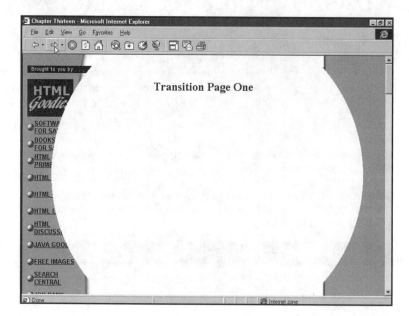

A good many tutorials come about because of e-mail letters I get from readers who drop a command in my lap and yell, as much as one can yell in an e-mail, "What the #$*% does this do?" That's where this topic came from, although Heath C. Ice had it pretty much figured out by the time he showed it to me. Thanks Heath, you're a gentleman.

Setting Up the DHTML Transition

It kills me that this is so simple. This is the code that creates the effects. They are META commands so they go between your document's <HEAD> commands, below the <TITLE> and </TITLE> commands. Here they are:

```
<META HTTP-EQUIV="Site-Enter" content="revealTrans
(Duration=1.0,Transition=23)">
<META HTTP-EQUIV="Site-Exit" content="revealTrans
(Duration=1.0,Transition=23)">
```

I only do the top command. You can take it from there to figure out the bottom one. I have not found any other levels of these commands other than the Site-Enter and Site-Exit attributes.

- ● META   Means that this command tells about the page.
- ● HTTP-EQUIV   Stands for Hypertext Transfer Protocol Equivalent. That's a fancy way of saying, through HTTP, "Make an equal to this page." In simpler terms, do something to this page's display.
- ● "Site-Enter"   Means to do the transition when someone enters the page. I think this is why you cannot get the effect when simply reloading.
- ● revealTrans   DHTML script denoting that the page should be revealed.
- ● Duration=1.0   The duration of the effect, set to one second right now.
- ● Transition=23   To randomly choose from 22 other transitions.

What was that last one again? And why? It doesn't make perfect sense to you that 23 is the perfect number for a random transition? I don't understand it either, actually. I base my statements on a totally unscientific process of entering the numbers 1 through 46 (2×23) into the transition statement and recording what happened.

You're right. I have no life. The next section shows what I found.

Specifying Transition Effects

You can try this for yourself. Just plug the numbers in and see. This is also pretty helpful knowledge if you want to set a specific transition.

The page is revealed by the following:

1. Opening from the inside out
2. Scroll in from outer edges
3. Scroll out from center
4. Scroll up from button
5. Scroll down from top
6. Scroll left to right
7. Scroll right to left

8. Vertical blinds left to right

9. Horizontal blinds top to bottom

10. Combination of 8 and 9

11. Looks a lot like 8

12. Comes in pixels

13. Scrolls in from outer parts

14. Scrolls out from center

15. Closes from both top and bottom

16. Opens from center to top and bottom

17. Diagonal roll from right to left

18. Different angle diagonal roll right to left

19. Number 17; the other way

20. Number 18; the other way

21. Random horizontal lines

22. Random vertical lines

23. Completely random

Cycle appears to start again after this...

FAQs from the HTML Goodies Web Site

Q. Do you see Netscape getting into DHTML soon?

A. Oh yeah. This is popular enough that it happens. But that's not the concern. What's next *is* the concern. What will one browser do that's new and not supported by the other?

 See these transition effects at `http://www.htmlgoodies.com/book/transitions.html`.

So, You Want Your Own Bookmark Icon, Huh?

This tutorial only works with Internet Explorer 5.0 (and higher when they come out). As of this writing, no other Netscape or IE browser supports this event. However, I would suggest using the effect because those browsers that do understand the commands display the icon and those that do not understand the command simply ignore it with no errors. What a deal, huh? On to the tutorial you go.

So, I get this letter one day asking why an error log was showing requests for something called favicon.ico. I had never heard of such a thing and neither had the person sending me the e-mail. An investigation ensued.

If you haven't heard about it yet, MSIE 5.0 has a great feature that allows you to create a small (16×16) icon and place it on your site so that when people bookmark using the 5.0 browser (or higher), their bookmark shows your little icon. Goodies is set up to do it right now. So, if you have IE 5.0, bookmark any page on the Goodies site. A little orange "HG" pops up in your Favorites Menu next to this page's link. Strangely, sometimes the icon shows right away, and other times it pops up the next time I open the browser.

 You can try out the bookmark icon for yourself at `http://www.htmlgoodies.com/book/` `favicon.html`.

So, follow along with me here and let's get you up to speed. You've got icons to place.

The Icon

The hardest part of this little exercise is getting an icon. The parameters are pretty simple. Your icon must be:

- 16 pixels by 16 pixels
- in the ".ico" Win32 format
- named "favicon.ico"

I talk about placement in a moment, but for now, I get into the daunting task of saving something in ico (icon) format.

I own three graphic editors. They are all full versions. None had the ability to save something in .ico format. So, I went looking. I found two hits.

The first was at `http://www.favicon.com`. The search engine text said that I could make an icon there. Well, when I showed up, the icon maker was down. However, they enable you to sign up for a mailing list that alerts you when their Java-based icon software comes out. It may be available when you read this.

Because I have no patience, I went looking for some other program that would enable me to create an icon. Bingo...Microangelo. This is a shareware program that enables me to either create the icon right to the screen or to create a 16×16 in Photoshop, save it as a .gif, open it in Microangelo, and then save that as an icon. I did the latter. Grab your own trial version of the Microangelo software at `http://www.impactsoft.com`.

As you can probably guess, 16×16 does not enable you to use much detail, so I went with a simple orange square surrounding a red "H" and a brown "G". You see it when you book-mark the page noted previously.

Okay, now let's assume you've got the icon in hand. What do you do with it?

Placing the Icon

MSIE 5.0 is set, by default, to look at the root directory for something called "favicon.ico" every time something is bookmarked. That's why my e-mail letter-writer noted previously kept getting errors. She didn't have this icon installed and people running MSIE 5.0 were bookmarking her pages. Thus, it threw an error.

Take your new favicon.ico and upload it to the root of your site. You should be able to reach it through this URL: www.yourdomainname.com/favicon.ico. Obviously, yourdomain-name is the name of your domain.

Believe it or not...that's it. You're good to go. Henceforth, MSIE 5.0 browsers bookmark your site with that little icon.

Wait! I Don't Have A Domain!

Not to worry. Let's say you have a site something like http://www.joesite.com/~joepages/. You can still use this method of setting the icon, but it requires one more step. You need to put the following code on every page that can be bookmarked:

```
<LINK REL="SHORTCUT ICON" HREF="http://www.domain.com/~joepages/favicon.ico">
```

Or, if the icon is in the same directory as the page that's calling for it:

```
<LINK REL="SHORTCUT ICON" HREF=" favicon.ico">
```

Put that code in between the HEAD flags on the page(s). The URL that alerts the browser to the icon is just your Web address with the domain taken off and a leading slash. See that? If you want, you can put in the entire URL, but that wears the fingers out faster. Just make sure that where you say the icon is found is actually where the browser can find it.

You can change the icon as many times as you want. Just know that after a person has bookmarked, the icon that was present when they bookmarked the first time is the one that displays.

The one downfall of all this is that the icon is held in the IE browser cache. If the user clears his cache...no more icon. The bookmark stays of course...but no more icon.

Add Your Page to Favorites

What you're reading is a tutorial that works with Internet Explorer browsers version 4.0 or higher only. At the time of this writing, Netscape does not have a method equal to this.

The concept here is to make a button that, when clicked, gives the user the ability to simply add the current page to his Favorites list.

Add This Page to Your Favorites

I give you a couple of methods first, and then show you the code for each (see Figure 13.13).

 Try both of the formats shown in this tutorial at http://www.htmlgoodies.com/book/ addtofav.html.

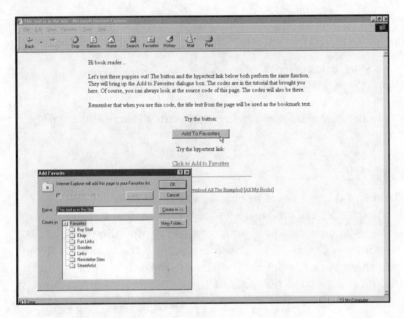

Figure 13.13
Opening the Add To Favorites dialog box.

If you got an error you're not using the correct browser. Later in the tutorial I show you how to make sure that this code only shows up on browsers that understand it.

The Code

Let's do the button code first because it's the easier of the two.

```
<FORM>
<INPUT TYPE="button" VALUE="Add To Favorites"
```

411

```
onClick='window.external.AddFavorite(location.href, document.title);'>
</FORM>
```

This is a basic HTML form button. The `onClick` Event Handler is what does the trick. The code is DHTML and is proprietary to Internet Explorer. That's a fancy way of saying only MSIE 4.0 or higher understands what the heck you're talking about. You know—like that smart kid in Spanish class.

This is what's happening:

- `window.external`   States that an external window is called upon.
- `AddFavorite`   Does just what it says. It adds something to your favorites menu.
- `location.href, document.title`   What it adds, the page's URL and the document.title.

When the command spawns the external Favorites window, you take it from there.

Now this is the basic text-based link code.

```
<a href="javascript:onClick=window.external.AddFavorite
➥(location.href, document.title);">Click to Add to Favorites</a>
```

The onClick Event Handler is exactly the same as it was in the button. Same effect. Different code.

Only in IE 4.0 or Higher

You really only want this "add to Favorites" code to be available to those using IE 4.0 or higher. Having the code pop up on Netscape 3.0 is useless as it only throws errors. However, you still want people to bookmark or add your page to favorites. Bookmarking is done on all other browsers by hitting Ctrl-D. So let's make it so that if the browser is IE 4.0 or higher, the code for one of these buttons pops up and if the browser is anything other than IE 4.0 or higher, text pops up asking the user to hit Ctrl-D. Okay?

Click Here *Try out this script at* `http://www.htmlgoodies.com/book/addtofav02.html`. *Try looking at the page with both an Internet Explorer and a Navigator browser so you see both effects.*

The Code

```
<SCRIPT LANGUAGE="javascript">

//This code is for IE v4 or better
if (navigator.appName == "Microsoft Internet Explorer" && navigator.appVersion >=
➥"4.0")
```

```
{
document.write("<a
➥href=javascript:onClick=window.external.AddFavorite(location.href,")
document.write("document.title)>Click to Add to Favorites</a>")
}

//This code posts text if not
else
{document.write("Hit CTRL-D to bookmark this page")}

</SCRIPT>
```

Note that I broke the JavaScript line into two document.write lines. This happens because of the comma. If it was all on one line, the comma would break the line and an error would display. This way the comma has no effect and the entire line prints and runs error free. This is just a little something I learned through trial and error.

This is a quick test of the browser. If the browser meets the criteria, the code or the text is written to the page. This is simple.

Setting Your Page as the Browser Home Page

At the moment, this is an Internet Explorer 5.0-only deal. Netscape does not have anything equal to this. You have to be running IE 5.0 to see this effect.

With the advent of IE 5.0, a lot of events that had been beyond a programmer's reach became available. Now, for example, users can place your page in their Favorites lists, or you can offer to print your page, all with the click of a button. With CSS, you can even state where the page breaks occur within that print.

In addition, you can now use one short line of DHTML to set your page as the home page for your users. I don't mean on their site, I mean in their browser. Look at the top of your browser. See that button that reads "HOME"? By using this little script, you are able to set it so that when the user clicks on that button, he comes to your page.

The Code

I show you how it's done, but a word of warning first. Only offer this as something the user can click to enact. Yes, it is possible to set this script to an onLoad event handler so that it happens as soon as the user logs into your page. Don't do that. For one thing, the process doesn't happen without your users knowing. A little box pops up after the script runs, asking if the user really wants your page set to be the home page. Don't make them click "no" every time they come in. Keep everyone happy and enable them to choose whether to set your page as their home page or not.

There. Now that I've put the soapbox away, let's get down to code.

Try out these scripts at `http://www.htmlgoodies.com/book/homepage.html`. *Remember that you must be running Internet Explorer 5.0 or higher to see the effect. Any other browser throws an error.*

The effect described previously looks like Figure 13.14.

Figure 13.14
The Home Page dialog box.

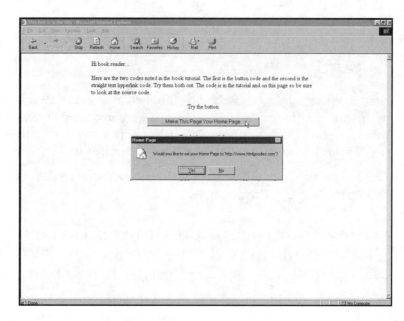

When you test it, when the home page dialog box opens choose yes. Then click your Home button to prove that the system works.

You can always change your Home settings back to whatever you had before by choosing Tools, Internet Options, and then changing your home page address at the top of that new window.

I have my own browsers set to open to blank pages. I just like it that way. But enough about me. On to the text code.

I want to start with this because it uses a new command included in HTML 4.0 (see Appendix A, "Everything You Need to Know About HTML 4.0"). The command is <SPAN> and its only job is to act as a transport mechanism for style sheet commands. Note that the following code produces something that looks like a hypertext link but really isn't. This is text that's made up to look like a link. At the moment, the SPAN flag is only understood by Internet Explorer, which is actually okay, because this effect is only understood by Internet Explorer. See how this all works out for the good of mankind?

Get this all on one line:

```
<SPAN STYLE="cursor:hand; color:blue; text-decoration:underline"
onClick="this.style.behavior='url(#default#homepage)';
this.setHomePage('http://www.htmlgoodies.com');">
Click Here to Make HTML Goodies Your Home Page
</SPAN>
```

Alter It

The code is fairly stable. To use it on your page, you really only need to make two changes:

- Change the URL http://www.htmlgoodies.com to your page's address. If you don't change it then, even though the code is on your page, it sets the browser's home to HTML Goodies.

- Change the text of the phrase "Click Here..." to be appropriate to your page

Other than that, just make sure you get the entire code on one line or you get some nasty errors.

Some Other Changes

You can also play with the cursor, the color of the text, and whether the text is underlined or not. See that in the STYLE= section? You find a list of 17 different cursors in Chapter 8. You can set the color to any one you want. Just remember that if you use a hex code, you need to put the pound sign (#) in front (for example, #FFCCFF). Word color codes do not need the pound sign.

How About a Button?

Don't mind if I do! Notice this effect is achieved via an onClick Event Handler. Because the Event Handler sets it in motion, you can use the code pretty much anywhere an Event Handler comes into play.

```
<FORM>
<INPUT TYPE="button"
VALUE="Make This Page Your Home Page"
onClick="this.style.behavior='url(#default#homepage)';
➥this.setHomePage('http://www.htmlgoodies.com');">
</FORM>
```

Get that entire INPUT line on one line in your code.

This is a fun piece of code, but remember to set it up so that your users are offered the choice to click or not. Don't fire this from an onLoad.

Also keep in mind that this code only works with IE 5.0. If you intend to use it, think about setting it to a JavaScript that only displays the code if the user is running IE 5.0 or higher. Any other browser would get some text.

 The code to get this effect is really a handful. Try going to http://www.htmlgoodies.com/ book/homepage02.html *and copying the code from there. You are less apt to make a mistake. Remember that you must be running Internet Explorer 5.0 or higher to see the effect. Any other browser gets the text "Have a nice day."*

This is the code you see online:

```
<SCRIPT LANGUAGE="javascript">

//This code is for IE v5 or better
if (navigator.appName == "Microsoft Internet Explorer"
➥&& navigator.appVersion >= "4.0 (compatible; MSIE 5.0b2; Windows 95)")

{
document.write("<SPAN STYLE='cursor:hand; color:blue; text-decoration:underline'
➥onClick=this.style.behavior='url(#default#homepage)';this.setHomePage
➥('http://www.htmlgoodies.com');>
➥Click Here to Make HTML Goodies Your Home Page</SPAN>")
}

//This code posts text if not
else
{document.write("Have a Nice Day")}

</SCRIPT>
```

Make a real point of getting the long lines on a single line in your code. You see it online in the correct configuration. Keep that configuration at all costs. Otherwise the errors fly.

Oh, and in case you're wondering, I know it reads 4.0 where you call for the version number. The text in the parentheses actually sets this script apart as being for Internet Explorer 5.0.

Wacky, huh? Welcome to the Web.

Chapter 14

Building Web Site Banners

I have been getting e-mail from people asking how to create an advertising banner for their home page for a while now. This chapter walks you through the process. The purpose is to introduce you to the basic theory behind banner creation and to enable you to comfortably create your own.

Software Tools Needed

You're going to need a lot more than a text editor and knowledge of HTML to build banners for your Web site—you're going to need some additional software. Before you begin, please go out and get the software described in this section.

Graphics Program

This chapter uses Paint Shop Pro (PSP). Those who are already in the graphics creation biz are immediately going bonkers saying that any number of programs are better choices. Well, to each his own.

I use Paint Shop Pro because it has what college professors call a *good learning curve*. That means that if you learn this graphics program, it is quite easy to get up and running on another. The menus are very basic and quite close to other great graphics programs such as Photoshop or CorelDRAW, which I also own. The biggest problem moving from one program to another, I've found, is that the commands are in different menus. For instance, the crop function in Paint Shop Pro is under the Image menu, whereas in Photoshop it's under the Edit menu. That's a good example of the concerns you face going from this tutorial using Paint Shop Pro to using another graphics program. This is not a big jump.

That said, the best reason I can give for using Paint Shop Pro is that it's shareware. You can go and grab a copy and follow along. No, Apple does not have a PSP yet, but use what image program you can get or already have. I taught at Bowling Green State University for three years using Macintoshes and the learning curve is equally as easy.

Get your 30-day evaluation copy here:

- http://www.jasc.com (JASC, Inc. makes PSP.)
- http://www.shareware.com

Shareware.com lists a lot of download sites. When you arrive, you are asked for your system type (Windows 95, Macintosh, or Windows 3.11). You can then search for the name of the product. Apple users can also use this site to look for graphics programs compatible with their system.

"I already have a graphics program," you say. You mean like MS Paint? Or maybe you have a more advanced program through all that great preloaded software. That's where I got CorelDRAW. If that's the one you want to use, great. The one downfall of MS Paint and the like is that they save images as bitmaps. That's a very vanilla format. I deal with GIF format in this tutorial. You are probably able to follow along all the way until it's time to animate the images you create. At that point you would need to find a program that converts the bitmap (denoted by a .bmp extension) into GIF format. Such as Paint Shop Pro...

GIF Animator Program

The purpose of these advertising banners is to attract attention. People seeing them is nice, but you also want them to be clicked. An advertisement that isn't acted upon is not doing its job. In the four years I have run Goodies, I have seen maybe three static banners. The animation is what really makes a solid banner come alive—even if the animation is only two cells flipping back and forth. It just adds to the effect. So you're going to need an animator program.

For more on animation see Chapter 3, "Adding Images and Backgrounds." If you've read it, you may already have the GIF Construction Set program. If not, grab it now.

Again, a lot of other animation programs exist. I learned on this one and I feel it's the best, plus that whole learning curve thing. You can grab a copy from
http://www.mindworkshop.com/alchemy/gifcon.html.

Banner Primer 1: Getting Started

This banner's main effect is a movie ticket that shows up in the middle of the banner. It tears in half as the two sides of the ticket pull away to the left and right ends of the banner. The text rolls by that and reads Admit One—To My Web Page—Click Here!. What you are seeing in Figure 14.1 is the very end, where the banner blinks Click Here. Please note that Figure 14.1 is a still picture. You need to see the banner online to get the full effect.

 You should see the banner in action at least once before you plunge into this series of primers. Point your browser to `http://www.htmlgoodies.com/primers/banner_1.html` *to see it. You need to scroll down a bit to get to it after you've logged into the page.*

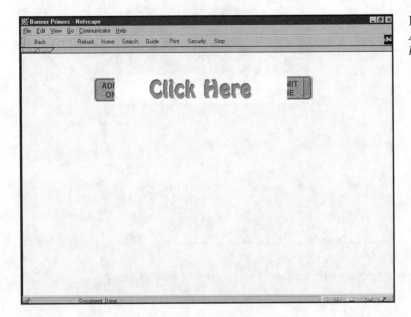

Figure 14.1
An animated Web site banner.

In the process of building this example, you perform six functions that are crucial to the creation of a good ad banner. Besides, I didn't expect that you would simply grab this one off the page and use it. But if you want to, go ahead.

This is the plan from this point on:

- Banner Primer 2: Creating New Images
- Banner Primer 3: Learning to Crop
- Banner Primer 4: Importing Images—Copying and Pasting
- Banner Primer 5: Adding Text and Shadows
- Banner Primer 6: Animating the Images
- Banner Primer 7: Activating the Image—Show Time

The banner in Figure 14.2 was created using the exact same steps I am going to cover here. I used Paint Shop Pro to create all the images except the original ticket. I got that from the WebSpice Images provided for free on the HTML Goodies site. See `http://www.htmlgoodies.com/freeimages` *to get them for yourself.*

The animated image in Figure 14.2 requires 13 different images to complete. The first group of images creates the tearing ticket animation.

Figure 14.2

Images needed for animated tearing-ticket GIF.

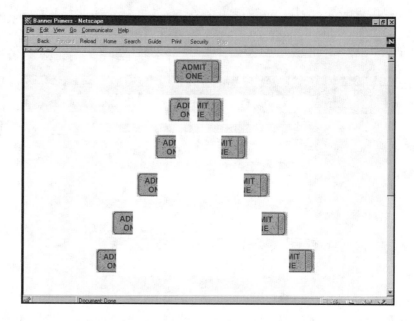

Figure 14.3 shows the second group of images used to create the text that appears.

Don't bother to go to the HTML Goodies site and download any of them now. Create each one as you go along. The only image you really need from me is the ticket image, and you get that at the start of Banner Primer 3.

FAQs from the HTML Goodies Web Site

Q. Are you making the banner you did in the banner primers or do you want us to make one for ourselves?

A. Both, actually. Make the one I am showing first to get the hang of it and then make one for yourself.

Figure 14.3
Images needed for text animation.

First of all, grab the two programs noted earlier. Install them on your computer and make sure they work by opening and playing around with the buttons. If you don't get any errors, they work.

Next, start thinking about what your banner is going to look like. I know you don't have the skills yet to create it, but so what? I'm not the president, but I still know what I'd do if I got into office. Sketch it out. Use arrows to show the motion you want. Create a sort of storyboard of your idea, but keep it simple. The more animation cells you have, the more bytes this takes and the slower it loads and runs. If your banner doesn't run, no one sees it anyway. Show your idea to a couple of people and see what they think. This little image is your site's welcome mat. It had better be nice—why would anyone visit otherwise? Get feedback on it. Creating a banner for your site should not be something you throw together in an hour or so. Because this is your representative in the real world, it should be given some thought.

Think about your site. What is good about it? Why should people come? Ask yourself what is so darn wonderful about your site that someone should take time out of their busy life and come see it. Whatever you land upon, that's what your banner should say, either in text or images.

Speaking of text, what does your banner say? The text needs to be very short. Only 10 words are on this banner (including those on the ticket). Furthermore, this banner rotates fully in just under six seconds. That's not a lot of time to read things over. So make your text big, exciting, and a very quick read.

And so you start.

Banner Primer 2: Creating New Images

At this point, you should have Paint Shop Pro (PSP) installed on your computer (or have the program you intend to use installed). If you are using PSP, you should have a screen that looks something like Figure 14.4.

Figure 14.4
JASC's Paint Shop Pro.

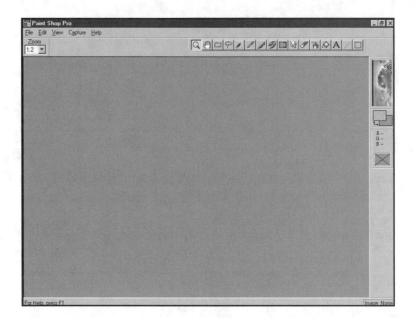

Creating a New Image

First off, you need to learn how to create a new image. Think of this as a canvas. You create one image that is the correct size of our banner and then, using PSP, you add items to that palette.

The banner you are creating in this series of primers is the generally accepted size for an advertising banner. The size banner sits on top of each HTML Goodies page. I don't know how these numbers were determined, but the banner size you want is 468 pixels wide by 60 pixels high.

A *pixel* is a little colored dot. You see, computer images are not like photographs, where the color is consistent and smooth. Computer images are a lot more like the images you'd find in a newspaper. Up close it's a lot of little dots, but when you move away and your eyes get the opportunity to blur the little dots together, it makes a picture. Your television works the same way. Tonight, go right up to your TV, lick your thumb, and drag the spit across a small section of the TV screen. The liquid offers enough of a "lens" that you can see the individual dots.

When I say the image is 468×60, that means 468 colored dots are across and 60 colored dots are up. You are going to create an image made up of all white dots. It looks like just a big white rectangle.

A menu called File is in the upper-left corner of PSP. Click it and choose the New option.

When that is done, you should get a dialog box that looks like Figure 14.5.

Figure 14.5
The New Image dialog box.

I doubt that the numbers in the width and height sections read 468 and 60 as the image does, so do that now. The fastest way is to click the number. It highlights in blue. Press your Backspace key. The number disappears and you can type the number of pixels you want.

Notice the background color section. You have multiple colors to choose from, but you want to stay with white because this banner is mostly white. Don't worry about the image type section. PSP takes care of that aspect.

Choose OK—ta da!—you have the new image. It should look like Figure 14.6.

Figure 14.6
Paint Shop Pro's new image.

Now, let's save it right away.

Saving the Image

You want to save this image in GIF format. Choose GIF because you want to animate this image, and a few others, later. The animator requires that the images be in GIF. Click the

File menu again and choose Save As. You get a familiar dialog box that looks like Figure 14.7.

Figure 14.7
Paint Shop Pro's Save As dialog box.

First, you need to choose where you want this image saved. Follow the same format you would to save any text file. Notice in the image that the section marked Save as Type is open. You open it by clicking the little down arrow at the end of the line. Now you have a scrolling list where you can see all the different types of image formats you can use. You want to save in GIF—CompuServe format. Scroll up or down to that format and when it is highlighted click to select it. You are now set to save in GIF format.

In case you're wondering, the reason GIF format has the word CompuServe after it is because the format was created by CompuServe. Now look just above the Save as Type box at the File Name box. This is where you give the image its name. To stay consistent with this chapter, call this image banner.gif.

FAQs from the HTML Goodies Web Site

Q. When I save the image, should I put the .gif at the end or will the computer do it for me?

A. Don't ever rely on a computer to do something for you. Be safe—put the .gif on the end.

Q. Why can't you save these images as JPG? Wouldn't that make the bytes smaller?

A. Because you're going to animate the images later and the animator program requires GIF format.

That's it! Success! You created and saved your first image. That wasn't so hard, was it?

You're creating and saving images like a pro. If you feel up to it, head to the next banner primer. Or take the night off and start again tomorrow. You do look a little tired.

 If you're having trouble making the template image, I have it for you to download at http://www.htmlgoodies.com/book/banner2.html.

Banner Primer 3: Learning to Crop

You are going to take the movie ticket image you should have downloaded from my site and cut it into two images. In technical terms, you *crop* two sections. First you need the image. After you have downloaded the image, open it in the PSP program by choosing Open from the File menu and looking for the image in the dialog box. This is the same process you follow when you look for a text document in a word processor.

Cropping an Image

 Grab the ticket image at http://www.htmlgoodies.com/book/banner3.html. *When you get it open, it should look something like Figure 14.8.*

Figure 14.8
Ticket image in Paint Shop Pro.

Make sure you have saved the ticket image in the same directory in which you saved the image you made in Banner Primer 2. In fact, make sure you save all the images you make during these primers in the same directory.

Crop it! Crop me? Crop you! (Sorry, easy joke.)

This is so easy you may not believe it. You are going to turn the ticket image into two images. Let's put PSP in the crop mode. Look at the screen. There should be a little button that looks like a dotted rectangle. It looks like Figure 14.9 on the PSP screen, the pointer is on it.

Click it. Now you have placed PSP in the mode to crop out a section of the picture.

After the crop button is clicked, place your mouse pointer over the ticket1.gif image. The pointer should change as shown in Figure 14.10.

Figure 14.9
The crop button on Paint Shop Pro's toolbar.

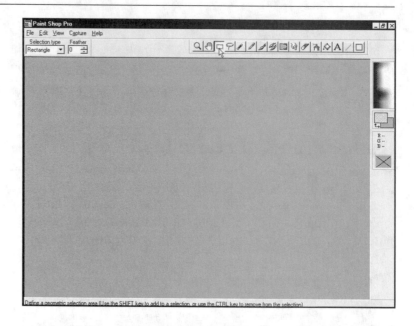

Figure 14.10
The Paint Shop Pro pointer in crop mode.

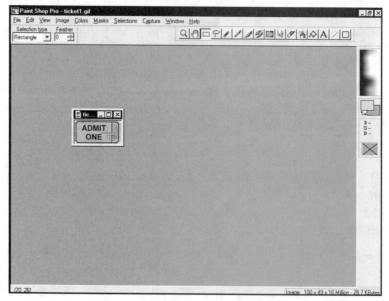

Put the cross in the upper-left corner of the image. Click and hold, and then drag the mouse down and to the right. See the box forming? Try to cut the ticket perfectly in half. After you have one half of the image set aside, let go of the mouse button. The box becomes a dotted line. It should look like Figure 14.11.

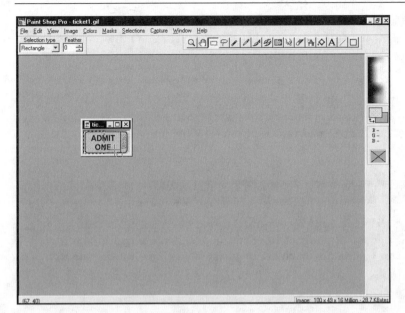

Figure 14.11
See the ticket image crop outline?

Got that? Good! Now let's perform the actual cropping. Look again at the top of the PSP window. There should be a menu called Image. Click it. Crop is a few commands down.

After you choose crop, your image should look like the one in Figure 14.12.

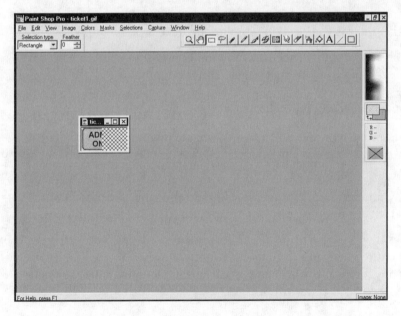

Figure 14.12
Cropped ticket image.

How about that? Now follow the same instructions from Banner Primer 2 and save that half image as `leftticket.gif`. After you've saved that new image, close it by clicking the gray X in the left corner of the image (not the X on the PSP program, but the X on the image).

Open the `ticket1.gif` image again and perform another crop, only this time crop the right side of the image and save it as `rightticket.gif`. Do your best to get the crop line in the same place as the last one. I did it by making the crop follow the left vertical line of the *m* in the word *Admit*.

You now have the two ticket images you need to animate the ticket opening up.

Now you can crop with the best of them. I use this function constantly. This is a very basic of image creation, but you also have importing images. Thus you move on...

Banner Primer 4: Importing Images—Copying and Pasting

If you're following along at home, you should have four images in your banner folder by now: `banner.gif`, `ticket1.gif`, `leftticket.gif`, and `rightticket.gif`. Those four images are your building blocks. Now let's construct the sections.

This should be a fairly easy primer to follow because you have probably used this method a thousand times. What you intend to do is copy one image and paste it into another.

This is the same method as if you were writing a text document in a word processor. Let's say you want to move an entire paragraph from one section to another. You would highlight the text, choose to copy (or cut) it, and then paste it in the section you feel is a better fit. This is the same thing, except it's done with images.

Copying and Pasting

Here you go. First, you need to open PSP if you haven't already. Now open two images: ticket1.gif and banner.gif. Both of the images should now appear in the PSP window. They might be on top of each other. If that's the case, place your pointer on the blue bar at the top of one of the images, click, hold, and drag the image away from the other.

Notice that even though two images are on the screen, they are not seen as equal by PSP. One of the images is in the *forefront*, meaning that is the image that is being acted upon at the moment. Look at the screen in Figure 14.13 that was taken from my own PSP while both images were open.

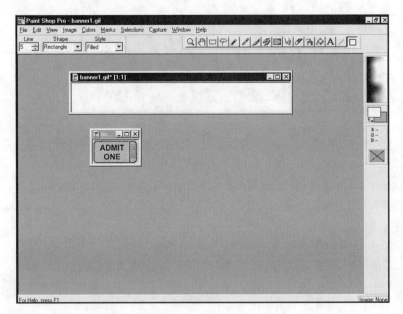

Figure 14.13
The banner image is in the forefront (the active window).

See how the banner.gif has a blue bar at the top (brighter) and the ticket1.gif image has a gray bar at the top (darker)? Look at your two images—one is one color and one is another. Your computer may be set to a different color scheme than mine. Usually one color is brighter than the other. The one with the brighter color bar at the top is the one that is in the forefront. That means that if you perform a copy, a cut, or a paste, that is the image that is acted upon. If you want the other image to be the one acted upon, click it. You see the colors flip. Click back and forth between the images to see them work that way.

Now you take those two images, banner.gif and ticket1.gif, and combine them to create a third image called banner1.gif. It looks like Figure 14.14.

Figure 14.14
Ticket image pasted into banner.

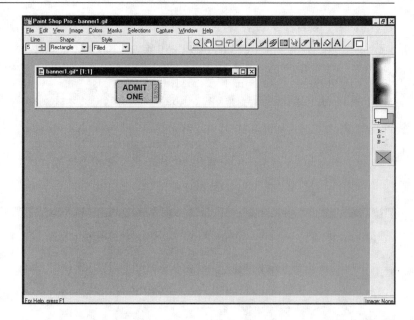

Performing the Copy

You copy one image, the ticket, and paste it into the other image, the banner. Now you want the copy to act upon the ticket because that is the image you copy. If it isn't already, click the ticket image to bring it to the forefront.

When it is at the forefront, click the Edit menu at the top of the PSP window. You find Copy under that menu (see Figure 14.15).

The ticket image is now copied to a section of your computer's hard drive called the Clipboard. Think of it as having a Xerox of the image standing by.

FAQs from the HTML Goodies Web Site

Q. **You might want to tell your readers that they can speed their copying and pasting by pressing CTRL+C to copy and CTRL+V to paste.**

A. I do that, too. I find that older computer people like you and me who came up from DOS-based programs seem to do that more often. Thanks. I pass it along.

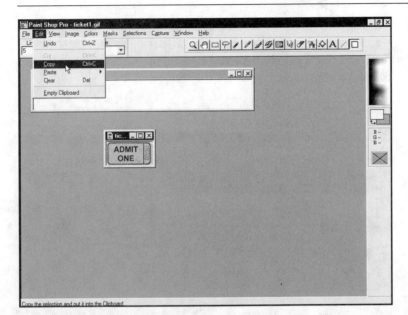

Figure 14.15
Copying an image in Paint Shop Pro.

Performing the Paste

Now you need to bring the banner image to the forefront. Be careful about jumping to paste at this point. When you go back to the Edit menu, you notice that the Paste command has three options. Those options are shown in Figure 14.16.

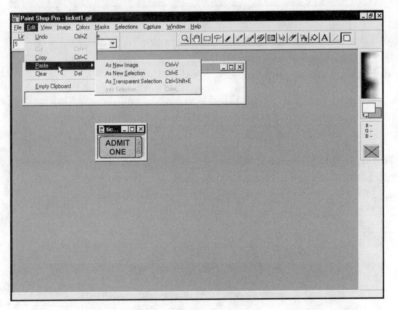

Figure 14.16
Paste menu options in Paint Shop Pro.

You are interested in pasting the copied image As New Selection. If you paste it As New Image, it pastes all by itself—and not into the other image. If you paste it as a transparent image, your effect is altered and you don't get what you're looking for. Go with the middle one. If the banner image is in the forefront, choose As New Selection.

You should now have something that looks like Figure 14.17.

Figure 14.17
Ticket image pasted into banner image.

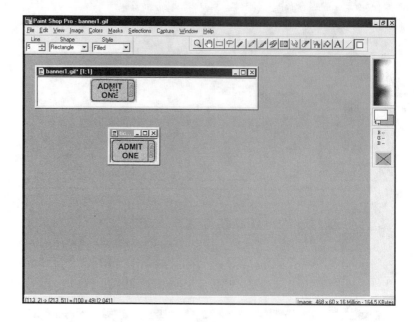

Go ahead and move your pointer around a bit. You see that the cross with arrows on the ends allows you to move the image wherever you want it. Try to get it right in the middle. When you have it right where you want it, click but don't hold—just click it.

The image now locks into place and the same dotted line you saw in the crop function appears. Click again anywhere outside of the pasted image. Don't click inside or you get the arrows again. The dotted lines should disappear.

You see your new image. You now need to save it with the same commands you used to save the images you created. Make sure you choose Save As. You see, if you choose Save, you save right over `banner.gif`. You don't want to do that. You want to make a whole new image, so choose Save As and name it `banner1.gif` in the same directory you have been saving all your other images in.

Tearing the Ticket

Now you have the first banner with the full ticket right in the middle. The process now is to create the next five images where the banner splits and pulls to the outer walls of the image. That is done by creating five new banners that look like Figure 14.18.

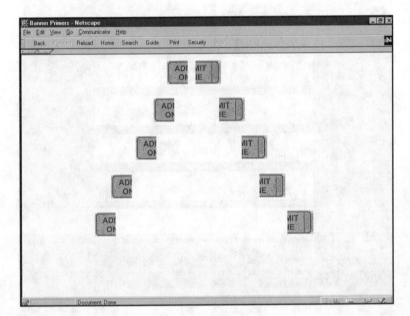

Figure 14.18
Tearing ticket sequence of images.

You already have the tools to create the five images. You need to open four images in the PSP window for this: `leftticket.gif`, `rightticket.gif`, `banner.gif`, and `banner1.gif`. After you have all those images open, place `banner1.gif` just above `banner.gif`. The PSP screen should look like Figure 14.19.

I am having you do this because you use `banner1.gif` as a guide to create the next image. Notice how I have one lined up right under the other. Copy and paste `leftticket.gif` and `rightticket.gif` into `banner.gif` so that you get a little bit of a tear. It should look like Figure 14.20.

Save it as `banner2.gif`. Now leave `banner2.gif` open and reopen `banner.gif`. Place `banner.gif` below `banner2.gif`. Now you can use `banner2.gif` as a guide to make the next image, which is `banner3.gif`. The screen looks something like Figure 14.21 when you finish making `banner3.gif`.

Figure 14.19
Four images opened in the Paint Shop Pro window.

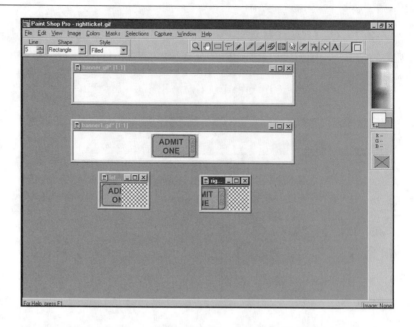

Figure 14.20
Pasting the left and right ticket halves.

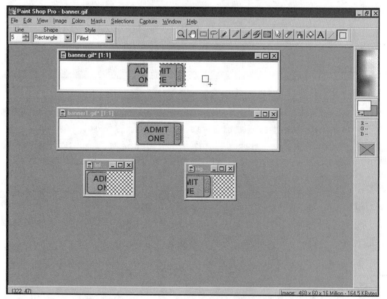

See how I am using one image as a guide to create the next image in the sequence? That's why I am asking you to create the images by looking at the image that comes before it. What you need to do now is create `banner4.gif`, `banner5.gif`, and `banner6.gif` so that they closely resemble the five images in Figure 14.18. They are all made by copying and pasting repeatedly, until the image is finished. Save the image by using the Save As command.

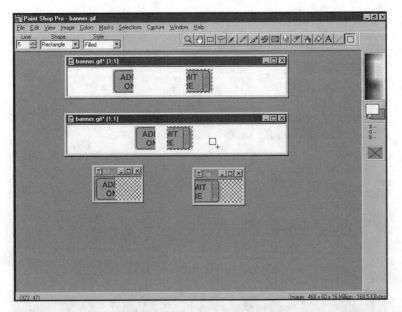

Figure 14.21
Pasting next sequence of left and right ticket halves.

FAQs from the HTML Goodies Web Site

Q. I accidentally hit Save instead of Save As. I keep trying to choose undo, but it doesn't un-save.

A. And it doesn't. Saving something is altering it on the hard drive. You can't undo it. Next time save a backup of the item you're working on.

The banner.gif image is your canvas, the blank space that all other items are placed upon. You use the image that came before it as a guide to creating the next image. Remember, these images are all going to be animated and need to be somewhat related to each other; otherwise the final animation looks way too jumpy to be enjoyed.

Make sure that banner1.gif through banner6.gif also end up in the same directory as the other images you have made. This is a little time consuming, but not as scary as you first thought, right?

If you'd like to download the images created in Banner Primer 4, go to http://www. htmlgoodies.com/book/banner4.html.

Banner Primer 5: Adding Text and Shadows

Now the text. You are going to create four more images with text. They are shown in Figure 14.22.

Figure 14.22
Banner text images.

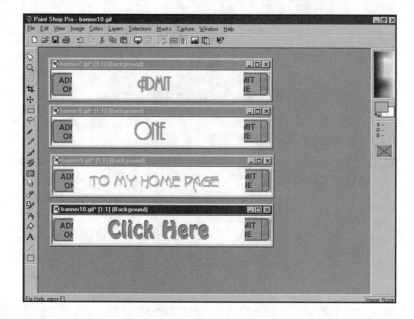

You're concerned about three things when doing this: the text's color, font, and size. Let's take them in order.

Text Color

I know in the book these images are all shades of black and white. However, if you've seen the images online, you see I went with shades of purple, mainly because the ticket is purple. If you feel another color is better on the eyes, knock yourself out. To get started, you need to play with the rainbow color block. Known as the *color palette*, it is on the far right side of the PSP screen. The pointer is just below it in Figure 14.23.

That's the designated area to pick colors. The rainbow item on top allows you to choose from a wide range of colors. At the moment, you can see the two colors that are chosen. One is a little lighter than the other. You don't want those two colors. You want shades of purple. You can do one of two things on your PSP—run your mouse over the rainbow until you find the color you like or do what I do and click twice on the box beneath the rainbow box that appears to be most forward. This is the one that is white. You should get a box that looks like Figure 14.24.

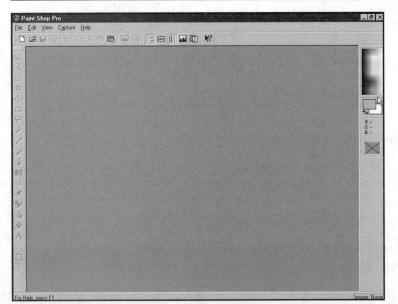

Figure 14.23
Viewing the color palette tool in Paint Shop Pro.

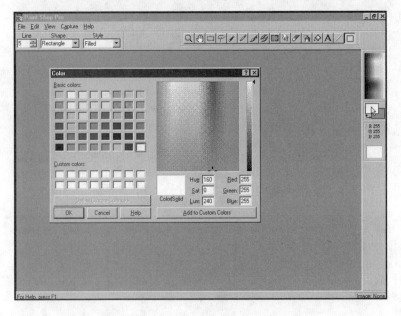

Figure 14.24
Paint Shop Pro's Color dialog box.

The colors in the small boxes are the most popular. I use them unless I need a really specific color. Choose a light shade by clicking the color. I don't care which. Choose OK. That shade should now appear in the little box to the right. Did it? Good.

Let's look at the color area again where you clicked to get the dialog box.

See the little arrow pointing to both of the small boxes below the rainbow box? Click it. Notice the two colors flip back to front? You just set background and foreground colors. You use both.

Click the arrow so that the color you just chose is in the background. Now click the foreground box twice to again open the color palette. Now choose a dark shade of the color you just chose. Again, I went with shades of purple.

Make sure the dark box is forward. You are going to first lay down a dark shadow and then lay the lighter color over top. You paste the same text twice, one dark and one light. They are just a bit offset from one another, giving the effect of a shadow. You have the text's color. Now choose the text's font.

FAQs from the HTML Goodies Web Site

Q. How small can I go with text on a banner?

A. Not very. Remember that these words are read on-the-fly. You may only get one shot at it. You might make supporting text smaller, but the main text should be big as life.

Text Font

To start this process, you need to once again display the image you intend to place this text upon. If you've been following along, remember that you created `banner.gif` for the sole purpose of acting as a template so that you could paste other items onto it, namely the two halves of the ticket. Now you need a different template.

Notice that all the text appears between the two ticket halves when they are at their farthest point. The image you created that has that look now becomes our template. If you've been following my format, that is `banner6.gif`. Does that make sense?

Open `banner6.gif` in PSP and put PSP in text mode. Remember the cropping section of this primer series (when you clicked the button with the dotted square to place PSP into crop mode)? Same deal here. The button that places PSP in the text mode is near the crop button. My pointer is on it in Figure 14.25. Notice that a ToolTip box opened up, telling me that button deals with text.

Now move your pointer over `banner6.gif`. It should look something like Figure 14.26.

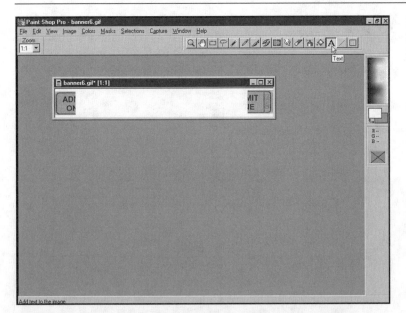

Figure 14.25
The text button on Paint Shop Pro's toolbar.

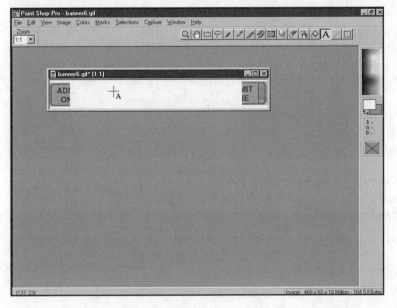

Figure 14.26
The text pointer over a banner image.

That little A means that you are ready to place text on the image. Make sure your darker color is in the foreground. I need to repeat that. Make sure your darker color is in the foreground. Remember that you are laying down the darker shadowing first. Click the banner. You should get the dialog box shown in Figure 14.27.

Figure 14.27
*Paint Shop Pro's Add Text
dialog box.*

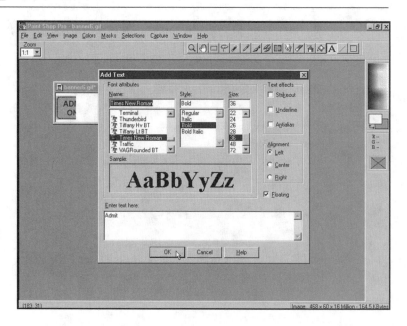

Now the fun part—choosing the type of text. The upper left of the dialog box lists the
available fonts. The example image uses Times New Roman font. That's not the font I used
to create the first image that says Admit. I changed the font to something called Party. You
don't have to use that font. In fact, you may not even have it available. The shareware version of PSP offers far fewer fonts than does the full version, which is what I have. If you
dislike this font, or don't have it, look at some others. Click the highest font available in
your own upper-left section. You see an example of the font in the gray window just below
it. Now use your arrow keys to scroll down. You see fonts just whizzing by. Find one you
like.

FAQs from the HTML Goodies Web Site

Q. Should I use the fonts you use on your primers?

A. You can use any font you'd like, but remember that these words have to be read and
read fast. Make them large enough and choose a font clear enough that people can
read them in one shot.

When you find the font you like best, type the text you want to appear on the image in
the box marked Enter Text Here. In the case of this first image, you only want the word
Admit. Click OK. You should now have something that looks a lot like Figure 14.28.

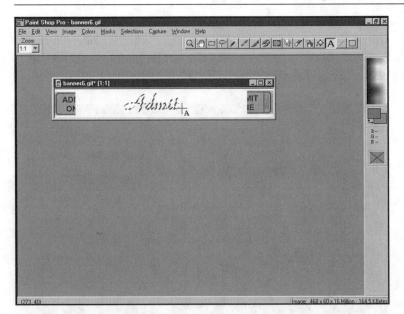

Figure 14.28
Selected text on the banner image.

The text you put in should be there, surrounded by those familiar dotted lines and that same four-pointed arrow. Move it around. You can place the text wherever you want. Click the mouse to set it.

I hate it! That happens. I never get my text just right on the first try. To delete the text you just posted, go under the Edit menu and click Undo. That brings back the dotted lines. Go right back under the same Edit menu and choose Clear as it shows to the left. The text should be gone. Click the banner again to get the text dialog box and try another font.

Text Size

You can just about guess at this. Two more areas are on the Add Text dialog box (see Figure 14.27). One is marked Style and the other is marked Size. Both affect the look and size of the text. I have found that the Example box is helpful, but rarely my final authority on how large or small text is. I always have to mess around trying nine or so looks before I arrive at the size and style I like most. Just keep posting text and erasing until you love it.

Adding Shadow

This is the fun part. If you have followed the instructions, you should have laid down dark text somewhere on `banner6.gif`. That is the shadow text. Now go back over the color palette and click the arrow between the two color boxes. This flips it so that the lighter color now resides in the foreground box.

Make sure PSP is still in text mode and click the image again. The settings you used to lay down the dark text should still be there. Choose OK. Now you should have a light color version of the same text. Click the mouse, hold it, and lay the lighter text across the darker text (slightly offset). It should look something like Figure 14.29.

Figure 14.29
Text shadow overlay.

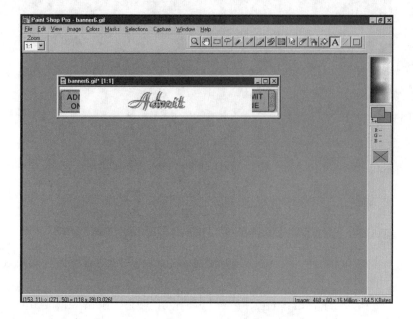

See the shadowing occurring? How much you set the light text off denotes how much shadow you get. After you have the shadow where you want it, click, put PSP into the crop mode, and click the image once to set the text in place.

FAQs from the HTML Goodies Web Site

Q. Why don't you use the shadowing tool on the image program rather than double pasting?

A. Habit. This is the way I do it, so this the way I teach it. I also think it's easier because I can play with the two levels rather than resetting and looking again and again.

Check out an outstanding book called *Paint Shop Pro Web Techniques* by T. Michael Clark (New Riders Publishing) if you want to delve deeper.

Now save the image using a Save As command. Remember: You just pasted two layers of text onto banner6.gif. If you simply choose Save you destroy banner6.gif. You need to save this as banner7.gif.

You only need three more banners. They are each created the same way as the banner you just finished. You use banner6.gif as a template for each, so you need to keep opening banner6.gif each time you want to create a new one. Just be sure to do a Save As each time you save a new image. The last three and a little about each follow.

Figure 14.30 shows banner8.gif. It uses the same colors as banner6.gif, but I flipped it so that the dark color is in the forefront. I also changed the font to Prom.

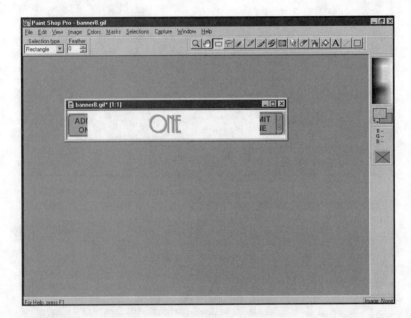

Figure 14.30

Text Image for banner8.gif.

Figure 14.31 is banner9.gif. It uses the same colors, but the font is Isadora.

Figure 14.32 is banner10.gif. I have changed the colors for impact and made the text a little bigger. The font is Hobbit.

You're probably wondering what you thought was so hard about creating images. After you create the last three images, make them all one. See you then.

 You can download the text banner I created for this chapter at http://www.htmlgoodies. com/book/banner5.html.

Banner Primer 6: Animating the Images

I should state right up front that if you haven't yet read the original Goodies animation tutorial in Chapter 3, "Adding Images and Backgrounds," you may want to do that. I am going to assume you have read it as you start this tutorial. This primer is for the creation of a banner. Because I have already written a piece on creating animation in general, I am not going over it again here.

Figure 14.31
Text image for
banner9.gif.

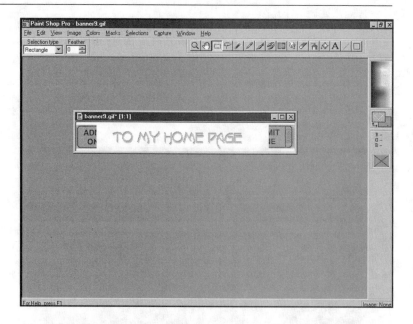

Figure 14.32
Text image for
banner10.gif.

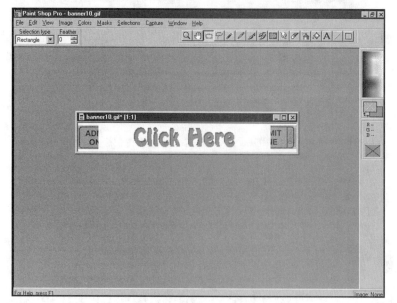

Creating an Animation List

You have all the bricks and mortar. Now let's build the house. In my opinion when you are using a long series of images, it is best to write out what images are used in the order they are used. Remember in the first banner primer I said for you to draw out your ideas? This is where you try to make your vision come true.

 You may want to jump online again and look over the finished product again at http:// www.htmlgoodies.com/banner.gif.

You should be quite familiar with the images that make up the animation. Here they are in the order they are used:

banner1.gif (full ticket)

banner2.gif (torn ticket)

banner3.gif (torn ticket)

banner4.gif (torn ticket)

banner5.gif (torn ticket)

banner6.gif (most torn ticket)

banner7.gif (Admit)

banner8.gif (One)

banner6.gif (most torn ticket)

banner9.gif (To My Home Page)

banner10.gif (Click Here)

banner6.gif (most torn ticket)

banner10.gif (Click Here)

Adding Time Sequence

Next take that list and denote how long you want it to be between each animation cell. The GIF Animator Set works in tenths of a second. However, because you don't have the cells actually denoted in the animation program, I do it through a simple method of s (short span of time), M (medium span of time), and L (long span of time). I consider short around a quarter second, medium around a half a second, and long a full second or longer. The time is how long it is before moving to the next animation cell.

This is what this banner looks like with times:

banner1.gif (full ticket)

(M)

banner2.gif (torn ticket)

(S)

banner3.gif (torn ticket)

(S)

banner4.gif (torn ticket)

(S)

banner5.gif (torn ticket)

(S)

banner6.gif (most torn ticket)

(M)

banner7.gif (Admit)

(L)

banner8.gif (One)

(L)

banner6.gif (most torn ticket)

(S)

banner9.gif (To My Home Page)

(L)

banner10.gif (Click Here)

(L)

banner6.gif (most torn ticket)

(S)

banner10.gif (Click Here)

Notice that the time is longer when text is on the screen. I have found that a good second is required. Remember that you know what this says. The person who is seeing it for the first time does not. They have to read it. Give them time. Don't hustle through this.

FAQs from the HTML Goodies Web Site

Q. Why do you have banner 10, then 6, then 10 again?

A. Going from one to the other and then back again creates a sort of blink. Watch the animation roll through again online at `http://www.htmlgoodies.com/primers/ banner_1.html`.

Q. I thought an animation was supposed to be equal, with the same amount of time between each image.

A. No. You want certain parts to go faster than others, so you get a good show and it doesn't become boring.

Creating an Animated GIF

I have found that nothing wastes more time than trying to set times as you place each image in the GIF Construction Set. My suggestion is to get them all in the animator without setting any times. Just remember to have a control before each image and the LOOP command at the beginning. Yes, you want the banner to loop. Those that just go through the animation once do not attract as much attention. You may also want to set the final control to a longer time. That gives the impression that the banner is pausing before starting again. Nice effect.

Again, don't worry about setting control times yet, just get it all in there. Let's set times after this step.

Now that you have the skeleton, you can start to enter actual times. I wrote out all the images with an S, M, or L between each image; that resembles what is showing in the GIF Construction Set. All you need do is click each control and enter 20 for the short changes, 50 for the medium changes, and 100 for the long changes. Run it by clicking the View button.

Watch it run a few times, and then go in and jimmy the times that look too long or too short. Believe me, doing an animation following this method saves you a bunch of time. Trying to enter the times while entering the control items to the GIF Construction Set very seldom works out right. I say go with the big picture first and whittle away after you have it.

After you have it set to your liking, save it as `banner.gif`. Yes, I know that is the name of your original template, but you don't need it anymore and `banner.gif` is a really good name for a banner.

Now you have this thing. Now what? That's what Banner Primer 7 is all about.

Banner Primer 7: Activating the Image—Show Time

At this point it's likely that you haven't created your own banner. My guess is that you have done a re-creation of what I did for this series of primers. Maybe you simply took this design and changed a few words around. If that's the case, start again. In all honesty, this is not a stunning banner. It says nothing about the page you are to visit. It doesn't have a whole lot of information on it, and it's kind of dull. However, it is a great example for teaching you the basics of banner creation.

Again, this is what I did in Banner Primer 1. Take some time to think about what makes your site great and what colors would be most eye catching without blinding the viewer. Try to come up with something that would make someone stop and watch your banner instead of scrolling down the page they came to visit.

To tell the truth, your banner is a bit of an intrusion. Think of your banner as a television or radio commercial. You're sitting there watching your favorite show when all of a sudden the show stops and you're expected to watch five or six 30-second commercials.

I teach advertising. I know. People see commercials in a poor light...until they see a really good one. Then they wait for it to come on. One of the main attractions during the Super Bowl is the commercials. I actually used to wait to see who would win Bud Bowl.

So don't just copy what I've done here. Take a day or two—or three—and think about your site. Make the banner that people stop and watch. Don't just hand them the same old, same old.

Getting Your Banner Out There

The purpose of the banner is to act as an advertisement for your site. It sits on pages other than your own. This banner is to bring people from other sites to your site. I think you can all agree on that. The question is, how do you get the banner on someone else's site? These are a few methods.

Paying for Page Space

"Ugh!" you scream, "Money?! No way!!" Don't be so quick. Yes, I know that sites that pull in millions of people a month ask for big money—but tons of sites are out there that are just like you, trying to build an audience. They would like to make a couple of bucks in the process.

The key to the entire process is finding your target audience. Let's say you have a page about watercolor painting. You want to get your banner on sites that have similar topics, sites that sell supplies, have artists displaying their work, display pages about oil painting, and so on. The topics do not have to be exactly the same, but close enough that someone who would visit that page might like to investigate your site as part of their surfing.

FAQs from the HTML Goodies Web Site

Q. You say to find a target audience for your banner. Isn't the point to reach the largest audience so you have a better chance of hitting people who might want to come to your site? Just because someone likes art doesn't mean they'll come, and just because someone doesn't surf arts sites doesn't mean they don't come.

A. You are attempting to make the exception the rule. Any advertiser tells you that a mass audience is a shot in the dark. A targeted audience is far better hunting.

Now, the part about price. I constantly receive requests from people asking me to advertise HTML Goodies on their site. And the prices are very low. I once got on a page with top center placement for a year for $30. Thirty bucks!! Unbelievable.

I have it a little easier finding advertisers because I own a site that pulls in millions per month. Many sites come to me regarding advertising.

You might have to seek out the sites yourself. Do it. Look around. Even if a site isn't displaying advertising at that moment, it doesn't mean they don't want any. Ask the Webmaster if she is willing to accept your banner for a small sum. Work out a deal. You may get your own $30 yearly rate, and then again you may not. See what you can get.

Above all, remember that the pages you place your banner must hit people that might have an interest in coming to your page. If not, it's wasted money and ad space.

By the way, Goodies has advertising representation and I am not supposed to buy my own advertising anymore as part of my contract.

Trading Banner Space

What a brilliant idea! Go surfing for sites that are most like yours and write to the owners of those sites suggesting that you start trading banners. You put their banner on three of your best pages and they do the same for your banners. Great! And it's free! If you get together with five or six sites, you can create a solid amount of cross-traffic. This is a great way to build your own visitors, maybe to the point where a real money-paying advertiser wants to get a banner on your site. Go figure. (Again, I am represented by a company to sell advertising. I cannot accept any banner trades.)

Joining a Banner Exchange Network

These things are really popular. What happens is that when you join you submit your own banner and in return you are given a bit of code to place on your page. That code is attached to the computers of the people who exchange banners. It keeps track of how many times your site displays banners. Some exchanges display your banner once for every 10 or so times you display a banner, while others just do a straight random display of banners. Either way, the number of displays is not guaranteed, and you must be running their banners to get yours displayed. Furthermore, you often do not have a say in which pages your banners display; you may be missing the target audience completely. You may also get on pages that you wouldn't want to be on. Then again, it is free. Just be sure to read over the parameters of how large your banner can be and how may bytes it can contain. This is their banner exchange; they set the rules and you have to follow them.

I was a member of a couple banner-swap programs for a short time and have since left. I wasn't happy with the number of displays and clicks (people clicking the banner to come to my page) I was getting. You may have more luck. Some people swear by these things. The number of banner exchange sites has grown since I used them and many are quite targeted. Heck, one is just for people with pages devoted to needlepoint.

The banner-swap program I hear about most is Link Exchange, but look at a bunch before you decide to place your banner. You can find banner exchange networks everywhere by going to search engines and searching for the topics you think would make for good target audiences.

Offering Your Banner for Free

This sounds a little goofy, but it has been fantastic for HTML Goodies. People who come to Goodies often ask if they can post the banner on their page as a link to the site. When they ask, I give them one. I can't tell you how many banners I have out there just from people posting them out of the kindness of their hearts. If you're one of those people, I can't thank you enough for doing that. I truly appreciate it. You have been quite helpful in building this site into what it is today. Word of mouth and links on other pages built the site. I didn't pay for the traffic. The traffic came because other posted links and banners said it was worth seeing. Go to the HTML Goodies home page and look toward the bottom of the page. See that link? Take a banner for your page.

Placing Your Banner on a Page

This is a good point of debate. The most popular placement is the top center, but I don't know if that's always the best place. You see, these things take time to load, especially if they are animations.

If the banner does not load quickly and the page has set aside all images with HEIGHT and WIDTH commands, all the page's text comes in and a hole is where your banner should be. Users simply start scrolling downward without ever seeing the image. It comes in and if you're using a program to count the number of times the banner displays, a count is made. But did the user really see the banner?

I offer these suggestions to get your banner seen as often as possible:

- Go as small on the bytes as possible. The lower the bytes, the faster the load.

- Make the first image in the animation an eye grabber. It might make them stay for the rest.

- Try a placement lower on the page. See the CNN home page for a lesson in this. I always wait to see the top story. By the time I read the headline and start scrolling, the smaller advertisements halfway down the page are up and ready for my viewing. Yes, banners are across the top, but I wonder if the banners down the pages aren't the better buys. This is a great method of placement, but you have to have a page design that stops people for a moment and then gets them to scroll.

- Try to get on more than one page per site. If you are only on the home page and someone misses your banner, you're done. If you are on three or four pages, your banner is cached from its having been loaded on the home page. Now you pop right up when the user goes to the next page with your banner on it.

- Be sure to use the ALT attribute. If you don't know about the ALT command in images, read about it in Chapter 3. This command allows for the little yellow box, called a ToolTip, which pops up when you roll your mouse over an image. In addition to the rollover, the ALT command places text in the boxes set aside by the HEIGHT and WIDTH commands. Even if your image doesn't pop up, there is at least some text there to catch some attention.

    Be sure to use the HEIGHT and WIDTH attributes so that you have a box for the ALT text to pop up in.

- Run your banner off the server that is displaying the page. This isn't always possible, but do it when you can. It gives you fewer possible problems and speeds the display.

FAQs from the HTML Goodies Web Site

Q. You say to go low on the bytes but then have us create an animated banner that can get huge. Which is it?

A. Both. Yes, a static banner might be smaller on the bytes, but many studies have shown that it doesn't catch the eye half as much as an animation.

Q. How about the bottom of the page? You didn't mention that.

A. Well, the bottom of the page might be a good placement if the page isn't very long. I say that because I go into ESPN's SportsZone just about every day to see how the Cleveland Indians are doing, and I don't think I have ever seen the very bottom of the page. I would shoot for the middle if I couldn't get the top.

Keeping Track of Visitors

How do you do it? Good question. If you have your banners on five different sites, how do you know which sites are being good to you and which are not? The method is so simple and so good, I shook my head in amazement that I hadn't thought of it earlier.

Let's say you are advertising on three sites: A, B, and C. What you do is have four home pages that are exactly the same. The first page is the original home page. This is the page you see if you came to the site through a Yahoo! search or by being given the address.

The next three home pages should be labeled in accordance with the three pages you are advertising on. The advertising banners you are running on site A should all be pointed to a home page called indexa.html. All the advertising on site B should be pointed at a home page called indexb.html, and site C should have all its advertising banners pointed to indexc.html. Put a counter on each page. Now you can keep a fairly straight record of which advertising is doing best for your site. You can also see if the advertising is working at all. If the original index page is bringing in the most traffic, you know the sites running your advertising ain't working.

You need to rely on the site you are buying advertising space on to provide you with simple information such as number of displays versus number of clicks. HTML Goodies has two separate programs running to keep track of that data. Smaller sites might not be as well equipped.

FAQs from the HTML Goodies Web Site

Q. What do you consider a good showing by an advertising banner?

A. I would like to see a 10%–15% increase if I am a low-visited site (2,000 or so people a month) and around a 5%–7% increase if I have more people coming through (10,000 or so a month).

Activating Your Banner

Okay, you have a site that offered a price you can afford (or wants to trade with you). The site asks for the code to run your banner on their site. What do you send them?

I first suggest you set it up so that you can run your banner off their site. A ton of things can go wrong if your banner is being run on their pages from your server. Things can still go wrong if you are running your banner on their pages from their server—just not as many things.

Don't get fancy with the code. Don't try to run an applet or fancy image flip deals. Simple is easiest. The following is the basic code. I feel this is sufficient:

```
<A HREF="www.yoursite.com/yourpage.html">
<IMG SRC="banner.gif" BORDER="0" WIDTH="468" HEIGHT="60"
 ALT="Come to my page!">
</A>
```

A lot of people like the onMouseover look, where text pops up in the status bar. I think it's a bit much and might cause problems, but here it is before you ask:

```
<A HREF="www.yoursite.com/yourpage.html"
 onMouseOver="window.status='TEXT IN STATUS BAR'; return true">
<IMG SRC="banner.gif" BORDER="0" WIDTH="468" HEIGHT="60"
ALT="Come to my page!"></A>
```

You now have the basics of banner creation and use. Is there more? Oh, yeah. Will Paint Shop Pro do more than I showed you? Oh, yeah. But that's for you to find out on your own. You have the basics. Now go and make your site a banner.

 Want to put the HTML Goodies banner on your site (blatant plug)? Go to http://www. htmlgoodies.com/book/somebanners.html.

Chapter 15

Other Stuff You Should Really Know

People e-mail me concerned about what they can and cannot do in terms of copyright. I know some of the answers and others I do not. After contacting a copyright expert at a local university, I was able to put together the answers to some of these common questions.

Please note that copyright law and copyright applications change. What is true in some cases may not be true in others. These are a series of questions with, to the best of my knowledge, the correct answers.

What Is a Copyright, Anyway?

Copyright is a form of intellectual property law. Copyright law protects an author or creator from his or her stuff being pirated and used without permission.

Keep in mind that it does not, however, protect the idea, system, or method of the information. For instance, I have a copyright on HTML Goodies. That copyright covers my writings. It does not cover the idea of teaching HTML on the Net, the fact that I used English to do it, or that hypertext is employed. Obviously, other places on the Net are trying to teach you how this stuff is done.

The Internet Is Public Domain, so Isn't Everything Fair Game?

No. The copyright laws that apply to written material, photographs, and myriad items apply on the Internet too. You cannot just take and use whatever you feel like.

This topic has already been addressed by the Clinton administration's Information Infrastructure Task Force (IITF). The task force is attempting to shape existing copyright laws to apply more fully to the digital age. However, until laws that deal specifically with the Internet are on the books, existing copyright laws are the yardstick for existing pages.

So, Is Making a Link to Another Copyrighted Page Against the Law?

For the most part, no. You are only making a link to the page rather than displaying the information. That doesn't create a violation per se. However, because owners of copyright also own the rights to what can be done with their items, they do have the ability to deny you permission to create a link. Please understand that denying someone a link happens in very rare cases, but it has happened.

In fact, it has happened to me. I was sent a letter one day from a fan of the site. He told me that he had placed one of my banners on his home page and offered me a login and password to see it. I thought the need for a password was strange, so I went to the site. There was my banner sitting above tons of hard-core pornography. "Gaaaah!" I screamed. I then contacted the author and called upon my copyright law right and told him to take down my banner.

How Do I Get My Stuff Copyrighted?

It technically already is. The law states that a copyright can be placed on an item as soon as it is placed into tangible form (a Web page, for instance). There have been many cases where an implied copyright has upheld in court.

But don't test those waters. Put up a copyright insignia and text.

What Do I Put on the Page?

You should place the circle (C) © and the word *Copyright*, the year, and the name of the author. Like so:

> This page © Copyright 1997, Joe Burns, Ph.D.

You may think you only need the circle C or the word *copyright* alone, but remember that the circle C is created in HTML through this command: `&copy;`. That does not show as a circle C when the source code is printed. Put them both to be safe.

Make a point of placing it on at least the main page. That's what I did. I made a blanket statement that everything inside `htmlgoodies.com` was written by me, except where noted. Whether you put the copyright on every page, or just the top page, make a point of putting it in the text so that it shows when the page is displayed. You should also put it in the HTML code. Like so:

```
<!-- This page copyright 1998 by Joe Burns Ph.D. -->
```

Wait, Don't I Have to Send a Form to the Government?

That is voluntary. The Copyright Office catalogs your site if you want it to. It costs 30 bucks plus some shipping. No, this is not required to be able to bring a civil suit against someone else for copyright infringement. You can still claim money for damages and lost profit. However, you can only attempt to get punitive damages (punishment money) if you are registered with the Copyright Office.

How Do I Register with the Copyright Office?

You need to fill out the application form TX. Other forms exist, but this is the one a Web site uses. The form is available from the Copyright Office home page at `http://lcweb.loc.gov/copyright` (Specifically: `http://www.loc.gov/copyright/forms/formtxi.pdf`).

Fill it out, print a copy of your Web site, and send it in with a $30 check to this address:

> Register of Copyrights
>
> Copyright Office, Library of Congress
>
> Washington, D.C., 20559-6000

You should receive confirmation in five to six months. Please note that the Copyright Office does not want two separate sheets of paper for the TX form. If you get the form from its site, it prints as two sheets. You need to photocopy them so they make one sheet, front and back.

Can I Just Send in a Disk?

No. A compact disc, yes. A floppy disk, no.

Do I Have to Register all My Pages Separately?

You mean like $30 a page? No. I registered HTML Goodies in one fell swoop. Updates go later. I looked at it as chapters in a book.

How Long Does My Copyright Last?

Until you've been dead 50 years. Don't sweat it.

I'm Just a Kid. Can I Get a Copyright?

Yes. Minors are allowed copyright protection. Follow the same procedure I just described.

The Internet Is Global. What About Someone in Another Country Using My Stuff?

That depends on the country's policies. Some countries recognize a U.S. copyright and help with violators. Some don't. I don't have a list of what countries do and don't. I have yet to find one.

What If I Copyright Something and Someone Else Copyrights the Same Thing?

You mean in pure coincidence, right? If it comes to a lawsuit, it is up to you and the other person to decide who did it first. That's why you register with the Copyright Office. You then have a solid alibi for when you copyrighted the item. Not registering the item makes it harder to prove the date of copyright. It can be done, however. Some people mail their items to themselves so that a date is stamped on the item. Others take their items to a notary public.

If you are not talking coincidence, and you mean that the person has simply stolen your idea, I hope you're quite sure you can prove the date you copyrighted your stuff. If you can't, I doubt the court is simply going to take your word for it. HTML Goodies is fully registered with the government Copyright Office. I don't want any misunderstandings.

I Call My Site "Dog Breath." Can I Copyright That?

No. Titles, names, and logos are not protected under copyright. You need to get into trademarks for that. Even then, you cannot trademark a word—just the design of the logo and the fact that the words represent your company. If you could copyright a word, I'd copyright the word *the*. I'd be rich.

This One Site Has a Great Image, But It's Copyrighted. Can I Use It?

Not without written permission. Period. I can't be more clear on that.

Can I Use Anything from a Site?

According to the Fair Use Doctrine (Section 110 [5] of the Copyright Act of 1976), it is allowable to use "limited portions" of a copyrighted item for works such as commentary, news reporting, academic reports, and the like. But you still have to give credit to the source; you cannot claim the work as yours. You must cite where it came from.

The tricky part is that no set number of words equal "limited portions." This is a tough call. My suggestion is to be fair to the person with the copyright. Don't post the whole site and give credit on only one page. I would fight someone posting a healthy portion of Goodies and only citing once. I also believe that on the Net the cite should include a hypertext link. (That's not law, I just believe that.)

I'll Just Post Everything and Cite to My Heart's Content

Wrong. Fair Use (17 USCS Sect. 107) has limitations. Several factors are taken into account: whether you are attempting to make a profit, the nature of the work, the size of the portion you use, and the effect on the marketplace.

For example, say you re-post a large section of the HTML Goodies site and write some of your own stuff around it. You then register it with search engines calling people to come. Even though you cite me all day long, I would still have a hairy. You are putting a dent in the number of people who visit my site and trying to use my work to bring people to you. Even if you quote a small amount of my work to gain visitors, I would still get upset because you are using my words to bring people to your site.

Now, before you ask, I am talking about direct quotes and the use of my language ("tutorials," "primers," and the like). If you read the tutorials and use the information to create your own page, great! That's the purpose. Here, I'm talking about a direct theft of my site. Feel free to use my ideas to death. Just don't use my exact words to attempt to get more people to your site.

What if I Take the Person's Page and Change It a Little. Can I Copyright It?

No. The changes must be "substantial and creative." In effect, there may be very few remnants of the original work. You might as well write it from scratch before trying to steal and alter. Editorial changes just do not cut it in a court of law.

The one possible exception to this rule is if you are creating a satire of a site. That is protected under the First Amendment. However, the satire must be obviously a satire. Subtle hints may get you in trouble. Make it blatant.

What Can I Do if Someone Uses My Copyrighted Stuff Without Getting Permission?

You can file a civil lawsuit in federal court to get an order stopping the person from using your material. A copyright attorney can get you started in the process. The U.S. Attorney can get involved if the person has used your work and is attempting to make a profit with it.

What Do You Do when Someone Posts Part of HTML Goodies Without Permission?

Usually I write a calm e-mail letter asking the person to stop and take the pages down. If he has registered the pages with search engines, I ask him to place a redirect on the page so that hits come to the right place.

If that doesn't work, I contact the server's Webmaster and tell her to shut down the user's site—the entire site—or civil action is brought against the server people for allowing copyrighted material to be pirated on their site. The next step would actually be to file a suit.

Has This Ever Happened?

A few times. I've only had to go to the server people once. When I did, the site was offline in a matter of hours. I've never filed a lawsuit.

Would You?

Yes. In fact, filing suit is an obligation. If you are not willing to defend your copyright, the courts can rescind it.

What if I Use Something I Didn't Know Was Copyrighted?

Take it down when you are asked to take it down. No one wants a lawsuit—they cost money. Usually you are asked to stop first. Just apologize and stop.

What if I Am Using Something That Is Copyrighted and I Know It?

You know you're breaking the law. The same answer applies from the previous question—take it down!—but don't be upset if you get served. You knew you were doing wrong to begin with.

I'm Just a Kid. I Don't Have Anything to Take. Go Ahead! Sue Me! You Can't Do Anything to Me!

You're right in one aspect. Because you are young and don't own a great deal, you have very little someone could take from you. What can be done is a conviction of a federal crime. Have you ever gone in to fill out a job application? Remember that line that asked if you had ever been convicted of a federal crime? You are checking Yes for the remainder of your life. Just try to get a job even related to computers with a conviction for copyright infringement.

In fact, in some states, your parents can be held responsible. You do something dumb and they pay. No kidding.

What if I Don't Take the Image, but Make a Link?

You know, a link to the real site so that the image shows up on my page, but is coming from the actual copyrighted site? No go. You are still displaying it and you are breaking the law.

I Want Music or Video from My Favorite Group on My Site

You might be able to get that. ASCAP and BMI are the two big music licensing firms. They sell what are known as *blanket fee licenses* to servers. That fee allows the server to reproduce any song under BMI or ASCAP representation. If your server has paid the fee, go for it.

Without that fee being paid, you are breaking the law by playing the song.

But I Only Play a Portion, Like in the "Fair Use" Deal

You're walking a thin line here. The purpose is entertainment in this case and might be a problem.

I Play My Version of the Song on My Keyboard and Post That

That's being done a lot and I didn't find much on it. Just remember that a song is more than just the performance and the recording. The melody is also under copyright. Your playing the song might still get you into trouble.

I Play a Recording of an Old Beethoven Piece

"He's been dead for 50 years! The song's out of copyright and in the public domain," you say. Not always so. Authors can claim copyright on the sheet music, arrangement, and even performance of the song. Whereas you may not be upsetting Beethoven, you may be upsetting the person who arranged it.

Same deal with old pictures and paintings. Just because the artist has been dead and gone since the age of no indoor plumbing doesn't mean that a museum or a collector doesn't own the rights.

What Is in Public Domain?

As far as I could find, no government list, or any other kind of list for that matter, exists. You have to be careful about playing and posting.

What if I Scan Something That's Copyrighted?

That's not yours. That would mean you are trying to copyright the method. That's not allowed.

How Can I Be Sure Nothing on My Site Is Copyrighted?

Make it all yourself or ask permission at all costs. Some sites out there check for you, but I think doing it all yourself is much safer and more gratifying.

If you want to post something that is not yours, get permission from the owner. If the owner says no, too bad. If the owner says yes, get it in writing and hold onto it. You may also want to build good relations with people by giving them credit on the page in addition to asking permission.

Do You Do That?

Completely. Every time something appears on HTML Goodies or Java Goodies that was not written by me, I make a point of giving credit. If someone sends me a letter and I think it's postable, I ask if I can. Some people don't want any other names on their sites other than their own. I don't buy that. I cannot possibly know everything. When others help, I am happy and put a link. It is an equal relationship. The only thing I frown upon is someone else writing a tutorial. I like to do that.

I only accept JavaScripts from their authors. Now, it's rather easy to fool me, and a couple have. They took someone else's work and put their name to it. I was then contacted by the real author and told to take it down. I did.

Another time, an author placed his copyright on the HTML page, but did not place it in the code. By posting the code without the copyright, I was breaking the law. It was brought to my attention rather sternly. I apologized for what was truly an innocent mistake and took the page down.

Those are the only two times I ran into trouble. I try to be very careful.

Final Thoughts

The Internet is not wide open. The laws still apply there. Just because you can take it does not mean you should. Give credit as you would want credit given to you. That image may be really cool, re-posting my site and claiming it as your own may impress your friends and a couple of visitors, and playing your favorite band's music may show you're a great fan.

...but none of it is worth a lawsuit.

Net Notes

These are a few great links with much more detailed information:

U.S. Copyright Office: `http://lcweb.loc.gov/copyright/`.

The Copyright Web site: `http://www.benedict.com`. This is a great, great site.

Copyright Clearance Center, Inc.: `http://www.copyright.com`. This site allows automated rights clearance on the World Wide Web.

Copyright and Fair Use—Stanford University: `http://fairuse.stanford.edu/`.

Thomson & Thomson: `http://www.thomson-thomson.com`. These guys offers services to determine whether your trademark or copyright can be adopted and protected.

For more, search copyright on Yahoo!: `http://search.yahoo.com/bin/search?p=copyright`.

What Are Cookies?

A cookie, huh? Either you are a real Web-head or you have stopped by to get the ingredients for that Neiman Marcus cookie that has been shuffled around the Net. If you're actually looking for a food item, you're out of luck. (Okay, maybe I explain the cookie story at the very end of the tutorial.) This is a tutorial dealing with electronic cookies.

Cookies, Joe?

Yeah. *Cookies* are a small computer-generated text file (no larger than 4K) that you receive when you stop at certain sites. Unless you make a point of setting your browser's preferences to not accept cookies, write-protected your `cookie.txt` file, or have installed a JavaScript to do the same, you probably have a cookie sitting in your browser's directory right now. The use of cookies is quite widespread.

I have heard a few reasons the little file servers and browsers are called cookies. Each is probably less creditable than the last, but these are a few for entertainment purposes:

> In UNIX, files of this type had a name something like k00k.z. Thus the strange pronunciation as *cookie* (uh-huh...).

> The guy who got really, really, really rich by creating Netscape digs these particular chunky cookies—thus the name (hmmm...).

> Because distributing cookies is like leaving crumbs all over (uh...).

> Just because (which is probably the most likely).

But Wait!

Ben Buckner offers what sounds as if it could be a true story about the term's origin:

> This is a very old bit of programmer slang (usually) for a piece of data stored to communicate between two processes, typically separated in time, and often as some kind of flag. The fuller form is "magic cookie." I know I've heard it used as far back as the late '80s anyway. The real defining point of the magic cookie is that some part of the data is unique to the process(es) so that the receiver can ensure that it's getting the message from the expected source. In the HTTP cookie, the server domain name serves that purpose, though in this case the client actually performs the verification to prevent server-based hanky-panky. I've heard that the term "magic cookie" was originally coined in reference to one of those old adventure games (perhaps "Adventure" itself) in which you had to give some character a magic cookie to get something from it (analogous to cookie verification), but that's just a vague memory.

Eh...I buy it.

What Do Cookies Do?

They themselves do nothing. Please do not be concerned that a virus or an evil program of some sort has been placed on your computer. The cookie is a text file. It is not executable. That means it can't run like a program.

The cookie was placed on your machine because you gave the server placing the cookie access to that section of your computer. Don't be alarmed. You have to give permission. Without it, you couldn't display any World Wide Web files or pictures. (I am talking a SLIP or a PPP connection to the Internet here. AOL is a different story. You are not connected directly to the Internet on AOL.) And no, the server does not have access to other sections of your computer. Contrary to what some believe, HTTP servers cannot go into your computer and reconfigure unless you enable it. Again, don't be alarmed. Chances are very, very slim you allowed it by mistake.

But, as I said earlier, you do have the ability, by going into your browser's preferences, to disallow the placement of cookie files. How does your computer know to enable all the regular image and text files, but no cookie files? The file's named cookie. Easy enough.

Getting Back to Cookies...

Remember that a cookie is used almost as a tag on your computer. You know, like they tag bears on those Saturday morning wildlife shows that play right before the football games. That "tag" holds information that the server that gave it to you would like to know. Such as the following:

- How many times your computer has stopped in—The server may post to a page a message welcoming you back for the nth time.

- What your computer did while you were in the site—Let's say you go into a shopping site. You order six things from four different pages. The cookie records the purchase and the price. At the end, you click a button and your total is displayed. In addition, the server knows you have purchased before when you return and may then send you directly to items you are interested in or offer a special as a return customer. You often hear this type of cookie usage referred to as a *shopping cart*.

- Keep track of a special name and password—No, I do not mean that the cookie has the ability to grab your actual server-side name and password. Let's say you join a sports page, and that you need to pay a bit of money to get very fast stats results on the games. This is common. After you paid the money, you are given a code word and password to log on with. After you log on the first time, those two bits of information are posted to the cookie. In the future you can then go back into the special site without having to fill out the logon form again and again. Plus, your favorite team's name may be added so that you are taken straight to the section you want without clicking.

Please remember that the cookie denotes your computer, not you. The server that uses cookies has no idea who you actually are unless you tell it by offering your name or e-mail address.

Do You Hand Out Cookies on Goodies, Joe?

Yep. You see those advertising banners at the top of the HTML Goodies pages? I use a rather expensive program to keep track of them. That program ensures that when you log in to a new page, you get a new banner. For that to happen, I assign every page a code word. This page's code word is "flook." To get you a new banner on each page, that little program needs to keep track of the code words. It does it by placing the current page's code word in your cookie file. Then, when you go to the next page, if the code word doesn't match, you get a new banner.

So, do I use cookies? Yes, but I am gathering nothing from you. I am only using your cookie file to keep track of code words. What I set is a "temporary" cookie.

Temporary Versus Persistent Cookies

A temporary cookie is a cookie that exists only during your time in the site, or erases soon after. A `persistent cookie` is one that, when placed, stays on your computer until you take it away. You see, I don't sell anything to the people who stop by. Everything on my site is free for the taking. Yes, I could place full cookies and use them for simple return visits data, but none of my advertisers have ever cared to know that.

Another reason I don't tag your computer for good is that it makes some people nervous. I don't want that.

But I guess the best reason is that I just don't need to do it. You see, every time you request files from my server or any server, the path back to your computer is recorded. It has to be. Without knowing where to send the files you request, you'd never get them. If you have a Web site, do the same thing.

(Before someone explains to me that anonymous surfing sites are out there, please remember that although the site that offers the information may not get the actual path to your computer, the anonymous surfing server does. It has to or you would never get the file. You're never going to do this totally anonymously.)

All the paths back to all the computers my server recorded are held in a file. Usually the file is called "logs." You have one of these yourself. You just may not have access. What I do is use a little program (it costs $500) to take the contents of the log files and jumble them into a useable form. This is what I get without using any cookies and just looking at my log files:

```
Total completed requests: 170 240 (88 879)
Average completed requests per day: 11 869 (12 697)
Total failed requests: 1 425 (752)
Total redirected requests: 3 007 (1 593)
Number of distinct files requested: 89 (86)
Number of distinct hosts served: 24 258 (13 456)
Number of new hosts served in last 7 days: 12 227
Corrupt log file lines: 172
Unwanted log file entries: 2
Total data transferred: 1 016Mbs (537 710kb)
Average data transferred per day: 72 515kbs (76 816kb)
```

And so on.

The following is my domain report:

```
Printing all domains, sorted by amount of traffic.


    #reqs: %bytes: domain
    ----- ------- ------
    38409: 21.74%: .com (Commercial, mainly USA)
    35007: 20.82%: [unresolved numerical addresses]
    31507: 18.54%: .net (Network)
    30149: 18.06%: .edu (USA Educational)
    5941:  3.58%: .ca (Canada)
    3301:  1.99%: .uk (United Kingdom)
    2636:  1.51%: .au (Australia)
    2509:  1.41%: .fr (France)
    2221:  1.38%: .se (Sweden)
    1808:  1.01%: .nl (Netherlands)
    1594:  0.86%: .us (United States)
    1191:  0.74%: .no (Norway)
    1153:  0.65%: .gov (USA Government)
    1069:  0.65%: .jp (Japan)
```

And so on.

This is information general enough that I can give advertisers good information about the amount of traffic that comes through my site and from where they came. I don't know a darn thing about any one computer or person specifically, just the total population.

> **Note**
>
> In case you're wondering, as of July 1998, the HTML Goodies site is bringing in between 50,000 and 65,000 different surfers per day. Those surfers look at an average of between 90,000 and 100,000 different pages. The home page itself is viewed more than 9,000 times a day. Do some quick math and you see that the Goodies site offers more than 3 million page views per month by close to 1 million people.
>
> Midweek is the heaviest usage time. The lowest surf time is weekend days, and the most popular time for surfing Goodies is lunchtime and early evening before 8 p.m.

I Want to See a Cookie

You can look at your own if you haven't altered your browser to stop receiving them. My guess is that if you've done any kind of surfing into any major sites such as ESPN, Yahoo!, or WebCrawler, you've received a cookie.

Where Would I Find My Cookie?

You need to travel into the guts of your computer to find it. It is somewhere in your browser's directory. Look at the entire directory first. In later models it'll be sitting at the top level...and yes...it'll be named "cookie." In earlier model browsers, you find it in your cache. Internet Explorer browsers store them in the Temporary Internet Files folder under the Windows directory. You could also do a search on your hard drive for "cookie." If you can't find it, no problem. This is what mine looks like. I just cut and pasted it from my personal computer:

```
# Netscape HTTP Cookie File
# http://www.netscape.com/newsref/std/cookie_spec.html
# This is a generated file!  Do not edit.
.sportszone.com      TRUE /FALSE      876509359
.netscape.com   TRUE /FALSE      946684799
NETSCAPE_ID     1000e010,138f8fd5
www.webcrawler.com   FALSE      /      FALSE      852076799
webcrawlerad    46162
```

What It All Means

You can pretty much see who has given me a cookie. I have one from Netscape and one from ESPN's SportsZone and others. The long numbers are actually dates, or time until expiration of the cookie in milliseconds. Those numbers were most likely placed by a JavaScript cookie script.

Are Cookies Bad?

I guess that depends on whom you speak to.

To be fair, the use of cookies does infringe on privacy. The server does know if someone stopped by before and knows what that person did while they were there.

If you haven't taken this tone from me yet, I don't believe cookies are all that awful. I also don't mind someone using them on me. A computer wizard with far more knowledge than me might prove me wrong, but I don't think you can expect to move around public phone lines and personal servers totally anonymously.

Let's look at some of the actual concerns people have written to me about cookies. I comment on each one.

- Do people know I'm in their site?—Yes, and K-Mart knows you're in their store. However, you're not being video-taped in a World Wide Web server. You are in a lot of K-Marts.

- Does server know what I'm doing when I'm there?—You bet. Where else other than your home can you have complete domain over all that is inside, taking whatever you want, while remaining totally anonymous?

- Do they know who I am?—To a point. Your login or e-mail login may be gathered because it's listed in the browser's general information, but it's not gathered by the cookie. The cookie can't do that. An applet can, and then it can be written to the cookie. This is a bit unnerving, I agree. But as I said before, it's hard to go around this web of computers totally anonymously.

- Will they spam me?—If they do, a line has been crossed and the person who is using the unauthorized e-mail addresses should be prosecuted.

- Will they get my picture?—Not unless you offer it.

- Will they get my home address?—Not unless you offer it.

- Will they get my Social Security number?—Not unless you offer it.

You really shouldn't be giving your Social Security number, name, phone number, or whatever else to anyone who doesn't need it. In this world of telemarketers and nasty people, giving your address to something as simple as a grocery story shopper's card can get you piled under with junk mail. I always try to sign up for items with my name only. If they refuse, I make a decision on whether the item is required for me to live a long and healthy life. Usually it isn't.

I agree to a point that surfing is invasive to your privacy, but it might be a trade-off you are willing make to have this web of computers.

I've been informed that a fairly successful method of surfing anonymously is to enter false information into your browser, such as an incorrect e-mail address and a fake name—but stop and think. Phone bills, power bills, cable bills—each of those also gathers information about you. Plus, they probably asked for your Social Security number. Should you also be anonymous to them? If nothing else, it's a good debate. Whether the cookies are good or bad is up to you.

On another note: Just for fun, I enjoy asking people if they would ever give a credit card number over the Internet even though great steps have been taken to ensure encryption of the numbers. Although most people have a rather violent reaction against doing it, they hand their credit card to the waiter who walks into another room with it.

Is That It?

Well, yeah. I can't cover much more than what I've already told you. To go further, you need to get in touch with your own server people. They'll be able to place the CGIs or show you what is already being done log-wise for you.

What About That Neiman Marcus Cookie Story?!

Oh, that. This is what popular culturalists term an *urban legend*. It probably isn't true, but it gets told so often that people think it's true. Plus, it's always told as if it happened to someone's older brother's former friend's roommate, so it has to be true! One of my favorites is the story that the Mikey kid, who liked Life cereal so much, died in the early 80s by eating Pop-Rocks and chugging a Coke. This is not true, but the story goes around.

I also like the one where a woman, always distantly related, gets on an elevator with a very large, gruff-looking man who's holding tightly the leash of his huge growling dog. The woman is quite nervous. The large man yells, "Sit!" And she does.

On to the cookie story. It seems that someone's brother's former roommate's friend took his daughter (wife, friend) to Neiman Marcus for lunch (dinner, breakfast). My version of the story had the daughter purchasing a scarf and a wool hat. Details make for a more compelling tale!

The people ordered and ate and were served three small cookies at the end of the meal. They liked the cookies so much the gentleman asked if he could purchase the recipe. The waiter said yes and told the price as 250. The man agreed. When his credit card statement arrived, he noted that it was $250 rather than $2.50. Apparently he'll sign anything at the restaurant.

Inflamed with cookie passion he said he would give the world the recipe if they didn't take the charge off the card. They refused and he set to spamming this story all over the Net through BBS servers and e-mail.

The recipe I received was actually pretty good. It called for finely ground coffee and oat-meal. In reality, it could be true but probably isn't. It is another reason to make cookies, and it's my opinion that you could all use a few more reasons to make cookies.

Using META Commands with Search Engines

META what? Unless you are loopy into this HTML stuff like I am, you probably haven't heard about META commands until now. I would guess the reason is that the commands don't put anything on your page. No visual is associated with them, but they can be quite helpful to the search engines that look over your page and tell others about it.

> As of this writing, many of the big name search engines have stopped accepting free submissions. They now want to be paid to list a site. I get further into it when I talk about registering pages with search engines.
>
> I wanted to mention it here simply because even if you pay to be on a search engine, you still must follow the meta rules set up by the search engine. Pay careful attention to the text in this tutorial. Now you might be paying to be able to use it.

Search Engine...What's That?

A *search engine* is a program that takes keywords from you, searches a database of Web pages, and gives you a list of pages that might be helpful. Yahoo! is a search engine, as is Excite.

When you submit your page to a search engine, or *register* the page as Web-heads like to say, you are asking the people who keep the page to place your page's text into a huge database.

You enter *keywords* when you use the search engine. Let's say you are interested in fishing; you might enter "rod reel salmon." The database is searched and returns any pages that contain those words.

When you register a page, some search engines ask you to enter a few keywords. What you are allowed to offer is limited. Wouldn't it be nice if you could send the search engine a page that has all the keywords written out in the HTML text? This way you could make the search engine's job a lot easier and get your page brought onscreen a lot more often. That means more people click your link and more people visit your site.

What You Can Do with META *Commands*

In terms of search engines, you can do a few different things with META commands. You can:

- Offer keywords to the search engine.
- Offer the name of the computer software, herein known as the *generator*. You used this to make the page—it helps.
- Offer a description for use when your page is displayed. Some search engines do not show descriptions, so this doesn't work on all engines.
- Offer the author's name.
- Offer a copyright statement.
- Offer an expiration date so the search engine's database stops opening your page after a certain amount of time.

Let's remember that you are playing against a search engine here. You play by its rules, not the other way around. These items do not work on all search engines, but are successful on most.

I say this again later in the tutorial, but I do it here anyway: All META commands go between the HEAD commands, immediately following the TITLE commands. Just list one right after the other.

Offering Keywords

Follow this format:

```
<HEAD>
<TITLE>Page title</TITLE>
<META NAME="keywords" CONTENT="bring,my,Browns,back,Baltimore">
</HEAD>
```

Sorry Ravens fans. I like who I like and I can't change for anyone. I grew up in Cleveland. No jokes!

See what I did? I offered keywords, all separated by a comma. No space. Some servers don't like an added space and may not open the page because of the space being seen as part of the word. Offer words in the format shown here.

Some servers bring up one page over others because the keyword appears more than once in the page. Why not offer 10 or 12 of each of the keywords you are using? That tells the search engine that the keyword appears many times inside the document. Something like "Browns,Browns,Browns,Browns,Browns,Browns,Browns."

You get the idea.

Just don't overdo it. Some search engines see excessive multiples of keywords as spamming and do not post your page specifically because of that.

Offering Your Page Generator

I don't get this one, but I always put it in anyway. This is another thing the search engine can use to isolate your page; it's simply the program you used to make your page. This is what mine always looks like:

```
<HEAD>
<TITLE>Page title</TITLE>

<META NAME="Generator" CONTENT="NotePad">
</HEAD>
```

Use it in good health.

Offering a Description of Your Page

If you use search engines to any great extent, you no doubt have seen those that return the title of the page and then something like the first 25 words. Most of the time, the text makes no sense. Wouldn't it be great if you could tell the search engine what description to place on the search-results page? Yes, it would! (This is a sign the mind is starting to go when you keep answering your own questions.)

This is the format:

```
<HEAD>
<TITLE>Page title</TITLE>
<META NAME="description" CONTENT="Come to my page please!">
</HEAD>
```

Pretty self-explanatory.

Author, Copyright, and Expire

These follow the basic format as given earlier.

- `<META NAME="author" CONTENT="Joe Schmoe">` Tells search engines who wrote the document.
- `<META NAME="copyright" CONTENT="Copyright © 1997 Me">` Tells search engines the copyright.

● `<META NAME="expires" CONTENT="15 September 2000">` Expires the document automatically in the search engine's database.

Where Do I Place These on My Page?

Between the HEAD commands just after the TITLE commands.

Make sure your page's title come first because that is the first item many search engines use. WebCrawler does that. Also, don't put something in the title that is different from the rest of the page when you submit a page to a search engine. It may be clever, but it's messing up the search for your information. Change it on your server, but be sure to submit a copy that is done correctly.

What if I've Already Submitted the Pages?

What to do now depends on the search engine people. Many only take a submission once. Some might take updates, but they are last on their list of priorities. Go to the search engine you submitted to and read their policies and take it from there.

Good question. I should write a full tutorial on just that. In fact, I did—next. Enjoy!

How Do I Register My Pages with Search Engines?

Why this tutorial? Didn't you sort of cover this in a few other places?

Yes. I cover registering pages a bit in the META commands tutorial and in the database tutorial, but I'm still getting e-mail letters asking how this is done, so I thought I'd put something together. This is a fairly simple process.

Registering Pages—What's That?

My guess is that you've used a search engine if you've used the World Wide Web to any extent. You go to the site, put in some keywords, and the server searches a database and returns pages that contain your words.

"Wouldn't it be nice If I could put my pages on the search engine?" you ask. "You can," I answer happily. To *register* your page is to place it in the database of the search engine. That's what I talk about here.

A long list of search engines is located in Appendix C, "Valuable Links," in case you want to register with more than one engine. I register my pages with 25.

It Isn't Always Free

I'm sorry to have to inform you that since the first edition of this book, many of the big name search engines including Yahoo!, WebCrawler, and AltaVista have all gone to a pay-for format.

Prices certainly change but the going rate when I wrote this update (May 2001) was $199 USD if you want your site posted within two days. Some sites also offered a $99 USD rate to post pages within a week or two.

Why many search engines went to this format varies from site to site. The general reasoning was that they couldn't keep up with the huge number of sites being submitted every day. The back log on many sites was pushing a month and a half to even have your page listed on the engine.

What I tell you in the remainder of this tutorial still applies to numerous search engines. There still are many out there that accept submissions for free and you should use them.

However, for a site to gather real traffic through the search engines, you must be on the big names. That means paying for the service. If you are starting an e-commerce company I suggest you bite the bullet and pay the fees. You need traffic. If you are starting a personal site, I leave the choice up to you.

For more on the change from free to pay-for, please visit my newsletter on the subject at `http://www.htmlgoodies.com/letters/124.html`.

How It's Done

You can register your pages in two ways. You can either head to each search engine separately and register your page, or go to a registration site or a registration program that allows you to register your page with many different search engines at once.

Registering at Each Page

I've registered my pages at a few different search engines. The following is a general idea of what you're going to find:

- Hierarchy sites—Sites that build pages of lists. Yahoo! (`http://www.yahoo.com`) is a hierarchy site. As such, Yahoo! wants you to help a bit. You log on, look for the category (or page) you feel you should be on, and then click the Submit icon at the top of the page. Magic occurs—you are asked to enter your URL address, a few other fine points, and that's that. Yes, you can apply your same page to more than one category page. You usually don't receive a letter saying you've been accepted.

- Webs—Databases that do not have a certain hierarchy about them. It is just one huge group of pages. WebCrawler (`http://www.webcrawler.com`) is one of these databases. These are fairly simple to register with. Usually you see an icon that says something such as Submit URL on the main page. Click it and answer the same question you answer anywhere else.

Sometimes you don't even have to answer any questions.

What Are These Questions?

Usually they want things like this:

- Your name—Good luck with this. Please use your real name. It feels silly returning an e-mail to someone named Snoogums Face.
- Your e-mail address—Give it to them straight.
- Keywords—Much, much more can be found on these in the META commands tutorial just before this one. Quickly, these are words some (stress *some*) search engines use to locate your page. Choose broad topic words. Also use the roots of words. Use "dog" instead of "doggie." If you use "dog," "doggie" is found because it's a root word. Using "doggie" eliminates "dog" because "dog" is smaller than "doggie." That may have been the dumbest example on this site.
- Description—Tell us all about your site in 15 words or less. Again, see the META tutorial for loads on this.
- Payment—Some search engines offer higher-level searches, certain placement, or more input text if you pay a bit. That's up to you.
- Passwords—Some ask you for passwords so that you can go back in and edit your entry later.

Please keep in mind that each search engine is different. Some ask for information, some don't. Some enable you to resubmit or edit, some don't. Some ask you to put a link to their search engine in return, some don't. I could do this for days.

Again, you probably don't get any letters telling you your site was cataloged. Sometimes you get a little return letter thanking you for registering. What you need to do is wait a couple of weeks and go back and search for your site. If it doesn't show up, try again in another week. If you still don't get an answer, resubmit.

Registering at Many Pages from One Page

This is how your old buddy Joe does it every time. I go to a site named Submit-It! (`http://www.submit-it.com`). Other sites do this, but this is the only one I've ever used. I have a list of Web sites in Appendix C that do multiple registrations. Many are pay-for deals, as is now Submit-It!.

You also run into sites that offer to sell you a program that helps you submit. You may also get letters from companies that submit and check for you. The downfall of these methods is that they cost a little money. I know people who have paid for both. Some were pleased, some were not. I've never paid to submit a site to a search engine.

That's about it. Go and register a page just for the heck of it. Let one of the engines walk you through the process. You find that the number of visitors to your site goes up a bit, if not a lot. Mine did. See you on the Net...

Getting Them all the Same: Cross-Platform Tips for HTML Artists

Ever since the advent of the browser wars, I have been inundated with questions about why one Web page looks so different on Internet Explorer and Netscape Navigator (and now Opera and others). This question never seemed to go away: How do I get my pages to look and work the same in all browsers?!

This is the short answer: You can't. The browser creators have seen to it. Internet Explorer and Netscape Navigator are very different animals. They have different margin settings, different browser screen sizes, and different methods for rendering tables, just to name a few fun problems to come.

Why are they so different? This is an attempt to create a browser that has something the others don't in an effort to get you to use that browser. I believe it comes down to marketing, pure and simple. Create the different, and hopefully better, mousetrap and users surf a path to your door.

Some might state that the easiest way to go about getting pages to look the same across browser platforms is to use a browser choice JavaScript. I have one for you in Chapter 11, "Java Applets and JavaScript."

I don't buy it. The real solution is to create a Web page that looks good across all browsers.

Here, in no particular order, I give 21 basic tips that help make your pages presentable, no matter what browser you choose.

Tip One: Put Multiple Browsers on Your Computer

If you have the hard drive space, install a version of Netscape Navigator (NN), Internet Explorer (IE), and Opera (O) on your computer. I have all three on mine and they don't interfere with each other. That way you can open your HTML document in multiple browsers to see what they look like before posting them to the Web.

Tip Two: Write for the Browser That Is Pickiest About Coding

That is Netscape Navigator. If your page looks good in Navigator, it probably looks good elsewhere. This is especially true in terms of tables. IE allows you to get away without ending every <TD> and <TR> command. NN does not. Everyone must be closed, otherwise the table doesn't render properly. If NN requires a certain coding, that's the coding scheme you go with.

Tip Three: Enable the Browser to Decide When Long Pieces of Text Wrap

If you have paragraphs, do not break the lines yourself—just write the text and enable the browsers to wrap it. If you break the text yourself, you may run into trouble when people have smaller screen settings. You get that lovely one long line and one short line look all the way down the page.

Tip Four: Force Text Issues

Do not assume that if you use one <FONT COLOR> command that every table cell's text is altered—it isn't. NN sees to that. Make sure that every table's cell data is defined with HTML flags.

Simple rule: When in doubt, add the flags. Make a point forcing every text alteration you want.

Tip Five: You May Want to Stay Clear of Style Sheets and Hard Code Most Elements

According to the brochures, both NN and IE support style sheet commands. If you've ever tried writing with them, you know that isn't always true. The scoop is that the World Wide Web Consortium adopted Microsoft's template of creating pages using style sheets, which made it standard in the industry. Netscape then adopted the standard for its browser. That should have done it, right? Wrong. As you have probably noticed, many non-standard commands are out there that do not work cross-browser. Case in point, the <BLINK> command works in NN, but not in IE.

Furthermore, style sheet commands are fairly new. Believe it or not, people are still out there browsing with version 2.0 (and earlier) browsers. I'm not kidding. Even if you do use standard style sheet coding, they are left out in the code.

Everything that standard style sheet commands can do can be done with HTML flags. Either create your page so that it doesn't matter if the style sheet commands don't render or use the HTML flags.

Tip Six: Be Kind to Those Who Are Surfing Without Images and Use ALT Commands

Many people surf without wanting to see images—really. I do it now and again. All browsers that support graphics also enable you to shut off the inline images. That means just the text displays. I still know people who surf with LYNX and CELLO, which are text-only browsers. You can find links for them in Appendix C.

ALT commands place text with an image. Read all about ALT commands in the height, width, and ALT command tutorial in Chapter 3, "Adding Images and Backgrounds." If the browser displays the image, you can get a ToolTip box to pop up using an ALT command. For those who are not using images, the ALT commands make their surfing life so much easier by telling them where the images are.

When you use ALT commands, set the image text aside by at least surrounding it with square brackets, and maybe adding the word IMAGE in all caps, like so:

```
<IMG SRC="image.gif" ALT="[IMAGE: A dog running across the lawn]">
```

You should also know that using ALT commands helps surfers who are blind. Now some computers can read text aloud. ALT commands enable the user to know where and what the image is.

Tip Seven: If You Use Imagemaps Offer Hypertext Links Too

Offer hypertext links to everything that is linked in the imagemap for all the reasons outlined earlier. Use an ALT command to denote that it is an imagemap.

Tip Eight: Do Not Use Frames Unless You Have a Very Good Reason

Frames are supported by most browsers, but that's not the concern—speed, download time, monitor screen settings, and text wrapping are. Remember, you are trying to enable all people to see your pages. Not everyone has your 56K dial-up or your Ethernet-driven G3 chip. Many are still attached to AOL with 14.4 modems. Be kind. Unless frames are required, go with single pages.

Tip Nine: JavaScript—I Love It, But Don't Get Crazy with It

JavaScript is another item that is supported by most, but not all, browsers. If you use JavaScript, make sure it is not a pivotal part of the page. Your page should run just fine without it. I find you can use event handlers without messing anyone up. See the advanced JavaScript tutorial in Chapter 11 for more on event handlers.

If you do have a JavaScript marvel you want to share with the people, put it on its own page and offer a link to it. Make sure the link tells the user what is coming. If it's cool enough, people click.

Tip Ten: Only Use Applets If It Is Necessary—And It Probably Isn't

Follow the same rules as outlined with JavaScript. Use an applet only if it is truly needed, and even then put it on its own page and enable people to click to it.

Tip Eleven: Always Use both the EMBED and BGSOUND Commands

Neither the EMBED command nor the BGSOUND command is supported by all browsers. If you are going to put background sound on a Web page, use both commands. That way both NN and IE users are able to hear it. In fact…you know what…most users don't like background music. You may want to skip it altogether.

Tip Twelve: Force Your Page's Layout and Design

The best way to accomplish this is to always place your page's elements inside table cells; it lays the page out beautifully. You can then always make the table cell's borders invisible by adding BORDER="0" to the main TABLE command. Read all about tables in Chapter 5, "Tables."

Tip Thirteen: Force Your Page's Width

Remember that computer monitors can have many different settings. This plays havoc with Web pages. Use the TABLE method to force your page to stay within certain parameters. I do this by placing every page inside one large table cell set to a specific width. This is the code:

```
<HTML>
<HEAD>
<TITLE></TITLE>
```

```
</HEAD>
<BODY>
<CENTER>
<TABLE WIDTH="750" BORDER="0">
<TD>
****Content of page goes here****
</TD>
</TABLE>
</CENTER>
</BODY>
</HTML>
```

I choose 750 as my width. That forces my page to display nicely in screen setting of 800×600, which is the most popular screen setting on the Web.

By the way, the same thing can be done using FRAME commands. Make one frame a certain pixel width and set everything else to 0. Put the HTML document into the larger frame and a page with the same color background into the other. This is what the code might look like:

```
<FRAMESET COLS="750,*"  MARGINWIDTH="0" MARGIN HEIGHT="0"
FRAMEBORDER="0' BORDER="0' FRAMESPACING="0">
<FRAME SRC="page.html">
<FRAME SRC="page2.html">
</FRAMESET>
```

If you want it centered, you can always change the code to COLS="*,750,*. It works, but again, you are incorporating multiple pages.

Go with the table commands version I showed you earlier.

Tip Fourteen: If Possible, Use Pixels When Forcing Widths

Attempt to build your page so it fits neatly into smaller screen settings. If you can build your page so that it fits nicely into 620 pixels wide, then it displays nicely on all screen settings 640×480 and higher. Get it?

If it doesn't fit nicely into 620, try 750. If it doesn't fit into 750, pick another design.

Tip Fifteen: Use GIF Format for Icons and JPEG Format for Larger Pictures

This is the way I have found it works best. GIF helps the smaller items keep their detail and JPEG helps the larger items load faster by being a compressed format.

Tip Sixteen: Try to Avoid META *Refresh Tags*

You can read about META refresh tags in Chapter 2, "Creating Links." These are the tags that create what I call "dynamic pages," by jumping to a new page after a set amount of time. I love the look, but a text-only browser cannot support the command.

If you decide to use META refresh commands, make sure you have also posted a hypertext link so that people who do not get the effect can then click to go on.

Tip Seventeen: Always Double-Align Text and Images

Never assume that using an ALIGN="###" command does the trick. Even if your table cells include an ALIGN="center" command, still surround the text with <CENTER> and </CENTER>.

The same goes for ALIGN="left" and right. Use <P ALIGN="left"> and </P> too.

Tip Eighteen: DHTML Is only Supported by IE 4.0 and Higher

Only those IE 4.0 users can see it. Make a link to the page using DHTML so that the user can choose to go. Don't simply assume they are using the correct browser.

Tip Nineteen: When Denoting Colors, Try to Use the 216 "Safe" Colors

Appendix B, "Useful Charts," has the 216 non-dithering color chart, which includes the 216 colors that most operating systems support fully. You might notice they are all hex command color codes made up from the values 00, 33, 66, 99, CC, and FF. You can use any one of the colors and be pretty darn sure the end user's browser supports it.

Tip Twenty: If You Need to Pick a Screen Resolution to Design for, Choose 640×480

Yes, that's small, but pages conform better to larger environments than they do to smaller ones.

The easiest way to do this is to set your own monitor resolution to 640×480. You can always change it back when you're done. This is your computer.

Tip Twenty-One: Write Simply

Yes, I know that animations, JavaScript, applets, and background are really cool. I like them just as much as you do. But go easy on the flash. Content should be your main concern.

Text and static images make a very good page if the user is interested in what you've written.

Look, you've seen MTV. If you're my age, it's VH1. If you're my wife, it's CMT. You know that no matter how great a video is, if the song it's set to stinks, forget it. You may look once, maybe twice, but after that the flash is not worth that poor content you have to listen to. See the analogy here?

If you want your pages to render well across browser versions and screen settings, you have to reign in your want to go for the latest thing. I love DHTML, it's great, but not everyone can see it.

Stay with the basics. Many people do not dive on the next browser version the day it comes out. Their version 3.0 browser works just fine. Heck, their version 1.0 version browser works just fine. I still have Netscape Navigator version 1.0. I really do. This is great to surf with. Just text and images, nice and fast.

Some may not like that reasoning because it means you cannot fill your pages with bells and whistles and the latest scripts that make images jump around. Don't assume the user has computer or browser to run the fancy formats. Always enable the user see your simpler cross-browser page. Enable them to choose whether they have the correct equipment and to see the latest thing.

So think about your users, not those you want to impress. You may not be as flashy, but I bet you get more hits.

How Do I Get Advertisers on My Site?

Note to you: The following is a tutorial that people have been asking me to write for some time now. This consists almost entirely of my opinion. Most of the information comes from my slant having gone through the process. You can do this in other ways. This is my way of doing it. So far, it's worked. The topics discussed are from different e-mails I have received.

What Do You Have That People Want?

That's a bold question, but it's a pretty good one. I get letters all the time saying they want to advertise on their home page. I say great! How many people are coming in a day? I'm not talking hits mind you, I'm talking visitors. How many? Furthermore, does that warrant someone paying money for your site?

Hits Versus Visitors Versus Impressions

When you are talking to a possible advertiser about the number of people that roll through your site in a day, month, or year, the advertiser usually wants to know about impressions or visitors. Too often this gets confused with the concepts of hits. The following are the differences:

- Hits—A *hit* is a request of the server. Let's say, for example, that you have a page that has five graphics on it. That page is equal to six hits, the page and the five graphics. Sometimes people report hits to a possible advertiser. This is wrong because it creates an inflated report of site traffic. If I could report hits alone, I could create graphics-filled pages and report numbers well into the millions, no sweat.

- Visitors—*Visitors* are the number of actual people coming into the site. This is a count of actual people. This is also sometimes called a Unique Visitor.

- Impressions—Also called *page views*. This denotes the number of pages viewed, or more specifically, the number of ad banners viewed. Where this differs from visitors is that one visitor can create multiple impressions by seeing many different pages. A thousand visitors might create 30,000 impressions.

What Is the Magic Number?

Ten thousand visitors per month.

The question I am asked time and time again is how many people must come through the site for it to be worth selling to an advertiser. When I first was interested in gaining advertisers, the number I kept hearing was 10,000 visitors per month. Not 10,000 hits, but 10,000 visitors. This appears to be the threshold where a serious advertiser begins to talk to you.

How Much Do I Ask For?

How much do you need? I don't mean that to be clever, either. What does it cost you in both hardware and time each month to run your site? I add time to that list because you must put in time. People want to be able to talk to, or e-mail, a real person. People also want to see change and improvement. It is my opinion that a site must evolve or it dies. I am forever answering e-mail or writing a new tutorial.

Now stop and think how much profit you want to make. Yes, you'd all like to make 500% profit, but that's not always possible. You may price yourself right out of contention.

Finally, be flexible. You know what you want, but maybe an advertiser would like a break in price. You might say okay if they then offer to buy for five months rather than one, or pay up front. A deal can always be made.

Flat-Rate CPM, Click-Throughs, or Impressions?

Your choice. I always go with a flat rate per 1,000 impressions, called a *CPM* (cost per thousand). I think it is most fair to the advertiser. As I suggested, I often give more impressions than I offer. That's good for the advertiser and shows good faith on my part. The advertiser also has it easier with flat rate because he can budget easily and forecast whether he can remain on my site next month.

If you go by exact number of impressions, you make the cost a floating number and that makes it harder to forecast dollars. It may lead to the end of an advertiser relationship. Plus, with a floating rate you need to prove exact numbers, which are far more difficult to provide than simply hitting a plateau of visitors.

Selling by click-throughs is another popular method. A click-through is when someone clicks the advertiser's banner to see what it links to. I've seen contracts anywhere from .20 cents to $1 per click-through.

The problem with click-through advertising is that you need to be able to keep track of the clicks. I do it with a program I purchased that rotates my advertising banners and records impressions and clicks. The program is from Central Ad Pro (`http://www.centralad.com`) and cost me around $600. You have to decide if that is worth it to you. If it isn't, how do you track people?

How Much Does HTML Goodies Ask For?

None of your business. Just kidding. I used to have different costs for each of the pages. When I created `htmlgoodies.com`, I asked for $500 if you wanted to be at the top of the main page. Each tutorial was $200. That was for one calendar month.

That meant I could offer 150,000 impressions for $500. Maybe that helps you decide on the amount to charge as you're getting off the ground.

As I said, I am now using a CPM rate. I also have someone selling for me. The site has more than 3 million impressions a month. Those are numbers I can't begin to think about. I actually stay pretty far away from the money side of the site. I believe the rates now run about $30 or better for a thousand impressions, depending on the deal. The site's pretty profitable.

How Do I Get Started?

After putting together the Web site, of course, I would suggest putting together two things:

- ⬤ A description of the site—Make this detailed. This is a PR-type thing. Say someone asks you to send some information about your site and what it offers. This is the information you would send them.

- A rate card—This is a listing of every page and its price, or how much per 1,000 impressions, or however you are going to do it. You may only be selling the main page. If so, great. List it.

Getting Advertisers

There a couple ways of doing this. I only use one.

- Sell yourself.
- Hire someone to sell for you.

Selling Yourself

Get out there! Press the flesh! Shake a few hands! Slap a few backs! Sell! Sell! Sell!

Not much I can say here, but to sell where you might find clients. Head to Internet shows, write to advertisers over the Net, put your pages on every search engine you can find, and post a rate card for all to see.

I've never really done this, outside of people asking about advertising simply because the site was there. I have never solicited for an advertiser outside of a return e-mail now and again.

Hiring Someone to Sell for You

This is what I did. I felt I put enough time in working on the site. I'd head to the poor house before I made any contacts, so I hired a company to sell for me. I think it's the best way.

The one downfall is that you don't get to keep all the money. These people don't work for free, you know! A commission is always involved. In my case, it's 30% of the gross. Also, usually a statement says you don't get paid until the advertiser pays. You may run a banner for a while, the advertiser doesn't pay, and you lose out. It happens. It's part of doing business.

What About Advertising to Get Advertisers?

I guess you can. The only problem with that is that they want to post a banner, which takes away from space you may sell in the future, and it appears that you have banners already and might not need advertising.

I'm just a big believer in "build a better mousetrap and they come." Just make a point of registering all your pages so that you are fairly easy to find when someone goes looking for what you offer.

Read my tutorial in this chapter on registering your pages. It describes search engine databases and helps you learn more about getting people to your page with engines' aid.

How Many Advertisers Should Go on One Page?

That depends on you and your advertisers. Some advertisers want to be the only one on the page and write that directly into a contract. Other advertisers want to be around other banners if they are at or close to the top. My limit was four when I had the old format of one long page linking everything, two at the top, one in the middle, and one at the bottom. I offered special prices to the one at the bottom.

Now that I use a program to rotate my banners for me, I go a few per page. Notice from your surfing that ad banners come in different sizes. Smaller banners enable for more per page and less intrusion. This is always going to boil down to your choice; it's a delicate balance between making money and cluttering your pages.

If you do start selling ad space on your site, let me suggest that you also purchase a program that posts banners to pages on-the-fly. If you assign specific ad banners to specific pages, it tends to make the site look static. The CentralAd program I use works well for posting on-the-fly ads.

Final Thoughts

It is my opinion that undertaking advertising is more than a hobby on the side. You must look at this as a small business. Not only must you offer something nice to attract people, but you need to continually update and add to what you offer. You need to keep balance sheets for tax purposes. Making money on the World Wide Web is hard to hide—everyone can see it.

Most important of all, ask yourself what you have that people want. The purpose should be providing something people come to see. The advertising comes easily after that.

Finally, I can give no better thought-provoking information than this: This site was up and running for five months before I made a penny in profit. Now that it is getting established, I am making enough for the site to pay for itself, and a dinner out with my wife once a week...and that's about it.

May you become rich! I'm certainly not...not yet, anyway.

So You Want a Web Ring, Huh?

Like most really good ideas, Web rings are simple and effective. Anyone can set one up on any topic and it doesn't take rocket science brain power to get it up and running. "Me do Web ring good," as I like to say.

Web Ring?

Yup. Easy concept. Let's say you have a Web page that discusses your overt love for collecting foam rubber from couches and sofas produced in the mid 1970s. Let's also say, and this is a long shot, that 10 other people out there have a similar page. One guy does foam rubber from La-Z-Boys. Another guy collects foam rubber from chairs that were sat on by famous Americans. Whatever.

Now you, the main foam rubber guy, decides it would be nice if others who are foam rubber-inclined could just jump from one page to another, all dealing with foam rubber. You set about creating a Web ring.

Web Ring Method One: Linear Rings

A Web ring is just what it is named—it's a series of pages, all with a common theme, that are all linked to one another.

Let's say 10 pages are in all. One person sets herself up as the "ringmaster" and takes charge. With a little bit of planning, all you really need is a section of the page denoting that the current page is part of a ring. Provide a link to the page preceding you in the ring, and the page following that page in the ring. Just make sure the last page in the series then links back to the first page. Done: Web ring.

The only hard part about all this is when a new page joins the ring. Whether it should be added at the end or somewhere in the middle or nearer a page it couples with is up to the ringmaster. Either way, the links have to be kept up-to-date and those in the ring have to be willing to make updates when you ask.

Web Ring Method Two: Generated Rings

This is a better way of setting up and mastering a ring. You have one central location for the ring and those who want to attach simply put a line of code into their page. A JavaScript, or some other type of interface, is contacted every time someone clicks to go to the next page in the ring.

I'm seeing rings now that have options for Previous Page, Next Page, and Random. I guess that's good, but isn't going for a random page sort of killing the whole concept of moving through a ring? This is just my opinion; take it for what it's worth.

 *With a little thinking, you can use myriad random and linear JavaScripts to set this all up. I went through Java Goodies and found a couple that would do the trick. The one by Qirien Dhaela (*http://www.htmlgoodies.com/JSBook/webring.html*) is set up to do just that— be a Web ring. It places three buttons on your page allowing you to choose next, previous, and random. This is slick and can be run on all Web ring pages, or as an external JavaScript, so members only have to place a simple* SCRIPT *code on their page.*

Web Ring Method Three: Let Someone Else Handle It!

If you haven't been already, you should head to http://dir.webring.yahoo.com/rw if you have any interest in joining or creating a ring. The site provides more than 22,000 rings for you to join. If you can actually think of a topic that isn't already covered, they'll let you become your own ringmaster. Gosh!

Now this is the good part. This is free (at least it was at the time of this writing).

To go through the process, I signed the online version of this tutorial up with a Web ring. I still write the bulk of my HTML stuff in NotePad, so I attached this page to the "Made with NotePad" ring. This is what happened:

- I went to http://dir.webring.yahoo.com/rw and looked at the full list of available rings, did a search, and ended up wanting to join the Made with NotePad ring.
- The NotePad ring (was) kept at http://www.pvideos.demon.co.uk/notepad/. I got to the page by clicking a link that appeared when I saw the full list of all the sites that are part of the ring.
- I clicked the link that said I wanted to join the ring and got my general issue stuff.
- I was asked to take a banner (you see it in a minute) and a few lines of code to put on my Web page. I had to alter the code slightly so that the image was being called for correctly, but that was very minor. I also had to put in my e-mail address.
- Next I filled out a short form giving my page's address, its title, and a few other items, such as a description and keywords.
- You are also asked for a password. Write it down—don't forget it.
- I clicked to submit all this to Webring.com.
- You're registered if you do not get any errors.
- For this particular NotePad Web ring, I had to e-mail the owner and tell him that I had posted the items. He took a look at the page and had the final yes or no as to whether it would become part of the ring. He chose yes.

I can't say that each and every one of the ring-joining experiences are just like this, but I bet they're all pretty close. By the way, this is the exact HTML code I received when I signed up:

```
<!-- Begin NotePad Ring Fragment-->
        <font size=2>
        <center>
                <CENTER>
        <br><IMG SRC="notepad.gif" HEIGHT="50" WIDTH="340"
        border="0" usemap="#notepad.map"><br>
```

```
            </CENTER>
<br>
This <a href="http://www.pvideos.demon.co.uk/notepad/"
        target=_top>NotePad Ring</a> site is owned by
        <a href="mailto:jburns@htmlgoodies.com">Joe Burns</a>.<br>
        Click for the [
        <a
        href="http://www.webring.org/cgi-bin/webring?
id=308&ring=notepad&next"
        target=_top>Next Page</a> |
        <a
        href="http://www.webring.org/cgi-bin/webring?
id=308&ring=notepad&skip"
        target=_top>Skip It</a> |
        <a
        href="http://www.webring.org/cgi-bin/webring?
id=308&ring=notepad&next5"
        target=_top>Next 5</a> ]
        <br>
        Want to join the ring? Click here for
        <a href="http://www.pvideos.demon.co.uk/notepad/"
        target=_top>info</a>.
        <br></center></font>
        <map name="notepad.map">
        <area shape="rect" coords="0, 0, 60, 70" target="_top"
        href="http://www.pvideos.demon.co.uk/notepad/">
        <area shape="rect" coords="465, 0, 549, 75" target="_top"
        href="http://www.webring.org/cgi-bin/webring?
id=308&ring=notepad&next">
        </map>
        <!-- End Webring Fragment-->
```

Figure 15.1 shows the image and what appeared on the page when I posted that code into a Web page.

And that's that. As you can see, it goes from super simple to pretty involved, depending on if you want to be a member or actually run your own Web ring. Like I said earlier, the best ideas are usually the simplest.

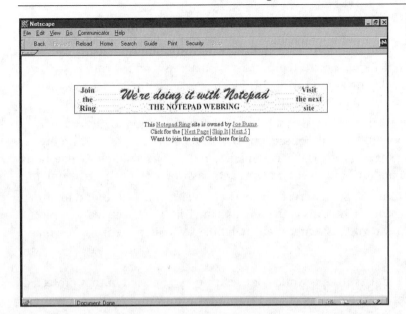

Figure 15.1
Web ring code.

So You Want a Password Protected Page?

Ever since word got out that I was working on this tutorial, I have been bombarded with requests to "Hurry up!" Well, here it is. You may not be happy with the answers I give you. Then again, you may. I don't know you.

The answer is that you can't do this with HTML commands alone. Password protection is done at the server level. You see, I was not waiting all this time to write a large tutorial, but rather for my Webmaster to arrange a protected directory in my account.

Here's What Happens

First, tell your Webmaster, server tech, or the guy who takes your checks each month that you want to do password-protected pages. He immediately asks what you have that is so darn important that you require these pages. You say, "None of your business" and ask again.

A protected directory is created for you after a short time. Not a page-by-page protection, but a directory. Basically, the technical people set aside a whole section of the server hard drive as protected. Every page you put into that directory requires a login and a password.

Some new files are added to that directory. These are the three most common files:

- `.htpassword`   A password file (duh). It contains one password for each login you denote to the server. It should be created initially with a password for you, its "owner." If you start playing around with this file, never delete the initial password. If you do you can't get in again to make changes.

- `.htgroup`   Contains the logins you denote. How you change or add logins or passwords depends on how the technician sets up your server. I have to Telnet into my server directly, enter some cryptic UNIX commands, and answer a couple of questions to prove I am who I am. I can then enter logins and passwords to my heart's content.

- `.auth`   A possible third file. Some servers enable you to enter passwords and logins directly to an HTML document. This is that document. This way is very easy. A nice form page comes up and you just enter it all straight away. I didn't get this. You may not either.

When you enter a login and password, it works for everything you placed in that protected directory. That means that the server doesn't continue to ask for passwords when a new page is requested.

Do all Servers Work This Way?

My tech informs me that any system can be configured a hundred ways, but no matter what the files are named, what I have just described is what happens. At least two files, one password and one login, are added to your accounts and you configure them to give only certain people access.

You need to call your Webmaster and ask for the protected directory to get things started. I'd ask before he does: What exactly do you have that is so important that must be protected? I know. None of my business.

What Is XML?

XML is beginning to pop up all over the Net, as well as in the Goodies e-mail box. People are wondering about this language and how it's going to affect the way people write. To be honest, I was wondering the same thing until I started looking into it.

You find XML mentioned in Appendix A, "Everything You Need to Know about HTML 4.0," and in Chapter 13, "Explorer-Specific Tutorials and DHTML." The language is starting to make a few in-roads into the Web and that makes a few people nervous. As one Goodies reader put it, "I just got pretty good with HTML, and now they're bringing out this thing." I feel your pain. It means I need to learn it all first so that I can teach it to you.

Here you go. This first tutorial is an introduction to what the heck this XML thing really is.

What Is It?

You mean in five words or less? That can't be done. XML stands for eXtensible Markup Language. Seems strange that the first word is eXtensible, yet they use the *X* to denote the word. My guess is that XML looked a lot cooler than EML.

Lineage

You may not know this but HTML and XML are brother and sister. Their mother is SGML. SGML (Standard Generalized Markup Language) is the overriding language that sprang both XML and HTML.

SGML is not a language per se, but a series of commands that are all understood by another program. JavaScript is a similar example. By itself—not much to it. However, if you use the JavaScript commands in a particular order, and then enable a Web browser to read it, you get some neat effects.

DTD—Document Type Definition

SGML is what is known as a *meta-language*. It allows a programmer to write a DTD (document type definition) that numerous pages can follow. For example, with JavaScript you use a word processor. Say you type the letter *j*. Something inside that word processor must understand what you did and display that letter. That's the DTD. You then alter the letter's size, font, and color. Again, the commands the word processor used were all understood and acted upon by using the DTD as a guide.

HTML uses DTDs. Ever seen one of these at the very top of a page's source code?

```
<!doctype html public "-//w3c//dtd html 4.0//en">
```

That's a *document declaration*. It states that the DTD being used is HTML 4.0 is English. See that? Where is the DTD actually located? In the browser. Yup, Netscape Navigator, Internet Explorer, Opera, and Mosaic are more than programs that display pretty little pictures—they are actually carrying a DTD so that the browser knows how to handle it when you type a command such as <B>, <UL>, or <CENTER>. The browser sees the command <B>. It goes to its DTD to check what that command is supposed to do. It sees that the command makes things bold. The effect is then generated.

The one drawback with a word processor, and HTML, is that you cannot set up your own DTDs. HTML is a very stable markup language format; the commands mean the same thing everywhere. The language is easy to learn because, to some extent, it is like playing blocks. The tools you use are never changing. JavaScript is more difficult because you are actually creating the blocks before you play with them.

Actually, that's XML's purpose: to enable you to create your own blocks to play with.

Making Your Own Blocks

Say you want to create a document where a certain type of text is going to bold, italic, red, 25 point, Arial font, and a few other fancy things. And this type of text appears a great many times. In HTML you need to write out the start and end flags every time you made the text, or you can set up a style sheet to do that. That's the general idea here. You set up a giant style sheet type document that acts as "mother" for all the other documents. What's the difference? Style sheets work inside HTML documents. You have to create one to use the other. Creating your own DTD eliminates one whole step in the process—the HTML.

Fine, but What Is XML?

XML is a simplified version of SGML intended to enable people such as you and me a pretty good shot at learning it. SGML is wide open. It is a 10,000-piece jigsaw puzzle with double-sided pieces spread all over the floor. XML is the same jigsaw puzzle with big sections already put together.

So What's Wrong with HTML?

My personal opinion is that nothing is wrong with it. It was the first computer language that could be understood and used by the masses. It gave the Web to the common person. Those in the XML know claim that HTML is clunky. They say it's become static. Not a lot more can be done with it. Supposedly, XML enables a lot more flexibility in your Web pages. Your HREF links also have more flexibility. You are able to create cross references, threads, and other fun stuff. At least that's what the brochure says.

HTML is not dead, nor is it breathing funny. HTML is around for years to come, if not forever. It is still a solid format and too many people know it. I believe I am able to write HTML and post Web pages as long as I live using HTML alone. They just might not be as fancy as other pages.

Two Kinds of XML Pages

The two main types of XML pages are the standalone and those that use a DTD. The *standalone* is just what it says: The page stands alone, relying on the browser to have the XML DTD. In the XML language, the browser is the XML processor. The other type of page offers the DTD to the browser so that it can run the page.

The Standalone

The standalone can be created by simply making some alterations to your current HTML document:

- Lose the current declaration statement and replace it with this one:

  ```
  <?XML version="1.0" standalone="yes"?>
  ```

- Remember that XML is case sensitive. If you use caps to start the command, use caps to end the command.

- This format of caps or no caps must continue throughout the document. If you use IMG first, you must continue to capitalize it the rest of the way through. If you don't the XML DTD sees it as two different commands.

- All tags that do not require end tags (such as <IMG> or <P>) must now be given one.

- All tags that did not require an end tag must also be given a slash before the final >. Like so:

  ```
  <IMG SRC="pic.jpg" /></IMG>
  ```

- Each subcommand must be surrounded by quotation marks, such as TEXT="brown".

- Lose all & commands and ASCII code characters.

- Make sure you are running the page in a browser that supports XML.

If you have followed all these rules, you have created a document that is termed *well-formed*. That means it runs. You see, XML is nowhere near as forgiving as HTML.

Creating the DTD

The second type of page uses a DTD. In XML, you need to set up your own DTD items called *entities* in the business. Each entity allows you to create your own tag in a traditional HTML format. Entities do nothing. They simply block off sections of the page. Any text that happens to be captured inside that space is then affected by the parameters assigned to the entity. Sound familiar? HTML works the same way. For example, say you wanted to create the tag <SUPER> that would make text red and underlined. (As far as I know that one doesn't exist in HTML.) The basic format is given here. Please understand that there's a bit more than this, I am just trying to stay basic at first to keep us all on the same page.

- You would create a basic text file with a DTD extension. This file would hold all the entities.

- Create an entity like this one in the DTD file:

  ```
  <!ELEMENT SUPER (#PCDATA|u|ff0000)*>
  <!-- Tag attribute - red and underlined -->
  ```

- Now save the DTD text document as joe.dtd.

- Put up a declaration like this one on the XML document you are writing for display in the browser window:

```
<?xml version="1.0"?>
<!DOCTYPE SYSTEM "joe.dtd">
```

The SYSTEM command denotes that the DTD can be found on the system running the XML document.

- Now you are prepared to add the command to the XML document, like so:

```
<SUPER>this is the effected text</SUPER>
```

- Again, this is a very simplistic offering. If you would like to view an honest and true DTD, try http://www.oasis-open.org/cover/xmlspec-19980323-dtd.txt. This is frightening, to say the least.

Is There More?

Yupper! In fact, much more. I don't know how goofy into this stuff you are, but if this is your bag, XML certainly offers some enjoyable reading before bed. A lot is not written on the subject (I mean in a relative fashion, like when compared to the number of pages available on the music group Hanson), but what is written is very thick—very technical. It takes some plowing through, but you start to see it all come together after spending the time.

I relied on five main sites when putting this tutorial together:

- W3.org—eXtensible Markup Language (XML): Part I. Syntax. This is a very technical site.

  http://www.w3.org/TR/WD-xml-lang-970331.html

- XML.com—Fantastic site, very helpful. It takes the technical document from W3.org and explains each section in greater detail.

  http://www.xml.com

- Robin Cover's XML Page at sil.org.

  http://www.oasis-open.org/cover/xml.html

- Frequently asked questions about eXtensible Markup Language. This is written a lot like I write; you will understand it.

  http://www.ucc.ie/xml/#FAQ-GENERAL

These authors deserve far more of the credit than I. For a great deal more than is given here, try the Yahoo! XML page: http://dir.yahoo.com/Computers_and_Internet/Data_Formats/XML/ .

So Now What?

Well, nothing really. XML is still in the test stages. The XML Working Group, a body created to set the language somewhat in stone, has not quite arrived upon the golden goose (as of the time of this writing, at least). But they are soon enough.

XML is still a ship on the horizon. You can see it coming, but goodness only knows when it hits the docks, and yet you can start XML right now if you'd like. Internet Explorer 4 already has some limited capabilities to act as an XML processor when you incorporate its active channels.

My personal plan of action is to hurry up and wait. I am a big fan of watching to see if the new wave of the moment hits hard. Those people who are advanced enough at this game to program a bowling ball and three packs of bubble gum to play Pac Man jumps on this right off the bat. I want to see if this is the DHTML or the VRML of the future. I can only offer help in case of an XML landslide.

So You Want to Screen Capture?

This is a quick tutorial about screen captures, thus the title. If you're not sure what a screen capture is, think about the pages you've seen lately: Maybe some of them have had specific sections of the desktop or a program made into an image. It was almost as if they captured part of the screen as an image.

Well, the person did capture part of the screen—it is a *screen capture*.

Be Careful of Violating Copyright Laws!

What I'm about to show you is going to give you the ability to copy anything your computer displays, like those little Microsoft icons, among other things—but remember that those images are copyrighted. Make sure you either give credit when using the image or ask permission. Yes, you can just copy and post, but that doesn't mean it's legal.

I should say that Windows operating systems enable this type of screen capture by simply pressing the Print Screen button on the keyboard at any time. You can then paste the image you've grabbed into a graphics editor by choosing Edit, Paste. However, I suggest following this format. It works with a graphics program open, you can save in multiple formats, and it edits straight away.

Here's How You Do It

1. Get Paint Shop Pro. That is the program I outline here, so go get it and install it. It is shareware. This means you are asked to send in your bucks after a month or so.

But go grab it for now. The best place to download it is at http://www.shareware.com or http://www.jasc.com.

2. Open the program. You get a screen that says you're starting your 30-day trial. Click OK. There should be a screen with a bunch of brightly colored buttons in the upper-left or -right corner. Notice also the menu items. One of them is Capture; click it. From the Capture menu, select Setup. It should look like Figure 15.2. That opens the dialog box shown in Figure 15.3.

Figure 15.2
Choosing Setup in Paint Shop Pro.

3. The Capture Setup dialog box allows you to set up how you want your capture to take place. The far-right groupings denote what is captured. I almost always leave it on Full Screen. The only other one I find helpful is the Area selection. That allows you to draw crop lines around the area you want to capture. Stay with Full Screen for now.

Buttons are on the other side of the dialog box. Click to include (or exclude) the cursor or to make multiple captures.

The area in the middle is what you're interested in as far as initiating the capture goes. That is where you set up what key grabs the screen. I have never used the right mouse button. I like the F11 button—but feel free to choose. You can also delay it, but I never understood why.

Click OK to set your wishes in motion.

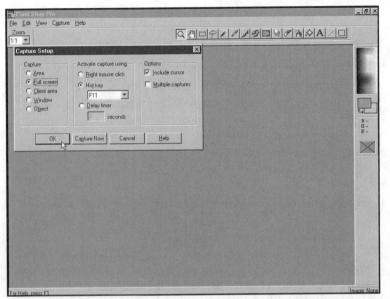

Figure 15.3
The Capture Setup dialog box.

4. Start the process; now you have the hotkey setup. To perform the capture, go back to the Capture menu and choose Start. It should look like Figure 15.4.

Figure 15.4
Starting the capture process.

The Paint Shop Pro program minimizes and becomes a small graphic at the bottom of the screen.

5. Capture! When what you want is on the screen, hit your hotkey or click your right mouse button. Paint Shop Pro becomes full screen again, but now the screen is there as an image. Crop out what you want. Now you have it as an image. Save it as a GIF or JPEG and put it on your page. Figures 15.2, 15.3, and 15.4 were made this way.

That does it. Enjoy and be sure to not break any laws by posting copyrighted stuff without credit or permission. It can really get you into trouble.

But wait...

This is another method of grabbing a screen from Arnar Thor Oskarsson, Web Designer from Selfoss, Iceland:

> *Joe,*
>
> *With some window open (Netscape, your desktop, whatever), press the "Print Screen" button on your keyboard (on my keyboard it's the one on the right side of the F12 key). Open some drawing program (Windows95 native Paint do), click "Edit" then "Paste"... BINGO! ;-) I know this just freezes a picture of the whole screen, and if you save it as .bmp in its original size, you're going to get a HUGE file, but it's a neat trick nevertheless. Feel free to use this on your excellent page if you like.*
>
> *Greetings from Iceland,*
>
> *Arnar*

But wait...

This is a bit more information from Jose Manuel Dias

> *Joe,*
>
> *In your tutorial about "screen capture" an addendum by Arnar Thor Oskarsson mentions the use of the "Print Screen" key to make a capture of the screen. He also mentions that the key only "freezes a picture of the whole screen," but you can capture only the current active window in the Windows 95 environment. For that, use "ALT" + "Print Screen" (press the "ALT" key and at the same time the "Print Screen" key), and you put an image of the active window in the clipboard; from there you can paste it in any place you want.*
>
> *Thank you very much, Joe, for an excellent site. An indispensable bookmark in my browser.*

How to Use Telnet

Ever since I posted the three CGI tutorials to the HTML Goodies site, I have been getting mail asking what I mean by "Telnet into your system." I put this quick lesson together to explain in a bit more detail.

Telnet

The term *Telnet* is a mushing together of *telephone* and *network*. The term means to use telephone lines for the purpose of contacting and entering another network computer. For example, let's say I am on joe.net and a file I want is on fred.com. When attached to the Internet, I use the Telnet program to work from joe.net on fred.net. It works much like a remote control.

Please note that just because I am discussing Telnet does not mean you are guaranteed Telnet capabilities with your account. You may not be able to connect your own system. Giving you access is up to the server people.

Even if you can log onto another server from yours, you still may not be able to do all the things I talk about in the CGI tutorials (see Chapter 12, "Common Gateway Interface (CGI)"). Again, it's up to your server people to give you the ability to do anything. Hopefully you have full access, but if not, contact the people you pay each month and see if your account can be altered to include full access.

Where Do I Find Telnet?

If you are running Windows 95 or Windows 3.*x*, you already have it on your system. Windows 95 people find the program by clicking Start, Programs, Accessories, and choosing Telnet. The icon looks like the one in the heading text. You could also jump right to it by clicking Start, Run, and typing in Telnet. The program pops right up. You can shorten the process by simply typing the name of the server you want to attach to right after the word Telnet (for example, Telnet joe.com).

You should get a telnet program from the people who act as your service providers if you are running Windows 3.*x*. The operating system doesn't always come with the Telnet program loaded.

Those of you using Macintosh systems need to grab Telnet programs, which are plentiful and small. You should have no trouble finding one. See either http://www.shareware.com or Yahoo!'s Telnet page. If you want a specific program to shoot for, I suggest NCSA Telnet (http://www.ncsa.uiuc.edu/SDG/Homepage/Platform.html). Telnet programs are usually very small. All they do is make the connection from one server to the next. The two servers do the rest.

How Does It Work?

Well, now I'm into an area that isn't so exact. The programs all work just about the same way, so I'm going to talk in generalities here and use screen captures of my Windows 95 Telnet program to explain.

First off, you have to attach to your server just like you do when you want to surf or get your e-mail. After clicking the Telnet icon to start the program, you get some kind of blank screen where text commands appear. Mine looks like Figure 15.5.

Figure 15.5
The Telnet screen.

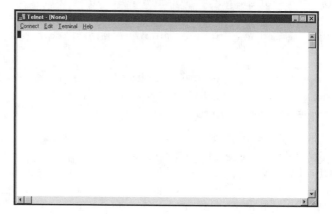

A series of menu items are somewhere along the top of the screen. One of them should give you the ability to connect. Your connection command might be under one of the menus. It is fairly obvious when you run across it. Sometimes it says Connect to Another System or words to that effect. My connect command is right along the top (see Figure 15.6).

Figure 15.6
The Telnet Connect menu.

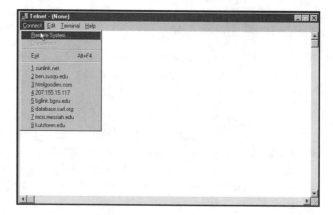

After clicking Connect, you are given a way to enter the name of the machine you want to attach to (see Figure 15.7). Usually you are good to go by entering the URL without the `http://`. I can get away with just putting in the domain name. You may also be asked for a port and a terminal type. The settings shown here are the most common. They are usually chosen for you.

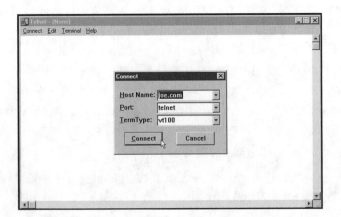

Figure 15.7
The Telnet Connect dialog box.

Putting in just the domain gets you to the server's front door. If you are given a longer address including some directories, place them where you enter the attachment directions. They get you right to where you want to go. Click Connect or press the Enter key to initiate the connection.

Magic happens, and hopefully a connection is made. You know it happened when the screen comes alive and asks for a login and password. Put in the correct pair and you're good to go.

That's about it. After you're attached, you can make directories and change modifications to your heart's content.

Writing for Disabled Assistant Browsers

Can everyone read your Web page?

I don't just mean that fact that you're using dark blue text on a black background either (lousy color choice). I mean all people, even those who are using disabled browsers.

I've known for a while that people who are using disabled browsers need everything on a Web page to have a text equal. Depending on the person's disability, the special browser reads the text to them, creates the text in Braille, or somehow relates the information to the user. I had a few tips to tell people, but now it's been laid down for all the world to see...and hopefully use.

On May 5, 1999, the World Wide Web Consortium (W3C) came out with their "Checklist of Checkpoints for Web Content Accessibility Guidelines v1.0" (Guidelines). You can travel to see the page yourself by going to: `http://www.w3.org/TR/1999/WAI-WEBCONTENT-19990505/`.

The Guidelines are the consortium's help page to Web developers to offer tips on how to make your pages more accessible to a disabled assistant browser. I've read the page a couple of times and it all looks pretty straightforward and easy to follow. If you write your HTML is a traditional manner, you're a big part of the way there.

The W3C breaks the tips down into three priorities. Priority 1 items must be done in order for your page to be read by disabled assistant browsers (the W3C refers to the browsers as "User Agents"). Priority 2 items should be done, and Priority 3 items may be done.

Let me hit some of the high points for you. Then you can go and read the page for yourself. Although it's a little dry, it's a great source of information.

Reading the document, I took away two major rules of thumb:

1. Absolutely every image, movie, icon, or any other non-text element on the page must have a text equivalent. The easiest method is to always offer an ALT command. Like so:

   ```
   <IMG SRC="image.src" ALT="Image of my father">
   ```

I go into more detail regarding the ALT command in Chapter 3, "Adding Images and Backgrounds."

Imagemaps (see Chapter 4) not only require the ALT command, but also require that you offer text links in addition to the map itself. Movies should offer audio tracks or the text right on the page so that the text can be read. The simplest method is to offer a second page that has the movie's elements. The user can go to the page to get the information.

2. Write your HTML code in a traditional fashion. That means flags in capital letters and attributes lowercase and in double quotes. Again, like so:

   ```
   <FONT SIZE="+3">Hello There</FONT>
   ```

Yes, I know that the double quotes aren't needed and that HTML is not case sensitive. However, remember that I'm talking about getting your pages to the point where the disabled assistant browser has the best shot at reading them for someone else.

Priority One Tips

These are a few other very good Priority one tips. Remember, Priority one tips are those that must be done to ensure your page can be read by a disabled assistant browser.

- Do not make color such a part of the page that without the color the page loses meaning.

- Avoid causing screen flickering or blinking.

- If style sheets are used, use the style sheet command right on the page rather than using an external CSS page.

- Use a client-side imagemap rather than server side.

- Give all frame and source pages a title.

- Make sure that your page is useable if the scripts and applets do not come into play because many disabled assistant browsers do not work with applets or scripts.

- Write with the simplest coding possible.

Those are all good tips. In fact they're good tips for whomever you're writing for, especially that "no blinking" thing.

Priority Two Tips

These tips are those that you should try to include in your page. This is a sampling. Many more exist than this. To see the complete list, visit the W3C pages noted earlier.

- Make sure your background and foreground colors differ so that people with poor eyesight can make out your text and are not inhibited by a clash in color.

- Use the HTML flags to get an effect before you use a style sheet or script equal.

- Use relative rather than absolute positions for your page's elements.

- Do not use auto-refreshing pages. Most disabled assistant browsers do not support the scripts that perform the refresh.

- Avoid pop-up windows as many disabled assistant browsers disallow the user to shut the window.

- Clearly identify what each link points at through text or ALT text.

- Make your navigation consistent. Use all active images or all text...that kind of thing. (That means across pages, not just page to page.)

- Layout should be done with style sheets rather than tables. If you use tables, provide a version of your page for the users.

Priority Three Tips

You may want to incorporate these into a Web page although they are not generally required. Again, many more than this exist. I just thought these were very good tips across the board.

- Identify the natural language of the document in a META or a commented-out line.
- Use style sheets to get links to highlight so that visually impaired persons can quickly realize the link.
- Group related links.

The W3C has offered all its Priority one, two, and three tips in a printable checklist at `http://www.w3.org/TR/1999/WAI-WEBCONTENT-19990505/full-checklist.html`. You can use it to roll down through your pages and test your work against the checklist.

So there you have it, some basic tips to make your Web page accessible to everyone who stops by. If you've been writing in good HTML form, you've probably already created useable pages.

Charset

In all my years of writing tutorials, I can't remember ever receiving an e-mail and spinning right around and posting a tutorial off of it. A first time for everything I guess.

I was working on a new site and asked some people to beta test it. I didn't know many of the people. They were all subscribers to my design newsletter. One gentleman happened to be an American now living in Japan and working as an interpreter. He also does Web design.

Well, when he entered the site using his Microsoft Internet Explorer browser, the page just looked horrible. The reason was that his browser was set to display Japanese characters by default. My page, however, was in English (more correctly, Western European text). Many characters could not be displayed, so he received the little boxes. Some text popped up, some didn't. It was a mess.

Some who actually know about this little problem might suggest that anyone running a browser not set to English as default can simply reload using the "encoding" function and the page displays in English (ASCII/Western European) text. I guess that's true but it's not being overly nice to the viewer. Every page has to be reloaded and encoded.

What's interesting about this problem is that it doesn't have to happen. You, the designer, can add one simple META command that alerts most browsers, using any language, that the page that is about to display is to be displayed using an English set of characters, or a character set, or a "charset."

The Code

I know you look at other people's code, right? Come on, admit it. Have you ever seen one of these:

```
<META http-equiv="Content-Type" content="text/html; charset=iso-8859-1">
```

That line of text saves people using browsers not set to display English a lot of reloading. This is what it is saying:

- `http-equiv` Should be viewed as meaning "name." It is most often accompanied by:
- `content` Equal to a value. The name/value pair here works much like it does in a `form` element.
- `charset` States what set of characters should be used to display the code within the document.

The command goes between the `<HEAD>` flags.

Other Charsets

The first thing that popped into my mind when I began really looking at this command was how many other charsets are there? The most complete list I found was one that described the charsets understood by the Netscape Navigator browser. Source: `http://people.netscape.com/ftang/meta.html`.

For English:

- us-ascii

For Western-European Languages:

- iso-8859-1
- x-mac-roman (only for Macintosh version)
- iso-8859-9 (3.0 and higher)
- x-mac-turkish (3.0 and higher only for Macintosh version)

For Traditional Chinese:

- big5
- x-euc-tw

For Japanese:

- Shift_JIS (3.0 or higher, 2.0 only know x-sjis)
- x-euc-jp
- iso-2022-jp

For Korean:

- euc-kr
- so-2022-kr

For Simplified Chinese:

- gb2312

For Eastern (or Central) European Languages:

- iso-8859-2
- x-mac-ce (only for Macintosh version)

For Cyrillic:

- iso-8859-5 (3.0 and higher)
- koi8-r (3.0 and higher)
- x-mac-cyrillic (3.0 and higher, only for Macintosh version)

For Greek:

- iso-8859-7 (3.0 and higher)
- x-mac-greek (3.0 and higher, only for Macintosh version)

Why iso-8859-1 Rather Than us-ascii?

I think I have to hit on this or I'm going to get e-mail asking the question. If you look at the previous listing of charsets, notice a charset for "English." Well, my pages are in English so why not use that? Why use the iso-8859-1?

The reason is that the us-ascii charset only contains the 128 ascii characters. Look at your keyboard. See all those letters and numbers and such? You have 128 of them. Count upper and lower case as two. That's not enough.

The iso-8859-1 charset is greatly expanded over us-ascii to include ASCII equals to special characters like ¥, ®, Ø. You can see a full list of the special characters in my `ASCII Command` tutorial.

For a short answer, the iso-8859-1 charset is standardized, more dynamic, and carries more information. For pages written in English it's the best choice.

If your pages are in English, I would suggest that you make a point of adding the previous META command in between your HEAD flags. You may never know it, but you probably are making someone's surfing life a whole lot easier and more enjoyable.

So, You Want A 404 Error Page, Huh?

Ah, the aggravating 404 error page. You've seen it. There you are, surfing in your favorite search engine when you come upon just the thing you're looking for. You click: (***Raspberry Sound Effect***) You see nothing, but a white page with the words "404 Error" and some other techie-sounding speak beneath.

What's even more cheesy about the error code is that it really doesn't tell you what the problem is. Basically you've been informed that the server cannot find what you want. It doesn't tell you why, how to fix it, or where to go from that point. You really don't have much choice but to hit your BACK button, call the computer a dirty name, and try again.

But then you see it—a server that's set up with its own special 404 error page that politely apologizes and offers you links to e-mail site administrators and maybe a site search engine. Now that's class!

This is the 404 Error page at HTML Goodies:

So I waltzed into the office of the Webmaster at work and asked how it was done. I was stunned at how easy it is to set up.

Want one of your own? This is how.

You'd Best Ask First

I'm going to offer you a very basic fix to this problem, but you'd best ask your system people if they want you doing this first. Better yet, ask them if you might mess things up by doing this.

Your .htaccess File

This is the file that does the trick for you. You should already have one waiting inside of your Web site directory. If you don't, you need to create it.

Figure 15.8
I'm sorry...I can't find that page.

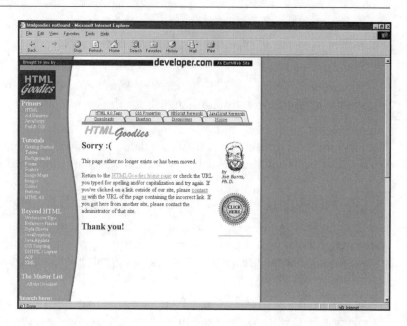

FTP into your server, so you're looking at the top level directory where you store your Web page files. This should be the directory that contains your home page document. Look for the .htaccess file there. Again, if you don't find it (it should be one of the very first files), you need to create it.

Please notice the dot (.) starting it off.

Here again is where you might have to get in touch with your systems people and ask them how they want you to edit or create this file. Some may enable you to do it like you would any other Web page, by creating a text document and uploading it, while others might want you to use a PICO editor and do it right on the server. It might be best not to guess at it.

Let's Edit It

Add this to the .htaccess file:

```
ErrorDocument 404 http://www.domain.com/404page.html
```

That's it. Write just that line. (Yes, it should all be on one line. Some smaller computer screens may bump it down to two, but get it all on one.) Where I have http://www.domain.com/404page.html is where you place the full URL pointing to that new, fancy 404 Error page you've created.

...you have already created an error page, right?

Let's Turn It On

If you already had an .htaccess page in your directory then chances are it's already turned on. If not, you need to do that. If you're using a UNIX server then you need to Telnet into the server and type this command at the prompt:

```
chmod 644 .htaccess
```

If you're not running a UNIX machine, I believe the file is ready to go, but again, contact your server people to see if I'm on the money or not.

That's it!

Upload your new 404 error page, if you haven't already, and log into your site. Then try to go to a page that doesn't exist. You should get the page you denoted in the .htaccess file. If you don't, first try the CHMOD again to see if the file is turned on. If you still get nothing, get back in touch with your system people and ask them for more specific help.

You are the envy of people who go to nonexistent pages everywhere.

Part V

Appendixes

A   *Everything You Need to Know About HTML 4.0*

B   *Useful Charts*

C   *Valuable Links*

Appendix A

Everything You Need to Know About HTML 4.0

As of this writing, HTML 4.0 has become the accepted HTML format. In fact, just before these pages were sent to print, version 4.01 came out. You can read all about it here: http://www.w3.org/TR/html401/. You don't find a great deal of change from what is below. Rather than incorporate this appendix into the full text of the book, I thought it would still be helpful to set it apart. By setting it apart I can, again, get into discussions of versions and some of the new elements of the new version.

Just keep in mind that HTML is dynamic and ever changing, whereas this book is static. Maybe by the third edition, I'll feel it's correct to incorporate these commands into the tutorials themselves, but not at this point.

Enjoy this tutorial for what it is—an overview of the latest version.

I guess if I were to wrap HTML 4.0 up in a nutshell, it would be that there is more user interactivity and more use of style sheets. In fact, style sheets are supposed to rule the roost, but don't sweat it. HTML is completely backwards-compatible. You can write pages that never use any of these commands and they display just fine. If you never actually use a style sheet, your pages will look fine. This tutorial is simply to introduce you to new commands, new subcommands, and three dead commands that I bet you've never used, anyway.

Add the commands you like to your arsenal of HTML. Those you dislike, leave for someone else. Here we go...

Readers Questions Regarding HTML 4.0

I thought I would teach you about the new HTML 4.0 commands by addressing the question I hear most often on my HTML Goodies Web site.

What Is HTML 4.0? Should I Be Concerned About It?

Concerned? As in HTML 4.0 might steal away in the night with your good china? Nah. From everything I've found, it will actually make writing a bit easier for you and on the search engines. The people at the World Wide Web Consortium stepped up to the plate and agreed, in late 1997, that the next version of HTML, version 4.0, should be the accepted version. Now, this *by no means* indicates that it is so. HTML is not fully adopted yet. Even so, remember who you are writing for. Contrary to what many Web-heads believe, the vast majority of Web users are still around the version 2.0 level. Watch the level of your writing. You may be above some heads. Most heads, actually.

I Use Netscape 4 (or Explorer 4). Does That Mean I Should Be Writing in HTML 4.0?

Ah, logic! Man, that sounds like it should be correct, I know. But it ain't. Version numbers of the two main browsers have nothing to do with what version of HTML they use. Now, someone is going to go bonkers at this point and tell me that some elements of HTML 4.0 are available for use in browsers version 4. True—but the manufacturers of the browsers did not wait for their version 4 number to incorporate HTML 4.0. This is one of those strange scientific synchronicities called a coincidence.

With that said, some of these commands can be run using the 4.0 (and some earlier) browsers. When we actually get to the commands, I'll offer some additional examples; then you can see if they actually work for your browser.

On Versions...

Now might be a good time to discuss what all these version numbers mean. There are no hard or fast rules to this, but here's the generally accepted method for giving version numbers to software:

- If there is a major change to the product, step up the number by one.
- If there are tweaks to the product, add a point something (1.1, for example).

With good writing like that, it's a wonder I wasn't hired at Microsoft years ago, huh?

For instance, say I create a software program that counts the number of times you curse at your computer screen while writing HTML code. I call it Cursor. The first version out of the gate is version 1.0. I offer that version for free over the Net so I can get fine people like you to test it out for free—you are my R&D (research and development) team. This is what companies call a *beta version*. It's something they assume will be replaced by a better version. Kind of like beta video tape. Remember that?

You play with it and find a few bugs. I fix the bugs. Now I have Cursor version 1.1. This is probably the one I sell.

Six months later I decide I hate the *interface* (the look of the screen) and decide to make major changes to my Cursor program. The changes are substantial, so I change the version number. I now have Cursor 2.0. Again with the beta testing. You find a few bugs, I fix them. Ta da! Cursor 2.1. But wait! You suggest an extra function for the program. I add it. We now have Cursor version 2.2. Get it?

What Version of HTML Are We Currently Using?

Version 4.0 is now the accepted mainstream format. Have you ever seen one of these?

```
<!DOCTYPE HTML PUBLIC "-//W3C//DTD HTML 4.0//EN">
```

That's a *declaration statement*. It sits at the very top of the page and proclaims to the browser that displays the page that the following page is using HTML 4.0. The EN stands for English.

Now, just because HTML 4.0 is the accepted format does not mean that you must incorporate new HTML 4.0 commands into your pages. You don't. In fact, you never have to incorporate any new commands into your pages.

Remember that the most important part of any Web page or site is content. If all you ever use on your pages are simple images and text, but the content is stunning, you're going to be a success.

Who Decided We Should All Go to HTML 4.0?

The World Wide Web Consortium, and it actually doesn't decide at all. Among other things, it is the governing body of HTML. It makes suggestions and hopefully the browser-makers follow, but not always. Case in point: The <BLINK> command works in Netscape, but not in Explorer. Go figure.

Every Time I Hear About HTML 4.0, I also Hear About SGML and XML. What Are They?

And you have these conversations with whom? You and your friends are either really, really up on the future of code or you need to get out more.

SGML Stands for Standard Generalized Markup Language

And you already use it. SGML is the mother of HTML. Think of it this way: By using SGML, you have the ability to create your own tags. I want the tag <ZORK> to represent text that is bold, italic, and Arial font. I can set it up with SGML code. HTML is simply a set standard of tags under the huge SGML umbrella.

XML Stands for eXtensible Markup Language

XML is a subset of SGML, just as HTML is. The best description of the language comes from Ken Kopf, computer specialist at Susquehanna University. He denotes XML as a very simplified version of SGML. It is a version of the language that people can understand. If SGML is a bear, XML is a kitten. It allows you to set up your own tags and mathematical equations using commands that you can understand. If you'd like to fill your brain cells regarding XML now, see the tutorial earlier in the book.

The concern I see coming out of all of this fancy new stuff is that it might do damage to the Web. You see, HTML was a stunningly easy language that took computer programming out of the hands of men with slide rules and gave it to you and me—the weekend silicon warriors. We understood it. It made some sense.

Introducing SGML and XML, in my mind, is the first real shot the higher-ups have of driving people away. It's something new and most people are comfortable now. Introducing it might stratify the audience or make people drop out altogether.

The full incorporation of these languages is still years away. By then there will probably be good, solid, programming software that does most of the XML work for you.

Will You Puh-Leeze Get to HTML 4.0!?

Stop yelling. I'm there. I should say up front that the majority of my research came from the World Wide Web Consortium's pages on HTML 4.0. There are miles of data available. Here's where I attempt to boil it down to the basics.

There are four sections here: "New Commands," "New Attributes," "Deprecated Elements," and "Dead Elements." After the first two sections, there is a URL to a page containing the commands. Some are actually available today for use. You'll see if your setup does the trick or not with these HTML 4.0 commands.

New Commands

The following 22 commands are "new" and are incorporated into HTML 4.0:

● `<ABBR>`

This indicates an abbreviated form of a word. Example:

```
<ABBR TITLE="National Football League">NFL</ABBR>
```

The `TITLE` command produces a rollover title like the `ALT` command does on pictures.

● `<ACRONYM>`

This works the same way as `<ABBR>` except it denotes an acronym. Example:

```
<ACRONYM TITLE="Self-Contained Underwater Breathing Apparatus>
SCUBA</ACRONYM>
```

● `<BDO>`

This is difficult to explain. Text goes left to right and sometimes right to left. The `BDO` command denotes to the computer to leave the text in the direction it is currently in. If you write in Hebrew, a language written right to left, using `BDO` ensures that other elements such as spelling checkers won't be incorporated and flip text around. It is most often used in the `<PRE>` tags. Example:

```
<PRE> <BDO DIR="LTR">hello</BDO> </PRE>
```

`LTR` means "left to right." Guess what "right to left" is represented by? Yup: `RTL`.

● `<BUTTON>`

This becomes standard code for creating link buttons, in a Guestbook form, for example. Example:

```
<BUTTON name="submit" value="submit" type="submit"></BUTTON>
```

What's more, this format easily allows an image to be placed on the button.

● `<COLGROUP>`

This command allows for an entire column of data in tables to be affected by one command rather than using a separate command for each cell. Example:

```
<COLGROUP WIDTH="30%"></COLGROUP>
```

● `<DEL>`

Surrounding something with this command provides a strikethrough over what it deleted. Example:

```
Version <DEL>3</DEL><INS>4</INS>
```

Now you have a jump on what the new command `INS` does. You'll get to it in a few.

● `<FIELDSET>`

This allows people to group controls on a page together, like grouping buttons that affect a certain JavaScript so there won't be any interaction between other scripts on the same page or sections of a guestbook. It works in tandem with the `LEGEND` command. An example is waiting there with that command's explanation.

● <FRAME>

This works the same way as the FRAME command we have today except it has been delegated new powers. These powers include denoting specific traits to each frame cell. It allows for many more abilities when working with style sheets. This is listed because it will be a specific subset of commands for use with SGML format styles.

● <FRAMESET>

Ditto this one except this deals with larger sections of frame pages. For instance, you have a page with four frame cells. You want only those on the left to have green borders. You use this command to set aside those two vertical frames and assign traits to that section. This is listed because it will be a specific subset of commands for use with SGML format styles.

● <IFRAME>

This again works much the same way as the inline frames we currently use. Again, this is listed because it will be a specific subset of commands for use with SGML format styles.

● <INS>

You saw earlier how this works. It sets something aside as having been added or "inserted" at a later time. It is denoted via an underline.

● <LABEL>

This command attaches a label to form commands. Example:

```
<FORM ACTION="--">
<LABEL for="email">Email Address</LABEL>
<INPUT type="text" name="email_address" id="email">
</FORM>
```

● <LEGEND>

Now we get to the example denoted earlier from the FIELDSET command. FIELDSET groups form items together. LEGEND denotes those sections. Example:

```
<FIELDSET>
<LEGEND>Personal Information</LEGEND> Name: [Input Text Box]
EMAIL: [Input Text Box]
AGE: [Input Text Box]
</FIELDSET>
```

It keeps it all straight for the computer.

● <NOFRAMES>

This denotes text content that displays whether the user has frame capabilities. This has been around for a while, but is now being officially brought into the fold.

⬤ `<NOSCRIPT>`

Ditto from `<NOFRAMES>`.

⬤ `<OBJECT>`

This command replaces IMG, ISMAP, APPLET, SCRIPT, and myriad other "objects" that appear on the page. This one command represents that something is going to be placed on the page. The computer then decides what kind of object it is due to its extension. Example:

```
<OBJECT data="image.gif" type="image/gif"></OBJECT>
<OBJECT classid="applet.class"></OBJECT>
<OBJECT data="movie.avi" type="application/avi"></OBJECT>
```

⬤ `<OPTGROUP>`

How this will be handled is still a little fuzzy, but it appears that it allows multiple groups of information inside pull-down menus, much like the menus produced by the W95 Start button.

⬤ `<PARAM>`

This command is used with applets to set parameters. It's already in use, but is now being brought into the fold.

⬤ `<SPAN>`

Think of the span element in terms of its being an equal to the `<DIV>` command. It denotes a certain division of the page or span of text that can then be altered to your heart's content. Example:

```
<SPAN CLASS="green">This would be green text</SPAN>
```

⬤ `<TBODY>`

This command surrounds a block of table cells so that you can affect just that section. Keep reading...

⬤ `<TFOOT>`

This enables you to place a footer below each TBODY section of a table. Notice that all the commands are TR rather than TD. This is an example for both TBODY and TFOOT:

```
<TABLE>
<TBODY bgcolor="--">
<TR> text
<TR> text
</TBODY>
<TFOOT>
<TR>The above cells...
</TFOOT>
</TABLE>
```

● <THREAD>

This is header information for a group of cells, used the same way as TFOOT—above the group of cells set apart by the TBODY command. Example:

```
<TABLE>
<THREAD>
<TR> The following cells...
</THREAD>
<TBODY bgcolor="--">
<TR> text
<TR> text
</TBODY>
<TFOOT>
<TR>The above cells...
</TFOOT>
</TABLE>
```

● <Q>

The difference between the Q command and the BLOCKQUOTE command is that the Q command is much easier to write. Use them exactly the same way.

Take Them for a Test Drive

 I've set up a page online that demonstrates these new commands in action. When you go see it, make sure you're using a version 4.0 browser, otherwise you won't get any of the new effects. Please remember that even though you may have the 4.0 browser, some of the commands are still not supported. You should make a point of looking at the source code. The latest HTML 4.0 declaration statement is used. That said, go to http://www.htmlgoodies.com/tutors/newcommands.html.

Some New Attributes

In my opinion, this is where HTML shines—the attributes. The attributes allow a simple table cell to have color and size. It allows an image to have text and set sizes, and there are a few new ones to be concerned with in HTML 4.0. Here you go:

● <CLASS>

This is already in use in Explorer versions 3 and 4. First you set up a class with a style sheet command. (See my tutorial on classes and IDs for how to do it http://htmlgoodies.earthweb.com/beyond/classid.html.)

Then you call for the style sheet using the CLASS command. Example:

```
<SPAN CLASS="purple">Affected text</SPAN>
```

○ <DIR>

This was touched on in the BDO command explanation. The DIR subcommand denotes whether the text is to be read LTR (left to right) or RTL (right to left).

○ <ID>

The ID can be used in the same manner as the CLASS subcommand, but in HTML 4.0 it is also being used to denote sections of the page. In short, it acts like a page jump. Example:

```
<A HREF="#sectionone-id">Jump to Section One</A>
```

The command jumps to this:

```
<SPAN ID="sectionone">section One
```

This method is a little better than the page jump because it jumps to a section of text rather than to the page.

○ <LANG>

This is clever because it helps the search engines understand different languages as being different languages rather than just misspelled English. Example:

```
<SPAN LANG="es">Hola! Como esta?</SPAN>
```

Those of you who remember your high school Spanish know that phrase loosely translates to "Hi, how ya doin'?" Contrary to what you might be thinking, the LANG subcommand does not translate. You must still write the text in the native tongue. The LANG command allows the search engines to recognize that section as Spanish text. In case you're wondering, here are some other codes: ar (Arabic), de (German), el (Greek), fr (French), he (Hebrew), hi (Hindi), ja (Japanese), it (Italian), nl (Dutch), pt (Portuguese), ur (Urdu), ru (Russian), sa (Sandskirt), and zh (Chinese). Yes, there is also a code set aside if you want to denote a language that doesn't really exist, like Pig Latin or Klingon. Follow the same form as earlier but add x- before the name. Like so: LANG="x-ubbee dubbie". The x indicates that it's an experimental language.

○ <TITLE>

This title command works just the same as the ALT command in an IMG command. It enables you to place a title onto just about anything so that a text box pops up when the mouse remains stationary for a second. Example:

```
<SPAN TITLE="National Football League">NFL</SPAN>
```

Now every time someone places his mouse on that set of initials, the box pops up saying "National Football League." It can be very helpful.

Now Take These for a Test Drive

 Same deal as before: There's a page set up for you to go look at these subcommands in action. Make sure you're using a version 4.0 browser. Remember to look at the source code. Go to `http://www.htmlgoodies.com/tutors/newsubcommands.html`.

Deprecated Elements

Table A.1 contains commands that are still good, but have better ways of getting the effect. When a command is deprecated, it also means that the next version of HTML might not support it. That means you run a risk of the next-generation browsers not recognizing it.

Table A.1   Deprecated Elements

Deprecated Command	What to Use Instead
<APPLET>	<OBJECT>
<BASEFONT>	Style sheet commands
<CENTER>	The ALIGN="center" sub command or style sheet commands
<DIR>	Create lists through <UL>
<FONT>	Style sheet commands
<ISINDEX>	Create various <INPUT> commands to create the text box ISINDEX creates
<MENU>	Create lists through the <UL> command
<S>	Create strikethrough text using style sheet commands
<STRIKE>	Create strikethrough text using style sheet commands
<U>	Create underlined text using style sheet commands

Dead Elements

In with the good, out with the bad. These three puppies are gone for good:

R.I.P.	Now What?
<LISTING>	<PRE>
<PLAINTEXT>	<PRE>
<XMP>	<PRE>

That's the Scoop

Now you know far more about HTML 4.0 than I'm sure you cared to know. If I were to put it all into a few simple sentences, I would say that this is not yet something to get all excited or nervous over. Let me again say that you should be taught the value of understatement in any Web page design class. Just because you have all these fancy commands doesn't mean you have to use all of them.

Think of your audience. If they are real Web-heads that simply go gah-gah over the newest stuff and have the latest browsers and all the stunning plug-ins, maybe you should get involved with this. If your audience is a mass of people with greatly varying browsers and platforms, maybe you should stay at a lower level. No matter how cool your page is, I can't be impressed by it if I can't display it.

There. I've now put my soap box away.

Useful Charts

Color Codes

Table B.1 contains a list of popular colors along with their hex code equivalents. You can see this chart online in full living color at `http://www.htmlgoodies.com/tutorscolors.html`.

Non-Dithering Color Chart

As if there isn't enough to be concerned about in terms of colors, here's one more little deal. It's called *non-dithering*. In layman's terms, non-dithering colors look the same when displayed by all browsers with all computer screen resolution settings.

"Doesn't that happen with all colors?" Nope. Have you ever seen a color created by what appeared to be one solid color and then a few lighter-colored dots placed across the top? It didn't blend at all, but the two colors together sort of created another color. Or have you ever printed something in color, and instead of being one color, it appeared to be a series of different-colored dots? That's called *dithering*, and it's not pretty.

See this tutorial online, in color, at `http://www.htmlgoodies.com/tutors/non_ dithering_colors.html`.

Table B.1   Color Codes in Word and Hex Form

Color Code	Hex Code	Color Code	Hex Code	Color Code	Hex Code
Aliceblue	F0F8FF	Darkmagenta	8B008B	Hotpink	FF69B4
Antiquewhite	FAEBD7	Darkolive green	556B2F	Indianred	CD5C5C
Aqua	00FFFF	Darkorange	FF8C00	Indigo	4B0082
Aquamarine	7FFFD4	Darkorchid	9932CC	Ivory	FFFFF0
Azure	F0FFFF	Darkred	8B0000	Khaki	F0E68C
Beige	F5F5DC	Darksalmon	E9967A	Lavender	E6E6FA
Bisque	FFE4C4	Darkseagreen	8FBC8F	Lavenderblush	FFF0F5
Black	000000	Darkslateblue	483D8B	Lawngreen	7CFC00
Blanchedalmond	FFEBCD	Darkslategray	2F4F4F	Lemonchiffon	FFFACD
Blue	0000FF	Darkturquoise	00CED1	Lightblue	ADD8E6
Blueviolet	8A2BE2	Darkviolet	9400D3	Lightcoral	F08080
Brown	A52A2A	Deeppink	FF1493	Lightcyan	E0FFFF
Burlywood	DEB887	Deepskyblue	00BFFF	Lightgoldenrodyellow	FAFAD2
Cadetblue	5F9EA0	Dimgray	696969	Lightgreen	90EE90
Chartreuse	7FFF00	Dodgerblue	1E90FF	Lightgrey	D3D3D3
Chocolate	D2691E	Firebrick	B22222	Lightpink	FFB6C1
Coral	FF7F50	Floralwhite	FFFAF0	Lightsalmon	FFA07A
Cornflowerblue	6495ED	Forestgreen	228B22	Lightseagreen	20B2AA
Cornsilk	FFF8DC	Fuchsia	FF00FF	Lightskyblue	87CEFA
Crimson	DC143C	Gainsboro	DCDCDC	Lightslategray	778899
Cyan	00FFFF	Ghostwhite	F8F8FF	Lightsteelblue	B0C4DE
Darkblue	00008B	Gold	FFD700	Lightyellow	FFFFE0
Darkcyan	008B8B	Goldenrod	DAA520	Lime	00FF00
Darkgoldenrod	B8860B	Gray	808080	Limegreen	32CD32
Darkgray	A9A9A9	Green	008000	Linen	FAF0E6
Darkgreen	006400	Greenyellow	ADFF2F	Magenta	FF00FF
Darkkhaki	BDB76B	Honeydew	F0FFF0	Maroon	800000

Table B.1   Color Codes in Word and Hex Form continued

Color Code	Hex Code	Color Code	Hex Code	Color Code	Hex Code
Mediumaquamarine	66CDAA	Peru	CD853F	Wheat	F5DEB3
Mediumblue	0000CD	Pink	FFC0CB	White	FFFFFF
Mediumorchid	BA55D3	Plum	DDA0DD	Whitesmoke	F5F5F5
Mediumpurple	9370D8	Powderblue	B0E0E6	Yellow	FFFF00
Mediumseagreen	3CB371	Purple	800080	Yellowgreen	9ACD32
Mediumslateblue	7B68EE	Red	FF0000		
Mediumspringgreen	00FA9A	Rosybrown	BC8F8F		
Mediumturquoise	48D1CC	Royalblue	4169E1		
Mediumvioletred	C71585	Saddlebrown	8B4513		
Midnightblue	191970	Salmon	FA8072		
Mintcream	F5FFFA	Sandybrown	F4A460		
Mistyrose	FFE4E1	Seagreen	2E8B57		
Moccasin	FFE4B5	Seashell	FFF5EE		
Navajowhite	FFDEAD	Sienna	A0522D		
Navy	000080	Silver	C0C0C0		
Oldlace	FDF5E6	Skyblue	87CEEB		
Olive	808000	Slateblue	6A5ACD		
Olivedrab	688E23	Slategray	708090		
Orange	FFA500	Snow	FFFAFA		
Orangered	FF4500	Springgreen	00FF7F		
Orchid	DA70D6	Steelblue	4682B4		
Palegoldenrod	EEE8AA	Tan	D2B48C		
Palegreen	98FB98	Teal	008080		
Paleturquoise	AFEEEE	Thistle	D8BFD8		
Palevioletred	D87093	Tomato	FF6347		
Papayawhip	FFEFD5	Turquoise	40E0D0		
Peachpuff	FFDAB9	Violet	EE82EE		

Non-dithering colors always give a nice, smooth color on Web pages and in graphics. That's because these are the 216 colors chosen by Windows and Macintosh operating plat-forms to make up their palettes of colors. The colors that aren't represented here are the colors that these try to make up by dithering. Get it?

The color list comes from a mathematical formula using the shades 00, 33, 66, 99, CC, and FF from hex codes. Using just those six hex combinations—over red, blue, and green hues—gives us a total of 216 colors that render perfectly on your screen. Obviously this isn't going to show up too well in a black and white book, so I suggest you go to the HTML Goodies Web site at `http://www.htmlgoodies.com/non_dithering_colors.html` to get a good look.

An Explanation of Hexadecimal Codes

The word color codes are pretty easy to understand, but those hex codes are rather strange. This is a quick explanation.

The three primary colors are red, blue, and yellow. Remember that from high school art? They are called the *primary colors* because there are no two "lesser" colors that make them up. Purple is not a primary color because it can be created through combining equal parts of blue and red.

In the world of mechanical things that make a color by using light, like a television or computer screen, color is created through mixing three basic colors. It's a process known as *additive color*.

You would think that the TVs and computer monitors of the world would simply use the three primary colors to start with, but nothing in life can be that easy. The three colors used to start additive color mixing are red, green, and blue. Why? Because by starting with one composite color, green, you can still create yellow because it's contained in the green. In addition, now you are actually starting with four colors: red, green, blue, yellow. Stay with me here...

To go on, I need to explain a second process of working with colors—subtractive color. *Subtractive color* is the concept of combining colors to make another, like mixing red and blue paint to get purple. That may sound like additive color, but in reality colors are made by subtracting a hue from the color scheme and by adding more of another. Adding more white to black makes it more silver, subtracting more black as more white is mixed in. Get it?

One other big difference between additive and subtractive color—and this is the key—is what you get when you add them all together.

If you add all the colors together in a subtractive color method, you get black. Why? Because you added them all together and all those colors subtracted from all the others leaves no set color: black.

A computer, on the other hand, works with light, not paint or any other goopy stuff. Mix a computer's additive colors—red, green, and blue—together and you get white.

No kidding, you really do. Shine a white light at a prism or a lead crystal glass. You'll get a rainbow of colors. Actually, that's how a rainbow is created. White light is being shown through water droplets in the air. That separates the white light into the "rainbow" of colors.

Now on to the six-digit representation of color known as the *hex code*.

Basic Hexadecimal Notation

Hex numbers use 16 characters:

0 1 2 3 4 5 6 7 8 9 A B C D E F

Zero (0) is the smallest representations of a color. It's almost the total absence of color. F is 15 times the intensity of the color 0. Combinations of these digits create different shades of a particular color. Double zero, 00, is equal to zero hue; FF is equal to a pure color.

This color representation is done three times, once for red, once for green, and once for blue, in that order. Put the three two-digit codes together and you get a six-digit hex code. The hex code is just a representation of the red, green, and blue intensity, in that order. The computer creates the three intensities, mashes them together, and you get a single shade of color.

For an example, here are the opposite ends of the color scale:

```
FFFFFF
```

The code is equal to white. Why? Notice the three colors are all set to FF. That means the highest level of red, green, and blue. As I said, the combination of all three primary colors creates white in a computer or television. Now here's black:

```
000000
```

This is just the opposite. All three settings of red, green, and blue are set to a total absence of color: black.

Now, here are a few other codes and their breakdown:

```
FFFF00
```

Let's start with yellow. This code produces pure yellow. Notice that the red and the green are at full tilt? There is no blue. By mashing the red and green up against each other, the red cancels out the blue and all that is left is the yellow. It's actually a subtractive color method being employed in an additive world. This gets loopy, huh?

DC143C

The code creates a shade of red called crimson. The red setting, DC, is pretty intense. There's not much green. Blue is set a little less than halfway up.

EE82EE

That's violet. The red and the blue are at pretty high levels. The green is there, but at a lower level. Now, this is not purple, but violet. Again, purple is a combination of red and blue alone. The code is 800080. Notice there's no green at all, just an equal amount of red and blue.

FFA500

That's orange. There's lots of red, not quite an equal level of green, and no blue.

That's how the hex codes work. This lesson probably won't make you an expert in color creation, but at least you'll be able to understand the creation of color in a computer.

So, are there more hex code colors than what I showed? Oh, yes. There are thousands upon millions, covering every color in the scale from pure black to pure white. When you set your computer monitor to 16.7 million colors, you're not kidding. You're setting it to the number of shades available in the computer universe. Every time you change even one of the red, green, or blue levels, you change the color. Most changes are so subtle you'll not recognize it, but it's there.

Ampersand Commands

Ampersand commands are quite useful, especially to me. I use them all over my HTML tutorials to create the characters not found on the keyboard or to make command characters show up on the page.

Let's say you want a copyright insignia. Well, there isn't any copyright on the keyboard. That means you'll need to either create it as a graphic or use an & command to place it. Have you also noticed a World Wide Web page that shows HTML commands like <HTML>? Don't you find it strange that if I enclose HTML in brackets (< >) that it shouldn't show up on the page? It's done using an & command to create the greater than and less than signs.

Here's How It Works

Your browser reads commands inside greater than and less than brackets. But did you know it also reads commands inside & and ; (semicolon) insignia?

Those who create the HTML code have created a slew of these commands that sit inside an ampersand and a semicolon. All you need to know is the little three- or four-letter code that goes between the characters and you'll be placing little insignias all over your page.

Figure B.1 shows as many ampersand commands as I could find. Remember that you do not place these codes inside < and > commands. These just sit as they appear in the chart shown here. They always begin with an & and end with a ;.

Each chart cell is set up with the ampersand command, as it should appear on your page, and then what the command created. Remember, capitalization counts here!

® ®	± ±	µ µ	¶ ¶	· ·	¢ ¢
£ £	¥ ¥	¼ ¼	½ ½	¾ ¾	¹ ¹
² ²	³ ³	¿ ¿	° °	¦ ¦	§ §
< <	> >	& &	" "	 (A Space)	&Ccdil; Ç
&ccdil; ç	Ñ Ñ	ñ ñ	Þ Þ	þ þ	Ý Ý
ý ý	ÿ ÿ	ß ß	Æ Æ	Á Á	Â Â
À À	Å Å	Ã Ã	Ä Ä	æ æ	á á
â â	à à	å å	ã ã	ä a	Ð Ð
É É	Ê Ê	È È	Ë Ë	ð ð	é é
ê ê	è è	ë e	Í Í	Î Î	Ì Ì

Ï Ï	í í	î î	ì ì	ï ï	Ó Ó
Ô Ô	Ò Ò	Ø Ø	Õ Õ	Ö Ö	ó ó
ô ô	ò ò	ø ø	õ õ	ö ö	Ú Ú
Û Û	Ù Ù	Ü Ü	ú ú	û û	ù ù
ü ü	« «	» »			

Figure B.1
Ampersand commands and the characters they print.

ASCII Commands

When writing a Web page you want to have as much flexibility as possible in placing characters. If you have read the preceding ampersand command section, you know you can create characters not found on the normal keyboard using an & and a ;. Well, you can do the same using &# and a ; and a command in between. They are called *ASCII commands* and are very similar to what your computer uses to display the text you type.

What are listed here are the ASCII commands that produce certain characters not readily found on the keyboard (some are though, just to keep the flow of the numbers).

Some are repeats from the ampersand command tutorial. Just follow the format to place any of these on your page. Do not enclose these in the brackets commands; they sit just as they look in the boxes.

Because these are ASCII commands, there must be an equivalent for all the characters already found on the keyboard. There are:

- Numbers 33–47, 58–64, 91–96, and 123–126 are the non-letter and non-numerical characters on the keyboard—things like a $ and an *.
- Numbers 48—57 are the numerals 0 through 9.
- Numbers 65—90 are the capital letters *A* through *Z*.
- Numbers 97—122 are the lowercase letters *a* through *z*.
- 127 is the Delete key entry.
- 128–159 are not in use.
- 160 is the spacebar.

The other numbers are shown in Figure B.2. You'll see what the command creates in each cell and the command you use to create the symbol below it.

Figure B.2
ASCII commands and the characters they print.

‚	ƒ	„	…	†	‡
&#0130;	&#0131;	&#0132;	&#0133;	&#0134;	&#0135;
ˆ	‰	Š	‹	Œ	'
&#0136;	&#0137;	&#0138;	&#0139;	&#0140;	&#0145;
'	"	"	•	–	—
&#0146;	&#0147;	&#0148;	&#0149;	&#0150;	&#0151;

˜	™	š	›	œ	Ÿ
&#0152;	&#0153;	&#0154;	&#0155;	&#0156;	&#0159;
	¡	¢	£	¤	¥
	&#0161;	&#0162;	&#0163;	&#0164;	&#0165;
¦	§	¨	©	ª	«
&#0166;	&#0167;	&#0168;	&#0169;	&#0170;	&#0171;
¬		®	¯	°	±
&#0172;	&#0173;	&#0174;	&#0175;	&#0176;	&#0177;
²	³	´	µ	¶	·
&#0178;	&#0179;	&#0180;	&#0181;	&#0182;	&#0183;
¸	¹	º	»	¼	½
&#0184;	&#0185;	&#0186;	&#0187;	&#0188;	&#0189;

¾	¿	À	Á	Â	Ã
&#0190;	&#0191;	&#0192;	&#0193;	&#0194;	&#0195;
Ä	Å	Æ	Ç	È	É
&#0196;	&#0197;	&#0198;	&#0199;	&#0200;	&#0201;
Ê	Ë	Ì	Í	Î	Ï
&#0202;	&#0203;	&#0204;	&#0205;	&#0206;	&#0207;
Ð	Ñ	Ò	Ó	Ô	Õ
&#0208;	&#0209;	&#0210;	&#0211;	&#0212;	&#0213;
Ö	×	Ø	Ù	Ú	Û
&#0214;	&#0215;	&#0216;	&#0217;	&#0218;	&#0219;
Ü	Ý	Þ	ß	à	á
&#0220;	&#0221;	&#0222;	&#0223;	&#0224;	&#0225;

â	ã	ä	å	æ	ç
&#0226;	&#0227;	&#0228;	&#0229;	&#0230;	&#0231;
è	é	ê	ë	ì	í
&#0232;	&#0233;	&#0234;	&#0235;	&#0236;	&#0237;
î	ï	ð	ñ	ò	ó
&#0238;	&#0239;	&#0240;	&#0241;	&#0242;	&#0243;
ô	õ	ö	÷	ø	ù
&#0244;	&#0245;	&#0246;	&#0247;	&#0248;	&#0249;
ú	û	ü	ý	þ	ÿ
&#0250;	&#0251;	&#0252;	&#0253;	&#0254;	&#0255;

Valuable Links

Links to Search Engines

This appendix includes a list of some of the more popular search engines, each of which accepts submissions of personal pages. Whether they will post them is another story.

If you do submit your pages, you should check back within a month to see if it has been posted. If not, you will want to resubmit.

Ahoy!

http://ahoy.cs.washington.edu:6060/

AltaVista

http://www.altavista.com/

Apollo—The Web's Advertising Catalog

http://www.shopathome.com/

BizAds Business Locator

http://bizads.2cowherd.net/

ComFind—A Business Directory

```
http://www.allbusiness.com/directory/index.jsp?
```

EuroSeek

```
http://www.euroseek.net/page?ifl=uk
```

Excite

```
http://www.excite.com
```

Galaxy

```
http://www.galaxy.com/
```

Google

```
http://www.google.com
```

Humor Search Comedy Search Engine

```
http://www.humorsearch.com/
```

HotBot

```
http://hotbot.lycos.com/
```

Human Search—Real Humans Do the Search for You

```
http://www.humansearch.com/
```

Go.com

```
http://www.go.com
```

Inktomi

```
http://www.inktomi.com
```

Internet Sleuth

```
http://www.isleuth.com/
```

Lycos

http://www.lycos.com

MoneySearch—Geared to Small Business and Investment

http://www.moneysearch.com/

Nerd World Media

http://headlines.nerdworld.com/

PedagoNet—Geared to Teaching and Learning Sites

http://www.pedagonet.com/

Planet Search

http://www.planetsearch.com/

Rescue Island

http://www.rescueisland.com/

SoftSearch—Geared to Finding Software Programs

http://www.softsearch.com/

Webcrawler

http://www.webcrawler.com/

Websurfer

http://www.gowebsurfer.com/

What-U-Seek

http://www.whatuseek.com/

WWWomen—Geared to Finding Sites Regarding Women's Issues

http://www.wwwomen.com/

WWWW (The World Wide Web Worm)

http://www.goto.com/

Yahoo!

http://www.yahoo.com/

Search for Search Engines

If you couldn't find what you were looking for, don't fear. There are well over 500 search engines on the World Wide Web covering every imaginable topic. Here are a few links to pages that can help you search for search engines:

Beaucoup's Search Engines—Close to 600 at Last Count

http://www.beaucoup.com/engines.html

Dr. Webster's Big Page of Search Engines

http://www.drwebster.com/search/search.htm

Search.Com—From C-Net Central

http://www.search.com/

Yahoo!'s Search Engine Page—The Mother Lode

http://search.yahoo.com/bin/search?p=Search+Engines

Registering with Search Engines

To get people to your site, you must let them know your site is there. The best way to do that is to register your site with search engines. Here are a few sites you might find helpful in your quest for more visitors:

@Submit!

http://uswebsites.com/submit/

1–2–3–Register Me!

http://www.123registerme.com/

AnsurWeb Services

http://www.e-accountant-pro.com/

Add Me!

http://www.addme.com/

Linkosaurus

https://secure.rt66.com/swestart/linkosaurus.html

Postmaster

http://www.netcreations.com/postmaster/

Register-It!

http://register-it.netscape.com/

Submit-It!

http://submitit.bcentral.com/

Sites Offering JavaScripts

This is a list of sites offering JavaScripts for downloading:

Danny Goodman's JavaScript Pages

http://www.dannyg.com/javascript/index.html

HotSyte

http://www.serve.com/hotsyte/

JavaScript Authoring Guide

http://developer.netscape.com/docs/manuals/index.html

JavaScript FAQ

http://www.sqrl.com/

JavaScript Planet

```
http://www.geocities.com/SiliconValley/7116/
```

JavaScript World

```
http://www.mydesktop.com/internet/javascript/
```

JavaScripts.com

```
http://webdeveloper.earthweb.com/pagedev/webjs
```

Yahoo!'s Java Script Page

```
http://www.yahoo.com/Computers_and_Internet/Programming_Languages/
```

Pages Offering Java Applets

This is a list of sites offering Java applets for downloading:

Gamelan

```
http://www.gamelan.com
```

Jars.Com—A Massive Site with Links and Reviews

```
http://www.jars.com/
```

Java Boutique

```
http://javaboutique.internet.com/
```

Java Centre

```
http://www.java.co.uk/
```

SneakerChat—Applets for Creating Chat Rooms

```
http://www.sneakerchat.com/
```

Yahoo!'s Applet Page

```
http://www.yahoo.com/Computers_and_Internet/Programming_Languages/Java/Applets/
```

HTML Helper Applications

Try these sites for HTML assistant programs. Some are free, some are shareware, and some want the money up front.

MS FrontPage

http://www.microsoft.com/frontpage/

Globetrotter Web Assistant

http://www.akimbo.com/globetrotter/index.html

HotDog

http://www.sausage.com/default.php

HoTMetaL

http://www.akimbo.com/globetrotter/index.html

HTML Assistant

http://www.exit0.com/ns/home.html

HTMLpad

http://www.intermania.com/htmlpad/index.html

Web Director

http://www.webdirector.com/

Yahoo!'s HTML Editors

http://dir.yahoo.com/computers_and_internet/software/reviews/internet/web_
authoring_tools/html_editors/

Yahoo!'s HTML Editor Review Page

http://www.yahoo.com/Computers_and_Internet/Software/Reviews/Titles/Internet/Web_
Authoring_Tools/HTML_Editors/

Internet Browsers

More than one or two browsers are out there. There may also be a newer version of the browser you are currently using. You have to know where to find them. These are the download sites for some of the different World Wide Web browsers:

Cello

ftp://ftp.law.cornell.edu/pub/LII/Cello/

HotJava—A Java-based Browser from Sun Microsystems

http://java.sun.com/products/hotjava/index.html

Lynx—A Text-only Browser

http://lynx.browser.org/

Microsoft Internet Explorer

http://www.microsoft.com/windows/ie/default.htm

Mosaic for Windows

http://archive.ncsa.uiuc.edu/SDG/Software/WinMosaic/HomePage.html

Mosaic for Macintosh

http://archive.ncsa.uiuc.edu/SDG/Software/MacMosaic/MacMosaicHome.html

NetCruiser

http://www.earthlink.net

Netscape Communicator—A Suite of Programs Including the Navigator

http://home.netscape.com/browsers/index.html

NetTamer—A DOS-based Browser

http://people.delphi.com/davidcolston/

Opera

http://www.opera.com/

Voyager—Made for the Amiga Computer

http://www.vapor.com/voyager/

WinWeb

http://www.galaxy.com/

Yahoo!'s Browser Page

http://dir.yahoo.com/Computers_and_Internet/Software/Internet/World_Wide_Web/
Browsers/

Index

Symbols

& (ampersand) commands, 532-533

* (asterisk), frames, 207

: (colon), style sheet commands, 252

[cw] (copyright) symbol, placing on Web pages, 456-457

{ } (curly brackets), style sheet commands, 252

> (greater than sign), flags, 17

< (less than sign), flags, 17

(pound sign), internal page jumps, 81

? (question mark), link buttons, 221

; (semicolon),
    frames, 213
    style sheet commands, 252

~ (tilde), absolute paths, 372

!-- --> flag (comments), 58

!-- //--> flags, hiding text (JavaScript), 334-345

  code, 67

  attribute, layering images, 280

1x1 images, 105-106

1–2–3–Register Me! Web site, 540

404 error pages, 509-511

A

<A HREF> flag, 29-30, 78. See also links
    code words for internal page jumps, 81-82
    imagemap command, 151
        client-side imagemaps, 156-157
        server-side imagemaps, 150-152
    mailto command, 31-32

<A NAME> flag, 81-83

<ABBR> flag (abbreviated text), 56, 518

absolute paths (hit counters), 372-373

Acclaim Web Services Web site, 541

<ACRONYM> flag, 56, 519

ACTION attribute, link buttons, 220

activating banners, 452-453

active (clickable) images, 84-86. See also thumbnails, 108
    creating, 36-38, 84-85
    HTML Goodies Web site examples, 36, 86
    imagemaps. See imagemaps
    removing blue borders, 85-86

active channels (Internet Explorer), 388-390
    creating, 390-391
        flags, 394
    creating links to pages, 390-394
        creating Channel Definition Format (.cdf) files, 391-392
        <ITEM> flag, 393
        <SCHEDULE> flag, 393-394
        <USAGE VALUE=> flag, 393
    FAQs
        animated images, 392
        automatically giving channels to visitors, 389

547

location of pushed files, 389
screen appearance, 390
Add Me! Web site, 541
Add To Favorites buttons
HTML Goodies example, 412
HTML Goodies tutorial, 411
additive color, 530
addresses
<ADDRESS> flag, 56
links, 31
source code, search engines, 239-240
Web pages. *See* URLs (Uniform Resource Locators)
advertising, 483-487
costs, 484
click-throughs, 485
flat rate CPM, 485
HTML Goodies, 485
number of impressions, 485
obtaining advertisers, 484-487
advertising banners, 417
activating on pages, 452-453
animating images, 443-447
adding time sequences, 445-447
creating animation lists, 444-445
finishing the animated GIF, 447
cookies, 466
FAQs
animation, 447
copying/pasting images, 430
cropping images, 428

file size, 451
fonts, 440
image formats, 424
location on page, 451
revenues, 383
saving images, 435
shadowing tool versus double pasting, 442
target audience, 449
text size, 438
tracking visitors, 452
HTML Goodies Web site
Banner Primer 4 image downloads, 435
example banners, 419, 445
free images, 420
HTML Goodies banner, 453
template image download, 425
text banner download, 443
ticket image download, 425
images
animating, 446-447
copying and pasting, 433
creating, 422-425
creating different versions of images for animation, 433-435
cropping, 425-428
images needed for text animation, 420-421
importing (copying and pasting), 428-432
saving, 423-425
placing (other sites)
banner-swap programs, 449-450
buying page space, 448-449

offering banners for free, 450
trading page space, 449
positioning, 450-451
software tools required, 417-418
text, 436
color, 436-438
font, 438-441
shadow, 441-444
size, 441
tracking visitors, 452
Ahoy! search engine, 537
Alchemy Mindworks, Inc. Web site, 117
alert event handler (JavaScript), 325, 328-329
using with onClick, 329
using with onMouseOver, 328-329
ALIGN attribute
<HR> flag, 126-127
<IMG> flag, 39-41, 99-101
tables, 98-99
wrapping text, 96-97
inline frames, 400
layering images, 280
scrolling marquees (<MARQUEE> flag), 387
alignment
cross-platform browser tips, 482
fake imagemaps, 161
horizontal rules, 126-127
images
placement on page, 39-40
table cells, 172-173
with text, 40-41, 96-102. *See also* images, alignment with text
inline frames (Internet Explorer), 399-400
link buttons, 221-224

tables, 169-170
text, 25-26
ALT attribute
  cross-platform browser tips,
    479
  <IMG> flag, 103-104
AltaVista Web site, 241, 537
American Standard Code for
  Information Interchange.
  See ASCII
ampersand (&) commands,
  532-533
animated images
  animated GIFs, 116-118
    animating the images,
      120-123
    banners. *See* banners
    creating GIF images,
      118-120
    placing animated
      images on pages, 124
    SMPTE Code (Society of
      Motion Picture and
      Television Engineers
      Code), 116
    software, 117-118, 418
  banner ads, 443-447
    adding time sequences,
      445-447
    creating animation lists,
      444-445
    finishing the animated
      GIF, 447
Apollo Web site, 537
applets (Java), 311-313
  compiling, 315
  copyright infringement,
    313
  cross-platform browser tips,
    480
  dancing text applet,
    314-315
    downloading applet,
      315-316

HTML code, 316-317
  modifying parameters,
    317-318
  uploading modified
    applet, 319-320
recognition of applets by
  browsers, 313
Web sites, 542
<APPLET> flag
  dancing text applet, 316
  HTML 4.0, 522
ASCII (American Standard
  Code for Information
  Interchange), 49
  commands, 533-535
  FTP transfer mode, 48-50
  iso-8859-1 charset versus
    us-ascii, 508-509
  transferring files, 49
  versus binary, 49
asterisk (*), frames, 207
attributes, 24-26. *See also*
  commands; flags
   , layering images,
    280
  ACTION, link buttons, 220
  ALIGN, layering images,
    280
  BGPROPERTIES=*fixed*,
    static backgrounds (IE),
    384
  BORDERCOLOR (<TABLE>
    flag), 186
  CENTER, layering images,
    280
  COLS
    <FRAMESET> flag,
      191-192
    text area box forms, 227
  HEIGHT
    banner ads, 450-451
    resizing images, 109

HTML 4.0, 520-521
  <CLASS>, 522
  <DIR>, 523
  HTML Goodies tutorial,
    524
  <ID>, 523
  <LANG>, 523
  <TITLE>, 523
LEFT, positioning images,
  279
METHOD, link buttons,
  220
NAME
  AutoComplete (Internet
    Explorer), 246-247
  drop-down box forms,
    232
  layering images, 279
  radio button forms, 229
  text area box forms, 227
  text box forms, 226
ROWS
  <FRAMESET> flag,
    193-194
  text area box forms, 227
SELECTED, drop-down box
  forms, 232
SIZE=
  drop-down box forms,
    232
  text box forms, 226
TABINDEX, 242-243
<TD> flag
  COLSPAN, 174-175
  ROWSPAN, 175-177
  WIDTH, 176-177
TOP, positioning images,
  279
TYPE, radio button forms,
  229
VALUE
  eliminating VALUE text
    automatically, 244-245

link buttons, 220
radio button forms, 229
WIDTH
    banner ads, 450-451
    resizing images, 109
    sideline images, 134
audio. *See* sound
audio/video interleaved (AVI),
    304. *See also* video
    helper applications, 309
author META command,
    using with search engines,
    473
AutoComplete, 245-248
    clearing saved responses,
        247-248
    disabling, 247
    HTML Goodies Web site
        example, 245
        tutorial, 245
AVI (audio/video interleaved),
    304. *See also* video
    helper applications, 309

B

Back and Forward buttons,
    creating with JavaScript,
    329-330
backgrounds, 128
    color
        onClick event handler
            (JavaScript), 328-329
        onMouseOver event
            handler (JavaScript),
            327-328
        style sheets, 270
        text background,
            262-263, 270
    HTML Goodies Web site
        examples, 131
    sideline backgrounds,
        131-135
        color, 133

placing items on the
    stripe, 133-135
removing text from the
    stripe, 133
right-side borders, 135
text, 133
sound
    cross-platform browser
        tips, 480
    Internet Explorer, 384
    playing background
        MIDI files with
        JavaScript, 338-339
    static, 384
    style sheet definitions, 254
tables
    cell color, 182-183
    images, 184
wallpaper, 128-129
    creating, 129-130
    guidelines for use, 130
bandwidth, 301
banners, 417-422. *See also*
  advertising
    activating on pages,
        452-453
    animating images, 445-447
        adding time sequences,
            445-447
        creating animation lists,
            444-445
        finishing the animated
            GIF, 447
    banner exchange network,
        450
    cookies, 466
    FAQs
        advertising revenues,
            383
        animation, 447
        copying/pasting images,
            430
        cropping images, 428

file size, 451
fonts, 440
image formats, 424
location on page, 451
saving images, 435
shadowing tool versus
    double pasting, 442
target audience, 449
text size, 438
tracking visitors, 452
HTML Goodies Web site
    Banner Primer 4 image
        downloads, 435
    example banners, 419,
        445
    free images, 420
    HTML Goodies banner,
        453
    template image down-
        load, 425
    text banner download,
        443
    ticket image download,
        425
images
    animating, 446-447
    copying and pasting,
        433
    creating, 422-425
    creating different
        versions of images for
        animation, 433-435
    cropping, 425-428
    images needed for text
        animation, 420-421
    importing (copying and
        pasting), 428-432
    saving, 423-425
placing (other sites)
    banner-swap programs,
        449-450
    buying page space,
        448-449

offering banners for
free, 450
trading page space, 449
positioning, 450-451
software tools required,
417
GIF animator programs,
418
graphics programs,
417-418
text, 436
color, 436-438
font, 438-441
shadow, 441-444
size, 441
tracking visitors, 452
<BASE HREF> flag, 286-287
<BASEFONT> flag, 57
HTML 4.0, 522
BBS (billboard server), 379
downloading CGI script,
379
emptying BBS.html pages,
381
FAQ, 381
HTML document, 380-381
personalizing the script,
379-380
<BDO> flag, 57, 519
Beaucoup's Search Engines
Web site, 540
begin (open) flags, 19
BEHAVIOR command,
scrolling marquees (<MAR-
QUEE> flag), 387
beta versions, 517
BGCOLOR command
scrolling marquees (<MAR-
QUEE> flag), 387
table cells, 183
BGPROPERTIES=*fixed* com-
mand, 130
static backgrounds (IE),
384

<BGSOUND> flag, 298
<BIG> flag, 57
billboard server (BBS), 379
downloading CGI script,
379
emptying BBS.html pages,
381
FAQ, 381
HTML document, 380-381
personalizing the script,
379-380
binary
bits (binary digits), 48
FTP binary transfer mode,
49-50
versus ASCII, 49
bitmaps, 35, 139-140
compression, 140-142
bits, 48
BizAds Business Locator Web
site, 537
blank lines (<P> flag), 101
blanket fee licenses, 461
<BLINK> flag, 57
<BLOCKQUOTE> flag, 57. *See
also* <Q> flag; <SPAN> flag,
61
.bmp (bitmap) images. *See*
bitmaps
<BODY> flag, 322
frames, 190-191
bold text, 18-19
<B> flag, 56
<STRONG> flag, 62
bookmarks
Add To Favorites buttons,
411-413
bookmark icons (Internet
Explorer), 408-409
HTML Goodies Web site
example, 409
icon, 409-410
non-personal domains,
410
framed pages, 198

BORDER command
<FRAMESET> flag, 201
sideline backgrounds, 135
BORDERCOLOR command
<FRAMESET> flag, 214
setting for Internet
Explorer, 385
<TABLE> flag, 186
borders
frames
color, 213-214
preventing resizing,
202-203
resizing, 201
imagemaps
client-side, 155
fake, 161
server-side, 153
images
active (clickable) images,
36-38, 85-86
increasing border size,
38
inline frames (Internet
Explorer), 397-399
sideline backgrounds, 135
tables, 168-169
color, 184-186
<BR CLEAR=*all*> flag, 101
breaks
<NOBR> flag, 61
text, 20
<WBR> flag, 63
browsers, 544-545
charsets, 506-509
HTML code, 507
iso-8859-1 versus us-
ascii, 508-509
commands that don't work
in certain browsers, 76
cookies. *See* cookies
cross-platform tips, 477
aligning text/images,
482

ALT commands, 479
background sounds, 480
colors, 482
DHTML, 482
frames, 479
GIFs versus JPEGs, 481
imagemaps, 479
JavaScript, 480
META refresh commands, 482
monitor resolution, 482
page layout, 480
page width, 480-481
simple page content, 483
style sheets, 478-479
testing pages on multiple browsers, 477
text formatting/wrapping, 478
widths, 480-481
writing for pickiest browser, 478
disabled assistant browsers, 503-506
DTDs, 493
e-mail preferences, setting, 31
frames display, 195
opening frames in a new, full browser window, 198
helper applications, 294-295
HTML 4.0 support, 514
Java applet detection, 313
links that open new browser windows, 87-88
loading different pages for different browsers (JavaScript browser choice script), 345-347

non-frames compatible browsers, 198-199
opening Web pages, 13
overriding browser default fonts (<BASEFONT> flag), 57
plug-ins, 295-296
RealAudio. *See* RealAudio
pop-up windows. *See* JavaScript, opening new windows
refreshing pages automatically (meta-refresh command), 88-90
setting home pages, 413-416
sideline backgrounds, 133
viewing cookies, 468
Web site URLs, 544-545

 flag, 20
buffers (RealAudio), 301-303
bulleted lists, 68-70
bullet formats/images, 69-70
combining with numbered lists, 72-73
FAQs, 68, 73
buttons
Add To Favorites, 411-413
HTML code, 411-412
HTML Goodies Web site example, 412
HTML Goodies Web site tutorial, 411
adding colored buttons with style sheets, 271
Back and Forward, creating with JavaScript onClick event handler, 329-330
e-mail, creating with JavaScript onClick event handler, 332-333

Guestbook image submit buttons, 237
inline frames (Internet Explorer), 397-398
link buttons, 219-220
? (question mark), 221
creating, 220-221
HTML Goodies Web site examples, 221, 224
HTML Goodies Web site tutorials, 219, 221
lining up, 221-224
radio buttons, 228-229
Reset, 232-233
Send, 232-233
setting browser home pages, 415-416
submit buttons
forms, 232-233
Guestbooks, 237
<BUTTON> flag, 519
buying page space for banners, 448-449
<B> flag, 18-19, 56

C

C-Net's Table of Style Sheet Commands Web site, 258
calendars, creating with tables, 179-182
Campaign Against Frames Web site, 189
<CAPTION> flag, 167
capturing video, 307-308
cascading style sheets. *See* CSS
case sensitivity of flags, 18
.cdf (Channel Definition Format), 391
creating .cdf files, 391-392
Cello browser Web site, 544
CELLPADDING command, sideline backgrounds, 134.
See also tables

cells (tables)
background color, 182-183
background images, 184
cell width, 176-177
column span, 174-175
creating, 167
creating links, 170
calendars, 181
images in cells, 171
centering, 172-173
framing images, 172
padding, 169
row span, 175-176
HTML Goodies Web site
examples, 177
spacing, 169
text color, 183-184
CELLSPACING command,
sideline backgrounds, 134.
See also tables
centering
images, 39
layering images, 280
table cells, 172-173
in text, 97-98
text, 25-26
<CENTER> flag, 26
HTML 4.0, 522
images, 39
Central Ad Pro Web site, 485
CGI (Common Gateway
Interface), 150, 363
billboard server (BBS), 379
downloading CGI script,
379
emptying BBS.html
pages, 381
HTML document,
380-381
personalizing the script,
379-380
FAQs
billboard servers (BBS),
381

Guestbook return pages,
378
Guestbook trou-
bleshooting, 378
hit counters, 364, 367,
373, 375
Guestbooks, 375-376
activating Guestbook,
378-379
adding Guestbook script
to Web pages, 377
cgi-bin directory, 375
downloading Guestbook
script, 375-377
modifying Sendmail
portion of script, 377
return pages, 378
hit counters, 364-368
creating directories with
FTP, 369
creating directories with
Telnet, 370
creating CGI directories,
371
disadvantages, 364
downloading counter
script, 371
finding counters on
Internet, 365-368
finding absolute paths,
372-373
format, 365
installing, 373
placing HTML on pages,
373-374
preparing the script,
371-372
protecting from outside
use, 374-375
starting counter from a
certain number, 374

HTML Goodies Web site
billboard server (BBS)
example, 379
billboard server (BBS)
HTML document, 380
billboard server (BBS)
script, 379
counter script down-
load, 371
Guestbook example,
375-376
hit counter tutorials,
364, 368
primers, 363, 375,
378-379
server-side imagemaps,
150-152
shopping cart order forms,
353-354
Channel Definition Format
(.cdf), 391
creating cdf files, 391-392
<CHANNEL> flag, 392
characters
creating with ampersand
(&) commands, 532-533
creating with ASCII com-
mands, 533-535
charsets, 506-509
HTML code, 507
iso-8859-1 versus us-ascii,
508-509
check bits, 48
check box forms, 229-230
CineWeb Web site, 309
<CITE> flag, 58
CLASS attribute (HTML 4.0),
520
classes, style sheets, 264-267
clearing AutoComplete forms
(Internet Explorer), 247-248
click-throughs (advertising
costs), 485

clickable buttons. *See* link buttons

client-side imagemaps, 155-156
 HTML Goodies Web site tutorial, 155
 imagemap command, 156-157
 making maps, 155-156
 map coordinates, 157
 placing images on pages, 156-157

close (end) flags, 19

closing
 pop-up windows, 338
 Web pages, 20

code. *See also* HTML
 HotBot, 241
 Webcrawler and Excite searches, 239
 Yahoo! search, 239

CODE command, Java applets, 316-317

<CODE> flag, 58

code words
 <A HREF> flag, 81-82
 <A NAME> flag, 81-83

COLGROUP> flag, 519

colon (:), style sheet commands, 252

color
 additive color, 530
 backgrounds
  onClick event handler (JavaScript), 328-329
  onMouseOver event handler (JavaScript), 327-328
  style sheets, 270
 buttons, adding with style sheets, 271
 cross-platform browser tips, 482

FAQs, 64-65
frame borders, 213-214
hexadecimal codes, 63-64, 527-532
 hexadecimal notation, 531-532
 HTML Goodies chart Web site, 527
 tables, 183
Java applet color codes, dancing text applet, 317
non-dithering, 527, 530
 HTML Goodies chart, 530
 HTML Goodies tutorial, 527
scrollbars, 276-277
scrolling marquees, 387
sideline backgrounds, 133
subtractive color, 530
tables, 182-186
 borders, 184-186
 cell backgrounds, 182-183
 Internet Explorer, 385
 text, 183-184
text, 63-65
 banner ads, 436-438
 <FONT COLOR> flag, 59
 HTML Goodies tutorial, 64
 links, 64-65
 multiple words, 64
 setting with style sheets, 262-263, 270
 single words, 65
 style sheets, 253
COLOR attribute, <FONT> flag, 59
COLS attribute
 <FRAMESET> flag, 191-192
 <MULTICOL> flag, 76
 text area box forms, 227

COLSPAN attribute, <TD> flag, 174-175
 HTML Goodies Web site examples, 177
 using with ROWSPAN, 177
columns
 FAQ, 76
 frames, 191-192
  combining with rows, 193-194
 HTML Goodies Web site, 76
 <MULTICOL> flag, 60, 75-76
 <SAMP> flag, 62
 tables. *See also* cells (tables), 175
  span, 174-175
  width, 167
combining
 flags, 19
  <FONT COLOR> and <FONT SIZE>, 65
 lists, 72-73
ComFind Web site, 538
commands. *See also* attributes; flags
 & (ampersand) commands, 532-533
 © ([cw] symbol), 456
 ALIGN=*###*
  inline images, 400
  scrolling marquees (<MARQUEE> flag), 387
 ALT, cross-platform browser tips, 479
 ASCII commands, 533-535
 BEHAVIOR=*###*, scrolling marquees (<MARQUEE> flag), 387

BGCOLOR, scrolling marquees (<MARQUEE> flag), 387

BGPROPERTIES=*fixed*, 130

BORDER, sideline backgrounds, 135

BORDERCOLOR=*###*, setting for Internet Explorer, 385

CELLPADDING/CELLSPACING. *See also* tables, 135
   sideline backgrounds, 134

CODE, Java applets, 316-317

DIRECTION=*###*, scrolling marquees (<MARQUEE> flag), 387

FRAME=*###*, setting for Internet Explorer, 385

HEAD commands, HTML Goodies Web site examples, 288

HEIGHT
   inline images, 399
   Java applets, 317
   scrolling marquees (<MARQUEE> flag), 387

HSPACE=*###*, scrolling marquees (<MARQUEE> flag), 387

HTML 4.0, 516-520
   <CLASS>, 522
   <DIR>, 523
   dead commands, 524
   deprecated commands, 524
   HTML 4.0 attributes tutorial, 522
   HTML 4.0 flags tutorial, 520
   <ID>, 523

<LANG>, 523
<TITLE>, 523

HTTP-EQUIV, page transitions, 407

IFRAME, 395

imagemap (<A HREF> flag)
   client-side, 156-157
   server-side, 150-152

Internet Explorer, 386

JavaScript event handlers
   alert, 325, 328-329
   onClick, 325, 328-329
   onClick, Back and Forward buttons, 329-330
   onClick, e-mail buttons, 332-333
   onClick, links within pages, 330-332
   onLoad, 322-323, 333
   onMouseOut, 325
   onMouseOver, 325-328

layering images, 277-280

LEFTMARGIN=
   Internet Explorer, 384
   sideline backgrounds, 133

LOOP, scrolling marquees (<MARQUEE> flag), 387

MAP NAME=, 158

MARGINHEIGHT/MARGINWIDTH, inline images, 400

META commands, 285-286
   cross-platform browser tips, 482
   meta-refresh, 88-90

NAME
   multiple inline frames, 396
   shopping carts, 352

NORESIZE=*###*, inline images, 400

onLoad
   JavaScript, 345
   usage as JavaScript event handler, 333

RULES=*###*, setting for Internet Explorer, 385

SCROLLAMOUNT/SCROLLDELAY, scrolling marquees (<MARQUEE> flag), 387

SCROLLING=*###*, inline images, 400

style sheets, 251-252
   classes, 264-267
   defining flags, 252
   FONT/TEXT definitions, 252-253
   handling the same flag different ways, 256
   IDs, 264-268
   MARGIN/BACKGROUND definitions, 254
   positioning/division definitions, 255
   scrollbar color, 276
   using STYLE command on individual items, 257, 263-264
   Web site resources, 258

TABINDEX, 242-243

TITLE, 271

TOPMARGIN=, Internet Explorer, 384

TYPE=, shopping carts, 352

VALUE=, shopping carts, 352

VSPACE=*###*, scrolling marquees (<MARQUEE> flag), 387

WIDTH
   inline images, 399
   Java applets, 317

555

scrolling marquees
(<MARQUEE> flag),
387
<COMMENT> flag, 58
Common Gateway Interface.
See CGI
compiling Java applets, 315
compression
images, 140-142
JPEG, 35
video, 307
FAQ, 307
Intel Indeo, 305
cookies, 463-470
banners, 466
concerns, 469-470
HTML Goodies site,
467-468
security, 469-470
shopping carts (JavaScript),
349-350
temporary versus persis-
tent, 466-468
viewing, 468
coordinates, client-side
imagemaps, 157
copying
banner images, 428-433
Java applets, 313
copyright META command,
using with search engines,
473
copyrights, 457-463
artist been dead 50 years,
462
blanket fee licenses, 461
changing existing Web
pages, 459
defending, 460
Fair Use Doctrine,
459-461
global, 458
HTML code from Web
pages, 15

images, 36, 93, 458
infringement
applets, 313
avoiding, 462
knowing, 460
minors, 461
without knowing, 460
without permission, 460
Internet, 455-456, 463
sounds, 293
length, 457
links
copyrighted pages, 456
to images, 461
minors, 458
placing copyrights on
items, 456
© symbol, 456-457
registering with
Copyright Office, 457
placing copyrights on Web
pages, 456-457
public domain, 462
same item, two different
people, 458
satires, 459
scanning, 462
screen captures, 497
sound
FAQ, 293
music and video, 461
titles (Web pages), 458
Web resources, 463
costs
advertising, 484
Web page hosting, 46
counters, 364-365
disadvantages, 364
FAQs, 364, 367, 373, 375
finding counters on the
Internet, 365-368
ISPs, 366
obtaining permission,
366-367

private sites, 366-367
public domain, 366-368
format, 365
installing counters, 368
creating CGI directories,
371
creating directories with
FTP, 369
creating directories with
Telnet, 370
downloading counter
script, 371
finding absolute paths,
372-373
placing HTML on pages,
373-374
preparing counter script,
371-372
protecting counters
from outside use,
374-375
starting counter from a
certain number, 374
tracking banner visitors,
452
cropping images for banners,
425-428
cross-platform browser tips,
477
aligning text/images, 482
ALT commands, 479
background sounds, 480
colors, 482
DHTML, 482
frames, 479
GIFs versus JPEGs, 481
imagemaps, 479
JavaScript, 480
META refresh commands,
482
monitor resolution, 482
page layout, 480
page width, 480-481
simple page content, 483

style sheets, 478-479

testing pages on multiple browsers, 477

text wrapping/formatting, 478

widths, 480-481

writing for pickiest browser, 478

CSS (cascading style sheets), 249-250

classes, 264-267

commands, 251-252

defining flags, 252

FONT/TEXT definitions, 252-253

handling the same flag different ways, 256

MARGIN/BACKGROUND definitions, 254

positioning/division definitions, 255

using STYLE command on individual items, 257, 263-264

Web site resources, 258

cursor properties, 272-274

forms, 268-270

background color, 270

colored buttons, 271

text color, 270

ToolTips, 271

<HEAD> flag, 287-288

HTML Goodies Web site examples, 250

IDs, 264-265, 267-268

inline, 250-251

Netscape Navigator versus Internet Explorer, 250

positioning items, 258

HTML Goodies examples, 258

images, 259-260

text, 261-262

scrollbars, 274-275

color, 276-277

main document scrollbar, 275

textarea scrollbar, 275-276

span, 256-257

text color, 262-263, 270

curly brackets { }, style sheet commands, 252

cursor properties, style sheets, 272-274

customizing pages by screen size (JavaScript), 359

redirecting browsers to pages with specific settings, 360-361

writing items to pages based on screen settings, 361-362

D

dancing text applet (Java), 314-315

downloading applet, 315-316

HTML code, 316-317

modifying parameters, 317-318

uploading modified applet, 319-320

Danny Gooman's JavaScript Pages Web site, 541

databases, 238

HTML Goodies JavaScript-based search engine, 241

HTML Goodies Web site tutorial, 238

searching

one's own site, 240-242

other sites, 238-240

date stamps (JavaScript), 343

calling .js files, 344-345

creating .js files, 343-344

Dave Central's FTP Web site, 47

<DD> flag, 74

dead commands, 524

declaration statements, 517

declaring HTML versions, 288-289

FAQ, 289

HTML Goodies Web site example, 289

definition lists, 73-75

definitions (<DFN> flag), 58

deleted text (<DEL> flag), 58, 519

deprecated commands (HTML 4.0), 522

<DFN> flag, 58

DHTML (Dynamic Hypertext Mark-up Language), 400-408

cross-platform browser tips, 482

FAQs, 401

building DHTML games, 403

Netscape errors, 402

Netscape support, 408

troubleshooting, 405

HTML Goodies Web site examples, 401, 405, 408

tutorials, 401, 404

interactive game, 402-405

page transitions

creating, 406-407

selecting effects, 407-408

placing on Web pages, 404-405

popularity of, 401-402

setting browser home pages, 413-416

HTML Goodies Web site examples, 414, 416

digital video, 306

DIR attribute (HTML 4.0), 521

557

direction of text (<BDO>), 57

DIRECTION=*###* command, scrolling marquees (<MAR-QUEE> flag), 387

directories

absolute paths (hit counters), 372

finding via Telnet, 372-373

creating, 291-292

CGI directories, 371

via FTP, 369

via Telnet, 370

pages without .html extension, 289-290

creating subdirectories, 291-292

FAQ, 291

HTML Goodies Web site tutorial, 290

index pages, 290-291

<DIR> flag, 524

disabled assistant browsers, 503-506

disappearing links, 64

dividing pages (<DIV> flag), 59. *See also* <SPAN> flag

<DL> flag, 74

document declarations, 493

Document Source command (Web browsers), 14

domains, 467

downloading

billboard server (BBS)

CGI script, 379

HTML document, 380

CGI counter script, 371

Guestbook script, 375-377

images, 93-96

HTML Goodies Web site, 36

Java dancing text applet, 315-316

RealAudio files, 301

shareware, 117-118

shopping cart pages, 351

drop-down box forms, 230-232

DTDs (document type definitions)

browsers, 493

HTML, 493-494

SGML, 493

XML, 494-496

<DT> flag, 74

Dynamic Hypertext Mark-up Language. *See* DHTML

dynamic pages (meta-refresh command), 88-90

E

e-mail

creating e-mail buttons with JavaScript onClick event handler, 332-333

creating e-mail links, 31-32

Guestbooks, 235

designating plain text messages, 235

e-mailing multiple addresses, 236

filling out subject line automatically, 236

sendmail command, 377

mailto flag, 31, 235

receiving from Web sites, 31

setting browser preferences, 31

embedding sound, 295-296

cross-platform browser tips, 480

EMBED command, 297-300

FAQ, 299

emphasis text (<EM> flag), 59

ending flags, 18-19

erasing AutoComplete responses (Internet Explorer), 247-248

error pages (404), 509-511

EuroSeek Web site, 538

event handlers (JavaScript), 312, 324-325

alert, 325, 328-329

onClick, 325, 328-333

Add To Favorites buttons, 412

Back and Forward buttons, 329-330

e-mail buttons, 332-333

links within pages, 330-332

setting browser Home pages, 415-416

onMouseOut, 325

onMouseOver, 325-328

banners, 453

Excite Web site, 538

search code, 239

searching Web sites, 240

expires META command, using with search engines, 474

eXtensible Markup Language. *See* XML

external JavaScripts, 342-343

browser choice script, 345-347

reasons for using, 346

the script, 346-347

uploading pages, 347

date stamp, 343

calling .js files, 344-345

creating .js files, 343-344

hiding text with <!-- //--> flags, 345

shopping carts, 348-349

accepting credit cards, 354

cookies, 349-350
downloading required pages, 351
modifying item pages, 352-353
modifying order page, 353
template, 350-351
using CGIs, 353-354
using multiple scripts in the same .js file, 345

F

FACE attribute, <FONT> flag, 59
Fair Use Doctrine (Copyright Act of 1978), 459
limitations, 459
music and video, 461
Fake Counter Home Page Web site, 367
fake imagemaps, 158-160
HTML Goodies Web site tutorial, 158
images
aligning/putting together, 161
creating, 160
FAQs
active channels (Internet Explorer)
animated images, 392
automatically giving channels to visitors, 389
location of pushed files, 389
screen appearance, 390
banners
advertising revenues, 383
animation, 447
copying/pasting images, 430

cropping images, 428
file size, 451
fonts, 440
image formats, 424
location on page, 451
saving images, 435
shadowing tool versus double pasting, 442
target audience, 449
text size, 438
tracking visitors, 452
CGI
billboard servers (BBS), 381
Guestbook return pages, 378
hit counters, 364, 367, 373, 375
troubleshooting Guestbooks, 378
color, 64-65
columns, 76
commands that don't work in certain browsers, 76
copyrights, 457-463
DHTML, 401
building DHTML games, 403
Netscape errors, 402
Netscape support, 408
troubleshooting, 405
flag attributes, 26
flags, 18-19, 22
fonts, 66
font images, 25
frames
<BODY> flag, 190-191
bookmarking framed pages, 198
color, 214
filling multiple frame windows with one page, 206

inline frames (Internet Explorer), 395, 400
multiple frames, 212
Netscape Navigator versus Internet Explorer, 195
page size, 192
seamless frames, 209
titles, 191
"_Top" target, 198
FTP transfer modes (Binary versus ASCII), 49
Guestbooks
e-mailing multiple addresses, 236
simply mailto Guestbook format, 385
<HEAD> flag, 284, 287
horizontal line size, 43
HTML declaration, 289
imagemaps
client-side coordinate text placement, 157
fake imagemaps, 160-161
image flips, 342
layering images, 279
server-side, 153-154
images, 34-36, 108
alignment, 40
ALT command, 103
animated GIFs, 117, 123-124
backgrounds, 128, 130
downloading, 94
horizontal rules, 125, 128
LOWSRC command, 112
placing images side-by-side, 96
shareware, 118
sideline backgrounds, 135

size, 42, 103
text wrapping, 98-99, 102
thumbnails, 108, 110
transparent images, 113
java
applet names, 316
<PARAM> flag, 319
resources for learning to write, 312
running multiple applets, 319
troubleshooting error messages, 319
JavaScript
cookies, 349
e-mail buttons, 333
image flips, 339, 342
onLoad command, 345
opening new windows, 334, 336
resources for learning to write, 312
shopping carts, 349, 353-354
troubleshooting error messages, 322
layering images, 279
links, 30-31, 78-82, 85-90
lists, 68-73
removing .html extension from URLs, 291
requirements for creating Web pages, 10
scrolling marquees, 388
sound
copyrights, 293
downloading RealAudio files, 301
embedding, 299
formats, 299
RealAudio servers, 301
recording, 297

style sheets, 258, 270
color codes, 271
image framing color, 272
inline commands, 265
Netscape Navigator versus Internet Explorer, 250
positioning, 260-263
ToolTips, 271
troubleshooting, 257
tables, 168
background images, 184
border color, 186
calendars, 182
cell width, 177
CELLPADDING, 176
color, 183
creating page layouts, 171
flags, 168, 170
table in a table, 179
using VALIGN="top", 175
Telnet, 369
video
compression, 307
RealVideo, 304
reducing file size, 307
Web site hosts, 302
XML FAQ Web site, 496
Favorites (Internet Explorer)
Add To Favorites buttons, 411-413
Favorites icons, 408-409
HTML Goodies Web site example, 409
icon, 409-410
non-personal domains, 410
framed pages, 198
<FIELDSET> flag, 519
File Transfer Protocol, see FTP, 47

files
.cdf, 391-392
.htm, 12
.html, 12
image formats, 35
naming, 12
sound files. *See* sound
.txt, 13
uploading to Web via FTP, 46-50
ASCII versus Binary transfer modes, 48-50
how FTP works, 47-48
video file size, 305-307
film versus video, 305-306
Film.com Web site, 187
finding
search engines, 540
Telnet, 501
fixed-width font (<VAR> flag), 63
flags, 17-18. *See also* commands; attributes
<-- //-->, hiding text (JavaScript), 334-345
<A HREF>, imagemap command, 150-152, 156-157
active channels, 394
<APPLET>, 316
<BASE HREF>, 286-287
<BGSOUND=*###*>, 298
<BODY>
frames, 190-191
JavaScript, 322

, 20, 101
<CAPTION>, 167
case insensitivity, 18
<CHANNEL>, 392
close (end) flags, 19
combining, 19
<FONT COLOR> and <FONT SIZE>, 65
<DD>, 74

deprecated (HTML 4.0), 522
<DL>, 74
<DT>, 74
<EMBED>, 297-300
    FAQ, 299
ending, 18
FAQ, 18
format, 17
<FORM>
    creating back and forward buttons (JavaScript), 330
    frames, 213
    link buttons, 220-222
<FRAME SRC>, 192
    RESIZE="no" attribute, 203
    SCROLLING attribute, 203-204, 209
<FRAMESET>, 192. *See also* frames
    BORDER attribute, 201
    BORDERCOLOR attribute, 214
    COLS attribute, 191-192
    FRAMESPACING attribute, 201-202
    MARGINWIDTH attribute, 202
    NAME attribute, 197
    RESIZE="no" attribute, 203
    ROWS attribute, 193-194
    TARGET attribute, 197-198
<HEAD>, 283-288
    BASE HREF command, 286-287
    FAQ, 284, 287
    JavaScripts, 287-288
    META commands, 285-286

style sheets, 251, 287-288
    TITLE commands, 285
<HR>, 19-20, 124. *See also* horizontal lines
    HEIGHT attribute, 43
    WIDTH attribute, 42-43
<HTML>, 20
HTML 4.0, 516-520
    dead flags, 524
    deprecated flags, 524
    HTML Goodies tutorial, 522
<IFRAME>, 395
images
    ALIGN attribute, 39-41, 96-101
    ALT attribute, 103-104
    <CENTER>, 39
    HEIGHT attribute, 42, 102-103
    LOWSRC attribute, 110-112
    WIDTH attribute, 42, 102-103
<IMG SRC>, 34
    hit counters, 373-374
    ISMAP command, 153, 157
    layering images, 279
    USEMAP command, 157
<INPUT>, 330
    link buttons, 220
    shopping carts, 352
    text box forms, 226
<ITEM>, active channels, 393
<LAYER>, 279
links
    <A HREF>, 29-32, 78, 81-82. *See also* links, 79
    <A NAME>, 81-83
<LI>, 68
mailto, 31

<MARQUEE>, 387
<META>, 285-286
    page transitions, 407
<NOFRAMES>, 198-199
<OL>, 69
    sideline backgrounds, 133
open (begin) flags, 19
<OPTION>, drop-down box forms, 232
order of use, 19
<PARAM> (Java applets), 317-319
Primer 2 Web page, 17
<P>, 20
<SCHEDULE>, active channels, 393-394
<SELECT>, drop-down box forms, 231-232
single flags, 19-20
style sheets, 252
subcommands, 24-26
<TABLE BORDER>, link buttons, 222
tables, 166-167
    <CAPTION>, 167
    <TABLE>, 167-170, 222
    <TD>, 167-168
    <TR>, 167-168
<TD>, 167-168. *See also* tables
    COLSPAN attribute, 174-175
    link buttons, 222
    ROWSPAN attribute, 175-177
    WIDTH attribute, 176-177
text, 55-63
    HTML Goodies Web site text codes tutorial, 56
<TEXTAREA>, 227
<TITLE>, 20, 285

561

<TR>, 167-168. *See also* tables
  link buttons, 222
<UL>, 68-69
uppercase, 18
USAGE VALUE=*###*, active channels, 393
flashing text (<BLINK> flag), 57
flat rate CPM (advertising costs), 485
focus, eliminating VALUE text automatically, 244-245. *See also* tab order
fonts, 65-67
  banner ads, 438-441
  <BASEFONT> flag, 57
  <CODE> flag (monospace font), 58
  FAQs, 25, 66
  HTML Goodies Web site font test, 67
  HTML Goodies Web site tutorial, 66
  images, 25
  <KBD> flag (keyboard-style font), 60
  overriding browser default fonts (<BASEFONT> flag), 57
  size, 24-25
    <SMALL> flag, 61
  style sheet definitions, 252-253
  <TT> flag (typewriter-style font), 63
  <VAR> flag (fixed-width font), 63
<FONT> flag
  COLOR attribute, 59, 65
  FACE attribute, 59
  HTML 4.0, 522
  SIZE attribute, 24-25, 59, 65

foreign languages charsets, 506-509
  HTML code, 507
  iso-8859-1 versus us-ascii, 508-509
formatting
  tables, 168-170
  text, 19. *See also* text; flags, text
    color, 63-65
    cross-platform browser tips, 478
    fonts, 65-67
forms, 224-225
  AutoComplete (Internet Explorer), 245-248
    clearing saved responses, 247-248
    disabling, 247
  buttons. *See* link buttons, 220
  check boxes, 229-230
  creating forms, 224-225
  databases. *See* databases
  drop-down boxes, 230-232
  focus onLoad, 243-244
  HTML Goodies Web site examples, 233
  HTML Goodies Web site tutorials, 219, 224
  radio buttons, 228-229
  Reset buttons, 232-233
  search engines. *See* search engines
  Send buttons, 232-233
  style sheets, 268-270
    background color, 270
    colored buttons, 271
    text color, 270
    ToolTips, 271
  tab order (TABINDEX command), 242-243
  text area boxes, 226-227

  text boxes, 225-226
    eliminating VALUE text automatically, 244-245
<FORM> flag
  creating back and forward buttons (JavaScript), 330
  frames, 213
  link buttons, 220-222
Forward and Back buttons, creating with JavaScript onClick event handler, 329-330
<FRAME> flag, 520
<FRAME SRC> flag, 192
  attributes
    RESIZE="no", 203
    SCROLLING, 203-204, 209
FRAME=*###* command, setting for Internet Explorer, 385
frames, 187-189
  advantages/disadvantages, 195
  bookmarking framed pages, 198
  borders
    color, 213-214
    preventing resizing, 202-203
    resizing, 201
  browser display, 195
  creating simple frames, 189-191, 199-200
    columns, 191-192
    combining columns/rows, 193-194
    rows, 192-193
  cross-platform browser tips, 479
  example Web sites, 187-189

FAQs
    <BODY> flag, 190-191
    bookmarking framed
        pages, 198
    color, 214
    filling multiple frame
        windows with one
        page, 206
    multiple frames, 212
    Netscape Navigator ver-
        sus Internet Explorer,
        195
    page size, 192
    seamless frames, 209
    titles, 191
    "_Top" target, 198
filling multiple frames with
    a single page, 205-206
fitting pages, 192
<FORM> flag, 213
<FRAME SRC> flag, 192
    RESIZE="no" attribute,
        203
    SCROLLING attribute,
        203-204, 209
<FRAMESET> flag, 192,
    520. *See also* frames
attributes
    BORDER, 201
    BORDERCOLOR, 214
    COLS, 191-192
    FRAMESPACING,
        201-202
    MARGINWIDTH, 202
    NAME, 197
    RESIZE="no", 203
    ROWS, 193-194
    TARGET, 197-198
HTML Goodies Web site
    examples, 217
    advanced frames,
        199-200, 206
    inline frames, 400
    multiple frames, 213
    seamless frames, 210

target hypertext links,
    197
HTML Goodies Web site
    tutorials
    frames, 187
    multiple frames, 210
    seamless frames, 206
inline frames. *See* inline
    frames
links
    changing content in
        multiple frames,
        210-213
    opening in a different
        frame, 196-197
    opening in a new, full
        browser window, 198
    opening in the same
        frame, 196
    opening non-frame
        alternative pages,
        198-199
margins, 202
multiple frames, filling,
    205
<NOFRAMES> flag,
    198-199
order numbers, 212-213
preventing pages from
    appearing in frame win-
    dows, 215
preventing pages from not
    appearing in frame win-
    dows, 215-216
proper use versus overuse,
    187-189
scrollbars, 203-204, 209
seamless frames, 206-210
    frame sources, 209-210
    main codes/commands,
        206-208
spacing between frames,
    201-202
framing images, 172

FrontPage Web site, 543
FTP (File Transfer Protocol),
    47
    creating directories, 369
    Dave Central's FTP page,
        47
    uploading Web pages,
        47-50
        ASCII versus Binary
            transfer modes, 48-50
functions, triggering
    (JavaScript), 338

G

Galaxy Web site, 538
Gamelan Web site, 314, 542
games (DHTML), 402-405
generated Web rings, 488
GIF Construction Set
    creating animated GIFs,
        120-123, 445-447
        adding time sequences,
            445-447
        creating animation lists,
            444-445
        finishing the animated
            GIF, 447
    program requirements, 119
    Web site URL, 117
GIFs (Graphics Interchange
    Format), 35, 142-143
    animated GIFs, 116-118
        animating the images,
            120-123
        animator programs, 418
        banners. *See* banners
        creating the GIF images,
            118-120
        placing animated image
            on pages, 124
        software, 117-118
    cross-platform browser tips,
        481

GIF89a format (transparent images), 113
interlaced versus non-interlaced, 143-144
global copyright, 458
Globetrotter Web Assistant Web site, 543
Graphical Interchange Format. *See* GIFs
graphics. *See* GIFs; images
greater than sign (>), flags, 17
Guestbooks, 233, 375-376
  activating Guestbook, 378-379
  adding Guestbook script to Web pages, 377
  cgi-bin directory, 375
  creating, 233-235
  designating plain text messages, 235
  downloading Guestbook script, 375-377
  e-mailing multiple addresses, 236
  FAQs, 378
    e-mailing multiple addresses, 236
    simply mailto Guestbook format, 385
  filling out subject line automatically, 236
  HTML Goodies Web site examples, 236
    image submit button, 237
  HTML Goodies Web site tutorial, 233
  image submit buttons, 237
  mailto, 235
  modifying sendmail portion of script, 377
  return pages, 378
  virtual pages, 236

GUTTER attribute, <MULTI-COL> flag, 76

H

<H#> flag, 23-24, 60
headings, 23-24, 60
<HEAD> flag, 283-288
  BASE HREF command, 286-287
  FAQ, 284, 287
  JavaScripts, 287-288
  META commands, 285-286
  style sheet, 251, 287-288
  TITLE commands, 285
HEIGHT command
  banner ads, 450-451
  <HR> flag, 43
  <IMG> flag, 42, 102-103
  resizing images, 109
  browser pop-up windows, 335
  inline frames, 399
  Java applets, 317
  scrolling marquees (<MARQUEE> flag), 387
helper applications, 294-295. *See also* plug-ins
  HTML assistants, 543
  video, 309
hex codes, 63-64, 527-532
  hexadecimal notation, 531-532
  HTML Goodies chart Web site, 527
  HTML Goodies Web site examples, 65
  table colors, 183
hidden values, search engines, 241
hiding text (JavaScript), 334-345

hit counters, 364-365
  FAQs, 364, 367, 373, 375
  finding counters on the Internet, 365-368
    ISPs, 366
    obtaining permission, 366-367
    private sites, 366-367
    public domain, 366-368
  format, 365
  installing, 368, 373
    creating directories with FTP, 369
    creating directories with Telnet, 370
    creating the CGI directories, 371
    downloading the script, 371
    finding the absolute path, 372-373
    how personal counters work, 369
    placing the HTML on your page, 373-374
    preparing the script, 371-372
    protecting counters from outside use, 374-375
    starting counter from a certain number, 374
  invisible (log files), 367
  tracking banner visitors, 452
home pages
  index pages, 290-291
    subdirectories, 291-292
  links to other pages, 80
  setting browser home pages, 413-416
    HTML Goodies Web site examples, 414, 416

horizontal lines, 19-20, 43, 124
  alignment, 126-127
  creating with images, 105-106
  height, 43, 125-126
  no shading, 126-127
  width, 42-43, 124-125
hosts for Web sites
  FAQ, 302
  Internet service providers (ISPs), 45-46
  uploading files via FTP, 46-50
    ASCII versus Binary transfer modes, 48-50
HotBot Web site, 241, 538
HotDog Web site, 543
HotJava browser Web site, 544
HoTMetaL Web site, 543
HotSyte Web site, 541
<HR> flag, 19-20, 124. *See also* horizontal lines
  HEIGHT attribute, 43
  WIDTH attribute, 42-43
HSPACE=*###* command, scrolling marquees (<MAR-QUEE> flag), 387
htaccess files (404 error pages), 509-511
.htm file extension, 12
.html file extension, 12
  removing from Web page URLs, 289-290
    creating subdirectories, 291-292
    FAQ, 291
    HTML Goodies Web site examples, 292
    index pages, 290-291
HTML (Hypertext Markup Language), 10-11. *See also* flags; commands; attributes
  comments, 58

declarations, 288-289
versions
  4.0. *See* HTML 4.0
  4.01, 513
  declaring, 288-289, 493, 517
versus XML, 494
viewing source code for a Web page, 14-15
Web page copyrights, 15
writing pages, 10, 20-22
  word processors, 11-12
HTML 4.0, 513-520
  browser support, 516
  dead flags, 524
  deprecated flags, 524
  new attributes, 522-523
  new flags, 518-522
HTML assistants, 50-51
  Web site URLs, 543
<HTML> flag, 20
HTML Goodies Web site
  Add To Favorites buttons, 411-412
  advertising costs, 485
  AutoComplete, 245
  banners
    Banner Primer 4 image downloads, 435
    example banners, 419, 445
    free images, 420
    HTML Goodies banner, 453
    template image download, 425
    text banner download, 443
    ticket image download, 425
  bulleted lists, 73
  CGI
    billboard server (BBS), 379-380

counter script download, 371
  Guestbook example, 375-376
  primers, 363, 375, 378
  tutorials, 364, 368
databases
  JavaScript-based search engine, 241
  tutorial, 238
declaration example, 289
DHTML
  examples, 401, 405, 408
  tutorials, 401, 404
directories tutorial, 290
disappearing links, 64
domain report, 467
FAQs
  active channels (Internet Explorer), 389-390, 392
  banners, 383, 424, 428-430, 435, 438-442, 447-452
  CGI billboard servers (BBS), 381
  CGI Guestbooks, 378
  CGI hit counters, 364, 367, 373-375
  color, 64-65
  columns, 76
  DHTML, 401-405, 408
  flag attributes, 26
  flags, 18-19, 22
  font images, 25
  fonts, 66
  frames, 190-192, 195, 198, 206, 209, 212, 214
  FTP transfer modes (Binary versus ASCII), 49
  Guestbooks, 236, 378, 385

<HEAD> flag, 284, 287
horizontal line size, 43
HTML declaration, 289
image alignment, 40
image size, 42
imagemaps, 153-154, 157, 160-161, 279
images, 34-36, 94-99, 102-103, 108-113, 117-118, 123-125, 128-130, 135
inline frames (Internet Explorer), 395, 400
java, 312, 316, 319
JavaScript, 312, 322, 333-336, 339, 342, 345, 349, 353-354
layering images, 279
links, 30-31, 78-82, 85-86, 88-90
lists, 68-73
removing .html extension from URLs, 291
requirements for creating Web pages, 10
scrolling marquees, 388
sound, 293, 297-301
style sheets, 250, 257-265, 270-272
tables, 168-171, 175-179, 182-186
Telnet, 369
video, 304, 307
Web site hosts, 302
focus onLoad example, 244
font test, 67
forms
    examples, 233
    tutorials, 219, 224
frames
    examples, 197, 199-200, 206, 210, 213, 217
    tutorials, 187, 206, 210

Guestbooks
    examples, 236-237
    tutorial, 233
HEAD command examples, 288
hex color codes chart, 527
IE bookmark icon example, 409
imagemaps
    client-side imagemaps tutorial, 155
    examples, 150, 158, 161
    fake imagemaps tutorial, 158
    imagemap tutorial, 150
images
    1x1 image tutorial, 105
    1x1 images examples, 106
    alignment tutorial, 93
    ALT command, 104
    animated GIFs tutorial, 116
    arrows, 119
    backgrounds example, 131
    bitmap examples, 139-141
    clickable images, 36
    determining size example, 104
    downloading example, 96
    free images for download, 36
    GIF examples, 142-144
    horizontal rule tutorial, 124
    image formats tutorial, 135
    JPEG examples, 145-146
    LOWSRC attribute tutorial, 110

LOWSRC command example, 112
    sideline backgrounds, 131, 135
    text alignment tutorial, 96
    thumbnail tutorial, 107, 110
    transparent images , 112, 115
inline frames, 400
Internet Explorer command examples, 386
Java tutorial, 314
JavaScript
    browser choice JavaScript, 347
    browser choice tutorial, 346
    displaying screen settings, 359
    event handler examples, 324
    example script, 320
    external JavaScript example, 345
    image flips tutorial, 339-340
    image flips imagemap example, 342
    onClick/onMouseover commands examples, 333
    opening/closing window example, 339
    primer, 312
    print function, 355
    reading screen settings, 362
    redirection based on screen settings, 360
    scrolling text example, 324

shopping cart example, 350

shopping cart tutorial, 348

link buttons
examples, 221, 224
tutorials, 219, 221

link examples, 31

links
active (clickable) images, 84, 86
dynamic pages (meta-refresh command) tutorial, 88
meta-refresh command (dynamic pages), 90
new browser windows, 87, 88
no underline, 91-92
page jump examples, 81-83

links examples, 80

log files, 467

manipulating images
examples, 39

marquees
example, 388
tutorial, 386

<MULTICOL> flag, 76

non-dithering colors, 530
tutorial, 527

pages with no .html extension, 292

PERL primers, 363, 375, 378-379

search engine fees, 475

setting browser Home
pages examples, 414-416

sound
examples, 300, 304
tutorials, 294, 300

style sheets
examples, 250, 258, 268-269, 272-274, 277-279
printing example, 354
tutorials, 249, 274

TABINDEX examples, 242-244

tables
examples, 173, 177, 182-186
tutorials, 177, 182, 185

text codes, 56

text color, 64-65

tutorials
1x1 images, 105
Add To Favorites buttons, 411
animated GIFs, 116
AutoComplete, 245
border color, 185
browser choice (JavaScript), 346
CGI hit counter, 364, 368
color tables, 182
databases, 238
DHTML, 401, 404
directories, 290
dynamic pages (meta-refresh command), 88
fake imagemaps, 158
fonts, 66
forms, 219, 224
frames, 187
Guestbooks, 233
horizontal rules, 124
HTML 4.0 attributes, 522
HTML 4.0 flags, 520
image alignment, 93
image alignment with text, 96

image flips (JavaScript), 339-340
image formats, 135
image links, 84
imagemaps, 150, 155
Java dancing text applet, 314
link buttons, 219-221
lists, 67
LOWSRC attribute, 110
marquees (Internet Explorer), 386
multiple frames, 210
new windows from links, 87
no underline on links, 91
non-dithering colors, 527
page jumps, 81
scrollbar color, 274
seamless frames, 206
shopping carts (JavaScript), 348
sideline backgrounds, 131
sitelinks, 77
sound, 294, 300
style sheets, 249
tables, 177
thumbnail images, 110
thumbnails, 107
transparent images, 112
video, 304

video
examples, 308
tutorials, 304

viewing/copying HTML source code, 14-15

Web ring example, 488

HTMLpad Web site, 543

HTTP-EQUIV command, 407

Human Search Web site, 538

Humor Search Comedy Search
Engine Web site, 538
hyperlinks. *See* links
Hypertext Markup Language.
See HTML

I

ID attribute (HTML 4.0), 521
ID, style sheets, 264-268
<IFRAME> flag, 395, 520
image flips (JavaScript),
339-341
  calling script, 341-342
  fake imagemaps, 342
  multiple flips on the same
    page, 342
  requirements, 340
  script, 340-341
  specifying graphics, 341
imagemaps, 149
  borders, 161
  client-side, 155-156
    borders, 155
    imagemap command,
      156-157
    making maps, 155-156
    map coordinates, 157
    placing images on
      pages, 156-157
  creating fake imagemaps
    with image flips, 342. *See
    also* image flips
    (JavaScript)
  cross-platform browser tips,
    479
  fake, 158-160
    aligning/putting images
      together, 161
    creating images, 160
  FAQ
    client-side coordinate
      text placement, 157
    fake imagemaps,
      160-161

image flips, 342
layering images, 279
server-side, 153-154
HTML Goodies Web site
  examples
    client-side imagemap,
      158
    fake imagemaps, 161
    server-side imagemaps,
      150
HTML Goodies Web site
  tutorials
    client-side imagemaps,
      155
    fake imagemaps, 158
    imagemaps, 150
  server-side, 149-151
    basic imagemap format,
      154
    borders, 153
    CGI (Common Gateway
      Interface), 150-152
    creating maps, 152
    imagemap command,
      150-152
    placing images, 153
    providing backup links,
      154
images, 33-38
  1x1 images, 105-106
  acquiring, 35-36
    copyrights, 36
  active (clickable) images,
    84-86. *See also* thumb-
    nails
    creating, 36-38, 84-85
    HTML Goodies Web site
      examples, 36, 86
    HTML Goodies Web site
      tutorial, 84
    imagemaps. *See*
      imagemaps
    removing blue borders,
      85-86

alignment, 39-41, 96-102
  centering images, 97-98
  cross-platform browser
    tips, 482
  single lines of text,
    99-100
  tables, 97-99
  two lines of text,
    100-101
  wrapping text, 96-97
animated GIFs, 116-118
  animating the images,
    120-123
  creating the GIF images,
    118-120
  placing animated image
    on a page, 124
  software, 117-118
backgrounds, 128
  guidelines for use, 130
  sideline backgrounds,
    131-135
  tables, 184
  wallpaper, 128-130
banners
  animating, 443, 445-447
  copying and pasting,
    433
  creating, 422-425
  creating different ver-
    sions of images for ani-
    mation, 433-435
  cropping, 425-428
  importing (copying and
    pasting), 428-432
  saving, 423-425
bitmaps, 35, 139-140
  compression, 140-142
borders
  active (clickable) images,
    36-38, 85-86
  increasing border size,
    38
bullets, 70

buttons
  active (clickable) images,
    36-38, 85-86
  Guestbooks submit but-
    tons, 237
compression, 140-142
copyright laws, 93, 458
counters. *See* counters
downloading, 93-96
editing, 147
FAQs, 108
  alignment, 40
  ALT command, 103
  animated GIFs, 117,
    123-124
  backgrounds, 128, 130
  downloading, 94
  horizontal rules, 125,
    128
  layering images, 279
  LOWSRC command,
    112
  placing images side-by-
    side, 96
  shareware, 118
  sideline backgrounds,
    135
  size, 42
  sizing images
    (HEIGHT/WIDTH), 103
  text wrapping, 98-99,
    102
  thumbnails, 108, 110
  transparent images, 113
fonts, 25
formats, 35, 135-136
  bitmaps, 139-142
  choosing formats, 146
  compression, 140-142
  cross-platform browser
    tips, 481
  GIF, 35, 142-144. *See
    also* GIFs
  JPEG, 144-146

Meta/Vector formats,
    138-139
  Raster image formats
    (RIFs), 137-138
  saving images, 147
framing, 172
hard drive location, 34
horizontal lines created
  with images, 105-106
HTML Goodies Web site
  examples
  1x1 images, 106
  ALT command, 104
  arrows, 119
  backgrounds, 131
  bitmaps, 139-141
  clickable images, 36
  determining size, 104
  downloading, 36, 96
  gifs, 142-144
  jpegs, 145-146
  LOWSRC command,
    112
  manipulating images, 39
  sideline backgrounds,
    135
  transparent images, 115
HTML Goodies Web site
  tutorials
  1x1 images, 105
  alignment, 93
  alignment with text, 96
  animated GIFs, 116
  horizontal rules, 124
  image formats, 135
  LOWSRC attribute, 110
  sideline backgrounds,
    131
  thumbnails, 107, 110
  transparent images, 112
imagemaps. *See* imagemaps
<IMG SRC> flag, 34
inserting, 33-34
layering, 277-280

loading low-res versions
  first, 110-112
not showing, 35
pixels, 35, 41
placing images side-by-
  side, 96
positioning with style
  sheets, 259-260
pre-loading (JavaScript),
  357-359
  advantages, 357-358
  command format,
    358-359
saving, 146-147
screen captures, 497-500
size, 41-42, 102-104
  determining image size,
    104
  loading speed, 106
table cells, 171
  centering, 172-173
  framing images, 172
text links to images, 108
thumbnails, 107-110. *See
  also* active (clickable)
  images
  text links to images, 108
  using two images,
    108-109
  using two versions of
    same image, 109-110
ToolTips (alternative text),
  103-104
transparent images, 112-
  116
  creating with LView Pro,
    113-116
troubleshooting, 35
<IMG SRC> flag, 34
  hit counters, 373-374
  ISMAP command, 153, 157
  layering images, 279
  USEMAP command, 157
<IMG> flag

ALIGN attribute, 39-41,
99-101
tables, 98-99
wrapping text, 96-97
ALT attribute, 103-104
HEIGHT attribute, 42,
102-103
LOWSRC attribute,
110-112
WIDTH attribute, 42,
102-103
importing banner images,
428-433
impressions, 484-485
indenting text, 67-68
<BLOCKQUOTE> flag, 57
<Q> flag, 61
index pages, 290-292
InfoSeek Web site, 538
Inktomi Web site, 538
inline frames, 394
altering, 400
buttons, 397
creating, 395
Internet Explorer,
394-395
alignment/size,
399-400
clickable buttons,
397-398
FAQs, 395, 400
HTML Goodies Web site
examples, 400
IFRAME command, 395
invisible frame borders,
397-399
multiple frames,
395-397
invisible borders, 399
multiple, 396-397
inline style sheets, 250-251.
See also style sheets
INPUT TYPE= attribute,
<FORM> flag, 213

<INPUT TYPE> flag, 330
link buttons, 220
text box forms, 226
<INPUT> flag, shopping carts,
352
<INS> flag, 60, 520
Intel Indeo compression rate,
305
interactive games, 402-405
interlaced GIFs, 143-144
internal links. *See* page jumps
Internet
bandwidth, 301
cookies, 463-469
banners, 466
concerns, 469-470
HTML Goodies site,
467-468
temporary versus persis-
tent, 466-468
viewing, 468
copyrights, 455-456, 463.
See also copyrights
finding CGI counters,
365-368
ISPs, 366
obtaining permission,
366-367
private sites, 366-367
public domain, 366-368
search engines, 471
registering pages,
472-477
sounds, 293
Telnet, 501-503
finding, 501
Internet Explorer
active channels, 388-390
creating Channel
Definition Format
(.cdf) files, 390-392
linking to pages,
390-394
FAQs, 389-392

flags, 393-394
Add To Favorites buttons,
411-413
AutoComplete, 245-248
clearing saved respons-
es, 247-248
disabling, 247
HTML Goodies Web site
tutorial, 245
background sound, 384
bookmark icons, 408-409
HTML Goodies Web site
example, 409
icon, 409-410
DHTML
interactive games,
402-405
placing, 404-405
HTML Goodies command
examples, 386
inline frames, 394-395
alignment/size, 399-400
altering, 400
button, creating, 397
clickable buttons,
397-398
creating, 395
FAQ, 395, 400
HTML Goodies Web
site, 400
IFRAME command, 395
invisible frame borders,
397-399
multiple frames,
395-397
marquees, 386-388
FAQ, 388
HTML Goodies Web site
example, 388
HTML Goodies Web site
tutorial, 386
page margins, setting, 384
setting Home pages,
413-416

HTML Goodies Web site examples, 414-416
static backgrounds, 384
table properties, setting, 384-386
Internet service providers. *See* ISPs
  hit counters, 366
  hosting Web sites, 45-46
  uploading files via FTP, 46-50
    ASCII versus Binary transfer modes, 48-50
    how FTP works, 47-48
Internet Sleuth Web site, 538
Internet Yellow Pages Web site, 188
<ISINDEX> flag, 524
ISMAP command (<IMG SRC=> flag), 153, 157
iso-8859-1 charset, 508-509
ISPs (Internet service providers)
  hit counters, 366
  hosting Web sites, 45-46
  uploading files via FTP, 46-50
    ASCII versus Binary transfer modes, 48-50
    how FTP works, 47-48
italic text, 19
  <ADDRESS> flag, 56
  <CITE> flag, 58
  <EM> flag (emphasis), 59
  <I> flag, 19, 60
<ITEM> flag, active channels, 393

J-K

Jars.Com Web site, 542
JASC, Inc. Web site, 418

Java, 311-312
  applets, 311-313
    compiling, 315
    copyright infringement, 313
    cross-platform browser tips, 480
    recognition of applets by browsers, 313
  dancing text applet, 314-315
    downloading applet, 315-316
    HTML code, 316-317
    modifying parameters, 317-318
    uploading modified applet, 319-320
  FAQs
    applet names, 316
    <PARAM> flag, 319
    resources for learning to write, 312
    running multiple applets, 319
    troubleshooting error messages, 319
  HTML Goodies Web site tutorial, 314
  versus JavaScript, 311-312
  Web sites, 542
Java Boutique Web site, 542
Java Centre Web site, 542
JavaScript, 311, 320, 322-324
  browser choice script, 345-347
    reasons for using, 346
    the script, 346-347
    uploading pages, 347
  cross-platform browser tips, 480
  customizing pages by screen size, 359

redirecting browsers to pages with specific settings, 360-361
  writing items to pages based on screen settings, 361-362
date stamp, 343
  calling .js files, 344-345
  creating .js files, 343-344
eliminating VALUE text automatically, 244-245
event handler commands, 312, 324-325
  alert, 325, 328-329
  onClick, 325, 328-329
  onClick, Back and Forward buttons, 329-330
  onClick, e-mail buttons, 332-333
  onClick, links within pages, 330-332
  onLoad, 333
  onMouseOut, 325
  onMouseOver, 325-328
example script from HTML Goodies Web site, 320-323
external JavaScripts, 342-343
  browser choice script. *See* JavaScript
  date stamp. *See* JavaScript, date stamp, 343
  hiding text with <-- //--> flags, 345
  shopping carts. *See* JavaScript, shopping carts, 348
  using multiple scripts in the same .js file, 345

FAQs
> cookies, 349
> e-mail buttons, 333
> image flips, 339, 342
> onLoad command, 345
> opening new windows, 334, 336
> resources for learning to write, 312
> shopping carts, 349, 353-354
> troubleshooting error messages, 322

focus onLoad, 243-244

HTML Goodies Web site
> browser choice JavaScript, 347
> displaying screen settings, 359
> event handler examples, 324
> example script, 320
> external JavaScript example, 345
> image flips imagemap example, 342
> onClick/onMouseover commands examples, 333
> opening/closing window example, 339
> primer, 312
> print function, 355
> reading screen settings, 362
> redirection based on screen settings, 360
> scrolling text example, 324
> shopping cart example, 350

HTML Goodies Web site tutorials
> browser choice, 346

image flips, 339-340
> shopping carts, 348

image flips, 339-340
> calling the script, 341-342
> fake imagemaps, 342
> multiple flips on the same page, 342
> requirements, 340
> specifying graphics, 341
> the script, 340-341

onLoad command, 322-323

opening new windows, 333-336
> closing pop-up windows, 338
> including new window inside main HTML document, 336-338
> playing background MIDI files, 338-339
> script format, 334-335
> window configuration, 335-336

pre-loading images, 357-359
> advantages, 357-358
> command format, 358-359

printing, 354-357
> attaching to user events, 356
> opening print windows, 355-356
> print method (window object), 354

requirements for JavaScript use, 323

search engine, 241

shopping carts, 348-349
> accepting credit cards, 354
> cookies, 349-350

> downloading required pages, 351
> modifying item pages, 352-353
> modifying order page, 353
> template, 350-351
> using CGIs, 353-354
> triggering functions, 338
> troubleshooting, 323-324
> versus Java, 311-312
> Web sites, 541

JavaScript Authoring Guide Web site, 541

JavaScript FAQ Web site, 541

JavaScript Planet Web site, 542

JavaScript World Web site, 542

JPEGs, 35, 144-145. *See also* images
> cross-platform browser tips, 481
> progressive JPEGs, 145-146

<KBD> flag (keyboard text), 60

keywords, search engines, 472-473

L

<LABEL> flag, 520

LANG attribute (HTML 4.0), 521

language charsets, 506-509
> HTML code, 507
> iso-8859-1 versus us-ascii, 508-509

layering images, 277-280

left aligning text, 25-26

LEFT attribute, positioning images, 279

LEFTMARGIN command
  Internet Explorer, 384
  sideline backgrounds, 133
<LEGEND> flag, 520
less than sign (<), flags, 17
linear Web rings, 488
lines (horizontal rules), 19-20,
  43, 124
  alignment, 126-127
  creating with images,
    105-106
  height, 43, 125-126
  no shading, 126-127
  width, 42-43, 124-125
link buttons, 219-220
  ? (question mark), 221
  creating, 220-221
  Guestbook image submit
    buttons, 237
  HTML Goodies Web site
    examples, 221, 224
  HTML Goodies Web site
    tutorials, 219-221
  inline frames, 397-398
  lining up, 221-224
Link Exchange (banner
  exchange network), 450
Linkosaurus Web site, 541
links, 29-32, 77-80
  <A HREF> flag, 29-30, 78
    code words for internal
      page jumps, 81-82
    mailto command, 31-32
  <A NAME> flag, 81-83
  active (clickable) images,
    36-38, 84-86. *See also*
    thumbnails
    HTML Goodies example
      Web page, 36
    removing blue borders,
      85-86
  active channels (Internet
    Explorer), 390-394

addresses, 31
buttons. *See* link buttons
color, 64-65
copyrighted pages, 456
creating, 77-80
  e-mail links, 31-32
disappearing links, 64
dynamic pages (meta-
  refresh command), 88-90
FAQs, 30-31, 78-82, 85-90
frames
  changing content in
    multiple frames,
    210-213
  opening links in a dif-
    ferent frame, 196-197
  opening links in a new,
    full browser window,
    198
  opening links in the
    same frame, 196
  non-frame alternative
    pages, 198-199
HTML Goodies Web site
  examples, 31, 80
  active (clickable) images,
    86
  meta-refresh command
    (dynamic pages), 90
  new browser windows,
    88
  no underline, 92
  page jumps, 81, 83
HTML Goodies Web site
  tutorials, 77
  dynamic pages (meta-
    refresh command), 88
  image links, 84
  new window, 87
  no underline on links,
    91
imagemaps. *See* imagemaps

internal page jumps, 79-83
  <A HREF> code words,
    81-82
  creating with JavaScript
    onClick event handler,
    330-332
  opening new browser win-
    dows, 87-88
  Primer 3 Web page, 29
  RealAudio meta files, 303
  removing underline, 90-92
  table cells, 170
    calendars, 181
  text links to images, 108
    copyrights, 461
  troubleshooting, 32
<LISTING> flag, 60
  HTML 4.0, 522
lists, 68-75
  bulleted, 68-70
  combining list types, 72-73
  FAQs, 68, 70-71, 73
  flags, 68-69, 74
  HTML Goodies Web site,
    73
    tutorial, 67
  numbered, 70-72
<LI> flag, 68
location= attribute, <FORM>
  flag, 213
locking out unauthorized
  counter users, 374-375
log files
  hit counters, 367
  HTML Goodies site, 467
LOOP command, scrolling
  marquees (<MARQUEE>
  flag), 387
low resolution images,
  110-112
LOWSRC attribute, <IMG>
  flag, 110-112

LView Pro
  creating transparent
    images, 113-116
  Web site URL, 116
Lycos Web site, 539
Lynx browser Web site, 544

M

Macintosh Telnet programs
  Web site, 501
Macromedia's DHTML Zone
  Web site, 405
MacZilla Movie Player
  (Macintosh) Web site, 309
Made with NotePad Web ring,
  489
mailto command (<A HREF>
  flag), 31-32
<mailto> flag, 31
  Guestbooks, 235
MAP NAME= command, 158
MapEdit Web site, 155
MARGINHEIGHT command,
  inline frames, 400
margins
  frames, 202
  pages, 384
  style sheet definitions, 254
MARGINWIDTH command
  <FRAMESET> flag, 202
  inline frames, 400
marquees (Internet Explorer
  <MARQUEE> flag), 386-388
  FAQ, 388
  HTML Goodies Web site
    example, 388
  HTML Goodies Web site
    tutorial, 386
<MENU> flag, 524
META commands
  frames, 216

refresh, 88-90
  adding sound, 89-90
  cross-platform browser
    tips, 482
  search engines, 471-474
meta files (RealAudio),
  302-303
Meta/Vector image formats,
  138-139
<META> flag, 285-286
  page transitions, 407
METHOD attribute, link buttons, 220
Microsoft FrontPage Web site,
  543
Microsoft Internet Explorer
  Web site, 544
Microsoft's DHTML Pages
  Web site, 405
MIDI (Musical Instrument
  Digital Interface), 297. *See
  also* sound
  playing background MIDI
    files with JavaScript,
    338-339
minors, copyright infringe-
  ment/protection, 458, 461
MoneySearch Web site, 539
monitors
  cross-platform browser tips,
    482
  customizing pages by
    screen size with
    JavaScript, 359
    redirecting browsers to
      pages with specific set-
      tings, 360-361
    writing items to pages
      based on screen set-
      tings, 361-362
monospace text (<CODE>
  flag), 58
Mosiac browser Web site, 544

Motion Picture Experts
  Group. *See* MPEG
mouse. *See also* mouse actions
  cursors (style sheets),
    272-274
  ToolTips. *See* ToolTips
mouse actions
  image flips (JavaScript),
    339-340
    calling the script,
      340-342
    fake imagemaps, 342
    multiple flips on the
      same page, 342
    requirements, 340
    specifying graphics, 341
  onClick event handler,
    325, 328-329
    Add To Favorites but-
      tons, 412
    Back and Forward but-
      tons, 329-330
    e-mail buttons,
      332-333
    links within pages,
      330-332
    setting browser home
      pages, 415-416
    using with alert event
      handler, 329
  onLoad event handler, 333
  onMouseOut event han-
    dler, 325
  onMouseOver event han-
    dler, 325-328
    background colors,
      327-328
    banners, 453
    using with alert event
      handler, 328-329
.mov file extension, 304

MPEG (Motion Picture Experts Group), 304. *See also* video
helper applications, 309
<MULTICOL> flag, 60, 75-76
multimedia. *See* sound; video
music copyrights, 461
blanket fee licenses, 461
Fair Use Doctrine, 461
FAQ, 293
Musical Instrument Digital Interface. *See* MIDI

N

NAME attribute
AutoComplete (Internet Explorer), 246-247
drop-down box forms, 232
<FRAMESET> flag, 197
layering images, 279
multiple inline frames, 396
radio button forms, 229
shopping carts, 352
text area box forms, 227
text box forms, 226
naming Web pages, 12
NCSA Telnet Web site, 501
Nerd World Media Web site, 539
NetCruiser browser Web site, 544
Netscape. *See also* browsers
Communicator Web site, 544
DHTML support FAQ, 402, 408
Navigator charsets, 507
NetTamer browser Web site, 544
new flags, 518-522
newspaper columns
FAQ, 76
<MULTICOL> flag, 60, 75-76

<NOBR> flag, 61
<NOFRAMES> flag, 198-199, 520
non-dithering colors, 527, 530
NORESIZE=*###* command, inline frames, 400
<NOSCRIPT> flag, 521
NotePad Web ring, 489
numbered lists, 70-72
combining with bulleted lists, 72-73
Roman numerals, 71-72
starting count after one, 72

O

<OBJECT> flag, 521
<OL> flag, 69
sideline backgrounds, 133
on-site links. *See* page jumps (internal links)
onClick Event Handler, 325, 328-329
Add To Favorites buttons, 412
Back and Forward buttons, 329-330
e-mail buttons, 332-333
<FORM> flag, 213
links within pages, 330-332
setting browser home pages, 415-416
using with alert event handler, 329
onLoad command
form focus, 243-244
JavaScript, 322-323
external JavaScripts, 345
usage as JavaScript event handler, 333

onMouseOut event handler (JavaScript), 325
onMouseOver event handler, 325-328
with alert event handler, 328-329
background colors, 327-328
banners, 453
opening
new windows (JavaScript), 333-336
closing pop-up windows, 338
including new window inside main HTML document, 336-338
playing background MIDI files, 338-339
script format, 334-335
window configuration, 335-336
Web pages, 13, 20
Opera browser Web site, 545
<OPTGROUP> flag, 521
<OPTION> flag, drop-down box forms, 232

P

page jumps (internal links), 79, 81-83
<A HREF> code words, 81-82
HTML Goodies Web site examples, 83
HTML Goodies Web site tutorial, 81
page transitions (DHTML)
creating, 406-407
HTML Goodies Web site examples, 408
selecting effects, 407-408

pages
  columns
    FAQ, 76
    HTML Goodies Web
      site, 76
    <MULTICOL> flag, 60,
      75-76
    <SAMP> flag, 62
  declaration statements, 517
  dividing (<DIV> flag), 59
  document declarations,
    493
  fitting to frames, 192
    filling multiple frames
      with a single page,
      205-206
  image loading speed, 106
  index pages, 290-292
  linking pages together,
    77-80
    directory structures,
      79-80
    home page links, 80
    using full URLs, 80
  loading low-res image ver-
    sions first, 110-112
  making pages accessible to
    disabled assistant
    browsers, 503-506
  margins, setting for
    Internet Explorer, 384
  password protecting,
    491-492
  refreshing pages automati-
    cally (meta-refresh com-
    mand), 88-90
    adding sound, 89-90
Paint Shop Pro
  banner text
    color, 436-438
    font, 438-441
    shadow, 441-444
    size, 441

color palette, 436
copying/pasting banner
  images, 431
creating banner images,
  422-423
  creating different ver-
    sions of images for ani-
    mation, 433-435
  cropping images,
    425-428
  saving images, 423-425
creating banners, 418
downloading Web sites,
  418, 498
screen captures, 497-500
paragraphs
  creating, 20
  indenting, 67-68
<PARAM> flag (Java applets),
  317-319, 521
parity digits, 48
password protecting Web
  pages, 491-492
pasting banner images,
  431-432
PedagoNet Web site, 539
Perl CGIs. *See* CGI
persistent cookies, 466-468
pictures. *See* images
pixels, 35, 102, 422
  1x1 images, 105-106
  image sizes, 41
<PLAINTEXT> flag, 61
  HTML 4.0, 522
Planet Search Web site, 539
plug-ins, 295-296
  helper applications,
    294-295
  RealAudio. *See* RealAudio
  sound files, 295-296

pop-up browser windows
  closing windows, 338
  creating with JavaScript,
    333-336
  including new window
    inside main HTML docu-
    ment, 336-338
  playing background MIDI
    files, 338-339
positioning
  banners, 450-451
  style sheets, 255, 258
    HTML Goodies exam-
      ples, 258
    images, 259-260
    text, 261-262
Postmaster Web site, 541
pound sign (#), internal page
  jumps, 81
pre-loading images
  (JavaScript), 357-359
  advantages, 357-358
  command format,
    358-359
preformatted text (<PRE>
  flag), 61
printing (JavaScript), 354-357
  attaching to user events,
    356
  opening print windows,
    355-356
  print method (window
    object), 354
privacy (cookies), 469-470
progressive JPEGs, 145-146
publishing Web pages. *See*
  uploading Web pages
push technology (IE active
  channels), 389. *See also*
  active channels
<P> flag, 20, 101

Q-R

question mark (?), link buttons, 221
QuickTime, 304. *See also* video
  Intel Indeo compression rate, 305
  Web site URLs, 309
quotes
  <BLOCKQUOTE> flag, 57
  <CITE> flag, 58
  <Q> flag, 61, 522
<Q> flag, 61, 522. *See also* <BLOCKQUOTE> flag; <SPAN> flag

.ra files, 302. *See also* RealAudio
radio button forms, 228-229
.ram files, 302. *See also* RealAudio
raster images, 137-138. *See also* images
RealAudio, 300-301
  buffers, 301
    creating meta files, 302-303
  downloading files, 301
  HTML Goodies Web site
    examples, 304
    tutorials, 300
  running files from HTTP servers
    creating meta files, 302-303
    creating sound files, 302
    disadvantages, 303
    linking to meta files, 303
    requirements, 301-302
  servers, 301
  streaming, 301

Web site URL, 302
RealVideo, 304
receiving e-mail from Web sites, 31-32
recording sound, 297
  FAQ, 297
  RealAudio files, 302-303
redirecting browsers to pages with specific settings, 360-361
refreshing pages (META REFRESH command), 88-90
  adding sound, 89-90
  frames, 216
Register-It! Web site, 541
registering
  copyrights with Copyright Office, 457
  sites with search engines, 474-477, 540-541
    fees, 475
    HTML Goodies Web site article, 475
    META commands, 472-473
    WebCrawler, 476
    Yahoo!, 475
requirements for creating Web pages, 9-10
Rescue Island Web site, 539
RESIZE="no" attribute
  <FRAME SRC> flag, 203
  <FRAMESET> flag, 203
resolution (monitors), cross-platform browser tips, 482
RIFs (Raster image formats), 137-138
right aligning text, 25-26. *See also* aligning
Robin Cover's XML Page at sil.org Web site, 496
Roman numeral lists, 71-72

rows
  frames, 192-193
    combining with columns, 193-194
  tables, 167
ROWS attribute
  <FRAMESET> flag, 193-194
  text area box forms, 227
ROWSPAN attribute (<TD> flag), 175-177
rpm files, 302. *See also* RealAudio
rules (horizontal), 19-20, 124
  adjusting length/height, 42-43, 124-126
  aligning, 126-127
  creating with images, 105-106
  height
  no shading, 126-127
RULES=*###* command, setting for Internet Explorer, 385

S

<SAMP> flag, 62
satire copyrights, 459
saving
  images. *See* downloading Web pages, 11-13
<SCHEDULE> flag, active channels, 393-394
screen captures, 497-500
  copyrights, 497
  creating, 497-500
screen size, customizing pages (JavaScript), 359
  redirecting browsers to pages with specific settings, 360-361

writing items to pages
based on screen settings,
361-362
SCROLLAMOUNT=*###*
command, scrolling mar-
quees (<MARQUEE> flag),
387
scrollbars
frames, 203-204, 209
style sheets, 274-275
color, 276-277
main document scroll-
bar, 275
textarea scrollbar,
275-276
SCROLLDELAY=*###* com-
mand, scrolling marquees
(<MARQUEE> flag), 387
SCROLLING attribute
<FRAME SRC> flag,
203-204, 209
inline frames, 400
scrolling marquees (Internet
Explorer), 386-388
creating, 387
FAQ, 388
HTML Goodies Web site
example, 388
tutorial, 386
seamless frames, 206-210
frame sources, 209-210
main codes/commands,
206-208
search engines, 471, 537-540
Ahoy!, 537
AltaVista, 537
Apollo, 537
Beaucoup's Search Engines,
540
BizAds Business Locator,
537
ComFind, 538
EuroSeek, 538
Excite, 538

Galaxy, 538
HotBot, 538
Human Search, 538
Humor Search Comedy
Search Engine, 538
InfoSeek, 538
Inktomi, 538
Internet Sleuth, 538
Lycos, 539
META commands,
471-474
author, 473
copyright, 473
expires, 474
offering keywords,
472-473
offering page descrip-
tions, 473
offering page generators,
473
placement on pages,
474
MoneySearch, 539
Nerd World Media, 539
PedagoNet, 539
performing searches,
238-240
searching one's own
site, 240-242
Planet Search, 539
registering pages, 474-477,
540-541
fees, 475
HTML Goodies Web site
article, 475
META commands,
472-473
registration sites,
540-541
WebCrawler, 476
Yahoo!, 475
Rescue Island, 539
Search.Com, 540
SoftSearch, 539

source code, 239
addresses, 239-240
on the Web, 540
Web site URLs, 537-540
Webcrawler, 539
Websurfer, 539
What-U-Seek, 539
WWWomen, 539
WWWW (World Wide Web
Worm), 540
Yahoo!, 540. *See also*
Yahoo! Web site
Search.Com Web site, 540
searching Web sites, 238-242
Excite search engine, 240
hidden value, search
engines, 241
HotBot, code, 241
HTML Goodies Web site
tutorial, 238
JavaScript-based search
engine, 241
searching one's own site,
240-242
searching other sites,
238-240
security
cookies, 469-470
password protected Web
pages, 491-492
protecting hit counters
from outside use,
374-375
SELECTED attribute, drop-
down box forms, 232
<SELECT> flag, drop-down
box forms, 231-232
semicolon (;)
frames, 213
style sheet commands, 252
server-side imagemaps,
149-151
basic imagemap format,
154

CGI (Common Gateway Interface), 150-152
creating maps, 152
imagemap command, 150-152
placing images, 153
providing backup links, 154
servers
directory structures, 79-80
running RealAudio files
RealAudio servers, 301
HTTP servers, 301-303
SFAN Experimental Multimedia Page Web site, 402
SGML (Standard Generalized Mark-up Language), 493-494, 518
shading horizontal rules, 126-127
shadow text, banner ads, 441-444
shareware, 118. *See also* software, 118
Web sites, 105, 418
shopping carts (JavaScript), 348-349
accepting credit cards, 354
cookies, 349-350
downloading required pages, 351
modifying item pages, 352-353
modifying order page, 353
template, 350-351
using CGIs, 353-354
sideline backgrounds, 131-132
color, 133
placing items on the stripe, 133-135

removing text from the stripe, 133
right-side borders, 135
text, 133
single flags, 19-20
sites. *See* Web sites
SIZE attribute
drop-down box forms, 232
<FONT> flag, 59
<HR> flag, 125-126
text box forms, 226
sizing
horizontal rules, 124-126
images, 41-42, 102-104
determining image size, 104
inline frames (Internet Explorer), 399-400
<SMALL> flag, 61
SMPTE Code (Society of Motion Picture and Television Engineers Code), 116
SneakerChat Web site, 542
SoftSearch Web site, 539
software
animated GIF programs, 117-118
GIF Construction Set. *See* GIF Construction Set
beta versions, 517
HTML assistants, 543
LView Pro
creating transparent images, 113-116
Web site URL transparent images, 116
shareware, 118
Web sites, 105, 418
version numbers, 516-517
video playback, 308-309

sound
adding to pages, 295
embedding, 295-300
background
cross-platform browser tips, 480
Internet Explorer, 384
dynamic pages (meta-refresh command), 89-90
FAQs
copyrights, 293
downloading RealAudio files, 301
embedding, 299
formats, 299
RealAudio servers, 301
recording, 297
helper applications, 294-295
HTML Goodies Web site examples, 300, 304
HTML Goodies Web site tutorials
embedded sound, 294
RealAudio, 300
MIDI (Musical Instrument Digital Interface), 297
playing background MIDI files with JavaScript, 338-339
plug-ins, 295-296
RealAudio, 300-301
buffers, 301-303
creating meta files, 302-303
creating sound files, 302
disadvantages to running files from HTTP servers, 303
linking to meta files, 303
RealAudio servers, 301

requirements for running files from HTTP servers, 301-302
streaming, 301
recording, 297
FAQ, 297
RealAudio files, 302-303
source code
search engines, 239
addresses, 239-240
viewing HTML source code for Web pages, 14-15
spacing
between frames, 201-202
text
  code, 67
style sheets, 253
span style sheets, 256-257
<SPAN> flag, 62, 521. *See also* <DIV> flag; <Q> flag; <BLOCKQUOTE> flag
special characters
creating with ampersand (&) commands, 532-533
creating with ASCII commands, 533-535
speed, image loading, 106
stacked buttons examples (HTML Goodies Web site), 224
standalone Web pages (XML), 494-495
Standard Generalized Markup Language (SGML), 493-494, 518
static backgrounds, 384
streaming RealAudio, 301
strikethrough text
<DEL> flag, 58
<S> flag, 62
<STRIKE> flag (HTML 4.0), 522

<STRONG> flag, 62. *See also* <BOLD> flag
style sheets, 249-250
classes, 264-267
commands, 251-252
defining flags, 252
FONT/TEXT definitions, 252-253
handling the same flag different ways, 256
MARGIN/BACKGROUND definitions, 254
positioning/division definitions, 255
using STYLE command on individual items, 257, 263-264
Web site resources, 258
cross-platform browser tips, 478-479
cursor properties, 272-274
dividing pages (<DIV> flag), 59
example Web site, 250
FAQs, 258
color codes, 271
image framing color, 272
inline commands, 265
Netscape Navigator versus Internet Explorer, 250
positioning, 260, 262-263
ToolTips, 271
troubleshooting, 257
forms, 268-270
background color, 270
colored buttons, 271
text color, 270
ToolTips, 271
<HEAD> flag, 287-288

HTML Goodies Web site examples, 250, 258
classes/IDs, 268
cursor settings, 272, 274
forms, 269
layering, 279
positioning, 258
printing, 354
scrollbar color, 277
HTML Goodies Web site tutorials
scrollbar color, 274
style sheets, 249
IDs, 264-268
inline, 250-251
positioning items, 258
HTML Goodies examples, 258
images, 259-260
text, 261-262
scrollbars, 274-275
color, 276-277
main document scrollbar, 275
textarea scrollbar, 275-276
span, 256-257
text color, 262-263, 270
troubleshooting, 257
subcommands, 24-26
subdirectories, 291-292
submit attribute, link buttons, 220
submit buttons. *See also* link buttons
forms, 232-233
Guestbooks, 237
Submit! Web site, 540
Submit-It! Web site, 476, 541
subscript text (<SUB> flag), 62
subtractive color, 530
superscript text (<SUP> flag), 62

surfing anonymously, 469-470
symbols
  creating with ampersand
    (&) commands, 532-533
  creating with ASCII com-
    mands, 533-535
<S> flag, 62
  HTML 4.0, 522

T

tab order, forms
  focus onLoad, 243-244
  HTML Goodies Web site
    example, 242
  TABINDEX command,
    242-243
<TABLE BORDER> flag
  link buttons, 222
tables, 165-166
  activating cells for links,
    170
    calendars, 181
  border color, 184-186
  calendars, 179-182
  cells
    background color,
      182-183
    background images, 184
    cell width, 176-177
    column span, 174-175
    creating, 167
    row span, 175-176
  color, 182-186
    borders, 184-186
    cell backgrounds,
      182-183
    text, 183-184
  column width, 167
  creating, 167
  FAQs, 168
    background images, 184
    border color, 186
    calendars, 182
    cell width, 177

CELLPADDING, 176
  color, 183
  creating page layouts,
    171
  flags, 168, 170
  table in a table, 179
  using VALIGN="top",
    175
flags, 166-167
  <CAPTION>, 167
  <TABLE>, 167-170
  <TD>, 167-168
  <TR>, 167-168
formatting
  alignment, 169-170
  borders, 168-169
  cell padding, 169
  cell spacing, 169
HTML Goodies Web site
  examples
    advanced tables, 177
    calendar, 182
    checkerboard, 184
    colors, 186
    table within a table, 177
    tables, 173
HTML Goodies Web site
  tutorials
    border color, 185
    color tables, 182
    tables, 177
images, 97-99
  centering images, 97-98
images in cells, 171
  centering, 172-173
  framing images, 172
rows, creating, 167
setting properties for
  Internet Explorer,
    384-386
sideline backgrounds,
  133-135
table within a table,
  177-179

<TABLE> flag, 167. *See also*
  tables
  attributes, 169-170
    BORDERCOLOR, 186
  link buttons, 222
tags. *See* flags
TARGET attribute, <FRAME-
  SET> flag, 197-198
<TD> flag, 167-168. *See also*
  tables
  attributes
    COLSPAN, 174-175
    ROWSPAN, 175-177
    WIDTH, 176-177
  link buttons, 222
Telnet, 501-503
  creating directories,
    291-292, 370
    CGI directories, 371
  FAQ, 369
  finding, 501
  finding absolute paths (hit
    counters), 372-373
  locking out unauthorized
    counter users, 374-375
templates, shopping carts
  (JavaScript), 350-351
temporary cookies, 466-468
testing cross-platform browser
  capability, 477
text, 55-56
  abbreviations (<ABBR>), 56
  acronyms (<ACRONYM>),
    56
  addresses (<ADDRESS>
    flag), 56
  aligning/centering, 25-26,
    482
  alignment with images,
    40-41, 96-102
    centering images,
      97-98
    single lines of text,
      99-100

tables, 97-99
two lines of text,
100-101
wrapping text, 96-97
banners, 436
color, 436-438
font, 438-441
shadow, 441-444
size, 441
blinking (<BLINK>), 57
bold, 18-19
<B>, 56
<STRONG> flag, 62
breaking, 20
citations (<CITE>), 58
color, 63-65
<FONT COLOR> flag, 59
HTML Goodies tutorial,
64
links, 64-65
multiple words, 64
setting with style sheets,
262-263, 270
single words, 65
table cells, 183-184
columns
FAQ, 76
HTML Goodies Web
site, 76
<MULTICOL> flag), 60,
75-76
<SAMP> flag, 62
cross-platform browser tips
alignment, 482
double-align, 482
formatting, 478
definitions (<DFN> flag),
58
direction (<BDO>), 57
dividing (<DIV> flag), 59
emphasis (<EM> flag), 59
flags
combining, 19
ending, 18

uppercase, 18
fonts, 65-67. *See also* fonts
<BASEFONT> flag, 57
<CODE> flag (mono-
space font), 58
HTML Goodies Web site
font test, 67
HTML Goodies Web site
tutorial, 66
<KBD> flag (keyboard-
style font), 60
size, 24-25
<TT> flag (typewriter-
style font), 63
<VAR> flag (fixed-width
font), 63
headings, 23-24
<H#> flag, 60
hiding
HTML comments, 58
JavaScript statements,
334, 345
HTML Goodies Web site
text codes tutorial, 56
image ToolTips (alternative
text), 103-104
indenting, 67-68
<BLOCKQUOTE> flag,
57
<Q> flag, 61
italic, 19
<ADDRESS> flag, 56
<CITE> flag, 58
<EM> flag (emphasis),
59
<I> flag, 60
keyboard (<KBD> flag), 60
links to images, 108
lists. *See* lists
paragraphs, 20
positioning with style
sheets, 261-262
preformatted (<PRE> flag),
61

Primer 3 Web page, 23
sideline backgrounds, 133
size
<BIG>, 57
<FONT SIZE> flag, 59
<SMALL> flag, 61
spaces,   code, 67
strikethrough
<DEL> flag, 58
<S> flag, 62
style sheet definitions,
252-253
subscript (<SUB>), 62
superscript (<SUP>), 62
typewriter, 19
underline
<INS> flag, 60
<U> flag, 63
wrapping
cross-platform browser
tips, 478
<NOBR> flag, 61
<WBR> flag, 63
text area box forms, 226-227
textarea, scrollbars, 275-276
<TEXTAREA> flag, 227
text box forms
creating, 225-226
eliminating VALUE text
automatically, 244-245
<TFOOT> flag, 521
TheCounter.com Web site,
367
Thomson & Thomson Web
site, 463
<THREAD> flag, 522
thumbnail images, 107-110.
See also active (clickable)
images
text links to images, 108
two images, 108-109
two versions of same
image, 109-110
tilde (~), absolute paths, 372

TITLE command, 271
    <ABBR> flag, 519
    HTML 4.0, 521
title copyrights, 458
<TITLE> flag, 20, 285
ToolTips
    abbreviated text (<ABBR>), 56
    images (alternative text), 103-104
    setting with style sheets, 271
    <SPAN> flag, 62
TOP attribute, positioning images, 279
TOPMARGIN= command (Internet Explorer), 384
tracking visitors
    banners, 452
    hit counters. *See* hit counters
trademarks, 458. *See also* copyrights
trading page space (placing banners on other sites), 449-450
transducing (video), 306
transfering files. *See* FTP; Telnet
transition effects (DHTML)
    HTML Goodies Web site example, 408
    pages
        creating, 406-407
        selecting effects, 407-408
transparent images, 112-116
    creating with LView Pro, 113-116
triggering JavaScript functions, 338
troubleshooting. *See also* FAQs
    images, 35
    JavaScript, 323-324

links, 32
style sheets, 257
<TR> flag, 167-168. *See also* tables, 167
    link buttons, 222
<TT> flag, 19, 63
.txt file extension, 13
TYPE attribute, radio button forms, 229
TYPE=button command, shopping carts, 352
typewriter text, 19
    <KBD> flag (keyboard-style font), 60
    <TT> flag (typewriter-style font), 63

U

U.S. Copyright Office Web site, 463
<UL> flag, 68-69
underline
    <INS> flag, 60
    removing from links, 90-92
    <U> flag, 63
Uniform Resource Locators. *See* URLs
UNIX, 368
unordered lists. *See* bulleted lists
uploading
    animated GIFs, 124
    Web pages, 46
        directory structures, 79-80
        FTP, 47-50
        Internet service providers, 45-46
URLs (Uniform Resource Locators), 14
    removing .html extension, 289-290
        creating subdirectories, 291-292

FAQ, 291
    HTML Goodies Web site examples, 292
    index pages, 290-291
    specfic Web sites. *See* Web site URLs
    using full URLs in links, 80
<USAGE VALUE=*###*> flag, active channels, 393
USEMAP command (<IMG SRC=> flag), 157
<U> flag, 63
    HTML 4.0, 522

V

VALIGN command, 102
VALUE command
    back and forward buttons, 330
    eliminating VALUE text automatically, 244-245
    <FORM> flag, 213
    link buttons, 220
    radio button forms, 229
    shopping carts, 352
Van Halen News Desk Web site, 207
<VAR> flag, 63
Vector/Meta image formats, 138-139
version numbers, software, 516-517
versions of HTML in declaration statements, 517
video, 304-306
    AVI format, 304
        helper applications, 309
    compression, 307
    FAQ, 307
    Intel Indeo, 305
    copyrights, 461
    digital video, 306
    FAQs
        compression, 307

583

RealVideo, 304
  reducing file size, 307
file formats, 304-305
file size, 305
  reducing, 307
hardware requirements, 307-308
helper applications, 294-295
HTML Goodies Web site
  examples, 308
  tutorials, 304
MPEG, 304
  helper applications, 309
playback software, 308-309
QuickTime, 304
  Intel Indeo compression rate, 305
  Web site URLs, 309
transducing, 306
versus film, 305-306
viewing HTML source code for Web pages, 14-15
virtual page Guestbooks, 236
visitors
  advertising requirements, 484
  hits versus impressions, 484
  tracking
    banners, 452
    hit counters. *See* hit counters, 452
Voyager browser Web site, 545
VSPACE=*###* command, scrolling marquees (<MARQUEE> flag), 387

W

W3C Web Content Accessibility Guidelines, 504-506

wallpaper (background images), 128-129. *See also* backgrounds
  creating, 129-130
  guidelines for use, 130
.wav files. *See* sound
<WBR> flag, 63
Web Director Web site, 543
Web pages
  addresses. *See* URLs (Uniform Resource Locators)
  bookmarks. *See* bookmarks
  closing, 20
  copyrights. *See* copyrights
  fitting frames, 192
  linking. *See* links
  naming, 12
  opening, 13, 20

  password protection, 491-492
  requirements for creating, 9-10
  saving, 11-13
    naming files, 12
  titles, 20-22
  uploading. *See* uploading
  viewing HTML source code, 14-15
  width, cross-platform browser tips, 480-481
  writing, 20-22
    HTML assistants, 50-51
Web rings, 487-491
  creating
    generated, 488
    linear, 488
    Web ring Web site, 489-490
  HTML code, 489-490
  HTML Goodies Web site example, 488
  ringmaster, 488

Web rings Web site, 489
Web site URLs
  1–2–3–Register Me!, 540
  Acclaim Web Services, 541
  Add Me!, 541
  Ahoy! search engine, 537
  AltaVista, 537
  Apollo, 537
  AVI helper applications, 309
  Beaucoup's Search Engines, 540
  BizAds Business Locator, 537
  browsers, 544-545
  C-Net's Table of Style Sheet Commands, 258
  Campaign Against Frames, 189
  Cello browser, 544
  Central Ad Pro, 485
  CineWeb, 309
  ComFind, 538
  Copyright Clearance Center, Inc., 463
  Copyright Office, 457
  copyright resources, 463
  dancing text applet download, 315
  Danny Goodman's JavaScript Pages, 541
  Dave Central's FTP, 47
  EuroSeek, 538
  Excite, 538
  Fake Counter Home Page, 367
  Galaxy, 538
  Gamelan, 314, 542
  Globetrotter Web Assistant, 543
  helper applications, 543
  HotBot, 241, 538
  HotDog, 543
  HotJava browser, 544

HoTMetaL, 543
HotSyte, 541
HTML 4.01, 513
HTML Assistant, 543
HTML Goodies. *See* HTML
  Goodies Web site
HTMLpad, 543
Human Search, 538
Humor Search Comedy
  Search Engine, 538
InfoSeek, 538
Inktomi, 538
Internet Sleuth, 538
Jars.Com, 542
Java Boutique, 542
Java Centre, 542
JavaScript Authoring
  Guide, 541
JavaScript FAQ, 541
JavaScript Planet, 542
JavaScript World, 542
JavaScripts, 541
Linkosaurus, 541
LView Pro (download), 116
Lycos, 539
Lynx browser, 544
Macintosh Telnet pro-
  grams, 501
Macromedia's DHTML
  Zone, 405
MacZilla Movie Player
  (Macintosh), 309·
Made with NotePad Web
  ring, 489
MapEdit, 155
Microsoft
  DHTML Pages, 405
  Front Page, 543
  Internet Explorer, 544
MoneySearch, 539
Mosiac browser, 544
MPEG helper applications,
  309
NCSA Telnet, 501

Nerd World Media, 539
NetCruiser browser, 544
Netscape Communicator,
  544
NetTamer browser, 544
Opera browser, 545
Paint Shop Pro downloads,
  418, 498
PedagoNet, 539
Planet Search, 539
Postmaster, 541
QuickTime, 309
RealAudio, 302
Register-It!, 541
Rescue Island, 539
Robin Cover's XML Page at
  sil.org, 496
search engines, 537-540
Search.Com, 540
SFAN Experimental
  Multimedia Page, 402
Shareware.com, 418
SneakerChat, 542
SoftSearch, 539
Submit!, 540
Submit-It!, 476, 541
TheCounter.com, 367
Thomson & Thomson, 463
U.S. Copyright Office, 463
Van Halen News Desk, 207
Voyager browser, 545
World Wide Web
  Consortium (W3C), 289
    W3C's Style, 258
    W3C Web Content
      Accessibility
      Guidelines, 504, 506
WebCounter, 367
Webcrawler, 539
Websurfer, 539
Web Director, 543
Web rings, 489
What-U-Seek, 539
WinWeb browser, 545

WUSAGE, 367
WWWomen, 539
WWWW (World Wide Web
  Worm), 540
XML.com, 496
XML resources, 496
Yahoo!, 540
  Applet Page, 542
  Background Image, 131
  copyright search, 463
  DHTML Games, 405
  HTML Editor Review
    Page, 543
  HTML Editors, 543
  HTML Formats, 405
  imagemap links, 155
  Java Script Page, 542
  Search Engine Page, 540
  Transparent Image, 116
  Web ring listings, 489
  XML page, 496
Web sites
  bookmarks. *See* bookmarks
  copyrights, 463
  copyrights. *See* copyrights
  directory structures, 79-80
  Film.com, 187
  GIF Construction Set
    download, 418
  hosts, 45-46
  HTML Goodies. *See* HTML
    Goodies Web site
  Internet Yellow Pages, 188
  JASC, Inc. 418
  linking pages together,
    77-80
    directory structures,
      79-80
    home page links, 80
    using full URLs, 80
  making pages accessible to
    disabled assistant
    browsers, 503-506

registering with search
engines, 540-541
searching, 240-242
Excite search engine,
240
hidden values, search
engines, 241
HotBot, code, 241
JavaScript-based search
engine, 241
search engines, 238-240
shareware, 105
style sheet example, 250
WebCounter Web site, 367
Webcrawler Web site, 539
registering pages, 476
search code, 239
Websurfer Web site, 539
What-U-Seek Web site, 539
width
table columns, 167
Web pages, cross-platform
browser tips, 480-481
WIDTH command
banner ads, 450-451
browser pop-up windows,
335
<HR> flag, 42-43, 124-125
<IMG> flag, 42, 102-103
inline frames, 399
Java applets, 317
<MULTICOL> flag, 76
resizing images, 109
scrolling marquees (<MAR-
QUEE> flag), 387
sideline images, 134
<TD> flag, 176-177
windows
frames. *See also* frames
opening frames in a new,
full browser window,
87-88, 198

JavaScript. *See*
JavaScript, opening
new windows, 336
preventing, 87-88
opening print windows via
JavaScript print method,
355-356
WinWeb browser Web site,
545
word processors, writing
HTML, 11-12
World Wide Web Consortium
(W3C) Web site, 289
W3C's Style, 258
W3C Web Content
Accessibility Guidelines,
504, 506
wrapping text
around images, 40-41,
96-102
centering images, 97-98
single lines of text,
99-100
tables, 97-99
two lines of text,
100-101
cross-platform browser tips,
478
<NOBR> flag, 61
<PRE> flag, 61
<WBR> flag, 63
writing HTML
HTML assistants, 50-51
word processors, 11-12
WUSAGE Web site, 367
WWWomen Web site, 539
WWWW (World Wide Web
Worm) Web site, 540

X

XML (eXtensible Markup
Language), 492-494, 497,
518

creating standalone Web
pages, 494-495
DTDs, 493
creating, 495-496
versus HTML and SGML,
494
Web resources, 496
XML.com Web site, 496
<XMP> flag, 63. *See also*
<PRE> flag
HTML 4.0, 522

Y-Z

Yahoo! Web site, 540
Applet page, 542
Background Images page,
131
copyright search page, 463
DHTML Games page, 405
HTML Editor Review page,
543
HTML Editors page, 543
HTML Formats page, 405
imagmap links page, 155
Java Script page, 542
registering pages, 475
Search Engine page, 540
Transparent Image page,
116
Web ring listings, 489
XML page, 496

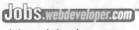